Kings of Disaster

Dualism, Centralism and the Scapegoat King

in Southeastern Sudan

Simon Simonse

FOUNTAIN PUBLISHERS
www.fountainpublishers.co.ug

Fountain Publishers
P.O. Box 488
Kampala, Uganda
E-mail: sales@fountainpublishers.co.ug
              publishing@fountainpublishers.co.ug
Website: www.fountainpublishers.co.ug

Distributed in Europe and Commonwealth countries outside Africa by:
African Books Collective Ltd,
P.O. Box 721,
Oxford OX1 9EN, UK.
Tel/Fax: +44(0) 1869 349110
E-mail: orders@africanbookscollective.com
Website: www.africanbookscollective.com

Revised, illustrated Edition
© Simon Simonse 2017
First published in 1992, as Volume 5 in the series Studies in Human Society, by E.J Brill,
Leiden, the Netherlands.

Cataloguing-in Publication-Data
Simonse, Simon
Kings of Disaster: Dualism, Centralism, and the Scapegoat King in Southeastern Sudan /
by Simon Simonse
Includes bibliographical references and index

ISBN: 978-9970-25-897-0 (Paper back)
ISBN: 978-9970-25-946-5 (ebook)

1. Political anthropology —South Sudan.
2. South Sudan—Kings and rulers— Case studies.
3. Scapegoat— Case studies.
I. Title. II. Series.

This book has been published with support of the IMITATIO FOUNDATION
www.imitatio.org

Dedicated to my father and Elias

«We must realize that war is bonding, and that order springs from conflict, and that all that comes into being, does so antagonistically and out of necessity.»

Heraclitus, *Fragments*, Diels-Kranz, No.80.[1]

désastrer   I. placer sous l'influence d'un astre défavorable
II. préserver de l'influence des astres

Edmond Huguet,
Dictionnaire de la langue française du seizième siècle.[2]

« Supported by the pages, the king was slowly ascending the stairway of the central tower. The stairs were lined by the vassals, one standing on each step. Each one held his drawn sword in front of him the handle turned towards the sovereign and the point resting on the vassal's throat as if they were impatient to be slaughtered. But the king did not even look at them...»

Camara Laye, *The Radiance of the King*, p. 32.

«...we must say that *power is something that is exchanged*. Not in the economical sense, but in the sense that power is executed according to a reversible cycle of seduction, challenge, and ruse (neither axis, nor indefinite relay, but a cycle).»
«There was a time when power allowed itself to be sacrificed according to the rules of this symbolic game from which it cannot escape, a time when power possessed the ephemeral and mortal quality of what had to be sacrificed. Ever since, it has sought to escape that rule, or has ceased being a symbolic power in order to become a political power and a strategy of social domination.»

Jean Baudrillard, *Forget Foucault*, pp. 52, 61.

«As he [the Rainmaker] was preparin' his potion the hearts were filled with love
And every eye was fixed on those cloudless skies above.
Hour after hour — but no rain came down
And they caught the old rainmaker — just as he was leavin' town.
Yeah, they hung the rainmaker beneath the dead oak tree;
As he cried and he pleaded, "Just wait! Wait — and you're gonna see!"

Things in old Dry Gulch haven't been the same.
When they hung the rainmaker, they walked home in the rain.
When they hung the rainmaker, they walked home in the rain.»

Hank Williams Jr., "The Rainmaker",
from the Album *Ballads of the Hills and Plains*

Notes on the front cover and the citations:

Front cover: The scene of the men spearing the tree evokes the ritual of simulated regicide performed during a drought crisis when it is not possible to put the blame on the king or another individual member of the rain clan. The tree, in this case, is the totem of the royal clan (see pp. 376–380).

First citation: This fragment of the philosophy of Heraclitus of Ephesus (540–480 BC), was preserved in a treatise of Origen written in defence of the truth claims of Christianity against a critical pamphlet written by the Greek philosopher Kelsos (AD 248). The Greek text reads:

> εἰδέναι δὲ χρὴ τὸν πόλεμον ἐόντα ξυνόν, καὶ δίκην ἔριν
> καὶ γινόμενα πάντα κατ᾽ ἔριν καὶ χρεών

In translating ξυνόν (ksunon) as *bonding*, I followed Frans Casimiri's Dutch translation of ξυνόν as 'verbindend' (https://nl.wikibooks.org/wiki/Heraclitus_over_de_natuur). This translation endorses Heraclitus' reported disapproval of Achilles' oft-cited exclamation at the news of his best friend's death: *"May discord be banished from among gods and men!"* (*Fragments* DK A22; Homer, *Iliad*, Book 18: 107). Postulating an intimate link between conflict and concord is in line with Heraclitus' *Doctrine of the Unity of Opposites*.

In the translation of δίκη (dikè) I opt for the meaning of the term in Heraclitus' days when δίκη referred to behaviour that was 'in accordance with the existing order of things' (Luschnig & Mitchell, 2007:35–36). In the Hellenistic period δίκη became the equivalent of Latin *justitia* 'justice', the term adopted by most translators of the Fragment. For Heraclitus δίκη did not have the moral and legal implications of our concept of justice.

With respect to ἔρις (eris), I capitalise on the full meaning of the word which ranges from a state of conflict, ('fight, battle, contest, rivalry') to the inclination to cause conflict ('incitement, eagerness, zeal, passion, anger') (Valpy, 1860:49–50). In his *Works and Days* Hesiod (ca. 800 BC) who was an unavoidable reference for Heraclitus, understood ἔρις as a compulsion that is at the same time destructive in that it leads to conflict and constructive as it yields prosperity through envious emulation (Hesiod, *Works and Days*, lines 11–24) .

In bringing 'passion', 'rivalry' and 'emulation' together in one concept, Hesiod's ἔρις prefigures René Girard's central concept of *mimesis*.

Second citation: The English word *disaster* is derived from the seventeenth century French word *désastre*, which is composed of the Greek prefix δύσ-(dys-) 'unfavourable' and ἀστηρ (aster) 'star'. Seventeenth century French had a verb corresponding to this noun: *désastrer* which, according to Huguet's dictionary had two meanings:

> I: to place under the influence of an unfavourable star
> II: to protect from the unfavourable influence of stars.

The obsolete French verb offers an adequate summary of the double role of the kings that are the subject of this book.

Contents

Models, Diagrams and Tables

Narratives from Various Sources Serving as Case Histories[1]

1　The first number of the case is the number of the chapter in which the case appears.

Foreword

Mark Anspach

Who is the king of this disaster? That is the question the Lulubo ask whenever a calamity of some kind strikes the village. It could be an invasion of locusts, an outbreak of contagious disease, or a string of attacks on livestock by lions or leopards. Whatever the nature of the misfortune, people want to know who is responsible. The 'king' of the disaster is the individual who will be blamed for maliciously bringing harm to other members of the community. In short, the king is the scapegoat.

Drought is the greatest scourge that can afflict the mountainous region of southeastern Sudan studied by Simon Simonse in this path-breaking work. Since the Rainmaker is thought to possess the power to cause or prevent drought, he is the most important king. Simonse draws on extensive field research and a wealth of archival sources to explore the pivotal role of the Rainmaker in the collective life of the Bari, Lotuho, Pari, Lokoya and Lulubo. This is the first detailed ethnographic portrait of these five Nilotic peoples and also the most systematic and successful attempt to apply the scapegoat theory of René Girard to an anthropological case study.

Girard traces sacred kingship and other ritual institutions to what he calls the scapegoat mechanism. In the face of a crop-destroying drought or other calamity over which people have no direct control, the existence of a scapegoat provides an irreplaceable focal point for collective action. When hunger threatens, tempers fray. An empty stomach will make people bitter and resentful even when no one is responsible. Directing their bitterness at the scapegoat may help keep them from jumping at each other's throats. The scapegoat mechanism defuses internal violence and promotes unity by channeling tension and hostility in a single direction. Although meteorological conditions may be left unchanged, an agreement to blame one person for bad weather might well stabilize the social climate.

Once a Rainmaker has been designated, everyone else can hold that person responsible for an uninterrupted dry spell. The Rainmaker's job is not just to make rain, but to absorb the community's pain when the rain fails and food grows scarce. At the installation ceremony for the Rainmaker of Ngangala, the people tell him, 'We give the bitterness in our stomach to you.' The Rainmaker is destined to bear the brunt of collective resentment when times are bad. Suspicion and accusation will centre on the king. As Simonse demonstrates, this is not merely an occupational hazard of kingship; it is what being king is all about.

In fact, a good king may also be a hated one. To do his job properly, the king should serve as a lightning rod for animosity. Among the Bari, the ability to inspire hatred is one of the virtues ascribed to an admired ruler. Simonse brings out the logic behind this paradoxical attitude. The king transcends the divisions within the community most effectively when he himself stands in opposition to the community as a whole. He unifies his kingdom by uniting his subjects against him. The quintessential king is the enemy of his people.

But the relationship between king and people is in no way a static one. It is an ongoing drama, an ever-shifting balance of power in which threats alternate with propitiatory gestures and each side resorts to a rich array of gambits and stratagems. Simonse brings this delicate ballet to life while introducing a brilliant new twist to the analysis: he shows that the adversarial relationship between king and people is strictly analogous to the adversarial relationship between rival groups in a system of segmentary opposition. Both display a comparable admixture of co-operation and competition, of positive and negative reciprocity, within the same basic framework of mutual antagonism. This means that a single organizing principle can elucidate the operation of both centralist and dualist political systems. Acephalous segmentary societies and those with an assertive central authority turn out to be variations on the same theme. 'In its simplest form,' Simonse writes, 'centralism is only a transformation of dualism with a different cast: one of the social segments is replaced with the king.'

This stunning insight is far-reaching in its consequences. By reducing to a single principle two apparently distinct forms of interaction — that between king and people and that between antagonistic social segments — it lays the basis for something like a unified field theory of African political systems. At the same time, it points the way to understanding the emergence of the state as one possible outcome of a dynamic process, the result of an irreversible shift of the balance of power in the direction of the king. Finally, applied to Girardian theory, the same insight suggests the interchangeability of two alternative scapegoat scenarios: one focused on a central figure such as the Rainmaker, the other entailing a dualist opposition with an enemy group. Modern politicians instinctively grasp this interchangeability; when faced with public wrath at home, their first reflex is often to stir hostilities against an enemy abroad. We never truly leave the shadow of dualism, centralism and the scapegoat king.

It is impossible to overstate the achievement of this book. With an exemplary combination of empirical rigor and theoretical daring, *Kings of Disaster* transforms the landscape of African studies while forcing us to think in new ways about the origins of political power and the state. The hardest thing to do in reflecting on any institution is to break free of the retrospective illusion that it always was what it appears to be today. If we are convinced we already know what a king is, we are likely to assume that a scapegoat king can only be a king who is scapegoated. The figure Simon Simonse describes will be much more surprising to modern Western eyes. In this case the scapegoat's role comes first. The ruler is a scapegoat *before* he is a king.

Simonse's findings lend weight to René Girard's views on African sacred kingship. In his pioneering study *Violence and the Sacred*, Girard defines the African monarch as a victim whose execution has been deferred: 'The king reigns only by virtue of his future death' (1977:107). Simonse characterises the king in similar terms as a 'victim in suspense'. Regicide is not every king's fate. If a monarch's reign is liberally sprinkled with rain, a grateful people will allow him to live out his natural life. This is the optimal outcome for all concerned. Yet 'the possibility of an assault on the king is never completely absent from the minds of his subjects.' It is a 'structural' and 'constitutive' feature of kingship, a dark cloud hovering over the Rainmaker's head. The sentence of death is only suspended for good behavior. Should a drought persist too long and the king stubbornly refuse to deliver the least precipitation, his exasperated subjects will eventually conclude that they have no choice but to lynch him. Simonse has compiled a number of cases, from the 19th century to the 1980s, in which rain kings or queens died at the hands of the collectivity.

The impressive evidence gathered by Simonse for his interpretation of the king as a victim in suspense should lead to a reconsideration of material from elsewhere in Africa. We will confine ourselves here to a single example. In his classic work *The Ritual Process*, Victor Turner quotes a long passage from the 19th-century explorer Paul Du Chaillu's account of the installation of a Gabonese king. The first stage of the 'ceremony' observed by Du Chaillu recalls the dramatic end that awaits an unlucky Sudanese Rainmaker. Having been secretly chosen by the village elders, the king-elect was 'kept ignorant of his good fortune' until the moment when his future subjects launched a surprise attack on him:

> As he was walking on the shore on the morning of the seventh day [after the death of the former king] he was suddenly set upon by the entire populace… They surrounded him in a dense crowd, and then began to heap upon him every manner of abuse that the worst of mobs could imagine. Some spat in his face; some beat him with their fists; some kicked him; others threw disgusting objects at him; while those unlucky ones who stood on the outside, and could reach the poor fellow only with their voices, assiduously cursed him, his father, his mother, his sisters and brothers, and all his ancestors to the remotest generation. A stranger would not have given a cent for the life of him who was presently to be crowned. (Quoted in Turner, 1969:170-71)

This outpouring of collective fury went on for about half an hour. Although the future king's life was spared, it would be misleading to describe the violence of the attack as purely symbolic. The force of the assault may have been calibrated to avoid serious injury, but the blows that rained upon the victim were perfectly real. He was entirely at the mercy of his future subjects.

Victor Turner sees this as a case of 'the temporary reversal of the statuses of rulers and ruled'. He says that Du Chaillu's account illustrates both 'the humbling of a candidate in a rite of status elevation' and 'the power of structural inferiors in a rite of status reversal' (1969:171). This implies that the hierarchical relationship between ruler and ruled is the real phenomenon while the reversal of statuses is merely symbolic. But there is something very paradoxical about interpreting this stage of the Gabonese ritual as an example of status reversal. At the moment the man on the shore was attacked by his fellow villagers, they were not yet ruler and ruled. According to Du

Chaillu, the most vigorous blows were accompanied by the cry, 'You are not our king yet.' How can a status be reversed before it even exists?

Simonse's study suggests an alternative approach: the role of victim comes first. To see the members of the crowd as the structural inferiors of their victim is an optical illusion produced by the future radiance of the king. In reality, the power of life or death originally lies with the collectivity. If it chose to finish off the recipient of its blows, the victim would be too helpless to resist. This bare material fact must be the starting point for any objective analysis. At first, the crowd holds all the cards; it has its way with the victim before ultimately ceding power to him. This is the reversal that needs to be explained. Why should people submit to the authority of a poor wretch whom they seemingly wanted to beat within an inch of his life? The real mystery is the dramatic elevation in the victim's status that follows the near-lynching.

One key to the mystery is the unanimous participation of the 'entire populace'. Everyone joined together in directing their antagonism at the victim simultaneously. René Girard contends that any such ritual of collective violence is modeled on long-ago actual lynchings that allowed the members of a strife-torn group to reconcile themselves with one another by unanimously venting their hostilities on a common scapegoat. The scapegoat thus became the source of social consensus, to use the term adopted by Simonse. The apparently miraculous role it played in restoring harmony led to its posthumous apotheosis. Later sacrificial rituals reenact the same event, replacing the original scapegoat with substitute victims who inherit its glory.

Indeed, so lofty is the victim's status that the community may eventually hesitate to put it to death. There will be a tendency to sacrifice lesser victims in place of the most important one. Over time, Girard suggests, those who play the central part in the ritual may succeed in postponing indefinitely the moment of their own execution, gradually parlaying the prestige associated with their role into a real power over the community (1978c:61– 62). In the installation rites of sacred kingship, ontogenesis displays the traces of phylogenesis, giving us a chance to witness first-hand the metamorphosis of victim into ruler.

The different Rainmakers studied by Simonse would appear to be located at points about half-way along the path hypothesised by Girard. Among these Nilotic peoples the king's status is still in flux. The relationship between ruler and ruled has not yet crystallized into the permanent structural imbalance posited by Victor Turner; it see-saws back and forth, now favoring one side, now the other in a politico-ritual arena where the sacred embodiment of central authority is but one pole in an unending dualist confrontation. Simonse shows how a savvy Rainmaker can play to his best advantage the cards he is dealt, but the end of the game will ultimately depend on the weather. Sooner or later, a dearth of rain leads to a reverse metamorphosis of ruler into victim.

Simonse's richly textured ethnographic account confirms many key tenets of Girard's scapegoat theory, from the recourse to sacrifice of substitute victims as a means of forestalling regicide to the preference for methods allowing unanimous participation once the effective killing of the king can no longer be avoided. But the lynching, when it comes, does not resolve the crisis. Unlike the natural death of a king, it is perceived as a deeply inauspicious event. Girard foresees the possibility that the good and evil aspects of victimage may be divided from each other in like fashion through a secondary elaboration. Nevertheless, Simonse's phenomenological description of the victimary process and its aftermath does not fully correspond to what a familiarity with Girard's ideas might lead one to expect. According to Simonse, it is the anticipation of collective murder and not the event itself that exercises a unifying effect. A feeling of *suspense* is a defining feature of the drama.

Suspense regarding the outcome of the high-stakes confrontation with the Rainmaker is the engine that keeps the group moving forward as it navigates its uncertain way through a crisis provoked by drought. In such a context, actually going through with the murder can bring only a fleeting release of tension that solves nothing. Unless a sudden downpour ensues, the crisis is bound to continue, this time without the central figure of the king to provide a focal point for collective action. The ruler's death will be anti-climactic if its sole result is the dissipation of suspense.

The concept of suspense does not simply add an interesting new wrinkle to the scapegoat theory. In the last analysis, it makes the hypothesis of a victimary origin of kingship considerably more plausible. As imagined by René Girard, the leap from victim to ruler remains somewhat mysterious. It is not at all clear how the transition would play out in practice. How could a scapegoat postpone his own lynching long enough to convert his sacred status into temporal power?

Here Simon Simonse fills in the blanks, not only by detailing the nuts-and-bolts political maneuvering of Nilotic Rainmakers, but also by showing that *the community itself may have an interest in deferring the collective murder as long as possible.* If maintaining suspense is an essential unifying factor, then one understands why everyone might collude in keeping the scapegoat alive, thus opening up a decisive interval for the progressive transformation of victim into king.

Acknowledgments to the First Edition

First of all I want to express thanks to the University of Juba for giving me the opportunity to do fieldwork alongside my teaching duties, and to the Netherlands Foundation for Research of the Tropics (WOTRO), for generously financing this research for a period of two and a half years.

I thank Prof. Dr A. Abu-Zayd and drs. Erik van der Sleen for having encouraged me to come to Juba and leave my teaching job in Amsterdam.

I am indebted to Prof. Dr K.K. Prah, Prof. Dr A. Kuper and Prof. Dr W.M.J. van Binsbergen for encouraging me to go ahead during the preparatory stages of this research, and to Prof. Dr J.M. Schoffeleers for not allowing me to lose momentum.

I have greatly benefited from the comments of Prof. Dr J.M. Schoffeleers, Prof. Dr P.L. Geschiere, and Prof. Dr A.F. Droogers who worked their way through a rather dense, largely unfinished manuscript and gave valuable suggestions for the improvement of its accessibility.

I am especially grateful to Roel Kaptein for deepening my understanding of René Girard's thought and for his generous, penetrating and refreshing attention to my text. I thank Bert van de Hoek for his enthusiastic comments drawn from a different Nilotic experience.

On the longer term I owe a debt to my teachers in Leiden, especially to Prof. Dr De Josselin de Jong who taught me that anthropology is about explaining cultural facts, a lesson to which I have tried to remain faithful in this dissertation.

Many people have helped me in the field and it is impossible to mention them all. I thank Paride Lado Tongun Lualla, Chief of the Lulubo, for introducing me to his people and for offering me hospitality in the early stages of my fieldwork; Pio Lado Okollo for adopting me into his lineage and associating me with his rain; and Lomini for tolerating my inquisitiveness.

I was sad when I received the message that on 17 February 1988 Chief Lolik Lado had died. I am grateful for the many hours I have spent with this exceptional man who has been an inspiring example for his people and, within the limits imposed on him, a wise statesman of the southern Sudan, from the days of imperial pacification, through the colonial heydays and the first civil war, right into the present troubles.

I am grateful to the members of the Lulubo Tribe Development Committee, especially to Mr Eluzai Mogga and Mr Vitalyano Wani, for the moral and practical support they have given to my research. I hope they will forgive me for having made them share 'their book' with neighbouring peoples.

From the many men who have let me into their lives in Lokiliri I only mention my friend Tombe Kenyi. I hope he, and the others, are well.

I thank Mr Valeryano Orrege and Mr Vitale Aburi for giving their precious time to the historical expert sessions on Lotuho dynastic history they were so kind to arrange during a period of great hardship in Juba.

I offer thanks to Chief Sebit Bedden, Mr Philip Yenkoji and Mr Epiphanio Wani who gave me valuable help in collecting information on the dynastic histories of the Bari, and to Matat Pompeio Lado for teaching me about his rainmaking art, and especially for arranging that wonderful shower on a cloudless day in March 1981 when he received me on my first field trip.

My work could not have been carried out without the help of interpreters. I owe a lot to *turjuman* Israel Lado Busei who helped me in communicating with speakers of four different languages. He was a meticulous worker, always critical of the reliability of the information that was being dished out to us and sincerely dedicated to the preservation of Lulubo traditions.

Israel Lado Busei, whose work as a research assistant from 1981–1986 contributed much to this book, died tragically on 12 December 2009.

Adriano Jacob Ohirek's enthusiasm for his work as a translator was contagious. I have good memories of the days spent together in the Lokoya villages.

I thank Toby Martyrio for introducing me to the Lotuho and the Pari. I hope Trueman and Freeman will live up to the expectations expressed in their names.

Peter Duku Wani has assisted me in interpreting from Bari to English from my first field trip in March 1981 until my unforeseen departure in 1986. I am grateful for his conscientious work and lasting pleasant companionship.

I thank Mr Venansio Ongom for his resourceful assistance in the Uganda National Archives, especially for the information forwarded after my departure from Entebbe, and Father Franceschini and Mrs Lesley Forbes for their efficient help in the Comboni Archives in Rome and in the Sudan Archives of the Oriental Library in Durham respectively.

Mrs Domenica Ghidei, Mr Con Obura Bartel and Mr Bol Deng Chol gave excellent help in translating archival texts from Italian, Lotuho and Arabic respectively.

With Eisei Kurimoto I have shared most of the uncertainties that surrounded my fieldwork. I feel fortunate for having found a friend like him. His sober empiricism was often a good antidote to my more speculative leanings. Much of the data on the Pari stems from him, or has passed his critical eye. I am especially grateful to him for translating and allowing me to publish part of his article in Japanese on the regicide case in Lafon.

I express my warm appreciation to Ydo Jacobs for his help in keeping some of my research activities going after my departure, for forwarding my fieldnotes, and above all for his genial cynicism about my academic pursuits.

I thank my colleagues in the Research Centre of Sriwijaya University in Palembang, especially Dr Zainab Bakir, for 'dosaging' my workload in such a way that I could finish my manuscript.

Mercedes, however great the contributions of all of these people, it was you who created the environment needed to get the job done—thank you.

Palembang, March 1990

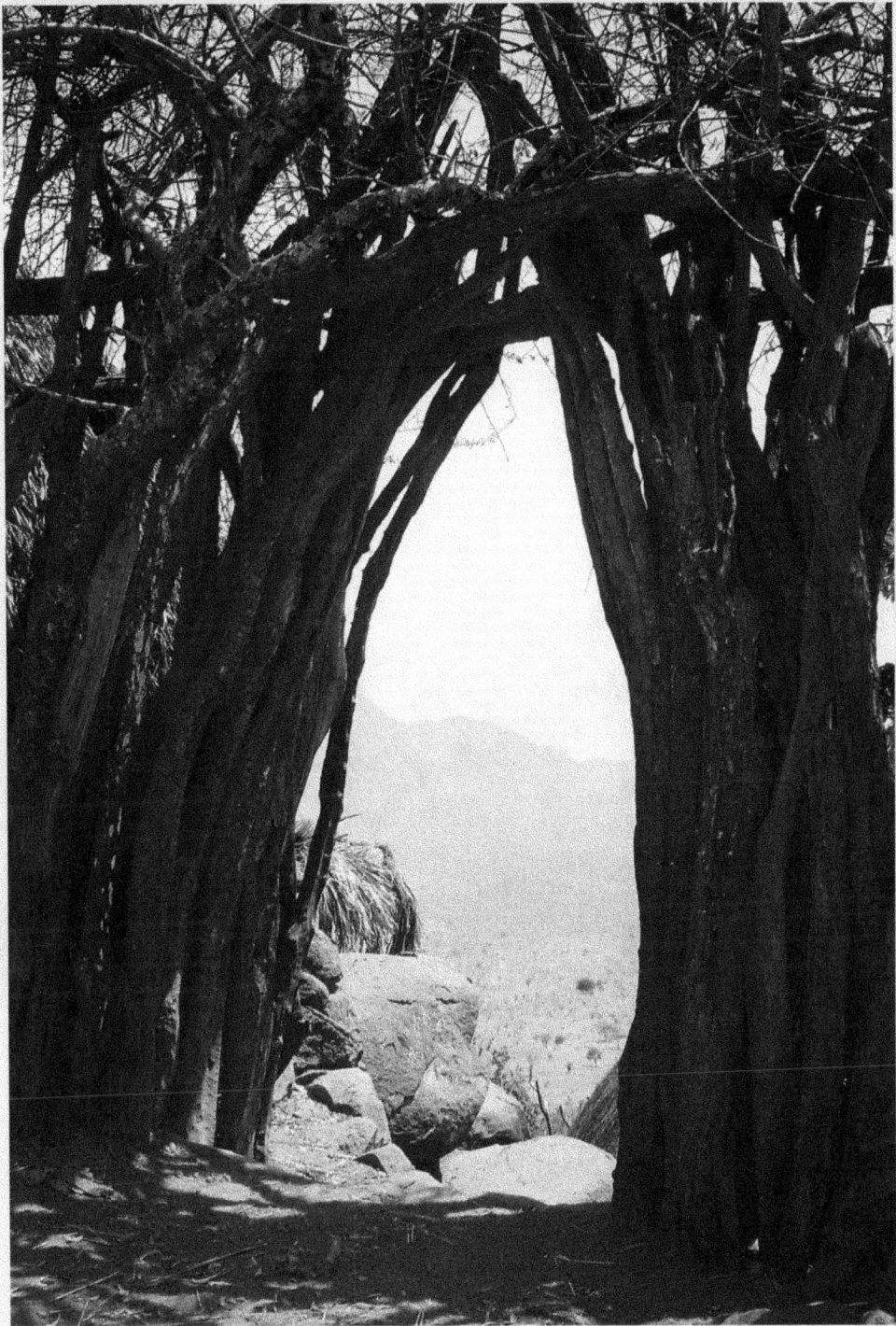

"No country presents such a field to a philosopher as this country does."
Charles Gordon, Governor of Equatoria 1873–1876, commenting on the Bari
(G.B. Hill, 1881: 100).

Lopit village

Introduction

The aim of this study

Most recent studies on African political systems have been guided by two methodological premises. The first is the dichotomy between the sacred and the political dimension of power as separate fields of investigation. The second is the dichotomy between systems with centralised authority or 'states' and acephalous, segmentary political systems. Both methodological dualisms were set out as guidelines for research by Fortes and Evans-Pritchard in their introduction to *African Political Systems* (1940:1–23), a work which has in many ways been programmatic for political anthropological research in Africa.

Although the work done from this perspective has resulted in a rich harvest of new insights into the political aspect of African social order — which had been obscured by the unilateral emphasis on the symbolic and the divine by the school of Frazer — the contention of this book is that these insights provide us with but a partial view of the operation of power in African political systems. They postulate an unbridgeable gap between centralised and non-centralised systems, and obscure the intimate connection between the sacred and the political dimension of power in African polities.

This study departs from that now-hoary tradition. I attempt to develop an angle of observation of African political systems in which this double dichotomy is suspended, which allows us to see the common ground from which central authority and segmentary competition emerge, and grasp the interrelatedness of power, consensus and the sacred in the institution of kingship.

The nature of the polities in the Nilotic Sudan which I investigated in the field between 1981 and 1986 compelled me to look for such a theory. The way political power was socially embedded in these societies baffled the two methodological premises mentioned above. While the societies I studied had kings, it would be misleading to describe them as 'states'. Their kings were far from possessing a monopoly of the legitimate use of physical force. Kingship itself often seemed a plaything of forces similar to those which regulate social order in segmentary societies. Although central power in these societies was defined as 'rain', i.e. in a symbolic way, it was the object of intense political rivalry. The inseparability of the sacred and the political was particularly manifest in the way regicide — that 'most mystical' dimension of divine kingship, according to the Frazerians — was practised. In the instances that I investigated, this highly sacralising act was the outcome of a series of public decisions, that is, of a political process.

The theory which I am offering as an instrument to elucidate these facts derives from the ideas of the French thinker, René Girard. His fundamental assumption is that social consensus is based on shared antagonism to a third party. In its most

3

elementary dramatic form, the joint antagonism expresses itself as the aggression of a lynching mob against its victim. The consensual mechanism coincides with the transfer of potential or actual violence inside the group to a victim placed outside it. As a result of this transfer, the victim acquires a positive quality and may eventually turn into a symbol of the group's unity and identity. According to Girard's theory, the power of the king derives from his identification as a public scapegoat.

The idea that the king is a scapegoat is by no means new. It is one of the main themes of Frazer's *The Golden Bough*. The idea that social consensus and scapegoating are two sides of the same coin is not new either. As a common sense notion, most of us are familiar with it. In sociology, the idea is common currency in the sociology of deviant behaviour and the study of race relations. The combination of the two ideas into the systematic theory of sacred kingship presented here, however, is a novelty.

To be able to see the connection between the victimary dimension of kingship and the generation of consensus, we have to define a new angle of observation and analysis from which the interactions corresponding to Girard's scapegoat mechanism become visible. This angle is not provided by the current approaches to the study of African kingship. These either study the facts synchronically, as elements of a system existing at a particular moment of time, or historically, as part of long-term processes of change. To establish the kind of coherence that is postulated by Girard's scapegoat mechanism, we need to observe recurrent processes of interaction between the king and his subjects, and to analyse these interactions or 'dramas' we require a kind of model that describes a regular pattern that unfolds over time: a scenario.[1] If one adopts a system-oriented approach, one is inevitably forced to choose between two levels of coherence within which to study the empirical facts: the symbolic level or the political level. The alternative focus on either of these defines two clearly distinguishable groups of researchers: the political and the symbolic anthropologists. The former group includes scholars working in the structural-functional tradition of *African Political Systems* and those drawing from a Marxist inspiration. These study the symbolic aspect of kingship as a means to legitimise claims to power.

For the symbolic anthropologists, power is a corollary of the association with or possession of sacred symbols. The symbolic approach to kingship, which draws on a Frazerian inspiration and was therefore considered outmoded for some decades, is undergoing a swift rejuvenation as a result of an injection with structuralist comparative methodology. The study of the symbols of kingship among the Bantu carried out by De Heusch (1981, 1984, 1985), is an impressive step forward in our understanding of the symbolic aspect of kingship among the Bantu. Still, in both systemic approaches the level of meaning and that of the distribution of power remain

---

1   Processual models have been used in the study of conflict settlement (Comaroff & Roberts, 1981:11ff; Swartz, Turner & Tuden (eds.), 1966: Introduction; Turner, 1957) and in the study of ritual (Turner, 1969).

external to one another. The king is either a politician who cleverly manipulates sacred symbols, or a ritual or theatrical puppet.

Other studies, carried out from a historical perspective, are not hampered by these straightjackets. Here, too, important advances have been made, again mainly in the field of Bantu studies (Willis, 1981; Van Binsbergen, 1992). Yet the temporal framework within which events are placed in these studies is long-term. The interactions between king and people that we need to study — power contests, conflicts over rain and drought, collective assaults on the king and reconciliations between king and people — have a more short-term character and are not cumulative. The coherence of these interactions cannot be studied by a systemic approach and they fall outside the scope of the historian.

This book intends to show that when we study kingship as an ongoing drama in which the king, the different sections of the society, enemies and rivals are the main protagonists, fixed patterns emerge that correspond to the scapegoat mechanism postulated by René Girard. Defined as a 'scenario', this mechanism will help us to account, in a single model, for the political and the symbolic dimension of kingship.

Secondly, I intend to demonstrate that analysis by means of the same victimary scenario enables us to describe political systems based on complementary segmentary opposition and those based on central authority as transformations of a single underlying structure.

The testing ground for this approach is formed by a number of neighbouring ethnic communities in the southeastern Sudan on the east bank of the Nile. Most of these communities speak languages of the Eastern Nilotic family, notably Bari and Lotuho, and dialects of these. One feature that distinguishes these polities from others in that part of Africa is the coexistence of an age-class system and institutions of central authority. I have used this feature as the main criterion to delimit my area of study.

This is the first systematic study dealing with these polities, despite their evident originality and the fact that anthropological studies of the political institutions of other Nilotic peoples have often functioned as eye-openers in the development of the discipline.[2]

The evidence produced in this study is drawn from some twenty political units and has a comparative character. For the study of kingship, a comparative approach proves particularly appropriate. While most social institutions define many individual relationships, which can be studied as cumulative evidence of the nature of the institution, kingship defines one relationship at a time only: that between a people and its king. While no social scientist would think of basing a study of marriage on investigations carried out on a single couple, in the field of kingship studies, this sort

---

2   The information received from Seligman on Shilluk kingship played a decisive role in the development of Frazer's idea of divine kingship (Frazer, 1913, Part III: 14–33). Evans-Pritchard's work on the Nuer (1940b) was a breakthrough in the study of acephalous political systems, while his and Lienhardt's studies of the Anuak political system (Evans-Pritchard 1940c; Lienhardt, 1957 & 1958a) shed new light on the nature of African kingship.

of thing has been done frequently. Although the information collected on different kingdoms in our field of study is necessarily unequal in depth and detail, the variation in the cultural forms of kingship in different societies has allowed me to penetrate to a more fundamental level of coherence in the phenomena studied.

By taking a well-defined 'anthropological field of study' as my point of departure, I place myself in a tradition of research that has been particularly cherished at the University of Leiden, where I received my training.[3] The societies selected fulfil, I believe, the requirements needed to be considered an 'anthropological field of study'. Although the field I have staked out is relatively small, it shows a rich blend of resemblances and differences, quite enough to embark upon fruitful comparison.

The evidence presented is partly first-hand ethnographic material, partly written material from published and unpublished sources. Fieldwork was carried out during different periods between 1981 and 1986 while I was lecturing at the University of Juba. My most intensive field experience was in Lokiliri (Lulubo) where I had a second house. I also carried out extensive field trips in most of Eastern Equatoria Province, from the villages of the Avukaya in Yei River District in the west to the Toposa of Kapoeta District in the east. During periods when my teaching duties or the security situation in the field kept me in Juba, I conducted interviews with informants of different ethnic groups, most of which had sizeable migrant communities in Juba.

Archival research was carried out in the Southern Records Office in Juba, in the Central Records Office in Khartoum, in the Uganda National Archives in Entebbe (the research area was part of the Uganda Protectorate from 1898 to 1914), in the Sudan Archives of the Oriental Library in Durham, and in the Comboni Archive in Rome, where the manuscripts of Missionary Fathers A. Pazzaglia and C. Muratori proved to contain valuable information on the Lotuho kingship. Published written documents were obtained from all over Europe through the help of the Interlibrary Loan Desk of the Free University of Amsterdam.

The plan of the book

The book is divided into four parts. The first part provides a more precise formulation of the theoretical problem to which the book is meant to contribute and of the social setting addressed. The first chapter discusses the victimary theory of consensus and its possible application to the study of sacred kingship. It assesses Girard's victimary thesis from a sociological perspective and shows some of its advantages in relation to the major anthropological and sociological schools of thought. Next I systematise and elaborate his thesis in such a way that it suits the needs of the analysis that I want to carry out. Three models articulating the relationship between violence, consensus,

---

3   The founding statement of this methodology is the inaugural lecture of J. P. B. de Josselin de Jong in 1935 'The Malay Archipelago as an Ethnological Field of Study'. The lecture, together with studies applying the method, was included in P.E. de Josseling de Jong, 1977; see also Kuper, 1977, 1982; Ridder & Karremans, 1987; Claessen. 1988.

and the sacred are formulated, each of which corresponds to definite forms of social organisation.

The second chapter presents the peoples which constitute the anthropological field of study. It provides an overview of the various ethnic groupings and their principal cultural and linguistic similarities and differences. Chapter Three provides basic background information: on the livelihood of the people, their settlement pattern and their political and social organisation.

Chapters Four, Five and Six offer a summary history of the major events and changes in the kingship institutions of the peoples studied, from their first contacts with the wider world up to the present time. A comparison is made regarding the way in which the peoples reacted to the imposition of foreign rule. According to their political organisation, three groups are distinguished: the Bari (Chapter Four), the Lotuho (Chapter Five) and the Pari, Lulubo and Lokoya (Chapter Six). The historical accounts are only meant to serve as background information. For this reason, and because of limits of space, no attempt is made to interpret accounts relating to earlier periods and to other aspects of socio-political evolution.

The historical information contained in this book is not limited to these introductory chapters. Accounts of past events occur in other parts of the book as well. These are, if at all feasible, recognisably formatted as numbered and named case histories. A list of these cases has been appended.

Parts II, III and IV each treat one of the main aspects of the central argument of this study. Part II, *Dualism*, describes and analyses the political organisation of the peoples of the Equatorian east bank of the Nile in terms of what I call the enemy scenario. Chapter Seven is an analysis of the political relations at different territorial levels (regional, village and village-section). Chapter Eight applies the same analysis to the age organisation.

The first two chapters (Nine and Ten) of Part III, *Centralism*, argue the structural similarity of the relationship between king and people and that between dualistically opposed groups. Chapter Eleven reviews the economic and political strategies at the king's disposal to strengthen his power *vis-à-vis* his subjects. Marxists and structural-functionalists maintain that economic and military power is the 'basis' of the king's position which, in a second movement, is legitimised by a 'symbolic superstructure'. My conclusion in this connection is quite the reverse: economic and military institutions function to reinforce the king's position in a pre-existing balance of power, such that the king wins a more or less permanent ascendancy over his people.

Processes of territorial expansionism and fragmentation are examined in Chapter Twelve. The result of both processes in my field of study are two typical sizes of territorial scope of political units: in the mountainous areas polities are limited to a single conglomeration or to a string of settlements on or around the same mountain, and in the plains there are much vaster territorial units comprising a larger number of villages.

The king's divinity, which is defined by his power over disaster, is the subject of Chapter Thirteen. A comparison is drawn between the Lokoya and Lulubo, on one side, and the Bari and Lotuho, on the other. Among the former, the powers to shield the community from disaster are divided over a large number of offices, while among the latter most of these powers are concentrated in one office, that of the king. Chapter Fourteen examines the symbols that express the oneness of kingship: the rainstones and the Rain Queen. Both are shown to play a central role in the rivalry over the succession.

The last chapter of Part III shows how dualism resurges within centralist political organisation in the form of dynastic rivalry. Taking the well-known Nilotic story of *The Bead and the Spear* as a starting point, two case histories are presented that show how opposed dynastic factions have a destructive polarising effect on the communities they are supposed to unite.

While Part III can be said to focus on the antagonism emanating from the king in the direction of his people, Part IV, *The Scapegoat King*, concentrates on the other side of this oppositional relationship: popular antagonism directed against the king. Chapter Sixteen, *The King as Victim in Suspense*, describes the confrontationist character of the relationship between king and people. In this power contest with his subjects, the king uses his cosmic power to punish his subjects, while his subjects use appeasement and force in order to press the king to relent and to release the cosmic blessings expected from him. If these blessings are not forthcoming, the antagonism between king and people escalates and passing through successive stages of increasing suspense and violence culminates in regicide — the subject of Chapter Seventeen. Chapter Eighteen offers an interpretation of royal installation, funeral and exhumation ceremonies in the light of the victimary scenario. The last chapter answers the question why rain plays such a preponderant role in the symbolism of central power in our area of study. Through the analysis of different mythical and ritual themes, I show how rain, as a symbolic element, is part of a cosmology centred on the opposition between peace and violence. Rain is a metaphor of the human disposition that allows people to live together without violence. The chapter ends with a discussion of the digestive symbolism of the process by which violence is converted into order.

A note on terminology: *kings, chiefs, masters, rainmakers*

Some may find it inappropriate that I use the term *king* for men who control only a few villages, or just a single village. They may want to reserve this title for rulers governing more numerous populations and vaster territories. These same readers would probably not hesitate to accord the distinction of the royal title to the pre-colonial rulers of the Bari and the Lotuho, just as the early travellers to the area did.

I have decided to use the word *king* throughout, because this word expresses, better than any other, the idea of sovereignty, which is a defining characteristic of the pre-colonial Nilotic king in relation to his following, whatever its size. In so doing I take Hocart's advice into account:

> If a distinction is to be made it must be based on the whole structure, because the structure reflects the meaning; not on an accident such as the extent of square miles ruled, or the size of the civil list (A.M. Hocart, 1970:86).

The main alternative in the English language: *chief,* has acquired the connotation of a local-level official whose authority depends both on a long-standing connection with his subjects and on recognition by a more powerful, encompassing, state. The idea of sovereignty is absent. I shall reserve this term for the grass-roots government official whom the people in the area of study refer to as the *government chief.*

The other alternative to *king* which has gained wide currency in studies on central authority in the southern Sudan is the term *Rainmaker* — in colonial days often written with a capital 'R' a convention I have followed. It has the disadvantage of too narrowly focusing on one of the cosmological attributes of the ruler and giving these a distinctly magical flavour. I use the term *Rainmaker* for persons believed to have power over rain, but whose following need not include an entire community, or who perform their duties on behalf of a more powerful *Rainmaker* or king elsewhere. The sovereignty of the kings has been usurped by the modern state and their political power on the local level has shifted to the government chief. Their position still has a political element in the rare places where they serve as government chiefs. Weighing these different considerations, I have chosen to refer to the contemporary descendants of the old royal families who have been selected by their communities to take care of the 'rain' as *Rainmakers* and call only kings those persons who combine juridical and administrative responsibilities within the modern state with the inherited ritual responsibility for rain.

Apart from the *kings of rain*, sometimes called *kings of heaven*, the societies on the east bank of the Nile have a whole range of other office-holders who are also invested with cosmological powers and who, in some cases, may be addressed with the same title as the king. The various blessings and disasters over which they exercise power include: the fertility of the soil, health in man and beast, epidemics, plagues of insects, birds and monkeys, safety from attacks by predatory animals, and so on. These controllers of disaster will be referred to as *Masters* — adding the attribute they are believed to control: *Master of Leopards, Master of the Land, Master (also Mistress) of the Mountain*, and so on.

Technical notes

On spelling:

c	is realised as *ch* in English *ch*arm
h	is a glottal fricative realised as Arabic *kha* in *Kh*artoum, or *g* in Dutch *goed*
ö	a Bari vowel, as *ö* in German k*ö*nnen, or *u* in English l*u*st
ny	as in French Espa*gn*e
'b	is an implosive voiced bilabial consonant
'd	is an implosive voiced dental consonant

My untimely repatriation prevented the completion of a comparative cultural vocabulary of Bari, Lokoya, Lotuho, Acholi, Madi, Lulubo and Pari — a joint plan by Eisei Kurimoto, who carried out anthropological fieldwork on the Pari, Torben Andersen, a specialist of Nilotic and Central Sudanic languages, and myself. Only Bari has a generally accepted spelling and an accessible dictionary (Spagnolo, 1960), which I have adopted in this book. Lotuho has at least two rival spellings. Muratori's English-Bari-Lotuxo-Acoli Vocabulary uses obsolete spelling and is impractical and incomplete. The Lulubo, Lokoya and Pari languages have not been developed for writing. The transcriptions of local terms offered are, therefore, far from perfect, especially as regards the distinction between open and closed vowels.

PART I

The Problem and the Setting

The pole-shrine and ceremonial ground of Mura-Hatiha

"Religion *in its broadest sense, then, must be another term for that obscurity that surrounds man's efforts to defend himself by curative or preventative means against his own violence.*"

(René Girard, 1977, p. 23)

The villages of the communities discussed in this book have a variety of public spaces: meeting points with benches in wood or stone for debate, bamboo platforms for conversation and relaxation, as well as spacious grounds for ritual and festive occasions. The photo shows a square with meeting facilities of one of the sections of Ilyeu, Lotuho.

1

The King: Focus of Suspense, Lever of Consensus and Inventor of the State

Girard's scapegoat mechanism

Before touching on ethnographic material a brief presentation of the model of the scapegoat mechanism is necessary. The scapegoat mechanism is a corollary of Girard's mimetic anthropology.[1] The cornerstone of this approach is the idea that human behaviour is essentially imitative, motivated by *mimesis*. Human knowledge and the ways of acquiring knowledge, human desires and ambitions originate in the imitation of the knowledge, desires, ambitions, etc. of others and not in natural instincts or in the individual psyche. There is a direct connection between the mimetic character of human motivation and man's propensity for conflict. Since imitation also governs the choice of the object of individual desire, the desiring person inevitably manoeuvres him-or herself into situations which lead to conflict with the model.

This situation in which the individual is torn between two contradictory imperatives, one saying "Imitate me!" and the other "Never imitate me in what I want and who I am!" constitutes a *double bind* which no socialisation process can avoid. Girard has borrowed the concept from the anthropologist Gregory Bateson but gives it a wider application than the Palo Alto school that Bateson inspired (Bateson, 1958 & 1972; Girard, 1978:316–319). In Girard's view, the double bind defines the human condition. Social life begins in conflict and the primary challenge for human societies is to reduce its destructive potential. This, according to Girard, is what religion is about. Like Durkheim, Girard attributes a central role to religion in the constitution of society.[2] At the heart of religion are two complementary operations that deal with the destructive potential of the mimetic process and transform it into a socially cohesive force. The first builds on the conflictual and ultimately violent dynamism of the mimetic process by allowing it to run its full course in a controlled environment, while the second pre-empts mimetic escalation and redirects its conflict potential into a togetherness that is characterised by peaceful sharing.

---

1   Girard's own work is the best introduction to his anthropology, especially *Violence and the Sacred* (1977), *Things Hidden since the Foundation of the World* (1987), *The Scapegoat* (1989) and *Evolution and Conversion* (2008). Girard's contribution to Hamerton-Kelly (ed.), *Violent origins* (1987:73–145) is a good summary of the ideas that concern us in this study.

2   Girard acknowledges this Durkheimian influence in various passages in his work, e.g. 1977:306–7; 1987:43, 63, 82. For epistemological parallels between the two scholars see: Livingston, 'La démystification et l'histoire chez Girard et Durkheim', in Dumouchel (ed.), 1985:191–200).

In the first operation, mimetic rivalry is left to escalate and intensify to a violent climax. During this crisis, the general discontent and disorder converge against an enemy or scapegoat who is blamed for the intolerable situation. Collective aggression discharges itself in a single mimetic drive against a shared victim. The unanimity generated in the act of collective aggression gives a sense of relief to the group which discovers that it is now no longer divided. When later faced with another crisis the group will reproduce the effect of deliverance from violence. Reproduction of the act by which divisiveness is transformed into unity is the core of all religious ritual.

In the second operation, violence is forestalled; and mimetic rivalry is redirected into non-violent channels. The potentially violent, mimetically reinforced competition for the possession of a desired object is brought to a halt by a sudden awareness of the threat of violence, and of the absolute need to stop. The arrested desires and the aborted competition make the object of attraction free for a new way of jointly enjoying it. Competition for the object is replaced by its non-violent distribution and consumption. This operation is the basis for all taboos. These two ways of resolving mimetic conflict correspond to Durkheim's categories of *negative* and *positive* rites (1976:297–350), a dichotomy also used by Girard: "The things you must not do are called *prohibitions* and the things you must do are called *rituals*" (Hamerton-Kelly, 1987:9).

Both ways of dealing with mimetic tension can be modelled as dramas, sequences of interaction between groups or individuals that bring about a change in the nature of the relationship between the groups and individuals involved. The models are *diachronic* and are best rendered as the unfolding of a story with a beginning and an end. Girard uses the words *scene* and *scenario* for this narrative model, probably in imitation of the Freudians who refer to their primeval event as a *scene*, a *drama* or a *tragedy*. The first, and in Girard's conception most fundamental of these models, is the *scapegoat mechanism*.

A.	The scapegoat mechanism
1.	*mimetic rivalry* escalating into a violent *crisis*;
2.	*polarisation* of the violence driven by *antagonistic mimesis,* turning rivalling individuals into symmetric *doubles,* effacing social differences and, ultimately, pitting the group as a whole against a single member or minority;
3.	the *transference* of the discontent in the group onto the targeted other resulting in his or her *negative transfiguration*;
4.	the *elimination* of the thus designated victim in a collective mimetic drive in which the group experiences a new sense of unity and a relief from internal violence; and
5.	the *transference* of this sense of unity and relief onto the eliminated victim, bringing about its *positive transfiguration*.

The process accounted for by this five-step model is self-regulatory[3]: a crisis unfolds, escalates and is resolved without intervention by extraneous factors. Because of the self-contained, inescapable way in which the process unfolds, Girard speaks of a *mechanism*. A similar sequence of interactions was, according to René Girard, the course of events that led to the emergence of modern humans. Exactly how the mechanism developed over time is an open question. It is worth emphasising that Girard never envisaged the collective murder as a single event — as Freud did and as some of Girard's interpreters do — but as a frequent occurrence during the early stages of our development as a species.[4]

Girard then makes it plausible that this five-step sequence is, first, the *model for ritual action*. In ritual the community, or rather, the individuals wanting to establish or restore their community, repeat the above sequence in order to obtain the deliverance from violence and the achievement of communal peace.

The combined effect of the negative and positive transfiguration of the victim is what students of religion know as *the sacred*. Its ambivalence, the mysterious fact that the sacred is both dangerous and beneficial — which has long been noted as one of the defining characteristics of the sacred (Otto, 1917; Caillois, 1950) — is now given a straightforward explanation by the scapegoat mechanism.

Sacrifice, according to Girard, is nothing but a repetition of this original scenario. It is 'the production of the sacred' (corresponding to the literal meaning of the Latin word *sacrificium*).[5] It consists of a process in which the negative sentiments in the group are elicited and projected on a human being, animal or object that is cast away. The success of the sacrificial operation depends on the amount of social negativity the victim captures as it is eliminated. The more forceful and generalised the negative transference, the more radiant and convincing the positive transfiguration of the victim.

The victimary model offers, secondly, a *model of representation*, i.e. a model for organising social experience cognitively. To the group involved in the collective act of expulsion, the victim signifies the return of consensus. The victim, its substitute (name, emblems, totem) or what remains of it (the body, the tomb) functions as the *signifier* for the power that has saved the community from destruction. This power, says Girard, is the essence of the sacred. The sacred is fundamentally ambivalent

---

3   A discussion of this aspect of the theory is found in Dupuy, 1982:125–184 and in several of the contributions to the Stanford International Symposium 'Disorder and Order' (Livingston, ed., 1984).

4   In a conference in 1983 Girard is quick to correct Burkert's allusion to the collective murder as something that "happened once". Girard says: "The collective murder I am talking about must be regarded as a 'normal' occurrence in pre-human and human groups during the whole pre-history of our species and some of its history as well. My idea is that violent forms of so-called scapegoating must put an end to a kind of intraspecific fighting that is normal, too, during the same stages of human development, but so intense and deadly that it would make human culture impossible if there were nothing to interrupt it" (Burkert, Girard & Smith, 1987:121).

5   The Latin word *sacrificium* is derived from Latin *sacer* (sacred) and *facere* (to make).

since in the positive transfiguration of the victim the negative charge is not nullified. Collective attention for the victim is the precondition for the elaboration of all other cultural signs, linguistic as well as aesthetic. Accordingly, Girard defines the victim as the *transcendental signifier* (1978:108–113).

Implicit in the community's ritual reproduction and mythical representation of the victimary event are three fundamental organising principles:

B.   Fundamental ordering principles deriving from the scapegoat mechanism

- *before* and *after*:
  the miraculous transformation from a condition of intolerable violence to a state of salutary peace confronts the human group with its first question of causality. The awareness of the transformative role of the victim is the anthropological backdrop for all later causal connections and the condition for the human faculty of establishing causality;

- *inside* and *outside*:
  the inside is the sphere that has been purged of violence by means of the elimination of the victim while the outside is the sphere to which the violence has been driven out and where the victim in its negative and positive transfiguration dwells ; the opposition between inside and outside is a fundamental structuring device in group formation and intergroup perception;

- *good* and *evil*:
  the contrast between the intolerable violence before the elimination of the victim and the experience of peacefulness afterwards generates the distinction between good and evil, the precondition for all moral and ethical notions.

In the third place, the scapegoat mechanism provides a *model of social organisation*. Although Girard explicitly includes social organisation in the range of phenomena to which his theory applies (1972:305–345), he hardly elaborates on this aspect. In the passages in his work on kingship, no distinction is made between kingship as a form of political organisation and kingship as ritual. Political power is treated as a mere spin-off of ritual action. Social organisation and ritual are different in important respects. Ritual is a form of collective symbolic action that reproduces and reinforces the cohesion of already existing groups. Social organisation is about the way relationships between groups and segments of groups are structured and about the division of roles between these groups and individuals.

Girard's victimary model is silent about the social organisation of proto-humans before the first eruptions of mimetic crisis. It figures a single group that suffers endemic conflict and that by arbitrarily picking on one its members (an individual or a sub-group) and driving him or her out, finds peace. The proto-humans, however, were not clean slates. Like other primates, they must have lived in territorial groups that were in contact with other groups. Recent primatological research shows that demonstrations of hostility are part of inter-group relations of primates. Chimpanzees even engage in warfare including acts of killing and cannibalism (Goodall, 1986).

It is plausible that the proto-humans who acquired the capacity to use symbols incorporated existing pre-human behavioural patterns when they started reproducing the salutary victimary event. It is likely that the first mimetic crises after the primeval event were resolved by discharging the urge of salutary scapegoating on groups competing for the same territory and resources.

The worst fear of human communities is a descent into a crisis that could entail the chaos of the raw scapegoat mechanism. The controlled reproduction of the scapegoat mechanism in sacrificial ritual is one way of preventing the community from slipping into crisis. Warfare is another outlet that pre-empts the escalation of internal conflict. It captures the emerging negative mimetic dynamic and mobilises it against outsiders. In a roundabout way, the initial threat of division is ultimately transformed into a boost of internal cohesion and sense of identity. This kind of warfare is particularly effective in areas where otherwise independent communities have a shared understanding of what wars are about. In the literature, such warfare in which victimisation is controlled by a code of conduct is known as *ritual warfare*.

Relations between different groups inside communities benefit from the same mechanism by organising group interactions on the basis of competition. To be sustainable, such internal competition should remain non-violent. In the societies that form the topic of this book, controlled warfare and social competition are central to social organisation. To distinguish this *modus operandi* from the scapegoat scenario where the discontent achieves focus in a confrontation with an internal scapegoat, or in a sacrifice, I have called this type of dramatisation of the victimary mechanism the *enemy scenario*.

The victimary mechanism is embedded in many institutional complexes. Two of these stand out in their morphogenetic impact on the profile of society: war and kingship. This study will show that war is a powerful force for order as long as hostile groups are able to maintain a balance in the toll of victims that their warfare imposes. A fundamental requirement for maintaining a balance of power is an unequivocal, bi-polar definition of who an enemy is, and who is not. The universal principle *my enemy's friend is my enemy* and *my enemy's enemy is my friend* serves that purpose. It allowed communities to engage in war in such a way that each camp gathered a maximum of glory at the cost of a minimum of unnecessary bloodshed.

In contrast to war, kingship channels the negative sentiments in the community onto a single person. The suspense that the collective expression of anger creates provides the king with the leverage necessary to make demands on the people. These demands offer an action perspective to the people as well as hope in facing the crisis. However, if the crisis is not resolved the accusations will bounce back to the king. They may mean his end — at least if the people do not give him another chance. They often do since they know that without a king they are likely to start blaming one another, the consequences of which are difficult to control.

Kingship and war are equally effective dramatisations of consensual antagonism but their morphogenetic impact on social organisation is different. War organises the society in symmetrically polarised groups while kingship organises the society around a centre. In this book, I will use the term *enemy scenario* when referring to the consensual mechanism as it is activated in warfare and the term *dualism* to refer to the organisational principle that channels and maximises the consensual potential of the enemy scenario. The term *scapegoat scenario* is used when the consensual antagonism is played out between a group and one of its members while the term *centralism* refers to the organisational principle that channels and maximises the consensual potential of the scenario of the single scapegoat.

The enemy scenario

It is possible to summarise the enemy scenario of the victimary model in the same format as the scenario of the individual or minority victim of Girard's scapegoat-mechanism:

C.	The enemy scenario
1.	a *crisis* driven by mimetic rivalry threatening the survival of the group;
2.	a *polarisation* process, driven by antagonistic mimesis resulting in the alignment of groups into opposed hostile camps;
3.	the *transference* of the discontent between and inside the hostile groups onto the opposite party resulting in a *negative transfiguration* of the adversary;
4.	the *elimination* of adversaries (individuals or groups) in one or more violent group confrontations resulting in a new sense of unity and collective destiny within the enemy camps; and
5.	the *positive transfiguration* of victim(s) and/or victimiser(s) associated with the violence that enhanced group cohesion.

The precept that 'my friend's enemies and my enemy's friends are my enemies and my friend's friends and my enemy's enemies are my friends', channels the *mimesis of the antagonist* towards a polarisation of the political arena into two neatly opposed camps. Since the antagonists seek to ensure — by way of coalitions with similar groups, for instance — that they are able to meet the challenge posed by a potentially superior adversary, the system tends towards equilibrium.

The scenario of the internal scapegoat and the scenario of the external enemy run parallel till the fifth and last step. The fifth step is different in two ways: confrontations between enemies have a variable outcome — one party becoming the winner and the other the loser; while the outcome of the scapegoat scenario is fixed — the scapegoat being the victim and the community being the actor in charge of the killing. The sacralising effects primarily impinge on the victim but they may also reflect on the community and on the official in charge of the killing.

War hero making a mock-charge at the camera. The wild cucumbers hanging from his bow and those squeezed on his head protect the people he interacts with from contamination with the violence this killer of one or more enemies is associated with. In the Nilotic world the wild cucumber is a common substitute of a sacrificial victim.

In the enemy scenario, we have two sets of victims and two sets of victimisers. Cultures differ in their choice of who among the four is to be sacralised. In the societies studied in this book, it is the victimiser of one's own group who attracts the effects of sacralisation. The dead bodies of victimised group members are left in the battlefield to be eaten by predators. They are not given funeral rites, nor are they taken to the village of the killer. Yet, the names of the enemy victims will survive in self-aggrandising songs of their killer, his age-group, and his community.[6] The killing will mark the killer for the rest of his life. He is a celebrated member of the community but he will also be expected to protect his entourage and himself from the dangerous sacred charge that henceforth taints his person.

In other cultural contexts, it is the enemy-victim that attracts the sacralisation. This is the case in societies practising head-hunting and cannibalism. In *La Violence*

---

6   The Toposa, Didinga, Boya and Acholi have the custom of giving 'victim-names' to men who have killed an enemy. The names recall the situation of victimisation e.g. Toposa: *Goromoi* 'the enemy was crying'; *Rumamoi*: 'the enemy was caught by the hand while running away'; *Lotoparamoi*: 'the enemy was killed in a pool', etc.

et le sacré, Girard provides us with an analysis of Tupinamba cannibalism. The enemy-victim, normally a war captive, is eaten by the community in a collective orgy which intimately associates the well-being and integrity of the community with the enemy. The eating is believed to have healing powers. Being killed and eaten by one's enemy is the preferred way of dying. In fact, the passage through the enemy's stomach is a means of achieving immortality. Since the enemy will later be revenged and eaten by one's own people, a never-ending lineage by digestion is established that assures the integrity of their respective hostile communities.

Not only the victim but also the captor, who is responsible for killing the captive at the orgy, is affected by his deed. Like his Nilotic counterpart, he is impure and a danger to others as well as to himself. He does not take part in the cannibal meal. After the killing, he leaves the group and goes into seclusion, he fasts (while others are eating the victim), undergoes scarification and bloodletting, has his properties taken from him, and takes up a new name, a scenario not fundamentally different from what one finds in South Sudan. While the Sudanese victimiser may include his victim's last words in his war cry and in songs of self-praise, the Tupinamba hero cuts the lips of his victim and carries them around his wrist as a bracelet to remind himself of his victim's last words and of his own future violent death that is usually announced in these words.

There are also cases where the enemy in his quality of victimiser is sacralised by the victimised community. The Arawete, related to the Tupinamba and studied by Viveiros de Castro (1992), believe that after death, they will go to a heaven where divinised enemies will eat them. After being eaten, they will be resuscitated to join these cannibal gods and stay with them.[7]

In other cultures, including that of the modern nation-state, the victims fallen at the hands of the enemy are, if possible, taken home and transfigured into heroes or martyrs . The commemoration of their *sacrifice* is an important source of inspiration for their compatriots and a key reference in the narratives that underpin national unity. It is the only form of sacrificial death that survives even in nations and under regimes that define themselves as strictly secular.

Dualism as the institutional embedding of the enemy scenario

Dualism and dual organisation are classic topics in social anthropology. Although anthropologists generally recognise that dualism is associated with antagonism and competition, they have mostly been studied as institutions that facilitate marriage transactions and other 'positive' exchanges. Dual organisation makes possible one of the most straightforward applications of the rule of exogamy. The society is divided into two halves (called moieties) whose men exchange their sisters and daughters — a practice called 'restricted exchange' by Lévi-Strauss (1967). Cognitive anthropologists,

---

7   Girard based himself on Métraux's work (1967). The Huguenot Jean de Léry (1578, 1994) who
      stayed in Brazil from 1556–1558 is the most important eyewitness of Tupinamba cannibalism
      and a source for Métraux.

among them the later Lévi-Strauss, relate these structures to the binary operation of the human mind. No anthropologist, to my knowledge, has looked at classical moieties as vehicles of consensual antagonism.

Most of the communities in this study are divided into named territorial and antagonistic moieties. They compete in sports, hunting and in the discharge of community work. They confront one another in stick fights. These confrontations are strictly non-violent, in the sense that spears are forbidden and bloodshed should be avoided at all cost. The community thrives on the mimetic energies that are mustered in the many forms of competition. Many daily activities are staged as occasions for competition: from fetching water to composing songs and dancing. During feasts, villages, sections and age-sets compete in keeping the floor to make their own tunes and songs heard. Although the risk of violence is never completely absent, the ambiance during contests at the lower levels of social inclusiveness usually remains playful.

The territorial and age-class organisation of the communities being studied is systematically structured in polarised pairs: successive age-sets facing one another; the two senior age-sets of a generation-facing the two junior ones; while alternating generation-sets form opposed blocks; the retired elders and aspiring young men forming one block against the ruling generation-set and its alternates. Among the Lotuho, the resulting pair of permanent generational moieties carry proper names. In many communities, women are organised in the same way, their age-sets mirroring those of the men. There are institutional settings where the men and the women of the community act as competing political blocks, for example, in the investigation of the cause of drought.

The victimary drive in dualism becomes visible when we turn to inter-communal relations. There, the polarisation has not crystallised into stable pairs of moieties or named corporate groups. Inter-communal relations in our area of study are ruled by what the British anthropologist, Evans-Pritchard, has called "complementary segmentary opposition". The characteristic feature of this system is the existence of several levels of hostile polarisation. Polarisation on one level is superseded by polarisation on a higher level. People who face each other as antagonists on one level are allies when faced with a higher level common outsider. This outsider, in turn, may be an ally on a more inclusive level when a remoter outsider has to be confronted.

The classic description of this type of political system is Evans-Pritchard's study, *The Nuer*. Between the village and Nuer society as a whole (an entity which is defined in opposition to other peoples such as the Dinka), there are at least five different levels: tertiary (not in all tribes), secondary and primary sections, tribes, tribal coalitions and Eastern versus Western Nuer. Evans-Pritchard uses the following diagram to represent the mutual inclusion and exclusion of segments on different levels.

D.   Complementary segmentary opposition (based on Evans-Pritchard, 1940b:144)

A	B		
The complementary tribes A and B are united in their opposition to external enemies (*the enemies are not represented in the diagram*)	**X1** The primary sections X and Y occasionally fight thus unifying their secondary sections X1 and X2 and Y1 and Y2.	**Y1** The tertiary sections of Y1 (not shown here) and of Y2 stay united because of the antagonism of Y1 and Y2	**Y 1**
The antagonism of tribe A and B (and others not shown) leads to occasional warfare that keeps the primary sections of both (only X and Y of B shown here) united.	**X2** The antagonism with X1 keeps the tertiary sections of X2 (not shown) united	**z1** The tertiary sections of Y2 occasionally fight	**Y2**
		z2 The fights between z1 and z2 strengthen the cohesion between local descent groups that make up z2	

When the tertiary sections z1 and z2 have a conflict, they will be left to fight it out by themselves. In a conflict between z1 and Y1, all of Z unite as Y2. Similarly in a confrontation between villages belonging to the primary sections X and Y, all of Y will take the opposite camp from X. In a conflict between the two tribes A and B, X and Y must unite to face A, and so on.[8]

From the village level to the tribal level, restrictions on the use of violence in settling conflicts gradually diminish. In the village, only wooden sticks or clubs may be used in fighting; between tribes spears are the rule. The relations between sections are expressed and defined by feuds and occasional violent clashes, on the one hand, and by routine procedures to settle conflicts, on the other. War, feuds and stick fights define the boundaries of the groups that make up Nuer society. Which group identity is relevant in a particular encounter and which level of consensus an individual social actor should comply with depends on the situation of the moment.

Evans-Pritchard is very brief in his description of the interaction between killer and victim and on the social consequences of the killing for the killer. He obviously considers it an issue which requires a different, symbolic, type of analysis. The

---

8   Other classics in the study of 'complementary segmentary opposition' are: Barth on the Pathans of Pakistan (1959) and Gellner on the Berbers of the Moroccan Atlas (1969); important contributions to the discussion on the nature of segmentary systems are Smith (1956), Sahlins (1961), Sigrist (1967), Holy (1979) and Kelly (1985).

information that the killer, before being allowed back into normal life, has to have his upper arm cut with a fishing-spear[9] by the 'Master of the Land'[10] to remove the blood of the victim from his body, is evidence of the victimary significance of the Nuer system of complementary opposition (1940b:152).

I propose to study the volatile, situational groupings that emerge from hostile polarisation in societies organised on lines of complementary opposition as outcomes of the same morphogenetic principle as the more permanent 'dual organisations' that form the choice evidence of the structuralists. This means a departure from Durkheimian, structuralist analysis where dual organisations are studied as part of all-embracing cosmological classifications that derive their dualism from the way the human mind works, not from a social necessity (Durkheim & Mauss, 1963; Lévi-Strauss, 1958:147–180, 1962).

From a passage in *Violence and the Sacred*, it appears that Girard initially considered dual organisation as not being amenable to victimary analysis.[11] Yet, a few pages down, he provides us with an admirable analysis of ritual hostility at the occasion of weddings between intermarrying Tsimshian sections. He concludes: "In sum, the [intermarrying] groups agree never to be completely at peace, so that their members may find it easier to be at peace among themselves." (1977:249)[12]

Girard is here more direct to the point than in his analysis of Tupinamba cannibalism. To apply the scapegoat mechanism to Tupinamba cannibalism, Girard feels obliged to explain how an external enemy becomes an internal scapegoat. He, therefore, puts great emphasis on the 'domestication' of the enemy during the period between his capture and execution when the captive receives VIP treatment from his host community. It is only after this assimilation to his captors that he can stand in as a victim for the benefit of the community.

While the concepts of 'enemy scenario' and 'dualism', as developed here, would have saved Girard the detour of a preliminary domestication to turn the captured enemy into an effective victim, Girard's analysis pointedly shows the equivalence of the enemy victim with a domestic scapegoat. When analysing the relationship between the Nilotic king and his people, we shall see that the reverse is also true: the king deals with his subjects as if both parties to the interaction were enemies.

---

9   The symbolism underlying the use of the fishing-spear should be understood in the contrasting values Nilotic cosmology attributes to water and blood. More on this in Chapter Nineteen.

10   The *kuaar muon* is in the literature known as the 'leopard-skin chief'.

11   "There are perhaps two fundamental types of society which overlap to some extent: those that have central authority essentially monarchical in character and those having no such authority, disclosing no trace of generative violence in their political institutions — the so-called dual systems" (1977:305). The French original (1972:424) has *'organisations duelles'* for 'dual systems' . Again in *Des choses cachées* Girard reaffirms this dividing line: "...in the so-called dual societies, central authority has never existed and no one has ever thought of making it up" (1978:63; my translation).

12   The French original is more pointed: *"...on s'entend pour ne jamais s'entendre, afin de s'entendre un peu mieux au sein de chaque groupe"* (1972, in 2007b:602–603).

Centralism as the institutional embedding of the scapegoat scenario

The main aim of this book is to demonstrate that kingship is an institutional complex that is powered by the scapegoat mechanism. In contrast to war, kingship follows a scenario in which collective aggressiveness is discharged onto a single member of the group. In times of collective distress, the person or group designated as a potential victim receives the blame for disaster and disorder, and provides the group with opportunities to affirm its threatened integrity. Whatever affirmative transactions may take place in times of good fortune, the default relationship between king and people is one of hostility. If a community suffers disaster or defeat, the king is held responsible for not having protected his people, even of having unleashed the disaster. An exchange of accusations follows in which the king will try to shift the blame to the people and seek solutions that de-escalate the crisis. The king will not deny that he is angry or upset but accuse his people of having caused his anger. This opens the door for negotiations. The king's demands may vary from restorative sacrifices or payment of tribute to a plea for a change of heart of his people, for forgiveness and reconciliation. If the people choose to negotiate, they will take measures that mitigate the hostility and re-engage the king as their benefactor. If they do not, force will be used to break the king's stubbornness. Kings who fail to avert the crisis will eventually die as victims of the fury of their people. Their bodies will be left in the bush just like those of enemies slain on the battlefield.

In many societies, including those in our area of study, natural disasters figure prominently among the crises the king is called to deal with: drought, epidemics, plagues. The recurrent character of certain natural disasters makes for frequent opportunities for king and people to come to grips with one another. As kings grow more versatile in leading their people through crises, their rule will become more permanent. They will find ways to consolidate their rule and avoid an untimely death.

Confrontations between kings and their subjects carry lots of suspense. It is not accidental that some of the greatest works of literature are king's dramas. Long before these dramas were canonised by the authors of the Mahabharata, the Greek tragedians and Shakespeare, they were the life blood of politics in the first centralist formations. To understand the nature of kingship, the volatile centralist formations studied in this book are more telling than the stable states that later evolved out of these formations, let alone contemporary constitutional monarchies. States only offer a frozen and lopsided reflection of the vigour and dramatic reversibility of roles in early kingship. In contemporary constitutional monarchies, the king has almost completely been insulated from real political drama. The drama has shifted to the arenas of democratic decision-making, elections and street protests.

Lokoya age-mates in festive attire on the way to the New Year celebrations, Liria, 1986; note the syncretistic elements. Photo by Eisei Kurimoto.

This book relates and reconstructs the dramas played out by the historic kings of the Bari, Lotuho, Lokoya, Pari and Lulubo. Since these societies did not have writing, we have to rely on oral traditions and on the observations of explorers, traders, colonial officials and missionaries who dealt with the kings before the colonial administration drastically curtailed their freedom to deal with their subjects as they felt fit, and vice-versa. Almost 80 years elapsed between the first contacts of explorers, traders and missionaries with local royalty and the effective establishment of colonial rule which only occurred when the Lotuho, Lokoya, Lulubo and Pari were incorporated into the Anglo-Egyptian Sudan in 1914. Only the Bari underwent a measure of administration under the Uganda Protectorate (1898–1914). The Turco-Egyptian (1871–1885) and Mahdist administrations (1888–1898) hardly interfered in the relationship between local rulers and their subjects.

In order to obtain a relatively unbiased picture of events, I brought together, and cross-checked, accounts from oral history with reports of explorers, colonial officers and missionaries. For a number of kings, it proved possible to draw a picture of their careers as victims and idols of their people that is sufficiently complete to serve as evidence for the argument of this study.

In understanding sacral kingship, anthropologists have often had recourse to the concepts of 'god' and 'divinity' — as if these referred to self-evident phenomena. James Frazer coined the term 'divine kingship' to refer to kings whose installation was staged as a capture of the new king by a spirit. His key example was the king of the Shilluk of

South Sudan who was captured by Nyikang, the spirit of the founder of the dynasty (Frazer, 1913, Part III, p. 14–34). Frazer, however, excluded from this category the kings who are the subject matter of this book. They were classified as 'magical kings' and were supposed to represent a more primitive stage in the development of the institution of kingship.[13] At their installation, they were not captured by a spirit but, in Frazer's view, imposed themselves claiming cosmological powers and abusing the credulity of their subjects. In fact, as we shall see later, the kings in this study were installed after being either captured as a wild, predating animal — a leopard (Lokoya), or a crocodile (Lotuho), or selected as a sacrificial animal (Bari, Lulubo) that will take diseases and disasters with it in its death.

With Girard's victimary theory, it is possible to overcome Frazer's artificial distinction. 'King' and 'god' are personifications of different, successive stages of the unfolding of the scapegoat mechanism. The 'king' dramatises the events preceding the elimination of the victim while in the worship of divinity, the aftermath of the elimination is highlighted: the victim-saviour being worshipped in his accomplished transcendence.

Compared to the cult of divinity, the living king lends itself far more easily to lively and dramatic enactments of the original scenario. Kingship puts a live victim centre stage. Divinity, as the apotheosis of something absent, must always be *re-presented*. For this reason, sacred kingship is one of Girard's favourite institutions to demonstrate the explanatory power of the scapegoat mechanism (1978:64–65).

According to Girard, modern thinking narrows the conception of the divine to the *supernatural* and *non-empirical*. It conceives God-like qualities attributed to kings are envisaged as something separate, added on later in an attempt to make the monarch look more important, or to legitimate his power:

> Everyone repeats that the king is a kind of 'living god' but no one says that the divinity is a kind of dead king, which would be just as accurate. In the end, there is a persistent preference for viewing the sacrifice and sacredness of the king as a secondary and supplementary idea, for we must beware of rocking our little conceptual boat. Yet what guides our interpretation is only a conceptual system dominated by the idea of divinity, a *theology*. Scepticism about religion does not abolish this theological perspective. We are forced to reinterpret all religious schemata in terms of divinity because we are unaware of the surrogate victim.[12] If one examines psychoanalysis and Marxism closely it becomes evident that this theology is indispensable for them. (1987c:57)

The conception of the separate existence of worldly and divine power in sacred kingship, denounced as "theological" by Girard, is still characteristic of most of the

---

13   "Among the tribes which cherish these beliefs [in the magical powers of the king] and observe these customs [killing of the rainmaker if he fails to perform] are the Latuka, Bari, Laluba (*sic*) and Lokoiya" (Frazer, 1913, Part I, Vol. 1:p. 345). The Pari who are the fifth group studied in this book would certainly have been included in Frazer's list if, at the time, they had also been under the administration of the Uganda Protectorate one of whose officials Frazer is quoting, and not under the Anglo-Egyptian Condominium of the Sudan.

work done on African kingship. The structural-functionalist position in this respect is very similar to the Marxist one. Research is focused on the establishment of correspondences between the 'religious level' and the 'politico-economic level' which are conceived as separate entities in which the latter as the infrastructure, shapes the profile of the former, the superstructure.

An illustration of the contradictions this theoretical stance leads to is offered by Evans-Pritchard's and Fortes' introduction to *African Political Systems* considered a classic text in the development of anthropological theory on political systems. The authors present the 'mystical' and 'ritual' values 'attached' to offices of central authority as 'the ideological superstructure of political organisation' (Fortes & Evans-Pritchard, 1940:3, 17). This superstructure is conceived as a duplication of the social structure 'on a mystical plane, where it figures as a system of sacred values beyond criticism or revision' (p.18). The authors advise researchers to keep ideology and political organisation strictly separate in the course of investigation 'because the nature of the connexion is a major problem in sociology' (p. 3). At the same time, they concede that the members of an African society do not look beyond the symbols in which their institutions are immersed because 'it might well be held that if he [the subject of the African king] understood their objective meaning they would lose the power they have over him (p. 18). So we reach the paradoxical theoretical position of two identical political systems: one, profane, examined by anthropologists but overlooked by the participants, and the other, 'mystical', of primary importance to the participants, but considered as a secondary elaboration by anthropologists.

Frazer's scapegoat king

Following a period during which Frazer functioned as a kind of scapegoat of modern anthropology (Boon, 1983:149), a number of anthropologists working along structuralist precepts again admit indebtedness to Frazer's inspiration.[14] Luc De Heusch even speaks of "Frazer's camp" in anthropology (1984:301–314' 1985:98). In addition to De Heusch, this group includes, Alfred Adler, the author of a detailed study of Moundang kingship in Chad, and Jean-Claude Muller, who investigated kingship among the Rukuba in central Nigeria. Adler considers the research programme set out by Evans-Pritchard and Fortes a failure (1978:29, 1982:15). In traditional Africa, the political is immersed in symbolism and can be isolated from it only at the cost of a serious distortion of the facts. Whatever exists in the way of competition for power coincides with "heraldry: insignia, coats of arms, sacra, regalia, etc." (1982:402). While distancing himself from Frazer's evolutionist views and from his work on magic, Adler avows that without Frazer's 'dogma' of regicide, his material on Moundang kingship could not have been deciphered (1979:194). Nowhere, however, do we find a discussion or explicitation of this dogma.

---

14   For a general discussion of the present Frazer revival see also: Douglas, 1978; Wood, 1982; Boon, 1983.

What Adler retains of *The Golden Bough* are a few themes. In his major study (1982), for instance, he makes use of the theme of the 'magical king' whose power is demonstrated by his control of nature. In his analysis of the annual ritual cycle (1979:193–207) he retains the Frazerian idea of the king as 'scapegoat'. According to Adler this scapegoat role is meant to counterbalance the overestimation of his power during the rest of the year (1982:394) — a conclusion which rather deviates from Frazer's 'dogma'.

Jean-Claude Muller also reckons himself part of the new generation that has divested itself of the structural-functionalist prejudices against Frazer. In his '*Le Roi bouc émissaire*' (The Scapegoat King) Muller describes how the Rukuba blame and depose their kings for allowing disasters to befall the country, and how they kill a royal substitute as part of the installation ceremony. Despite the inclusion of a brief presentation of Girard's theory (1980:164), Muller refuses to look beyond the interpretations which the Rukuba give of their royal institutions (1980: 473).

De Heusch has criticised Girard on several occasions by referring to particular African rituals and myths of kingship as evidence contradicting the alleged general applicability of the victimary thesis (1985:98–124). It is not necessary to discuss this evidence, since De Heusch's assumption that Girard's scapegoat mechanism should be directly manifest in ritual practice and myth is wrong. In Girard's theory, the scapegoat mechanism has the status of a structuring device which is not *represented* but organises practice and belief while being *misrepresented*.

The way cultures represent victimary violence is, according to Girard, necessarily distorted, since no society can afford to admit explicitly its violent origins. Instead, each culture produces a deliberate misinterpretation of the process, throwing light on some of its aspects while obscuring others.[15] These misrepresentations follow directly from the negative transference of the group towards the victim before his elimination — the victim being portrayed as evil while the victimisers pretend innocence — and the positive transference afterwards — which results in the attribution of superhuman powers to the victim.

Since the 'Frazerian structuralists' limit themselves to the study of the inner coherence of representations and do not ask the question of their genesis and function, their interpretations leave the victimary content largely implicit. This content can only be brought to light by a hermeneutic tool that interprets the beliefs and practices that constitute 'divine kingship' as part of a larger whole that is cognisant of their origin and function. Such a tool is the victimary model. It does greater justice to Frazer's intuitions than the authors just mentioned. Let us list the main characteristics attributed in Frazer's *The Golden Bough* to divine kingship and set them off against the victimary model:

---

15   "To keep its structuring power intact, the founding violence should not come to the surface. Misrecognition [*méconnaissance*] is indispensable for any religious and post-religious structuring" (Girard, 1972:430; my translation).

E.	Frazer's themes that connect kingship and scapegoating
1.	The idea that the king has power over nature and the related practice to aggress and kill him when this power fails (Part I, *The Magic Art and the Evolution of Kings*, esp. vol.1);
2.	The idea that, in a later stage of intellectual development, the king's power is believed to emanate from a divinity incarnate in the king (Part I, *The Magic Art and the Evolution of Kings*, esp. vol.2);
3.	The idea that the community rids itself of evil by transferring it onto a scapegoat who may be a king (Part VI, *The Scapegoat*);
4.	The idea that the king is equated with a *dying god* who through his death regenerates the forces of nature (Parts III, *The Dying God*; IV, *Adonis, Attis, Osiris*; and V, *The Spirits of the Corn and the Wild*).

In *The Golden Bough*, these themes are not brought together in an organic whole. Once Frazer's scheme is shorn of its evolutionist and intellectualist assumptions the listed dimensions of kingship easily reveal their victimary coherence:

F.	The scapegoat model as a construct integrating Frazer's concepts of the *magical* and *divine king*, the *scapegoat* and the *dying god* as moments in a single transformational sequence
1.	*Mimetic crisis*: for Frazer, human behaviour, including conflict, is determined by ideas; he lacks a theory of the pre-reflective origin and nature of conflict;
2.	*Polarisation*: Frazer is not interested in social processes of escalating tension that lead to the designation of a scapegoat, but he perceives the link between collective misfortune and the aggression against scapegoats including *magical kings*–although in the latter case he tends to considers the magical kings' fate as the just reward for their bluff (Theme 1);
3.	*The transference of collective evil* onto a scapegoat who may be a human being (witch, king), a demon, a god and even an inanimate object. It is a great achievement of Frazer to have identified, for the first time, a wide range of practices from all over the world as the single phenomenon of scapegoating (Theme 3);
4.	*The victimisation of the scapegoat* (Frazer 1, 3 and 4);
5.	*The positive transfiguration of the victim* The death of kings is a source of blessings. Most of Frazer's *dying gods* are transfigured, divinised, scapegoat kings. Instead of killing the king or waiting for his regenerative death, the ruling king, at his installation, is invested by his ancestors' healing and cosmic powers, thus becoming a *divine king* (Frazer 2 and 4).

On the last point, Frazer's presentation is unnecessarily cumbersome, since most of the dying gods that Frazer comes up with are originally murdered kings (Dionysus, Adonis, Osiris).

Unequal exchange

Our discussion has focused on the negative dimension of the relationship between king and people. I have argued that the fundamental role of the king — that of keeping his people united and at peace — is a function of the antagonism between the two. When the tension mounts in a period of crisis and people look for its causes, the blame will ultimately be directed to the king and, if the crisis is not resolved, this may lead to his expulsion. However, in times of peace and plenty, the same principle of attributing accountability will be used by the king to make claims for the good he is doing. The relationship between king and people cannot just be a series of confrontations. To be sustainable, king and people should also be able to understand and operate their relationship as an ongoing exchange in which the blessings operated by the king are reciprocated by demonstrations of appreciation by his people and vice-versa.

First launched in 1924 in Marcel Mauss's famous *Essai sur le don*, the notion of reciprocal exchange is central to the work of the structural anthropologists. Lévi-Strauss, in *Les structures élémentaires de la parenté* (1967), demonstrates that reciprocity is the fundamental morphogenetic principle that accounts for the wide variety of forms in which kinship is organised worldwide. In *Les structures élémentaires de la parenté*, Lévi-Strauss presents the rule that a man should not marry from his own group but give his sisters and daughters to men of other groups as a strategy that avoids conflict and builds bridges of peace with actually or potentially hostile groups (1967:68–69; 98-101). Instead of satisfying his desire to get a woman in his own group, a man has to approach strangers and engage in negotiations to obtain one of their women as his wife. On the other hand, he has to treat the women in his own group as 'peace capital'. Radicalising his argument Lévi-Strauss comes to defend the thesis that the incest prohibition is just a corollary, the flip side, of the injunction to exchange.

In *Violence and the Sacred*, Girard devotes a whole chapter to a refutation of this subordination of the negative incest prohibition to the positive obligation to exchange (1972:305–345). According to Girard, before any transaction qualifying as an exchange of women can take place, there has to be a set of ordered relationships based on the distinction between relations of alliance (husband-wife), consanguinity (brother-sister) and filiation (parent-child). These distinctions can only emerge as a consequence of the incest prohibition. Without it, there are no clear-cut fathers, brothers, husbands and sons, no wives, daughters and sisters, only males — some dominant, others subordinate — competing over the possession of females. By arguing the primacy of prohibition over exchange, Girard defends the decisive role of the victimary mechanism in the emergence of human culture. Prohibiting any conduct that triggers or even evokes the violence of the mimetic crisis is an obvious step only when the community has experienced the peace of the scapegoat mechanism. Girard sticks to the Durkheimian distinction between 'positive' and 'negative' religious practices, things you should do and things you should not do, rituals and prohibitions.

Eric Gans, one of the first students of Girard to carry out his own research in victimary theory, has given an interesting elaboration of his master's insistence on the independent socio-morphogenetic role of prohibition. He developed a processual model that shows how cultural practices of exchange and sharing emerge in a situation when heightened tension over the possession of an attractive object is cut short by a group's sudden awareness of the violence that will follow if all individuals reach out for the same object. Like Girard's scapegoat mechanism, Gans's primeval drama can be summarised as a sequence of five moments:

G.	The scenario of aborted violence
1.	*nascent mimetic rivalry* provoked by the simultaneous desire of a number of individuals for the same appetising object;
2.	a *premonition of imminent violence* followed by an *alarming gesture* make the group shrink away from reaching out for the attractive object;
3.	in the shared fearful attention following the alarm the object appears dangerous; it undergoes a *negative transfiguration;*
4.	the deferral of a violent crisis relieves the fearful tension and transforms it into a sensation of *non-violent togetherness* resulting in a *positive transfiguration* of the object;
5.	the doubly transfigured object is now available for a non-violent appropriation by the group of individuals that is transforming itself into a *community* that will reproduce their non-violent co-existence in events in which the object (or its substitutes) is ceremonially shared and celebrated.

Gans's model is the mirror image of the scapegoat mechanism. The two models describe symmetrically inverse operations. While the scapegoat mechanism transforms an abhorred victim into a sacred 'subject' in a violent conjunction of rivals, prohibition transforms a focus of mimetic attraction into a sacred object by a non-violent disjunction of the rivals. While the object of prohibition is ultimately internalised by the community in an act of sharing, the scapegoat ends up as an object of worship external to the community. The non-event of the abortion of violence is the condition for a social praxis of the exchange of real values, while the scapegoating event is reproduced in a ritual praxis that addresses an imaginary transcendence.

This model makes it possible to build a bridge between mimetic theory and the intuitions of the early Lévi-Strauss who understands gift exchange as a strategy to avoid and overcome conflict but does not spell out how institutions of reciprocal exchange could have emerged in an essentially conflictual context. The object of appropriative mimesis that Gans had in mind when designing his model was an object shared in a group at the same time and place, for example, a game animal. (Gans, 1985:14). I believe the model works just as well, or maybe even better, when applied to other exchangeable values, including a partner for sex and procreation. The sacred horror with which society reacts to incest may even evoke the drama of the abortive gesture more vividly than the scorn that hits the hungry hunter who reaches out to the forbidden heap of flesh. It is clear that the joint involvement in networks of matrimonial exchange establishes a moral presence between the partners which is structurally of the same order as that of the participants in Gans' ceremonial meal. The fact that the 'consummation' of marriage does not necessarily take place in the physical presence of the group, does not, of course, place it outside its moral presence.

While safeguarding the connection between prohibitions and the imminence of violence from being subordinated to Lévi-Strauss's exclusive focus on exchange, Gans, in turn, underrates the fundamental role of the scapegoat mechanism in the generation of social consensus by subordinating it to his 'model of the aborted gesture' — or 'aborted violence'. Gans argues that the extreme polarisations that are assumed in Girard's scapegoat mechanism could only have occurred among mimetically advanced hominids, already endowed with the faculty of speech, representation, and with a sense of the nature of prohibition not among the hominids still protected by their instinctual dominance patterns, that Gans stages in his scenario of the aborted violence. Girard's reply to this is that prohibitions can only take hold when a group knows what extreme polarisation is. How, otherwise, can one explain the extreme apprehension of an outbreak of violence among Gans' proto-humans?

Anthropological studies of systems of exchange have demonstrated that marriage transactions (such as Lévi-Strauss, 1967), the exchange of valuables (such as Malinowski, 1922) and the distribution of food (such as Rappaport, 1968) depend on principles which cannot be derived from political and economic considerations. They are procedures to maintain *sociality* where otherwise *hostility* would reign. The gift, in its quality as symbol of the social relationship, is often more important than the material satisfaction the given object provides. In many objects that are exchanged, the symbolic value prevails over the use-value.

Exchange has its own dynamic of creating social inequality. As Mauss has convincingly argued, the process of exchanging gifts creates inequality between the giving and the receiving party. The giver puts the recipient under an obligation to acknowledge his gift by reciprocating it. As long as the gift is not reciprocated, the recipient is indebted — putting the giver in a superior position. This superiority does not derive from commonplace considerations of credit and debt but from the fact that the gift is a move in a strategy to avoid, contain and replace potential violence. As long as the gift has not been reciprocated, the sole credit for having taken the 'social' option of exchange against keeping the option of conflict open, goes to the giver. This double character of the gift — affirmation of peaceful intentions of the giver and its potential to become a cause of conflict if disregarded by the recipient — provides the gift with a sacred charge.[16]

As long as the partners in the cycle of transactions are capable of reciprocating, the inequality created by the gift exchange will only be temporary. But if one of the

---

16   The Maori, who call this sacred quality of the exchanged object *hau*, attribute a revenging power to it when the partners in the exchange betray the friendship of which the object is the material symbol (Mauss, 1990:10–12).

partners is not or only partly able to reciprocate, the relationship will gradually turn unequal. The power of the anthropological figure of the *Big Man* is rooted in this inequality.

The two sources of the king's power

The victimary scenario of kingship puts king and people face-to-face, exchanging hostilities, the people accusing the king of their troubles, the king — while returning the blame and seeking ways out of his predicament — a potential victim for scapegoating. As a purely victimary institution, kingship would not be sustainable. In a society where military might is defined by the number of able-bodied men a leader can put into the field, the primeval king, being a minority, would normally be the loser. Kingship only becomes a sustainable option when king and people have other mechanisms at their disposal to build their relationship. This is where gift exchange comes in. When it is possible to manage routine conflicts by gift exchange and the payment of fines, the relationship of king and people has a chance to stabilise and it becomes possible for both to engage constructively.

In fact, in the communities in our field of study, the day-to-day interactions between king and people revolve around exchange. The king is believed to be the provider of rain, an unparalleled gift creating a perpetual indebtedness among his people. His subjects acknowledge their debt by giving him wives; cultivating his field; providing him with firewood and other daily necessities; pampering him with choice cuts of game and all sorts of seasonal delicacies (termites, honey), and so on.

Since the rains are unpredictable, they can be the occasion for a lot of drama. When the rains are prompt, the king is spoilt with gifts. But if they persistently fail, a problem in the relationship of king and people is suspected. Investigations are carried out. Both sides will consult diviners who will come up with unresolved issues (unpaid debts, unwarranted violence by an age-set or section, an offence against the king, a destitute widow left to her own devices, and so on) and give advice on ways to address the problem. When the rains are regular and people start taking their king for granted, the king will use a spell of drought as an opportunity to remind the people of his powers and claim his due. People will first oblige but if the drought persists, they will conclude that the fault must lie with the king. A point will be reached when the community will fall back on its default response to crisis. The king will meet his fate as envisaged by the scapegoat model.

As the pivot of the cycles of exchange inside his community and as the main interface of his community with outsiders, the king has all that it takes to become a *Big Man*. The Oceanist anthropologist Marshall Sahlins is the main architect of the concept of *Big Man*. He describes him as a 'social entrepreneur' whose aim it is to 'amass a fund of power' with which he can 'create and use social relations which give him leverage on others' production and the ability to siphon off an excess product (1962–63:292). This excess product is normally spent on the organisation of feasts and food distributions with which the *Big Man* obtains more 'social credit' and 'prestige'.

Sahlins contrasts the *Big Man* which, according to him, is a typical Melanesian phenomenon, with the Polynesian *chief*. The *Big Man* is the product of a personal career, in which he is 'a fisher of men' always trying to increase the number of his dependants. He competes with other men for pre-eminence, using economic, political and magical powers in this struggle. In contrast to this, the authority of the Polynesian 'chiefs' is ascribed. Chiefs related to a well-defined section of the society. Their power is not the end-product of a career but is believed to reside in the office and in the *mana* ['charisma'] inherent in the chiefly line.

The power of the Nilotic king is a combination of both. While his royal power depends primarily on the chancy operation of his inherited rain-charisma, it is sustained by exchange practices that turn him into a *Big Man*. The two types of power compare as follows:

H.   The power of the king compared to that of the Big Man

KING	BIG MAN
Office: source of power is transcendent to social give and take;	Status: source of power is immanent to social give and take;
Selection to office ascribed and endorsed by community in a collective sacralising act, either a curse or a blessing;	Power of status achieved as a result of the accumulation of wealth that is invested in the mobilisation of dependants (wives, clients) who enable him to accumulate even more wealth, and so on;
Position defined in opposition to all other members of the community;	Position defined in competition with other *Big Men* as a function of one's number of dependants;
Typical relation to others: bless and curse, leader in war and interlocutor of the enemy in peace negotiations;	Typical relation to others: patronage and protection;
Power conceived as separate of the incumbent;	Power closely associated with personal career.
Continuity of office by succession to office	Continuity of status by inheritance of one's wealth;
Tendentially centralist.	Dispersed, competing, foci of power.

In the myths about the origin of kingship, the king's power comes from a location outside the community, from heaven (for example, among the Bari), from the bush (in the staging of the inauguration rituals of the Lokoya) or from the depths of the water (in Lotuho dynastic myth). The fact that succession is conceived as the result of the conjunction of a transcendent power with the concrete person of the king opens the possibility for the king to be false. His relationship with the transcendent could be a sham. This explains that the succession to the kingship is normally subjected to all sorts of restrictive rules, not only aimed at reducing the number of competitors for the throne but also to ensure that no 'false' king ascends the throne.

In Lotuho, for example, the successor should be a child from parents both of whom are of rain descent. Before nominating the prince-elect, the biographies of candidates are scrutinised for indications of extraordinariness. If there remains doubt, communities may force their would-be Rainmaker to undergo an ordeal or to engage in a rainmaking contest.[17] Once there is a candidate who fulfils the criteria and shows hints of extraordinariness, the kind of circular mimetic process ensues that is as admirably described by Ernest Gellner for the selection of the *agurram*, the charismatic leaders in the Moroccan Atlas:

> *Agurram*-hood is in the eye of the beholder. But that isn't quite right: *agurram*hood is in the eyes of the beholders–all of them in a sense squint to see what is in the eyes of other beholders, and if they can see it there, then they see it also. Collectively this characteristic is an ascription, but for any one man, it is an objective fact, an inherent characteristic: if all others see it in a man, then, for any single beholder, that man truly has it (Gellner, 1969:74).

The *Big Man* Polynesian or Nilotic is the product of an entirely different, more down to earth process. From among his peers, he rises to a position of prestige by clever use of manpower, social connections and wealth. He is a product of upward mobility.

The benefits the subjects receive from their king, and the way in which these are received, contrast with the advantages the dependents and clients receive from their *Big Men*. In the case of the latter, the advantages are distributed individually; they are tangible and often have an important material component (food, bridewealth, prestige goods). In the case of the king, the benefits accrue to the collectivity as a whole. They often have a cosmological or sociological dimension (protection against disaster, the unity of the group, national glory).

Big man dynamics are active in all societies covered in this study. Only in exceptional circumstances does a *Big Man* make the leap to kingship. But a king is always a *Big Man*, having more wives (from his people's gifts) and children, benefiting from the collective labour of his subjects. Being the lynchpin of regional trade[18], the king has more to offer as a patron of the poor and will have more clients than *Big Men* who are commoners. While his power of kingship comes from the beyond, he is likely to be the 'biggest man' around.

---

17   This custom is practised by the Logir, one of the Lotuho-speaking groups in Eastern Equatoria.

18   For example: Polanyi, 1944:43–55; Ekholm, 1972:128ff; Claessen, 1984:30.

The royal drums of Loronyo, the capital of Lotuho kings of the Mayya Dynasty, 2009

Early kingship and the genesis of the state

An unintended spin-off of the endeavour to apply Girard's scapegoat theory to the analysis of kingship in the southern Sudan was the discovery, during the analysis of my field data, of the structural homology between the consensual antagonism played out in the relationship between king and people and the oppositional dynamics underlying territorial and age organisation. As I shall demonstrate in Chapters Seven, Eight and Ten, in all three cases — territorial organisation, age-organisation and kingship — the interactions between the antagonists follow a confrontational, potentially violent scenario that results, in principle, in one or more victims.

As I have argued above, dualism is institutionalised on two levels, on the inter-communal level as warfare in which descent-based and/or territorial groups of matching scope of inclusiveness are mobilised as adversaries with the aim of making victims among their opposite number, and secondly, on the intra-communal level, as competition between equivalent, fixed sections and moieties in which the use of violence is strictly controlled and victimisation prohibited. The latter situation is what anthropologists usually label as *dual organisation*. Centralism institutionalises around a central actor (individual or group) confronting a larger, surrounding, peripheral group — consisting of devotees, supporters, dependents who may, at times, turn into persecutors — and results in formations that are marked by social inequality.

The question presents itself whether this homology between dualist and centralist consensual antagonism offers a clue as to how centralist formations, including kingship and the state, developed out of more egalitarian, dualistically structured, social formations. The origin of social inequality and the emergence of the state have been key questions in anthropology since Rousseau. Anthropological studies have mostly examined external conditions that correlate with the emergence of central authority and the state, such as the development of the productive forces resulting in a surplus production that can feed an upper class, long distance trade, the rise in population numbers, or else looked at systemic functions performed by the new institutions of central control (coordination of production, adjudication, safeguarding the position of the ruling class). Little attention has gone to the political dramas that must have been part of this transformation of social relations from relative equality to inequality.

I believe that the kingdoms that are the subject of this book offer us a glimpse of these dramas of transition. We are dealing with kings whose sovereignty had an extremely volatile character. In fact, every rainy season was a test of their royal legitimacy, not only of their effectiveness as Rainmakers but also of their capacity to maintain internal peace and keep enemies at bay. Rivals, from the ruling rain family or from rain clans of neighbouring communities, were always waiting around the corner to take over. Popular suspicion that the king had turned against his people led to head-on confrontations in which the king's life was at stake. As we shall see in Chapter Nine, the nervousness with which moves of enemies were monitored often also characterised the community's dealings with the king, and vice-versa. The outcome of the confrontations was not predetermined. They could mean the king's demise, but they could also work in the king's favour. If the rains were timely, the enemies suffered defeat and internal peace prevailed, his success was likely to breed more success culminating in recognition by an ever widening range of communities including former enemies.

The relationship between the early kings and their 'subjects' was full of suspense. In fact the people these kings were ruling had not been transformed into *subjects*, they had not been *subjected*. Yet, if we study the interactions of these kings with their people, it soon becomes apparent that their main purpose was to strengthen their grip on the people. Chapter Eleven shows that the kings did everything they could to tip the balance of power to their side and become irrevocable, omnipotent, *sovereigns*[19]. They did this by economic means using the possibilities offered by the *Big Man* scenario, by manipulation of their dynastic antecedents and — last but not least — by allying themselves with the builders of commercial and political empires that appeared on the Nile in the middle of the nineteenth century.

So the kingdoms studied in this book may offer a unique window on a crucial phase in the evolution of political systems: one in which the control of the use of physical force is 'not yet' monopolised by the king, or in other words, in which the use of force by the people against a king perceived as obstructive to their interests was not less *legitimate* than the king's use of force against some of his people who were perceived as disobedient.

---

19 'Sovereign' is derived from Medieval Latin *superanus* an adjective meaning 'on top'; cf. *soprano* derived from the same root, meaning 'the top of the vocal range'.

I qualify this window as unique because once a king can more or less credibly claim the monopoly of the use of physical force, the window will quickly be shut and may remain so for centuries. Hinting at the king's power as a reversible reality will remain forbidden as subversive propaganda while any activism to restore the old situation will count as a *rebellion*, to be met with royal counter-insurgency measures.

Within the mosaic of political systems — more or less 'centralised kingdoms', 'segmentary states', 'generation-based gerontocracies', acephalous societies practicing complementary segmentary opposition — that emerged in the Upper Nile basin, the societies studied in this book — possibly together with the Anuak and Shilluk[20] — , most patently built their political institutions on the reversible polarity between king and people.

From the point of view of the emancipatory activism that sustained the democracies that developed from the absolute monarchies in Europe and that has continued to inspire democratisation world-wide, it is tempting to consider these political systems as 'democracies *avant la lettre*'. This is, in fact, what local ethnographers (Lomodong, 1995) argue in an attempt to inspire pride in the dynamic complexity of the traditional political set-up. Without belittling the political sophistication of the *monyomiji*-systems, I think the use of the term *democracy* is better reserved for mechanisms of popular representation that control the exercise of power by *states*, that is polities where the government has full control of the use of physical force.

The polities built on the king-*monyomiji* polarity were definitely not *states*. While their capacity to form larger, more cohesive and more enduring political units must have been manifest to both the kings and their peoples, their weaknesses often outweighed their strengths. The main weakness was the interminable rivalry between pretenders to the throne. The coexistence of centralist kingship with dualistically structured territorial and age-based groups that offered opportunities to competing rivals to promptly mobilise followers made things worse.

The Lotuho version of the myth of the bead and the spear (Chapter Fifteen) can be read as an expression of the misgivings that existed about the capacity of kingship to sustain a unified political community. The story concludes with a curse by a dying king which forever prevents his subjects from having kings. The curse is pronounced when his people are ready to hand him over to his enemies to be killed.

There are indications that such a re-conversion from centralism to dualism is not just a story. As I suggest in the concluding chapter, the radical egalitarian dualism of the Nuer may very well have been the outcome of a collective rejection of kingship. Abnegating centralist kingship was not necessarily a step backwards as rigid evolutionists may be tempted to think. The rapid expansion of the Nuer at the cost

---

20   Because of the similarities of their political system, the Anuak, some of whom are ruled by kings and others by village headmen who are moreover targets of rebellion (Lienhardt, 1958a:31–5); the Shilluk with their peculiar mix of dualist and centralist institutions (Lienhardt, 1954: 151–4) and the regicide practicing Shilluk-Luo of the Bahr-el-Ghazal (Santandrea:1938; Santandrea & De Giorgi, 1965:24–30), together with the groups who form the focus of the book, may be grouped as members of the same class of political systems.

of their more centralist neighbours proves that the dualist option was, in terms of its capacity of ensuring collective survival, not inferior to centralist options.

The state as an evolving cybernetic system

What can this genealogy of the state teach us about contemporary states? Assuming that the mechanisms that produced the first states continue to be at work in present-day state formations, be it in a transformed way, I will try to answer this question by approaching the operation of the state as a cybernetic system consisting of a number of superimposed feedback loops:

The bottom of the multi-layered structure corresponds to the scapegoat mechanism. We should imagine a scene where a group of individuals caught up in an uneasy, conflictual, relationship is edging to the brink of violence. One individual sets himself apart from the wrangling and confronts the others. The pent-up negativity now directs itself at him. He becomes the focus of the hostility of all. At that very moment the scene changes. The disgruntled lot turns into a group because of the common focus. The impasse is broken.

The longer the stand-off lasts, the stronger will be the bonding of the group. The emerging sense of togetherness does not go unnoticed nor does its association with the figure who triggered it. The group may welcome its new state of being and realise that it is in its interest to make the suspense triggered by the exceptional figure last. The group — or the exceptional figure — may also realise that the new cohesiveness gives it an edge over similar, less cohesive, competing groups. This configuration may be the springboard from which the earliest forms of kingship were launched. What is important here is that the bonding was not the result of a deliberate agreement between individuals or the outcome of mutual compatibility, nor the side-effect of the pursuit of a common interest, let alone an expression of group solidarity. The unity is the product of the suspense of the stand-off between the group and its antagonist.

It will be clear that the dependence of these proto-kingdoms on a combination of defiance, trust and admiration does not make for a very stable political entity. We must imagine the early forms of kingship as volatile and in need of being propped up by practices that bridge and transcend the confrontational character of the relationship between the group and its proto-royal antagonist. As we have seen in the discussion of the powers of the king and the *Big Man*, the exchange of gifts, courtesies, favours and other signs of mutual appreciation open up a space for constructive management of the relationship between king and people for diplomacy.

On this second cybernetic level the role of the king is being defined as that of a partner in a cycle of exchange. The peoples in this book have integrated their kings in the cycle of exchange as givers of rain, in many ways the most crucial condition of survival. In return for this gift they marry him wives, perform services (the men clearing his land and building his residence; the women weeding the crops and collecting firewood) and provide him with all sorts of attentions. At this level of complexity, the relationship of king and people is ruled by the norm of reciprocity.

The king can count on his people's gifts and attentions as long as he continues to regularly deliver his blessing of rain.

However, when the flow of blessings emanating from the king is interrupted, the cycle of reciprocal exchange will begin to falter. The usual services are performed reluctantly. Reciprocal demands will be made but not granted. Mutual accusations escalate into violent scuffles. The bridge of peaceful exchange and diplomacy caves in and a crisis driven by negative reciprocity ensues. The system slips into regression, falling back on its basic operational level: that of the scapegoat mechanism.

While recovering from the crisis, the new king and the surviving people have good reasons to look for ways to remedy the fragility of their political arrangements. The people, on one side, may decide to mitigate the regicidal violence by ritualising it into mock-charges and verbal abuse during periodic festivals — as do the Swazi in their *ncwala* ritual. (H. Kuper, 1944; Gluckman, 1954; Makarius 1973; Apter, 1983). Alternatively, the killing of the king can be postponed until the time when his natural death is imminent, as in the case of the Shilluk.

The survivors of a crisis may also decide to make a completely new start, doing away with kingship, leaving the responsibility for internal order and external relations to lineage elders or to an assembly of age-mates. In the case kingship is abnegated after the crisis, its unifying, consensual dynamic should be expected to shift to other institutions: warfare, witchcraft.

In case the community emerging from crisis sticks to the centralist option, its new king — whose life could be at stake in a new crisis — will muse on alternatives that prevent another slippage into scapegoating. An obvious objective from his point of view will be a firmer control over his people. Chapters Eleven, Twelve and Thirteen show the many strategies used by kings to achieve ascendancy over their people, from the creation of armies, the control of trade, and the levying of tribute to the concentration of all ritual powers in the hands of the king.

Manifestations of this royal will to power are the Bari king Logunu who, in 1841, did not hesitate to try out the gun, which he had just received from the Egyptian explorers, on subjects who happened to be within range (*see* p. 209); King Alikori of the Pari, who at the turn of the nineteenth century, relentlessly continued to fight the smaller and weaker moiety of his kingdom to the point that its members massively fled into exile (*see* p. 143–144); and the excessive rage of King Lomoro, observed by the American explorer Donaldson-Smith, against one of his subjects (Case 9.2). A common reason for the Condominium Authorities to fire chiefs, who were usually from royal families, was their proneness to homicide. They had no qualms to kill commoners opposing their commands.

From regicidal kingdom to sacrificial state

To support my argument that the early kingdoms on the Upper Nile offer us a window on a crucial phase in the evolution of the state, I propose to take a closer look at what the transformation from non-state kingship to state-framed kingship means in terms of empirical practices and institutions. A suitable field to make relevant observations for this purpose is the kingdom of Buganda. While it is strictly speaking outside the Nilotic ethnological field of study, there have been regular historical contacts between the societies in our research area and the Buganda kingdom, and the founders of the royal dynasty of Buganda are believed to have Nilotic antecedents. Claessen, an international authority on the study of early states worldwide, counts Buganda among the most centralised and differentiated state formations that emerged in Sub-Saharan Africa before the colonial period (Claessen & Skalnik, 1978; 1981; Claessen, 1987).

What strikes first when examining Buganda kingship is the important role of violence in the exercise of power. This has puzzled anthropologists. Lucy Mair (1934:177–8), for example, ponders thus: "The question of precisely how the cruelties [...] by the last independent kings were reconciled with the conception of a 'good' king expressed at his accession is one that cannot be answered." And Audrey Richards (1964:291) remarks that 'many African chiefs are formally praised for their ferocity to enemies but the insistence that the Kabaka [the king] can and should destroy his own subjects is, I think, unusual.'

In fact, executions were a regular feature of the king's rule. While the king's court, at the apex of Buganda's finely meshed network of local courts, settled cases according to the principles of customary law, many of the death sentences ordered by the king were not the outcome of jurisprudence but were made by royal decree. Foreign visitors to the pre-colonial royal courts frequently reported on people being sentenced to death for trifles, often minor infringements of the court etiquette (sneezing, laughing, touching the throne, showing a piece of naked flesh, etc.).

While the executions decreed or confirmed by the king included criminal cases, most of the sentencing had a sacrificial or political objective. This is especially true for the mass executions called *kiwendo*, a term that refers to the fact that the number of victims required for this type of execution was fixed in advance. Roscoe (1911:333), who wrote an extensive monograph on the Baganda, following instructions given by Frazer, mentions a number between two and five hundred. The number was fixed by the king, often in compliance with the oracle of a spirit medium linked to one of the temples of the Ganda gods. Mediums also identified dangers to the well-being of the kingdom and reported suspected insurgents.

To complete the required numbers, commoners were randomly and in large numbers captured by the king's executioners from the roads leading to the capital. The work of the executioners was supervised by the king's police. When the desired number was reached the king's police chief would sound the drums to stop the arrests.

There were thirteen mass-execution sites in the kingdom. Some sites were specific for certain categories of victims: for chiefs and dignitaries; for princes accused of planning a rebellion (they would be burnt or starved since royal blood could not be shed) or for wives and friends of the king (a category of victims that was only executed some days after arrival to give the king time to change his mind); other sites catered for a mix of convicted offenders and innocent captives. The victims of these executions were generally co-operative, at least if Roscoe is to be believed:

> Those who have taken part in these executions bear witness how seldom a victim, whether man or woman, raised his voice to protest or appeal against the treatment meted out to him. The victims went to death (so they thought) to save their country and race from some calamity and they laid down their lives without a murmur or a struggle. (1911:338)

Before being killed — usually by spear or club — they were made to drink a potion that gave the king control of the victim's ghost. The bodies were left where they fell, for wild animals or birds to prey on. Relatives did not dare to bury the corpses because they had been given to the gods (*idem*: 336) or to the king (*idem*: 112).

The kings measured their power in terms of the capacity to victimise subjects. When King Muteesa (1856–1884) was shown a photograph of Queen Victoria by the missionary Felkin, the king not only asked him "how she lived, what she wore, and how many servants she had, but also whether she killed many people" (Wilson & Felkin, 1882, Vol.II:18). The thirty priests of the *lubaale* (Ganda divinity) cults who were decapitated during the audience given by Muteesa to Chaillé-Long, Gordon's envoy charged to convince the king to agree to the annexation of Buganda to Egypt (see the illustration on p. 447), were also meant to send a signal of the king's power to Egypt's *Khedive*. Mass executions took place at different occasions, at the inauguration or renovation of a king's tomb — with one of the largest known executions taking place at the renovation of King Ssuuna's (1832–1856) tomb in 1880 when thousands were killed. The frequency of such mass executions was estimated by Mair as once every ten years (1934:179). The missionary Mackay writes that the massacres had been more frequent during the last years of King Muteesa's reign and suggests that they were carried out to help restore the king's health (Ray, 1991:176). His fellow missionary, Felkin, reports that the number of massacres was rather an indicator of the king's good health. Once Muteesa would be well, so he had been assured, the frequency of executions would again go up (1882, Vol. 2: 23).

The executions were ordered when the king or the mediums felt that disorderliness was on the rise. Signals of such disorder could be dirty roadsides covered with excrement, young men loitering in the capital, a rise in adultery cases, especially those involving princesses, as well as reports of a planned insurrection. Executions were meant to counteract any tendency to entropy. They served, according to Mair, 'to set the land right' (1934:233).

Buganda as a country could be said to alternate between two conditions. On the one hand during an interregnum, it was '[a] wild state of disorder [...], where anarchy reigned, people tried to rob each other, and only chiefs with a strong force were safe, even the smaller chiefs being in danger from stronger chiefs, who did as they liked during the short interregnum' (Roscoe: 1911:103). On the other hand was 'the king's peace' (*mirembe*), always vulnerable and in need of sacrificial propping up. The forces of disorder were imagined to be permanently on the lookout for opportunities to undermine the peace. The king was permanently on the alert for signs of insubordination. Brothers of the king were the primary suspects. While Speke, in 1862, met with an estimated thirty brothers of Muteesa, the missionary Ashe, in 1883, is told that only one brother was still alive (Claessen, 1987:226). The Queen-Mother played an important role in protecting the king from the political aspirations of his brothers by arranging for their elimination (Roscoe, 1911:188).

The mass executions kept everybody on their toes. They were *sacrificial* in the sense that Girard gives to this term: they served to channel any uncontrolled discontent and hostility in the country in a single direction, in this case away from the king onto victims that were arbitrarily selected from among the people. Though these killings followed the opposite direction they fulfilled the same function as the regicidal confrontations played out between the Nilotic Rainmakers and their people some five hundred kilometres down the Nile and analysed in Chapter Seventeen.

There are two important differences between the Buganda kings and their Nilotic counterparts: the far higher cost in human lives of the state-framed mass executions in Buganda, and secondly, the fact that in Buganda, commoners were killed in order to establish, maintain or restore 'the peace of the king', while in the societies downstream the king was killed to remove epidemics, droughts and other misfortunes from his people. Between the state of Buganda and the regicidal Nilotic kingdoms, the direction of victimisation was inverted, Buganda representing an extreme case of the tipping of the balance of power between king and people, as discussed in Chapter Eleven, to the advantage of the king. While in the Nilotic kingdoms the king is the focus and point of attraction of internal discontent, in Buganda all violence is taken out on the king's subjects. At no point during his rule is the Ganda king brought into a situation of confrontation with his subjects, as is commonplace between the *monyomiji* and their king (Chapter Sixteen). The Ganda king is never summoned to account for his deeds. He is legally immune — together with a selected few of his top dignitaries. He is practically inaccessible to his people unless mollified by significant gifts such as a number of nubile women (not just one), a gift that is out of reach for monogamous commoners (Roscoe, 1911:333). People hid from the king and from his police when they encountered a royal party on the road. Their mere gaze could be considered a provocation, and a reason for execution (Speke, 1863:272).

The remoteness of the Ganda kings from their subordinates was underscored by the funerary arrangements. While among the Bari, Lotuho and Shilluk the closest associates of the king accompanied him in his grave, in Buganda all the staff in charge of the king's personal needs — chamberlain, cooks, fire-maker, dairymen, water fetchers including the wives of these officials — followed the king in his death. They were not buried alive alongside their dead master but killed at the inauguration of the tomb, weeks later, their bodies being left to decompose in the fenced compound surrounding the tomb (Ray, 1991:166).

A similar contrast is evident in the installation ceremonies. At his installation the Nilotic king is reminded of his eventual victimhood. The Bari transfer their most feared diseases on him while the uncle of the new Lulubo king demands payment of damages for putting his sister's son in the "centre of evil". The Lotuho and Lokoya take a lot of sacrificial trouble to domesticate the feline foundling they will convert into their ruler.

The installation of the Buganda king follows an opposite scenario. While he is believed to be a feline predator like his Lotuho and Lokoya counterparts the installation rite is aimed at intensifying his feline ferocity, not at taming it. Dressed in a fresh leopard skin, he is given a symbolic knife to kill rebels. Using metaphors that liken the king to a queen-termite eating the drones fertilising her, the top dignitaries counsel him not to refrain from using violence since "commoners (*bakopi*) are like sorghum: whoever judges them owns them" (Ray, 1996:171). Later, during a nine-day induction tour of the central districts of the kingdom (*okukula*), the new king, who was often only an adolescent, was made to witness killings, to give orders to kill, and even to kill himself (Roscoe, 1911:210–4; Ray, 1996:171–5; Wrigley, 1996:147–54).

Statehood implies an end to reciprocity in the conduct of affairs that are a common concern to king and people. The actions of the king are no longer contingent on those of the people and vice-versa — as this is to a large extent the case in the Nilotic kingdoms studied in this book. The norm of reciprocity is replaced by the *de facto* complementarity[21] of two distinct sets of roles. One set of roles is reserved for the king and his entourage and the other set defines the behaviour expected from the people. The two sets match like a dovetail joint but their fit is externally imposed and to the advantage of the king and his group. The key rules in the role relationship are that only the king has the right to decide on the use of violence and that he is immune to acts of violence himself. The complementarity of roles opens the possibility of organised repression and exploitative forms of mobilisation of people outside the orbit of reciprocity. As the complementarity of the state-subject relationship sinks in, it becomes increasingly difficult to re-convert the asymmetrical relationship into a reciprocal one. History teaches us that most rebellions and revolutions against the state, even when successful, ultimately result in another statal arrangement. Statehood is forever because of its capacity to deeply transform the society. It results in forms of demographic, economic and military expansion that social systems organised according to principles of reciprocal exchange cannot accommodate.

The inbuilt tendency of the state to violent repression demands feedback mechanisms on a fourth level of complexity: democracy and the rule of law. Because there is no way back, the transformation of polities based on early kingship into asymmetrical states has historically been exceptionally rapid despite the unequal and intrinsically violent nature of the power exercised by states. The capacity of the state to expand and incorporate foreign political entities has no other limit than the ambition of other states to do the same — with the result that today there are hardly any humans left that have not been brought within the orbit of state power. The challenge put before contemporary state-builders is to domesticate the state's violence and to create institutions that enable citizens to participate in political life — as was

---

21   For my use of the concepts of 'reciprocity' and 'complementarity', see Gouldner, 1960.

the case before the advent of the state. The uneven achievements in this direction over the last two and a half millennia have proved that this transformation will be far more difficult than the emergence of the state itself.

The state as crystallisation of the mimesis of the antagonist

If kings are the founders of the first states, then the state is ultimately an outcome of what Girard called the 'mimesis of the antagonist' and not of some kind of 'positive mimesis' as the founding fathers of sociology assumed. Both Durkheim and Weber described society as being primarily held together by positive imitation. Durkheim called that cohesive force 'solidarity by resemblance', the sharing of a common identity, beliefs and moral attitudes of which the king is an incarnation:

> If [society] happens to fall in love with a man and if it thinks it has found in him the principal aspirations that move it, as well as the means of satisfying them, this man will be raised above the others and, as it were, deified. Opinion will invest him with majesty exactly analogous to that protecting the gods. This is what has happened to so many sovereigns in whom their age had faith: if they were not made gods, they were at least regarded as direct representatives of the deity (1915:213).

Society cultivates 'the principal aspirations that move it' by 'falling in love with a man' who has the means of turning these aspirations into reality. For Weber, too, the charismatic bond between a leader and his following is the stem cellular prototype of all forms of political authority. Charisma is defined as:

> ...qualities of a person which are held to be extraordinary (originally magically determined, as in prophets, war-heroes, leaders in the hunt, healers and peacemakers) by virtue of which that person is accepted as a leader, while he is either believed to have a supernatural or superhuman effectiveness, or to be sent by God, *or to be someone to be imitated* (1985:140; my italics).

As for Durkheim, the special qualities of the charismatic leader are in the admiring eyes of his followers. Weber is aware of the scapegoat kings of the past. He discusses the case of the Chinese emperor (1985:656) who was made to do penance in times of disaster when people believed he underperformed, and that of the *Verschmäherkönige* ('kings of scorn') of the Germanic tribes (*idem*: 140; 670).

For both thinkers positive imitation was the foundation of the social bond, negativity being incidental, prompted by disappointment and anger about failure. Marx implicitly shared this viewpoint. For him the state had no social substance of its own. It was an extension of the dominant classes in the political realm. Once the proletarian revolution settled the class struggle, the state would perish and an era based on positive reciprocity could return.

Girard's theory reverses the classical view of the primacy of positive attachment as the cement of social life. This study demonstrates that Girard's scapegoat mechanism provides a plausible explanation of the practice of regicide in early kingship, and thereby of the dynamics that transformed early kingdoms into states.

The central point of each village is a bunch of ebony poles planted in the middle of an open space that serves as ceremonial ground. The pole-shrine is the main community shrine. During important celebrations (war dances, New Year, the handing over of generational power) the poles serve as drum posts. They are not used for profane festivities such as courtship dances. When they are first erected, a sacrifice is made over the hole in which the poles are planted. They are maintained with libations of oil and beer. More details in Chapter Nineteen. On the edge of the ceremonial ground are the drum house, the sitting platforms of the ruling generation and the residence of the king/rainmaker. The village in the photo is Lohutok, Lopit, in 1995.

2

Ethnological Connections Between the Nile and the Kidepo

After a tour of the geography of our field of study during which the different peoples that provided the data for this book are introduced, this chapter lists the arguments in favour of treating the area between the Nile and the Kidepo as a single field for comparative anthropological research.

The geographical setting

The traveller who navigates the Nile upstream from Khartoum enters the area selected for this study when the first mountain comes in sight. This is Mount Nyerkenyi marked on most maps as *Jebel Lado* after the name of the Bari chief who controlled the surrounding area when Charles Gordon chose it as the location for the site of the capital of Egypt's Equatoria Province, also named Lado. After one has spent several days navigating channels which cross the papyrus swamps, it is a pleasant change to enter Bariland with its well-marked, firm river banks, its park-like, undulating plains interspersed by rocky outcrops and mountains. The land of the Bari extends for some 150 kilometres along both banks of the Nile — locally called *Supiri*. Half-way this territory, rapids on the Nile prevent further navigation. This is why the administrative capitals of the southern Sudan have always been located in Bariland, on the stretch of Nile between the rapids to the south and the swamps to the north.

The Bari lived along the banks of the Nile and along its tributaries where these had perennial water, up until the beginning of this century when they were moved inland as part of the campaign against sleeping sickness.

Although Bariland was divided into many rivalling chieftaincies ruled by Rainmakers of various origins, all Bari recognised the supremacy of the Bekat dynasty by the time the first travellers set foot in Bari territory. The rulers bore the title of *Mor*, meaning "King of the Rainmakers" (in Bari: *matat lo kimak*). Their oldest and most powerful centre was Shindiru, some seventy-five kilometres south of Juba on the east bank of the Nile. The second most powerful centre was Bilinyan, also located on the east bank opposite the town of Juba. In the nineteenth century, Bilinyan surpassed Shindiru in political importance partly because of its contacts with the traders, missionaries and empire-builders that arrived from the north.

Travelling in southeasterly direction away from Bilinyan, one notes that the land rises. Once mountains and mountain ranges enclose the horizon in all directions, we have entered the land of the Lulubo and Lokoya. The Lulubo[1] are the most north-easterly extension of the speakers of languages of Madi-Moru stock, while the Lokoya are the most westward extension of the Lotuho languages. Nowadays, many of the Lokoya and Lulubo live along the main roads — the one from Juba going south to Uganda and the east road to Kenya. In the past, Lulubo villages were tucked away in the valleys of the Lulubo hills, while the Lokoya villages were right on top of the mountains and impressed the explorer Samuel Baker as "a series of natural forts" (1866, vol.I:168). Each valley or mountain formed the location of a separate kingdom. If we proceed further east, in the direction of the land of the Lotuho, we have to traverse the narrow pass near Mount Opone where Liria, the largest Lokoya village, is located. Its strategic position near the pass has made it a historic battlefield.

The ceremonial ground with the pole-shrine and monyomiji *assembly point (here consisting of* megaliths*) of old Loguruny on top of the mountain. Here is also the shrine with the pots containing the bones of the kings of Tirangore (see the illustrations on p. 342).*

We enter Lotuholand when we cross the Kinyeti River.[2] The horizon is wider again and the landscape of larger scope. Most of the Lotuho villages are located in the plains

---

1   Nowadays, a growing number of Lulubo prefer to present themselves to outsiders as *Olu'bo*, their name in *Olu'boti*, the language of the Olu'bo. When this book was first written, the name *Lulubo* was commonly used in English. In older documents 'Luluba' is common.

2   It has become more common for the Lotuho to use *Ótuho*, the name of their ethnic community in their own language. In older documents we find 'Latuka' and 'Lotuko'.

which are surrounded to the northeast by the long Lopit Range and to the south by the Imatong and Dongotono massifs whose peaks rise to 3,187 and 2,623 metres, respectively. The Lotuho live in about twenty large-sized villages, the majority of which are located along the banks of the Kinyeti, a river coming down from the Imatong Mountain, and the Hos, which flows between the Imatong and Dongotono massifs along the foothills of the Lopit Mountains north-westwards into the uninhabited floodplain to the north.

Before the Lotuho dispersed into their present villages, the majority of them are believed to have lived at Imatari, in the plains of the Hos, not far from present-day Loguruny. Imatari was destroyed by the Toposa who had been called in by the king to put down a rebellion of the young generation. Although this event took place in the first half of the nineteenth century, Lotuho recollections of Imatari are still vivid and its layout and organisation still serve as a blueprint for later villages.[3]

The Lotuho are surrounded by a number of smaller peoples which speak dialects of the same language. To the west and the south are the Horiok or Ohoriok, 'the black people',[4] a group which includes the Lokoya. The name Lokoya was given by the Bari to the Ohoriok and Lulubo villages immediately bordering on them. It is now generally accepted as an ethnic label for the people of the western Ohoriok chieftainships. Like the Lokoya, the Ohoriok live in polities based on the common habitation of a mountain.

In the past, the Ohoriok also lived further north at the foot of a few hills in the middle of the plains between Liria and Lopit. Segele, their main centre, was Imatari's major rival. As a result of increasing desiccation of the plains and because of the relentless warfare with Imatari, these locations were abandoned in the middle of the nineteenth century; most of the people fled to Liria, Loudo and Lopit.[5]

---

3   A map of Imatari that I found in the archive of the Comboni missionaries is the frontispiece of Chapter Five (p. 124).

4   According to Driberg (n.d.) the name was given by the Lotuho because they were struck by the black appearance of the Ohoriok when they approached them in battle as they did not carry shields. Since the Ohoriok do not have an alternative endonymic name, Driberg's explanation may very well be a popular etymology. The designation 'black people' (*omoliha* in Lotuho, Lokoya, and Lulubo; *col* in Pari) is widely used as a self-appellation. My informants were at a loss for an explanation once they realised that the appellation 'black people' was in common use before European whites appeared on the scene. Maybe the fact that the Lotuho designate their queens with rain ancestry on both sides as *red* queens, and those who lack rain ancestry from one or both parents as *black*, points at a contrast between two population strains of different skin colour, the reddish strain possibly referring to the Eastern Cushitic groups whose earlier existence in the area was hypothesised by Ehret (1974, 1982), or to Oromo traders known as *Gala* or *Ogala* to the Lotuho speakers and *Gela* to the Bari and Lulubo (see note 9 of this chapter). Note that the Murle also have *red* chiefs. (Lewis, 1972:48)

5   The depopulation of the area near Kurla hill, the one-time location of the villages of Faciti and Hullai, was an important factor in the westward push of the Ohoriok. When Vinco passed Liria and the Kurla hill on his way to Lafon in 1851, Kurla and the adjacent Icuda hills had been deserted only three years earlier. He was told that the inhabitants had fled to Liria and

The upper reaches and the northwestern slopes of the Dongotono massif are inhabited by the Dongotono. The eastern and southeastern slopes are occupied by the Logir who are organised into two rain kingdoms, each consisting of four villages. Their villages look out over the land of the Toposa, Boya[6] and Didinga — enemies who live on the other side of the Kidepo Valley. In a high valley in the mountain there is a stretch of high altitude rain forest which is the location of Sawa or Asawa, the Sacred Grove which the Logir and Dongotono share to perform their annual rain rituals. The land south and west of the Dongotono Mountains towards the Uganda border is the home of a collection of communities speaking dialects of Lotuho, the Lokwa, Ketebo and Lorwama, together with the Dongotono and Logir loosely called 'Lango'.[7] They will play only a minor part in this book.

The Lopit range is the northeastern extension of the area inhabited by communities that speak languages of the Lotuho group. At its southern tip are the Lotuho villages of Otunge, Chalamini and Ilyeu, according to Lotuho tradition the cradle of the Lotuho people. Together with Lobera, located on a promontory protruding from the Dongotono massif, these villages control the valley which gives access to Lotuholand from the east. Up to the present day, this gateway is a battleground between the Lotuho, on the one hand, and the Toposa and Boya, on the other.

The Lopit range is the abode for seven rain kingdoms varying in size from one to nine villages. Some of these political units are the result of fairly recent secessions. The Lomiya, living at the southern end of the Lopit range, used to have six villages, each village consisting of two sections. After the death of King Musingo, sometime in the middle of the nineteenth century, his two sons competed for the succession and the kingdom fell apart into two: Iboni, the old centre, was ruled by Ayiru, and Lohutok on the eastern slope was ruled by Ohule. A division similar to that of the Lomiya divided the Ngotira, ruled by the Twari rain clan and occupying the central part of the Lopit range, into the chieftaincy of Imehejek (only one village) and that of Mura (nine settlements). The Twari rain clan dates its arrival in Lopit to the destruction of the villages of Segele, Faciti, Hullai and Longulu in the plains between Liria and Lopit. North of the Ngotira are the villages of the Dorik, divided into two rain areas, Logunuwati and Acarok. At the northern tip lies Ngaboli.

Loudo after numerous attacks by enemy tribes (Vinco, 1974:87). Lilley and Arber report that the people of Segele were dispersed towards Lowe, Liria, Ohila, Longairo, Ngulere and Bilinyan (1937:85).

6   The Boya who—like the Didinga, Tenet and Murle—speak a language of the Surma group, call themselves Narim and are called Longarim by the Didinga. Irenge is the name used by Lotuho speakers for Murle, Didinga, Tenet and Boya together.

7   'Lango' is a supra-ethnic label that includes the Logir, Dongotono, the Lokwa (living around Ikotos), the Ketebo (living around Bira near the Uganda border), the Lorwama (in Lotome) and the Imotong (who are sometimes also counted as Horiok) on the eastern slopes of the Imatong massif (Nalder, 1937:82, 113–4; Huntingford, 1953:94–98; Alban, 1922; Lord Raglan, 1923). There is no immediate relationship with the Lango Lwoo speakers in Uganda. The origin of the use of this ethnic label is not clear.

Bordering on the Dorik and on Ngaboli lives a minority of 'Irenge', the name the Lotuho give to their neighbours of Surma stock. They call themselves 'Tenet' and are said to have placed themselves under the protection of the Ngaboli king to offset the imbalance in numbers with the Pari, the traditional enemies of Ngaboli. Like the Pari, the Tenet played an important role in the cross-plain trade, especially between their Boya relatives to the east and the Murle to the north.

Some twenty kilometres north of Ngaboli lies Lafon hill, a small outcrop which is home to some 10,000 Pari[8] who are speakers of a Lwoo[9] dialect closely related to Anuak. In the 1920s, the village covered the terraced hill. Nowadays, its six sections are located around the foot of the hill. Lafon's protruding position into the floodplains made it into a natural port of call for trade with the peoples living across the plains to the north and to the east: the Murle, the Anuak and also with traders known as 'Gala'[10] to the Anuak coming from Ethiopia. In the middle of the nineteenth century, Lafon was the main link between Ethiopia and the societies in the Nile valley from the Mandari in the north down to Bunyoro in the south.[11] Trade, especially the illegal arms trade, continued to be an important activity throughout the colonial period.[12]

---

8   I have adopted the spelling *Pari*. It is the spelling most commonly used by the Pari themselves and by their ethnographer Eisei Kurimoto. 'Berri' and 'Beri' are written in most of the early accounts; Driberg (1925) writes 'Fari' or 'Feri'; 'Föri' is used by Evans-Pritchard (1940a); Crazzolara (1951) refers to them as 'Pääri' while the Bari and Lulubo use 'Böri' or 'Böri-Lokoro' to distinguish the Pari from the 'Böri-Acholi'.

9   Following Joseph Crazzolara, I use the spelling *Lwoo* when referring to the speakers of a number closely related languages that form a branch of 'Western Nilotic' of which Dinka and Nuer constitute the other major branch, and *Luo* when referring to the Luo (or Jur-Luo or Luwo) and the Shilluk-Luo (different from the Shilluk) of Bahr-el-Ghazal and the Luo of Kenya and Tanzania.

10   The terms *gala* (Lotuho), *ogala* (Lokoya), *gela* (Bari, Lulubo) which the people in our area of study used to apply to all foreigners of lighter skin, including Europeans, probably dates from this period of contacts with Oromo traders (Kurimoto, 1995). 'Gala' used to be the name under which the Oromo were known to outsiders including Europeans. In South Sudan *gala,* and related words are used to denote the sphere of modern government. For example the Bari term for government chief is *matat-lo-gela*.

11   Werne (1845:299, 308, 314) mentions salt and copper as articles imported by the Bari via Lafon in exchange for iron objects. D'Arnaud (1842:379) reports on textiles originating from Surat (India). Brun-Rollet (1855:116-120) informs us that the Pari were also in contact with Bunyoro ('Kuenda'), and Vinco (1874:90) writes that the glass-beads found in Lafon had arrived there from Fazogli on the Blue Nile via the Anuak and were, therefore, named *dinyagi*.

12   Lafon continued to have direct contacts with Ethiopian traders up to the last decade of the colonial period: see: *Correspondence respecting Abyssinian raids and incursions into British territory and the Anglo-Egyptian Sudan,* Foreign Office Correspondence: Abyssinia No.1, 1928:1–20; *Lotuko Intelligence Reports,* August 1923 & March 1924. As late as 1944, Anuak rifle traders were arrested from among a Pari raiding party returning from Ngaboli (Equatoria Province Monthly Diary, November 1944, Central Records Office, Khartoum, CIVSEC 57/20/43). During the current war Lafon once again plays the role of transit port between the Ethiopian Highlands and the banks of the Nile.

The geographical area which constitutes the scene for my comparative study has well-defined boundaries, except on its southern flank, where it borders on Madi and Acholi chieftaincies. The vast, uninhabited flood-plains north of Lafon, which stretch on for more than two hundred kilometres before one finds other settlements, make for a formidable natural boundary. It can be crossed only during the turn of the seasons when drinking water is available and the plains are not flooded. To the east, the Kidepo River marks the boundary between the Lotuho and the Toposa, Boya and Didinga who have been their long-standing enemies. The western limit of the Bari is not far west of the Nile.

Delimitation of the 'ethnological field of study'

The peoples we have just passed in review have in common a number of cultural characteristics which distinguish them from their neighbours. The most important one for the purpose of this study is the coexistence of a developed age-class system (which usually consists of four age-sets spanning three to six years each) and institutions of kingship.

The kings in our area of study are Rainmakers, like those of the peoples to the east and south. The most conspicuous feature of the age-class organisation of the peoples east of the Bari is the prominent role of the *monyomiji* (a Lotuho word meaning 'owners' or 'fathers' of the village) in running the affairs of the village. The *monyomiji* rule their community for a fixed period (usually between 12 and 22 years). After this, the power is transferred in a polity-wide ceremony to the next 'generation'. A more detailed discussion of the age-class system will be given in Chapter Eight.

The *monyomiji* system is, first of all, associated with the Lotuho-speaking peoples. From there, it has been adopted by some other groups: the Lulubo, the Pari, the Tenet and a number of Acholi communities bordering on the Lotuho and Horiok. The Lulubo and Pari adopted the system during the second half of the nineteenth century. In Lulubo, its introduction is associated with Okale, Rainmaker of Lokwe, who is said to have 'divided the villages'[13] while the list of successive *monyomiji* sets of Lokiliri also takes us well into the nineteenth century.

Among the Pari, the *mojomiji* system — as the Pari call it — was introduced from neighbouring Lopit by King Alikori whose long rule ended in 1908. At the same time, Alikori, who was only the *rwath* (king) of the Boi moiety, proclaimed himself Rain King (*rwadhi-koth*) of all the Pari, thus raising his status above that of the other *rwadhi*. (Kurimoto, 1988:10–11). The Pari helped spread the *mojomiji* system further afield. During the 1890s, the Kor moiety — tired of the many stick-fights with Boi — went into exile to Pajok (called Parajwok by the Pari) in Acholi. By the time they

---

13   The sectional division of the villages is a feature that is intimately connected with the *monyomiji* system as we shall see in the next chapter.

returned, after Alikori's removal from power ten years later, the Pajok had adopted the *mojomiji* system.[14]

The Tenet adopted the system even more recently. Interestingly, only adolescents are *monyomiji*. The maximum age of the members of the generation taking over in 1984 was about 20 years. Their authority over village affairs is limited, since, contrary to practice in the other communities, the elders can impose fines on the *monyomiji*. The gerontocratic bias, typical for the political organisation of the Boya, Toposa and Didinga, has apparently persisted among the Tenet emigrants, leaving only room for the elaboration of a 'boy-scout variety' of the *monyomiji* organisation.

The Bari age-class system, of which little is left today, was, more like that of the Dinka and Nuer to their north, connected with the activities in the cattle camps away from the village.

Lotuho monyomiji *in gala uniform;* note the syncretistic elements.

---

14 According to some informants, they stayed for only three years, according to others, longer. The case is an interesting example of the speed with which political innovations can be adopted in a 'traditional' society.

If we compare these political systems with those of their immediate neighbours, we find that the Bari-speaking peoples to the west[15] and the north[16], and the Madi[17] and Acholi[18] to the south, possess institutions of kingship but lack an age-class system, while the peoples to the east, the Boya, Didinga and Toposa, have an elaborate organisation based on age and generation but lack institutions of kingship.[19]

Broadly speaking, the central feature of the political organisation of the peoples to the west and south of the area of study was a dominant, royal rain clan surrounded by a number of associated or dependent clans, each clan occupying a clearly defined territory. Political unity of different local groups under a single centre was realised through the attachment of a number of local descent groups to a leading clan. Among the Madi, the basic political unit usually coincided with the village. Among the Acholi, especially in the polities on the Uganda side of the present border, a successful *rwodi* might create large followings consisting of many villages and find himself and his clan at the top of a pyramid with an ever-widening base. His less successful successor might see this domain fall back into its constitutive units.

---

15   According to Nalder's ethnographic survey among the west bank Bari speakers only the Nyepu had age-classes (1937:227). The only detail given—that initiation equals tooth extraction — suggests that the author refers to age-grades. The Nyepu are a small group which shared the river bank with the Bari before the latter were removed inland, as part of the sleeping-sickness campaign.

16   The Western Mandari have only recently taken over their bead sets from the Atuot as an adaptation to their interaction with the Aliab Dinka who also have age-sets. Buxton (1975:311) mentions that in copying from the more remote Atuot, the Mandari avoid being ridiculed by their Aliab neighbours: an interesting instance of managing inter-ethnic mimetic rivalry! The riverine Mandari, the Koböra and Tsera have age-sets which resemble those of the Bari. They had a military function in the past. During the 1950s when Buxton conducted her fieldwork, this function had lost most of its former significance (Buxton, 1963:123–4).

17   The Madi of Moli, the northernmost Madi in close contact with the Lulubo, Lokoya and Bari, had age-classes in the past (information provided by Chief Ageri-Geri Tombe of Moli).

18   Age-classes, including *monyomiji*-sets do exist in a number of Acholi communities: in Omeo, Magwi, Agoro, Pajok, Panyikwara and in the Agago chiefdoms in Uganda. The age-class systems of Omeo, Magwi and Agoro are continuous with those of the neighbouring Lotuho-speaking communities from which some of the vocabulary, including age-set and generation names, has been borrowed. The same may be true for the age-classes in Panyikwara although they are less Lotuho-ised. The Pajok age-class system, as described by Allen (1984:40), appears to be fairly faithful copy of that of the Pari *see* p.52 and note 14 of this chapter). The age-class systems elsewhere in Acholi had but limited significance. Nothing is reported on age-classes in Girling's (1960) comprehensive account of the socio-political organisation of the Acholi.

19   A ten-day visit in May 1985 to Toposaland was instructive with respect to the major similarities and contrasts between Toposa social organisation and that of their westerly neighbours. Müller-Dempf (1989, 1991) is a sophisticated ethnographic account of Toposa age-class organisation. Tornay (1979, 2001) offers a comprehensive description of the socio-political organisation of the Nyangatom, the eastern neighbours of the Toposa also belonging to the Karimojong cluster.

Southall's study of the Lwoo speaking Alur of northwestern Uganda is an analysis of a political system of this kind. He introduced the concept of *segmentary state* to account for the specific articulation of social segmentation and centralism that characterises these polities (1956, esp. 229–266; 1965; *see* below p.270–271). Perhaps, it can be seen as an ideal-typical model of political organisation of the peoples to the west and the south of our field of study.

To the east, across the Kidepo, the age-class and generation organisation is the vehicle for the formation of political blocs transcending the boundaries of village and descent-group. In the territorial sections into which the Toposa and Nyangatom are divided, matters of war and peace are decided by the sectional council of the age-class of the elders. Some of the sacral powers which in our field of study are the prerogative of the king, such as the power over rain and drought, are vested in the ruling *Generation of Fathers* among the Toposa.

The capacity of the last type of political organisation to unify its constituent sections and to centralise its command in confrontations with outsiders was considerable. To their western neighbours, the Toposa and the Boya were, and to some extent they still are, formidable enemies. They were responsible for the destruction and disintegration of the Lotuho Kingdom of Imatari which in Lotuho tradition represents the highest degree of political unity ever reached by their society.

Didinga political organisation is described by Nalder as weak: "it seems certain that until recently they had no chiefs as such, though individuals might attain to temporary eminence, but that tribal guidance was in the hands of elders" (1937:143). In an article published two years later, Driberg, author of a well-known monograph on the Didinga (1930), points at a number of similarities between the Didinga political system and that of Bari and Lotuho. Like the latter, they have a ritual-political leader (*kabu*) with power over rain, a Master of the Land (*bang ti lotu*) and a Master of Health (*bang t'olu*). But unlike his equivalents to the West, the Didinga *kabu* lacks sovereignty over clans and clan territory other than his own (Driberg, 1939:71). Kronenberg who studied the Didinga between 1958 and 1960 does not mention the *kabu* at all. His study emphasises the role of the age-class system in the distribution of authority. Rainmakers appear in his study as charismatic persons not linked to a particular office or clan. They are not appointed; they do not succeed but "reveal themselves" (1972:139).

The Eastern Nilotic connection

With the exception of the Lulubo, Pari and Tenet, all peoples in our sample are speakers of languages that are classified as 'Eastern Nilotic'. This grouping, based on linguistic criteria alone, was designed by Köhler in 1948 and was made to replace the old-fashioned category 'Nilo-Hamites',[20] the old-time 'Nilotes' (Dinka, Nuer, Lwoo)

---

20 The use of this classificatory label by early anthropologists is based on the assumption that these peoples are the genetic, cultural and linguistic mixture of agricultural 'Negroes' and pastoralist Caucasian 'Hamites'. The Hamitic strain was believed to account not only for such diverse

being classed by him as 'Western Nilotes'. Sutton's geographic classification in Plains, River-Lake, and Highland Nilotes for respectively, eastern, western and southern Nilotes coincides with that of Köhler, the last category including the Kalenjin peoples and the Pokot of Kenya and the Sabiny of Uganda.

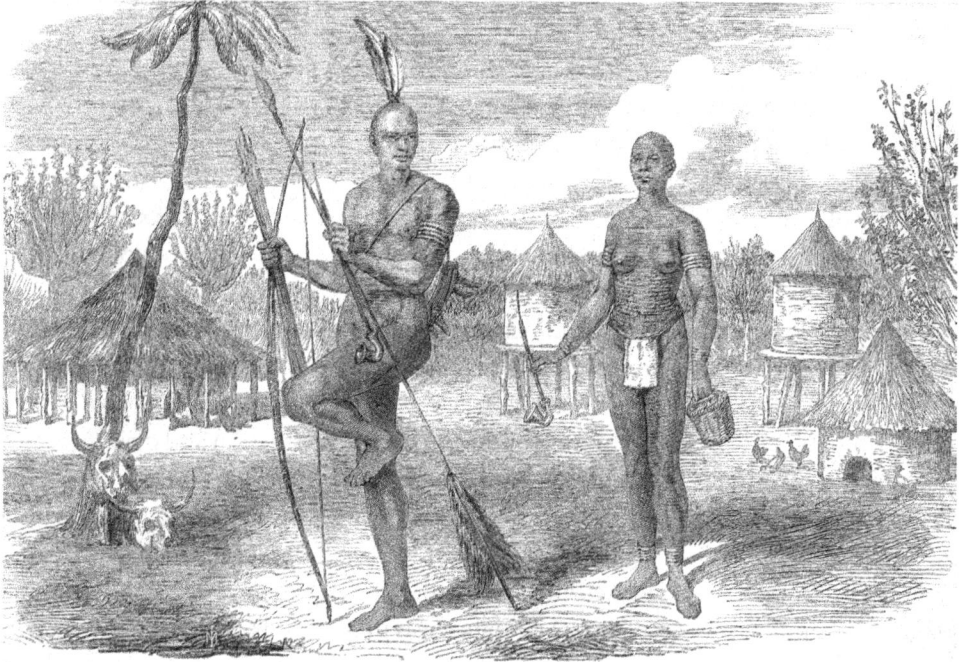

Bari couple sporting typical artefacts; note the typical Nilotic posture of the man (Cutting from an unidentified British newspaper, 1860s)[21].

The Ethnographic Survey of Africa of the International African Institute (Huntingford, 1953) groups the Bari, Lotuho, Lokoya and Lulubo as one block of 'Northern Nilo-Hamites' while Murdock (1959:330) and Greenberg include the

characteristics as pastoralism, centralised political institutions, nominal gender, long stature and pointed noses, but also for the 'noble' impression these peoples made on romantic European observers. Because of the mixing up of racial, linguistic and cultural criteria and its racist bias, anthropologists now consider the term unacceptable. An example of this mixing up is Lord Raglan's reaction to Seligman's inclusion of the Bari in the Nilo-Hamitic group: "as if Bari were a pure dolichocephalic language. As a fact it is a hybrid language, in which mesaticephalic elements probably predominate" (1926:23). Nevertheless, the term Nilo-Hamite is still popular in the Sudan and eastern Africa, often to vindicate an intimate connection to the founders of the Abrahamic religions. For a scholarly refutation of the Hamitic hypothesis, I refer the reader to Ehret, 1974.

21   A drawing in the same individual artistic style with the same homestead in the background but showing a couple with different physical features, yet holding the same artefacts, appears as an illustration in Baker's *Albert N'Yanza*, 1866, Vol. 1, facing p. 85.

Lotuho-speaking communities in the 'Bari cluster' of the Nilotic family.[22] In the last three classifications, the Pari are included among their Western Nilotic Lwoo brethren (the Acholi, Anuak, Belanda Luo (Jur-Luo), Shilluk-Luo and Shilluk, to mention only the main groups present in South Sudan).

The Bari speakers include the Fajelu, Kakwa, Kuku, Mandari, Nyangbara and Nyepu, all with the exception of the Bari and Mandari exclusively living on the west bank of the Nile. The riverain Mandari include the Tsera ('Shir' in 19th century travelogues) on both banks and the Böri or Köbora on the east bank of the Nile.

According to recent linguistic research by Ehret and Vossen, Bari and Lotuho, although members of the same language family, are as far apart as two members of that family can be. On the basis of a lexicostatistical study, Ehret proposed a new internal ramification of Eastern Nilotic, which was largely confirmed by the more detailed work of Vossen (1982:41–57, 1983:177–208). Eastern Nilotic is divided into two primary branches: Bari, on the one hand, and Teso/Lotuho-Maasai, on the other. The Teso group includes the Toposa, Nyangatom, Turkana and the Karimojong while Lotuho and Maasai find themselves together as members of one subgroup. Ehret (1982) distinguishes four dialects in the Lotuho group: Plains-Lotuho; Lopit, including the dialects of the Lomiya, Ngotira, Dorik and Ngaboli; Lokoya, including Horiok; and Dongotono, including the dialects of the Imotong, Ketebo, Logir, Lokwa and Lorwama. I am not aware of scholarly research on the relationships between these different dialects.

The age-class system of the Maasai betrays its common origin with that of the Lotuho. It includes an age-set leader who is a scapegoat figure: the *olutono* or *olaunoni*. The Maasai leader, however, is not supposed to meddle in politics and does not position himself in opposition to age-class leadership as does his Lotuho counterpart.[23] Among

---

22   Greenberg (1963) based himself not on phonological criteria and basic vocabulary, but on common borrowed vocabulary (Ehret, 1974:40, n.4). For a summary of the generally accepted relations of linguistic affinity of the communities figuring in this book, see the linguistic chart attached as Appendix 2.

23   The *olutono* or *olaunoni* is the ritual leader of a Maasai age-set. He is 'seized' by his age-mates unawares (like when the Lotuho and Lokoya pick their *hobu*) during the *eunoto* festival when junior warriors are promoted to senior warriorhood. He is respected by his age-mates who, after his designation, no longer interact with him as an age-mate but as a respected elder. There is a strong belief that he will die young 'since he is expected to suffer on behalf of his age-set' (Jennings, 2005:29). However, this transference of suffering from the age-set to its leader does not express itself in acts of violence, verbal or physical, but only in the belief that this transference takes place and that the leader will die relatively young as a consequence. The man selected for this dark fate should be without any moral or physical blemish; he should not have killed a human being (unlike the Lotuho *hobu*) and he is not expected to meddle in politics (unlike the Lotuho *hobu*). In compensation for his premature death, his age-mates marry him a wife (like the Lotuho *hobu*). Among the Parakuyo Maasai, the *olaunoni* has the privilege of marrying multiple wives free of charge. That the *olaunoni* should be innocent of violence and without physical blemish is a typical requirement for sacrificial victims, animal as well as human (see Case 16.5). The influence of the *olaunoni* over his peers is that of a role model whose

the Maasai, as among the peoples of the Karimojong Cluster, ultimate authority is unilateral and gerontocratic, and is vested in the senior elders, the 'Generation of Fathers' or in the prophet.

While the Nilotes belong to the Eastern Sudanic Branch of the Chari-Nile group, the Lulubo and their southern neighbours, the Madi, belong to the Central Sudanic Branch. Most of the speakers of this group live west of the Nile, in Sudan (Moru, Käliko, Avukaya), Uganda (Lugbara) and Congo (Lugbara, Lendu, Logo). The Tenet, living on the Lopit range, are an offshoot of the Boya and belong to the Surma group of the Eastern Sudanic Branch together with the Didinga and Murle and other people living in the Sudan-Ethiopia borderlands.

Although the region shows considerable diversity from a linguistic point of view, I believe there are good reasons to treat the area which I staked out as a single field of comparative study. The existing cultural resemblances appear to be based on reciprocal influence and borrowing rather than on the common 'Nilo-Hamitic' origin assumed by Huntingford. Despite the other inputs, the Eastern Nilotic Connection is the dominant one. This state of affairs is acknowledged in the following story, recorded by Spagnolo among the Lokoya:

2.1 *The origin of the Bari, Lokoya and Lotuho* (Lokoya story, Spagnolo)

A father had four wives, all of whom had sons. When he was about to die, he called for the oldest son of each wife. Tombe, the elder son of the second wife, came the same evening and was given all the cattle of which he gave a portion to his younger brother (by the same mother) Lado.

The next morning the sons of the first wife arrived, and the father said: "Why so late, my first begotten son? All the cattle already belong to your brother! Here is some iron so that you can do work in order to get some sheep from your brother in exchange. But you cannot have any cows except by stealing them from your brother."

To the son of the third wife the father gave a horn ladle to be fixed on his head, and of the fourth son he strengthened the nose so they could defend themselves against their enemies.

Tombe became the owner of countless herds and is the father of the Bari. Lado with a smaller portion of the paternal herd became the father of the Lotuko while Iparan and Okare[24], the sons of the first wife, went to the mountains to look for iron, and became the fathers of the Lokoya. The last two brothers became the fathers of the buffaloes and the elephants respectively and settled in the forests (Spagnolo, 1933: XIV, abridged).

The story offers an explanation for the difference in cattle wealth of the Bari and Lotuho and of the contrasting lifestyles of the Bari and Lokoya, respectively: the Bari live in the plains, own cattle and are the victims of raids, while the Lokoya are goat owners, raiders and mountain dwellers.

---

disapproval is feared like a curse. There is no acting out of antagonism as among the Lotuho. Yet among the Parakuyo Maasai, the *olaunoni* used to be a member of the war-council together with the prophet and the spokesman of the age-set (Spencer, 2003:157; Jennings, 2005:28).

24   A large clan found all over Lulubo and in the Lokoya villages of Ilyangari and Ngulere.

In addition to the Eastern Nilotic culture shared with the peoples of the east bank, there is a less conspicuous Madi and Lwoo connection. Furthermore, there are indications that iron played an important role in inter-ethnic and inter-dynastic relations. We shall look into these connections now.

The Madi connection

According to the lexico-statistical investigations of Christopher Ehret, none of the current inhabitants of the area predate the Madi-Moru-speaking group.[25] They were there when the proto-Eastern Nilotics arrived. The various Bari-speaking ethnic groups resulted from cultural convergence with these Madi-Moru speakers.

Lulubo young men in dancing gear; note the head-dresses made of bullet cartridges.

---

25   According to local tradition, the first inhabitants of the area were people of small stature, called *Ongadule* or *Cangadule* by the Lotuho speakers, *Tongotole* by the Lulubo, and *Guruguru* by the Pari. Emin Pasha was told that such small people, called *Njan njani*, could still be found in the forests west of the Nile (Emin Pascha, *Tagebücher*, Vol. I: 215). Emin suggests a connection with the 'Namnam', the name given by the ancient Egyptians to peoples of short stature. Although the stories told about them have an obvious legendary ring, some details—the practice of silent barter, the fact that they survived on meat and fruits, their bearded and brownish physiognomy—may betray a factual core which suggests cultural and racial continuity with the pygmoid peoples of the rainforest.

In the case of the Bari proper, we may assume that these Madi-speakers were the ancestors of the present Lulubo, who are now their eastern neighbours.[26] This is confirmed by several Bari traditions. In the first place, there is the tradition of the few Lulubo clans that claim to be autochthonous in the Lulubo hills "that their ancestors were found in the caves". The story adopts the viewpoint of the immigrant clans who constitute the majority in Lulubo and many of which have Bari antecedents. Two Bari traditions collected by Beaton confirm the ethnic proximity of the Bari and the Lulubo. One states that the Bari, Lulubo and Fajelu once dwelt together at Shindiru and separated after a conflict, the Lulubo going east and the Fajelu to the west (Beaton, 1934:169).[27] The other tradition mentions three brothers who lived in the vicinity of Rejaf, separated and became the ancestors of, respectively, the Bari, Nyangbara and Lulubo (Nalder, 1937:193). Although I have not found Lulubo traditions of shared residence with the Bari, the Lulubo consider the Bari as their closest cultural relatives.

A Pari tradition also puts both groups in one category: a local man who wanted to join Dimo, the leader of the first migration to Lipul hill, used a bow (unlike Dimo's other followers who used spears). When questioned by Dimo who he was, he answered "Nan Dubi" which is Bari for "I am Dubi". Dubi is believed to be the ancestor of the present Bupi clan (also 'Dubupi' or 'Dubi' clan) which the Pari consider as being of Lulubo origin—an opinion which is supported by Dubi's use of non-Nilotic archery. The use of Bari by the Dubi may point at the close association these groups have had for a long time.[28]

The people known as Omoholonye or Ongole in Liria may also indicate early Madi presence. They are considered to be the first settlers and the 'Masters of the Opone Mountain'. There is a Madi as well as a Liria tradition which connects these people with the Odukwe rain clan in Loa (Madi).[29] The name 'Ongole' is similar to 'Ongolu'. The 'Ongolu' in Lulubo occupy an outlying section of Lokiliri and are said to speak the purest Lulubo, uncontaminated with Bari and Lokoya elements.

It is significant that King Ringwat of Liria at an early stage of the occupation of Liria Mountain acquired his rainstones from Madhaira, the Ongole king, the rainstone complex being most developed among the peoples speaking languages of Central Sudanic stock.

---

26   As far as the other Bari-speaking ethnicities are concerned, the following assimilation processes could be hypothesised: Nyangbara with Moru, Kuku with Madi, Kakwa with Käliko and Lugbara, leaving the Fajelu as the group that has stayed closest to its Eastern Nilotic roots.

27   The Fajelu Malari Rainmakers indeed trace their origin to Shindiru (Nalder, 1937:196).

28   The similarity between the name Dubi and *du'pi*, the term the Bari use for their servile class, may also be significant. According to several Bari informants the *du'pi* have a different origin.

29   Both the Madi and the Liria tradition connect these people with Ngangala, while the members of the Odukwe clan now living in Loa say they are of Lokoya origin. This, however, may be due to the recent 'Lokoya-isation' of Liria. The Eru language, the Lulubo dialect of Aru which was formerly more widely spoken, is associated with the Odukwe, their first ancestor being an Oru. These last facts would argue against the Anuak ascendancy Rowley postulates for the Odukwe (Rowley, 1940:283–5).

The Lwoo connection

Oral tradition, names of ethnic groups and loan words indicate that today's Pari are the remnant of a formerly more widespread population of Lwoo speakers on the Equatorian east bank. Since the Lwoo are known to have played an important role in pre-colonial processes of state formation in the interlacustrine area[30] and since the most widely accepted theory of their migration there assumes that at one stage they marched via Lafon or via the Nile valley into present-day Uganda, Lwoo antecedents in our area of research have relevance for the reconstruction of the past over a more extensive area. The oral traditions indicating a previous Lwoo presence come from different areas and different ethnic groups. They show a considerable degree of congruence.

Most of the Pari clans trace their origin to Wi-Pari. Contemporary Pari informants locate Wi-Pari in an area between present Anuakland and Lafon — in the direction where, they know, their closest linguistic relatives live. There are, however, several different accounts. The first one is from Pugeri, the oldest section of Lafon:

> **2.2 The separation of Pari and Shilluk** (Pari story from Pugeri village, Kurimoto)
>
> Dimo, the founder of Pugeri, and his brother Nyikango, the ancestor of the Shilluk dynasty, once lived in the Nile valley. Some say the place was called Terkekke (Terakeka in present-day Mandariland?), others say it was Tindiru (Shindiru?). One day, they had a quarrel. According to one version, the quarrel was about succession to the throne: Caai, the father of the two brothers, favoured Dimo because he used to provide him a share of fish and milk every time he got some. Nyikango became jealous and both brothers fought with bows and arrows. Then Nyikango left.
>
> The other version says that Dimo's daughter swallowed a bead belonging to Nyikango's daughter. Nyikango insisted on getting the bead back since his daughter did not stop crying over it. Dimo was forced to cut his own daughter's stomach to retrieve the bead. Then Dimo left the place; accompanied by two sister's sons, Juro and Nyiggilo, he crossed the Nile and moved via stops in present-day Lulubo and Lokoyaland to Lipul hill, where Dimo became the owner of the hill by playing a trick on the people he found living on the spot (Kurimoto, 1988:2).

A significant detail in the migration story of Pugeri is the name of their place of origin, 'Tindiru', a name closely resembling that of 'Shindiru',[31] the Bari rain capital and the place from where they believe to have originated. Two traditions collected by Buxton among the Bari-speaking 'Böri' of the east bank of the Nile, north of the Bari, whose close relationship with the Pari is admitted by both parties, support this location. One tradition says that the Böri split from the ancestors of the present-day

---

30 The ruling dynasties of the kingdoms of Bunyoro and Buganda claim Lwoo descent.

31 'T' and 'S' are sometimes interchangeable on the east bank. A Lotuho child which was named after me was called Timon, nobody seeing anything wrong with the change of sound so evident to speakers of European languages. Kurimoto also gives as an alternative spelling of the same name 'Dindiru'. One informant told him that the place was east of Lafon, but this seems an adaptation to the now dominant idea that the Pari came from Anuak (1988:2).

Anuak at Wi-Pari, which this tradition locates close to the Kit River. The Kit River flows through the southern part of Bariland into the Nile, not far from Shindiru. From there, the Böri tradition says, the Anuak went east via Liria and Lafon, while the Böri went to their present location (which is not far from Terakeka on the east bank of the Nile).

Pari junior age-sets waiting for their turn in a stick fight. Photo by Eisei Kurimoto.

The second Böri tradition collected by Buxton at Kösumba tells about the successive separations of four brothers who originally lived in Liria (present-day Lokoyaland). When the brother who controlled the rain withheld it from the others, the three moved away and became the founding ancestors of the Böri, dwelling alongside the Nile, the Köbora (another Mandari group) and of the Pari of Lafon (Buxton, 1963:5).

The presence of Pari in Liria is well attested by oral tradition. Their expulsion from the mountain is one of the highlights of Lirian history, each of the invading clans claiming a crucial role in the event. One of these stories runs as follows:

2.3 *The expulsion of the Pari from Liria* (Liria oral history)

Before the arrival of Hatulang, the leader of the Ohoyo (Lotuho-speaking invaders from the East), the Pari and Omoholony (the later Ongole) lived on Opone hill. The Onyake — who, according to some informants, spoke Bari — lived on the hill across the pass. The Pari and Onyake had interminable fights over the use of the water of the Hicoroi stream. The Pari had sharpened sticks, the Onyake fought with iron weapons.[32] Hatulang united the Onyake and the clans that followed

---

32   The clan tradition of the Masters of the Bow of Liria (Acu clan) tells how the Onyake used bows and arrows to fight the Pari. When the Acu arrived with their iron spears they concluded an

him and ordered fires to be lit in a large semi-circle at the foot of the mountain so that the Pari believed they were outnumbered. Many of the Pari who tried to break through the cordon were killed, the others fled to Lafon. Only a few blind people were left behind in Liria where their descendants live up to the present day.

The same story was collected by missionary Morlang on his visit to Liria in 1860 as an account of events that had recently taken place. His story adds the detail that the Pari surrendered because of hunger and thirst (Morlang, 1862/3:117). The following Bari tradition makes a connection between the Pari and the Bari:

2.4 *The separation of the Bari and the Pari* (Bari story, Haddon)

Under the rule of King Tombe of the Nyori clan, a dispute broke out about the question whether a particular woman was going to bring forth a single child or twins. The chief could not find a solution that satisfied the disputants. The belly of the woman was cut open to see. When the woman died, the Bari, under Tombe, moved away towards the Nile after having divided the rain-stones and the cattle (Haddon, 1911:468).

It is worth having a closer look at the Nyori clan as a possible link between the Lwoo groups and the Bari. The Nyori are the largest Bari clan. They provide the Rainmakers for a large number of communities both inside and outside Bariland: Tombur, Kelang, Gumosi in Southern Bari, an area called 'Nyori' on the west bank in northern Bari (this last place is associated with the origin of the Nyori), Edemo, a Lulubo village where they are called Panyangiri, and in Moli, Madi. A tradition collected by Haddon suggests that they were the kings of Shindiru before the Bekat took over (Haddon, 1911).

The Bari chronicles collected by Beaton — almost certainly from Bekat spokesmen — do not refer to such an event. But the fact that several early ancestors in the genealogy of the Bekat have the same names as the ancestors of the Nyori dynasties of Tombur and Pager suggests that the early Nyori kings were included to give more depth to the list of Bekat kings.

If we read Beaton's Bekat chronicle closely there is a clear indication when the change of rule occurred. The diviner Lokuryeje acquired a powerful position during the rule of King Pintong, a name also figuring in the Nyori genealogies. According to Beaton's text, the diviner Lokuryeje disappeared while Pintong was succeeded by his son 'Lokureje'. By spelling the two names in a slightly different way Beaton supports the Bekat claim to the antiquity of their descent, or at least makes it more difficult for Nyori Rainmakers to bring rival claims forward.[33]

---

alliance with the Onyake. Since then the latter have never again been defeated.

33   Beaton, Notes, 'Histories of Kogi', 'History of Tombur' and 'History of Pager'; Southern Records Office, Juba; Beaton, 1934:198–200, Beaton:1936:120. The rule of Lokuryeje is also connected with the invasion of the Lomukudit ('numerous as grass', a typical age-class name, cf. my discussion of age-class names in Chapter Eight; see also: Beaton, 1936:139). They are connected by Crazzolara with the Lwoo migration wave rolling southward (1951:54–57). From the point of view taken here they should rather be identified as Eastern Nilotics, organised

The fact that the men of Opwalang, the moiety of Liria from where — according to Lirian tradition — the Pari were chased, refer to themselves as 'Nyori', the fact that the Toposa call the Pari 'Nyoro', and the coincidence that the Nyori place of origin is a location close to the area where, according to Shilluk and Pari myths, Nyikang and Dimo separated, would lend further support to the assumption that the Nyori were a Lwoo rain clan.

In addition to oral tradition, there is the widespread use of the name Pari and its equivalent forms (Böri, Pöri, Vari, and possibly even — why not? — Bari). The name Böri is used by the Lulubo and southern Bari both for the Lafon Pari and the Acholi, an indication that these groups were once considered a single people. The Didinga call the Acholi *Vari* (Driberg, 1925:27) while the Logir call *Pari* the Lotuho-speaking Lokwa who, according to Driberg, show signs of considerable assimilation to the Acholi.[34] The presence of the 'Böri' rain clan among the Kakwa and Moru indicates that the same Lwoo population possibly also extended westwards of the Nile (Baxter, 1952:111; Huntingford, 1953:55). The existence of Lwoo loan-words in Bari, Lotuho, Lokoya, and Lulubo for central religious and social concepts, for example, *juok* ('divinity'), *cien* ('posthumous curse'), *ker* ('royal'), and *bong* ('commoner'), points in the same direction.

This evidence confirms Evans-Pritchard's hypothesis — based on Anuak traditions — according to which the Shilluk and Anuak have spread from a location in present-day eastern Equatoria (Evans-Pritchard, 1940c:54–55). There is no need to define this Lwoo homeland very narrowly as being limited to Lipul hill, as Evans-Pritchard does. To the contrary, the available linguistic and historical evidence suggests a fairly even spread of Lwoo-speakers — mixed with other linguistic groups — between the Nile valley and the Kidepo River.

The hypothetical 'march south' of the Lwoo through Bariland, the idea of Father Crazzolara (1951:52-58) which has found wide support especially among students of Lwoo history in Uganda and Kenya,[35] should, I think, be replaced by a different view. My hypothesis is that the Lwoo have been present on the east bank between the 6th and the 4th parallel for a considerable length of time, coexisting with other ethnic groups. They were either absorbed, or pushed away from their original settlements by later Bari, Lotuho and Surma speakers, who drove wedges in what was formerly a continuous Lwoo and Madi speaking area. One such wedge (Surma) separated the Pari and Anuak, another (Lotuho) the Pari and the Acholi, while the different Bari-speaking ethnic identities were formed in a process of mutual acculturation of Madi-, Lwoo- and Bari-speaking groups. It should be noted that this hypothesis takes

---

in age-classes with a military function, possibly the introducers of the Bari language along the banks of the Nile. The rapid expansion of the language could be explained by its use as the language of the age-class organisation. Cf. the use of Lokoya by the *monyomiji* of Lulubo described below.

34   Driberg, 1932:601, note 1. The assimilation suggested by Driberg could have been the other way around: the 'Lotuho-isation' of a Lwoo population.

35   Ehret (1982) also implicitly accepts this view. At least, he works from the assumption that the Lwoo are latecomers on the Equatorian scene.

a middle position between the northern origin of the Lwoo postulated by Crazzolara and their southern origin, near Bunyoro, proposed by Wrigley in a recent article (Wrigley, 1981).

More research into the archaeology and history of eastern Equatoria, which takes into account new evidence from Upper-Nile and Bahr-el-Ghazal,[36] is needed before we can reach more definitive conclusions concerning the suggested population movements and the resulting interactions of speakers of Madi, Lwoo, Bari and Lotuho languages.

The iron connection

According to oral tradition, iron working played an important role in the formation and consolidation of new kingdoms. Its introduction to the area is associated with the Bari and with the Pari (names which in several stories seem to be interchangeable).

Both Shindiru and Bilinyan were important iron-working centres.[37]

Blacksmith's workshop Bongilo, Lokiliri.

In Bilinyan, it must have been a pillar of the royal economy. In 1841, the traveller Werne witnessed how in Bukö (Tsera), iron rings were bartered for slaves by deputies of Logunu, king of Bilinyan. These slaves were put to work in his iron mines.[38]

---

36 Recent finds in Upper Nile and Bahr-el-Ghazal indicate a formerly wider distribution of Lwoo-speaking communities (Johnson, 1980:84ff; Robertshaw & Siiriäinen, 1985).

37 Although the Bari are now considered 'bow and arrow people' like the Lulubo and the Madi, in the past their large spear blades were notorious. Morlang was informed by King Legge of Liria that "the people in the country of the Bari to the South have spears three times as big as ours" (Morlang, 1862/3:117). Gordon relates that the fact that the Southern Bari used spears with blades that were two feet long, forced him to distribute spears to his Makaraka troops whose bayonets were ineffective against the large Bari spears (G.B.Hill 1881:116).

38 The cheap availability of iron from Khartoum in the years following Werne's visit must have meant a serious blow to the position of the Bari kings. It may have been the main reason for

All over the east bank, blacksmiths were closely associated with the king. Among the Bari, blacksmiths were slaves of the king. Among the Lulubo, Lokoya and Lotuho they had prestige, as they were generally respected as part of the king's retinue.

In Lotuho, at least two stories circulate that point at Bilinyan as the origin of Lotuho blacksmithery. The *hang-Pari* ('Pari clan') claim to be the oldest blacksmiths in Lotuho. They state that their ancestor came from Bilinyan to Chalamini, where he was attached to the royal clan. From there, the *hang-Pari* dispersed to other centres: Mura-Hatiha, Lopit, Lafon and Ifwotu.[39] The other legend associates the foundation of Imatari with the introduction of new iron working techniques, again from Bilinyan:

2.5 *The foundation of Imatari and the introduction of iron working* (Lotuho oral history, collected in Hiyala)

Imuhunyi, the son of Attulang, the king of Chalamini, had been cursed by his father. He went to Bari (other versions say to Pari) to look for a spell that would deliver him of the curse. When he arrived at the palace of the Bari king of Bilinyan, the king expressed his doubt about Imuhunyi's royal powers and decided to subject him to a test. First, Imuhunyi was asked to make rain during the dry season. After Imuhunyi had produced a good shower, the king wanted to test him again. Imuhunyi was requested to sit on top of a skin suspended above a pit in which spears were fixed pointing upwards. The spear blades gently bent under Imuhunyi's weight. As a third test, the king asked him to keep a pipe burning under water. Imuhunyi disappeared for four hours before he re-emerged from the river with the tobacco burning. Lastly, he was asked to cut a huge mahogany tree with his ebony spear. In one blow Imuhunyi cut the tree in half. When the Bari tried to do the same with an iron spear it remained stuck half-way in the tree. After this miracle the Bari king conceded that Imuhunyi was really a king. To seal their relationship he gave Imuhunyi a two-bladed iron spear in exchange for his wooden spear. He also gave him a bull and a number of blacksmiths to accompany him, the *Cor*. He told Imuhunyi to build his town where the bull stopped walking. When the bull stopped, the *Cor*, whose descendants still live in Loguruny, made the first fire of what was to become Imatari. *Asalak*, the spear given by the king, became the most sacred royal spear of the Lotuho.

The Bari-speaking blacksmiths of Lokiliri unequivocally state that they are 'Böri-Lokoro' (= Pari) by origin but they simultaneously admit a genealogical link with the blacksmiths of Bilinyan.

The language and culture of the Lulubo, Lokoya and Lotuho blacksmiths was, and — in the case of those of Lokiliri (Lulubo) and Ifwotu (Ohoriok) — still is largely

---

the people of Bukö to secede from the Bilinyan Kingdom shortly after the trade with Khartoum had started (Lafargue, 1845:159–160; Werne, 1848:365–6). Whatever was left of the mining industry remained under the king's control, at least in Shindiru. When crossing the Kaya River in 1905, explorer Powell-Cotton came across a group of blacksmiths who were working for the king of Shindiru. They made hoes from iron which they were smelting themselves. These, they said, were given to their king who gave them sorghum flour in exchange (Powell-Cotton, 1908:156). They combined their blacksmithing with fishing; the women doing much of the iron smelting.

39   Personal communication by Andreas Grüb of the University of Frankfurt.

Bari. In the past, blacksmiths from all over eastern Equatoria used to have annual festivals attended by blacksmiths from as far away as Haforyere (Lotuho) in the east and Bilinyan in the west. During these festivals, the special blacksmiths' dance would be danced (Bari and Lulubo: *tibidi*; Lokoya: *ojibidi*) and marriages would be arranged, a practice suggesting a previous endogamy of the blacksmiths.

Melting-pot

Far from being a collection of neatly arranged, different ethnic communities each with its own language, culture and migration history, the east bank of the Nile proves an area where processes of cultural assimilation between various groups of peoples have gone on for a considerable period of time. A reconstruction of these past interactions encounters important difficulties, because of the tendency of these societies to create uniform images of themselves. This self-image in turn affects cultural behaviour, which, as a result, tends to acquire a homogeneous character. Three factors play a role in this homogenising process.

The first factor is the 'dualistic' principle whereby groups define themselves primarily in opposition to other, potentially hostile, groups: clan origins that do not match the polarisation are mystified; language use and cultural practices may be made to follow lines of political convenience.

Secondly, traditions are adapted in such a way that they retain their explanatory value to the people which keep them. The relation between place names and the locations to which they refer may be adjusted in a way that suits the conditions of the time. Today, it makes little sense for the Pari to say that they came from Bariland or lived in Liria. The Bari have lost all of their old-time glamour while the Lirians have defeated the Pari. It is understandable that most Pari clans adopt the Boi viewpoint that they came from Anuak, a story which at the same time explains the singularity of their language amidst other tongues. Similarly, most Lirian clans now claim an origin that emphasises their association with the invaders led by Hatulang.

A third factor promoting uniformity is the more rapid numerical increase of groups which have a political and economic advantage, and the concomitant decrease in the numbers of those who are at a disadvantage as a result of the difference in opportunity to acquire wives. The institution of clientship — by which a poor man adopts the clan identity of the patron who provides him with a wife — reinforces this tendency, so that clans of conquered groups gradually disappear from the scene.

Finally, we should mention the homogeneity effected by the colonial administration which put an end to war and froze ethnic boundaries. At the turn of the century, a large part of the Acholi communities were still bilingual, speaking both Madi and Acholi. When Peney visited Liria in 1862 he remarked: "In fact, the Lokoya people speak the Bari, Pari or Shilluk, and Lotuho idioms interchangeably."[40]

---

40 *"Les gens de Lokoyia parlent en effet indistinctement les idiomes barry* [Bari], *berry* [Pari] *ou schlouk* [Shilluk] *et lotouka* [Lotuho] *"* (Malté-Brun, 1863:59).

The cultural heterogeneity of the past still persists among the Lulubo, especially in the village of Lokiliri, their main centre. The village may serve as an example of what many communities in eastern Equatoria presumably looked like at some stage of their history.

Apart from the Lulubo language, which is used in all daily activities, Bari and Lokoya also play an important cultural role. Up to the turn of the twentieth century, Bari was used by the Kursak rain clan, not only for internal but also for external communication. Bari was, and to some still is, the language of the blacksmiths. The present blacksmith still considers Bari as his first language. Most of the terminology relating to animal husbandry, to kingship and to the age-sets of the girls is Bari. The commonly used birth-order names, the songs of the girls (*nyale*), of the courting dance (*kore*), the obscene songs of blacksmiths (*tibidi*), and many of the songs that in-laws sing as part of their joking relationship are still sung and composed in Bari.

Most of the Lulubo terminology of the male age-class system has been borrowed from Lokoya, while most of the war songs (*ira*) are sung and composed in that language. Some are also sung in Pari.

Although Juba Arabic has now become the *lingua franca* in contacts with neighbouring communities, Bari, as the language of first literacy and of the church, still plays an important role, next to Lulubo. The importance of Lokoya is rapidly decreasing since the wars are over and the joint Lulubo/Lokoya chieftainship is a thing of the past.

The people of Lokiliri plainly admit the diversity of their origins. They have as many origins as there are clans. In a list of clans composed by the Lulubo Tribe Development Committee in Juba, thirty-three clan names are enumerated with their respective origins. Only four clans claim autochthony: they say "they were found in the caves". The others come from Bari (8); Ori ('Ohoriok', Lokoya) (6); 'Böri-Lokoro' (= Pari) (3); Madi (2); 'Böri-Acholi' (2); Fajelu (1); 'Uganda' (1), while other origins are not known (Mogga Lado, ed., 1981:11). In times of misrule or crisis, the Lulubo upset their chief by saying that they will return, each clan to its own place of origin.

Here ends the initial introduction to the peoples who are the subject-matter of this book. Hopefully, it has become clear that the area between the Nile and the Kidepo River between the 6th and the 4th parallel is a field suitable for a comparative study of the institutions of kingship. We have seen that, while the cultural origins (Central Sudanic Madi, Western Nilotic Lwoo, Eastern Nilotic Bari, Eastern Nilotic Lotuho) of the people in this area show considerable variation, processes of reciprocal cultural assimilation have created enough common ground to expect that a comparative study may be fruitful.

Typical homestead, Lopit.

3

Modes of Subsistence and Social Organisation

In this chapter, I present a brief sketch of the economic and socio-political organisation of the societies located between the Nile and the Kidepo. The information on economic life and the organisation of descent is mainly drawn from my fieldwork in Lulubo and may not necessarily apply to all other areas. Still, since Lulubo, more than any other area in our sample, is a meeting point of different influences, the resulting picture may be more representative than it would be if another locality had been the source of information.

The territorial and age-class organisation of the Bari was destroyed during the wars of the last twenty years of the nineteenth century, and has been replaced by a rather dispersed mode of settlement. The Bari, far more than the other peoples in the area, have been affected by processes of rural depopulation and urban migration, especially to Juba.

The information concerning their social system prior to its destruction is very limited, so that only general inferences can be made as to its structure. As far as village organisation is concerned, the mainstay of this presentation of the social organisation concerns the *monyomiji* systems to the east of the Bari.

Sorghum, 'life-giver'

The cultivation of sorghum is the principal economic activity all over. Although millet (and recently also maize, sweet potatoes and cassava) is an important additional staple, sorghum remains the food *par excellence* and plays a symbolic and ritual role comparable to bread in the Mediterranean and rice in East Asian cultures.

A large number of varieties of sorghum with dissimilar qualities (length of maturation-period, resistance to drought, hardness, taste, yield, etc.) are grown on different types of fields: clearings in the forest, with or without fire lines[1] terraced fields (on the mountain slopes in or near the village, often manured with cattle or goat dung), and wet fields in swamps and near streams, to which drainage techniques are applied.[2] With the possible exception of the Bari, the importance of agriculture for the society is not played down as among the semi-pastoralist Dinka and Nuer to

---

1   Along these fire lines, all bush and high grass is removed in order to stop the bush fires at the end of the dry season from burning the area within the lines. The vegetation within the area circumscribed by the lines will be burnt at sowing time so that the ashes are used as fertiliser.

2   A description of the drainage techniques practised by the Pari is provided in Kurimoto, 1984.

the north. A keen interest is taken in agricultural achievements, especially among the Lulubo, Lokoya and Pari. The men prepare the field for cultivation and are responsible for the sowing. The women weed, harvest and store the grain, and gather wild fruits and vegetables if necessary. The children herd the smaller livestock and scare off the birds when the grain is ripening.

Sorghum flour used as a vehicle of blessing

There are two sorghum harvests per year. The first one is sown on wet fields in the last weeks of March and is harvested in July. The second is cultivated on the plains and harvested, depending on the time of sowing and the maturation period of the variety, between October and January. June and July is the period of greatest hardship; the demand for labour is at its peak while the reserves of the previous year have run out.

Work-parties and the *Big Man*

The basic productive unity is the household, which may comprise quite a large number of agnatic and affinal kin. A considerable amount of agricultural labour takes place in work groups recruited from outside the household. There are different arrangements to mobilise people for work parties. According to the economic power of the organiser, the size of a work group may range from a few neighbours to a complete village section. The work party may be for a full day or for half a day. According to the nature of the party (full or half time) and the number of people attending, a bull, a goat or only beer is provided. Organisers who have no grain for beer may receive labour on loan, but in this way, no large-scale parties can be organised.

To organise work parties is the main avenue to the accumulation of wealth. If natural conditions are favourable, work parties result in an upward economic spiral for the household concerned: a household which has recourse to outside labour is likely to have a bigger harvest than others, which in turn increases its capacity to organise work parties the following year.

As surplus grain is convertible into goats, and goats into cattle, the most important items in the bridewealth (namely the wealth transferred from the bridegroom's family to that of the bride), there is a fairly direct relationship between a household's surplus production and the number of wives the household head will marry. Polygamous households are likely to have more children who, when of age, increase the productive capacity of the family. The staging of work parties is, therefore, an important element in the career of the *Big Man* (Bari: *ngutu duma*, Lulubo: *modi nagwi*, Lokoya: *ohobarani*, Lotuho: *asamani*, Pari: *ngati duong*) who is culturally defined as a man with many dependants, a large herd and many granaries. Poor people find themselves in a reverse economic spiral. Lacking the capacity to call for a work party this year, their harvest is likely to be too small to afford one the next year. If natural conditions are adverse a poor man may have to put himself in debt, and find it impossible to find a wife for his son.

Work party of Lulubo youngsters clearing bush for cultivation using the tilo, *the long traditional hoe*

In the past the most important option open to the son of such a father was to attach himself to a *Big Man* and serve him in the expectation that he would eventually provide him with a wife. Other options were: to become a warrior or a big-game hunter — the latter were usually 'loners' — or to work hard in the production of the few local export goods (red ochre and tobacco). In recent years, new forms of agricultural co-operation, introduced from Uganda via the Acholi, are gaining ground. These are regulated in such a way that the input of each participant, measured and given a monetary value, is roughly equal.

Cattle and the fly

All the peoples between the Nile and the Kidepo have kept cattle at some stage in the past, but due to the spread of the tsetse fly, only the Northern Bari, the Pari, Eastern Lotuho, and Lango nowadays own sizable herds. These are kept in the village or in cattle camps at a short distance from the village.

Of the people in this study, the Bari are the most cattle-minded. An indication of the size of their herds in the past is the value of the bridewealth. In the middle of the nineteenth century, it varied from seventy head of cattle for a princess to ten head of cattle as a minimum for a woman of low birth.[3] After the drought of 1855–1860, the maximum bridewealth dropped to ten (Kaufmann, 1974:188). At the end of the century, chiefs could again afford fifty head of cattle (Seligman, 1934:242). In this century, the average bridewealth has been ten to fifteen head of cattle.

The Bari were the main victims of the cattle raids on which, between 1870 and 1910, the Egyptian, Mahdist and the Belgian local state apparatus depended. The large-scale destocking of the area as a result of the rinderpest of 1898 and the depopulation caused by continuous warfare at the end of the century reopened Bariland for large game animals which brought the tsetse fly in their wake. According to missionary Kaufmann, there were no game-animals left in 1860 (Kaufmann, 1974).[4] Eighty years later, it was a common hazard for the inhabitants of the newly established colonial centre of Juba to find an elephant or lion roaming in their backyard.

The patrols carried out by the Sudan government between 1914 and 1920 to subjugate the Lokoya, Lopit, and Dongotono had disastrous consequences for their herds (Hødnebo, 1981:110). Although restocking during the period of Condominium

---

3   Werne, 1848:325; Brun-Rollet, 1855:242; Buchta, 1881:86. Werne regards this as a very high amount even after taking into account the large herds he had seen. Comparing it with Brun-Rollet's figures: fifty cows for a high-ranking healthy bride down to a minimum of ten for women lacking these attributes, we may draw the conclusion that Werne's figures refer to the bridewealth paid among chiefs and *Big Men*. Buchta, who visited Bariland in 1878, gives exactly the same figures as Brun-Rollet. In comparison, Werne gives the amount to ransom a captive as thirty oxen.

4   All observers describe Bariland as very densely populated: Thibaut, 1841:129; Baker, 1874, Vol. I: 371; Kaufmann, 1974:183; Vinco, 1974:79 and 96. Around Rejaf Baker saw "innumerable villages ... as far as the eye could reach".

rule had some success, the sleeping-sickness boundary was not pushed back.[5] Southern Bariland was definitively lost as cattle-grazing area. The increase of the herds of the Lulubo and Lokoya[6] came to a halt during the first civil war (1955–72). Owing to the desertion of villages and their surrounding grazing grounds, new areas were invaded by the tsetse fly. At present, no cattle are seen in that area.

Cattle have an important nutritional value, both the milk and the blood — tapped by shooting a small arrow in the cow's neck — are consumed, although the latter practice is being abandoned nowadays. One rarely slaughtered one's own cattle for meat, but the capture of cattle from the enemy formed the occasion of festive meals. In view of recurrent warfare, they must have represented a far from negligible source of animal protein. Obtained through violence, they were taboo for sacrifice and matrimonial transactions.

Women grinding sorghum in holes in the rock, Loguruny

The main uses of cattle were social and religious: as payment in bridewealth and bloodwealth (the compensation paid by the family of the killer to that of the victim), to be eaten during work parties, and for sacrifice.

The cow is the most highly valued sacrificial animal. For the most important sacrifices, such as those marking the transfer of power to a new generation or the burial of a chief, cattle are prescribed, even where they have disappeared many years ago. In places where cattle is no longer available, their social function has usually been taken over by goats. In Lulubo, Lokoya and Southern Bari, values are still frequently expressed in heads of cattle, but the actual transaction takes place in goats, and lately,

---

5   Compare the maps (no.13, 1880, no.14, 1910, no.15, 1930 and no.17, 1950 in Hødnebo (1981a).

6   In Hødnebo's view an entrepreneurial success story (1981b:116).

also in cash. Other elements of the 'cattle-complex' (Herskovits, 1926): an elaborate set of names for colour-configurations, praise-oxen, ox-songs and ox-names, are known to all the peoples between Nile and Kidepo, whether they have cattle or not. Here too, goats are a substitute.

A custom apparently not recorded among the other Nilotes, is the Bari and Lulubo practice that rivalling owners of praise-oxen (or favourite goats) make their animals fight one another.

In the past, the Bari had wet-season cattle camps located away from the Nile. They were guarded by the warrior age-sets (*teton*). By the 1920s, these had disappeared (Whitehead, 1929:96), possibly because of the reduced pressure on the available grazing-land near the river.

Unlike their eastern neighbours, the Bari considered hunting of minor significance. It was delegated to a special, stigmatised class, the *tomonok*, who gave part of their catch to the king or the Rainmaker (Seligman, 1928:428–434; Whitehead, 1953:269–271).

Hunting and egalitarianism

For the Lulubo, Lokoya and Lotuho, hunting was and, if there is sufficient game, still is an important activity, both economically and socially. Early travellers describe their countries as abounding with game. Different techniques and different forms of co-operation are put into practice during the hunt. They vary from individual spearing of elephants and buffaloes from trees, to large-scale inter-village hunts encircling a large area, often more than ten kilometres in diameter. During the dry season, sectional and village hunts are frequently organised. They are occasions during which large groups of men test their capacity to co-operate.

From the point of view of the organisation of labour, there is an obvious parallel between these large-scale hunts and cultivation parties, especially those in which the *monyomiji* of a whole section join in.

From the point of view of social organisation, there is an important contrast. The work party starts from a situation of inequality (host/guest) and normally leads to the consolidation of the inequality in favour of the host. As long as he observes certain minimum standards of generosity, he will benefit from the labour of others.

The point of departure of the hunt is egalitarian. It leads to temporary prestige for the individual who shoots the deadly arrow or captures the fugitive animal, but this prestige does not crystallise into a permanent advantage. The expertise of the individual hunter has to be proved anew in every chase, and throughout the hunter's life, prestige will continue to depend on his agility and luck. While the modes of co-operation in agriculture reproduce the socioeconomic inequality in the community, communal hunting promotes a more egalitarian spirit.

Livestock and agricultural produce, especially sorghum, are convertible. They belong to the same 'economic sphere'. The rights to land and livestock and the distribution of agricultural produce are basically the concern of the household and the lineage. Hunting and warfare are outside this sphere and based on a different premise of co-operation. Rights to hunting grounds are held by the community as a whole, while the distribution of game is independent of relationships of descent.

This socio-economic contrast may explain the difference in social stratification between the Bari and the peoples east of them. Hunting is not part of the communal pursuits of free men; hence, the social nexus based on the *Big Man* is more pronounced among the Bari. Since they lack the levelling effect of collective hunts, their society can also afford to include a permanent servile class, the *'dupi'*. Inequality of the *Big Man* type is mitigated among the peoples where the age-class system goes together with hunting. Among the Lotuho, Lokoya, Pari and Lulubo, the king dealt with the *monyomiji* as a single body. In Bari, the king's most important interlocutors seem to have been the *Big Men* and the elders (*temejik*), while the warriors (*teton*) lived away from the village in the cattle camps, running their own affairs.

The balance between people's needs and nature's provender was — and remains — precarious. Many of the factors determining economic success are beyond the control of the community: rain, plagues, epidemics. The main economic strategy to reduce this uncertainty is the simultaneous dependence on different productive activities, each of which exploits different niches of the environment: agriculture (on different types of field), hunting, animal husbandry, fishing and foraging.

Despite this 'multiple subsistence-strategy', the community remains vulnerable to the whims of nature. Drought is always the gravest threat to the survival of the community since it simultaneously affects its grazing, its agricultural and foraging activities. This explains partly why in the political cosmology of the east bank, rain plays such a central role

The village: size, layout and defence works

The villages east of Bariland strike the newcomer, first of all, by their size and compactness, especially the few that have remained intact since the establishment of colonial rule, like the Lotuho villages of Hiyala, Loming and Ilyeu. The impression of compactness is even stronger in villages located on terraced mountain slopes. The dense mode of settlement led, among the Lokoya, Lulubo and Dongotono, to the construction of sophisticated amenities like stone urinals inside the village, a building practice which fell into disuse during the colonial period (Driberg, *typescript*, p. 30). Inside the villages, compounds are stockaded and located side by side along narrow streets, often just wide enough for cattle to pass. The population of a single village frequently exceeds a thousand inhabitants.

At present, in areas that are safe from attack by cattle raiders and more open to modern economic influences, such as Lulubo, the villages have tended to fall apart in a number of separate settlements which often coincide with the sections (see below). In the case of Lokiliri, these are more than an hour's walk apart.[7] The villages in the east, where the colonial and postcolonial governments were less able to maintain

---

7   During the civil war, many villages reverted to their old mode of settlement — moving back from the feeder roads into the mountains.

security, have retained the fortified compact mode of settlement. Elsewhere, only the compounds of *Big Men* are still surrounded by palisades of ebony. The less well-to-do may build a bamboo fence while the poor have no fence at all.

Informants agree that in the past, their villages were larger. This is confirmed by the great number of open spaces in today's villages and by written sources. In 1863, Baker counted 3,000 large houses in Tirangore (Baker, 1866, Vol. I: 207). Emin Pasha was told that the male fighting force of Loronyo was 1,000 (Emin Pasha, 1882:267), while Peney estimated the population of Lokoya District, in which he probably included the villages of Liria, Ilyangari and possibly also Kamuturu, at 10,000 (Malté-Brun, 1862:57–58).[8]

One of the largest agglomerations in the area may very well have been that of Imatari, the centre from which many of the villages of the Plains Lotuho originate. A hand-drawn map found among the papers of the Verona Fathers in the Comboni Archive in Rome reproduced opposite the first page of Chapter Five of this book, shows the location of Imatari and its constituent sections in relation to present-day villages. The map must have been drawn in the period that Carlo Muratori and Augusto Pazzaglia were collecting information on the history and ethnography of Lotuho—between the war and the expulsion of the missionaries in the early 1960s. According to the map, the total population would have amounted to 43,700. This figure is calculated on the basis of an estimate of the number of *monyomiji* in each section multiplied by 3 for women, children, elders and young men. Considering that a *monyomiji*-set coincides with an age-cohort spanning between 20 and 25 years, the ratio of three to one may be on the low side. Since the map was probably drawn to glorify the past, it is likely that the number of *monyomiji* per section has been exaggerated. The fact remains that the old-time settlements were larger than those in the colonial and postcolonial period.

The little we know of the traditional Bari village indicates that they have always been more loosely structured than the villages of their eastern neighbours. According to Emin (*Tagebücher*, Vol. II:111) and Mountenay-Jephson (1890:139), who made observations before the old settlement pattern was upset during the Mahdist period, the Bari villages consisted of a number of separate homesteads, each surrounded by dense thorn and Euphorbia fences. Nowadays, the houses are far apart.

Some of the old Bari villages were very large. Angelo Vinco, the first European to travel to the southern boundary of the Bari, describes the agglomeration of Makedo, in the area of the present chieftainship of Koggi, as "the largest town (*città*) in the

---

8   Peney refers to the population of 'Lokoya District' which he says covers six square miles. Since he estimates the population of Orinyak (one of the moieties of Liria) at 2,000, to which we should add a roughly equal number for Opwalang, the opposite moiety, we should assume that Peney's 'Lokoya District' also included Ilyangari which is located at five kilometres distance from Liria on the same mountain and is ruled by the same king, and possibly also Kamuturu, at its old site of Mount Ningere, which in 1862 had not separated yet from the Liria Kingdom. Other Lokoya villages were too remote to be included in the six miles range. The separation story of Kamuturu/Langabu is part of case history 14–6.

Bari country situated on both banks of the White Nile. It takes two days to cross it." (Vinco, 1940:320).[9] The only village of comparable size nowadays is Lafon which, according to the 1983 census, had 11,017 inhabitants (Government Census, 1983; Kurimoto, 1985).

Climbing the fortifications of Loming, Lotuho

The traditional villages were surrounded by palisades consisting of tightly planted ebony poles tied horizontally with bamboo. They have gates, in many cases more than one for the same entrance. Baker and Emin both described the gate of Ohila, which is located in the plains. It gave access to the village through a number of palisades and thorn-hedges erected inside a grove of huge trees:

---

9   The distance of two day-marches would indicate that between the confluences of the Kaya and Karpeto rivers with the Nile there was a continuous string of settlements. Making an extrapolation from the distances covered by Vinco on other days of his journey, Makedo must have covered a distance between twenty and thirty kilometres. Brun-Rollet, whose information may be based on Vinco's, speaks of "*les nombreux villages des Makédo*" (1855:206). This phrasing again suggests the dispersed character of the settlement pattern. The size attributed to Makedo by Vinco strikes the contemporary observer who knows the deserted state of the Bari countryside as a gross exaggeration. From his other writings, however, Vinco strikes us as a rather sober reporter.

> The entrance to this fort is a curious archway, about ten feet deep, formed of the ironwood palisades, with a sharp turn to the right and left forming a zigzag (Baker, 1866, Vol. I:186).

Emin estimates that the width of the wall of thorn-bush, trees and palisades was at many places more than a thousand metres, and judges that "this natural fortress could successfully withstand an artillery attack for a long period" (Emin Pascha, 1882:264).

Away from the village wall, there were heavily fortified enclosures for the cattle. Emin, who visited Loronyo in 1881, not long after King Mayya for security considerations had moved the village from a location near the River Hos to a mountaintop almost an hour's walk away, mentions that the king's palace was built right on top of the mountain and next to the principal cattle enclosure which was surrounded with watch-towers (1882:268). In the villages facing east — towards the Toposa and Boya — these stockades, fortified cattle-enclosures, gates and other defence works still exist.

Elsewhere, the villages are no longer stockaded. Those formerly located on the top or the slopes of a mountain have come down to its foot. Bringing the villages down was one of the key strategies in the pacification policy of the Condominium government. Many old villages were burned down in order to force their inhabitants to rebuild downhill. Once the old infrastructure was destroyed and the *Pax Brittannica* had proved its effectiveness, a less defence-oriented and, especially in the west, a more dispersed mode of settlement developed. The location at the foot of the hill also had advantages: it made fetching water a lot easier.

Outside the fence of the village at varying distances are the fields, those that are rain-fed and left after three of four years and the 'wet fields' that are flooded during the rainy season. Members of the same section usually own adjoining fields.

Monyomiji *waiting at* orek *at their return from a ceremonial hunt for their wives* (arriving on the picture from the left) *to welcome them with beer. Each of the four age-sets that together constitute a* monyomiji-*set is seated under a separate mango tree* (Liria).

Not far from the entrance of the village, there is an open space shaded by trees and used as a meeting place of the *monyomiji*. It is called *orek* by the Lokoya, *rek* by the Bari and *re* by the Lulubo. Here, they regroup when they return from the forest, from hunts or from war, to be met by those who stayed behind. Here, the spoils of war and hunted animals are divided. Here, also, do the *monyomiji* meet when matters of life and death have to be discussed. Deeper into the bush, there are other meeting places where issues are settled that will certainly entail violence, such as the killing of the king.

Bloodshed should be kept at a distance from the village. It is a particularly bad omen when violence occurs inside the village, especially in its centre. This centre is a wide, open space (Lotuho: *afwara*; Lokoya: *avwata,* Pari: *thworo*) with a bundle of ebony poles (Bari: *'bilili* or *wore;* Lulubo: *gbwilili,* also *kaci,* Lokoya: *alore* or *odilir,* Lotuho: *balacar,* Pari: *avalacar*). The open area is the dancing ground. The bundle of ebony poles (among the Bari often only a single stake) is the central shrine of the community. The pole-shrine has a proper name and is the object of sacrifice and libation. During communal dances, when the drums are attached to it, the pole-shrine serves as the pivot around which the community rotates during dances. The sacred character of the pole-shrine and of the dancing ground surrounding it precludes dances which are aimed at courting and entertainment. For these purposes, there are other dancing grounds without a shrine.

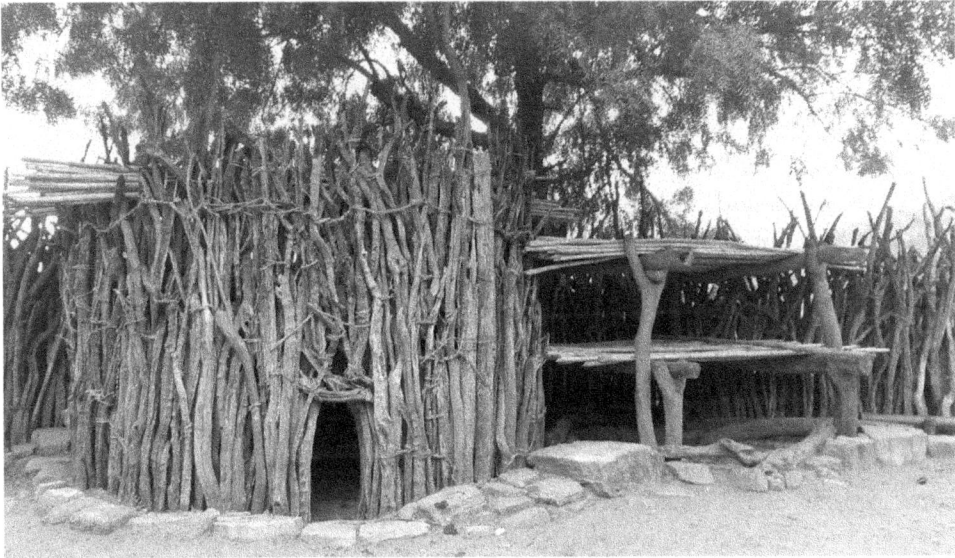

Assembly platforms (amangat) *with a partitioned off section for the members of the senior* monyomiji *age-sets, Loming, Lotuho.*

Next to the ceremonial ground is the meeting place of the *monyomiji* and the central drum house. If the king has a residence in the village, it is located there as well. The meeting place consists of a number of bamboo platforms (Bari, Lulubo: *'bali,* Lokoya, Pari: *obale,* Lotuho: *amangat*), usually tiered, so that the men sit in accordance to their seniority. Sometimes, rocks or the natural steps in a mountain slope are used as seats — in some Lotuho villages, ancient megaliths form the *amangat*. On the occasion of the transfer of power to a new generation, the new *monyomiji* build towers consisting of up to eight ascending platforms (*olobele*) which simultaneously serve as watch-towers.

The meeting place of the *monyomiji* has a hearth on which meat of collectively hunted game is roasted. Next to it is a forked stake from which the trophies of animals killed by the *monyomiji* are suspended.

A meeting place, a dancing ground, a drum house and a pole-shrine also are the visible structures of the organisation of the section, the level of social segmentation immediately below the village. The pole-shrine of the village as a whole is often the shrine of its most ancient or most central section. Before I discuss the section, let me add some descriptive details about that most important corporate group in community life: the *monyomiji*.

The *monyomiji*

In the minds of the people, the village is defined by three characteristics: a common locality, a common assembly of *monyomiji*, and a common politico-ritual leadership. The latter may consist of a single Rainmaker, a Master of the Village (Lotuho: *amonyemiji*), a Master of the Land (Bari: *monyekak*), or, in the case of the Lulubo/Lokoya area a Rainmaker/king together with one or more other Masters of Disaster.

The core institutional framework of the village is, however, the body of *monyomiji*, the adult men responsible for the defence of the village. *Monyomiji* are all the members of the generation which took over power in the village from the previous ruling generation in a great ceremony, held every so often, which may vary from about twelve years in Lulubo up to twenty-two years among the Plains-Lotuho. *Monyomiji* is a word from the Lotuho language group which literally means 'owners' or 'fathers' (*monye*) of the village (*miji*).[10]

A generation usually consists of four successive age-sets, each age-set spanning between three and six years. Age-sets are formed in stages: in Lulubo and Lokoya, boys sharing the same village section give themselves a group name during the period that they are herding the goats (7–12 years). When the boys are old enough to start thinking of one day taking over the responsibility for the village, the sectional age-sets band together, adopt a collective name for all the juniors in the village and begin to campaign for recognition by showing exemplary behaviour (in the areas of public works and bravery) and by pointing at the weaknesses of the ruling *monyomiji*. The period of transfer of power is full of tension and excitement. I describe the ritual and political scenarios of the transfer of generational power in Chapter Eight.

The *monyomiji* are responsible both for the daily running of public affairs, and for the long-term well-being of their community. They should keep the internal peace, settle disputes and, in a general way, prevent the occurrence of violence in the village. They should also take the necessary precautions to keep drought, epidemics

---

10   The Bari term for the same body of people is *monyejur*, from *jur* 'village' and *monye* 'owner'. The Lulubo occasionally use *jururi ate*, *juru* meaning village, *ate* fathers or owners. The Pari say *mojomiji*, a loanword derived from *monyomiji*.

and plagues away from the village. To keep the hearts of the people 'cool' and the skies above the village 'clouded' would summarise their duties nicely.

To achieve these ends, the *monyomiji* are vested with a wide range of powers. A typical power is that of declaring *edwar*, a word which English-speaking informants readily translate as 'state of emergency'. 'State of non-violence' would also be an appropriate translation. During *edwar*, no fighting is allowed; no unnecessary noise should be made; and dances and the sounding of drums are prohibited. *Edwar* is annually proclaimed when the first sorghum harvest is about knee-high and lasts until the time the crop can be harvested. The death of a Rainmaker, the New Year festival, or exceptional misfortune may also be reasons for the proclamation of *edwar*. If it is disregarded, the *monyomiji* impose fines on the culprits and usually order a sacrifice to purify the village.

The *monyomiji* further issue regulations concerning the rates of exchange between the goods that are bartered in the village. They fix the maximum value of the bridewealth and the bloodwealth. Lomini, the generation in power in Lokiliri when I conducted my fieldwork there, regularly campaigned against the excessive use of alcohol.

The *monyomiji* have the right to appoint and dismiss the Rainmaker and the other Masters protecting the community against disaster. In Langabu, at the occasion of the New Year festival on 26 December 1985, the *monyomiji* dismissed two such officers because of unsatisfactory performance and replaced them with others. In disputes between ritual specialists, they have the power to redefine his rights. A typical case in the last category is the following:

3.1 *The disputed calabash of the Master of the Land, Lokiliri* (contemporary case)

In 1986, a conflict arose in Lokiliri over one of the three sacred calabashes used by the Master of the Land and his two assistants to anoint *Tukure*, the central pole-shrine of Lokiliri, on the occasion of the New Year festival. One of the two ritual assistants (*jai*) had used the calabash to anoint the shrine of his own section when he brought home his father's skull (a second funeral for a person who died away from the village). Although it was only February, the people of Lokiliri, because of the drought of the previous year, were very tense about the coming rains and felt that nothing should go wrong this year. During the meeting which was attended by elders who gave advice on the past division of responsibilities, there were those who wanted to cancel one calabash kept by an assistant-Master so that there could be no confusion anymore. This idea was supported by the assistant who had used one of the calabashes for 'private ends' and who apparently felt sure of his case. The other assistant-Master then offered his resignation. After a long discussion and much advice from the elders — who felt that a conflict between two clans could have worse effects for the rain than the anomalous situation of having two ritual assistants and three calabashes — it was decided that each assistant should keep his position and his calabash but that the calabash over which the conflict had arisen should only be used for *Tukure*. The decision was accepted by both assistant-Masters and the peace was kept.

In Lokoya and Lulubo, it is customary that the *monyomiji* issue statements of general policy at the New Year festival. In1986, in Ngulere, the *monyomiji* demanded more respect for the Rainmaker (Case 9.9); and in 1983, the *monyomiji* of Lokwe ordered the villagers to settle their debts prior to the start of the cultivation season (Case 16.3). They feared that the accumulated debts would be a ready cause for conflicts, which in turn might affect the rain.

The *monyomiji* are concerned with all conflicts that endanger the peace in the village, whether they be between families over the bridewealth or bloodwealth or between village-sections concerning violence during a communal dance. The *monyomiji* use their influence to force the parties to negotiate and to press them to arrive at a settlement. If the slowness with which the debtor pays the compensation agreed upon endangers the village peace again, the *monyomiji* may confiscate his goods and livestock and transfer them to the offended party directly.

Tukure, the central pole-shrine of Lokiliri with drums and a calabash for libations

A special category of offences dealt with by the *monyomiji* are insults to the Rainmaker, the Master of the Land, and the other ritual specialists on whose intervention the well-being of the village depends. They monitor the Rainmaker's state of mind and take action if they see that he is aggrieved. Insults to the Rainmaker or his family should be settled at short notice for fear that the rain will be affected. If the rain fails, the *monyomiji* call for a general assembly to find out the cause and take the necessary measures.

The *monyomiji* are responsible for the execution of all projects on the level of the village: war, village-wide hunting parties, the maintenance of public utilities (drum house, ceremonial ground, and lately also the roads leading to the village). They arrange the cultivation of the Rainmaker's field; oversee the collection of tribute; and the building of the Rainmaker's palace. If the interest of the village as a whole is at stake, they have the right to levy fines and to raid the house of an individual who is unwilling to provide what is needed in the interest of the community.

The village-wide assembly of the *monyomiji* ideally represents the cause of public interest as opposed to the private interests of descent-based groups and the divisiveness that often characterises relations between the sections. All men sharing the same generation name are supposed to have a common cause. *Vis-à-vis* the elders, they have to live up to their claim that they are better rulers. Towards the next generation, they have to project an image of resolve and steadfastness and must demonstrate that they are able to keep the village united. If a village-wide meeting is convened, it is the duty of the *monyomiji* to reach a unanimous decision that overrules sectional and clan interests. Village-wide general assemblies are only held at special occasions. Most of the time *monyomiji* spend together is spent with members of the same section, either at its place of meeting or during communal work parties or hunts.

Monyomiji and sections

The term for village sections (Bari, Pari, Lulubo: *'bali*, Lotuho: *amangat*, pl. *amangatim*, Lokoya *obali*, pl. *obandak*) is the same as that for the bamboo platforms that function as meeting places of the *monyomiji*.[11] The number of sections in a community may vary from only two in smaller villages to a dozen in larger ones. This is where the *monyomiji* of the section spend their leisure time, discussing village topics, planning joint activities such as hunts and dances, or doing some handiwork, like making hats or repairing hoes and bows.

The *monyomiji* of a section act as a corporate group on many occasions. They join in work parties in the fields of members as well as non-members of the section. They act as a unit during dances in which different sections participate. They organise a sectional hunt at least once a year. They form a team in village and inter-village hunts

---

11   The Pari 'sections' are called *paajo* (pl. *mieri*). This term is used to refer to any residential unit
        from the homestead to the village as a whole. In the anthropological literature on the Dinka,
        Nuer and Shilluk, 'section' is used for the supra-village territorial units (Evans-Pritchard, 1940b;
        Lienhardt, 1958b:122). In this study, it is used to denote sub-village residential units.

and in time of war. The sections are fairly permanent social units with a territorial reference similar to villages. Sections that have moved or that have become scattered in recent times still remember the location of their original meeting point and maintain an ideology of common brotherhood. Sections occupy distinct areas with clear boundaries. *Monyomiji* of the same section usually cultivate adjacent fields on the plains.

When sections of the same village fight they should not use spears. They should limit themselves to the use of sticks and whips. Rivalry is usual between sections of the same village. 'Good' rivalry expresses itself in sports (wrestling), dances, during hunts and in songs. Every section has its own dance songs and drum beats which it loves to impose on others by monopolising the floor or the drums during dances. The dualist character of this sectional rivalry will be discussed in more detail in Chapter Seven.

Most sections have their own shrine, ceremonial ground, drum house and drums, each of which have proper names. Drums may be named after important events in which they were used, or after the traditional enemy. A popular drum name among the Lotuho is *Akara*, the Lotuho name for the Toposa, their most redoubtable enemies (Novelli, *thesis*: 614). The drums are usually well maintained. They may become very old and are the principal heirlooms of the section (or the village for that matter). The construction of the drum house and the repair of the drums are typically tasks carried out by the young generation before its rise to power.

The most important sectional office is that of guardian of the section or guardian of the shrine (Lotuho: *amonyemangat*, Lulubo: *kaciri modi*), usually a hereditary office. When violence erupts during dances, it is the guardian's responsibility to collect the drums and stop the dance that has turned 'bad'.

In most villages, the sections are grouped into two opposed territorial blocs, located at opposite sides of the river or along an east-west or north-south axis. Although these groups have proper names (such as in Liria: Orinyak and Opwalang, in Lokiliri: Kworijik and Lokwe), there is no local term for this combination of sections. They play an important role in the organisation of competitive sports. Local authorities of the modern state (colonial and post-colonial) have often put this competitive spirit to use in forced labour and self-help respectively.

Inter-clan relations

Sections are associated with a limited number of descent-groups whose members have lived in it of old. One of these clans usually has a senior position in relation to the others on the basis of its earlier settlement in the place.

The normal procedure for immigrants from elsewhere was to associate themselves with one of the resident clans: either as clients or as an allied satellite group. Dependency relations between clans are of little importance nowadays. An individual who wants to settle in a section only pays a goat as fee to the *monyomiji* of that section.

Descent is patrilineal. The local clan group (the members of the same clan sharing the same village) and the lineage (among the Lulubo and Lokoya about five generations deep, and named after its ancestor) form clan segments that act as corporate groups.

The main interests shared by the members of the lineage are matrimonial transactions and the payment of compensations for lost life. A typical situation when the male members of a lineage take corporate action is when one of its nubile girls is abducted, or when one of its male members elopes with a girl.

The length of time it takes before a lineage splits into two or more new groups depends on its size and the capacity of its elders to resolve conflicts. The moment of fission should be postponed as long as possible, since the larger the lineage the stronger its position within the clan group and in the village. Small lineages usually remain intact over more generations than larger ones.

In each village around ten to twenty different clan names may be found. Some names are spread over a wide area and are found in different ethnic groups, especially among the Bari, Lulubo and Lokoya. Other names may be found in only one or two villages. Among the Lotuho, the number of clan names is limited: not more than four or six.

Clans are exogamous. In Lulubo, women of one's mother's clan and of one's father's mother's lineage are also prohibited as brides. The relationship between mother's brother and sister's son is in many ways the opposite from that between father and son. While the relationship between father and son is characterised by a rivalling disposition kept in check by attitudes of authority and obedience, the mother's brother is expected never to refuse whatever his sister's son may ask, and *vice versa*. The bond between mother's brother and sister's son, therefore, plays an important role in ventures which cannot bear the light of day, such as intrigues for power.

Working party moving a roof, Langabu

Clan members sharing the same village have a responsibility to one another when a fellow member finds himself in difficulties. In fact, the physical security of the individual villager is in the first place guaranteed by his local clan brothers. They support him if he is brought before the *monyomiji* to account for his deeds. They defend him if he is physically threatened. If different clans of the same village fight, they should only use sticks and whips. From the moment the *monyomiji* are aware that some trouble is brewing they are supposed to intervene to prevent or stop a fight.

Clans may entertain different types of relationship with one another. These can be roughly classified in three types: they may be allied by marriage; involved in a short-term conflict; or separated by long-term feuding. The two cases of conflict involving bloodshed that occurred during my stay in Lokiliri took years to solve. One of the cases which occurred in 1983 had not been brought to a conclusion yet when I left in 1986. The culprit had to seek refuge in another village to be safe from attack. The father of the victim broke all relations with the clan of the accused to the extent of causing his sister's son to divorce his wife who was from the clan of the accused and whose bridewealth had been paid by the father of the victim. His demand for bloodwealth was so high that the relatives of the accused — who were poor — could not be expected to meet it. There was worry that the case might be insoluble and that a state of *gi* might ensue.

Gi (Bari: *giko* or *gik*) could be defined as 'a state of non-relationship between clan groups'. When a conflict remains unresolved for a long time or when settlement or attempts at settlement have been repeatedly frustrated by renewed outbreaks of violence, the conflicting parties may decide that henceforth they will be 'taboo' to each other. Such a 'non-relationship' may last for generations. The clans in Lokiliri that were in a state of *gi* no longer fought but they did not intermarry either. *Gi* then refers to a halfway freezing of the processes of conflict resolution described by our models: the violence between the antagonists has stopped but as it has not been expelled through the immolation of a shared victim; a resumption of the give and take that constitutes social life remains blocked.

It was a fundamental rule in these societies that families should intermarry in such a way that as many clans as possible would become part of the family network. A brother should not marry to a clan to which his sister had already been given in marriage. Every marriage should fit into a strategy of gaining new allies or of reaffirming old ones. If questioned on the matter, people declare that this is the best prevention of division in the village. Like sections, clans are conceived as rival groups. There is good and bad rivalry between them. Good rivalry or 'joking' characterises the relationship between in-laws. It is typically expressed in the mocking songs that in-laws address to one another. Many of these songs are composed, sung and danced during the period following the first harvest (June-August). Adolescent boys and girls position themselves in opposite rows singing in turns. Out of a collection of eighty-nine of these songs I recorded, thirty-seven challenged the in-law's food and drink habits: greediness, stinginess, the consumption of animals that are not supposed to be eaten, etc. Nine concerned oppressive behaviour by the mother-in-law (with whom the son-in-law is expected to reside during the years after marriage). Four songs criticised the in-law's laziness; and four his slowness in paying the bridewealth. The remaining twenty-six were on a diversity of other issues.

An interesting aspect of the authorship of these songs is that they are not necessarily composed by, or on behalf of, the in-law who is the challenging party in the song. In practice, any person can compose a mocking song. The person using the song should preferably be an in-law to the composer. Sometimes, a person challenges his own clan-relatives by adopting the viewpoint of one of his in-laws. In that case, the joke is on both, since the composer mocks his in-law for mocking his own brothers. The songs weave a network of safe competitiveness among the families allied by marriage. The same people — it should be added — are divided with regards to commensality. The son-in-law should under no circumstances accept food or drink from his mother-in-law. Four of the songs I collected were mockeries of men who were suspected of having done so.

Good rivalry can in principle always turn bad. The boundary between a good joke and a bad one is — as elsewhere in the world — sometimes difficult to draw. At one occasion during my stay in Lokiliri, when a Rainmaker who had recently died was the target of the mocking, worry about the rain led the *monyomiji* to intervene and to ban the song. The possibility that a conflict may break out between clan groups sharing the same village or the same section is never completely absent. A clan group should, therefore, be ready to face the challenge when it presents itself, which means: to be ready for a fight. The number of men the contenders can bring into the field determines the outcome of a fight more than anything else. A local clan group should, therefore, make sure that the discrepancy between its own numbers and that of its potential opponents is not too large.

Oral tradition indicates that in the past, small clan groups merged with similar groups to be able to counterbalance the more powerful clans in the village. A ritual sealed the clan merger. The two parties that wanted to unite positioned themselves at opposite sides of a stream. Each of the two parties slaughtered the goat presented by the other group. After the sacrifice the two goats were eaten in communion by the new clan brothers, who could henceforth not marry each other's sisters.

A symmetric opposite of this ritual which is still carried out occasionally, splits a clan into two parts that are allowed to intermarry. Only one goat is taken, cut lengthwise and divided between the two parties, each one allowed to eat only the half it receives.

The arena for clan rivalry is limited to the village. I did not come across cases of conflicting clans mobilising members living in other villages. Of course, a man who happens to visit his clan brother living elsewhere will be expected to rally when the latter is attacked in his presence, but if the fight takes place while he is at home he is not expected to go and join his clan brother.

Similarly, in a fight between villages, all *monyomiji* of the villages should join, regardless of their clan. However, it would reflect badly on a man if he were to kill his clansman in battle. Hence, clan brothers living in separate villages should keep out of each other's way when their villages fight. The same rule applies to in-laws, mother's brothers and sister's sons. The ties of the latter, which cross complementary opposition, may be precious in the ensuing peacemaking process, just as they may have been a source of intrigue during the jockeying for war.

The Rainmaker/king

The king is the symbol of village unity *par excellence*. As sovereign, his decisions are expected to transcend sectional and clan interests. Nevertheless, the fact that he is the leader of the most powerful clan in the village and a member of its central section are important assets to his *de facto* authority.

The king is the chief peacemaker in the village, in conflicts between sections as well as in clan disputes. An agreement that has the blessing of the Rainmaker is less easily abrogated than one which was arranged 'privately'. The king is, further, ultimately responsible for war and peace and is the guardian of the war drum, which is used to call the *monyomiji* to war. He is responsible for the foreign affairs of the community and maintains relations with neighbouring kings. Such relations are usually underpinned by matrimonial exchange and trade. He is the highest ritual authority in the village. Rituals performed at village-level, such as the ceremony of transfer of power between generations, are in most places presided over by him.

Last but not least, the king plays an important cosmological role. He is believed to protect the village against disaster — against drought most of all. He asserts his power in his relationship with his subjects. Especially when he is offended or aggrieved, drought and other plagues are sure to follow. His anger may also be aroused when harm is done to others; when the peace in the village is not kept; or when agreements achieved under his auspices are broken. There are, however, limits to the king's use of his cosmological power to castigate and harass his people. If drought persists, the *monyomiji* will call him to account for his deeds. If there is no excuse or improvement, they may kill him.

This sketch should suffice for the moment. The sectional and age-class systems are discussed in more detail in Chapters Seven and Eight, respectively, while the role of the king will be the subject of the third and fourth part of the book.

May 26, 1871—The hoisting of the Ottoman flag in Gondokoro (named 'Ismaïlia' in honour of the Khedive) marking Equatoria's annexation to Egypt, (Baker, 1874, Vol. I, p. 249)

July 21, 1871 — Night attack by a joint force of Bari, Lulubo and Lokoya on the Egyptian government post in Gondokoro, (Baker, 1874, Vol. 1, 309)

4

The Passing of the Glamour: The Bari

In the following three chapters, I present an overview of the historical background of the peoples between the Nile and the Kidepo. I begin with the onset of foreign intervention along the Upper Nile, not only because this is the period from which most of my evidence is drawn, but also because the oral tradition relating to events in this period can be checked against written sources. Although I will occasionally refer to the kingdoms practising *monyomiji* rule located on the Lopit range and in the foothills of the Imatong and Dongotono Mountains, no attempt is made to provide a historical background of these groups for reasons of space and because little has been recorded on the individual histories of these kingdoms.

Depending on how they were incorporated into the modern world, three groups of peoples can be distinguished. The first are the Bari, whose exposure to foreign influence has been the longest, the most intense and the most violent. They contrast with the Lotuho whose transition to colonial rule went without any major armed confrontations with the invading power. The third group consists of the polities of the Lulubo, Lokoya and Pari, which maintained their independence up to the second decade of this century. Their villages were conquered one by one in violent confrontations with the colonial power.

Before beginning this comparative historical sketch, I would like to review and comment briefly on the anthropological features that seemed particularly striking to nineteenth century visitors to the area.

The beautiful, the brave, and the earthly

The impression the people in this area made on the first travellers, missionaries and representatives of Western imperial power was generally favourable. Their attitudes and lifestyle conformed to the romantic European image of the 'noble savage'. Four themes dominate in the discourse concerning the human type living along the Nile between the Dinka to the north and the Acholi and Madi in the south: (1) racial beauty, (2) the warrior ethos and bravery, (3) the excessive rivalry, (4) the lack of religion.

Werne, a member of the first group of Europeans to see the Bari, compared their physique favourably with both the black and the white members of his crew. His hosts were tall (6.5 to 7 feet), and he was impressed with their classical features which reminded him of Roman aristocrats and Egyptian murals, and made him think that the Bari constituted "a protoplasm of the black race" (1848:288). He described Prince Nyiggilo, his Bari interlocutor, as having "a beautiful Roman head ... with half-long, curly hair tied with a fur strap instead of a laurelwreath."(*idem*: 292, my translation).

Veterinary Professor Lafargue, who visited the Bari three years later, in 1844, did not hesitate to qualify them as "the most beautiful human race that exists on the earth" (1845: 159–160). Similar assessments of their physique and health were common throughout the nineteenth century (Brun-Rollet" 1855:257; Wilson and Felkin: 1879, Vol. II: 96; Buchta, 1881:85) and are summarised in Hartmann's statement "that the Bari might very well provide us with a model of the authentic noble savage" (1884:129).

The Lotuho, rarely visited by Europeans before the turn of the century, enjoyed a similar reputation. For Samuel Baker, they were both in physique and in civility of manners "the finest savages [he] had ever seen" (1866, Vol. I: 204–205). Emin Pasha shares this judgement which he, like Werne and Baker before him, supports with anthropometric data (1882:269).[1]

A number of travellers and missionaries contrast the cheerful and gallant way they are received by the Bari and Lotuho with the uncomfortable, shy and clumsy approach of the Nuer and Dinka.[2] For Baker, and many British officers coming after him, the Lotuho stood out: "Far from being the morose set of savages that I had hitherto seen, they are excessively merry, and always ready for either a laugh or a fight" (1866, Vol. I:204).

In contrast to the Bari and Lotuho, the Lokoya had a most unfriendly reputation. This was partly due to the fact that they were the long-standing enemies of the Bari who had described their eastern neighbours as "man-eaters" to Werne (1848:318). The negative impression was reinforced by the disastrous defeat the Lokoya villages of Liria, Ilyangari and Ngangala inflicted on an army of Nile traders sent out to punish them in 1860. Out of 150, men 117 were left dead, not counting the casualties among the Bari auxiliaries. French medical officer, Peney, and Maltese trader, De Bono, who visited Liria one year after the battle, were treated with disdain by King Legge, although they were accompanied by 120 men armed with firearms. Their soldiers were made to parade in honour of the king after the latter had flatly refused them the passage to Lafon. No wonder that Peney characterises the Lokoya as "more arrogant, more insolent, more intractable than any people of their colour placed in different circumstances." (Malté-Brun, ed., 1863:57).

---

1   "The Lotuho people are a very special lot, completely different from the other Negro tribes here. With an average height of 1.70–1.75 m, they have a slender — I would say — elegant physique….." (Emin Pascha, 1882:269, my translation).

2   "I look at these people, people like us, they show modesty when they meet us but without that fearfulness and awkwardness that we observed for example with the Cic." (Emin Pascha, 1882:292). And Mitterrutzner, the author of the first Bari Grammar, quoting an observation by the missionary Kaufmann, writes: "One does not see the timidity and fear of the Dinka who quickly withdraw at the sight of strangers. Here everybody runs en masse to the ships" (1867: xiii). The diffident attitude of the Nuer and Dinka, and especially the Cic, may be explained by the particularly violent way in which the first encounter with the invaders from the North took place. Many Cic were arbitrarily killed by the first expedition sent by Mohammed Ali to discover the source of the Nile (Thibaut, 1856:141–153).

Baker, after a similar unhappy experience with Legge in 1863, did not spare invective in describing the man: "the greatest rascal that exists even in Africa" who has "ferocity, avarice and sensuality stamped upon his face" (1866:176).[3]

Because of their fierce reputation, the Lokoya and Lulubo were long left undisturbed by successive governments on the Nile, even though this independence often caused great inconvenience to the maintenance of regular contacts with the Lotuho. At the time of the border rectification with the Uganda Protectorate, they were included in the Anglo-Egyptian Condominium (1914) and subjugated in a number of bloody patrols. Once they became colonial subjects, a less hostile, more patronising stereotype emerged:

> ...a very wild and attractive crowd of naked savages who have an inherent dislike to do anything but dance, drink and cultivate, all of which they do well.[4]

Travellers who reached the Upper Nile from the Indian Ocean were struck by the similarity of the Bari,[5] Lulubo[6] and Lotuho[7] with the East African Maasai who, up to the present day, are called upon to uphold the nineteenth century myth of the noble savage. The warrior ethos of the Bari, Lokoya and Lotuho compelled the admiration of the Europeans. Courage was seen as the key to Bari culture:

> As with *virtus* of the Romans, courage is the common denominator of all their virtues, to which all other qualities springing from their pure, uncorrupted, nature are subordinated (Werne, 1848:295).

Gordon, whose attitude to the people he was mandated to conquer was marked by feelings of guilt, was impressed by the "show of great courage" of the Bari who succeeded in eliminating a full company (27 out of 30 men) of his Nubi soldiers while

---

3   A portrait of Legge, drawn by Baker, opens Part Four of this book.

4   Report of Captain Cooke on Abilli, Chief of Liria, in National Records Office, Khartoum, *Juba District Files* 1/1/2, 'Chiefs Evaluations'.

5   Milne (1899:482): "[the Bari] strike one much as the Masai do further south with the cattle plague robbing them of their only means of support."

6   "The people who inhabit the first range of hills behind Gondokoro are called Lokoya under a great chief called Lewala [Lualla]. They are possibly akin to the Bari, but present at least a superficial resemblance to the Masai. Like that tribe, they paint themselves red and wear their hair in curls and like them they have rainmakers, who are important political personages." (Report by Sir C. Eliot. Through the Uganda Protectorate down the Nile to Gondokoro, Uganda National Archives, *Foreign Office Correspondence*, 11/9/1902).

7   MacDonald, who was asked by the Intelligence Department to write a proposal concerning the future boundary between Uganda and the Sudan, uses the resemblance between Maasai and Lotuho as an argument in favour of their inclusion into Uganda. Lt Col J.R.L. MacDonald, 'Memorandum respecting Proposed Boundary between Egyptian Soudan and Uganda Protectorate', (Uganda National Archives, *Foreign Office Correspondence*, 2/12/1899). Capt. Barlow on his journey in 1903 also comments on the resemblance of the Lotuho to the Maasai ('Report on the Latooka and their country', p. 8. Uganda National Archives, *Foreign Office Correspondence*, 1904, East Africa Confidential, 8 Jan., Section 1, No. 1:8, also in the *Uganda Protectorate Intelligence Report* No. 21).

he struggled to pull his steamer upstream from Rejaf to Lake Albert. The courage of the Bari exposed the "wretchedness" of his own soldiers who, although armed with firearms, were no match for the spears and bows of the Bari (G.B. Hill, 1881:107, 112). The Lotuho, "where altogether everything looks like fighting" (Baker, 1866, Vol. I: 213) were viewed as "superb warriors somehow resembling their lofty forests" (Hassan, 1893:25–26).

The rivalry that was at the root of this military ethos was sometimes positively valued, as in the appraisal by Lieutenant Jennings-Bramly regarding the morale of the Lotuho of Queen Tafeng's as "sportsmanlike", in contrast to the Lotuho of Tirangore who, because of their more frequent contacts with the outside world had become an "unsportsmanlike and unenterprising lot". [8] The rivalry existing among the Bari chieftains received mainly negative comments. It looked pointless to Gordon, "since no chief thinks of annexing his rival's territory to his"; moreover, it prevents the Bari from uniting against the intruders: "They are far too jealous of one another to combine their forces against us" (G.B. Hill, 1881: 98, 102). The Bari are often described as excessively quarrelsome: [9]

> …being slaves of their passions, without inhibition, without law, they abandon themselves to excess. the least quarrel often ends in spearthrusts, and sometimes leads to serious wars (Brun-Rollet, 1855:250).

The missionaries in Gondokoro noted on several occasions that more Bari men died as a result of violence than of disease. [10] There was, however, one redeeming quality, noticed by Brun-Rollet: their respect for a beloved authority:

> …they are just as quick to surrender to good reason as they put themselves in anger. After a few words from Don Angelo [the first missionary to stay among the Bari] I have seen them become meek as lambs, however furious they were; they said: It is true, you are right, and all was finished (*idem*).

Several authors contrasted the Bari and Lokoya with their northern and southern neighbours. The Dinka were characterised as comparatively "soft" (Lejean, 1865:85), more "sociable" (Kaufmann, 1974:180), and "less noisy" (Kirchner, Comboni Archive, *typescript*: 272). Dinka men were said to reach advanced ages, while the Bari men died young in fights (Beltrame: 1881:203). Baker, having taken his leave from the Bari ("that incomprehensible tribe"), is struck by the Madi of Labore (Moli) as being "exceedingly quiet and orderly" (1874, Vol.1:48). When Linant de Bellefonds entered Madiland, after having failed to arrange negotiations with the prophet Moyok, the leader of the anti-Egyptian resistance in southern Bari, he expressed similar relief in

---

8   A.W. Jennings-Bramly, 'Report on a Journey to Latooka and back, July 13 to August 3, 1903', Uganda National Archives, Entebbe, *Foreign Office Correspondence*, East Africa Confidential, July 29, 1904, Appendix I: 23.

9   Brun-Rollet, 1855:250; Von Harnier, 1866:48; Beltrame, 1881:303; Kaufmann, 1974:180; Kirchner, Tagebuch p. 272 (Comboni Archive, file A/5/3, *typescript*).

10   Brun-Rollet (1855:250) quoting oral information by Vinco, and Beltrame (1881:302–303) quoting oral information by Morlang.

a letter to Gordon: "the Madi are softer and more intelligent than the Bari" (Shukry, 1953:230).

The same contrast applied to the Acholi who, in Baker's view, projected a "picture of true harmony" and were "of all the negro tribes the most moral and the most honest" (1874, Vol. II: 189, 459). His favourable judgement on the Acholi was shared by later colonial administrators and postcolonial development workers, who found the Acholi and Madi much easier to deal with than the Lotuho.

Kenrick, who served as an Assistant District Commissioner in Torit District in 1937— the district which is the home to Lotuho and Acholi — explained their difference in attitude to the government in a letter to his parents:

> The Acholi willingness to cooperate with the government was purely on an individual or family basis and if they resisted it was passively rather than openly. The Lotuho were openly obstructionist to the government and would comply only after a confrontation and a showdown.

But, he added:

> …once the Lotuho had agreed to a policy they would be committed to it, so that their courts functioned better than elsewhere.

Kenrick characterised the Lotuho when facing the colonial administrators "as a football crowd", thereby pointing at the unanimity that marked their attitude to the colonial administration.[11] Using the concepts and terminology developed in the first chapter, Kenrick could also have said that the Lotuho were more given to consensual antagonism.

In fact, Kenrick's observations signal the contrast between the polities of the 'segmentary state' type in which centralist power follows the bedding of relations between individual members of clans and lineages, and the polities described in this study in which power is a function of the antagonism between the king and the body of *monyomiji*.

The religious beliefs of the peoples of the east bank, or rather their presumed absence, has puzzled many nineteenth century observers, especially the Austrian missionaries in Gondokoro who, in a period of twelve years, paid with twelve missionary lives for the baptism of only 47 Bari converts (Beltrame, 1881:312). Wilson and Felkin, missionaries to Uganda, suggested that this lack of success was due to the absence of a belief in a Supreme Being. Kaufmann, one of the Austrian missionaries, writing at the end of the famine that had decimated the Bari, sarcastically remarked that, except for a vague knowledge of a Creator and the domestic cult of the black viper, the only religion among the Bari is that of the belly. Hansal, the Austrian consul in Khartoum, put the same idea in hardly more sophisticated language, when he characterised the Bari as:

---

11   I interviewed Mr Kenrick at his home in England in July 1987. He donated the letters he sent from Torit to his parents to the Durham Oriental Library for its Sudan Archive (647/5/191).

..neither religious nor superstitious, and not an idolator either but an absolutely irreligious earthly human being, who only strives for transitory goods: women, cattle and glassbeads (Hansal, 1876:302).

The image projected here is a far cry from the immersion in symbols and mystical values attributed to the African mind by Frazer and continuing through Evans-Pritchard and Fortes (1940:18) up to Adler (1982:250). Baker is astonished by the defiant nihilism articulated by Prince Kamiru of Tirangore when he is interviewed:

Baker: 'Do you think that a good man and a bad must share the same fate, and alike die, and end?'

Kamiru: 'Yes. What else can they do? How can they help dying? Good and bad all die.'

Baker: 'If you have no belief in a future state, why should a man be good? Why should he not be bad, if he can prosper by wickedness?'

Kamiru: 'Most people are bad; if they are strong they take from the weak. The good people are all weak; they are good because they are not strong enough to be bad' (1866, Vol. I: 250).

Prince Kamiru of Tirangore (Baker, 1866, Vol. II, p.212)

But there is also an element of admiration in Baker, who must have shared some of the rationalist skepticism about religion of his days:

…there was not even a superstition upon which to found a religious feeling; there was a belief in matter; and to his [Kamiru's] understanding, everything was *material*.

It was extraordinary to find so much clearness of perception combined with such complete obtuseness of anything ideal (*idem*).

The missionaries Morlang and Kirchner both commented on the Bari belief that 'Ngun', the name the Bari use to denote the Supreme Being, is essentially evil:

They could not be convinced that God (of whom they had a vague idea) was good. To the contrary, they maintained that He was evil (*aloron*), because He sends death, and is responsible for the sun, which burns all their crops (Morlang, 1974:112).

Hansal contrasts the Bari indifference to 'God' and the lack of a sacrificial cult in his honour with the high expectations they have with regard to their Rainmakers, to whom they ascribe omnipotence and who receive a great number of sacrifices in order to placate and thank them. A diary entry of the missionary Kirchner also wryly states that the Bari talk a great deal about the miracles wrought by King Nyiggilo, but have no more than a most obscure notion of 'Ngun':

Whenever I inquire about Nyiggilo, one miracle is related after the other, he makes the sun, the rain, etc. But of God, they don't have any knowledge, not even of His name; only a few people near the river know of an evil *Ngun* who kills people and animals"[12]

Finally, he points at the same, to him paradoxical, fact:

These savages, utterly devoid of belief in a Deity, and without a vestige of superstition, believed most devotedly that the general affairs of life and the control of the elements were in the hands of their old chief (Baker, 1866, Vol. I: 322).

The main objective of this study is to describe, analyse and explain this central role played by the king, while doing justice both to the king's *earthiness* and to his *divinity*.

The Bari: The collapse of the hegemony of the Bilinyan Bekat

We now turn to the history of the kingdoms which are the focus of this study. I limit myself to the period that commenced with their first direct contact with the world at large. I begin with the Bari who were the first to be confronted with the intrusion of 19th century empire builders.

From the point of view of the local political leadership, Bari history, since the encounter with the Egyptian expedition in 1841, can be divided into four periods:

up to 1859:   local hegemony based on rain: Rain kings;

1859–1883:   local hegemony based on trade: cargo chiefs;

1883–1899:   local hegemony based on the gun: warlord-chiefs;

1899–present: administration by government chiefs; chiefly power based on the fact that the chief is an extension of the modern state (colonial or postcolonial).

---

12   Kirchner, Tagebuch, 281–2 (Comboni Archive, file A/5/3, *typescript*).

The first encounter with the foreigners from the north, on 19 January, 1841, with the members of the second expedition sent by Mohamed Ali, the Viceroy of Egypt, to discover the source of the White Nile, was a very festive one, at least for the Bari.[13] The German geographer, Werne, who accompanied the expedition, described their reception by the Bari as a "triumphant procession". On both banks, the boats were followed by singing and dancing crowds. While some people helped pulling the boats, others swam after them and tried to hold on to the boards — something the crew sought to prevent by hitting their fingers. Glass beads were traded for cows, spears and Bari ornaments while the boats moved on slowly.

King Logunu of Bilinyan, of the Bekat rain clan, who claimed sovereignty over both Nile banks over a distance of eleven days of marching from the north to the south (1848:315), came to meet the travellers, dressed in a blue cotton gown and accompanied by thirty singing women (his own according to the French trader Thibault, 1841:130), a band of drummers and blowers of horns and whistles, and other members of the royal family, including two sons: prince royal Subek and his younger brother Nyiggilo. He approached the vessels dancing, his arms spread wide in welcome "as the eagle with its wings superbly spread" (Thibault: 1841:130). Boarding the ship without any hesitation, the king immediately identified Selim Capitan, the leader of the expedition, as his compeer and performed the respectful Bari greeting of sucking Selim's index finger.[14] After the introductions, the king sang a praise song to welcome the foreign guests. To both Werne and Thibaut, the commanding and unperturbed posture of the sovereign and the social sophistication of his entourage contrasted favourably with the diffident attitude of the Shilluk king and the timid way the Dinka and Nuer had approached them on the way. Selim offered the king a big bronze cowbell weighing some 25 pounds. The king showed great satisfaction and reciprocated the gift with a newly made iron stool and a female statue. The stool put the spotlights on the local iron industry, the source of Bilinyan's power; the statue may have been associated with the fertility cult.[15]

---

13   Not for all the Bari. During the first day, a shooting incident took place in which at least eleven Bari were killed (Werne, 1848:276–277; see also p. 209).

14   The fact that Logunu pretended not to notice the army commander, Soliman Kashef, who also offered his finger to be sucked by the king proved to Werne that Logunu knew his worth as a monarch. That Subek, Logunu's son, noticed Soliman's disappointment and anger, and offered to suck his finger instead while perfectly hiding his disapproval of the commander's outward show of feelings, constituted another demonstration of authentic royal courtesy in Werne's eyes.

15   The Bari no longer make figurines (*nyimuyö*). All the Bari figurines in museums were collected during the 19th century. According to an elderly informant they used to be owned by Big Men who applied oil and ochre to them in order to enhance the family's prosperity. Male and female clay statues are used by the Lokoya of Liria and Ngulere in their fertility cult while Lotuho tradition relates that King Okomo placed two clay figurines armed with spears opposite one another when he cursed the Lotuho dynastic rivals to perpetual hostility (Case 12.5, Round 2).

Bari figurines, such as the one given in 1841 by King Logunu to Selim Capitan, the leader of the Khedive's second expedition to discover the source of the Nile (Catalogue, Museum für Völkerkunde, Vienna). The same two statues also appear on the oldest known photograph of Bari figurines, in Frobenius (1923), Tafel 171; see also Pugach, (1993).

Ten years later, when missionary Don Angelo Vinco attended a rainmaking ceremony in Bilinyan, he noticed that the same bell was used as the receptacle in which the rainstones were washed (1940:307; Brun-Rollet, 1855:229). The fact that the Bari kings perceived the presence of the white man as a means to increase the efficacy of their rain powers shows the high expectations they had of the newcomers.

These expectations, however, were soon frustrated. After Logunu's death, his sons, Subek and Nyiggilo,[16] emerged as rivalling leaders of the Bari.[17] Nyiggilo established close contact with the Savoyard trader, Brun-Rollet, who took Nyiggilo to Khartoum in 1844 at his own request.[18] Nyiggilo acquired a key position in the trade in goods from Khartoum with the eastern hinterland of Bilinyan and travelled widely to Pari,

---

16   Nyiggilo was legally the son of Muludiyang, Logunu's father. He was begotten by Logunu from a wife he inherited from his father. The village of Nyiggilo's mother, Ferica, almost became the location of the first missionary post on the Upper Nile. It was known to Nile travellers as Umm Nikla, after the warm welcome given by Nyiggilo's (Nikla's) mother to her son at his return from Khartoum (Brun-Rollet, 1855; Duc d'Aumont, 1883; Pedemonte, 1974).

17   The full story of this rivalry which went on for several generations is told in Case 15.2.

18   The request is rendered in the typical literary fashion of the time by Brun as follows: "I leave myself in your hands. I want to know the country that produces the fruits and drinks that you have given me to taste; I want to see how woven fabrics and the other objects in your possession that I admire are manufactured. They prove that your people are superior to us who cannot produce anything of the like. If you give me some of these articles, I will return to my country as a rich and powerful man either with you, if you wish so, or with the people you confide to me to buy ivory" (Brun-Rollet, 1855:188).

Loudo and Lotuho. He was also the local protector of the Austrian missionaries who ran the mission post in Gondokoro from 1852 to 1860.[19]

Vinco was hospitably received by the king and accompanied him on one of his trading expeditions. The missionary gained a reputation as a *juök*, a divine person. As such, he played an important role as peacemaker in his friend's kingdom, not only in the mediation of its internal conflicts, but also in its relations with external powers. On one occasion, the peace and trade between Bilinyan and the Pari was restored due to his intervention. Another time, Vinco successfully negotiated peace between Bilinyan and the alliance of Liria, Loudo and three other Lokoya villages, the names of which are not mentioned. The Lokoya refrained from their planned attack on condition that Vinco would soon come to visit them (Vinco, 1974:96). When Vinco delayed, they responded with a series of assassination attempts on the man who was such an important asset to their enemy.

When Vinco finally paid his long-promised visit to King Legge of Liria and became his friend, he manoeuvred himself in an impossible position. After his return, the Bari wanted him to lead them in a war against the Lokoya. When Vinco refused, they faced him with an ultimatum: be our leader or die. Vinco narrowly escaped to Khartoum in one of the merchant's boats (Vinco, 1974:100). Soon after he had fled from Bilinyan, the war with Liria broke out (Brun-Rollet, 1855:198). The war with the Pari had resumed earlier on (Vinco, 1974:96).

Vinco does not give us a very precise idea about what the Bari wanted from him as their leader in the war against the Lokoya. From the context of Vinco's own account, one would conclude that it was his quality as a *juök* that the Bari wanted to deploy in the field. His divine powers had been demonstrated in an earlier event: when Vinco bypassed Liria on his return journey from Lafon, the Lirians who had been waiting to attack him during the night, had fallen victim to a sudden panic and had dispersed. In the panic, they had even killed six of their own men. After this incident, King Legge swore never again to chase "a spirit, a demon, a god against which his arms were powerless" (Brun-Rollet, 1855:198).[20]

---

19   In 1846 Pope Gregory XVI founded the Vicariate Apostolic of Central Africa in order "to spread Christianity under the pagan negro tribes and at the same time counteract the slave trade". In 1850, the earliest missionaries — Vinco is among them — made a first exploratory visit to the Upper Nile.

20   There is another context for the Bari demand and Vinco's escape: In 1850, Knoblecher, the Pro-Vicar of the Vicariate Apostolic of Central Africa had promised Nyiggilo firearms to defend himself against the Lokoya in return for permission for two missionaries to settle with the Bari. After the agreement had been reached, agents of the Governor in Khartoum had influenced King Subek, the official heir to the throne and Nyiggilo's rival, not to allow the missionaries to settle. Knoblecher and his team returned to Khartoum without a conclusive agreement. Thereupon, Knoblecher had travelled to Europe to mobilise support from the Austrian Emperor. Vinco, evading the orders of the Governor, had embarked on one of the ships of Brun-Rollet, to follow the developments in Bariland (Gray, 1961:25). With the knowledge that Subek and Nyiggilo were rivals to the kingship, it becomes clear why Subek was driven into the camp of the Khartoum Government when the missionaries promised Nyiggilo firearms to fight the Lokoya.

By the end of the 1840s, two factions had formed around the missionary and trading interests in Bariland. On one side, there was a group of traders from Khartoum, supported by the government. These indulged in slave trade[21] and had found an ally in King Subek. The other faction consisted of the missionaries and trader. Brun-Rollet, who opposed the slave trade and were prepared to rally international opinion against it. Their local ally was Nyiggilo, Subek's half-brother and rival.

Werne noted the rivalry in existing within Bari society. On two occasions Bari chieftains had confided in him that they did not think much of the powers of King Logunu (1848:283, 299); while Logunu himself had asked Selim Capitan to launch a joint punitive expedition against the west bank Bari who, for some years, had refused to pay the customary tribute (*idem*: 323). Selim Capitan had no time for this, but many of the traders who followed in his wake took up the venture willingly. According to Brun-Rollet, by the middle of the 1840s, many traders' armies were involved in local wars between Bari chieftains, taking possession of the war captives to sell them as slaves to Omdurman.

In 1852, the antagonism between the two factions escalated in an open row between the missionary Vinco and the trader Vaudey, who was also Vice-Consul of Sardinia. The quarrel between the two men — both of whom aspired to discover the source of the White Nile[22] — further polarised the relations between the two factions and culminated in a violent clash which cost the trader-explorer Vaudey his life.

4.1 *Confrontations between the traders, the missionaries and the Bari, 1852–1854* (distilled from various published accounts)

Vinco had travelled further south than any explorer before him. When Vaudey asked Vinco for information that would help him in planning his own expedition (Brun-Rollet, 1855:203),[23] Vinco — who must have condemned Vaudey's trading practices among the Bari — refused. In response, Vaudey began a whispering campaign against Vinco and openly accused him to his superior, Knoblecher. Vinco was called to Khartoum to explain himself.[24] Although Knoblecher acquitted him of the suspicions that had been raised against him, Vinco's life among the Bari was henceforth full of obstacles. At the end of 1852, Vinco died, according to Brun-

---

A military success against the feared enemy would certainly have tilted the legitimacy of the claim to the throne in favour of the conqueror of the Lokoya.

21   Gray argues that the slave trade was only of minor importance compared to the ivory trade. The profits on ivory were incomparably higher while slaves could be obtained with less effort in the Nuba Mountains and in Blue Nile Province (1961:28).

22   "Ever since I had decided to remain among the Bari, I had also made up my mind to try and discover the source of the White Nile and to this end, I left nothing undone" (Vinco, 1974:94). Vinco did indeed provide Vaudey with important information, as Vaudey acknowledges in his replies to a questionnaire put to him by geographer Antoine d'Abbadie (published under Vaudey's name in 1852).

23   Accounts that have only come to my attention in 2016 (Buet, 1887) justify a re-interpretation of the events.

24   This request coincided with the Bari demand to lead them in war against the Lokoya. It offered Vinco a good excuse to leave the scene for a while.

Rollet, as a result of the stress caused by the continuous harassment and intrigues of the traders and their Bari allies.

Don Angelo was given a Bari royal funeral. Eight days of mourning were observed and 3,000 to 4,000 people came to his tomb to wail, dance and sacrifice. A touching detail is the fact that Vaudey, who had been a major cause of Vinco's distress, joined the Bari in digging his grave in the middle of Marju, a section of Ilibari. He publicly begged Don Angelo for forgiveness at his grave (Brun-Rollet, 1855:203).

However, on 4 April 1854, while the consul was still busy with the preparations for his expedition to the sources of the Nile, he met his death in a bloody clash with the Bari of Ulibo, another section of Ilibari. A crowd of about 5,000 Bari from both banks of the river had gathered at the riverbank near the Mission station to welcome the Pro-Vicar Knoblecher who had just arrived from Khartoum when a ship of Vaudey's trading firm happened to pass by Gondokoro on its way from Rejaf (about 15 kilometres upstream) to Ulibo (half an hour downstream from the Mission). Mohammed Effendi, the captain, fired a salute in honour of the Pro-Vicar, which accidentally killed a Bari boy in the waiting crowd and hit another one in the leg. The Bari immediately reacted by shooting arrows at the ship. To this, Mohamed Effendi responded by firing into the crowd. Vaudey, who was in Ulibo, immediately came to Mohammed's aid, taking fifteen soldiers with him, chasing anybody in his way by gunfire.

Prince Nyiggilo, who understood Arabic and the way the gun worked, was among the welcoming crowd. When he heard Vaudey shout that his gunpowder was finished he opened the counterattack and had all of the soldiers killed.

Vaudey met his fate while trying to escape by swimming. He was killed at the hands of Mödi-lo-Busok, the Master of the Land in that part of Ilibari and a relative of Nyiggilo. *Matat* killed *matat*, a proper match according to the local ethics of warfare.[25]

Only eleven years after the arrival of the first explorers, Bari and traders stood face to face as enemies. From the written accounts it is not clear what kind of support the traders received from the Bari. It seems as if the majority had joined the fight in Gondokoro — although the possibility that the people who came to welcome Knoblecher may have been from one faction only should not be overlooked.

The chain of revenge and counterrevenge did not stop with Vaudey's death, at least not in the eyes of the Bari. One year later, the great drought set in that ravaged the Bari for five years and that appears to have been especially disastrous for the Gondokoro-Bilinyan area.[26] The Bari attributed it to the wrath of le *grand chef blanc*

---

25   This summary of the events is based on a critical reading of the three following accounts of the events: Brun-Rollet, 1855:292–296; Poncet, 1864:56–62; Lejean, 1865:78. Two more accounts, which I have not seen, are mentioned by Gray: a letter by Hansal, the Austrian Vice-Consul in Khartoum, published in: *Neueste Briefe aus Chartoum in Zentral Afrika*, Vienna, 1855, and an unpublished letter by Knoblecher kept in the Oesterreichischer Staatsarchiv in Vienna (Gray, 1961:43 notes 1, 2).

26   All accounts of the travellers who came before 1855 speak of numerous villages and a dense population. Vinco, who moved from Gondokoro to Bilinyan in 1851, speaks of Marju and

(Lejean: 1865:78).[27] As a result of the drought, violence in Bariland intensified. "One only hears of robbery and burglaries, theft and homicide" wrote missionary Kaufmann (1974:180). Kirchner, another priest, wrote in his diaries how the regular provisions of the Mission from Khartoum attracted the envy of the Bari and the thieves.[28] As early as 1855 the missionaries built a "strong encircling wall to defend the Mission from Bari attacks".[29] Morlang, who stayed in Gondokoro until 1860, gave a distressing description of the general mood of despair in 1859, the fourth year of the famine: dead bodies everywhere, mothers who threw their babies whom they could no longer feed into the Nile and vain attempts of the chieftains of Ilibari to stop widespread robbery and violence by summary executions (1862/63:115).

Different groups and persons were successively blamed for the drought. At one point, the missionaries were designated as its cause. The smoke of the chimney of the brick kiln of the Mission was believed to blow the rain away.[30] The chiefs who had allowed the Mission to build on their land were forced to bring several sacrifices to neutralise its effect (Hansal, 1876:300). The person who was to become the ultimate scapegoat of the long drought was Nyiggilo, who, since he became Brun-Rollet's agent in 1844, had been the local champion of foreign influence. After putting up considerable resistance, he was killed on 21 June 1859 by a band of young men. His belly was ripped open and his body thrown into the Nile.[31]

The cargo chiefs (1859–1885)

Upon the death of Nyiggilo, the political initiative in Bariland passed to another type of men. Throughout the 1850s trade in ivory with the Bari had expanded.[32] The increase in the number of trading houses operating in Bariland multiplied the opportunities for local chieftains to become middlemen in the collection of ivory and the distribution of trade goods. This fragmentation of the relationship with the

---

Bilinyan as forming a continuous series of settlements (Vinco, 1940:304). But when the missionary Morlang visited Gondokoro in June 1859, only three houses were left (Morlang, 1862/3:116 note).

27 The Bari must have explained the drought as the posthumous vengeance of Vaudey, not as the punishment by a heavenly power (*châtiment céleste*) as Lejean suggests. Examples of the significance of posthumous vengeance (*cien* in Pari, *epit* in Lotuho, *sendya* in Bari) are found in Case histories 9.6, 12.5, 15.1 and 17.11).

28 Kirchner's diary on his stay in Gondokoro in 1858 is one long litany of incidents of theft of food belonging to the Mission. The Bari pupils in the mission school "were instructed by their elders to steal .... The main occupation of the missionaries was to sit on their boxes and cabinets to guard their provisions" (Tagebuch, *typescript*: 275, Comboni Archive, Rome, file A/5/3).

29 Gray, 1961:39, quoting an account by F. C. Tappi.

30 If one knows that pipe smoking, especially the smoking of an empty pipe, is believed to be a method to cause drought we can imagine the worries of the Bari that the giant pipe of the brick oven must have represented to them.

31 Nyiggilo's death is treated in more detail in Case 9.7 and Table W. (p. 384).

32 In 1851, twelve boats left Khartoum for the ivory trade on the White Nile. In the year 1856, there was a total of forty boats; and in 1859, about eighty (Gray, 1961:31).

outside world was an important factor that helped to undermine the sovereignty of the Bekat kings in Bilinyan.

Between 1860, the year of the withdrawal of the Catholic Mission from Gondokoro, and 1871, when Baker hoisted the Ottoman flag near the old location of the Mission, the Egyptian firm of Aqqad, locally managed by Muhammad Abu Sa'ud al-Aqqad, was the most important foreign presence in Bariland. 'Presence' in this case meant that Abu Sa'ud and his boats spent about two months of the dry season at the stations of Gondokoro on the east bank and Rejaf on the west bank of the Nile. The rest of the year his interests were handled by local chieftains. For Gondokoro, this was Loro-lo-Lako, a commoner, who had started his career as a *turjuman*, an interpreter and middleman assisting the traders. Through Baker's and Emin 's writings, he became better known as *Alloron*. In Rejaf, on the opposite bank of the Nile, the main middleman was Laku-lo-Rundyang, nicknamed *Abu Kuka*,[33] a man without rain, as was Loro.

These two men, backed by Abu Sa'ud, became the main obstacles to the establishment of the Egyptian state in Bariland when Baker was sent by the Khedive to annex Equatoria. Loro was an in-law and ally of Bepo, the son of Nyiggilo, who was in power in Bilinyan when Baker arrived on the scene. Loro refused to cooperate with Baker in building his camp, while Bepo, assisted by Lokoya warriors,[34] carried out attacks on the camp of the Egyptian Governor (see the frontispiece to this chapter). Baker's counteroffensive against the triple alliance of Loro, Bepo and Abu Sa'ud was the siege of Bilinyan which lasted for thirty-five days, an extraordinarily long period according to local conceptions of warfare (Baker, 1874: 300–340). It is still remembered in Bilinyan as "the war of Ali Bey and his Sitti".[35] Peace was finally sought by the Bekat Rainmaker of Mögiri, who controlled the eastern side of the mountain. The negotiations were carried out by a sister of the Rainmaker who said she represented the wishes of the women as against those of the men "some of whom had very hard hearts" (Baker, 1874, Vol. I: 377).

Even after raiding and taxing Bilinyan, Baker's main problem remained how to feed the troops that threatened to desert him. None of the surrounding villages were

---

33   Abu Kuka means 'possessor of an enlarged scrotum'.

34   Possibly the generation of *monyomiji* of Lokiliri named 'Dokonyo'. They are remembered to have carried out a raid in Ilibari, of which Gondokoro forms part. At their return from that raid, according to Lokiliri oral tradition, they raided the village of Douro, south of Bilinyan. Baker writes that the Lokoya were not satisfied with the spoils and, therefore, raided a village belonging to Bilinyan as a compensation for being used as a cat's paw (Baker, 1874, Vol. I: 377). The Lulubo are often classified as Lokoya by the Bari. Extensive trade and matrimonial relations existed between Lokiliri and Bilinyan.

35   "Ali Bey was the usual designation of any white officer in command, and among the Bari the Governor-General bore this title as well as myself" (Chaillé-Long, 1876:240). Beaton (1934:194; Southern Records Office, Historical Notes on Bari Chieftainships, *typescript*, p.75, 88) did not know this and thought that Ali Bey was a Dongolawi trader, although he rightly assumes that the *Sitti* could only have been Baker's wife. Chaillé-Long's remark also explains the wide distribution of the name in Equatoria.

willing to sell food. The royal family of Mögiri advised him to go raiding to solve his problem and indicated suitable targets while expressing their willingness to join. Among the targets proposed were the Lokoya (dropped as too dangerous) and Ferica (dismissed by Baker because of their past help to the Catholic Mission).[36] Baker finally chose to raid the populous area south of Rejaf, the only area where he could use river transport to bring the grain back to Gondokoro. He admitted that he failed to find a peaceful solution for the problem to procure food.

By reverting to raiding or *ghazwe*[37] to provision his troops, Baker set the pattern for future relations between the government (whether Egyptian, Mahdist or Belgian) and the surrounding communities. Although both Gordon and Emin Pasha attempted to stop the practice, it was continued as the principal means to feed the increasing numbers of soldiers and their dependants stationed in the many government posts in Bariland.

Baker's victory over the people of Bedden, the chieftain of the area south of Rejaf, was the reason for Chief Loro to come and sue for peace. With Loro's surrender, Baker considered the pacification of the Bari completed.

Abu Kuka, the other powerful cargo chief, was dealt with by Gordon four years later, after he moved the government station from Gondokoro to the more salubrious Rejaf. Abu Kuka resisted Gordon's policy of establishing an open market in Rejaf. All supplies by the people, if they were not extorted in *ghazwe*, had so far been channelled through the chiefs, who received textiles and beads in return which they could distribute at their own discretion. Gordon opened a local marketplace, introduced copper coins, and wage labour (half a *piastre* per day for work for the station instead of payment in trade goods) as an alternative to the raids and as a way to "break through the feudal system of chiefs" by allowing "their subjects to stand on their own feet". (Crabitès, 1933: 53). At the instigation of Abu Sa'ud (who had been appointed by Gordon as his second-in-command),[38] Abu Kuka closed the market confronting Gordon with a band of warriors in an act of open defiance. He did not kill him as Gordon feared for a moment. Gordon retaliated by sending Abu Kuka to Khartoum to impress him with the power Gordon represented (Douin, 1936, Vol I: 82–830). He returned as a loyal subject to the government.

The only remaining centre of resistance left was in the south of Bariland close to the Uma River. There, the subjects of six different Rainmakers had united under a *juök*, named Moyok.[39] In 1874, they had attacked the reinforcements from Khartoum that

---

36 The village of Nyiggilo's mother and of Bepo's classificatory mother's brothers! The selection of this village by the Rainmakers of Mögiri may have been a revenge for the difficulties into which Bepo had brought them by attacking Baker.

37 *Ghazwe* is the etymological root of the word 'razzia' in English and in many other languages. The term *koya* from Dongola Nubian was also used. *Koya* continued to be used by the Belgian officials of the Lado Enclave (Lotar, 1946:157).

38 Much to Baker's surprise and anger.

39 Informants called him a *juök*, a divine person with thaumaturgic powers or a *nabi* (prophet from Arabic). Anybody who disobeyed him was believed to meet certain death. The number of

were sent to Baker in Acholi, killing twenty-eight soldiers (Baker, 1874, Vol. II:460; Shukry, 1953:329). In 1875, after another attack, one of Gordon's officers had tried to open negotiations with the prophet, but the latter refused to meet him (Shukry, 1953:329). Later that year, Gordon's troops again suffered heavy losses (thirty out of the thirty-six men brought into the field) while the steamer he was trying to pull upstream to Lake Albert ran aground near Muggi. Two more punitive expeditions, the last one carried out by Makaraka irregulars (Junker, 1889:303), were necessary to break the resistance and to declare the Bari pacified,

In addition to the government stations of Gondokoro and Rejaf, four more stations were opened by Gordon: Lado in the north, used as the capital of Equatoria Province from 1875 to 1885 (and of the Lado Enclave from 1897 to 1906); Bedden, south of Rejaf; and Kiri and Muggi further south on the Nile bank. It is no coincidence that three of these stations (except Muggi) were named after the chief in charge of the surrounding area.[40] In exchange for privileged access to trade goods, these chiefs were able to offer their subjects a limited protection against the depredations caused by the troops.

Each of these stations hosted a garrison of considerable size during Emin's days. Despite Emin's attempts to make each station self-supporting, it is clear from his diaries and from the writings of travellers that the main method of procuring provisions remained *ghazwe*. During the period of the disintegration of Equatoria Province (1884-1888), during the Mahdiyya (1888–1897) and to a large extent also in the days of the Lado Enclave (1897–1906), plunder was the main or the only method for the state to acquire food (Hassan, 1896, Vol. I: 80/81; Junker, 1889, Vol.I:309–310; Lotar, 1946:157).

The destruction caused by these raids was enormous. Apart from the regular army (the *jihadiya*), the state apparatus relied on Danagla volunteers, recruited from the former traders' militias (*hutteriya*) often backed by private slave armies (*basingers*), and local auxiliaries known as dragomen in the Ottoman empire or in Arabic as *tarajma* (sg. turjuman, interpreter), who acted as intermediaries between the *jihadiya* and the local communities. All joined in the raids and took a share in the spoils. Gordon estimated that each of his soldiers had an average of eleven dependants (G.B. Hill, 1881, entry 22/9/1875) while one of Emin's officers had a household of not less than 95 persons (Yunis, 1905:227). There is no reason to believe that these numbers were very different for the *hutteriya* and the *tarajma*. So, the demands of a station such as Lado (In 1883: 300 *jihadiya* and 70 *tarajma*), or Kiri (70 *jihadiya*, 10 *tarajma* (Hassan, 1893, Vol.I:62) on the surrounding population must have been a heavy

---

Rainmakers more or less corresponds with the number of Bari rain-areas near the Karpeto and Uma rivers: Kelang, Nyongkir, Gwodiang, Muggi-Jenderu or Nyarbanga, Muggi-Remonyo and Gumosi. Moyok's tomb near Muggi is venerated for its healing powers up to the present day.

40   Lado, named after Chief Lado-lo-Möri whose name was also given to the nearby mountain; Kiri after Köri, the Chief of Kogi (Cf. Case 9.4); Bedden after Chief Bedden who was defeated by Baker in his first *ghazwe*.

burden indeed. In 1878, only two years after the establishment of Kiri and Muggi, all cattle, grain and sesame had disappeared from the area as a result of the frequent raids. In his diary Emin observed:

> ...this is the consequence of the system of plunder and robbery that is shamelessly carried out under the name of official provisioning. If no prompt and energetic measures are taken, the Government will lack the basis to maintain itself here within a period of two years. (*Tagebücher*, Vol.2:39).

The main cause for the breakdown of Emin's authority in Equatoria, however, was not the lack of food provisions, but the lack of trade goods caused by the blockage of the *sudd* since 1878. As a result, the number of steamers reaching Lado gradually decreased. In 1882, not a single ship came and in March 1883 the last steamer called on Lado for a long time to come.

The Steamer Cult

The advent of steamers such as the one depicted here was the obsession of the cargo cult that took hold of the Nile stations when the sudd *became blocked in the mid-1880s. The drawing shows the first steamer, the* Khedive. *It was assembled in Gondokoro in 1871 from parts transported from Alexandria on camelback and in sailing boats. After the introduction of the gun in the 1840s these huge (though not taking more workload than an average lorry today) noisy, self propelled, metal vessels were further evidence of the white man's technological power.* (Baker, 1874, Vol. II, p. 47)

In the reproduction of the relationship between the government and the group of chiefs that I have labelled as cargo chiefs, and between these chiefs and the rest of the community, the exchange of trade goods played an increasingly important role.[41] In

---

41 Before the Egyptian expeditions, goods that were considered especially valuable, such as beads and textiles, were obtained by young men who sometimes travelled as far as Ethiopia to get

his diaries, Emin frankly admitted that his rule coincided with a personal network of patronage in which the chiefs played the key role. At times he worried that his successors would not understand the rules of the game:

> If my eventual successor does not interact with the chiefs the way I do, he will have a very difficult time, since all the chiefs ... feel personal loyalty towards me because I am generous to them and I take care of them from my own pocket at times when the Government has no money (*Tagebücher,* Vol. 2: 114).

Emin's gifts consisted of cotton cloth, glass beads, copperware, and alcohol. These goods were used by the chiefs to maintain the loyalty of their followers and to reward them for services rendered, in particular the services required by the government and the traders (porterage).

It is understandable that the stoppage of the supply of trade goods had consequences for the relationship between the government and the chiefs. From the end of 1883, the signs of discontent multiplied.[42] The soldiers in Lado refused to maintain the stockade around the town and there were rumours of an impending revolt of Chief Loro and King Bepo with Lokoya support. Abu Kuka, Loro's principal rival, was quick to confirm the rumours concerning Loro's rebellious intentions to Emin. After some observations on the alleged conspiracy against his authority Emin ended his diary entry of 28 November 1883 with the following exclamation: "And all this because the steamer does not come!" (*Idem*: 362). Emin had considered Loro and Abu Kuka his pillars of strength among the Bari.[43] When, in May 1884, the news reached Emin of the siege of nearby Amadi by Mahdist troops, he decided to have Loro eliminated as a precaution to the extension of the rebellion to the Bari (Hassan, 1896, Vol. II: 12). Before he was beheaded, Loro is reported to have spoken the following words which prove that his warrior ethos had survived his association with cargo and *gela*[44]:

> Now that you have taken me prisoner, you are welcome to kill me. I have lived long enough. The fame of having been a source of despair for your Baker, who could never defeat me, is enough for me (Hassan, 1896, Vol. II: 112).

---

them. Brun-Rollet quotes a girl's courting song praising a young man who has returned after a long absence bringing home necklaces from Ethiopia (1855:112–113). In the years immediately following the Egyptian expedition, many young Bari men travelled to Khartoum with the aim of obtaining luxury goods. Unfortunately, as they had no means of subsistence in the town, most of them ended up as slaves, a fate that, according to Brun-Rollet, would also have befallen Nyiggilo, had he not helped him. With the coming of the traders and the government, the trade goods no longer entered the community via its enterprising young men but via the networks emanating from the cargo chiefs.

42　These signs coincided with the news of the revolt of the Agar Dinka against the government post in Rumbek (in July 1883) and the capture of El Obeid by the Mahdi (in January 1883).

43　In a diary entry Emin referred to Loro as "my great friend" (*Tagebücher*, Vol.2:12) and "my most trusted Bari chief" (*Idem*:110); while a family tradition of Abu Kuka's descendants claims that Abu Kuka and Emin had established a bond of blood brotherhood (Beaton, 'History of Tokiman East', *Unpublished Notes*, 1933, Southern Records Office, Juba).

44　For the concept of *gela* see Ch. 2, note 10, p. 51.

Instead of forestalling the outbreak of a revolt among the Bari, Loro's execution precipitated it. Bepo-lo-Nyiggilo, Loro's in-law, assumed leadership of the rebellion which was supported by all the chiefs between Rejaf and Kiri. Once more, the political initiative in Bariland passed into the hands of the Bekat of Bilinyan. A special dimension of this war was that it was carried out in an alliance with the Nyangbara and the Aliab Dinka who were led by a prophet named Deng Tonj.[45]

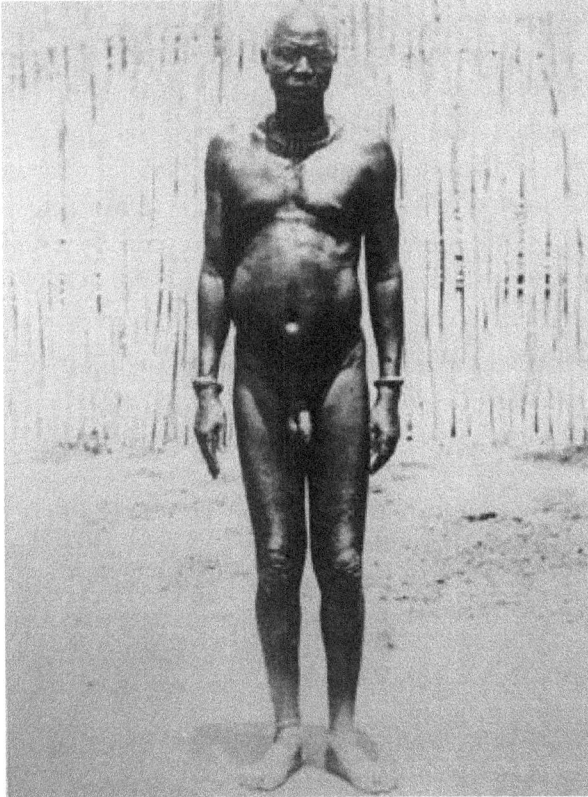

Loro-lo-Laku, the powerful 'cargo chief' of Gondokoro executed at the orders of Emin Pasha for undermining his authority (photo by Richard Buchta in 1878, kept in the South Sudan Internet Collection of the Pitt-Rivers Museum, Oxford).[46]

45   The prophet whose name first appears as 'Ben Tondj' in Emin's diaries, was according to Emin a Rek Dinka "who had been the soul of all the rebellions — from Bahr-el-Ghazal, Rumbek, Shambe, and now the Bari". His death was mentioned in the letter of the Egyptian Prime Minister that informed Emin of the death of Gordon. The prophet's name is given there as 'Dentón'. According to information received by Emin from the contingent left behind in Lado, the prophet had been captured alive. He would have been taken to Emin in Wadelay, had not angry soldiers pulled him from his place of detention and burnt him alive (*Tagebücher*, Vol.3, entries 14/12/85 and 26/2/86). However, according to the Prime Minister's letter and Casati (whose book has a picture showing the killing of the prophet), he died from a bullet wound while storming the ramparts of Lado (Casati, 1891:330–332).

46   Wilson and Felkin who met Chief Loro in Lado in September 1878 have the following comment on the chief's nakedness: "Although he is so great a chief and receives numerous presents of clothes, he absolutely refuses to wear any; the only article of European manufacture which he uses is a large sunshade, and it is an amusing sight to watch him strutting about with it" (Wilson and Felkin, 1882, Vol.2, p. 86–7)

Chief Abu Kuka, his major rival now dead, offered renewed signs of loyalty to Emin even putting fifteen of his men at Emin's disposal to fight alongside the government troops. In December 1885, Abu Kuka was killed by his own warrior age-class (*teton* in Bari) who had joined the anti-government rebellion led by Bepo-lo-Nyiggilo (Emin Pascha, *Tagebücher*, Vol. 3, entries 30/11/83; 31/7/85; 13/12/85).

In the period following the execution, the continued absence of the steamers was becoming a concern with religious dimensions. For more than forty years, the ships and their cargo had been the motor of change among the Bari. The changes had created a new local class consisting of chiefs, soldiers (many *jihadiya* had been recruited from among the Bari) and *tarajma*, which depended on their connection with the government stations. Prophets preaching that the steamer, bringing guns and a new leader, would be coming within one month were first heard of in Laboré (Moli in Madi), Dufilé (near Nimule) and Wadelay (in Alurland) (Emin Pascha, *Tagebücher*, Vol. III: 42). According to one prophecy, it was only because of one high official's dislike for Emin that the steamer had not come yet *(idem,* p. 103, 112). The message found ready belief among the troops. When Emin ordered the evacuation of the government stations in Bariland (Lado, Rejaf, Bedden, Kiri and Muggi)[47] in response to the approach of the Mahdists, his order was simply ignored by the officers.[48] Instead, they suggested to Emin to come and wait for the steamer in Lado (*Tagebücher*, Vol. IV: 236) or to march on Khartoum *(idem,* p. 188).

In the turbulent events surrounding Emin's withdrawal to the south, the role of this cargo cult has been overlooked by the historians. Most authors have taken Mountenay-Jephson's view that the soldiers were merely motivated by stubbornness. But even in the few lines by Jephson devoted to the question there is more than mere stubbornness:

> …they knew but one road and that road was by way of Khartoum, if the Khedive really wanted the people to come let him send up his steamers and they would go down to Khartoum. Were there ever such fools as these people, always harping on Khartoum? (Mounteney-Jephson, 1969:278).

The importance of the cult — which was directed against Emin and on which he, therefore, only received indirect information — and its spread among the local people, is attested to by Bari oral tradition. This is how an informant from Tombur summarised the tenets of the cult in its centre of Barajak, near Kiri:

> Queen Vendina was preparing to send many steamers filled with glass beads (called *suksuk*) and clothes up the Nile. In anticipation of the event people should collect ivory so that it could be exchanged for the goods brought by the steamer. But the steamers were stopped by the Muslims and the Christians who wanted to keep the goods away from the Africans.

---

47   Gondokoro had been given up shortly after the outbreak of the rebellion led by Bepo.

48   It should be taken into account that many *jihadiya* in these stations were Bari and were, therefore, unwilling to leave.

Equatorian officers molest Emin Pasha when he reads the instructions of the Khedive to them. They were given two choices: follow Emin to Egypt via Zanzibar and remain in the Khedive's army, or stay in Equatoria where they will no longer be Egyptian soldiers. The soldiers do not trust Emin. If they have to march it will be to the north, to Egypt, only. They believed that Effendina *would soon send them a steamer carrying the true governor as well as fresh commodities* (Mounteney-Jephson, 1890:146).

Queen Vendina can be nothing other than a merger of *Effendina*, the petname used by the Equatorian soldiers to refer to the Khedive,[49] and Queen Victoria.

The era of the cargo chiefs ended in a cargo cult at the time when the trade goods were no longer available. The cargo cult was the first religious reflection by the Bari on their new dependence on events in the wider world. But in the cult, there is also an element of continuity with the older rain cult. Like the rain, the coming cargo was believed to depend on the will of a living sovereign. When the desired cargo did not come, an atmosphere of increasing suspense developed in which a person or group was blamed for stopping the cargo. Like the rain, the advent of the cargo was in the hands of a benevolent sovereign. Like the absence of rain, the non-arrival of cargo was blamed on a person maliciously holding it back, The followers followed a life of military discipline collecting ivory for the imminent cargo event, behaving, as in rain rituals, as if the delivery of the cargo — and the resurrection of cattle — could

---

49   Zucchinetti mentions that the Shilluk King, Abdel–Mek (= Kuikon), who remained loyal to the Khedive and led the Shilluk in war against the Mahdists also called the Khedive by this title (1890:9). Vita Hassan (1893:ch.11–12) informs us that the soldiers rebelling against Emin also referred to the Khedive by that name. This lends further support to the connection between the mutiny and the steamer cult.

happen any moment.[50] The substitution of rain by cargo in cultic symbolism is exactly what should be expected if trade-goods had taken the place of rain in the operation of chiefly power and their influx would suddenly cease.

While large groups of Bari continued to wait for the cargo, others relied on their guns — many of which became available after the partial disbandment of the Egyptian army — to get what they wanted.

The era of the warlords (1885–1898)

Between Emin's withdrawal to Wadelay (1885) and the establishment of Mahdist rule (1888), security in Bariland deteriorated further. Bepo, who controlled a large part of the Bari countryside, continued to carry out attacks on the government stations and on the chiefs who had remained loyal to the government. Withdrawal of the troops from Lado in 1887, brought on by the attacks of the people of Ilibari on the road between Rejaf and Lado, and the rebellion of the Rejaf garrison against Emin, prepared the field for the Mahdists — or Ansar as the followers of the Mahdi were commonly called —, who finally arrived in October 1888.

While the Ansar besieged and defeated the Rejaf garrison, Bepo settled accounts with the people of Abu Kuka, the rival of his ally Loro, in nearby Tokiman. After their defeat at Rejaf, Emin's *jihadiya* were willing to withdraw to Nimule and Wadelay and join Emin. However, many of the troops and the *tarajma*, especially those recruited from among the Bari, chose to stay put. Some of these men professed allegiance to the new invaders and adopted the *jibba*, the patched robe of the Ansar, others relied on their guns alone and allied themselves to local Bari chiefs. In this situation of insecurity, the capacity to offer military protection and the distribution of booty became the decisive source of power. A new class of chiefs whose power depended on the gun came to dominate the Bari scene.

Like its predecessors, the Ansar government relied on *ghazwe* for its provisioning. To ensure the safety of the men when on *ghazwe*, it was necessary to deploy the whole force (1,500 men as they arrived in 1888). The main resistance against the Ansar came from the former *jihadiya* allied to Bari chiefs and from the adherents of the steamer cult.

After the withdrawal of Emin's troops from Kiri and Muggi, the main political factor in southern Bari became Barajak, the centre of the steamer cult at the confluence of the Nile and the Kaya River. The centre was led by the prophetess Zainib Kiden, a Fajelu by birth. She ordered her followers to collect ivory and store it in her house so that when the steamers would arrive, guns and other tradegoods could be received in return. She not only preached a return of cargo but also the resurrection of lost cattle. As long as the steamers had not brought real guns, her followers, who were made to believe that they were invulnerable because of having drunk Allah's water, had to

---

50   Compare this summary with the 'Basic scenario of a rain ritual', Ch. 16, Model R., p. 358 and with Case 16.13 on p. 362 and Table U, step 5 and 7 on p. 364, 365.

parade and fight with wooden ones. Until the arrival of the steamers, her followers were exempted from paying bridewealth.

The forces of the Ansar and those of prophetess Kiden clashed in Kelang in 1890 when Umar Salih, sent by Khalifa, the successor of the Mahdi, to clear the last remnants of the Turco-Egyptian presence, attempted to occupy the stations of Muggi and Kiri. During the attack of Kiden's troops, the former *jihadiya* who had joined the Ansar deserted. The Ansar suffered a disastrous defeat. Left with only seventy men, Umar Salih withdrew to Bor.

Two years later, the Ansar mounted a new offensive.[51] Kiden was captured and taken to Rejaf. In a letter to Khalifa in Omdurman, the Emir Ali Mukhtar explained that he had her executed because her presence in Rejaf caused generalised diarrhoea, shivering and fainting among the *abid* (Ar.: slaves) as the local population was referred to in the letters of the Emir.[52]

After Kiden's elimination, a number of Bari chiefs renewed their allegiance to the Mahdists,[53] who were to stay in Bariland for another four years. In February 1897, the Ansar were defeated by the *tukutuku*, the forces of the Congo Free State, in the Battle of Bedden. Belgian administrators were appointed in Lado and Rejaf to rule the part of the west bank of the Nile that was known as the Lado Enclave until the Belgian withdrawal in 1910.

On the east bank of the Nile, power fell into the hands of the various warlords. The most important of these was Mödi Adum, by descent a Nyori from Ilibari, who had made a career from *turjuman* (sg. of *tarajma*) in Emin's days to the rank of *emir* in the Mahdist state.[54] During the Battle of Bedden, he defected and left Rejaf

---

51 The comeback of the Ansar coincided with the attack by the forces of the Congo Free State —
known as *tukutuku* — on the Nile stations of Muggi and Laboré. The *tukutuku* were assisted by
the *jihadiya* of Fadl Mula, a breakaway group from Emin's army that had not followed him on
his march to the Indian Ocean. These attacks may have further weakened Kiden's position.

52 Letter from Ali Mukhtar Bakr to Khalifa, dated 13 Dhul Qa'dah 1310, Central Records Office,
Mahdiya files, I/32/9, translated by Mr Bol Deng Chol. Richardson wrote a short article on
Kiden (1933:181–6). Contrary to what he reports, Kiden was hanged by Ali Mukhtar, and
not beheaded by Arabi Dafa'alla. Shivering and fainting are symptoms of the trance into which
the adepts of the cult worked themselves. Trance also played an important role in the successor
Yakanye cult. On the symbolic dimension of diarrhoea, read the comments on the king's
stomach in Chapter Nineteen (p. 445).

53 Among the chiefs who came to declare their allegiance to Arabi Dafa'alla, the new Emir at Rejaf,
seven were selected to be sent to Omdurman to meet the Khalifa: Ibrahim Boreng of Tokiman,
the sister's son of Abu Kuka, in Arabi's letter to the Khalifa referred to as 'the paramount chief'
of the Bari; Lado Möri, from Lado, the son of the chief who had offered his daughter as a wife to
Emin; Kirba Lokola, chief of Logo at the confluence of the Kit and the Nile; Lualla, the Lulubo
chief (who must have refused to go since nothing is remembered in Lokiliri of such a journey),
and three others. Letter Arabi Dafa'alla to Khalifa, 12 Jumada 1311, Central Records Office,
Mahdiya Files, I/32:48; translation by Mr Bol Deng Chol.

54 According to another informant, he had started his career by being taken to Khartoum as a
slave. There, he had been enrolled in the army and sent to Equatoria Province.

with 1,500 followers of ethnically diverse Equatorian origins, clad in the *jibba* to seek refuge with Lualla, the chief of Lokiliri who had been a Mahdist ally.[55] When Colonel Martyr entered Bariland in 1898 on behalf of the Uganda Administration, Mödi Adum came to meet him as the leader of a delegation of Bari chiefs. He made a very favourable impression on the colonel who, in a letter to the Commissioner in Kampala, recommended to recognise Mödi as the overall leader of the Bari and offer him a paid government position.[56]

The condition of Bariland in 1898, after half a century of internecine war and *ghazwe*, was terrible. Martyr estimated the number of Bari living between the Uma River and Rejaf, the area characterised by Baker as "immensely populous" at not more than one thousand.[57]

> The warlike and troublesome Bari tribe, with whom Baker had so much trouble, are extinct, having been either murdered or taken off as slaves by the Dervishes [Ansar]. Formerly the country must have been thickly populated, for the remains of old villages are very numerous.[58]

The author even went so far as to suggest that the Bari area should be resettled by Lotuho and Lokoya.

The smallpox epidemic of 1894 (Yunis, 1905:227) and the Rinderpest at the end of the century added to the destruction due to man-made violence. Many Bari had, in fact, fled away from the Nile, east to Lafon and Lulubo, into Madi and Acholi to the south and west to the Kuku and Fajelu.

The government chiefs

By 1898, the Bari found themselves divided between three colonial zones: the Belgium-administered Lado Enclave on the west bank; the Anglo-Egyptian Condominium on the east bank north of the 5th parallel and the administration of the Uganda Protectorate south of it.

The policy of all three colonial governments was to rely on whatever strongmen were available, regardless of their antecedents.[59] Most of these strongmen, however, did not

---

55   Macallister, Sub-Commissioner of Nimule Province, 'Report on Nile Province, 1902', Uganda National Archives, Entebbe, *Shuli Correspondence* A162:52. The same report mentions that Mödi Adum is not immediately accepted by the other chiefs in the area. The *ghazwe* led by Mödi Adum from his refuge in Lokiliri are still remembered by the people of the neighbouring Lulubo villages of Aru, Edemo and Kudwo who called his followers *lowora* (robbers).

56   Lt Col Martyr, 'Report on the Nile District of the Uganda Protectorate', Inclosure 1, in Despatch 76 from Acting Commissioner Kampala; Uganda National Archives, Entebbe, *Foreign Office Correspondence, East Africa*, May 18, 1899.

57   Lt Col Martyr, *idem*.

58   Letter from D.Z. Carré from Dufile, 1/2/1899, Central Records Office, Khartoum, *INTEL* 5/5/49: 'Uganda Reports'.

59   Haddon, the Uganda administrator in Gondokoro, formulates the issues as follows: "When the Uganda authorities took over ... there was a chaotic confusion, but affairs were comparatively settled in so far as the balance of power based on might was concerned, and of necessity, the

have rain. Some of them were sons of the former cargo chiefs (Kwajo in Gondokoro, a descendant of Loro; Morbe Boreng in Tokiman/Rejaf, a sister's son of Abu Kuka). Others were new on the scene (Mödi Adum and Kirba Lokole of Logo who had been sent to Omdurman to meet Khalifa). One or two of them were Rainmakers, the most important being Könyi-lo-Jalinga, the Nyori King of Tombur, who had successfully survived the Mahdist period by relying on his army commander, Kulang.

The Uganda administration allowed these chiefs to keep their armies, some of which were of respectable size.[60] They were expected to take care of their own defence, especially in the eventuality of attacks from the Lulubo and Lokoya. The colonial administration limited itself to a peacekeeping role by providing arbitration in conflicts and offering military support in case of a serious threat. These chiefs were settled in a string of new settlements along a new road between Nimule and Gondokoro, which was constructed at some distance from the Nile in order to prevent the spread of the tsetse fly.

---

country was divided into administrative districts, of a size proportionate to the apparent power of the existing chiefs.... For further convenience ... the abler of the chiefs were put over their less able neighbours. As the axiom that power collects power, and might is right, is sound law with these people, the natives soon realised the equity of the present arrangement" (E.B. Haddon 1911:471).

60 The following are the chiefs recognised by the Uganda Administration in 1901, the number of houses in their chieftaincy and the registered number of guns. Counts of 1905 are given for comparison.

Name Chief	Area	Houses in 1901	Houses in 1905	Guns in 1901	Guns in 1905
Mödi Adum	Pager, most of S. Bari	469	201*	60	63
Kirba Lokole	Logo (incl.Shindiru)	84	269	25	61
Morbe Boreng	Tokiman	103	261	7	18
Könyi-lo-Jalinga	Tombur	70	169	44	50
Amoja	Nyarjua	100	87	11	17
Kwajo	Ilibari (incl. Bilinyan and Gondokoro	347	390	28	44

* The decline in the number of Mödi Adum's subjects is due to the fact that his subjects near the Uma and Karpeto rivers were placed under a new chief: Gumbiri, an ex-soldier. Some other followers returned to Ilibari, Mödi's original home (E. Haddon, 'System of Chieftainship amongst the Bari', Uganda National Archives, Entebbe, *Secretariat Minute Papers* 1232). See also note 64, on p. 118.

** When conditions improved in the Lado Enclave, Amoja's subjects returned to the sites of their old villages.

*** Source: 'Transport and Road Clearing Arrangements Nimule/Gondokoro', Uganda National Archives, *Shuli Correspondence A16, Inward,* Vol. I) and 'List of Chiefs on the Bari Dewan, 1905' *idem,* Vol. IV). The actual number of guns may have been much higher. In 1910 when Könyi's homestead was searched by the government not less than 132 guns were found, 65 of which were Albini rifles (Letter A/D.C. Gondokoro to Chief Secretary Entebbe, 21/10/1910, Uganda National Archives, *Secretariat Minute Paper* 1356, 'Arrest of Kenyi').

One of the main problems faced by the colonial administration in relation to these chiefs was the definition of their rights in relation to the older rights of the Rainmakers. Some of the Bekat attempted to make a comeback on the political scene after peace returned to the area. Three factions opened the competition for the succession in Shindiru: [61] Wani Yemba'dija (son of Pitia Yeng-ko-Piyong), Leju-lo-Lugör (senior son of the senior wife of Lugör) and Jada and Wani (sons of Lugör's second wife Möjukulu, the sister of Lualla, chief of Lokiliri).[62] To fight their war of succession the rain princes had to rely on their alliances with warlords who in fact turned out to be the decisive factor in the struggle.

The first round of fighting was between Wani Yemba'dija, supported by the warlord/ government chief Kirba Lokole, against Lualla, who fought on behalf of his sister's sons, and was helped by Mödi Adum who was also Lualla's in-law. Lualla's brother Pitia Lonyogo led the combined force of Mödi Adum's men and the *monyomiji* of Lokiliri in war against Wani Yemba'dija and Kirba Lokole. When Pitia Lonyogo was killed by Kirba, Mödi Adum, in a second round of fighting, took revenge, kidnapped Wani Yemba'dija and killed him. After Wani's elimination Mödi Adum chose to support the candidacy of Leju-lo-Lugör.

Stories about a war of succession in Bilinyan are absent, so that it seems as if the candidacy of Bambu, the grandson of Subek, went unopposed when he returned from his exile in Lafon.

The power of these new rain kings had little political content. Both Leju and Bambu found themselves under the tutelage of warlords/government chiefs. Leju is given the position of *mukungu* (headman)[63] under Kirba, the chief of Logo, while Bambu, the grandson of Subek, is made into a *mukungu* of Chief Kwajo of Gondokoro. Their position in the administrative hierarchy contrasts sharply with their ritual importance. Bambu, for example, continued to receive tribute from a large number of subjects, including Bari who lived at the other side of the Nile in the Lado Enclave.

In the first decade of this century, there were several conflicts concerning the delimitation of the competence of the Rainmaker and the new class of chiefs which were *böngön* (without rain). As early as 1902, there was concerted resistance against the large area given to Mödi Adum, which was a patchwork of not less than seven rain areas.[64]

---

61   The heir with the oldest rights was Wani Matat, a son of Pitia Yeng-ko-Piyong, who during the Mahdist period had made a living as a warlord allied to the Ansar. Because of his *juök* the Ansar always wanted him to follow them on their expeditions. Wani refused to take the responsibility for the rain shrine of Shindiru. The reason given was that he was still too young. He was killed for stopping the rain in Mankaro, across the Sudan border, 24 August 1909.

62   Lualla himself is a sister's son to the Bekat of Shindiru. By in turn supporting his sister's sons to the throne, a sequence of quasi matrilineal succession ensued.

63   This term, derived from the administrative hierarchy of Buganda, is still used in Eastern Equatoria.

64   "Adamadi of Fagiri who was made a chief by an Acting Sub-Commissioner ... is not acknowledged by the chiefs" (Macallister, Sub-Commissioner Nile Province, 'Report on Nile Province, 1902',

A resurgence of the steamer cult, now known as *Yakanye*, jointly led by Kajikir (an ex-soldier and descendant of the Pönyili Rainmakers of Muggi-Remonyo) and by a prophetess named Mursillah, was crushed by Mödi Adum's son Tombe Musa. Gumbiri,[65] an ex-soldier like Kajikir, brought the grievances of his followers from the rain areas of Muggi, Nyongkir, Kelang and Gwodiang to the attention of the Uganda authorities. As a result, he was given a separate chieftainship, first as *mukungu* under Tombe Musa, later as a chief in his own right.

With these difficulties in view, Haddon, a young Assistant District Commissioner in Gondokoro during the years 1909–1910, decided to make a study of the political system of the Bari. The study, which served as a Master's thesis in anthropology at Cambridge,[66] describes the distribution of power in Haddon's days. Haddon distinguished three levels of authority: that of the *temejik (*clan leaders; *temeji* in his text)*, the *matat*, (rain chief; *mata* in his text), and the *böngön* (*bongun* and *boñun* in his text, translated by Haddon as 'district chiefs'). *Böngön* in Bari is used in opposition to *kör:* people with rain and denotes the class of commoners without rain. This last connection escaped Haddon. In his writing, the word is obviously used to refer to the warlords/government chiefs.

According to Haddon, the *matat* represented the highest level in the hierarchy, although his role was strictly ritual. The only non-ritual role of the *matat* is that of judge of appeal, a right which, according to Haddon, is seldom exercised "as the case tried before a *bongun* was and still is conducted with a council composed of *temeji*." (Haddon, 1911:102–3). Since the death of Jangara, who was *matat* over all the Bari and some of the other Bari-speaking tribes (Fajelu, Nyepu, Tsera, Nyangbara), there are two *kimak 'duma* (big Rainmakers), the one of Shindiru and the one of Bilinyan, all others are *kimak nadit* (small Rainmakers) with the exception of Loke-lo-Rume, the Nyori Rainmaker of Kelang who, while dependent on Shindiru, has six Rainmakers subordinate to him. The *böngön*, Haddon continues, did most of the political work: he settled disputes between the people in his district and distributed land (cultivation, grazing, hunting and fishing rights) among the *temejik* in his district. The *böngön* did not usually pay a tax to the *matat*, although both *matat* and *böngön* received a day's agricultural labour from their subjects. *Böngön* were also war leaders.

Haddon was right in thinking that the position of the *böngön* chiefs was a later development, but he wrongly assumed that their position was the result of a gradual process of devolution of power to local leaders or to sons of rain chiefs sent to rule outlying villages. Haddon's study is an illustration of the need of historical research as a complement to ethnographic description.

Uganda National Archives, *Shuli Correspondence* A162:52).

65   Gumbiri claimed to be the son of the brother of the rain chief of Kelang. Others told Haddon that he was merely his 'boy' (probably Haddon's translation of the Bari *kölipönök*, meaning boy and client (Haddon, 'System of Chieftainship among the Bari', App. B, Uganda National Archives, Entebbe, *Secretariat Minute Papers* 1232).

66   The study also resulted in an official report and an article on the System of Chieftainship among the Bari published in the *Journal of the Royal African Society* (1911).

Haddon's study shows how in the fifty years after Nyiggilo's death, the position of the Bari king had been reduced from one which entailed considerable political, judicial, and economic power to a purely ritual role. What Haddon calls the king's 'right of appeal' and his competence to offer sanctuary to fugitives, were the last remnants of his role in settling disputes. Warlords/chiefs feared to use force to remove an asylum seeker from the Rainmaker's compound because of the possible consequences for the rain.

After the border rectification between the Sudan and Uganda in 1914, all the Bari were again united under one colonial administration. As a gesture of respect to the Rainmakers of Shindiru and Bilinyan, they were promoted to be government chiefs on equal footing with the warlords/chiefs. The independence of the chieftainship of Shindiru, which had a very small population, remained an issue of debate during much of the colonial period and thereafter.

Pitia Lugör, the 'King of the Bari Rainmakers' (1912–1949) whose rain in 1943 swept away the British Army pontoon bridge over the Nile. Note that Pitia Lugör's hair, like that of other Bari Rainmakers, has not been cut.

The long reign of Pitia Lugör (1912–1949) brought a revival of the ritual importance of the rain of the Bekat. In the 1930s, Pitia Lugör reinstated the solemn procession across the whole length of Bariland, a custom which, according to Whitehead, writing in 1929, had been abandoned. One year, the king travelled along the east bank, the other year the west bank, making rain, healing the barren, expelling evil from the Bari communities and accumulating big herds of cattle received in tribute.

The king's secular role, the settling of conflicts between chiefs, had long been taken over by the colonial administration. Pitia Lugör, in his days, was the living symbol of Bari identity, as opposed to *gela*, the ways and institutions the white man had brought to Bariland. Every Bari knows the story of the contest between Pitia Lugör and Captain Cooke, the District Commissioner of the Bari from 1929–1946. Cooke had built a pontoon bridge across the Nile in 1943 so that the allied troops, on their way from Leopoldville to the battlefields in North Africa, could cross the river. When he showed the bridge to Pitia Lugör, he boasted of his superior capacity in 'controlling water'. Pitia is said to have taken this as a challenge and, so the Bari say, made it rain for many days so that the bridge could not hold out against the force of the Nile waters and the debris carried by it.

The civil war and the rise to power of a new class of *gela* — the urban, educated government officials, many of whom were Bari — has stripped rainmaking of its importance as a 'national' or tribal symbol. The last journey along the Nile to collect the *doket* (tribute for rain) was undertaken by Pitia Lugör's son, Mauro, in 1964, the year before the civil war engulfed Bariland. His postwar successor, Pompeio Lado,[67] has never gone to collect tribute.

Gondokoro, from 1871 till 1874 the capital of Egypt's Equatoria Province. After the night attack of the Bari, Lulubo and Lokoya warriors (see the illustration on p. 92) *a wall, a moat and fortifications were built around the garrison.* (Baker, 1874, vol. II, p.478).

Conclusion

With Nyiggilo's death in 1859, the Bekat kings of the Bari lost the initiative in political affairs. Their leading role in foreign affairs and warfare was usurped by men whose power was based on their position as middlemen in the new trade and later, when the trade collapsed, by men whose power came from their possession of guns. Bepo's rebellion against the Egyptian state was the most important attempt to restore a degree of political initiative to the Bekat. If it had not been for the feud with the descendants of Subek, which cost Bepo his life,[68] he might have emerged from the Mahdist period as a warlord-king. When the Shindiru Bekat attempted to regain

---

67   See the photo of *Matat* Pompeio Lado standing with his assistants amidst the rainstones of Shindiru on p. 300.

68   The story of the rivalry between the descendants of Subek and Nyiggilo is Case 15.2 Round 1.

some of their power after 1898, they discovered that in political matters, they had become clients of the warlords and government chiefs and had to resign themselves to the fact that henceforth, a ritual role only was left for them to play.

It is clear that the power of the Bari king had an unequivocal political content before the cargo chiefs and warlords eroded it. In this chapter, we have noted his responsibility in the field of foreign affairs, warfare, trade and mining. Hence, there is no reason to think that his office was only *ritual* as Evans-Pritchard has argued for the comparable Shilluk kingship. Evans-Pritchard's statement on the nature of the Shilluk royal office has become the issue of a long debate with the result that the scholarly consensus today no longer supports the idea that the *reth*'s power had an exclusively sacral character (Evans-Pritchard, 1948; Mercer, 1971; Arens, 1979; Needham, 1980; Schnepel, 1986; Adelberger, 1987).

Nine-tiered watch-tower (olobele) *built by the* monyomiji-*set taking over power as evidence of their vigilant and constructive spirit, Mura-Hatiha, Lotuho, 1998.*

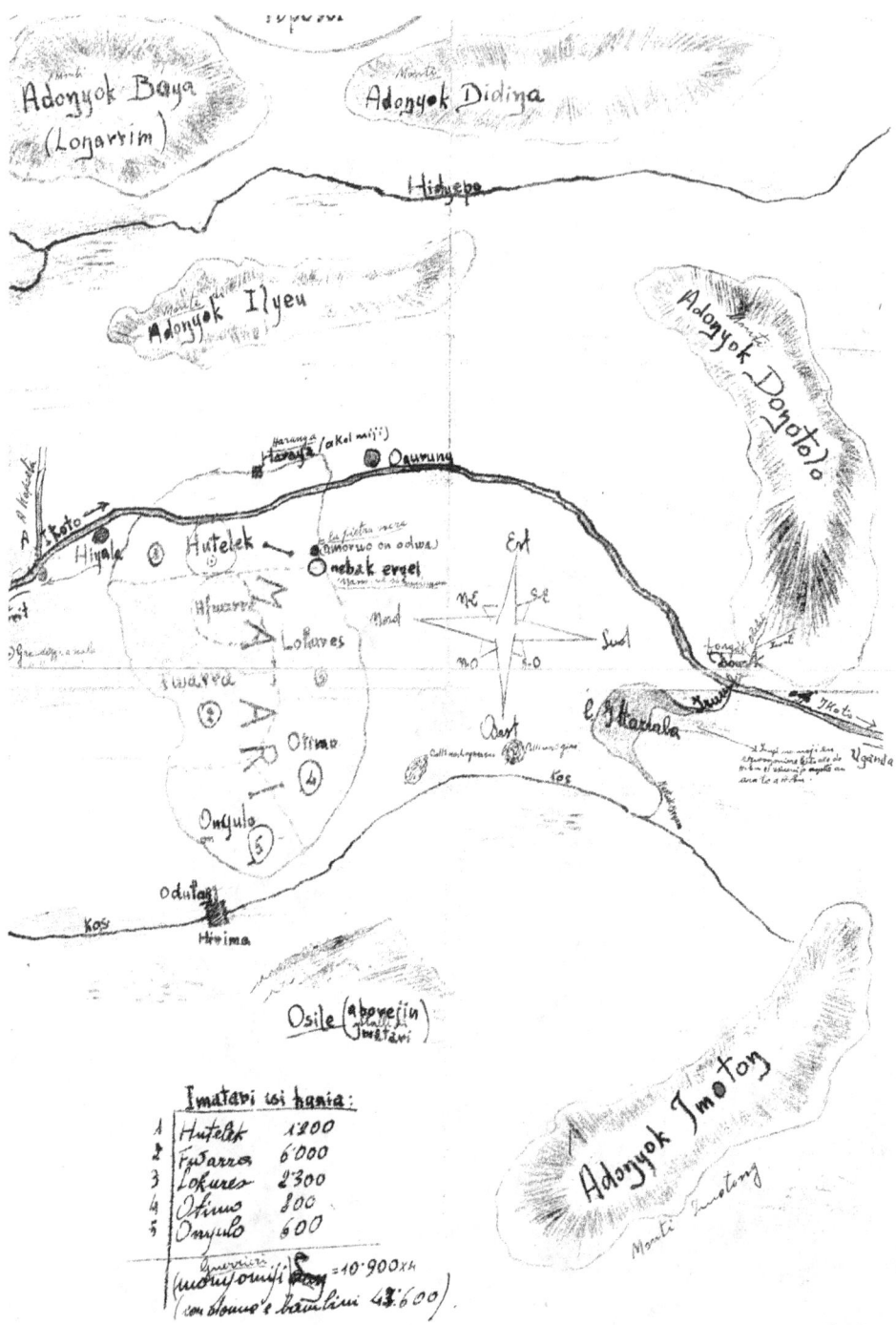

Pencil drawn map of Imatari specifying the numbers of monyomiji *of each of the five sections (Hutelek, Fwarra , Lokures, Otimo and Onyulo). The Lotuho words have Italian translations in lighter pencil strokes (Comboni Archive Rome, found among the papers of Father Pazzaglia, ca. 1950)*

5

The Twin Kingdoms: The Lotuho

Compared to the lasting and widespread violence of the Bari encounter with the modern world, the Lotuho seem to have experienced less of an ordeal. Although there are clear indications that the contacts first with the traders, and later with the agents of the Egyptian and Mahdist states, led to more frequent warring among the Lotuho, the armed confrontations tended to be contained in both time and space and, unlike among the Bari, the course of events remained largely under the control of the local kings.

The obvious factor explaining this difference is the lesser exposure of the Lotuho to outside influences, owing to their more protected geographic location. Things would have looked different if traders had sailed right up to the villages along the Hos and Kinyeti rivers.

The traders (1860–1875)

By the time the future of the Bekat rain dynasty of Bilinyan was sealed, no foreign trader had as yet set foot among the Lotuho. Until 1860, trade remained in the hands of local traders: Nyiggilo and his men, Legge of Liria and others. Without doubt, many Lotuho also went to visit *Kenisa* (Ar. 'church') — as the trading post of Gondokoro was known to the Lotuho.[1]

In 1860, Imatari had become a memory[2] and the Lotuho were divided into two kingdoms. The larger of the two had its centre in Loronyo and was ruled by King Mayya, known as Latomé or Lotomoi in the literature. The other kingdom was centred on Tirangore and ruled by King Hujang, alternatively known as Moy or Amoya. Trade relations in Tirangore were looked after by Prince Kamiru ('Commoro' in Baker, 1866), a uterine brother of Hujang and referred to in the previous chapter.

The first trading caravan reported to have penetrated inland towards Lotuho was that of the Coptic trader, Shenuda, in January 1860. The closeness of the date of Nyiggilo's death (June 1859) to that of the departure of the trader, and the fact that the destination of the caravan was Loronyo suggests that Shenuda usurped Nyiggilo's trading contacts. The expedition was attacked by Liria and five men were killed. Together with some fellow traders, Shenuda equipped an army of 155 men to punish the Lirians. Many Bari warriors joined the army, which mainly consisted

---

1   In oral tradition in Loronyo, it is recorded that King Mayya visited *Kenisa*. From Vinco (1974:77), we know that Nyiggilo received an important trading party from Lotuho.

2   Its memory was still fresh: when the French traveller Dr Peney climbed Mount Opone in Liria in 1861, his guide routinely showed him the location of 'Matari' (Malté-Brun, 1863, p.59).

of Danagla.[3] They were met with utter defeat. After burning and plundering Liria and already counting their expedition a success, the *monyomiji* of Liria, Ilyangari and Ngangala,[4] ambushed the party and killed 117 Danagla soldiers and almost all the Bari auxiliaries (De Bono, 1862:20).[5]

When Samuel Baker crossed Lotuholand at the beginning of 1863 in search of the sources of the Nile, Shenuda had established a trading post in the Lotuho kingdom of Loronyo. Two other firms entered the east bank trade shortly afterwards, namely, the Egyptian firm Aqqad which controlled the trade with Liria, Tirangore and the Acholi kingdom of Obbo. Its local agent was Khurshid Agha who allowed the Bakers to join his expedition to Lotuho in 1863. Their main trading partner in Tirangore was Prince Kamiru. The third trading firm was that of the Maltese trader, De Bono, who established control over the routes to southern Bari, to the Madi and to the part of Acholi that was reached via the Madi route.

The new rivalling monopolies coincided with and were duplicated by the dynastic rivalries in Lotuho: King Mayya and Shenuda's men versus Prince Kamiru and Hujang[6] with Aqqad's men. During Baker's stay in Tirangore, he was witness to one attack across this line of double polarisation: Kamiru, the Tirangore *monyomiji* and the party of Khurshid, on one side, against Hiyala which belonged to King Mayya and Aqqad's trading party, on the other. Despite the brave defence, in which both men and women took part, Hiyala suffered sixty-seven casualties (Baker, 1866, Vol. I: 349–355).

In the same month, King Mayya, together with the Danagla of Mohamed Her, Shenuda's agent, attacked the village of Imehejek in Lopit. The reason for the attack was trivial, at least compared to the losses. It was in response to a cattle raid by Imehejek, which in turn was in revenge of the rape of the daughter of the king of Imehejek by the young men of Loronyo (Hino, *M.A. Thesis*, Ch. II). The operation ended in a disastrous defeat for the attackers; about one hundred Danagla and two hundred Lotuho were killed (Baker, 1866, Vol. I: 221–223). The people of Imehejek still celebrate the victory over the first enemies using firearms by singing the following song:

---

3   *Danagla* (sg. *Dongolawi*) are natives of Dongola in northern Sudan.

4   Inferring from the location and the circumstance that the inhabitants are reported to speak the same language as the Tsera and Bari (De Bono, 1862:12), *Benguiren* in De Bono's account (1862:20), *Bondjourènn* in Peney (1863:55) and *Begiure* (Vinco, 1940) must be present-day Ngangala. *Bongojur*, the name of one's of Ngangala's sections, shows resemblance with these names.

5   Beltrame (1881:313) puts the number at 120 out of 150 soldiers. Lejean (1865:89) gives 96 out of 155. According to Baker, who passed the spot of the massacre in 1863 — three years after the event and not one as Baker writes — 126 men were killed (Baker, 1866, Vol. I: 166).

6   The trading network of Aqqad coincided with a wide network of alliances existing between the royal families in the area. The royal family of Tirangore was linked by marriage both to the Liria and Obbo royal families. Both Hujang and Kamiru were sister's sons to Kachiba, the king of Obbo (Acholi), while King Hujang had married into the Lirian royal family twice.

Gala[7] howled like dogs
The Lotuho howled like dogs
Gala let us go home
The valley [Loronyo] is far
It is so far!

Imehejek, the village that, in 1863, inflicted a terrible defeat on the joint forces of the soldiers of the trader Shenuda and the monyomiji *of Loronyo.*

Some years later, Tirangore itself became the victim of an attack by traders. During Baker's stay in Tirangore, the treatment of the women by the traders had caused considerable tension. It was only owing to a last-minute intervention of Prince Kamiru that an armed clash was prevented. According to oral tradition the traders were chased from the village not much later. In revenge, they set fire to the village and burnt most of it.[8] King Hujang fled to his mother's brothers in Obbo and stayed there for some years. This gave Mayya the opportunity to temporarily fill the power vacuum in Tirangore and preside for once over the *Nefira* (ceremony in which power is handed over from one generation of *monyomiji* to the next) of all the Lotuho (Novelli, *thesis*:184)

---

7   The name applied to foreigners of lighter skin. See footnote 2–9.

8   The identity of those responsible for the burning of Tirangore is a matter of debate (see Novelli, 1970: 182185; Hino, 1980, Ch. II). More investigations are needed to disentangle the existing contradictory information on the first contacts with the traders.

The Lotuho under Turco-Egyptian rule (1875–1884)

By 1865, the Egyptian firm, Aqqad, had acquired a state concession on all trade on the Upper Nile. This was the result of a measure of the Khedive to suspend all operations of private firms after Speke, the discoverer of the Nile sources, had reported on the continued existence of slave trade in southern Sudan (Gray, 1961:82). Abu Sa'ud was put in charge of the Gondokoro station and Taha Mahmoud, a Khartoumer and the former horseboy of Baker (Mountenay-Jephson, 1890:116–7), was given authority in Lotuho. Little is known of the way Taha conducted his business. We only know that Gordon continued to rely on him as his deputy until the Lotuho revolted against his methods of administration (Hino, *thesis*, Chapter III).

After the uprising, in 1878, the Englishman Lupton was appointed to replace him. Lupton built two stations: one in Ohila, near Loronyo, which was finished in October 1880, and the other in Tirangore (Emin Pascha, *Tagebücher*, Vol. 2, entry 20/10/1880). Lupton's presence did not stop the internal warfare as Emin had hoped it would. During his journey through Lotuho in April 1881, Emin spent one night among the ruins of Ibongijok where he counted more than a thousand destroyed houses. Emin blamed Lupton (who by that time had left his post) for the event.[9]

The Egyptian army in Lotuho consisted of one hundred *Hutteriya* (soldiers recruited from the disbanded traders' militias, mainly from Dongola) and only ten *Jihadiya*, a far lighter burden than the Nile armies for the Bari (Douin, 1939, Vol. III: 115). There is no reason to think that the methods of provisioning the troops were very much different in Lotuho.

By 1880, the frequent dealings of the royal families with the traders and the *Hutteriya* had resulted in some cultural assimilation — some princes, such as Ajaru, the prince-royal in Tirangore, adopting a northern Sudanese life-style:

> Chief Ladjuri [Ajaru], the son of the old Moje [Hujang] and the prince-royal, is just like Chief Ayuok [Ogwok] in Fadibek [Padibe, an Acholi chiefdom, now in Uganda] a naturalised Dongolawi, in language, as well as in customs and clothing. He even possesses donkeys to ride on which he has bought from the Lopit who have brought them from the Irenga [Tenet or Boya] (Emin Pascha, *Tagebücher*, Vol. II: 196).

Emin had the Lotuho garrisons evacuated in February 1884 soon after the information about the revolt in Rumbek and Shambe reached him (*Tagebücher*, Vol. III: entry 29/2/1884). So, the intervention of the Egyptian state in Lotuho was very short — especially if we assume that during Taha's administration, things went pretty much in the same way as before — and far more superficial than among the Bari.

---

9   "...shame on the Englishman!" (*Tagebücher*, Vol. II: entry 18/4/81. There may have been various reasons for the destruction of Ibongijok, see Hino, 1980, ch. III.

The 'Nacar' (1888 –1897)

Four years later, in August 1888, two months before the capture of Lado by the Ansar, Emin received word that Taha Mahmoud had reappeared on the Lotuho scene as the leader of a large Mahdist force with three hundred guns (*Tagebücher*, Vol. IV: entry 4/8/1888). The Ansar, who are remembered as 'Nacar' by the Lotuho, disembarked in Bor, entered Lotuholand from the north and established their first post at Lohiri, not far from Loronyo.

Prince Wani (the son of Mayya) and Lefuk, the king of Loudo, became the principal allies of Taha.[10] They provided him with porters to take goods to the Nile. A tradition collected by Abannik in Loudo tells how at the Nile, a group of porters was taken prisoner and shipped downstream. When King Lefuk saw that his men were taken into slavery, he committed suicide on the spot (Abannik, *thesis*, Chapter III).

King Lomoro Hujang of Tirangore, 1881–1906 (Cunningham, 1904: 368).

With the support of the Ansar, Wani succeeded in overthrowing his father who fled to Ilyeu, and was later killed there, for stopping the rain. The next opponent to be eliminated on Wani's list was Lomoro, the brother and successor of Ajaru in Tirangore (who had only ruled for one year after Hujang had died). The way Lomoro pre-empted this attack is still a well-known story in Tirangore. When Lomoro heard about Wani's plans, he ordered a general collection of cattle, goats, sheep, honey, limes[11], and other

---

10   Mountenay-Jephson writes that Taha is staying with 'Chief Elgir' (1890:116–9). This can very well be another name for Wani Mayya. Concerning the difficulty of identifying local actors who are known by multiple names see Ch. 14, note 32, p. 316.

11   The lime trees planted when Tirangore had a government station still stood during the visit by Spire and Jennings-Bramly in 1903 (Spire, 'Brief Journey from Gondokoro to Tarangole',

kinds of food and ordered all households to brew beer. When Wani and the Ansar reached Labalwa (half-way between Loronyo and Tirangore), he sent his interpreter, Jabir Obuyang, who was known for his excellent Arabic, ahead with gifts and choice foods. By the time the Ansar commander had started tasting the food, Lomoro arrived riding his white mule — probably using the same outfit as that described by Emin for his late brother Ajaru. For the commander (supposedly still Taha),[12] it was a pleasant surprise to meet a leader who, in addition to showing the outward signs of Sudanese Islamic culture, was generous and appeared to be rich. He called for Wani and took him to task for his plan to attack a person he had come to consider as 'his friend'. Wani's brother, Otuyek, unambiguously expressed his anger at the *volte-face* of the commander. Taha had him executed on the spot. Wani, together with thirty of his followers, was taken prisoner, sent to Rejaf, and was never heard of again. Wani's elimination and Lomoro's association with the Ansar made Lomoro the most powerful Lotuho leader. After the departure of the Ansar, Lomoro was able to maintain his strong position. Little is known of the military adventures Lomoro and the Ansar engaged in. But when Lt Col Macdonald appeared in Tirangore in October 1898, with the assignment of the British Foreign Office to liaise with the gunboats sent upstream from Khartoum, Lomoro claimed to be the king of all the Lotuho and of a number satellite polities as well.[13]

The Uganda Protectorate (1898 –1914)

The reception bestowed on Macdonald was similar to that given to the Ansar commander earlier. It is described by Macdonald as 'exceedingly warm' although only groundnut-paste could be offered as food since a locust plague had destroyed that year's crops. Macdonald and his officers each received ivory as presents.

Lomoro had an army of his own, the *Awusa*. The idea had been borrowed from his ally, Ogwok, in Padibe, who had a similar army called the *Bucura*. Next to Lotuho men, the army consisted of non-Lotuho elements, including five former Egyptian soldiers (who were recognised by Macdonald's *Nubi*), and a number of soldiers who

---

Uganda National Archives, Entebbe, *Foreign Office Correspondence*, East Africa Confidential, 24/7/1904, section 9, Appendix G:18).

12 It is likely that Taha and Lomoro had known each other before. This could have happened when Taha accompanied Baker as his horse-boy during his visit to Lomoro's father Hujang in Tirangore in 1863, and/or later when Taha was an agent of Gordon's administration in Lotuho. The story is mostly told as a triumph of Lomoro's diplomacy and generosity.

13 Muratori, in his short Lomoro biography, completely overlooked Lomoro's Ansar connection, possibly because it was still a taboo topic during the colonial period (1949:108). According to Muratori, Lomoro only fought two battles, one against the Lomiya and the other against the Logir at Ludwara. It would seem most villages surrendered to Lomoro without putting up a fight. A military expedition sent to Lotuho in 1893 carried out by the Ansar stationed on the Nile is mentioned by Collins (1962). Lotuho oral history and a popular song keep the memory alive of a battle that took place near Iloli between the Ansar, the Lulubo and Lomoro, on one side, and the Lotuho of Mayya, on the other. As a result, the Ansar and their allies were forced to withdraw from the kingdom of Mayya.

had served in the Mahdist army that had been defeated in the Battle of Bedden the year before (Donaldson-Smith, 1900: 620). Most of Lomoro's soldiers were clad in the *jibba*, the patched robe of the Ansar, which served as uniform. Lomoro possessed a complete store of them to be issued in time of war.

The argument that Lomoro had joined the Mahdists in order to save his kingdom was considered acceptable to Macdonald and on 23 October, without further questioning, a treaty was signed between "Lomor Moya, the king of the Latuka" and the British government. Lomoro undertook to put a force of thirty-five soldiers aside for the use by the British government "within his kingdom and its tributary states".[14] The soldiers were stationed in six army posts along a route into Uganda "to protect trading parties under the British flag."

The tributary states that Lomoro claimed as dependent on him were the Lokoya, Liria, Obbo, Loudo, Logire (a community living on the eastern side of the Imatong Massif) while Lomoro made Macdonald understand that through the treaty, the Pari[15] and some of the riverine Bari could be considered as being included in the British zone of influence.[16] The list included the old-time allies of Tirangore: Liria and Obbo. Loudo must have changed sides under King Issara after his predecessor had committed suicide. Logire probably submitted by force (Muratori, 1949:108), while the Pari were allies of Tirangore, by virtue of their longstanding enmity with nearby Loronyo. Which Bari Lomoro considered to be his, is not clear.

From 1898 to 1914, the Lotuho were formally included inside the Uganda Protectorate. No steps were taken to effectively control the area, far less to administer it. The Uganda authorities expected that the costs involved in pacifying the notoriously warlike peoples would be too high. They, therefore, limited their intervention in local affairs to the strategically important Nile banks.

The initiative to establish contacts with the colonial government in the first decade of the century came from the Lotuho kings themselves, who hoped to mobilise the government for their cause. Although the government kept aloof, afraid as it was to get involved in a political game from which it would be difficult to withdraw, it took a keen interest in developments among the Lotuho, which after all belonged to its zone of influence. The result of this interest is that for the period 1898–1914 we possess a corpus of archive materials, collected at close quarters, which document

---

14   Enclosure 2, in Letter Macdonald to Foreign Office, 28/7/1899, Uganda National Archives, Entebbe, *Foreign Office Correspondence, Inward*, Vol. III, East Africa, 1899.

15   Jennings-Bramly, A.W. (Uganda National Archives, Entebbe, Uganda Protectorate Intelligence Report no. 23, *Foreign Office Correspondence*, East Africa Confidential, 26/9/1904, Appendix D) confirms that relations between Lomoro and the Pari were friendly while those with Queen Tafeng in Loronyo were hostile.

16   Enclosure 5, in: Letter Macdonald to Foreign Office, Debasien River, 9/12/98 (Despatch 44); Enclosure 3, letter Macdonald to Foreign Office, 7/11/98 (Despatch 40), Uganda National Archives, Entebbe, *Foreign Office Correspondence*, Inward, East Africa, 1899; Report by Lt.Col Macdonald, of his Expedition from the Uganda Protectorate, 3 May, 1898, to 5 March, 1899, Africa, no. 9 (1899), London: H.M.'s Stationery Office.

events within the Lotuho kingdoms. These events, of which the succession struggles in Tirangore and Loronyo are the most relevant for the purpose of this study, are of special interest since they were hardly influenced by the colonial presence. From the ethnographic point of view, they took place under ideal conditions of observation. Both succession struggles — the one following Lomoro's assassination in 1906 and the rivalry between Queen Tafeng and Acalili — are examined below.[17]

The Tirangore kingdom during the Condominium (1914–1954)

The border rectification of 1914 brought the Lotuho back under the umbrella of a government based in Khartoum. In Tirangore, Lohide, a brother of Lomoro, was the king; in Loronyo, we find Acalili, a son of Mayya; and in Loudo, Lomoro's old-time ally Issara. The headquarters of the new Latuka District was established in Torit, a section of Hatiha, a village which at the time was divided in its support of the two Lotuho kings.

In a first move, the Condominium government recognised the *status quo*. To prove its support for the rulers in place, the government army was sent to punish Chalamini at Lohide's request shortly after the building of Torit had begun, in June 1914. Lohide had asked for this patrol because — so he said — the *monyomiji* of Chalamini, a village which belonged to the rival Kingdom of Loronyo, had attacked him and killed some of his people.[18] The people of Chalamini fled at the approach of the troops and only seventy heads of cattle were seized. Similar assistance was given to Issara in taking revenge on a rebellious section of Loudo (Hino, *MA Thesis*, p. 188).

Very soon, after the incident, Lohide lost the goodwill he had with the district administrators. He was suspected of being an accomplice in the desertion of some locally recruited soldiers. Lohide made things worse for himself when he cold-bloodedly killed an emissary who was sent by the *monyomiji* of Chalamini to the Inspector in Torit to negotiate a partial return of the seized cattle. He was arrested, together with Issara of Loudo, for refusal to cooperate in a government operation to collect firearms.

Upon his release, Lohide took immediate steps to acquire more firearms. He invited a party of Abyssinian traders to come and stay with him; offered them spirits so that they got drunk and then seized their guns. When the Inspector was informed about this, Lohide was summoned to come to the district headquarters to hand in the guns. Lohide tore up the summons, saying that the British should rather come to him. On 1 June 1917, a detachment of the Equatorial Battalion was sent to Tirangore to arrest Lohide. When it arrived in Tirangore, the *Awusa*, under their commander, Motong,

---

17 The succession of Lomoro is treated in Chapter Twelve (Case 12.5); the story of Queen Tafeng in Chapter Fourteen (Case 14.1).

18 In fact, the people of Chalamini had been the supporters of Ohuyyoro, the son of Ajaru, and therefore rivals to Lohide in the struggle for the succession of Lomoro (Case. 14.3).

at the last moment, deserted their king. Lohide died while fighting a one-man battle against the colonial army from the roof of his palace.[19]

His successor, Ibrahim Onyong, the principal Lotuho informant of the Seligmans during their tour of 1920/21 (Seligman, 1932:305–339), a less flamboyant character, was cooperative with the government and so was Queen Ikang, his childless wife, who, before being married to Onyong, had been the wife of three other sons of Hujang. For a short period after Onyong's death (1928–1930), the government chieftainship went to Otuyek, a posthumous son of Ajaru, begotten by Lomoro, born on the day Wani's brother Otuyek was killed by the Ansar after Lomoro had outwitted the two brothers with his hospitality and named by Lomoro after his main rival's brother. When Otuyek was found gambling with tax-money, the chieftainship was taken away from him and added to Ikang's rain duties.[20]

Ikang's administrative duties were gradually transferred to Lomiluk, the son of Lohide, who was also Ikang's uterine brother (Muratori, 1954:144–7). After Ikang's death in 1936, the rain was added to his responsibilities. Lomiluk continued to fulfil the combined duties of rain and government until May 1955, when the new Northern Sudanese District Commissioner of Torit suspended him as chief on suspicion of his having a hand in the acts of sabotage against the government. His role at the beginning of the civil war is the subject of Case Study 15.3.

The Loronyo kingdom during the Condominium (1914–1954)

Acalili, Mayya's son by a 'black wife', emerged victorious from the protracted succession struggle with Wani's widow Tafeng and with Wani's son. He came to terms with the government in a manner different from that of Lohide, although his early career was as full of violence as Lohide's. Before he became king, he had killed a lion, clubbed a man from Ohila to death in an argument about the rights of Rainmakers, as well as six other people, including the rivaling son of Wani.[21]

In 1918, the Inspector of Latuka District decided to prosecute him for killing an adulterous wife of his. Acalili escaped to Lafon and from there to Mongalla, offering a tusk to the Governor in the hope to be quits with the government. He was arrested nonetheless, imprisoned for three months and suspended from the government chieftainship of Loronyo. Loyyia, an immigrant from a Lopit rainmaking family, was appointed in his stead. In 1921, his chances of returning to the government chieftainship diminished further upon discovery that he was implicated in an affair of theft of ammunition from the arsenal of the Equatorial Battalion in Torit.

But in 1924, his fortunes changed on account of the rain. After a prolonged drought in Loronyo, the *monyomiji* chased the Lopit chief away and insisted that Acalili should

19   Hino, 1980: 188; Central Records Office, Khartoum, INTEL 6/8/25, Sudan Monthly Intelligence Reports, June 1917.

20   Southern Records Office, Torit Files, 'Tribal Appointments and Dismissals of Chiefs', T.D. 66:17.

21   Muratori, 'Accalili, the Lotuxo Rainmaker', *Typescript*, Comboni Archive, Rome A/126/4.

be reinstated. There were no further troubles with the government and Acalili's fame as a Rainmaker, and later also as a Master of Birds in Lafon,[22] reigned supreme. A last deed that had far-reaching consequences for the Lotuho was his conversion to Catholicism on his deathbed in November 1944. When their king — baptised as 'George' after his British counterpart — had gone over to the missionaries, many Lotuho no longer hesitated to join the new faith.

The ceremonial ground of Ilyeu with two pole-shrines, one for the village community and one for the Mayya Kingdom. Mayya chose Ilyeu as his residence when he was chased from Loronyo by his son Acalili and his monyomiji-*set.*

Acalili was succeeded by his son Patricio Ohucoli, who was appointed government chief four years before his father's death. Patricio was the last king in Loronyo to combine the responsibility for rain with that of government. His succession was disputed by the descendants of Wani. Since Patricio was never formally instated by the *monyomiji*, the rivalry with the lineage of Wani continues up to the present day.[23]

During his reign, which was marked by important developments — christianisation, opening of schools, independence and the beginning of the civil war — the rivalry with Tirangore and with its king persisted. The two kings, Lomiluk in Tirangore and Patricio in Loronyo, frequently took stands opposed to each other. While Patricio

---

22   He successfully chased the grain eating birds from the fields of the Pari at the invitation of the latter, receiving 46 goats in return for his services (Muratori, *idem*).

23   Southern Records Office, Torit District Files, Appointments, Dismissals of Chiefs, entry dated 23/1/1940; Chiefs Appointments and Dismissals 1942, 1943 and 1953, file TD.66:186. See also Ch. 18, note 24, p. 416–7 which discusses the amazement of F. Muratori about the limited family participation at the exhumation of Acalili's bones.

Ohucoli was considered to be an arch-traditionalist who obstructed social innovation, Lomiluk, whose leadership, in the eyes of the British administrators, had a distinctly charismatic quality,[24] was open to new ideas and took an active interest in the political developments leading to Sudan's independence.

Lomiluk openly opposed the amalgamation of southern Sudan with the north and from 1955 to 1959, he was the leader of the first and, at the time, only guerrilla group opposing the idea of a united Sudan. Patricio chose the opposite camp. In Case history 15.3 I examine this rivalry and its impact on the beginning of the civil war in the light of the Nilotic myth of the spear and the bead.

The rivalry between the dynasties of Mayya and Hujang persisted throughout the colonial period, be it in a far less violent way than in the Turkish and Mahdist periods. It was focused on the control of villages and village sections, both as parts of the administrative and of the rain domains of the kings. Up into the 1930s villages and sections continued to change sides. In June 1931, the *monyomiji* of Lalianga decided to swop Queen Ikang, with whom they had picked a quarrel, for Acalili.[25] In the same period, Imeni, a section of Hiyala, decided to move from Acalili to Ikang in protest of what it considered an instance of unfair arbitration on the part of Acalili.

Attempts by the government to incorporate villages located in the rain area of one king to the administrative area of his rival generally failed. The decision to amalgamate the southeastern Lotuho villages of Lobera, Ilyeu, Chalamini and Loming under the chieftainship of Lomiluk in nearby Tirangore in 1939 had to be reversed in 1943 when the separation of the office of rain and that of government proved unworkable.[26] At Patricio Ohucoli's death in 1959, the rain office was inherited by his widow, while the power of government went to one of his brothers. Queen Sabina Ihure still held the rain office in 1986 when I left the Sudan. A younger brother of Patricio, named Palatino Lobwor, inherited the queen. By virtue of his association with her, he enjoyed the material privileges of the rain kingship (tribute). Palatino's position as a prince-consort, however, was disputed by several other members of the royal family, each of whom supported by one of more villages and/or village sections. To prevent violence, the queen's palace has been moved away from Loronyo, where two other pretenders to her throne have a following, and is now in Hiyala.

Compared to the division among the descendants of Mayya, Hujang's political heritage presents an image of relative unity. Lomiluk was succeeded by Onyong's son Salomon Okong, who had been the dresser in the dispensary of Tirangore since 1931.[27] After his death in 1985 he was succeeded by Lomiluk's son, Victor Juma.

---

24 "Lomiluk has natural command and authority" (Tribal Appointments, etc.: entry 1942) and ["…he has] plenty of personality" (*Idem*: entry 1944).

25 *Idem*, p. 131.

26 *Idem*, entries 1937, 1942, 1943; see also letter D.C. Torit to Governor *d.d.* 19/5/1943, included in the same.file.

27 *Idem*, p. 225.

Conclusion

In contrast to the rapid decline of the power of the Bekat in Bari, the Lotuho kings continued to play a leading role in the events in Lotuho despite the changes of government. Although they had to deal with challenges to their power which were unprecedented in Lotuho history, there remained ample scope for them to take initiatives of their own and test their political ingenuity against the new realities they were faced with. They managed to remain the principal, if not the only interlocutors of the traders and administrators who entered their country. Their position was not undermined, as was the case in Bari, by the emergence of cargo chiefs and warlords without rain.

Sometimes — as in the case of Lomoro — the kings were able to bend new sources of power towards a consolidation of their own position over and against the *monyomiji*. The kings in fact remained the principal traders and warlords in Lotuholand. The power derived from their strengthened military and economic position, however, did not push their rain dimension to a subsidiary position. Lomoro, who must have been the most powerful Lotuho king, both in military and in economic terms, was chased from Tirangore by the *monyomiji* for stopping the rain shortly after 1898, the year his power had been confirmed by the British Empire.

In Lotuho, secular power and rain remained united in one person (in Tirangore up to the present day). In Bari, the division of the two was complete by the beginning of the twentieth century. At the establishment of the Uganda Protectorate Administration in 1899, the Bekat Rainmakers of Shindiru and Bilinyan were reduced to *mukungus*. Even their promotion to A-court chiefs by the Condominium Administration when it took over in 1914 was still a far cry from their former political relevance.

The final pacification of the Lotuho and their incorporation in the Anglo-Egyptian Sudan was achieved with a minimum of violence. The kings of both kingdoms had for some time tried to gain favour with the colonial authorities. When the latter finally came to settle in their midst, they were mainly interested in getting the better part of the alliance, rather than in opposing the invader. In addition to the Chalamini patrol in support of King Lohide, a force was deployed only twice and both times specifically directed against kings: the patrol that killed Lohide in 1917 and the arrest and imprisonment of Acalili in 1918.

The main dividing line in Lotuho until well into the first years of the civil war was that between the *Mayya* and the *Hujang* dynasty, that between the Lotuho as a whole and the invaders remaining of secondary importance. The Bari, in contrast, at several occasions, took up arms against the invaders and attempted new modes of political organisation that transcended the fragmentation of their political system: the movement led by *juök* Moyok-lo-Könyi in southern Bari which opposed Egyptian encroachment into the area; the rebellion of King Bepo against Emin Pasha's government, which had an inter-tribal character and was associated with Dinka prophetism; and the Steamer Cult led by the prophetess Kiden which succeeded in driving the Ansar out of Bariland.

The comparatively non-violent character of the pacification of the Lotuho also contrasts sharply with the way the people immediately bordering on them (Ohoriok, Lopit, Pari, Lokoya, Dongotono) were made to submit to the new colonial order. This is the subject of the next chapter.

Children mimicking a mock-charge in front of one of the gates of Ilyeu.

Governor Baker accompanied by his wife and son meet with a client ruler, here Chief Chama of Payira, an Acholi Chiefdom that is now in Uganda (Baker, 1884, vol. II, p.127).

6

The Bugbear of the Administration:
The Pari, Lokoya, and Lulubo

The polities in the zone between the Bari and the Lotuho were most difficult to deal with, both for the traders and for the governments on the Nile. They were a permanent threat to the security on the Nile bank, and it proved impossible to limit hostilities by concluding pacts with the kings as had been done with their Lotuho counterparts.

The Bari call the peoples to their east 'Lokoya' irrespective of the language they speak — Lulubo, Ohoriok or Bari (in Ngangala). Although the Pari were not included under the 'Lokoya' label, they had that kind of reputation among the northern east bank Bari and the Tsera. Moreover, the Pari warfare culture was similar to that of the Lokoya and Lulubo. Their age-class systems were linked. They used the same age-set names, the transfer of power from one *monyomiji*-set to the next followed the same intervals whereby the initial push for the change of guards was given by the Pari from where it spread to Liria and the other Lokoya and Lulubo villages. The first mention of the Lokoya in written documents is in connection with the threat they posed to the riverine Bari. Selim Capitan, the leader of the first Egyptian expedition to visit the Bari, was also the first white man[1] to receive a request from the Bari to help them against the Lokoya and the Pari. (Werne, 1940: 308). "Not only did [King Logunu] want us to undertake a war expedition to the copper-rich Pari, but also to the nearby 'Logajà' (or 'Lokonjà') mountains" (1848:324).[2] Later requests are addressed to Knoblecher (Gray, 1961:25) and Vinco (1974). When Vinco succeeded in arranging a temporary peace between Bilinyan and its Lokoya enemies in 1851, he was hailed by the Bari as their 'liberator' (Vinco: 1940:308).

Concerted military action against the Lokoya with the help of the foreigners on the Nile was undertaken only when the latter wanted to open the trade route to Lotuho. We have seen how this first punitive expedition ended in a crushing defeat for the traders and the Bari. The reputation of ruthless warriors that the Lokoya

---

1   To be precise: Selim Capitan was a Turkish subject of Russian ('Moscovite') descent.

2   The sound transcribed as 'j' in German is realised as 'y' in English: 'Logayà' and 'Lokonyà'. Since the ethnonym 'Lokoya' is documented as having been used in the communications of the Bari with the first Nile explorers, it cannot be derived from Nubian *koya* meaning 'raiders' as the Bari claim (*see also* Chapter 4 note 36). This is a popular etymology that must have arisen when the term *koya* was in common use. The name of the Liria rain clan 'Ohoyo' is a more likely candidate for the origin of the name if we take into account that an initial 'l' is routinely added to most proper names and that under the constraints of the three-vowel system of Arabic 'o' turns into 'a' while the guttural 'h', absent in Bari, turns into 'k'; cf. the derivation of Latuka from Lotuho.

earned by this feat was such that it took half a century before a new attempt was made to subject them.

The governors of Equatoria were afraid to risk a head-on confrontation. For ten years, overtures for a *rapprochement* were made. But most of the time they were kept in suspense, not sure of the attitude the Lirians were going to take. Until 1874, government caravans had to make a long detour through Acholi to reach Lotuho.

Shortly after his arrival in Gondokoro, Gordon reported with satisfaction that he made excellent progress in establishing good relations with the Lokoya and that as a result the route through Liria could be used again.[3] The progress must have been disappointing, because two years later, Gordon justified the construction of the government station in Muggi as a measure to deter Lokoya raids (Shukry, 1953:242), and in 1879, Emin reported on the imminent subjection of King Rugang of Liria "who so far resisted all peaceoffers and threats and remained independent" (*Tagebücher*, Vol. II, entry 25/1/1879). When Emin visited Liria in 1881, he had to conclude that Rugang, "the feared Lokoya chief ... should still be considered independent" (*Tagebücher*, Vol. II: 174). In the same diary entry, he also noted that Rugang was unpopular and did not even have the power to provide him with male porters, offering women instead to do the job — an indication that it was not so much the king but the *monyomiji* who formed an obstacle to co-operation with the government.

The Ansar, who are remembered by the people in the area for their long swords, entered Lulubo and Lokoyaland a number of times driven by famine. They raided several villages, taking food and slaves. Kudwo was raided and many of its people were taken.[4] The Ansar were guided to Kudwo by King Bepo of Bilinyan. Langabu was raided and burnt, while the people of Lokiliri claim they repelled the Ansar attack by first luring the enemy into a narrow up-hill path and then rolling heavy stones down on them. This tactic was also used by the Pari when the Ansar besieged their hill for thirteen days. In the attack, in which the Ansar were defeated, they lost thirty of their men and sixteen guns.[5]

The Lulubo were not just victims of the raiding that went on in the Mahdist period. Some of them were warlords themselves. Prince Langudwo (in Bari: Langudwöt), known as the first member of Lokiliri's rain family who worked with the government, was one of them. He undertook raids on behalf of third parties, who, my spokesman said, had been wronged in one way or another and could not take revenge by

---

3   "I am happy to inform you that I have made good progress in establishing good relations with the Lokoya ['Loquia' in the French text] tribes. If I succeed, the distance from here [Gondokoro] to Lotuho will be 4 days instead of the 10 days that were necessary to make the detour because of the hostility of the Lokoya" (Letter Gordon to Khairy Pasha, 21/11/1874, in: Shukry, 1953:198).

4   The villagers of Kudwo (Lulubo) tell the story how one of their men who was taken as a prisoner to Suakin on the Red Sea after the Torit Mutiny of 1955, met there with an old woman who spoke the Lulubo language. She had been taken there as a slave by the Ansar while still a girl.

5   Information given by a Bari follower of the Ansar to the Assistant Governor of Upper Nile Province in 1905 (Sudan Intelligence Reports, no.118, File INTEL 6/4/15).

themselves. The following case recorded from a Bari informant illustrates the way Langudwo operated:

6.1 *Langudwo, a Lulubo Robin Hood* (Lokiliri oral history)

The wife of a certain Loro had been taken by his *matat* who was a powerful warlord. When no Bari leader was prepared to help him get her back, he went to Langudwo. He approached him dancing. When he got near, he knelt down and grabbed Langudwo's leg. Langudwo told him "Move back and tell me your problem." Loro answered: "My *matat* has taken my wife. I have nowhere to eat. I have come to lick your calabash clean after you have eaten. Let me be yours." Langudwo ordered his warriors to go with Loro and surround the house where the woman was kept. The woman and the *matat* were called out. After the woman had been identified, the *matat* and many of his followers who ran to help him were killed. When they arrived back at Langudwo's, he questioned the woman: "Were you taken by force by that *matat*? Is this your husband? Do you still want him?" When the answer was affirmative, Langudwo told husband and wife to sit down and said: "You are now my soldier. Let your wife stay with you. Beautiful girls need not be the wives of chiefs exclusively."

Tongun Lobijo and Wani-lo-Jele, two sons of the Lokiliri rain family, also established a raiding army called the *Makatub*, a name betraying the Ansar connection of the group.[6] Their raids into Bariland continued up to 1911, when Wani was captured and hanged by the Ugandan authorities in Gondokoro.[7]

One of the largest warlord operations was launched from Lokiliri in 1897 or 1898, after the Ansar had withdrawn to Bor and before Colonel Martyr arrived with his Ugandan troops. The three most powerful Bari warlords, Mödi Adum, who was Lualla's guest at the time, Kirba Lokole, the Bari warlord in control of the mouth of the Kit River, and Könyi, the king of Tombur, combined with Ali Bey, the Lulubo rain king and the leader of the Limojo *monyomiji*, in an attack on the Lokoya of Lowe. They suffered a miserable defeat at the hands of the warriors of Hojovi, who lured the raiders onto a cliff and pushed them down from it. The event is still remembered in a saying the Lulubo use to dissuade a person from a military adventure that does not look promising: "Remember! The last war was with Hojovi!" (*Kili Kojopi naju!*)

---

6   The Ansar were called *Amakuta* by the Pari, a word which — taking local phonetic adaptations into account — is probably related to *Makatub* which must be derived from the Arabic root KTB: 'to write'. One informant gave as its meaning "those who have been registered to die".

7   Uganda National Archives, Entebbe, *Secretariat Minute Papers* 'Return of capital sentences, passed under H.M. High Court of Uganda, executed in the Uganda Protectorate during the year 1912', Enclosure in despatch No.49, 3/02/1913. The hanging took place on 20 November, 1912. Wani-lo-Jele's 'race' is given as Lokoya.

The first interactions between the Pari and the Sudan government

The Ansar had no intention of exercising permanent control or to win the support of the peoples in the area. Their intervention outside the immediate surroundings of their stations was purely predatory.

The Uganda and Sudan governments which replaced the Mahdists came to stay and had to establish an enduring working relationship with the polities in the area. In Lotuho and Bari, the selection of the men that could serve as a link between the colonial government and the people had been very obvious: the kings in Lotuho, the warlords in Bari.

The ceremonial ground, shrine and shaded monyomiji *sitting facilities in Wiatuo, the royal village of the Pari.* Photograph by Eisei Kurimoto.

Previous experiences with the Lokoya, Lulubo and Pari had shown that their kings were not reliable partners in government. Apart from the instability of office as a result of the rivalry over succession, the degree of authority their kings possessed over their following puzzled the colonial administrators. The first interactions between the Pari, who were included in the Sudan in 1898 (their settlements are a few kilometres north of the 5th parallel which formed the boundary with Uganda) and the Condominium government in Mongalla offer a good illustration of these difficulties. The available records of these contacts are fairly continuous, especially for the period that Captain Owen was Governor of Mongalla Province.[8]

---

8   Owen was an interested observer of local affairs and the author of a Bari Grammar and Dictionary (1908).

Shortly after the establishment of the Sudan Government Post in Mongalla in 1903, the officer in charge sent Captain Burton to Lafon to initiate contacts with King Alikori of the Pari who was reported to possess large stocks of ivory.[9] On his return, Burton reported: "Alikori is the chief of the tribe and holds absolute sway.... All disciplinary powers are vested in the chief" (Gleichen, 1905, Vol. II: 147). This intelligence was confirmed by some Pari who visited a village near Mongalla in September 1905:

> Alikori rules Lafon, his son Kud Dei [Kidi] is his *wakil* [deputy]. He will succeed him. There is *not* a council of old people. He seems more or less absolute.[10]

During the same period, relations between the Bari villages around Mongalla and the Pari were very tense. The Bari renewed the stockades around their villages in the expectation of a Pari attack.[11] In March 1907, an armed confrontation took place at Badingilo, a location between Mongalla and Lafon, the traditional battleground of the two peoples[12] and later that year the government refuelling station on the Nile at Gemmeiza was raided by the Pari.[13]

Not long before these events, strangely enough, King Alikori had sent a delegation to the Governor in Mongalla to pledge his support to the government promising that he would henceforth refrain from warfare in accordance with the wish of the Governor. He also used the occasion to report on an attack on Lafon by the Lotuho of Loronyo in which nine Pari had been killed — apparently Alikori hoped that the government would help him. He offered an enormous tusk to Captain Owen and invited him to come to Lafon, adding the following warning: "that whoever visited him should have sufficient escort, as otherwise he might have some difficulty in restraining his young bloods."[14] A few months after this invitation, Alikori requested government assistance again, not only against attacks of the Lotuho but also against the Murle.[15] In May 1908, Alikori came to Mongalla in person accompanied by his son Kidi. Since 1902 invitations had been sent to Alikori to come and meet the Governor, but without result. When Captain Owen received the two men, Kidi took the lead and made the surprising request to Owen to kill his father:

> … it was a custom of the tribe to do so when the son came to a certain age and also that his father was hated by the tribe, because he had kept the rain back.[16]

9   Central Records Office, Khartoum, Sudan Intelligence Reports, no. 98, September 1902, Appendix B.

10   *Idem*, Report, September 1905, Central Records Office, Khartoum, *Intel*, 6/4/15, Appendix B: The Beir and the Berri, by H.D.E. Sullivan, Act. Gov. Upper Nile Province.

11   *Idem*, Reports, no. 113, December 1903 and no. 141, App., July 1906.

12   *Idem*, Report, no. 151, Appendix, March 1907.

13   *Idem*, Report, no. 158, September 1907.

14   *Idem*, Report, September 1906.

15   *Idem*, Report 138, Appendix A, p. 151. There is no comment or explanation why the Murle (Beir) were raiding so far from home.

16   Sudan Archive, Oriental Library, Durham, *Reports on the Finance, Administration and Condition of the Sudan, 1908*, p. 608.

When Owen made it clear this was not sufficient reason for him to kill Alikori, Kidi suggested his father be sent to Khartoum.[17]

> This was altogether too much for the old man who hurled every invective against his son for suggesting such a thing. He seemed quite callous as regards being put to death, but to be sent to Khartoum was altogether too much.[18]

Owen then decided that Alikori should stay in Mongalla for protection. In a report to his superiors in Khartoum, Cairo and London, Owen presented the case as a sign of the success of his pacification policies. The fact that the Pari brought their problems with their king before the Governor instead of killing him was interpreted as a sign of their respect for the new government.[19]

To consolidate what Owen considered to be an improvement in the relationship between the government and the Pari, Captain Jennings-Bramly was sent to Lafon with an army detachment in October of the same year. When the army approached Lafon, a huge swarm of bees appeared, which continued pestering the troops and could not be driven off. This, added to trouble with the floods, made Jennings-Bramly decide to return to base. Soon, rumour spread that the swarm had been sent by Kidi in order to keep the army away from the hill. Before the departure of the troops, Kidi came to meet Jennings-Bramly briefly to receive the presents the latter had brought.

After spending half a year in Mongalla, Alikori was collected back from Mongalla by Kidi because the Pari had grown anxious that "if he didn't return, their rainfall might be stopped".[20] Alikori, together with his forty wives, was allowed to stay among the old people who, in Lafon, had the privilege to live on top of Lipul hill. King Alikori died in April 1911, shortly before Owen paid his long-promised visit to Lafon.

Despite the matter-of-factness of Owen's reporting, the sequence of events must have puzzled him and his staff: why can a ruler who is reported to be absolute not prevent the young men under his authority from attacking an official guest? Why propose an alliance and at the same time allow the would-be ally to be attacked? Why ask a foreign power for assistance to kill one's king?

With the knowledge of the political system of the Pari at our disposal now, it is possible to make sense of the events recorded by Owen. This is what must have been at issue: between September 1906 and May 1908: a new generation of *mojomiji* led by Kidi was ready to take over power. This generation wanted to remove Alikori, first of all, because of the drought he was believed to have caused, secondly, because of the simple fact that he belonged to, or was supported by, the generation of *mojomiji* that

---

17   Kidi may have taken the fate of King Wani of Loronyo who is believed to have been shipped as a slave to Khartoum as a precedent (see p.129–130).

18   *Idem*, p. 608.

19   "I tell this anecdote to show that the Berris, knowing the Government and their ways were afraid to carry out their ancient custom in this case and referred it to the Government to deal with" (*idem*, p. 608).

20   Sudan Archive, Oriental Library, Durham, *Reports on the Finance, Administration and Condition of the Sudan*, 1909, Annual Report, Mongalla Province, pp. 758–759.

had to be removed before the young ones — the later *Alangure* — could take over, and thirdly, because of his ruthless methods of government that had caused the moiety of Kor and a large group from the section of Angulumere to go into exile.[21] The exodus of Kor was the result of interminable stickfights between the larger moiety Boi, which was led by Alikori against the much smaller Kor. Taking his father to Mongalla may have been a way for Kidi, destined to be the leader of the new generation, to meet the demands of his age-mates and to save his father's life, or at least to let him die in a faraway place so that his *cien* (posthumous vengeance) would not disturb the Pari.

Along with dependence of the king's power on the rain and the *monyomiji*, the case documents three other typical aspects of the exercise of royal power in the area: the alternation of provocative ruthlessness ('absolutism') and powerlessness of the king in relation to his subjects, the association between the coming to power of a new king and the change of generation of *monyomiji*, and the willingness of the king to engage the invading powers against the wishes of the *monyomiji*.

First government interactions with the Lulubo and Lokoya

Alikori was not the only king in the area seeking support from the colonial government. The staunchest government ally in the area was Lualla of Lokiliri who succeeded Langudwo as contactperson with the government stations along the Nile. The first written record we have of him is in a letter by Arabi Dafa'alla to Khalifa, in which he is listed among the chiefs selected to meet Khalifa.[22]

Lualla who was a sister's son and in-law to the Bekat of Shindiru and an in-law to Mödi Adum played an active role in Bari politics. During the era of the warlords, he attracted many fugitives from Bariland. These were settled in a new section of Lokiliri which was created with Lualla's palace as its centre and named Gulumere, after the name of the high ground on which the district office in Gondokoro was located. The section was provided with its own pole-shrine and ceremonial ground named *Yengkulia*.

While Mödi Adum was the main interlocutor of the Bari with the government in the years after 1898, Lualla became its principal supplier of food and building-materials, first at the provisional garrison of Fort Berkeley, and later in Gondokoro.[23]

---

21 Soon after Alikori's dethronement these people returned from exile. (Central Records Office, Khartoum, *Sudan Intelligence Reports*, October 1909, App.C).

22 Central Records Office, Khartoum, Letter Arabi Dafa'alla to Khalifa, 12 Jamada 1311, *Mahdiya Files*, I/32:48; translation by Mr. Bol Deng Chol

23 In 1903 Lualla visited Gondokoro several times bringing food and bamboos (Uganda National Archives, Shuli Correspondence, Inward, A/16 Vol. III, Gondokoro Monthly Reports, November 1903). He brought timber for the roof of the house of the medical officer in Gondokoro (*idem*, January, 1904). The help was welcomed by the Collector Cooper: "Lualla and Ali Bey have in every way supported me throughout the year" (*idem*, Bari District Annual Reports 1905–1906. In the Bari District Annual Report 1906–1907 the Lulubo area is quoted as being the 'granary of the government station'. Early 1907 Lualla brought 100 baskets of grain for sale (*idem*, January 1907) and in October 1908 he is sending 187 baskets of grain in

As a result of his good relations with the colonial administrators who looked upon him as "a strong progovernment man ... very straightforward, honest and ready to give any assistance when necessary",[24] Lualla laid a successful claim as paramount chief over the six villages which today constitute the Lulubo chieftainship.

The office of the Commissioner of Bari District (under the Uganda Protectorate) for which King Lualla of Lokiliri provided the timber, 1903 (E.A. d'Albertis, 1908:177).

There was opposition to him from two Rainmakers who were from senior lineages of the rain clan: Ali Bey Okollo, the senior son of the senior rain lineage in Lokiliri and the successor to Tira, and Tongun Agora, the Rainmaker/king of Co'doni. The Rainmakers of Lokiliri had split off from these. All three rivalled to be recognised as the Supreme Chief by the government. Tongun even went to the extent of blocking the road to Gondokoro which passes via Co'doni to obstruct Lualla's emissaries.

To help to disentangle the situation, Spire, the Collector of Gondokoro, paid a visit to Lokiliri in 1903. In the presence of two hundred *monyomiji*, the following settlement was reached: Ali Bey was to be the chief, Lualla was given the management of all affairs connected with the station, and Tongun became Chief-Rainmaker to the tribe.[25] This distribution of offices between the lineages of Lualla, Ali Bey and Tongun remains in force up to the present day. The descendants of Lualla are the government chiefs of the Lulubo, those of Ali Bey and Tongun still hold the Rain in Lokiliri and Co'doni respectively.[26] However, the relative importance of their offices has changed to the advantage of the government chieftainship.

---

tax; (*idem*, October 1908). Gleichen (1905, Vol. II: 81) also mentions the role of the Lulubo in keeping the Gondokoro station supplied.

24   Assistant-Collector Reymes Cole, *idem*, Monthly Report, June 1905.

25   *Idem*, Monthly Report, December 1903.

26   The position at the top of the political structure accorded to Tongun has been nominal. Although everyone recognises the *gumö* (rain shrine) of Co'doni as senior, I have not heard of instances in

In contrast to Lualla's pro-government attitude, the Lirian kings adopted a hostile or at best a stand-offish attitude to the government, which is understandable if we know that Lokiliri and Liria were on hostile terms. No leader of stature emerged from among Rugang's sons who rivalled over the Rain of Liria for most of the first decade of the twentieth century.[27]

As it was, Lualla's alliance with the government did not help him very much against his enemies. In 1905, after an attack by King Lomiling of Liria on the Kabai section of Aru in which seven people were killed, Lualla immediately informed the Collector in Gondokoro, expecting that quick action would be taken against Liria. The initial response of the civilian authorities in Gondokoro and Nimule was favourable, but — as can be gleaned from the extensive correspondence on the case[28] — the army commander in Nimule procrastinated and finally cancelled the operation, mainly, it seems, because he feared that the operation might not be successful. The expedition was called off by the officer-in-command in Nimule at the last moment, when one detachment, led by the Collector, was well on its way, and the sub-Commissioner of Nile Province was about to liaise. Both men were furious, not only because of all the unnecessary trouble they had taken, but above all because of the loss of face in the eyes of their Bari and Lulubo allies and their Lokoya enemies. The incident extended by a few more years the Lokoya reputation as redoubtable warriors.

When in 1910 Lualla requested government help again, after twenty of his men had been killed by the Lirians, the Collector flatly told him to fight his own battles and not to look for government assistance.[29] The reason given was that both the Lulubo and the Lokoya were outside the area administered by the government.

---

which the Rainmaker of Co'doni imposed or tried to impose his will on villages outside his own.

27 This rivalry is described and analysed in case history 14.5.

28 The arguments of Capt. Fletcher, the Officer-in-Command, seem indeed flimsy and advised by fear: the possible factual inaccuracy of Lualla's report, the high grass, the lack of topographical knowledge, the beginning of the musketry course for the infantry, the difficulties of food supplies, etc. (Uganda National Archives, Entebbe, *Shuli Correspondence*, A/16/5, 1905/06, File 67/06/Pt.I 'Raid Lummelum on Rugun', Letter of Capt. Fletcher, Oc Nile District, to Sub-Commissioner in the field, Nimule, 9/1/06). On the other hand it is also clear that Cooper's (the Collector) and Fowler's (the Sub-Commissioner) military ambitions may have needed some mitigation: in his protest-letter to the Commissioner in Entebbe Fowler justifies the operation with the opinion — which he says is shared by many — that the Lokoya are '*nasr batal*' (Ar. 'evil people'). He also writes that he feels assured that two companies of the King's African Rifles (KAR.), helped by Lulubo auxiliaries, could easily have exterminated (*sic*) the isolated Lokoya (*idem*, Letter Fowler to Acting Commissioner, from Camp-Kiriloo, 15/1/1906. More information on Lomiling's attack on Kabai and its aftermath is found in the *Uganda Protectorate Intelligence Report* no. 28, August 1906, Appendix H, 'Notes on the Tribes in the Nile District', by Mr. P.W. Cooper; and in the Bari District Report for 1905/1906 (*Shuli Correspondence*, Inward, A/16 Vol. III).

29 Uganda National Archives, Entebbe, *Secretariat Minute Paper* no. 279. Monthly Diary, November 1910.

Shortly afterwards, the Commissioner in Nimule wrote to the Chief Secretary in Entebbe asking for wider powers to deal with the Lokoya "who have obtained the proud position of being *the bugbear of our administration* in the Gondokoro District".[30] It is ironic that when the Uganda Administration finally decided to take tougher measures against the Lokoya, the first group of 'Lokoya' these measures were applied to were Lualla's followers.

The Lokoya patrols (1910–1920)

On 13 June 1911, the *Makatub* of the Mögiri section of Lokiliri led by Wani-lo-Jele, burnt the Bari village of Lyeparang, killing two men, two women and two children and taking two hundred goats. Lualla had made it clear to Wani that he was against the attack, but since Wani was continuously harassed by his late brother's wife who nagged him by calling him *Ileko* (the name of a fourth born girl)[31] for not having revenged her husband killed in an earlier attack on Lyeparang, Wani had brushed Lualla's advice aside.

As it happened, the District Commander, Weatherhead, locally known as 'Logopelo' and considered by the Bari to be a good friend, was near the place of the attack, accompanied by a police force. The *Makatub* were pursued and eight of them were killed. Lo-Jele himself escaped. Troops were called in from the provincial capital Hoima (Bunyoro) for an immediate punitive expedition against Lokiliri. When the troops were on the way, the attack was called off and replaced by an ultimatum addressed to Lualla to extradite Wani, to return the stolen goats and three hundred more by way of a fine. If these demands were not met, the punitive expedition would carry on.

Actually, the troops were diverted to march on the Ohoriok of Iyire. In July of 1911, three months after the death of Alikori, the two moieties of Lafon had celebrated their reconciliation in a large-scale raid on the Acholi village of Obbo. The raid, justified as a revenge for the killing of one of the Kor returnees from Pajok by a man from Obbo, was carried out in co-operation with the *monyomiji* of Iyire. Obbo was burned down and fifty-eight people were killed, an exceptionally high number in Nilotic warfare. An unspecified number were taken captive.[32]

When the government troops returned from Iyire and it was found that the demands put to Lualla had not been met, an attack was launched against Lokiliri. Ten more Lulubo were killed and seven hundred head of livestock taken. Weatherhead took Lualla and his son Jada hostage, promising to release them if Wani-lo-Jele were produced. After some delay, the *monyomiji* (Limojo) collected Wani from his place

---

30   *Idem*, Letter D.C. Nimule to Chief Secretary Entebbe, *d.d.* 13/121910.

31   The use of *Ileko* in this context can be compared to that of 'sissy' in English.

32   Uganda National Archives, Entebbe, *Secretariat Minute Papers*, 2092 B/13, Northern Province Monthly Reports, July 1911; *Intelligence Report* no. 40, Appendix M. One of the captives, who was adopted by *rwath* Ulum of Kor, later succeeded his adoptive father as Rainmaker.

of refuge with Loli, the Rainmaker of Edemo. Lualla and his son were released and Wani was hanged in Gondokoro.[33]

The Pari, who were in the Sudan, had not been punished for the raid on Obbo, perhaps because their co-operation was needed in an operation which had higher priority for the Condominium government: the Beir Patrol, the large-scale military operation to subject the Murle who formed a permanent threat to the Dinka along the Nile.[34] Lafon was selected to provide food and porters for the southern column, which was to attack the Murle on their southeastern flank.

On the outgoing journey in January 1912, three sections of Lafon refused to provide the porters and food demanded. Instead of the one hundred and fifty porters planned, only eighty-seven could be recruited. The southern column failed to liaise with the central column because of shortages of food and water in the area east of Lafon, and reappeared in Lafon one month later, very tired and hungry. The only help forthcoming was from Wiatuo, the section of King Kidi. Major Drake, the leader of the column, and King Kidi then agreed that "the most truculent and obstinate of the three recalcitrant sections" should be given an exemplary punishment. A full day's fight only resulted in more daring acts of defiance from the side of the hostile sections.[35] The next day, a large-scale raid was carried out on the village as a whole. According to Captain Owen, the raid took place with the full consent of Kidi: "He said he was glad and hoped the government would punish them severely, as they would never believe or listen to him."[36]

Much grain was confiscated, and women and children were taken as hostages, to be released if and when porters were provided.[37] Kidi, accompanied by two chiefs of the sections loyal to the king — promised the government that he would replace the chiefs of the rebellious sections, and come to present them to the government.[38]

The Pari did not accept defeat easily. Two months after the incident, Pari envoys visited a Bari village north of Mongalla and informed its inhabitants that the Pari,

---

33   Uganda National Archives, Entebbe, *Secretariat Minute Paper* no. 2135A: 70–72, 'Northern Province Annual Report', 1911–1912; *Secretariat Minute Paper* 809/08, 'Return of Capital Sentences ... in the Uganda Protectorate during the Year 1912'. While 1911 had been a very dry year in Bariland, 1912 was excessively wet. In July 1912 the floods reduced the station of Gondokoro to an island. The army camp, where Wani was kept, was completely flooded and Weatherhead had to wade through waist-high water to get to his offices. The Bari, who had never before seen so much rain, attributed the drought and the floods to Lualla's anger. (*Secretariat Minute Paper* no. 1859, 'Monthly Report Bari District', July 1912).

34   For a brief description of this operation see: Lewis, 1972:7–9.

35   Sudan Archive, Oriental Library, Durham, *Reports on the Finances, Administration and Conditions of the Sudan, 1912*, Annual Report Mongalla Province 1912:198–203.

36   *Idem*, p. 199.

37   *Idem*, p.198–203.

38   There is no archival evidence that the chiefs have been replaced. The insights into the political relations between kings and the sections developed in this book make it highly unlikely that they were replaced.

Lopit and Boya had formed an alliance to sweep the Bari, the principal allies of the government, into the Nile.[39]

The Lokoya were forced into the new colonial order in a series of particularly violent patrols sent out by the new Sudan Administration after the border rectification of 1914. After a year of futile negotiations with several Lokoya chiefs, Beaumont, the Inspector of Latuka District,[40] advised the Governor of Equatoria Province as follows:

> Chiefs are willing to assist the Government, but their people utterly refuse to listen to them. The whole tribe should be dealt with and not only Chief Jada.[41]

The advice was taken and in the next four years, each of the Lokoya villages was visited by one or more patrols. The first village to suffer an attack was Liria, less than a month after Beaumont's letter. The Lirians had repeatedly cut the telegraph-line connecting Mongalla with Torit to use the wire for bracelets and anklets. They had refused to carry the government's mail; and no steps had been taken to build the government rest house. A company of the King's African Rifles (K.A.R.), accompanied by Beaumont, succeeded in making a surprise attack on Liria in the early morning of 5 January 1915. The fighting lasted for about six hours and left an estimated fifty Lirians dead as against two army casualties. The village was plundered and set ablaze; six hundred sheep and much sorghum were taken. The myth of Liria's invincibility was broken. Beaumont gave the Lirian delegation that came to negotiate for peace an ultimatum to bring King Jada Rugang, return the stolen mailbag, and formally surrender to the government. Only the bag was returned. Assurances that the Lirians were prepared to submit to government authority came one month later. The king stayed in hiding until 1917, when the government agreed to reinstate him formally as 'chief'.[42]

The other Lokoya took longer to accept their defeat. The patrol that forced Liria to its knees also attacked Lowe. Four villages were destroyed and King Tamut was shot in the leg. At the last moment, Langabu avoided a similar fate by adopting a friendly attitude to the patrol.

Two more patrols were sent against Lowe: one in November 1915 and the other a month later. Iyata and Hojovi — the sections that had defeated the warlord-army in 1897 — were taken under fire and destroyed by Inspector Somerset (better known as Lord Raglan, the anthropologist). Only seven casualties were counted, one ton of

---

39   Central Records Office, Khartoum, *Sudan Intelligence Reports*, no. 224, INTEL, 6/7/23. The threat was linked to the accusation that the Bari had stopped the rain over Lafon. Stopping the rain over one's enemy was a normal extension of warfare, or at least believed to be one.

40   Until 1930 the Lulubo, Lokoya and Ngangala were included in Latuka District. In 1930, they were transferred to Juba District (except the Lokoya of Lowe and Longairo).

41   Central Records Office, Khartoum, *Mongalla Files* 1/2/6, Letter *d.d.* 9/XII/1914, by Bimbashi Beaumont, Inspector Latuka District.

42   Central Records Office, Khartoum, *Sudan Monthly Intelligence Reports*, INTEL 6/8/25, January 1915; Mongalla *Files* 1/2/6, 'Report on the Lokoiya Patrol' by Governor Mongalla to War Office Khartoum, 31/1/1915. Southern Records Office, Juba, *Chief's Register*, Reports on Chiefs, 1923, File SCR/66.I/8.

sorghum collected and all the sorghum and beans in the field burnt. In this patrol Langabu was raided as well.

In the fourth and last patrol against Hojovi, the Maxim gun was used. After being shelled for some time, King Tamut and the other chieftains of Lowe and Longairo finally came to surrender to the government.[43]

The last Lokoya village to which a patrol was sent was Ilyangari. Minge, its Master of the Mountain, had declared his loyalty to the government even before the punitive patrol against Liria and had so saved his village from an attack. After repeated attacks by the young men of Ilyangari on the police, a punitive patrol was sent in July 1918 which killed forty-eight people. As in Lafon, there are clear indications that the resistance against the new government came from the young men, those who had not attained *monyomiji*-hood yet. The case is studied in more detail in Chapter Eight (Case 8.5).

Rainmakers and government chiefs

Administration through 'indirect rule' on which the Condominium Government increasingly relied,[44] was difficult to apply to the Lokoya. The Rainmakers were either too 'soft' on their people or too 'harsh'. Moreover, there was the complication that the acceptance of the Rainmaker by his people depended on his fortunes with the rain.

The existing chieftaincies were put in a hierarchical order, the Rainmakers of Liria becoming the paramount chiefs of the Lokoya while the Kursak of Lokiliri became the head-chiefs of the Lulubo. The Rainmakers in other villages were reduced to the position of sub-chief or *mukungu*. The Pari were included in the chieftainship of Tirangore, in accordance with the old alliance existing with that kingdom. Kidi became a sub-chief of the Tirangore chiefs.

Both in Liria and Lokiliri, a certain degree of division of labour had developed within the rain family. Lualla and Jada Rugang were in charge of relations with the government and Ali Bey and Lojing were responsible for the rain. This specialisation did not mean that the government chief was not concerned with the rain. Both Lualla and Jada Rugang were Rainmakers of some repute.[45]

The first two government chiefs in Liria belonged to the harsh category. In 1921, four years after his appointment as government chief of Liria, Jada Rugang was suspended for one year because of manslaughter. In 1925, he had to flee from Liria for reasons which are not mentioned.[46] As 'rain' was by far the most frequent reason

---

43   Central Records Office, Khartoum, *Sudan Monthly Intelligence Reports*, 1915–1916; *Mongalla Files* 1/2/8, 'Report Lotuko Patrol' no.19; *Mongalla Files* 1/2/9, 'Report Small Patrols Latuka'.

44   During the first period of Condominium rule, the office of *mamur* — in many cases held by Egyptians — was an administrative echelon between that of Inspector (the later District Commissioner) and the indigenous authorities. After the anti-Egyptian demonstrations in 1924, the office was gradually phased out. Liria had a *mamur*. According to Lirian oral tradition, the last person to occupy the post was a man of Acholi descent by name of Longinya.

45   Cole, 1910:91; for Jada Rugang's rainmaking record see Case 14.5.

46   Southern Records Office, Juba, *Chiefs' Registers*, File 66.I/8, 'Reports on Chiefs', 1921. Jada Rugang is remembered as a man wearing *oroso* — wild cucumber — during dances as a sign that

for Rainmakers to be threatened with death, we may assume that this was also the case here.

Jada's sister's son, Lohide Magar, was appointed as his successor. Like his mother's brother, he was deposed and imprisoned for manslaughter. The atrocities he committed during the construction of the road from Juba to Torit are remembered by the Lirians up to the present day.

After the depredations of Lohide, the Lirians were allowed to elect a new government chief by themselves. Their unanimous preference was for the Rainmaker Abilli Kömiru, the son of King Legge. Once again the powers of rain and government were united in a single person. Abilli, however, was of the 'soft' type, too willing to please the *monyomiji*. Whatever good he did in the eyes of District Commissioner, Captain Cooke, was attributed by the latter to his *mukungu* of Langabu, Lolik Lado.

During an inspection visit by Captain Cooke in 1933, Abilli had not shown up to meet the District Commissioner because of a duty connected with the rain.[47] This was a reason for Cooke to start looking for a solution which would break with the established policy to rely on rain families for the recruitment of government chiefs. At the time of the New Year Festival of 1934/35 (*Odhurak*) Cooke staged a 'coup' and replaced Abilli with his own man, Chief Lolik, the *mukungu* of Langabu. This is how Chief Lolik related the event to me:

6.2 *The appointment of Lolik Lado as chief of the Lokoya* (autobiographical; live recording)

I was called to the office of the District Commissioner in Juba. When I entered his office, Cooke put the chain of President of the Liria B-Court around my neck before I could say anything. When I tried to protest, he shouted: "Nonsense! Shut up! Khartoum has already decided that you are the chief. There is no need to speak." He got up and chased me out calling an attendant: "You see this madman, the government has made him into a chief and now he does not want it." I was taken by the man to a shop and given a khaki-uniform and a tropical helmet. An ostrich-feather was put on top. I was now dressed as a full chief.

The next morning, we left for Liria where people were already drunk because of *Odhurak*. Cooke took six policemen from Liria, all Lirians. We went to the rest house. A chair was brought and a table. They were put in front of the rest house. Both of us were sitting there, drinking tea. He said: "Bring Abilli!" King Abilli was brought with all his guards and the sub-chiefs. Abilli was arrested and later taken to Juba. Then, sub-chief Lokesuri (of Wurewure) was beaten, twenty-five lashes.[48] After him, Loso, also twenty-five lashes. Lanyoro was spared because of his age. He was put under arrest. All the chief's guards received fifteen lashes,

---

he had killed people. On the significance of the wild cucumber read the paragraph 'Hero and victim in warfare', Ch. 7, p. 167–9. The photo on p. 19 shows a war hero with wild cucumbers squeezed on his head and hanging from his bow.

47   *Idem*, 'Reports on Chiefs', 1925.

48   These whippings were known among the Lokoya as '*gubek*' because of the order 'Go Back!' after the required number of lashes had been administered.

without further comment or explanation. Then Cooke said: "I am tired of all of you, chiefs. From today on, Lolik will be your chief. Is that clear?!" The people murmured. One man spoke up in Bari [the language used by Cooke]: "Lolik is a stranger to us Lirians. Will he not rule us with prejudice? We reject him." He was lashed. Another spoke: "Lolik is our son but he has no rain. We want a Rainmaker as chief." He was silenced with a blow on the head. Five men spoke up and each one was beaten. Then, the speaker of Opwalang (the northeastern moiety of Liria) spoke: "The chiefs of Liria have always been mistreating you. How often did we not say that it would be better to bring someone from outside? Now, Captain Cooke gives us a chance. Let us not cause unnecessary suffering!" Opwalang dispersed. Not much later Orinyak (the other moiety) also scattered. The next morning the *monyomiji* came to me: "Boss, we have accepted you as the chief." I told them: "Captain Cooke wants you to build a new rest house at Opwalang." Opwalang built the rest house. Ovwara, the section of the kings, erected the dispensary and the people of Wurewure built my residence: six huts.

From there, Captain Cooke took me to Ilyangari. The Olyangari were tortured. The sub-chief and all the headmen were lashed many times. They were ordered and forced to build a rest house. Then, we went to Ngulere, the sub-chief was called and lashed. They were lashed without cause, believe me Pitia.[49]

Chief Lolik Lado, B-Court Chief of Liria, 1934–1988. At South Sudan's independence Chief Lolik was proclaimed a national hero for his stand against unification with the North during the Juba Conference in 1947 and for his role as an arbitrator between rebel factions during the first civil war. The photo is from 1985.

---

49   The researcher's name given by the Lulubo of Lokiliri.

The moment for this takeover was well chosen: right after the New Year discussions of the *monyomiji* at Nyamatuo, the sacred rock in the forest, after the first drinks had been tasted to celebrate the New Year.

From Cooke's point of view, the appointment — which remained in force up to chief Lolik's death in 1988 — was a great success: new roads were built and old ones maintained; court-clerks were paid out of the court-fees; the output of the compulsory cultivation of groundnuts increased rapidly; and so on. Owing to Lolik's remarkable qualities as a chief, Cooke decided to put the Lulubo under his authority as well. From the time of the inclusion of the Lulubo in the Condominium, power had successfully been shared between Jada Lualla, the government chief, and Ali Bey, the Rainmaker. The latter's role as a peacemaker was most effective. The Lulubo had the reputation of being a 'non-litigious tribe'. Yet, their area was still considered unsafe for travelers. They might be killed by young men wanting to make a name for themselves as 'killers'.

Cooke had put his hopes for the Lulubo on Jada's son Biajino Lado. He was baptised and had successfully completed primary education. In 1935, he succeeded his father. Cooke had waited for this moment to order the Lulubo to leave their well-hidden villages in the mountain valleys and to settle along the newly built feeder road to the east of the Lulubo hills. Biajino, however, executed the resettlement order in such a brutal way that he was ostracised by the community.

Since there was no other suitable candidate to the chieftainship, opposition among the Lulubo against their inclusion in the Lokoya chieftaincy was minimal, especially after Jada Lualla had given his blessing to the appointment of Lolik, who was related to him through marriage.

To support his authority, Lolik contracted marriages with women in most of the six Lulubo villages and pursued the development policies dictated by Cooke. By the end of the 1930s, the Lulubo and Lokoya had become the most successful cotton growers on the Equatorian east bank of the Nile (K.Hødnebø, 1981:55–59). The area experienced a relatively prosperous period. Hødnebø, who made a study of animal husbandry on the east bank, quotes reports that indicate that much cattle was bought by the Lulubo and Lokoya during that period. In 1937 and 1941, the first shops were opened in Lokiliri and in 1941, a shop was established in Aru.

By the end of the 1930s, the administration felt the need to replace King Kidi of the Pari as government chief by a person who was more open to modern ideas. Suggestions to give the government chieftainship to an ex-KAR. soldier, Suleiman Gubbar, who had no rain, met with fierce resistance. The Pari were afraid that Kidi might spoil the rain in revenge for being replaced. When Kidi had become very old and blind, a provisional solution was found by appointing Suleiman as deputy of Kidi who remained Paramount Chief—both men receiving half a chief's salary.[50]

---

50   Southern Records Office, Juba, *Tribal Appointments and Dismissals of Chiefs* file no. TD/66.D, Letters D.C. Torit to Governor Equatoria, 26/6/1945 and 17/11/1945.

At Kidi's death in 1949, his son Ongang took the responsibility for the rain while Suleiman continued with the government chieftainship — a division of powers similar to that prevailing in Lulubo and Lokoya.[51]

By 1950, the main government chieftainships among the Lulubo, Lokoya and Pari were headed by men without rain. Only at the level of the sub-chiefs and *mukungus* do we still find Rainmakers and other 'Masters' (for example, the Masters of the Mountain in Ilyangari and Ngulere). Between the powers of rain and government, the latter gradually grew in importance to the detriment of the former. The government office was attractive in virtue of the occasional glamour the empire bestowed on local leaders. In 1953, Chief Lolik was selected as one of the two representatives of the southern Sudan to attend the coronation of Queen Elizabeth.

A new code of honour developed in the relationship between the rain chief and government chief, the role of the government chief increasingly being defined as the protector of the Rainmaker. On several occasions during his career Lolik, saved Rainmakers from the anger of the crowds. The standard procedure he developed was to imprison the persecuted man. This satisfied the mob and at the same time put the man out of immediate danger.

Chief Lolik explained to me that after the crowd had dispersed, he would call the Rainmaker, give him some beer and perform a summary rain ritual. Both chiefs would spit in a calabash with water and throw the mixture up in the air in a joint attempt to make rain. Once the rain had come the man would be released.[52] The lives of Abilli and Ahimang[53] were saved in this way.

In the preparation for Sudan's independence, government chiefs were among the few Southern Sudanese that were consulted by the Condominium Government. Chief Lolik was one of the few participants in the Juba Conference of 1947 to take a clear stand against the inclusion of the South in a united Sudan, while King Lomiluk of Tirangore, also a government chief, played a leading role during the early phase of the rebellion that followed the Torit Mutiny. When the war was in full swing (1965–1972) and the rebels had organised themselves as Anyanya, Chief Lolik was

---

51   Southern Records Office, Juba, *Torit District Files* no. 4, 'Lafon Area Trek File', Reports on visits *d.d.* 5/4/48, 2325/8/48 and 1314/4/49.

52   Despite the fact that Lolik did not openly claim to possess rain powers, this practice shows that he and the people surrounding him believed that he did have rain. He limited himself to the simple ritual described above. He never resorted to using rainstones, although he could have claimed some stones that his father had inherited as a sister's son from a now extinct rain family.

53   Ahimang, the son of Lorwungo and the brother of the current Rainmaker of Liria, was accused of drought by the generation of Tome before it took over power in October 1955. This generation, which came to power during the two years of internal autonomy that preceded full independence and two months after the Torit Mutiny, presented itself as extremely bold and radical. Ahimang was dragged towards a large fire, his hands and legs tied. Lolik's police could only just save him from death. Tome were henceforth nicknamed *Akulyabantu*, a Swahili word brought by labour migrants from Uganda, meaning 'man-eaters'.

appointed as their Supreme Arbitrator. On several occasions, his intervention was crucial for maintaining the unity among the Anyanya fighters.

Despite the many changes brought about by the civil war — this is not the place to discuss them — the definition of the division of powers of rain and government after the war remained largely the same. Lolik returned as chief of the Lokoya. After the Addis Ababa Agreement of 1972, the Lulubo took a new look at their ethnic identity and demanded the restoration of the chieftaincy to Lualla's family. This was accorded to them in 1976 when Tongun Lualla, a son of the great Lualla, was appointed as chief.

After the Addis Ababa Agreement, the Pari returned to a system of undivided rule. When they were given a free choice to elect their government chief, they unanimously chose Rainmaker Fidele, the grandson of Kidi.[54] As his performance did not satisfy the government, he was replaced in 1977. He continued to be the Rainmaker until his death in 1980. In the absence of an adult son, the rain powers were given to his wife, Queen Nyiburu, who assumed responsibility at the onset of one of the worst periods of drought of the century. The story of her tragic death at the hands of her people is recorded and examined in Chapter Seventeen (Case 7.11).

Conclusion

What strikes us first when we compare the changes among the Lulubo, Lokoya and Pari with those of their neighbours to their east and west is the large degree of independence their polities were able to maintain up to 1914. This independence was due to the weakness of the position of their kings rather than to their strength. Because the kings were not able to impose themselves on the *monyomiji* to the same extent as their Lotuho counterparts could, they were hampered in concluding stable alliances with the new foreign powers. As a result they missed the opportunity to strengthen their power with the government's help.

We may assume that the pacts concluded by Vinco with the Lirians and the Pari were not broken by their kings but by the *monyomiji*. Similar interference by the *monyomiji* was noticeable in Alikori's attempts to get in touch with the authorities in Mongalla, in Kidi's failure to mobilise enough support for the Beir patrol and in Minge's unsuccessful policy to save his village from being the target of a 'Lokoya Patrol'.

The historical consequence of this structural weakness in the position of the king was, on the one hand, that, unlike the Bari, the peoples in this area were not easily lured into *de facto* dependence on the imperial and commercial interests that had penetrated the area since the 1840s. On the other hand, it made a head-on confrontation with these powers inevitable when the latter decided to permanently administer the east bank. Each village was subjected to one or more patrols, most of which were far more destructive than what people were used to in the way of local warfare. The patrols took many lives and caused great economic damage.

---

54   Southern Records Office, Juba, Torit Rural Council, *Torit District Files*, 'Lafon Trek Files', Report on Visit to Lafon, *d.d.* 14/3/1975.

The main exception to this pattern was Lualla of Lokiliri. Like Lomoro in Lotuho, he was able to use his foreign contacts to extend and consolidate his power. But internally, he had great difficulty maintaining control not only over his *monyomiji* but also over rival princes, as the case of Wani-lo-Jele shows. In the following chapter, I examine two more events in which his power was challenged by the *monyomiji*: the war against Ngulere (Case 7.1) and the rebellion by the generation of Limojo led by his sister's sons (Case 8.3)

Another common feature in the exercise of power by the Lulubo, Lokoya and Pari kings was the excessive violence occasionally used against their subjects. When they wanted to assert their power *vis-à-vis* the *monyomiji*, they easily overdid it. This may be the truth about Alikori's reported absolutism that resulted in the exodus of a whole section from his kingdom. It was certainly the case with later chiefs such as Lohide Magar in Liria and Biajino Lado in Lokiliri.

Disconcerting to a nationalist reading of African history is the promptness with which some kings were prepared to lend themselves to the interests of the foreign invader: Kidi who joined the soldiers of the Beir patrol in a punitive expedition against his own people; Biajino who had all the houses of Lokiliri burnt; Lohide Magar who, at the instigation of the District Commissioner, knew no compromise in forcing his people to build the road for the government.

In Chapter Nine, I argue that these cases, far from being just instances of individual excesses, reveal a fundamental characteristic of the structure of kingship in our area of study.

As a last point in this comparison, it should be noted that during the period described, none of the peoples to the east of the Bari had recourse to prophetism as a means to create a new consensus. Only the unmarried girls in some Lulubo and Lokoya villages were for one or two years during the 1930s affected by an offshoot of the *Yakanye* possession cult — a branch of the steamer cult of the Bari. When I asked a Lulubo informant how the cult had come to an end, he answered in typical no-nonsense fashion: "Oh, the *monyomiji* and the Master of the Land just cursed it away." Cursing (Lulubo: *rilemi*), the standard approach of the community to disaster and evil, prevailed over what was considered to be just another form of social disorder.

PART II

Dualism:
Generating Consensus from the Suspense of War

Monyomiji *of Edemo (Lulubo) charging*

"In our spear our manhood resides. In our manhood our spears are found."
Taban-lo-Liyong, 1970:3

Stick-fight between matching age-sets of opposed sections, Pari. Photo by Eisei Kurimoto.

7

The Dualist Structure of Territorial Organisation

In this chapter, I examine the dualist aspect of territorial organisation or (to use the current terminology in Nilotic studies) its dimension of complementary segmentary opposition. Territorial dualism, in most communities in the area, is operative on five levels: (1) between clan groups of the same section, (2) between sections of the same village or moiety, (3) between village moieties, (4) between villages, and (5) between inter-village alliances. In some cases, there are fewer levels: when sections consist of only a single clan group, and when the polarisation of village sections into more or less fixed moieties is less clearly marked.

I will show that the enemy scenario, presented in Chapter One, structures the relations between groups on each of these levels, by way of either a violent or a non-violent setting of the stage.

Violence and social distance

When two parties accidentally meet on the road, it is customary that both make a show of prowess. They shout war cries, brandish spears, level their bows, and aim arrow or spear at the opposite party, and adopt a generally ferocious mien. This exchange of aggressive mimicry and the accompanying reciprocal mock charges (Lulubo: *roka*, Lokoya: *egera*, *ewanga*, Lotuho *arremua*), quite frightening to an unsuspecting newcomer to the area, is the proper way to 'greet' equals who do not belong to one's own section or clan.

In encounters between parties of different seniority, the senior party has to take the initiative while the reply of the junior one should not be excessively challenging. Women are expected to ululate when a man makes a mock charge in their presence. At festive occasions, women also make mock charges at visitors. For men, it is the favourite posture adopted in front of the camera which, from the local point of view, is easily equated with a Western equivalent of the mock charge.

By polarising the men meeting on the way into two groups of opponents, the mock charge creates a situation in which further transactions can take place, either of a hostile or a peaceful kind. Peace, in the philosophy that underlies the greeting ceremony, is the result of a deliberate act of peacemaking. Hostility is the normal condition between strangers; each party is defined as 'fair game' to the other.

When persons know each other, the decision to use violence depends on the nature of the relationship of the groups to which the persons belong. Members of allied clans, sections or villages are expected to refrain from violence.

Three types of group confrontations can be distinguished, depending on the amount of violence allowed in the encounter: contests in which violence should be avoided, conflicts in which blood is shed, and confrontations in which physical violence is allowed as long as no bloodshed ensues.

Warfare is defined by the explicit intention of the opposed parties to make victims, to injure or kill. In fighting, lethal weapons (spear and bow) are used. The legitimacy of intentional bloodshed defines the boundaries between groups that are free to become enemies, namely communities defined by a common king, pole-shrine and *monyomiji*-set. Intentional bloodshed is forbidden between members of the same community. When sections, moieties or villages of the same kingdom fight, they should not carry spears or bows. Two sticks are carried instead, one to hit the opponent and one to ward off the opponent's blows. As soon as blood flows, the fight should stop and the case should be referred to the assembly of *monyomiji*, to the king or to the Master of the Land.

The occurrence of bloodshed between sections of the same village may have serious consequences, since it may lead to a chain of revenge and counterrevenge. If no solution is found, the losing section may decide to quit the community and leave, as the section of Kor left Lafon after losing many stick fights against Wiatuo.

Normally, sections rival in non-violent ways: in sporting events (wrestling matches, goat fights, running competitions and competitive hunts), dancing and by composing provocative songs. In Chapter Three, we have examined the role of songs between in-laws and, by extension, between clans allied by marriage. On the basis of the space given to the use of violence, the following social arenas can be distinguished:

I. Appropriate levels of violence according to socio-political arena

Socio-political arena	Appropriate level of violence
territorial communities (villages or groups of villages sharing politico-religious leadership which have become enemies	violent open confrontation in order to kill *(war)*
descent groups settling victimary accounts	furtive attacks in order to kill *(feud)*
sections, moieties, and successive generations	violent open confrontation without killing *(stick fight)*
groups at peace	open playful confrontations in which bloodshed is forbidden: mock-fights, wrestling, competitive sports and games, abusive songs, joking relationships.

The principle of clan solidarity may at times be in contradiction to that of sectional and communal solidarity. Feuds between clan groups, usually caused by homicide or marriage conflicts, may pose a serious threat to the unity of the section or the community. It is the task of the *monyomiji* or the king to contain and solve these conflicts. The opposition between village and sectional solidarity, on the one hand, and clan solidarity, on the other, coincides with the distinction between public and private interests. In their defence of public order, the *monyomiji* and the king should act in terms of the interest of the community as a whole. This point of view may often be at odds with the interests of one or even of both of the quarrelling descent groups. In clan conflicts mediated by the *monyomiji* or the king, there is an element, that of public interest, which transcends the idea of a fair deal between the two quarrelling parties.

In the perception of the people, a period of 'strong rule' by *monyomiji* or the king is marked by the absence of intra-communal rivalry. When their rule is weak, clan and sectional conflicts easily run out of hand and may ultimately cause the community to become scattered.

The desire of young men to make a name for themselves and so become heroes was a frequent cause for warfare between neighbouring communities. In some communities, a man gains immediate access to the *monyomiji* if he kills an enemy or one of the four dangerous animals (leopard, lion, buffalo or elephant). Young men used to organise themselves in small gangs to stalk an enemy in the bush. These actions, often undertaken against the will of the *monyomiji*, could easily provoke war.

In the following paragraphs, I will examine warfare, sectional fighting and non-violent forms of sectional competition. The chapter will conclude with a discussion of the east-west directionality of warfare between the Kidepo River and the Nile.

Warfare

The following case reveals a number of features which may be considered as typical for pre-colonial warfare. The fighting occurred prior to the establishment of effective colonial rule, and involved Ngulere (Lokoya) and Lokiliri (Lulubo), two villages located at a distance of about a two hours' walk from each other. I have accounts of the war from informants of both villages. There are no major discrepancies in the two accounts. My informants were around ten years old at the time (the age of goat-herds, *ca.* 7–14 years), which puts the war at about the year 1910.

> **7.1 *The war between Ngulere and Lokiliri*** (oral history from both communities)
>
> A man from Ngulere had disappeared in the bush not far from Lokiliri. The people of Ngulere suspected that he had been killed by a man from Lokiliri. A party from Ngulere visiting Bongilo, the blacksmiths' centre in the Kworijik moiety of Lokiliri, made accusing insinuations to the people of Kworijik. A few days later, a man from Kworijik was killed by a leopard. The people in Lokiliri were convinced that the leopard had been 'stage-managed'[1] by Alapa Kaleri, the Master of Leopards in Ngulere. Early the next morning, the *monyomiji* set out to attack Ngulere. The initial plan, to encircle the houses of the war-heroes of Ngulere so that the war-heroes of Lokiliri would face their counterparts in Ngulere, failed because the arrival

---

[1]   The phrasing used in Lulubo *odwe o'duni* and Lokoya *ayeyo ohwaru* means 'to make', 'to create', or 'to put a leopard down in front of a person'.

of the men of Lokiliri was discovered before they could enter the village. In the first round of fighting the guns of three of Lokiliri's war-heroes killed three men of Ngulere, among them the Master of Leopards himself and one famous warrior. Only Lokiliri possessed guns at the time. The guns used in this battle belonged to the son of King Lualla, to a *Big Man* of the rain clan and to Loriba, the leading warrior of the Okare clan, the second most powerful clan in Lokiliri.

The *monyomiji* of Ngulere regrouped themselves and ambushed a group of Lulubo while they were driving off the goats, and killed one person. Closer to Lokiliri, in a second ambush, both parties lost one man each.

At the end of the fight the leaders of the two groups addressed one another from a distance, each leader surrounded by his followers. Lopiti, the Master of the Mountain of Ngulere shouted to Loriba, the war leader of Lokiliri: "You go now, we shall not pursue you further, go well." Loriba answered, "Oh you, Lokudonge [nickname of Lopiti] we have beaten Otolo [the name of the location of Ngulere]. Yesterday you claimed Alapa [the Master of Leopards] had not staged the leopard. Oh Master, you have suffered a lot. We have really caught you by the balls! I am going now. Your goats have already reached Lokiliri!"

King Lualla of Lokiliri, who belonged to the Lokwe moiety, had opposed the war, which had been an initiative of the *monyomiji* of the opposite moiety, Kworijik. Moreover, Lualla belonged to a generation senior to that of the ruling *monyomiji* (Langure). Immediately after the fight, Lualla, whose main ambition was to find recognition for his kingship in the surrounding villages, whether they be Lulubo or Lokoya, and also in the eyes of the Uganda authorities, made arrangements for a reconciliatory sacrifice. He sent a message to Ngulere saying: "Since there has been a fight at your place, bring a bull, I shall also bring mine so that I unite you since you are all my children!"

Although the admitted purpose of battle is to inflict death upon the enemy, the killing in this war was not indiscriminate or unrestrained. By sending the great warriors of Lokiliri to the houses of their counterparts in Ngulere, a deliberate attempt was made to stage a 'matched battle' such that the aggressor and the victim were of equal strength and prestige. Great warriors (*buluka, otir*) were expected to select victims who would be a credit to them (*see also* Case 4.1). The tendency of both parties to 'match' their forces also put a limit to the number of victims made. Immediately after making their three victims, the Lulubo began to withdraw, carrying along whatever livestock they could get hold of, while Lopiti, the leader of Ngulere, abandoned the pursuit when two victims had been made among the Lulubo party.

The account of the war also shows that the acts of reciprocal killing were part of a wider scenario of rivalry and challenge. The armed conflict was preceded by challenges during the visit of the *monyomiji* of Ngulere to Bongilo and by suspicions concerning the assault by the leopard. They were concluded by the exchange of insults between Lopiti and Loriba. After all is over, the war was — and still is — commemorated in songs composed to retain the moment of glory for the *monyomiji*-set whose name will henceforth be associated with the event.

The sequence outlined above corresponds to what the nineteenth century Turco-Egyptian governors of Equatoria reported on warfare from their own experience or from hearsay, as in this account by Emin Pasha on Lotuho warfare:

7.2 *The conduct of war in Lotuho* (Emin Pasha)

The chiefs of the two warring communities gather all the men able to carry arms and meet in a large, open space, leaving a distance of about fifty to sixty metres between the two parties. The chiefs seat themselves in front of both lines of warriors and begin a long exchange of words during which they accuse one another of all sorts of injustices and crimes, using very strong language. The longer these discussions last the more restless the warriors become. Three or four impatient men from both lines break away. They leap on each other, using their spears and shields. Usually the whole fight is not more than this: a man is injured, sometimes quite seriously, and both parties return home. Sometimes, however, it escalated to a serious battle over the whole line. In that case it is usual that some men get killed and one party takes to its heels. During the real battle the chiefs gradually withdraw behind the battlefront (1894:777).

Verbal challenges as uttered by Loriba and described by Emin were also directed at Gordon and Baker in their fights against the Bari. This is how Gordon summarises the address by the war leader of the Muggi, while he made himself ready to attack Gordon's troops:

Sons of dogs, why are you going up and down? Come over here and we will sit under trees and send our children to destroy you." (G.B. Hill, 1881:147).

Baker is openly challenged by a Bari chieftain whom he has commandeered to provide grain for his troops in exchange for (raided) cattle:

In reply to this polite assurance [that one granary would be paid for with one cow] they used most insulting language and said: 'You will not offer us your cattle, as we intend to take them by force; therefore be off to Khartoum!'(1874, Vol.I:369).

There is no fighting immediately after this challenge. Only three weeks later, the tension escalates into a fully-fledged battle. Before the attack, the war leader of the Bari climbed an anthill to provoke his opponents with a war dance. Baker's reaction to the challenge was most unchivalrous:

7.3 *Dance of defiance by a Bari war leader* (Baker)

I observed a man painted red like a stick of sealing-wax [red ochre] with large ivory bracelets upon his arms. This fellow was in advance and he ascended a small anthill to obtain a better view. Monsoor [one of the 'Forty Thieves', Baker's elite corps] whispered "That is the Sheikh". He is shot at. A puff of smoke and the sharp crack of the rifle startled the enemy as the red sheikh rolled over. The yells increased on all sides, the whistles of antelopes' horns now sounded a shrill alarm during which the red sheikh recovered his legs and vainly attempted a dance of defiance (1874, Vol.I:393)

To return to the war between Lokiliri and Ngulere: there were two incidents during the fight which highlight the way people dealt with the conflicting loyalties of clan and village.

7.4 *Clan and village loyalty in the Lokiliri–Ngulere war* (oral history from both communities)

During the assault, a warrior of the Okare clan had entered the compound of a member of his own clan. When he realised where he was, he ordered his followers to go and fight elsewhere saying: "these are for me to be killed." When the fight was over he set his relatives free.

When during the pursuit two men of the Ngulere branch of the Okare clan were face to face with a clansman from Lokiliri, the latter shouted: "We are brothers; we are clansmen; we are Okare. We should not spear one another." At this, the two from Ngulere replied: "In war kinship is not considered." Then the Okare from Lokiliri threw the spear and hit one of the two in the hip so that he fell down. When approaching the fallen men to give him the final blow, the victim cried: "Leave it, my brother, please; it is me who forced you to kill me." So he was left.

The main issue in this war was not conquest or booty, but human victims. Both the cause and the conclusion of the war between Ngulere and Lokiliri were marked by its victimary aspect. The war was triggered by a misunderstanding concerning the 'balance in the count of victims' between the two villages, Ngulere suspecting that Lokiliri killed one of their men and Lokiliri believing that the leopard sent by the Leopard Master of Ngulere had killed one of theirs. The conclusion of the war was marked by the exchange of abuses and the songs that would be composed to commemorate the victimisers and the victims.

What about the connection between warfare and group consensus? If we study the data at our disposal carefully, we find several indications that at the moment of the attack, Lokiliri could very well 'use' a war. The attack on Ngulere was initiated by Kworijik, the moiety opposite to that of King Lualla (Lokwe), which suffered serious division at the beginning of the century (Case 12.2), and by the Langure *monyomiji* who looked for an opportunity to show their prowess in the face of the retired generations (Taruka and Limojo), which had solid reputations in warfare.[2] An element of intra-dynastic rivalry also played a role: first of all between father and son: Jada, son of Lualla (who was opposed to the war) was the leader of the operation. He was also one of the men who killed an enemy in the battle.

It is probable there was an element of brotherly rivalry as well. By the rule of primogeniture, Ali-Bey Okollo, the son of Lualla's father's senior brother, was the king in Lokiliri. Although his position as supreme authority of the Lulubo was recognised by the Uganda government, it is clear from the course of later events that Lualla — despite the drawbacks in his relationship with the government as described in the

---

2   It is probable that the attack on Ngulere followed a generational transfer of power, so as to 'seal' the consensus of those newly in power, such as the attack of the Langure of Lafon on Obbo, in which the recovered unity between Kor and Boi was endorsed (see Ch. 6, p. 148).

previous chapter — got the better share in the distribution of powers agreed upon in the presence of the Collector of Gondokoro. Ali-Bey's blessing of the operation may very well have been a move against Lualla whose policy was directed towards consolidation of his alliance with the British authorities in Gondokoro. Lualla wanted to appear as the chief authority among the Lulubo and Lokoya. The only way he could prove this was by effectively keeping the peace in the area. His call for reconciliation immediately after the war is consistent with this policy.

The pieces of evidence at our disposal suggest that from the Lokiliri point of view, the war was waged as an act of assertion of the unity and power of a new generation of *monyomiji* led by the prince-elect (Jada Lualla) and blessed by the King/Rainmaker, against the increasing power of government chief Lualla.

While the war was the culmination and the discharge of a number of parallel tensions, the account also shows that clan loyalties did not run parallel with the process of polarisation between the warring communities.

Relationships between in-laws and between mother's brothers and sister's sons played a similar role. My informant in Lokiliri told me that his father's brother's daughter, who was married to a man in Ngulere, was in Lokiliri while the attack was planned. When she heard about the plan, she was allowed by her father to run to Ngulere to collect her beer-flour which she had left outside to dry, on condition that she would not tell her husband about Lokiliri's plans. My informant said she was not the one who leaked the information to Ngulere.

Relations based on common descent or marriage often make for a bridge between hostile parties. They can also form a basis for intrigue and subversive manipulations, in particular the relationship between mother's brother and sister's son (for example, Case 8.3).

Hero and victim in warfare

The score of victims is the primary index to determine who won the war. The songs that are made to commemorate the war list the names of the victims together with the names of their killers and the circumstances under which the killing took place. Warfare is not a transaction between anonymous enemies. It is, rather, a reciprocal exchange of violence between social actors who are known to one another by name, one becoming a victimiser/hero and the other a victim as a result of the transaction.

The victims are claimed simultaneously by the community, the generation ruling the village, the age-set of the killer, the section or moiety of the village to which the killer belongs, and by the individual killer himself. On the group level, this claim is expressed in war songs (Lokoya: *etolu*; Lotuho: *erremoti*; Lulubo: *ira*; Bari: *iriyang*); on the individual level in self-praise songs (Bari *mamaret*; Lulubo: *mamare*) in which details of the act of killing are recounted. Often, the last words of the victim are quoted in the *mamaret*.

Celebrating the community's enemy victims with song and dance, ira *in Lokiliri.*

One of the songs celebrating the victory of the *monyomiji* of Lokiliri over Ngulere is the following. It is composed in Lokoya, the language of the victims: [3]

> Kaleri son of Ruruga,
> You were left dead with Lurwata,
> You, Alapa, son of Ruruga,
> Left dead were you with Lurwata,
> Otolo is very far now,
> Langure have killed Lobe,
> Lurwata was left dead.

Alapa Kaleri (the Master of Leopards), Lurwata and Lobe were the victims on the side of Ngulere. Langure was the generation responsible for the war. The line /*Otolo is very far now*/ should be understood ironically: "you dead men will never again enjoy the sight of Otolo, your home village", here referred to as Otolo.

To sing such songs in front of the vanquished party was an outright provocation which could lead to a renewal of hostilities. When, in 1976, a song happened to be played on Radio Juba, commemorating the killing of two men from Ilyangari in a fight with Lokiliri that had taken place earlier that year, intensive top-level diplomacy was needed to prevent a renewed outbreak of fighting between the two communities.

The war songs are sung and danced at the beginning of the dry season, after the last harvest, which is a period of heightened social activity, of warfare and hunting. In

---

3   In Lokoya, using my assistant's transcription: "*Kaleri lo Ruruga/karahini lo Lurwata/karahini lo Lurwata/Alama na na di Tolo/Alangure kobakunu Lobe/karahini lo Lurwata.*"

these dances, the community celebrates its past victories and, in a way, reappropriates the consensus rooted in fighting a common enemy.

The act of killing is not made abstract as in modern wars. It is positively valued and depicted in concrete detail. There is no bad conscience about the heroism thus achieved. By killing an enemy, a man becomes a hero in his own lifetime. By shouting his *mamare* at festive occasions, he will remind his entourage that he really is a hero.

The positive transfiguration operated by killing an enemy only reflects on the killer, not on the victim. For the winner, the victim is an object of ridicule and contempt. For the vanquished party, a source of embarrassment and a bad omen. Among the Lokoya and Lotuho, the victims of war were not brought back to the village for burial. They were left where they died, to be eaten by the vultures.

Although there was no reason for the killer to feel bad about his act, his heroism also had a darker side. The violence he had been associated with was believed to carry grave dangers for the killer and his immediate surroundings. Immediately after the act of killing, the Lulubo advise the killer to take some soil of a small anthill (*ituki*) and swallow it, so that he may not faint because of the bloodshed by his hand. Someone who has killed should not enter his house at his return. He should wait outside the fence and ask a neighbour or a brother to collect one of the killer's goats, sacrifice it to purify him of the enemy's blood and tie pieces of its skin around his legs. The hero should also ask for some wild cucumbers (Lulubo: *loroso*, Lokoya: *orese*) and have them crushed and smeared onto his body and on the gate of his house.

The day a man has first drawn human blood, a new stage in his life begins, even if the victim was a defenceless woman. He is eligible to enter the enemy's stables during raids, and, if he is brave, he may become one of the elite warriors protecting the king during battle. He is given a new calabash to drink water from and he no longer drinks from the calabash used by other members of his household. At dances, he crushes some fruits of the wild cucumber over his body, or hangs some fruits from his bow and his arrows, not only to neutralise any dangerous emanations from his person, but also as an emblem of his heroism.

Groups returning from war are subjected to similar purification rituals. Before entering the village, the returning warparty should step on an egg (a minimal sacrificial victim), which the Master of the Land placed on the path leading into the village. They are not allowed to approach the pole-shrine unless the Master of the Land has sacrificed a goat to ward off the blood of the enemy victims.

The dualist structure of sectional organisation

Social organisation and group formation on the level below the village is along dualist lines as well. To clarify the operation of consensual antagonism on the subvillage level, I shall use the sectional organisation of Liria as an example. Liria presents a particularly symmetric and balanced instance of dualist organisation.

Liria has nine sections, arranged in a semicircle from west to northeast at the foot of Oponi Mountain. Each of the sections has a named 'sitting place' (*obale*) and ceremonial ground. In Okimu, each of the three clans inhabiting the section has its own daytime sitting place under a tree, while for meetings at night, there are two separate places, one used by a single clan and one used by the two other clans. These groupings could be called subsections or 'minimal sections'.

J.   Divisions of Liria (*The population figures are those of the UNDP survey of 1980.*)

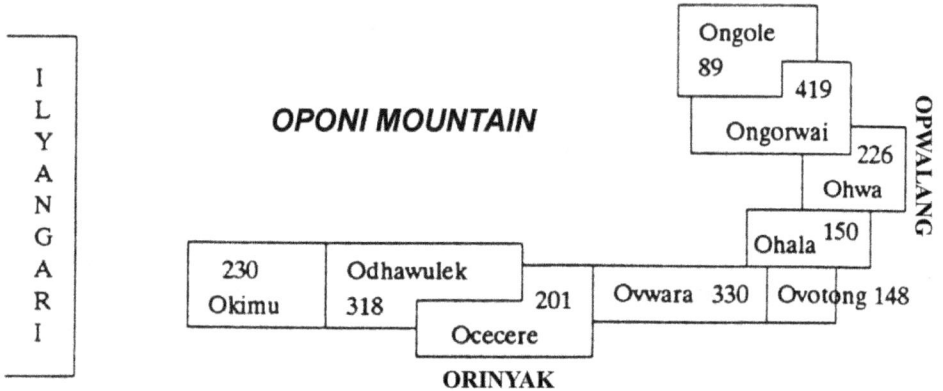

Before the rule of the generation of Boncuot at the beginning of the twentieth century, Odhawulek and Ocecere formed one section sharing the same sitting place and drums. They separated as a result of a fight over the sharing of an animal shot in a joint hunt. Their sitting places and drums have now been divided and they only share the ceremonial ground (named *Dhuma*). When they dance, they enter the ceremonial ground in separate blocs. Although Odhawulek and Ocecere consider one another as allies, its members feel that the risk of fights breaking out during the dances is always present. Hence, at the time of my field work, Ocecere was lobbying to have two separate ceremonial grounds suggesting that each section should take half of the poles of the existing shrine.

Ovwara is the residence of the king and the location of the central ceremonial ground with the central shrine of Liria named *Kujo*. Ovwara and Ovotong are close allies, Ovotong being small and, to a large extent, dependent on Ovwara.

Ongole, the last section in the ring, was characterised to me by informants who knew English, as an 'independent state'. It has its own Master of the Mountain and of the Land, Master of Bows and Master of Grain. Its Rain Office, however, was lost to the king of Liria (Case 13.5).

When a fight breaks out between two adjacent sections, each neighbour at the opposite side from that of the fight is expected to come and help. If, for example, Odhawulek and Ocecere fight, Okimu should come to the aid of Odhawulek and Ovwara should help Ocecere. If Odhawulek and Ovwara have a disagreement, the former can count on Ocecere while Ovwara would receive support from Ohala (not counting the small Ovotong). If Ongole and Ohala fight, they are joined by Ongorwai and Ohwa, respectively, etc.

The reason given by one informant for this system of mutual sectional support is that it prevents fighting sections from winning or losing. If such a thing would happen, he said, the sections next to the winner would, in a subsequent fight, be faced with a superior adversary, which is exactly what the system should prevent. Another informant stated that if your neighbour were defeated, the fight might easily spread to your own section. To prevent this, one should stop the aggressor from coming too close to one's own place by supporting one's neighbour. The gist of both explanations is that no section should be given reasons to believe that it is stronger than the others, and that no one should upset the existing balance.

In the period this information was collected, the *monyomiji* of Ohwa had made themselves unpopular with the other sections and had lost all their potential allies. The latter would go to the extent of saying that they no longer cared if Ohwa would be driven out of Oponi. If the smouldering conflict between Ohwa and Ongorwai were to develop into an open confrontation, the fate of Ohwa would be in the hands of the chief or of the elders (the retired *monyomiji*) so they said, mentioning the only political forces that could bring the fighting to a halt.

The sections at the outer ends of the semi-circle are at a disadvantage, since they have no section to back them when attacked from inside the circle. Moreover, they are more vulnerable to attacks from outside, especially Okimu, which is only one hour's walk away from the easternmost section of Ilyangari, the sister village of Liria on Oponi Mountain. In response to this factor of instability, the three western sections have concluded a pact. When two of them disagree, the third party is expected to mediate and bring the others together. The triple alliance of Okimu, Odhawulek and Ocecere which is known as 'Wurewure', functions as a device to avoid imbalance. The small Ovotong section is not counted as a full party in the balancing of power. Some informants simply omitted it when explaining the balancing mechanism to me, and treated it as belonging to Ovwara.

The nine sections of Liria are polarised into two moieties. The five western *obandak* (Okimu, Odhawulek, Ocecere, Ovwara and Ovotong) combine into the moiety 'Orinyak', the four others (Ohala, Ohwa, Ongorwai and Ongole) are 'Opwalang'. If sections of opposed halves of the village clash, the conflict might, in principle, escalate to a showdown between the two moieties. Fights which involve sections of opposed moieties are said to spread rapidly to the moieties as a whole.

The moieties play an important role in the organisation of competitions. They compete not only in sports manifestations and hunts, but also in the discharge of obligations towards the king (*amopwa*, maintenance and building of the palace). Since the colonial days, moiety competition is also put to use in the building of roads, churches and government offices. Although Orinyak and Opwalang recognise the same Rainmaker (who is also Rainmaker of Ilyangari), and share the Masters of the

Land, of Grain and of the Mountain, their Masters of Bows (*ohobwok latang*) are two different officials. Orinyak and Opwalang also have their own war-cry.[4]

Alongside this dual division, a triple division is used in other institutional contexts. For the purpose of the age-class system of girls and for the government administration, Liria has been divided into three divisions: Wurewure, Ovwara and Opwalang — each of them having its own girls' age-sets, and its own *mukungu*. This triple division corresponds to an opposition centre/periphery, since Ovwara is the seat of the Rainmaker and, nowadays, of the paramount chief of the western Lokoya.

The setting of Liria at the foot of Mount Opone helps the dualist principle to express itself in a very systematic way. A similar setting is available in Lowe where we find eight sections, divided in two moieties, arranged in a semi-circle at the foot of Lowe Hill, and in Lafon which has six sections grouped in a circle around the relatively small Lipul Hill. In contrast to Liria and Lowe, there is a marked imbalance between the moieties of Lafon: Boi consists of five sections and Kor of just one.

K. Divisions of Lafon (*The population figures are those of the Census of 1983.*)

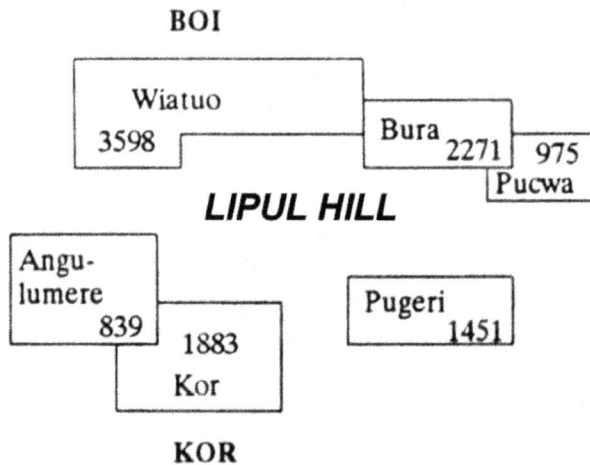

BOI

Wiatuo			
3598	Bura		
		2271	975
			Pucwa

LIPUL HILL

Angu-lumere		
	839	Pugeri
	1883	1451
	Kor	

KOR

This numerical imbalance is aggravated by the fact that the king of the Pari resides in Wiatuo, which is the most populous section of Boi.[5] The numerical discrepancy and

---

4   In order to boost their morale the warriors of Orinyak shout: "The spearshaft is red like *alyangi* (a reddish fruit)", while those of Opwalang yell: "We who comb the forest". The division in moieties may go back to a historical opposition between invaders and indigenous people. The proportion of clans in Opwalang which trace their origin to the Imatong Mountains is smaller than in Orinyak. The Ohala section consists of two clans one of which ('Ohala') claims to have always lived on Oponi Mountain.

5   The growth of Wiatuo into the biggest section is due to its being host to the kingship. Because of their greater wealth — acquired through tribute, booty and trade — kings marry more wives (Alikori had forty) and have more children. Kings are also the privileged recipients of war captives, and the favourite patrons of men who are forced by circumstance to become clients.

the fact that Wiatuo is the residence of the king was the major factor leading to Kor's mass exodus to Pajok around the turn of the twentieth century (see Ch. 6, p. 143–5).

Although only sticks are allowed in confrontations between sections, the conflicts between them are fought with as much zest as are the wars between separate communities. The number of casualties may be high; few dead but many wounded. In a stick fight between the two moieties in Lafon in 1942, not less than 35 men were seriously injured.[6] The violent confrontations are usually brief. A fight in 1985 between the junior age-sets (not yet initiated as *mojomiji*) of the sections of Wiatuo and Kor, witnessed by Kurimoto, lasted only five minutes, but cost the life of one of the boys of Kor. In the same affray, Wiatuo succeeded in burning the drum house of Kor, a customary target during such fights. The fight was stopped by the army detachment that was stationed in Lafon at the time to ward off a possible attack by the Sudan People's Liberation Army. A court consisting of the Torit Executive Officer and the chiefs of Loronyo, Magwi (Acholi) and Loa (Madi) sentenced Wiatuo to a fine of forty head of cattle for having killed the boy of Kor. When Wiatuo appeared reluctant to pay the whole sum, Kor remained absent at the New Year Festival (*Nyalam*), a particularly bad omen at the start of the New Year. Kor also refused Wiatuo further access to its fishing camps.

There are a number of factors that mitigate the imbalance in the sectional organisation of Lafon. In stick fights, not all the members of a moiety participate. In 1984, during a fight between junior age-sets of Pugeri and Kor, Kurimoto (in a personal communication) estimated that an equal number of about two hundred men joined the fight on either side, although Pugeri received support from men of Wiatuo, Bura and Pucwa. In this particular fight, the section of Angulumere, which is a neighbour to Kor, chose to remain neutral. In conflicts between Wiatuo and Kor, Pugeri normally takes a neutral position, so that its *rwath*, the descendant of Dimo and the Master of Lipul Hill, will be in a position to mediate between the two moieties.[7] Pugeri and Kor generally follow a policy of good neighbourliness; the incident of 1984 is considered an exception.

The fragile balance of forces in Lafon, and also the recent difficulties in Liria with the Ohwa section show that the dualist organisation of these villages is not a cosmological projection on society, as one might be tempted to think if one approached the facts from a Durkheimian perspective. On the contrary, it is the outcome of an open historical process in which the political actors frequently adopt attitudes which run counter to the ideal operation of the system.

Both in Liria and Lafon, there is, next to the dual opposition, also a tripartite division. The emergence of this third party can be understood in terms of the need of the two rivalling moieties for mediation. In Liria, the third party is the section of the

---

6   Southern Records Office, Juba, *Torit District Files*, Torit District Monthly Reports, 1942.
7   The role of the *rwath* of Pugeri in offering asylum is examined in Ch. 10, p. 234. On the photo on p. 323 the *rwath* of Lipul Mountain is seen performing the annual ritual of the blessing of spears.

king, in Lafon it is Pugeri, the oldest section led by the Master of the Mountain, the descendant from the first immigrants to the hill and the guardian of the reproduction of the Pari as a people.

To a considerable extent, sections decide and act on policies of their own. In Lotuho, it happened several times that sections chose to go over to the rival king when they felt unfairly treated, as Imeni in Hiyala did (see p. 135).

Sections may follow matrimonial policies of their own as well. In Lokiliri, the section of Loronyo has a special marital relationship with the section of Robbo in Kudwo, so that the two communities consider one another as in-laws. In the course of time, a rich repertory of reciprocally mocking songs has accumulated.

Sections and moieties make up the basic constituencies of rival princes. Often, villages are divided between different throne pretenders as in Loronyo during the 1880s, when the six sections divided their support between three descendants of Mayya. The present dispersal of the sections of the Kworijik moiety in Lokiliri goes back to a combination of sectional and dynastic rivalry that already existed at the end of the nineteenth century (Case 12.2)

A revealing application of the moiety principle is the practice in Langabu–and possibly in other villages as well — that overdue fines imposed by the assembly of *monyomiji* are seized by the *monyomiji* of the moiety opposite to the one of the debtor. Accordingly, seizure of goods or livestock from a household in the moiety of Ofiri is executed by the sections of Omiling, Omaranga or Okire, who constitute the opposite moiety. In return, Ofiri is called to collect overdue fines from Omiling, Omaranga or Okire. The justification for this rule is that there would be compromise between the bailiff and the debtor if both belonged to the same moiety.

The tightrope of non-violent competition

Members of different sections lose no opportunity to challenge and to compete with each other. Informants like to underscore the toughness of competition in the past. When, during a joint Lokiliri hunt, a stream was reached, it was standard practice that the two moieties first engaged in a wrestling match to decide who should drink first. The losers would have to wait until the others finished and would have to drink from the water muddied by the splashing of the others.

Collective work in the Lulubo and Lokoya villages is preferably carried out in a competitive way; sections or moieties are made to rival over the speed of the work. In 1986, when a new church was built in Lokiliri, the thatching was done on the basis of sectional competition, each side of the roof being thatched by one of the moieties.

Women's work is organised along the same lines. When fetching water during collective work, the three divisions of the girls of Liria compete in running to the stream. On their daily rounds to collect firewood, girls wrestle playfully. In Liria, there was an annual occasion at which the age-sets of different sections tested each other's strength. The symbolic prize of the wrestling match was a particular *obeleng* tree (*Lonchocarpus laxiflorus*) with budding leaves. The new leaves of the *obeleng* appear at the beginning of the dry season and so are harbingers of the coming wet season. The weeks after the match were spent in composing and singing songs against one another. Each female age-set had its champion wrestler and its champion runner.

In conflicts between the *monyomiji* of different moieties, the women also contributed their share by preventing the women of the opposite group from fetching water in the stream. The sectional rivalry between the women mirrors that between the men. A more recent introduction is the adoption of the organisational model of village administration to the girls' age-sets. At the time of my field work each girls' age-set had a 'chief', a *mukungu* (headman) and a *serikale* (chief's police).

The women are actively involved in sectional competition only during the years immediately preceding marriage and for a few years after marriage, until they have their first or second child. During the dry season (December-March) the neophytes stay together in the house of a *Big Man*. They select a name and a design for the beadwork of their headband, necklace and waist band which is not supposed to be copied by other age-sets. In the first year, the lower front teeth are extracted. In the subsequent three to five years, the girls are scarified, each successive year a new part of the body thus rendered more beautiful.

Among the Lulubo the girls' age-sets organise raids on girls of another section; the target is the conquest of the drums — used by the girls for dancing *nyale* (the special girls' dance), the flag, or the *mukungu's* whistle. The attacks take place at night in order to take the other group by surprise. By getting hold of the drums, playing them and starting to dance, the invading group has won. A successful attack calls for revenge, especially if the conquering group has taken the flag or whistle. Elaborate tactics are used to increase the chance of success. On one occasion when I was in Lokiliri, the girls of the attacking section had asked the boys of the same age to play the drums for *nyale* in their section so that the girls in the 'enemy' camp would assume they were having a dance and that there was no need to keep watch.[8]

Even though the raids are considered play, the fear of a possible outbreak of violence is always present. This factor is normally taken into consideration when selecting the target for the attack. The girls of Lokiliri who were interviewed in 1983 while they were preparing for a raid assured me that the section selected for the surprise attack could only be one with which relations were perfectly friendly.

Intersectional relations on the level of the *monyomiji* are marked by the ever-present possibility of an outbreak of violence. When different sections meet, the potential violence is the chief worry of those responsible for the organisation of the occasion. This is especially the case during dances. The excitement evoked by the dance is a constant threat to inter-sectional peace.

In Lulubo and Lokoya, different sections and allied villages join in dancing the war dance (Bari, Lokoya: *iriyang*, Lulubo: *ira*) held during the dry season and participated in by the whole community. *Kore* (a courting dance for young people, danced from

---

8   Bari girls had a similar age-set system (Spagnolo, 1932).

the first harvest up to the dry season), the New Year dance (after the last harvest) and funeral dances for commoners and for royalty are danced jointly as well.

There are many actions, incidents and misunderstandings that may cause conflict during a dance. It may be that not enough space is given to an arriving group of dancers that wants to join the ring. Perhaps drum-beats and songs belonging to one section are played for too long to the taste of other sections. Sections may misappropriate tunes and songs.[9] Groups and individuals who are on bad terms may run into each other. Then, there are accidental bumps, hurts with the weapons the dancers carry, expressions of competing claims on a particular woman–wishes that in the excitement of the dance are less easily suppressed than in daily life, and so on.

A frequent choreographic sequence in these dances is the conversion of the arrangement of the dancers from a positioning in two opposed lines into a unifying circle. When during a dance of *iriyang* a newly arriving section approaches the ceremonial ground of its hosts, it progresses in quasi-military fashion, waving its flags, brandishing its weapons and entering the ceremonial ground by storm. This is a critical moment, since the hosts are expected to reciprocate the challenge by a mock-show of defiance. Although the point of the whole exercise is that both parties display their ability to control the use of violence, the risk of an incident is never absent. After confronting the dancers from outside for a few rounds, the group of newcomers is supposed to merge gradually with the circle of the host group. *Iriyang* is usually concluded by a few rounds of *agba* or *igba*, a playful, frolicking dance in which the large group breaks up into couples dancing with arms locked, forming an appropriate transition from the intense, edifying unity of *iriyang* to scattered, day-to-day existence.

A similar opposition between competitive face-to-face dancing and the levelling of individual and group differences in the circle, is a main theme in the *kore* dance which is meant for entertainment and courting. *Kore*, as it is danced in Lulubo, is divided in two sequences: *budu*, in which the men and women form two circles moving anti-clockwise, the women forming the inner and the men the outer ring, and *tibidia*, the Nilotic jumping dance, executed by one young man and a girl at a time who both raise their arms and try to jump as high as they can. The two protagonists are accompanied and exhorted by alternating clapping and singing of those who stand in a circle around the two dancers. At the beginning of the dance and every time a group of youngsters from a different section arrives to join in, two or three rounds of *budu* are danced, as if to create a common social ground on which the competitive jumping can take place. Whenever I witnessed *kore*, there was continuous tension between the host-section and its visitors over the length of time each section monopolised the drums or the choice of tunes (which are section-owned).

---

9   In 1953, a series of clashes took place between the two moieties of Tirangore over a disputed drum-beat (Southern Records Office, Juba, *Torit District Files*, Torit District Monthly Diaries, September 1953).

Intersectional dances are like walking a tightrope. Their salutary effect is commensurate to the potential violence the dance is seen to absorb. The more 'realistic' the mock violence the more effective and enjoyable the eventual harmony, but also the more hazardous the event. The choreographic alternation between a dual, confrontationist mode of dancing and a centred, unifying mode reflects the two fundamental modes of group formation in these societies: the dualist mode that determines the division of the society into competing social units and the centralist mode that bridges these divisions. The contrast between dualist opposition and centralist mediation is also operative in the partly dual, partly tripartite arrangements of the sections of Liria and Lafon described in the previous paragraph.

The victimary directionality of warfare between the Kidepo and the Nile

To conclude this chapter on territorial dualism, I want to show how before the introduction of firearms the warfare between the communities living between the Nile and the Kidepo resulted in a number of successive lines of polarisation between aggressors overwhelmingly coming from the east attacking western neighbours.

In those days, the military strength of a community depended on four factors: the number of fighters it could deploy, its military organisation, its network of allies, and the effectiveness of its propaganda. To begin with the last factor: one reason given by informants for the ambition to become a 'killer' was that if a community was known to possess a large number of these men, its enemies would fear to attack it. The circulation of stories of heroic deeds and songs commemorating won battles were also believed to be a deterrent. The songs circulated in an area which was far wider than the community which composed them. In Lokiliri, for example, the repertory of war songs included songs from all over Lulubo, Lokoya and even from Pari, Bari and Lotuho villages.

The effectiveness of military organisation was a second factor determining military strength. It is probably one of the social domains where acculturation to more effective modes of organisation is quickest. The adoption of the *monyomiji* system by the Lulubo, Pari and the Acholi polities bordering on the Lotuho, in response to the military pressure of the Lotuho speakers was very quick. The case of Pajok shows that to assimilate the system only a few years sufficed.

Numbers are decisive when both antagonists have the same level of organisation and equal access to weaponry. Several standard policies existed which aimed at maximising population numbers: by attracting fugitives and poor men as clients (a policy followed by the Kursak of Lokiliri, and by Lomoro and Lohide in Lotuho) and the capture of women and children in war.

The conclusion of alliances with other communities compensated for lesser numbers. There are indications that militarily weak communities tended to be better at diplomacy. Of the two Lotuho kingdoms, Tirangore was numerically the smaller power for most of the time, but it was part of a more extensive network of allies which included Liria, Loudo, Lafon, and Obbo.

Moving from east to west in our field of study, we find that there were successive lines of military polarisation: the first line coincided with the Kidepo River across which the Lotuho-speaking peoples and the Pari opposed the Toposa, Didinga and Boya. A second line can be drawn to the west of the Lotuho, putting them face-to-face with the Ohoriok, and a third line put the Lokoya and the Bari in opposed camps.

The peoples facing one another across the Kidepo had different types of political and military organisation. Military alliances between the polities on opposite sides of the river were, therefore, rare. There is, as far as I am aware, only one documented instance of an alliance spanning the Kidepo River: the alliance between the Pari, Lopit, and Boya. The Pari used this alliance to threaten the Bari after the Beir Patrol of 1912.[10] This unique configuration which, as far as can be ascertained, never materialised into a combined attack, was the response to an unprecedented threat (the Beir Patrol). The fact that the different polities in the area were able — or at least claimed to be able — to transcend customary political bloc formation shows the creativity of the principle of complementary opposition in a situation when a new, vastly more powerful enemy appears on the scene.[11]

During the heyday of Imatari, the main line of polarisation to its west was that with the centres of Segele, Longulu and other Horiok communities. During the rule of Ngalamitiho in Imatari and Atafat in Longulu, the Horiok were pushed across the Hos River.[12]

After the fall of Imatari and the fragmentation of the Lotuho kingdom into two, the main line of polarisation among the Lotuho coincided with the antagonism between the kingdom of Mayya and that of Hujang. After the split of the dynasty, there is no further evidence of joint military endeavours of the twin kingdoms against outsiders. Instead, we see the rivalling Lotuho kings conclude alliances with non-Lotuho powers (for example, the Ansar) to fight one another. This introversion of the previous outward expansionism — to which the blockage of further expansion across the Nile as a result of the Zande pressure from the west may have been a contributing factor —removed the battlefields from the borders of Lotuho land to its heart.

The major dividing line to the west of the Ohoriok was that between the Bari, on the one hand, and the 'Lokoya', on the other. In fact, the coining of the Lokoya ethnic label by the Bari was in response to this division.

In the east-west orientation of warfare, the easterners generally initiated the attack while the westerners were the defenders and victims. The Lotuho speakers, as a whole,

---

10   Sudan Archive, Oriental Library, Durham, *Reports on the Finances, Administration and Conditions of the Sudan, 1912*, Annual Report Mongalla Province, 1912:200.

11   The mythical 'alliances' of King Facar of Otunge and King Ngalamitiho of Imatari who in their anger called the Toposa to destroy their own disobedient subjects should be interpreted in a different perspective: see Chapter Fifteen.

12   Novelli, 1970: 171; Nalder, 1937:84–86; Comboni Archive, Rome. A/126/10, Pazzaglia, 'Omuk eyabita to hobwok Otuho', pp. 39–41, translation by Constantine Bartel.

were pushed across the Kidepo River. Lotuho oral tradition is unanimous in asserting that, before they settled in their present territory, they lived further to the east near Mount Lotuke in the Didinga Hills. The role of the Toposa in Lotuho history is not unlike that of the Lokoya in the history of the Bari. The Plains-Lotuho of Imatari expanded at the cost of the Ohoriok and pushed the latter into the plains between Liria and Lopit. In 1841, when Mohammed Ali's expedition reached Bariland, the Lokoya had become an immediate threat to the Bari. Oral tradition I collected in Liria suggests that Bari-speaking groups staying near Liria started to emigrate towards Nyangbaraland west of the Nile in the beginning of the nineteenth century.

An important force behind this inter-ethnic pecking order seems to have been environmental: the gradual desiccation of the plains between the Didinga Hills and Lake Turkana. Mount Lotuke, the eastern tip of the Didinga Hills, is the first place with permanent water if one travels west from Lake Turkana. It is considered a starting point in many migration myths, not only to the east but also to the south (Webster, 1979).

The Bari, in turn, formed a military threat to their western neighbours. They initiated wars with the Kuku and Nyepu; while the Kuku, Kakwa and Fajelu expanded into territory occupied by speakers of Madi-Moru languages. The Fajelu finally 'collided' with the Adio (Makaraka) who formed the spearhead of the Zande expansion eastwards.

Expansion is reflected in the form of ethnic stereotypes among the people in the area. The people to the east are considered tougher, more warlike, but also less human — more leopard-like — than those to the west; while those to the west are seen as more effeminate and, therefore, as 'fair game'.

The military polarity was mirrored by another, symbolic, polarity. In purification rituals, in which evil (disease, hunger) is expelled from the community, the blight is invariably sent westwards, in the direction of the setting sun. At the celebration of the Logir New Year, mosquitoes and diseases are sent towards Lotuho. The Lotuho expel their evils towards the Horiok while the Lokoya and Lulubo send them to the Bari. At the Yangane festival all households deposit their ashes in a basket and present them to the elders to spit in. The Master of Ashes of the community (or in his absence the Master of the Land) empties the basket in the nearest Nile tributary while the children are ordered to pick a straw from the roof of the house and throw it, burning, into the same stream shouting: "Go away evil!"

Although the westward directionality of the expulsion of evil may have other cosmological roots, the use of the names of enemies in the annual purification ritual reveals the close connection between warfare and the expulsion of evil from the community.

Conclusion

From the level of local clan groups which make up the village-sections to the regional level, dualism is an important structuring principle in territorial organisation. If the principle is to function with a minimum of violence, it is important that the groups which face each other on the battlefield or in the arena of stick fights are of equal strength. Although it is in the interest of all parties that a certain equilibrium is maintained, this desirable condition is frequently not realised.

Apart from the regional disequilibrium along the east-west axis, severe and chronic imbalances also occurred on the level of sections and moieties, as in the case of the exodus of the Kor section of the Pari. The emergence of a third, mediating party is a way out. A more radical solution is the institution of kingship itself. In Chapter Nine, I shall argue that kingship in its most elementary form functions as a form of dualist antagonism which unifies the ranks of its opponents. Before turning to the discussion of kingship, I want to examine the age-class system — the other major field of social relations which is structured along dualist lines.

Four-tiered initiation-tower, Mak, Dongotono

Age-mates performing a mock-charge, yelling war songs and adopting a hooligan-like mien, Lokiliri, 1983.

8

The Dualist Structure of Age-class Organisation

The *monyomiji*, owners of the community

Up to the present day, the age-class system plays a prominent role in the organisation of community life, except in Bariland where the age-classes — in so far as they still exist—have largely been emptied of their meaning because of war, foreign domination, depopulation and urbanisation.[1]

I use the terms *generation* and *generation-set* to refer to a group of age-sets that jointly assumes responsibility for village affairs for a certain number of years — usually varying from twelve to twenty-two years. That is to say, I use it as an age-based category, not as a generation in the biological sense. There is no rule — as among the Toposa and related peoples — that members of a generation are, per definition, sons of fathers belonging to the same generation. It is possible, though improbable (except for Lotuho where the generational span is twenty-two years) that father and son are members of the same generation-set. In such exceptional cases, the father will belong to its most senior age-set and the son to the most junior one.

Within the age-class organisation, the men of middle age occupy the most prestigious position. They are the *monyomiji*: the *owners* or *fathers* of the community. They are *in power*. The young men who have not reached *monyomiji*-hood yet do everything in their power to hasten the day that they will control the affairs of the village, while the *monyomiji* who are about to 'retire' cling to their position as long as they can, to put off their reduction to the status of 'children', as the Lulubo say. The

---

1   The little that has been written on the subject by the Seligmans (1928:420), Spagnolo (1932) and Beaton (1936) offers insufficient clues as to how the Bari system worked. The lists of age-set names collected by Spagnolo, Whitehead and myself show a fair degree of continuity between the east bank Bari and the Lulubo, Lokoya and Pari. Spagnolo's article and Beaton's contribution to Nalder's ethnographic survey (1937:126–128) suggest a greater degree of subordination of the Bari age-sets to the power of the *matat* (chief) and of *Big Men* (*ngutu 'duma*). A *Big Man* usually hosted the initiation of a new set and his son would be the *matat-lo-ber*, the leader of the age-set. The Bari age-sets act as the chief's body-guard — a position similar to that described by Evans-Pritchard for Anuak age-sets. From the material at my disposal, it seems improbable that the Bari age-sets were ever combined to form 'generations' with responsibility in the running of community affairs. They were, rather, associated with life in the cattle-camps as were the age-sets of the Dinka (Lienhardt, 1958a:132; Zanen & Van de Hoek, 1987:182).

monyomiji system does not have the gerontocratic bias that according to Baxter and Almagor (1978, Introduction) defines the other Eastern Nilotic systems.[2]

The *monyomiji* are responsible for the well-being of the community in the broadest sense. They settle conflicts, organise hunts and wars, keep an eye on the Rainmaker, issue regulations limiting violent behaviour, fix the rate of the bridewealth and the price of village-produced commodities; and impose fines on those who trespass the rules. They are identified with the public interest and are expected to defend the community order against corruption from inside and dangers from outside.

Warfare and the typical 'virtues of manhood' are glorified by each new generation. This is especially manifest in the names of age-sets and generations, which frequently bespeak bravery, invincibility and acquaintance with violence. The following Bari names, recorded by Spagnolo (1933:449–50, 1932:395–6) and Beaton (1936:134 –142) may serve to illustrate:

Mukkonyen	eyes closed (during the attack)
Merkolong	intoxicated with the sun
Mirtiko	intoxicated with fury
	(The first three names are also found among the Lulubo and Lokoya.)
Pajutwan	despisers of death
Merkoka	drunk as leopards
Sesera	raiders of distant countries
Akupir	those with hair on their teeth (from devouring vast numbers of cattle)
Lumadak-konyen	red-eyed (of bloodthirstiness and excitement).

Names of peoples, tribes or political movements with a warlike reputation are also popular: *Nuer, Murle, Arabi, Nacar* (=Ansar, the Mahdists); *Akara* (=Toposa); *Agar* (a Dinka tribe), *Simba* (the Congolese rebel movement in the 1960s), *Mulele* (the leader of that movement), *Gala* (originally foreigners from Ethiopia, later also including Egyptians, Turks and Europeans, a name found in several places during the nineteenth century), *Orta*, (the Equatorial Battalion in Torit), *Anyanya II* (the popular name of the Sudan's People's Liberation Army at the onset of the second Civil War).

Other names refer to the membership of the age-class, or the degree of its rebelliousness (see following paragraphs). An age-class may also adopt a name by which it was abused or ridiculed by the generation in power:

---

2   Although today Lotuho informants are unanimous and emphatic as to this 22-year span, it seems plausible that the 22-year rule is a recent orthodoxy. Lord Raglan, who was D.C. of Latuka District in 1917–18 (as Fitz Somerset), gives a period of 16 years (Seligman, 1932:324), Lt.Col Lilley (D.C. Latuka District 1925–39) and H.A. Arber (Ass. D.C. Latuka District in 1936) give a period of 16 to 20 years (Nalder, 1937:86). Earlier, I pointed at the inaccuracy of Muratori's calculation of the year of Lomoro's assassination at 1912, which was based on the assumption of a 22-year interval between successive *Nefiras*. From various archival sources, we know that he was killed some weeks before 5 May, 1906 (Uganda National Archives, *Secretariat Minute Papers* 257, Letter F. Spire to Commissioner Entebbe, d.d. 5/5/1906).

Mura	immature (in Bari and Lokoya)
Salata	age-set that was ridiculed for eating salad like Arabs (in Hiyala)
Akulyebantu	man-eaters (in Swahili), a name given to the junior generation of Liria in 1956 after it had attempted to put the Rainmaker in the middle of a fire
Nyösukana	eaters who do not work (Bari), etc.

A person becomes a *monyomiji* by virtue of his membership of an age-set. Age-sets are formed from section-based gangs of adolescents which group themselves under one name on the level of the village. The average age-set spans between three to six years, the actual time-span depending on the number of adolescent boys. In Lulubo and Lokoya these 'gangs' are formed more or less spontaneously in the period that the boys acquire their first experience of technical and social skills. These youths spend much time on competitive activities (wrestling matches, goat-fights, running, etc.).

Four successive age-sets constitute what I have called a 'generation'. Power is transferred formally in a spectacular ceremony which takes place at more or less fixed intervals (varying from every ten to every twenty-two years). After they have become *monyomiji*, members of the same age-set continue to sit together at meals and share a specific part of the animal. Which part it may be, depends on the rank of the set. In Lulubo, the senior set of the *monyomiji* receives the neck (*gole*); the next senior one the breast (*juju*), etc. A set is often referred to by the name of the part of the animal it is entitled to.

The age-set provides the individual with a social status on which he can rely outside his own community. A fairly uniform system of dividing portions of meat among age-groups applies in the entire area between the Nile and the Kidepo. A man visiting a village where he has no relatives or affines receives the treatment due to his age-set. Upon arrival in a new environment, he should, first of all, find the group eating the part of the animal he is entitled to. Normally, this group will let him share in its meals or take him around to the houses of age-mates.

The duties of the *monyomiji* are divided on the basis of the age-sets; the most menial tasks (for example, running errands, fetching water) are given to the junior sets. During the years preceding the transfer of power, the members of the new generation are kept busy with all sorts of odd jobs and errands by the *monyomiji* about to retire.

At *monyomiji* meetings, the order of seniority of the age-sets is observed strictly. Members of junior sets are expected to keep a low profile. In the sitting arrangements at the *bali* (or *amangat*) the junior *monyomiji* occupy the higher platforms.

Generational succession as transfer of power

The ordered hierarchy of the age-sets, once they have assumed power as a generation, contrasts with the generalised competition that marks the period preceding the transfer of power.

Three varieties of generational succession can be distinguished. The differences between the three concern the flexibility in the recruitment of new members, the length of the period of rule, the overlap in the exercise of power by successive generations, and the relationship between the different territorial levels (section, village, kingdom) on which the transfer of power takes place.

The Bari, Lulubo and Lokoya have the most flexible system of recruitment. They do not stick to a fixed period of rule. The age-class system of the Pari and Lopit is characterised by a measure of overlap between the rule of successive generations, while the Lotuho system mainly differs from the others by staging formal recruitment to *monyomiji*-hood on the three different territorial levels of section, village and kingdom.

a) *Lulubo and Lokoya*

Among the Lokoya and Lulubo, power is handed to the young generation 'when they are strong enough'. This strength is measured in numbers. It is not conceived in absolute terms but as relative to the strength or weakness of the ruling *monyomiji*. As soon as the youths clearly outnumber those they want to replace, their intention to rule is taken seriously. Age-set names often reflect this. The current age-set of twenty-year-olds in Lokiliri calls itself *Kalororo* ('groundnuts') referring to their numbers, which are like groundnuts spread out in the yard to dry.

The retiring generation may refer to its own reduced numbers as an excuse for honourable early retirement. Plagues, defeats at the hands of the enemy and poor rain may be other reasons for a ruling generation to step down. Surviving members of Okwir, the generation that ruled Lokiliri from 1948 to 1958, admitted that they retired early because of a succession of droughts for which they were held responsible by their successors, Kwara.

Normally, however, power is handed over reluctantly. The older generation will not go unless ousted. The youngsters make propaganda for themselves and go around persuading others of the weaknesses of the old regime. They try to demonstrate the redundancy of the old rulers by showing exemplary conduct (for example, by repairing the drum house, the drums, the sitting platforms). They take a radical stand and accuse the ruling generation of laxity in public affairs, not unlike young radicals in the democratic systems of the West. They boast of feats of prowess in hunting and war and choose a name emphasising their fearlessness, manliness, wealth, invincibility or their sense of humour.

Among the Lulubo and Lokoya, normally, only the two senior age-sets are 'pushed out'. The recruitment of the new generation is subject to considerable lobbying and negotiation. There does not seem to be a strict, generally valid rule in the practices of the different villages. In the 1956 *obongoro* (transfer of generational power) of Liria, all of the four age-sets of the ruling generation were retired. The young men of the age-set Tangakwo who, strictly speaking, were not entitled yet to enter *monyomiji*-hood, were given the opportunity to be incorporated if they paid a fine in cash and provided a goat for purification (*avulyo*). Many Tangakwo preferred to wait for the next *obongoro*, because then they would hold the most senior and most prestigious positions within the body of *monyomiji*. One generation normally comprises four age-sets, but sometimes five (or four and a half, as in Liria).

Pressure for transfer of power may also come from a ruling generation beset by difficulties. In Lokiliri, Kwara (1958–1976) wanted to hand over power as early as 1970 because of the difficult war situation and because *de facto* control over the dispersed villagers was in the hands of non-initiated men who had joined the rebel movement. The young men preferred to wait because of the confused situation.

b) Pari and Lopit

Among the Pari and Lopit, a full generation has six age-sets, divided into three pairs. The *monyomiji* with daily responsibility never consist of more than four sets. The two sets opening a generation are called *wic* ('head') by the Pari and *lefirat* by the Lopit (*Efira* or *Nefira* is the name of the *New Fire Ceremony*, at which power is handed over.). The next four are called *lowatat* (Ngotira, Central Lopit: 'followers'), *lotuhot* (Lomiya, Southern Lopit: 'those who close the ranks') or *tengo* (Pari: 'rethatchers of the roof' complementing the name *jo-geedo* 'builders of the house' used by the *wic* before taking over power.

After *lefirat/wic* has ruled for a period of time (*ca*. ten years) with the help of the two senior *lowatat/lotuhot/tengo* age-sets, they are retired to make place for the *lowatat/lotuhot/tengo* sets reinforced by two newly recruited sets. The *wic/lefirat* sets continue to play an advisory role in *monyomiji* affairs. The take-over of power by new *lefirat/wic* sets is considered to be of greater significance than the transfer to the *lowatat/lotuhot/tengo* sets. "The *wic* really begin a new era; they are the real men," an informant assured me. The rule of *lowatat/louhot/tengo* is considered less promising as far as new initiatives are concerned, although I have also heard the opposite claim (from individuals who are *lowatat/lotuhot/tengo*). The last two age-sets never have full responsibility in the affairs of the village. They are just 'added' to the ruling *lowatat/lotuhot/tengo* when the latter take over. In Lomiya, they are exempted from paying the bulls that the other age-sets have to provide to acquire *monyomiji* status.

c) Lotuho

Among the Lotuho, the period of rule of a generation is nowadays fixed at twenty-two years. After this period, all *monyomiji* in the kingdom are retired and replaced by the new generation. Accession to the status of *monyomiji* is rather formal and takes place at three different levels: in the section (*amangat*), on the level of the village (*amiji*) and on that of the kingdom.

At the level of the section, a person is initiated to *monyomiji*-hood individually upon reaching a certain age (sometimes a number of individuals may be initiated together). A white he-goat is sacrificed by the guardian of the section (*amonye mangat*), who uses the goat's rumen to purify the neophyte before he introduces him to his section's drum house. The *monyomiji* who have been admitted in the course of one year are given a group name in a ceremony on the level of the section (*Najingana*) at the end of the ritual year.

Every four or five years, the newly admitted *monyomiji* are united in one village age-set in a ceremony presided over by the Master of the Village (*amonyemiji*).

About every twenty years, the four age-classes of the new *monyomiji* of the different villages are united into a single generation by the king in the great royal new fire ceremony (*Efira*). Only after the last ceremony does the Lotuho man reach the full status of *monyomiji* and is he entitled to count himself as one of the *efirat* (those to whom power has been handed over in the *Efira*) The *monyomiji* who have only been admitted on the sectional and village levels are called *olojingat* ('initiates': those who are *monyomiji* by virtue of having passed *Najingana* only). From the point of view of the *efirat* the *olojingat* are apprentices.

Banner fixed at the gate of a drum house of Mura-hatiha proclaiming that ARABI have taken over power. On the left side, a drawing of what appears to be a stick fight, on the right a man aiming his gun at a man who has his hands raised. The text is in Lotuho except for the third line which is Acholi. The translation is:
"Arabs,
Sons of thieves,
No cattle,
Taking power: 27–11–98"
The new generation proclaims its readiness for war by presenting itself not only as victims of robbery but also as doubles of their principal enemies whose name they adopt. On the notion of double see Model A, step 2, p. 14.

The three varieties of generational succession can be understood as different ways of coping with the antagonism between the generations. The Lulubo/Lokoya variety is the most open-ended alternative as the moment of transfer is made to depend on the actual balance of forces between the coming and the going generation. At the same time, it leaves considerable space for *ad hoc* manoeuvring before the transfer of real power.

The Pari and Lopit generations, which consist of six age-sets, have greater scope. After a *wiclefirat* age-class has assumed authority over the four age-classes following it, it is there to stay, even after they have handed over power to the *tengo/lotuhot/lowatat*. As advisers, the elders have a more formalised role in village affairs than their Lulubo and Lokoya counterparts, who are said to revert to 'childhood'.

The diffusion of inter-generational tension is perhaps greatest in the Lotuho system where a man goes through three stages before reaching full *monyomiji*-hood. He is accepted as a full member of his section at a relatively early age. But it usually takes longer before a man becomes a full *monyomiji* on the level of the kingdom. A compensation built into the system is that those who wait longest to become fully-fledged *monyomiji* will be among the most senior ones once they take over power.

Another institution mitigating the tension between generations is the classification of Lotuho generations in *Tome* ('elephants') and *Jifia* ('followers'). The generation following *Tome* is always *Jifia* and that following *Jifia* is always *Tome*. *Tome* was the last generation to rule in Imatari. The Lotuho say that *Tome* are 'sons' of the previous *Tome* and *Jifia* are 'sons' of the previous *Jifia*. In this way, solidarity is created between the generation aspiring to power and the retired elders. The latter are expected to use their influence to facilitate the rise to power of their 'sons' and to protect them against excessive demands issued by the ruling generation.

Generational succession as political antagonism

Whatever the exact organisational form given to the relationship between the generations, its fundamental dynamic is antagonism. The word choice of informants immediately betrays this. The older generation is 'pushed out', power is 'taken away' from the elders, and a 'new era' begins. The ceremony of transfer of power was repeatedly characterised to me as a 'revolution' and certain generations and villages claimed to be more 'revolutionary' than others.

The use of the word 'initiation', which refers to the incorporation of a 'passive' neophyte into an established order, is, therefore, out of place in this context—except perhaps for the Lotuho ceremony on the sectional level. To the participants, the transfer of power is an event in which the young men actively do away with an old, outlived order and replace it with something more vital and promising.

The larger the junior generation, the greater the antagonism. When, during the last years of rule of a generation the numbers of its successor-generation equal or surpass its own numbers, reciprocal challenges and clashes will become more frequent. Generational antagonism during that period is, in many respects, similar to territorial antagonism. Numbers play the same decisive role in the balancing of power between the generations, as they do in inter-village and inter-sectional relations. The importance of numbers is reflected in age-set and generation names: *Naboro*

(Lotuho: 'sand'), *Ama* (Lotuho: 'locusts'), *Dotiti* (Lotuho: 'a long line of people'), *Iru* (Lotuho: 'swarm of birds'), *Losiwa* (Bari: 'bees'), *Somba, Na'buyuk, Nyamunga* (Bari: 'multitude'), *Lomukudit* (Bari: 'grass'), *Muluri* ('red ants'), *Lo'duka* (Bari: 'too many to be punished').

Confrontations between generational groups are subject to the same restrictions with regard to the use of violence. In Lotuho, inter-generational stick fights are frequent in the five years preceding the *Nefira*. Before the last *Nefira*, which was scheduled for October 1976, the police had to intervene several times in clashes triggered by attempts of the ruling *monyomiji* to postpone the date of the transfer of power by one more year. In the end, the old generation compromised and agreed to have the *Nefira* in 1976.[3]

During the years preceding the *Nefira,* the junior generation tries to make a name for itself by carrying out raids, often against the will of the ruling *monyomiji* and the king. In 1952, three years before the *Nefira* of the Mayya dynasty at Hoding, the joint junior age-sets of Lalanga, Ilyeu and Loming carried out an attack on the Boya, capturing four hundred head of cattle and eight hundred sheep and goats. Their attack was the culmination of a series of raids on the Boya in which the Logir had also played an important part. Captain King, the Commissioner of Nagichot District, considered the matter sufficiently serious to ask the Governor to send the Equatorial Corps to carry out a punitive patrol against the raiders. But Lewis, the Governor, decided against it because he did not consider the punitive use of the colonial army opportune just then. The eyes of the world were focused on the Sudan, which at the time was negotiating for independence.[4]

The names of age-sets aspiring to power are often chosen to express defiance of the ruling generation or of authority in general. The *monyomiji* who took over power in Lowe (Lokoya) in 1959 called themselves *Thimomonye* ('Those who ignore their fathers'). Those in Ngulere in the same year called themselves *Lofohitu* ('Immune to Sorcery'), those in Liria *Akim* ('The Overturners'). In Beaton's list of Bari age-class names, we find names such as *Kanyikwara* ('the Disobedient Ones'), *Lo'dumun* ('those who take the wives of others'), *Losegga* ('those who will have nothing to do with the words of others'), *Wube* ('those who reply badly to the elders') — all of which testify to the same rebellious spirit.

The most common form of generational rivalry is the exchange of acts and words of defiance from the junior side and bullying and meting out punishments from the senior side. This is how a recently initiated *monyomiji* from Ohobohobo in Lopit described his position as an *inyarhalu* (member of the candidate generation):

3   Torit People's Rural Council, Monthly Report, January 1976, Southern Records Office, Juba, *Torit District Files.*

4   Letter Governor Equatoria Province to D.C. Torit and D.C. Nagichot, 11 July, 1952. File 'Border issues Torit District/Eastern District, Southern Records Office, Juba, file no. E.P. /66, B.41, vol.1:21–27.

8.1 *Bullying of the candidate* monyomiji (account by recent initiate, Iboni, Lopit)

If *inyarhalu* fail to do as they are told by the *monyomiji*, they are chased out of the village. This is in case the mistake is very bad. But if it is a simple mistake, you are not allowed to gather and laugh in any corner of the village. As soon as you have eaten your supper, you go to sleep. After five or six days, you, the *inyarhalu*, have to gather and ask for a tin of beer flour from any home in the village. When you have been given the flour, you call for anyone from among the *monyomiji*, apologise to him and inform him about the tin of beer flour. Then, he will go and advise the *monyomiji* to find a solution. If they accept, you are allowed to move freely in the village, except with girls. If you are found playing around with girls, your father's goat is killed. If the *inyarhalu* does not apologise for it within a period of a month or two, you will be asked to bring a bull in apology. And this bull will not be counted as part of your age-set's entrance fee to become *monyomiji*.

If the junior generation refuses to apologise or to pay the fine, the tension easily escalates into an open fight between the two generations. The following three case-histories show that generational rivalry may have serious political repercussions:

8.2 *Generational antagonism and the fall of Imatari* (oral history, Hino)[5]

When the rule of the generation of Miriyang and King Ngalamitiho did not seem to come to an end in the eyes of the young men, the latter grew rebellious. The song they composed to lament their perpetual adolescence is still being sung:

> We, the boys of Tome,
> When shall we ever be full men?

One day, the young men challenged the authority of the *monyomiji* by dancing with girls of their own age in the ceremonial ground: an act strictly prohibited for non-*monyomiji*. When the boys were found out, they fled with the girls to Dongotono, where, according to one version of the story, they obtained wives by way of sister exchange. In this way, they married bypassing their fathers' bridewealth and authority. Miriyang wanted to take revenge for the insult by attacking the Dongotono who had offered them refuge, but King Ngalamitiho, who wanted to keep the peace, stopped them. Songs were composed by the rebellious generation which challenged Ngalamitiho's weak attitude demanding his son Ohurak to become the king:

> Our King Imoi [=Ngalamitiho] is afraid of death
> Let the power go to Ohurak
> Our community is falling apart

---

5   This version of the story was recorded in Hiyala from the mouth of prince Luka, son of Queen Ihure. It corresponds to versions of the same narrative related by Hino (1980:56–59) and by Novelli, (1970:171–3). Novelli's story is based on material collected by A. Pazzaglia and C. Muratori. The episode of the dance and the flight to Dongotono is taken from it. The version in Paolucci's thesis (1970:518–523) was recorded by Muratori from the mouth of Mario Obura. It attributes the invitation of the Toposa to destroy Imatari to Ohurak after he had been challenged by his sons. The same Mario Obura (together with Mr Adelino) related a summarised version of the same account to me which was not significantly different from the version of prince Luka. I thank Messrs Obura, Adelino and Luka for their help. The third and the last song of the five songs are copied from Hino (1980:56, 57).

We want war with the Dongotono!

And:

King, prepare yourself for war against Dongotono
You are afraid, king!
Hand the power to Ohurak
Since a new generation is about to take over.

When Ngalamitiho heard the song, he cursed his son and his people:

Imatari, many as you are,
The enemies of your fathers are coming
The Toposa are coming
Let us hide ourselves in the corners of our houses!

And:

Lament for the *Tome* generation!
Which Ohurak will not survive
They will scatter building shelters like birds

Ohurak and *Tome* finally succeeded in expelling Ngalamitiho from Imatari. Ngalamitiho fled to Toposaland only accompanied by his Master of Ceremonies.[6] He returned later with a band of Toposa and encircled Imatari. The people fled to the compound of the king which had strong walls, the Toposa hard on their heels. When the invaders reached the walls of the king's palace the Toposa shouted. "Will they hold?" Ngalamitiho replied "Go ahead and push." While the wall was being pushed over, Ngalamitiho and his Master of Ceremonies disappeared in lightning.[7] Ohurak was killed in the battle and the Lotuho dispersed to different villages in the valley of the Hos and Hinyati. So ended the glory of Imatari.

Whatever the historical truth of these events, they offer a clue to the way a rebellion against the ruling generation by its junior is represented in Lotuho social consciousness: there is a demonstrative take-over of the main public facilities of Imatari: the ceremonial ground which includes the village shrine and drum house; there is an armed confrontation between the competing generations (which is stopped by the king at the last moment); and there is an attempt by the young men to circumvent the control of the elders over matrimonial exchange.

The following case of generational rebellion is from Lokiliri. It should be dated around the turn of twentieth century:

---

6   Lord Raglan (Somerset, 1918:153), Lilley (in Nalder, 1937:86) and my informants invariably speak of the 'dog' of the king. The term 'dog' is a common metaphor referring to the assistants of the king who are recruited from the Lomini clan and include the *labusuti hobu*, a title often translated as 'Prime Minister' or 'Master of Ceremonies'. He is the person closest to the king. "Dog" must have referred to this human companion of Ngalamitiho on his quest for help from the Toposa and not to the quadruped. The dog metaphor highlights the leader-follower nature of the relationship and the inseparability of king and the *labusuti hobu*. In the past, the *labusuti hobu* accompanied the king in his death. An account of the live burial of the *labusuti hobu* alongside the dead king is given in Ch.18, p. 413–4.

7   In the versions recorded by Pazzaglia and Muratori and summarised by Novelli (1970:173) and Paolucci (1970:518) Ngalamitiho is killed by the Toposa.

8.3 *Generational subversion in Lokiliri* (oral history)

Limojo felt its way to power blocked by *Taruka*, the powerful generation to which chief Lualla belonged. Although *Limojo* had already given proof of its intrepidity (for example, in the unsuccessful attack on Hojovi; see Ch. 6, p. 141), *Taruka* was not prepared to surrender its power. The bad feeling between the two generation-sets was such that *Limojo* established its own '*bali* (sitting platform), named Mododa, separate from that of *Taruka*.

Yugusuk Lowa, the younger brother of King Ali Bey, and Wani Lokume, the son of Lugör, the Bari king of Shindiru who lived in Lokiliri with his mother's brother, Lualla, decided to cause a drought in order to discredit *Taruka*[8]. In this way, they hoped to speed up the succession of *Limojo*. A bad drought affected the first harvest when the grain was waist-high. The conspiracy was discovered and both men fled. Wani returned to Shindiru and Yugusuk fled to Bilinyan.

Only by joining their rain powers and pooling their rainstones could Lualla and Ali Bey save the harvest and safeguard *Taruka*'s hegemony for at least one more year.

The case illustrates the way generational responsibility for communal well-being is conceived. A generation which fails to deliver the goods (rain, victory, health) has to quit sooner or later. This cosmological responsibility is also used as a stake in generational competition.

Accounts of rebellions by the junior generation are not confined to oral history. In Chapter Six (p. 145, 150), we noted the obstruction caused by the junior generation of the Pari and Lokoya to deals between their chieftains and the Condominium Government. The following case, which is based on archival records,[9] examines the resistance offered by the junior generation of Ilyangari to a settlement with the colonial authorities.

8.4 *Anti-Colonial Resistance by Ilyangari's 'young bloods'* (Juba Archives)

After most of the other Lokoya villages had surrendered, acts of sabotage against agents of the Condominium Government continued to be carried out by Ilyangari, despite repeated declarations of loyalty by Minge, the Master of the Mountain, who dealt with the external affairs of Ilyangari.

Minge had made formal protestations of allegiance to the Sudan Government–even before the punitive patrol against Liria in 1915. In the following years, he had shown his friendly attitude to the government by successfully restraining his people from attacking the mail carriers, the team constructing the telegraph line from Mongalla to Torit, and the passing government patrols.

However, in July 1918, a clash occurred when a police patrol demanded porters and the corporal-in-charge was shot by an arrow and killed. Another policeman

---

8   According to one informant, an empty tortoise shell rubbed with red ochre was hung in a high tree in the middle of the forest. According to the son of Wani Lokume, whom I interviewed, it was an antelope's tail and a broken potsherd with ochre. Yugusuk put a piece of bamboo smeared with ochre in the pipe of the elder Agiramu who was a heavy smoker.

9   Central Records Office, Khartoum, *Mongalla Files*: 'Report on Punitive Patrol no. 14', 'Mongalla Province Intelligence Reports' July, August and September 1918 (*INTEL* 2/48/408); G. Donne, 'Report on Punitive Expedition against Chief Minge at Ilyangari' (*INTEL* 91/57).

was wounded and three rifles and some ammunition were taken. One day later, the convoy taking the mail from Mongalla to Torit was attacked while the telegraph line passing near the village was dismantled over a distance of more than six hundred yards.

During the investigation by the Inspector of Torit, Brock Bey, the people of Ilyangari accused the corporal of having taken food by force and molesting women. Other witnesses revealed that the corporal had given an ultimatum to Minge to hand in a gun which he had received from 'Abyssinian Poachers'. Whatever may have been the case, on 29 July, a punitive expedition was sent to Ilyangari and forty-eight people were killed.

On 10 September, there was another attack of Ilyangari, this time on an armed convoy that carried mail and merchandise to Torit. In the affray, twenty men from Ilyangari were killed. No action was taken by the government before 16 September 1918, when news came in of an attack involving a postman and carriers. The men deemed to be responsible were a gang of seven 'ringleaders' who had taken to the bush between Ilyangari and Mögiri (at the eastern foot of Bilinyan). They were led by gun-armed Lokidi [Lohide], the son of Minge.

One more patrol was sent led by Brock to arrest Lohide and his friends. When neither Lohide nor Minge were found in Ilyangari, a search was begun with the co-operation of the headmen of Ilyangari. Two men who were found hiding along the road were killed as suspects. Further searches seemed futile to Brock and Donne, the Inspector of Latuka District.

In his statement on the situation in Ilyangari, the latter advised the Governor in Mongalla not to take further action since the majority of the people were most eager to behave themselves and that the cause of the disturbance was a few young bloods, desiring to gain distinction by committing a murder.[10]

Donne's interpretation, which may have been suggested to him by the collaborating headmen who were eager to help restore the peace, was probably only half the truth. The ringleaders must have had the support of most of the junior generation; otherwise they could not have exposed the village to the risk of repeated government reprisals. It is worth noting that, in the end, Minge, unlike the Imatari King Ngalamitiho (Case 8.2), chose to side with his son and with the rebels and not with the main enemy to Ilyangari's independence at the time.

Inter-generational rivalry continues to play a role in contemporary local politics. The radicalism that is characteristic for a generation that has recently taken power may, to some extent, have been responsible for the acts of sabotage against the government when, between 1954 and 1956, northern Sudanese were gradually replaced by the British administrators in Torit (Case 15.3). It may also have been a base of recruitment for the rebel movement that developed among the Lotuho in the late 1950s. During the second wave of fighting, around 1965, the Lulubo and

---

10   'Letter from Donne to Brock 6/10/18, in: G. Donne 'Report on Punitive Expedition against Chief Minge at Ilyangari', Central Records Office, Khartoum (*INTEL* 91/57).

Lokoya men who enrolled in the Anyanya belonged, on the whole, to age-sets which had not reached *monyomiji*-hood yet.

In the election campaigns for the Regional Assemblies in Juba, young candidates generally mobilised old-time generational antagonism by presenting themselves as protagonists of a new generational style of rule. Support for the Sudan People's Liberation Army (SPLA) in the mid-1980s in some places on the east bank, had a decidedly generational character. The support offered to the rebel army in Lafon, mostly came from the younger age-sets that were particularly dissatisfied with the rule of the *Anyua* generation-set which was blamed for the persistent drought.

The SPLA commitment of the young men in Lafon had its repercussions in the arena of inter-communal rivalry. Following dualist logic it led, at least during the early stages of the war, to a pro-government stance among the communities that had been targets of attacks by the Pari youth. These victims (Lokiliri, Loronyo[11]) now demanded that the government supply them with arms.[12]

In the scope given to the expression of open defiance between young and old, the societies in the area seem surprisingly 'modern'. In assessing this democratic openness of the *monyomiji* system, we should realise that not all the power is in the hands of the *monyomiji*. The ownership of wealth and the control of matrimonial exchange continue to reside with the clan and lineage elders. The *monyomiji* play a role in regulating the rate of the bridewealth only. The rebellion of the *Tome* of Imatari is interesting because it shows that the idea of the possibility of a reversal of this dimension of the power of the elders was not completely absent. It would be wrong, however, to interpret the inter-generational tension as resulting from a spirit of revolt of the younger generation against the oppression of the *monyomiji* or of the elders. First of all, the elders as the controllers of wealth and marriage mostly belong to the retired generation. Among the Lotuho, they are the natural allies of the ascending

---

11   When the pole-shrine (*alore*) of Loronyo was replaced in 2011, slippers and eating-bowls were unearthed and put on display. These, according to the informants of the Japanese anthropologist Naoki Naito, who happened to attend the event, belonged to Pari fighters who had been killed during the hostilities referred to here. The find incidentally confirms the close association of the pole-shrine with the cult of war as I will argue in Chapter Nineteen. I thank Dr. Naoki Naito of Tokushima University in Japan for sharing the information and his photographs (on p. 422 and 434) with me

12   The interplay of anti-government sentiment and generational ambition is not restricted to Eastern Equatoria. According to the thesis of Githige submitted at the University of Nairobi, generational frustration was one of the main forces behind the Mau-Mau movement among the Gikuyu. The Maina generation which should normally have taken over from Mwangi in the late 1920s failed to do so. The *Itwika* ceremony was first postponed because of sectional rivalry. When it was about to be held some years later, it was hit by a ban issued by the colonial authorities who feared disturbances. The Mau-Mau, according to Githige, was therefore to a large extent a rebellion of the Maina generation against the Mwangi generation which had ruled for most of the colonial period, collaborating with the British and losing the lands of the Gikuyu (Githige, *thesis*, 1978:53ff).

generation. Among the Lulubo, they are, again, 'children', that is, they are supposed to be outside the arena in which the *monyomiji* compete for power.

The many similarities in the way inter-generational and inter-sectional relations are institutionalised prove that both are modelled on the same dualist principles. Like sectional and moiety relations, inter-generational exchanges are characterised by reciprocal challenges expressed in songs. When tension rises, generations have recourse to stick fights. Throughout the period which precedes the transfer of power, the balance of power is a day-to-day concern of the two generations. The ruling group tries to cling to it until eventually the balance tips in favour of the youngsters.

There is also a victimary aspect to this form of dualism: during the period of build-up of tension, each of the antagonistic generations is constantly trying to 'score' to the detriment of the other. The ruling *monyomiji* do so by exercising a reign of terror over the young men; catching them for any mistake they make and making them pay for it. The young men, in turn, criticise whatever weakness they can detect in the ruling *monyomiji* (e.g. Ngalamitiho's compromising attitude with the Dongotono, Minge's collaboration with the colonial authorities), and are not averse to cheating (the case of Limojo in Lokiliri).

Generational succession as a rite of passage

In the ceremony which marks the transfer of one generation to the next three stages can be distinguished:

- seclusion, either in the bush or in a specially built enclosure in the centre of the village;
- conquest of the village by way of mock-battles with the retiring generation; and
- sacrifice of one or more bulls and the joint consumption of these animals by the incoming and outgoing generations in accordance with the meat entitlements of their new status.

a) Seclusion of the new generation

Some time before the ceremony, from one day to a week prior to it, the junior generation enters a period of seclusion. Among the Lulubo, Lokoya, Lopit and Tenet the candidates leave the village for the bush or the mountains, places outside and opposed to ordered village life: the abode of wild animals, expelled evil and of the enemy.

In the village *Nefıra* in Lotuho, the candidates choose a central location inside the village. The 'liminality' of their social position finds expression in the fact that they spend the night outside, in front of the central drum house, rather than inside as the *monyomiji* do. They build an enclosure (*kuku*) in which a miniature drum house, sitting platforms and a pole-shrine (*alore*) are erected, screened off from the villagers by a fence. Here, they spend four days of seclusion, after which they go hunting and build a new watchtower (*olobele*) for their sections.

In Lulubo and Lokoya, the period away in the bush is believed to be full of danger. A young man should be prepared to die when going there with his age-mates. If one of the aspiring *monyomiji* does die, it is considered a good omen for his generation. His body will be left in the bush (like the bodies of victims of war).

In Edemo (Lulubo), the candidates are on high alert all night long because they should be prepared for an attack from the *monyomiji*. These are believed to want to raid the bulls which the aspiring age-sets have obtained for the sacrifice. If a man of the retiring generation should succeed in merely touching one of the bulls the junior generation would be disqualified from ruling.

During the four days of seclusion in Lotuho, the young men should abstain from all violence (including beating animals and using the spear against them), from washing, smoking and from sexual intercourse. The period of seclusion is concluded by the 'hunt against the *noholot*' which Pazzaglia translates as 'hunt against evil' (Novelli, 1970:642–3). The first animal killed during this hunt is believed to prevent and take away all evil that might befall the rule of the new generation. After the hunt, the young men are allowed to wash and start building the watchtowers (*olobele*).

While the Lulubo and Lokoya version of the ceremony forces the initiates to identify themselves with the violence associated with the bush, the Lotuho ceremony takes an opposite course: the new *monyomiji* in their *kuku* form a model community in which violence, sex and stimulants are banned. To conclude their seclusion they test their corporate effectiveness in the collective hunt of the *noholot*, the beast that embodies the evil forces that undermine new rulers. The first kill, whatever the animal, counts as *noholot*. The kill will offer protection against smallpox, believed to be a serious threat during the transfer of power. While the Lotuho *noholot* brings the scapegoat scenario to mind, the way the Lokoya and Lulubo understand their seclusion in the bush evokes the enemy scenario.

In the Lokoya/Lulubo area, the scenario of the period of seclusion conforms with the enemy scenario. In Edemo, the relationship between the old and the new generation is conceived of as that of raiders and potential victims of a raid. The belief that an accidental death of a member of the new generation is a good omen is particularly revealing of the essentially victimary character of generational antagonism: while intentional bloodshed between generations cannot be condoned for obvious reasons, accidental death for which nobody in particular can be blamed is welcomed. In the Lotuho version of the seclusion period, violence is forbidden and inter-generational antagonism is directed away in the chase of the *noholot* monster.

b) *The mock-conquest of the village*

In the ceremonies as conducted by the Lokoya, Lulubo and Lopit, the new generation returns to the village as an invading force straight from the bush, as if they were enemies. In Lopit, they enter the village at daybreak and storm the ceremonial ground, which is defended by several lines of retiring *monyomiji* armed with sticks and shields. The target of the attack is control of the drums.

Although the victory of the new generation over the old is anticipated, the fight is not mere 'play'. I was told that a junior generation that would not put up a proper fight would not get hold of the drums. However, my informant added, the *monyomiji* are usually defeated by the youngsters "because they have eaten and the boys are wild since they have not eaten in the forest". Once the new generation has gained the upper hand, the bulls are given to the retiring group and both generations join in a war-dance circling the pole-shrine, thus expressing the end of the era of confrontation.

Among the Tenet — who practise what I called a 'boy-scout variety' of the *monyomiji* system — the young men have to pay spears to the elders who block their way so that they may reach the ceremonial ground. Once the dance has started, any of the retiring elders may stop it if he wishes to, and demand a spear, an axe or any piece of iron from the young men. The bulls are given after a number of rounds of dancing *ler*.

Among the Lulubo, the ruling *monyomiji* are called to the forest by their successors to receive the bulls of *ruli*. After one is speared and its head is severed, there is a tug-of-war over the bull's head. If the candidate *monyomiji* are defeated, they will not receive the power and the current *monyomiji* will continue to rule. I was told that in Lokiliri, the generation-set of Kalang was defeated in the fight over the bull's head by their predecessors, Limojo. Limojo chased Kalang from the mountain back to the village and, according to the story, added three more years to their rule.

If the younger generation wins, they will receive a name from the retiring *monyomiji* and march towards the village ceremonial ground singing *nyakurumong* songs — the songs which are also sung when coming home from the battlefield.

Monyomiji *storming the ceremonial ground, Liria, New Year (Odhurak) 1986.*

We have a written participant's account of the *obongoro* of Langabu of 1956 by Severino Matti (1973:187–202) who was one of the members of the Cololong generation which took over from Amukonyen. Early in the morning of the day of *obongoro*, the candidate generation had gone hunting. When they returned, they found that the retiring generation had taken up positions around the rock at a fifteen-minute walk from the village, where hunters and warriors meet before re-entering the village. Although the combatants were fully armed, only the shafts of the spears were used. This is Matti's description of the fight:

8.5 *Mock battle during* obongoro *in Langabu* (Matti)

All are in a kneeling position; everyone yells behind his shield; throws a handful of soil in the air to frighten the young generation-set. The young initiands, in their turn, come in full force like a wounded buffalo, breaking tree branches and twigs … and make ululations as they march forward. But their opponents remain firm and keep their places until they are in a hand-to-hand fight. As they strike each other with shafts, sticks and shields, the noise produced by these weapons roars like a thunderstorm. For more than an hour, the vigorous fight goes on until the new initiands are either overpowered by the retiring group or just allowed to reach the rock after a long struggle. Often this mock-fight escalates into a real fight and has to be brought under control by the elders of the two respective generations. (*idem*:190*)*

When both generations sat down on the rock, Matti writes, there was the following exchange of words between the spokesman of the senior generation ('S') named Bendewuye and the spokesman of the junior group ('J') named Ojang. Spokesmen use the first-person singular when making statements on behalf of their age-set or generation:

8.6 *The vows of the new* monyomiji (Matti)

S: Ojang, are you prepared to guard the ancestral shrine?

J: Bendewuye, I am fully prepared!

S: Do you think you are old enough to care for me?

J: I am fully grown. I can carry you on my back!

S: Do you think you will protect my chickens, goats and children from harm?

J: I am sure to keep your chickens, goats and children from any harm!

S: Do you think you can keep all the ancestral rivers flowing?

J: They will not just be flowing. They will be flooding!

S: Do you think you will be able to satisfy the ancestral Masters of Rain, the Master of the Land and the Master of the Mountain?

J: I will, I will, I will! They will all be happy!

S: Will you not forget the old and the poor in time of famine?

J: They will not be forgotten. Instead, I would rather forget my own stomach!

Etc. (*idem*: 191–192).

After the speeches, the older generation handed the firesticks to the new one. The two groups marched towards the central ceremonial ground, making two stops on the way. At the first stop, the new *monyomiji* received the ceremonial feathers in the colours corresponding to their new *monyomiji* status. After this, further mock-fights took place between the senior age-sets of the two generations.

At the second stop, the ceremonial bull was killed. Its head was eaten by the junior generation — the first time for them to enjoy this *monyomiji* prerogative.

When they arrived at the ceremonial ground, a last show of resistance was offered by the retiring *monyomiji*. I give Matti's vivid description:

8.7 *The conquest of the pole-shrine* (Matti)

At the royal grounds, a more frightful picture presents itself as the new initiands come closer.... The hot-headed members of the retiring generation have surrounded the ceremonial ground to prevent the young group from reaching the pylon (the pole-shrine) where the royal drums are hung. On their knees, they form a strong barricade by juxtaposing their shields. Their bodies are covered with *orose* [the wild cucumber which with those who have killed enemies sprinkle their bodies on public occasions].... They remain unmoved as their successors march forward with youthful force. Coming closer to each other, each opposing generation strikes at the shields of the other group. For moments, shields roar like waterfalls, women and children scream, dogs bark, spear shafts fall to pieces, headgears lose their masters, bells fly off the ankles and above the heads hangs a brownish umbrella created by the rising dust. After a sweaty struggle the new initiands penetrate and force the retiring group to leave the pylon. As a senior member of the new generation-set touches the royal drum and begins to play even the rocks and trees seem to dance; everyone runs wild ... girls run after male youths; the soil chief's [Master of the Land] wives empty baskets and baskets of beer flour on the heads of the drummers, on the pylon and on the drums. Widows leave the graves of their beloved ones and join the people; the old and the sick nod their heads in dark rooms; careless women are left naked by their flying off aprons as they skip up (*sic*); and the ankle bangles of the initiands' wives tear through the village like machine guns. Indeed this is the colour, the air and the spirit of Lokoya initiation! (*idem*:198–199).

This enthusiastic description by an initiate highlights the atmosphere of collective effervescence in which all forms of social antagonism and opposition merge into an undifferentiated, shared presence of all members of the community. In this excitement, a new era and a new order is born.

In Lotuho, mock-battles take place at all three levels of the *Nefira* section, village and kingdom. The newly initiated men, now *monyomiji olojingat*, enact fights against the enemy alternatingly playing the role of the attacking and the defending party. When the enemy has been beaten, they march to the ceremonial ground singing war songs and dancing the war dance (*etolu*) around the central pole-shrine. This dance that concludes the initiation is forcefully interrupted by the *monyomiji efirat*. The *olojingat* are chased away from the ceremonial ground with the message that they still have a long way to go before they are *efirat*.

At the *Nefira* presided over by the king, there is a mock-battle between *efirat*, on one side, and *olojingat*, on the other, from which the *olojingat* finally emerge victorious. This battle is fought with sticks and shields the day before the lighting of the new fire. The fight is said to be very fierce, since the younger generation is expected to take revenge for all the unfair treatment they have undergone during their minority as *olojingat*. Injuries are common and in the past, so people say, it was by no means rare if a few men were killed. In Tirangore, a second mock-battle takes place at the return of the new *monyomiji* from the *Nefira* at Loguruny prior to their first formal assembly in the central square of the village. The dualist character of these mock-battles needs no further argumentation.

Because of the occasional casualties, the colonial government officially discouraged the practice of mock-battles (Nalder, 1937:101). The way the *Nefira* of Loudo was held in 1932, of which we have a record written by Arber, the Assistant District-Commissioner in Torit at the time (*idem*:101), was a new adaptation that took into account the wish of the colonial authorities to reduce the violence in the conduct of the ceremonies: The first mock-battle was replaced by a dance during which the new and the retiring *monyomiji* first danced opposite one another in the central ceremonial ground of Loudo and after some time mingled into a single circle. The second mock-battle, staging the conquest of the pole-shrines and of the ceremonial grounds of the different sections, was replaced by a footrace between the two generations from the central to the sectional ceremonial grounds. Since the elders lagged behind because of their age, the new generation could take control of the public utilities of their section without any violence. The substitution of the mock-battle by a dance in opposite lines which subsequently fuses into a circle is an unexpected confirmation of the interpretation of this choreographic sequence as a rendering of the transformation of dualist opposition into centralist unity (see Ch. 7, p.176).

c)   *Reconciliatory sacrifice*

The sacrifice of one or more bulls marks the beginning of the new era. The provision of bulls is considered a precondition for access to *monyomiji*-hood, and among the Lulubo and Lokoya who do not have cattle, it has become a test of the co-operative spirit of the new generation.[13] Money is collected from all the members of the young generation, including from those who live in Juba and Khartoum to buy the bulls in the cattle market of Juba. In Lopit the young men obtain the necessary bulls by working in the fields of *Big Men* while among the Tenet, a bull is borrowed from the outgoing generation.[14]

The participants ascribe three major meanings to the sacrifice. First of all, the sacrifice marks the end of the period of conflict and opens the way for a new era of

13   In the *Nefira* of 1932 in Loudo which is also in a tsetse-infested area a he-goat was sacrificed (Nalder 1937:101).

14   From Spagnolo's notes, it would appear that among the Bari, the bull required for access to the status of *teton* was provided by a *Big Man* or by the Rainmaker. The son of the person providing the bull would so become the leader of his age-set (see also note 8.1).

peaceful coexistence between the generations. The new hierarchy which replaces the antagonism finds expression in a new distribution of the age-sets over the different meat-groups. From now on, the retired generation will receive the portion meant for the elders while the new *monyomiji* will, for the first, time consume the parts they are now entitled to, especially the head, which plays an important symbolic role.

Secondly, organising the sacrifice, providing the bulls and controlling the proceedings are considered a demonstration of the social competence of the new *monyomiji*. For the first time, they act as masters of ceremonies on the level of the village and for the first time they offer a sacrificial meal to the elders, thus reversing the hitherto existing order.

Lastly, the bulls are also considered a compensatory gift for the loss of power to the retiring elders, whose blessings for the new era are considered essential. In Lopit, the number of bulls paid in compensation varies with the number of age-sets of retired elders and the comparative importance of the transfer of power. Six bulls have to be provided by an *efirat* generation; four bulls are required in case of *owatat*. The last two age-sets who join the *monyomiji* do not have to provide any bulls at all. In the reconciliatory sacrifice that marks the transfer of power, the Lopit just kill a goat.

In Edemo (Lulubo), in 1975, the retiring *monyomiji* (called Kwara) of the two moieties, Oremi and Makaro, received one bull each. The bulls were given cross-wise. The bull provided by the candidate *monyomiji*, named Aringa, went to the Kwara of Oremi and the bull of the Aringa of Makaro was given to the Kwara of Oremi. In this way, both sectional and generational divisions were bridged in a sacrificial transaction. The bulls were speared by the spokesmen of the Aringa generation and prepared by the cook of Aringa. The ceremonial acceptance by Kwara of the meat from their juniors was considered to be the moment of transfer of power. The first portion — the left front leg and the hump — was given to the retiring group and was shared by everyone present without distinction of generation. The other parts were distributed according to age — the head being eaten by Aringa. After finishing the meal, Kwara smeared the rumen of the animals on the left side of the bodies of Aringa as a blessing. In concluding the ceremony, both generations knelt and approached each other in two opposite lines. They tore off some grass, and when both lines were near enough they threw it at one another, together with dust, as a sign of reconciliation. As they took their leave, the Kwara took the heads of Aringa in their hands and spat on them by way of blessing.

In Liria, each of the extant generations has to be provided with its bull, so that the total number of bulls is usually four (one each for two retired generations, one for the retiring one and one for the generation taking power).

The role of the sacrificial bull as a symbol of the positive bond between the generations and as the carrier of the blessing (or curse) of the retiring generation is particularly marked in the ceremony performed by the Pari. Before the bull is killed, it is rubbed with grain, beans and sesame seeds by the king. These crops represent the blessings expected from the new rulers. After the bull is killed, its mouth is opened wide. Each member of the retiring generation[15] comes near and spits into the mouth of the bull to convey his blessing to the next rulers who will eat the head afterwards. Before spitting, each man has to open his own mouth wide enough to show the new *monyomiji* that it does not contain any wild fruits — the latter symbolising a period of crop failure, during which the village has to rely on foraging for its subsistence. If the bull's mouth were to contain any such fruits, the rule of the new generation might be beset with drought and other calamities. After this, the head is severed, taken outside the village and eaten by the new generation.

The significance of the sacrificial animal as an omen of the new rulers' success also determines the choice of colour of the animal (black signifying rain), and the mode of killing. The Lokoya and Lulubo spear the bull "like a wild animal" as one informant put it. The new Lotuho *monyomiji* at the *Nefira* of the kingdom strangle and suffocate the bull. The animal is laid out in an east (tail) west (head) direction, the legs pointing southward, thus representing the direction of the Lotuho migration into the territory they occupy at present. The bloodless and noiseless mode of killing practised by the Lotuho emphasises the non-violent character of communal co-existence. No blood is shed in the act of killing; the candidate *monyomiji* push in unison to accomplish the bull's end. In the *Nefira* of Hoding in 1955, the bull was killed under the joint weight of the new *monyomiji* of Lobira, Buruny and Iloli. They collectively sat on it until it died after an agony lasting from 4.45 to 6.10 A.M. The position of the bull during this action symbolised the whole extent of the kingdom.[16] After the bull had died, the king slit its stomach and threw the rumen into the faces of the new generation.

The sacrifice of the bull of generational reconciliation corresponds in all respects to the function of sacrifice as outlined in the theory of Girard: to redirect social tension and violence towards a victim. The bull which is killed — with or without shedding its blood — is the prefiguration of the order of the new era: it should carry the spittle — a rainy and peaceful element[17] — of the elders. It should be black as rain clouds; and it should face west, the direction of the enemy-victims.[18] The way it is consumed marks the new ranking of age-sets and generations.

Conclusion

The sequence — seclusion, mock-conquest and sacrificial reconciliation — is common to the ceremony of the handing over of generational power in all societies of our area of study. The *Nefira* of the Lotuho stands out by its complexity. Its protocol incorporates a number of ritual themes that in the more decentralised societies of the east bank are

---

15 To bless a *wic* generation only the former *wic* perform the spitting ritual. For *tengo* both the retiring *wic* and the former *tengo* spit.

16 Eye-witness account of E.K. Mulla, Executive Officer Torit Rural Council, 'A Report on the *Nefira* of 1955', Council Monthly Diaries, May 1955; Southern Records Office, File TRC/24.B.1. I was told by one of the men who had been initiated that day that all *monyomiji* participated in the killing.

17 See the fundamental cosmological oppositions listed in Table.

18 See Ch. 7, p. 177–9.

the concern of separate calendrical festivals: the purification of the community as a whole, the making of new fire and the promotion of human fertility in the mountain ritual. The political significance of this concentration of several rituals in a single, nation-wide ceremony presided over by the king will be discussed in Chapter Thirteen.

In this chapter, we demonstrated the fundamental role of dualism in structuring the relationship between the generations. There is an unmistakeable homology with territorial organisation, not only in the two-fold division of society during the period preceding the ceremony of power transfer, but also in the two-fold sub-divisions of the generations. The ideal form of territorial organisation in the area seems to have been that of a three-tiered, nested polarity, exactly homologous to that of the age-class organisation.[19] The social organisation of the Logir, as an informant described it to me: two divisions led by a Rainmaker/King consisting of four villages each, might be exemplary in that respect. The Lotuho, who stand out from the societies surrounding them by only possessing a limited even number of clans (four or six depending on the classification of two units as sub-clans), seem to have also subjected the overall organisation of descent-groups to a dualistic restructuring.

However logical and systematic these dualist structures may look from the outside, I hope it has become clear that the structuring force at work is a polarising mimetic dynamic, feeding into the down-to earth need to maintain group consensus and not from the binary constraints of the operation of the human mind.

Explaining the antagonistic dimension of age-organisation by its underlying dualism is more economical and less involved than Spencer's recourse to the concept of 'ritual rebellion' in his study of the age-organisation of the Maasai (Spencer, 1988), who are the closest linguistic relatives of the Lotuho speakers. Spencer admits having difficulties in accommodating his data to Gluckman's concept because the rebelliousness of the Maasai *moran* lasts for years (*Idem*: 274) and is, according to Spencer, closer to a 'true' rebellion than Gluckman's blueprint (*Idem*: 278). Although Spencer characterises the antagonisms between the *moran* and the elders as a 'balance of power' which is continually being redefined by the bullying of the elders and the acts of insurgency of the *moran* (*Idem*: 273–4), he accounts for the uncompromising attitude of the elders by introducing the concept of 'ritual of counter-rebellion' (*Idem*: 148) while the solidarity and selflessness of life in the *manyata* (warrior-village) are interpreted with reference to the Freudian pact of peers (*Idem*: 272). The model of dualism would quite obviously provide a better tool to grasp, not only the political, ritual, and theatrical aspects of Maasai age-antagonism, but also the close consensus and the taste for heroism of the *moran*.

---

19   The Lotuho word *miji* is used for the village as a territorial unit, as well as for the local ruling *monyomiji*-set as an age-based corporate group.

PART III

Centralism:
The King as Aggressor of the People

The tall structure on the right is the royal palace, on the left an assembly point of the monyomiji
— well positioned to monitor the comings and goings of the royals, Hiyala, 1981.

"Their one idea was power."
Baker on the Tirangore royal family (1866, Vol. I: 241).

Mount Hoding, the ritual centre of the original Lotuho kingdom of Imatari and — after Imatari fell apart — of the Mayya kingdom. In one of its caves the bones of the descendants of Mayya are kept. In another cave Queen Nyadinga committed adultery with the brothers of king Irwangi, the act that eventually led to the split of the kingdom (Case12.5). Hoding is also the place where the king inaugurates the rule of a new generation of monyomiji *who celebrate their promotion to power by a galloping dance around the mountain.*

Mount Loguruny, the ritual centre of the Hujang dynasty. On top of the mountain is the shrine where the bones of the descendants of Hujang are kept (cf. the photos on p.48 and p.342).

9

The King as Enemy of his People

The core of this chapter is that dualism and centralism are not opposed principles of political organisation deriving from heterogeneous sources, as is often assumed in studies on the origin of the state. Both are transformations of the same fundamental mechanism by which social consensus is achieved. In developed states, the gap between centralist and dualist modes of political organisation has grown very wide. In the societies we are now looking at, the fundamental similarity in the operation of both principles is still manifest, or, at any rate, it was before their political systems were affected by incorporation in colonial states.

In the two previous chapters, I have argued that the basic corporate groups within the political system — sections, villages, generations — maintain and reproduce their identity as groups by continuously engaging in power contests with groups of the same structural order. We shall now see that the relationship between the king and people is reproduced in the same way.

The antagonism between king and people

The oppositional character of the relationship between the ruler and the ruled permeates most levels of their interaction. The most important and most conspicuous arena where king and people exchange acts of aggression is cosmological. Kings are believed to punish disrespectful subjects with drought and other ill fortune; while the people blame natural disasters and disorders on their king. Alternatively, peaceful relations between the king and the people are believed to result in good rains, abundant harvests, the absence of diseases — all of this attributed to the king. The people attest to peace in demonstrations of respect: obedience, gifts of food, livestock, game animals and women.

The king's discontent is believed to be aroused by any deed that shows a lack of respect, either to him personally or to members of his family, clan or following. If he feels neglected, not respected, or overlooked, he will burst out in anger and turn against his people, using his power over the elements. In fact, disaster follows upon acts of disrespect to the king even if they escaped his notice. One of the principal duties of the *monyomiji*, therefore, is to make sure that the Rainmaker, and the other Masters of Disaster, have no reasons to complain. Informants, when interviewed about the rights and duties of the *monyomiji*, invariably mention the supervision of the relations between the community and the king as one of the main responsibilities. The *monyomiji* should identify the causes of royal grudges and make the necessary arrangements to straighten things out by issuing orders to pay compensation, by demanding a sacrifice or the return of stolen goods — whatever course of action may be applicable. If the accused refuses to co-operate, the *monyomiji* will raid his house and take by force what is required.

If repeated attempts by the *monyomiji* to cool the king's anger fail — the success of these attempts is measured by the return of cosmic order — a more confrontationist course of action is adopted with regards to what is now defined as the king's stubbornness. Threats are uttered and the king is pressed to stop his obstruction, to release the rain. If the king remains insensitive to this, he may ultimately be killed.

Drought, disease, barrenness, crop failure, locust plagues, swarms of grain eating birds and insects and other major and minor disasters are the issues in which the antagonistic relationship between king and the people comes to expression. Both the king (and other Masters of Disaster) and the people take initiatives in this game of exchange of accusations and demands for compensation for suffered harm. One day, we see the *monyomiji* pointing their accusing finger at the king, the next day, it is the king's turn to take the community to task for negligence in the running of their affairs or in the respect due to him.

The attitude of Lomoro, King of Tirangore, at the turn of the twentieth century, provides a typical example of this game of reciprocal accusations. A colonial officer of the Uganda Protectorate wrote the following account of his meeting with him:

9.1 *King Lomoro's bluff* (Yunis)

I found Limoro [Lomoro], the big chief at Logguren [Loguruny] and I asked him why he was not residing at Tarangoli [Tirangore], his capital and usual abode. He gravely informed me that he had left Tarangoli to punish his people there who had disobeyed his orders. "And now," said he, "I will not give any rain until they all come here and beg for it, and then perhaps I shall return to Tarangoli and let the rain fall" (Yunis, 1905:228/9).

Informants from the Tirangore royal family whom I interviewed on this episode assured me that Lomoro had fled Tirangore for fear of his life after the *monyomiji* had accused him of drought.[1] So, we see the king and the people involved in a game of reciprocal acts of aggression and bluffing in which threats of regicide by the people are matched by royal threats of genocide by means of drought.

The antagonism between king and people was not limited to the concern about rain. It encompassed all interactions in which respect for the king was at stake. Any act which was considered to diminish this respect might become the pretext for a vengeful reaction. The king kept an eye on his subjects' behaviour and was permanently on the alert for signs of lessened regard, not unlike the way the movements of the enemy are followed for signals of renewed hostility.

The king's revenge was normally believed to manifest itself as disaster. But at certain occasions, his reactions could be very direct, bypassing the cosmological arena, as the following case history from 1899, again featuring Lotuho King Lomoro, demonstrates. The event was reported by the American explorer, Donaldson-Smith, who was greatly

---

1   This version of the course of events is confirmed by Father Muratori's account (1947:108).

impressed by the reception given to him by the king. He had offered the king his own leopardine blanket in which the king had shown a special interest:

9.2 *King Lomoro's anger* (Donaldson-Smith)

I am sure he has never owned anything which pleases him more than this rug, which resembles the skin of some marvellous species of the cat family. Not only did the king at once send for an escort and guides for us, but he insisted on having a large tusk brought to me from his village....This man [the person who had been sent for the tusk] had made a mistake, and instead of bringing the tusk the king had ordered, he arrived at midnight with two ridiculously small cow tusks. Amara [Lomoro] was so enraged that, picking up one of the latter he began beating the wretched messenger in a terrible manner. The smiling chief had suddenly turned into such a ferocious beast that when I endeavoured to prevent his killing his subject, he at first turned at me a pair of eyes so full of passion that I feared he might deal his next blow at me, but I pretended that I had only interrupted him to praise the two small tusks with which "I would be delighted", etc. and thus managed to quiet him. The unconscious body of his victim was almost hurled out of camp, and others sent to bring the proper tusk, which did not arrive till two o'clock in the morning (Donaldson-Smith, 1900:621).

Similar violent behaviour was reported of the Bari King Logunu in 1841 during his reception of the Egyptian exploratory expedition. When, after repeated requests, the Bari crowd that had followed the king on his visit to the ships of the explorers refused to collect the firewood demanded for the travellers, Logunu urged the Egyptians to shoot into the crowd. Against protestations that this would mean death for some of his subjects, the king insisted that they should shoot, "even if some would be left dead" (Werne, 1848:297).

The overt arbitrariness in the operation of royal authority was a source of puzzlement for the liberal Werne, who was looking for traces of the 'noble savage' among the Bari. When they entered Bariland, the soldiers of the expedition had arbitrarily killed an estimated twelve or thirteen people by shooting into a crowd from a distance of twenty-five metres. Many others, according to Werne, were wounded (1845:276–7). The king uttered no word of protest about the massacre. On the contrary, he condoned it and encouraged the Egyptians to kill even more people "since they always started to wage war on the people of the east bank" (*Idem*: 323).

When Werne observed that cattle were daily being driven across from one bank of the river to the other, he started to doubt Logunu's statement about the existence of hostility between the people on opposite banks of the river. He investigated the matter and soon found out that Logunu's quarrel with the west bankers had nothing to do with rivalry between his people. Its main cause was the fact that for two years, Logunu had not received tribute from the west bank.

Baker expressed similar puzzlement about the lightheartedness with which the Lotuho kings engaged in raids against subject villages which they consider rebellious:

9.3 *Prince Adang's raids on his subjects* (Baker)

On one occasion, Adda [Adang], one of the chiefs, came to ask me to join him in attacking a village to procure molotes [iron hoes used in bridewealth]; he said, "Come along with me, bring your men and guns, and we will attack a village near here, and take their molotes and cattle; you keep the cattle, and I will have the molotes." I asked him whether the village was in enemy's country. "Oh no!" he replied, "it is close here; but the people are rather rebellious, and it will do them good to kill a few, and to take their molotes. If you are afraid, never mind, I will ask the Turks to do it." Thus forbearance on my part was supposed to be caused by weakness, and it was difficult to persuade them that it originated in a feeling of justice. This Adda most coolly proposed that we should plunder one of his villages that was rather too 'liberal' in its views (Baker, 1866, Vol. I: 152).

The antagonism between the ruler and the ruled is expressed quite openly. The balance of power between the ruler and the ruled is maintained by reciprocal acts of violence, not unlike the power balance that exists between opposed social sections.

Accordingly, acts of 'insubordination' by the people were a common occurrence, and they did not escape the attention of the first travellers. In addition to his account of the refusal to collect firewood for Logunu and the state of rebellion among the west bank Bari, Werne mentions that on two occasions during the twelve days spent among the Bari, he was taken into the confidence of chieftains who spoke with contempt about the ruling king (1848:283, 299).

In 1851, the Austrian missionary, Don Angelo Vinco, delivered a speech during a meeting in Bilinyan at which King Subek was asked to account for not having produced rain within the time of the ultimatum set by the elders. The argument of Vinco's sermon focused on the thesis that rain was not given by the king in exchange for tribute but by God in exchange for a peaceful disposition. The speech meant a turning point in Vinco's acceptance by the Bari. Vinco attributed its success to its anti-royalist purport:

> My speech was particularly welcomed by the people who above all admired me for having thus spoken before Jubek [Subek] himself, as each year they had to hand over many oxen to him in his capacity as Rainmaker (1974:83).

Later, historical evidence confirms that the relationship between the Bari king and his people had at times an unambiguously exploitative character. During the drought of 1909, which occasioned the death of Wani Matat, King Bambu of Bilinyan reportedly terrorised his subjects with repeated and increasing demands for goats, sheep and cows.[2] Today, for the elderly Bari who still know the meaning of the now obsolete word *kör* (the class of the people controlling the rain), the word carries a connotation of disregard for the interests of the people. One informant defined it as "the class of

---

2   Central Records Office, Khartoum, Mongalla Intelligence Report, September 1909, *INTEL* 6/5/18.

those who spoil the land, those who cause drought to get their rights" and related it to the Bari verb *kör* (to spoil, to contaminate).[3]

Although the expression of negative attitudes is normally avoided in the king's presence, the negative side of the relationship is not repressed or mystified. In the Bari conception of kingship, a king, to be successful, should not only be admired but also *hated*. When the Bari talk about Pitia Lugör, their cherished 'national' symbol during the Condominium period, they acknowledge that he was truly *hated*.

The same negative image is present in the mourning songs recorded by Beaton at the funeral of Chief Yokwe Köri of Koggi[4] in 1931. Amidst the stanzas expressing the grief and the admiration of the survivors there is also a stanza reading as follows:

> Laugh and be merry, ye people,
> All of you laugh and rejoice,
> Rescue has come for the Scourger is dead
> (Beaton, 1932:90).

Beaton feels it is necessary to give an explanation for this odd stanza, and adds:

> This song may represent the thoughts of Yokwe's enemies, or may be a bitter railing against death, that could not distinguish between a Yokwe and a Scourger (*idem*, p.91).

The theory of kingship defended here offers a more direct interpretation: the 'Scourger' is Yokwe as seen by his own people in his role as antagonist, as King of Disaster.

Alliances of kings against their people

Rebellion against the king could be dangerous, not only because of the disasters the king might send, but also because of the possibility — imagined or real — that he might ally himself with the enemy against his own people. In the previous chapter, I discussed the alliance between King Ngalamitiho and the Toposa which led to Imatari's destruction. As a second example of an alliance between a king and the enemy, I relate one of the legends of the fall of Segele, Imatari's principal rival.

9.4 *The fall of Segele* (Lotuho oral history, various sources)[5]

Queen Mulak of Segele had two sons who were still *aduri horwon* (uninitiated juniors), both of whom were killed by the *monyomiji*. The second prince was killed in the following way: one day, the *monyomiji* ordered the young men to make the

---

3   This popular etymology is linguistically not plausible. *Kör* in Bari must be derived from the same Nilotic root as the Acholi word *ker* and the Shilluk *kwer* meaning 'pertaining to kingship'.

4   Yokwe Köri is the son of chieftain Köri who broke his pact with Lugör to deprive their respective subjects of rain (Case 9.5 below) and 'who had Kiri' one of the Egyptian government stations, named after him.

5   There are two more versions of the story of the fall of Segele. I thank Andreas Grüb for providing me with the version that is reproduced in the main text. The second version from Lilley and Arber (in Nalder 1937:84–86) runs as follows: "Two grandsons of Nyangeri, the founder of the dynasty that conquered the Horiok kingdom of Longulu, were kings of Longulu and Segele, respectively. One day, the brother who was king of Segele sent his brother in Longulu, named

necessary preparations for a meal and beer drinking. One of the princes who was of giant stature instigated his age-mates to refuse the menial tasks imposed upon them and to rebel against the *monyomiji*. During a joint hunt the *monyomiji* decided to take revenge on the prince. When he noticed the intentions of the *monyomiji*, the prince fled into a high tree at the edge of the river. The *monyomiji* then cut the tree and let the prince drown when the tree fell.[6] At the return of the hunt, the women of Segele, including the queen, went to meet the men at the entrance to the village to offer them beer. When Queen Mulak noted that her son was not among the group, the *monyomiji* told her to wait: "He is behind, he will soon arrive." When it became dark, a man came up to the queen telling her: "You had better go home. Your son is dead."

The queen was deeply aggrieved about the loss of her son, who was the second to meet his death at the hands of the *monyomiji*, and sought revenge. She first went to Longulu for help. The *monyomiji* of Longulu replied: "We are too few to fight Segele. You could go to Imatari." Imatari was of comparable size to Segele and its arch-rival. Queen Mulak entered Imatari, going straight to the *alore* [pole-shrine] singing mourning songs for her sons. She was taken to King Ngalamitiho and told him: "Segele has killed my sons. I have no sons left. Please, help me to destroy Segele as a punishment." The following morning, the war drum was sounded and all of *Ohonyemorok*, the ruling generation at that time, assembled. When Mulak saw the *Ohonyemorok*, she said that their number was too small. Then Ngalamitiho ordered the junior generation, the later *Miriyang*, to be added to the fighting force.

Nolong, a gift of poisoned tobacco. Longulu took a terrible revenge inviting Imatari to join in the destruction of Segele. This meant the end of Segele's glory.

A third version was recorded by Father A. Pazzaglia ('Omuk eyabita to hobwok Otuho', p. 39-41, Comboni Archive A/126/10): King Atafat of Longulu, who also controlled Loronyo, and Ngalamitiho, the king of Imatari, entered a magical competition over the control of the River Hos. Ngalamitiho speared the water, which became dirty and full of worms. Atafat could not change the condition of the water and had to call for Ngalamitiho to spear it clean again. Ngalamitiho took *Asalak*, the spear brought by his grandfather, Imuhunyi, from Bari, speared the water and all the worms disappeared. In this way, he proved his ownership of the water and Atafat and his people were obliged to move to the west side of the river. Ngalamitiho, who was not satisfied with this arrangement yet, ordered Labang, his son with Iteng, a Longulu princess, to go to his grandmother, also named Iteng, to set fire to Longulu. After staying with the queen of Longulu for a few days, Labang did as he was told. While leaving the palace, he set fire to its roof. The *monyomiji* ran after Labang, killed him and returned the body to the queen. In revenge, the queen called a drought over Imatari which lasted for two years and which caused many Lotuho to flee to Segele, where they survived on fishing and hunting. When the drought was over, Ngalamitiho sent his deputy to Segele to call his subjects back. When they refused, he asked his deputy to bring a fish from Segele. He took *Asalak*, cut the fish in two and said: "Whoever refuses to return to Imatari, will die of dysentery!" When this proved not enough, Ngalamitiho allied himself with Longulu and destroyed Segele." (Constantine Bartel translated this story for me from Lotuho into English).

6   The princes had provoked the anger of the *monyomiji* by their arrogance. Yet, once outside the village, the *monyomiji* carried the responsibility for the safety of the princes. So, according to a Lotuho informant, the queen's revenge was justified.

Ngalamitiho sent Mulak back with an escort promising to come with the bigger force after four days.

In the early morning of the fourth day, the *monyomiji* of Imatari sealed all gates of Segele except one. After letting her own relatives escape through the open gate, the queen addressed the *monyomiji*: "Those who killed my sons will have to face the consequences today." Segele was burnt and many people were killed. Queen Mulak thanked Imatari saying: "Now the death of my son is bearable. With so many men dead as against two princes, there is no reason for regret.

Segele never recovered from the destruction and was not rebuilt.[7]

Whatever the core of historical truth of this story, it clearly shows that the relationship between king and people is conceived in terms of an equilibrium of power which is repeatedly tested in open confrontations. All works well as long as the test of power takes place on the cosmological level of rain and drought. When the power contest takes a military character, severe imbalance between the two antagonists may result. The king is either too weak and becomes a mere scapegoat, or he turns out to be too strong and destroys his people.

His strength mainly consists in his ability to create alliances with fellow kings independently of his people. When the king chooses the side of the enemy, the centralist equilibrium is broken and the continued existence of the polity is in danger. The story of the fall of Segele — and also that of Imatari, recorded in the previous chapter — is more than merely an account of royal treachery. It demonstrates a major weakness of centralism when no monopoly on the use of physical force has been established and the maintenance of power depends on open trials of strength between king and people.

The following case story from southern Bari, which was recorded by Beaton, shows a reverse plot. Here, we have two kings who have agreed to join hands in teaching their peoples a lesson. One of them, at the last moment, takes the side of his people and betrays his royal ally.

9.5 *The secession of Koggi* (Beaton)[8]

Lugör [the king of Shindiru during the latter half of the nineteenth century] ... viewing with alarm the rapid increase of manpower at this centre [Koggi] went

---

7   Segele's fame outlasted its fall. On a map drawn in 1898 'Suguerlè' is still marked as an existing location east of Kurla Hill. (Map of Uganda, reproduced at Intelligence Division, War Office, from a map compiled by the Lt Col J.R.I. Macdonald, assisted by Maj. H.H. Austin and Lieut. R.T. Bright, from Surveys during the Macdonald expedition, 1897–1898 in: Brevet Major E.M. Woodward, 1902).

8   The historical core of this story may be formed by the establishment of the government station of Köri (spelled 'Kiri' in the colonial documents) by General Gordon in 1876 as a result of which Köri's village suddenly outflanked the old centre of Shindiru. Köri being Lugör's sister's son, the story is also an example of the kind of conspiracies mother's brothers and sister's sons engage in. Their plan, unsuccessful in this case, was clearly at odds with the interests of their communities. On the relationship between mother's brothers and sister's sons, see also Ch. 7, p. 167. In the version told by an informant from Koggi, Lugör's anger had been aroused because

to Köri, son of Sukiri [and more importantly Lugör's sister's son], the Chief of Koggi, with the suggestion that they, as Rain Chiefs, should cause a year's famine, in order to reduce the number of people inhabiting the land. Lugör naively hoping that the famine would harm his neighbour more than himself withheld the rain. He sent a spy to Köri's country to see if he was keeping his part of the pact. Rain had fallen and men were busy hoeing, but the spy was bribed to report that there was not even enough water to drink. The crops grew and Köri fell to reaping. A second spy sent by Lugör was bribed to report death and famine. The grain was gathered and safely stored when the third spy arrived. He was given a basket of grain with these words: "Take this to Lugör and tell him our granaries are full."

The story ends in the refusal of Koggi to continue performing the *kuruket* (the day of collective agricultural work for the king) for Lugör which was tantamount to a unilateral declaration of independence of Koggi. In the subsequent war, Lugör suffered a serious defeat which resulted in the severing of all ties between mother's brother and sister's son. The outcome of the power contest was the secession of Koggi.

The rain drama of Lowe (June 1981)[9]

The following case is the description of the conflictual relationship between a Rainmaker and the community receiving rain from him over a period of more than twenty years. It shows the operation of central power in a situation when the power balance between the Rainmaker and his people is maintained by confrontations on the cosmological level: as a series of struggles over rain and drought. In this case, the struggle ends with the killing of the Rainmaker. In many similar cases, the antagonism does not escalate to that extent. However, the killing of the Rainmaker as an ultimate step is never completely absent from the minds of the people who are dissatisfied with his performance. When I asked individuals who had taken part in the killing why they had done so, the answer invariably was: "He is killing us, so, why should we not kill him?" which, of course, is the basic postulate of dualism. The killing occurred on 17 June 1981 in Iyata, one of the sections of Lowe in Lokoya. My information on the events is based on interviews with participants in the drama, including the main protagonist, Aristo [a fictitious name], and on the report made on the case by the Torit police:

---

other men had slept with his wives (Beaton, 'Brief History of Kogi', p. 2, in: 'Historical Notes on Bari Chieftainships' *typescript*, Southern Records Office, Juba).

9　I collected the details of this case of simultaneous regicide and parricide during a visit to Lowe in August 1982. I later interviewed people who had been directly involved in the action. The police in Torit allowed me to read the reports based on the interrogations of the arrested *monyomiji*. The prison's officer in Torit kindly allowed me to interview the main protagonist in the drama, who is named Aristo for the purposes of this account. I thank Eluzai Mogga for his assistance at this stage of the investigation. Plans to pay another visit to Lowe were cancelled on two occasions because of the unpredictable security situation in the area. However, I had the opportunity to interview several persons from Lowe in Juba during the years after the murder.

9.6 *Regicide in Lowe, June 1981* (case history)

Rodrigo Loholiyang came from a family whose duty and privilege it was to provide one of the four *oihejek* (assistant-Rainmakers) of the king of Lowe. During the annual rainmaking ceremony, he pulled a ring made of the rain creeper from the central shrine of Lowe to the four sections of Omirai, the southern moiety of Lowe. Although, in theory, assistants are subordinate to the king, they are frequently believed to have rain powers and rain medicine of their own. because of their close association with rainmaking activities.

After completing primary school, Rodrigo spent some time in the Technical Training College in Torit but did not finish the training. Since he was one of the most educated villagers, he became a teacher in the 'bush school' for a while. His elder brother who also completed primary school became a catechist, a calling which the mission considered incompatible with that of Rainmaker. So, the rain responsibility went to Rodrigo, the younger brother.

Rodrigo is described as a man of huge stature, short-tempered, often provoking fights from which he usually emerged as the winner. He belonged to the generation of Thimomonye, 'those who ignore their fathers', which took over power in 1959 and which prided itself on being 'extremists'. During the first years in rain office, he impressed the *monyomiji* with his powers. He even enticed one section away from a rival *oihejek* so that he became the *de facto* Rainmaker of the moiety of Omirai. The *monyomiji* started to call him *ohobu* (Rainmaker/king), thereby challenging the authority of Ameri, the king who resided in a section of the opposite moiety.

But Rodrigo's relationship with the *monyomiji* was always tense. Rodrigo repeatedly tried to step up his demands for tangible signs of respect from the *monyomiji*. One day, he demanded the performance of *amopwa*, the customary day of cultivation for the Rainmaker, a privilege to which *oihejek* were normally not entitled. When the *monyomiji* refused, he demonstratively sold his rain medicine to Loselik, the king of Liria, for thirty piastres. When a period of drought followed, the *monyomiji* went to Liria to buy the medicine back from King Loselik. They performed the *amopwa* and ordered Rodrigo to perform the customary rain rituals.

During the civil war, there was a series of conflicts between Rodrigo and the Anyanya. More than once, Rodrigo was given a beating by the rebels. In this context, one informant said that nobody had been able to cut Rodrigo Loholiyang down to size — neither the *monyomiji* nor the Anyanya. After Thimomonye were retired in 1974, the *rapport* between the *monyomiji* and Rodrigo deteriorated even more. There were successive years of poor rain and when the *monyomiji* asked Rodrigo to do something about it, he stubbornly reminded them of their duties towards him, again stepping up his demands.

Rodrigo's private life had been very unfortunate. Six of his children had died and in 1980, his last surviving son was killed in a road accident under suspect circumstances. This son had been trained to use his rain medicine and was considered his successor. Rodrigo's misfortune was attributed to the vengeance of the *monyomiji*. Not long before the accident, they had reproached him: "We cultivate for you each year, yet you are keeping the rain away from us."

Rodrigo had another son who is called Aristo in this account He was begotten by Rodrigo in his late elder brother's name. Aristo felt he had always been put down by his father. After his brother's death, he felt his turn had come. He expected to inherit at least one of his brother's two wives, especially since his own wife had died a few years earlier. When Rodrigo did not take any steps to make arrangements for the transfer of one of the wives to Aristo, the latter started to suspect him of wanting to keep the wives for himself.

The early rains in 1981 had been poor and the tension between the *monyomiji* and Rodrigo had once again mounted. People pointed at Rodrigo's swollen arm and took it as a sign that he had poisoned the rain. In June 1981 Aristo who worked as an unskilled labourer in a neighbouring forestry reserve, received a message from his father to come home immediately. He took three days off and went home. Expecting a confrontation he went to his father's house accompanied by two *monyomiji*. His father told him that he might die soon and needed to discuss the responsibility for his late brother's children. Aristo, who had expected to finally discuss the inheritance of his late brother's wife, retorted. "How do you know you are going to die? Maybe you are planning to poison the rain once more? You called me as if you are the Central Intelligence Department!" Rodrigo then took his bow and aimed at Aristo but missed him. Aristo took a stick and hit his father twice on the head so that he fell unconscious. Aristo did not forget to take some water and pour it on his father, "in order [in his own words] that he could survive and that the rain could rain."

By that time, more *monyomiji* from the neighbourhood had arrived. Aristo explained what had happened. When the Rainmaker had regained consciousness, he was lashed by one of the men and subjected to interrogations relating to the drought. Rodrigo answered: "Since you are supporting my son who has beaten me, for seven years the four sections will not have rain! My son has already died, and this one here will follow me in my death!" The *monyomiji* answered: "If that is what you want, you will be the one to die first!" Aristo, assisted by a few others, then started digging Rodrigo's grave because, as he later explained to me, he wanted his father to die "since he had already made him suffer". One of the *monyomiji* tried to stop them, but Aristo answered: "Don't you want to eat food?" and to his father: "You will not survive this. Have you not heard of the Rainmaker of Obbo who was buried alive?"[10]

After this, the drum was sounded to call the *monyomiji* for an emergency meeting (*avaluho*). Rodrigo was put on a chair and further interrogated and beaten.[11] He

---

10   Statement by one of the men interrogated by the police. I have no information about the Obbo case.

11   According to one informant who was interviewed in Juba, the women led Rodrigo to Acholi. This piece of information confirms statements that the first day no meeting of the *monyomiji* took place although the drum had been sounded. It contradicts the detailed statement given to me by Aristo himself. The fact that the same informant told me that the tree was burnt by the women, raises the suspicion that an account of the ritual of simulated regicide, in which women symbolically kill the Rainmaker by burning a tree (see Ch. 17, p. 378–9) was taken to be a story of the actual killing of Rodrigo.

confessed that he had hidden some rain medicine in a tree in the bush, near an Acholi village at four hours of walking from Iyata. It was agreed that the *monyomiji* would accompany him there.

The next day, they were led to a dry tree which had been hit by lightning. Nothing was found. A goat, which had belonged to Rodrigo's late son, was sacrificed at the foot of the tree.

At the return of the party, the drum of *avaluho* was sounded again and the *monyomiji* of the three southern sections of Lowe assembled with the aim of burying their Rainmaker alive. While the digging of the grave was nearing its completion, Rodrigo was tied and made to measure the grave, to see if it was big enough. Before pushing him into the grave, Aristo reminded his father of his crimes, that his father had scorched the land by willingly "putting the sun" and that there was no way back since he had already beaten his father. Two of the *monyomiji* threw him inside with the rather abusive words: "Kumak" [Down with you]. Before he was completely covered with soil, Rodrigo ordered Aristo to stay at his father's house for seven days — the customary period for a funeral. All men present participated in the filling of the grave. When the tomb was completed, the *monyomiji* killed a goat on top it and smeared the *rumen* on the mound in order "to cool Rodrigo's heart so that his blood would not be on the survivors".[12]

Four days after the burial, it rained heavily in Lowe, a confirmation to the villagers that they had taken the right course of action.

The day after the murder, Rodrigo's elder brother, the catechist, alerted the police who came to the village and arrested twenty-two men. When the police arrived in Iyata, Aristo had already returned to the forestry scheme where he worked — counter to his father's injunction. He had told the *monyomiji* that the police should go and collect him there rather than cause confusion in the village. So the police did.

Some of the *monyomiji* were released after being interrogated; others were imprisoned, including Aristo. After a few weeks, all had escaped from Torit prison, the main reason being the lack of food there. Only Aristo opted to stay in prison. He was an exemplary prisoner and he was later made into a watchman in the prison. He stayed for more than two years despite the poor conditions and the opportunities to escape.

When I interviewed him there in June 1982, he emphasised that his fate was in the hands of the court. He added that, if he were acquitted, he expected that the *monyomiji* would carry him on their shoulders into the village, triumphantly, to be their *ohobu*. However, he was never tried, and his escape from prison in 1985

12   In the police statements there is mention of flour being put on top of Rodrigo before the grave was closed. I have found no confirmation from informants on this detail. According to one informant, the *monyomiji* of Iyata had thrown the rainstones into the grave together with the Rainmaker, thus causing the drought after Rodrigo's burial alive. I doubt whether this is the case since only the King of Lohera was known to own rainstones. Rodrigo, who was an *oihejek*, relied on rain-medicines which are usually purchased. Rodrigo's rain medicine consisted of a glass cylinder with water which had been removed from a levelling instrument.

during a period of general insecurity in Torit as a result of the SPLA operations in the area, may not have been unwelcome to the court.

The spells of rain that followed Rodrigo's burial alive were of short duration. The drought conditions returned and the *monyomiji* believed it was the vengeance (*acen*) of the dead Rodrigo. A sacrifice of apology (*aborongo*) was performed on the grave. This ritual is performed when someone has been killed by mistake. Rodrigo's skull was removed and transferred to a cave as is customary among the Lokoya. The removal of the skull is considered a last conciliatory act in relation to the deceased. It is also believed to make an end to any further act of vengeance of the dead person.

Yet, the rains did not become normal and the speculations on the possible role of Rodrigo in the drought continued. Some said he had swallowed his rain medicine before he was buried alive.

At his return from prison, Aristo claimed that the non-payment of blood wealth (*alunya*) for his father was the cause of the drought and demanded its immediate payment from the *monyomiji*. His father's brother, the catechist, who objected to Aristo becoming the next Rainmaker, led the opposition to this demand. He also refused to perform the customary purificatory sacrifice (*avulyo*) at Aristo's return from prison, which was his duty as a family elder.

Informants who had known the family for some time comment that the continuing violence inside the family, even after so much suffering, must be the result of a powerful curse.

The antagonism of the relationship between the Rainmaker and the *monyomiji* is particularly marked in this drama. It started with Rodrigo's request for *amopwa*, and continued after his death when the drought continues to be interpreted in terms of his hostility to the *monyomiji*. In this drawn-out struggle, the pendulum of triumph swung in either direction. There were periods when Rodrigo is 'on top' and the *monyomiji* are 'down' and other periods when the reverse was the case. When Rodrigo chose to risk the gamble and demand *amopwa* before agreeing to give rain, he won. The *monyomiji* complied with his demand and they got the desired rain. Later in the 1980s when he lost his children and when the rain was not forthcoming, Rodrigo became more and more a defeated man. But even in death, his drought-stricken people saw him once again as the winner in the power contest with the *monyomiji*.

After Rodrigo's death, Aristo followed a strategy similar to that of his father in his dealings with the *monyomiji*. At his return from prison, he confronted them with what looks, at first sight, as a rather spectacular demand: blood money for his father — in whose killing he himself had played the leading role. Although my informants disapproved of this move, they did not seem very surprised by it.

In line with the argument defended here, Aristo's demand should probably be interpreted as a manoeuvre to put him face-to-face with the *monyomiji* so as to achieve the antagonistic polarisation which is a prerequisite to a career as Rainmaker.

Kings as lonely heroes

The simple sacrificial interpretation of regicide as proposed by Girard is inadequate to explain these facts. It is unable to explain why the king should make things worse for himself by antagonising those prepared to sacrifice him. Girard's view of the king conniving with his executors by indulging in a variety of transgressions in order to become a victim worthy of punishment disregards the Nilotic king's will to fight until the bitter end and to win.

Kings who, like Rodrigo, stage a lonely fight against the majority of their people are a fairly common feature in the history of Eastern Equatoria. Although most kings, when faced with superior numbers, tried to escape or resigned themselves to their fate, some chose to die fighting. In the period immediately following the introduction of firearms, when kings formed a privileged minority possessing these new weapons, fighting back was a realistic option for the king. At least three kings in southeastern Sudan ended their lives in a gun battle of one against many: Nyiggilo of Bilinyan and Kamiru and Lohide of Tirangore.

Lejean gives the following account of Nyiggilo's death. The story is presented as told by Swaka, the blacksmith who claims it was his father who killed the king:

9.7 *The heroic death of King Nyiggilo* (Lejean)

"We asked Nyiggilo to give us rain. He made promises and demanded cattle as a payment. We gave them to him. Despite his spells, the rain did not come. So, we got angry: then Nyiggilo took his rifle and threatened to kill everybody. We had to leave him. Last year, the same thing happened for the third time: then we lost patience; we slit Nyiggilo's stomach open and threw him into the river: he will no longer make fun of us" (Lejean, 1865:75).

Nyiggilo, then, had resisted regicide by a show of force on three successive occasions. When his rain fortunes did not take a turn for the better, he tried to flee to Khartoum but was captured by a group of angry young men at the house of Mödi-lo-Busok, the Master of the Land of the area surrounding Gondokoro, who had offered him refuge. He was killed in the presence of missionary Morlang[13] whose account of the event is included in the list of 24 cases of accomplished regicide (List W, Case 6, p. 384).

Kamiru ruled Tirangore together with his half-brother and rival Hujang for some time during the middle of the nineteenth century. He was met by Baker in 1864 who was impressed by his intelligence and courage. According to Baker, Prince Kamiru was the most powerful man in Tirangore outstripping by far the more senior Hujang. The Lotuho remember him as a particularly ruthless member of the royal family, mainly because of the events that led to his death:

---

13   We know, from Von Harnier, who considered himself a friend of Morlang, that the latter was present at the lynching scene (Von Harnier, 1866:49).

9.8 *The heroic death of Prince Kamiru* (oral dynastic tradition)[14]

Kamiru aroused the hostility of Hatiha [the group of villages that include the location of the later Torit] when, on suspicion of Hatiha's complicity in his sister's death, he killed a number of its men who had come to Tirangore for *ekubo* [cultivation for the king] after having disarmed them. On a journey to the Nile, where he went to exchange ivory for guns, the people of Hatiha discovered him when he spent the night in Ibalany. The *monyomiji* surrounded the house where he slept. When Kamiru noticed he had been encircled, he rubbed the two aids who accompanied him with a slimy vegetal substance so that the hands of the enemy would have no grip on their bodies. They slipped through the enemy lines and took Kamiru's message to Tirangore: "Kamiru is a dying man." After the men had escaped, Kamiru, who was now alone, shouted: "I am coming out! We, kings, do not fear death! I know that my day has come! I am coming out!"

The *monyomiji* gave way to give Kamiru a chance to run. While he was climbing over the fence he was speared in the leg. Kamiru pulled the spear out and ran into a thick forest, from where he continued to defend himself with his gun for a whole day. At the end of the day, after Kamiru had lost much blood, one of his relatives convinced him to come out and surrender his gun. After he had done so a signal was given and all *monyomiji* present threw their spears at him and killed him. Not long after his death, the *monyomiji* of Tirangore arrived and destroyed Hatiha, dispersing its people over different settlements.

Nowadays there is perennial pool rich in fish even during the dry season at the very spot where he was killed.[15]

Although the story may be partly legendary, it shows the way a brave king is conceived by the Lotuho. There is no reason to suppose that the real course of events was very different from the trajectory described above, as is proven by the death of another king of Tirangore half a century later whose one-man stand is documented by archival sources.

Lohide, the successor of Lomoro in Tirangore, also had a reputation for his violent character. Because of his frequent raids and provocative behaviour, considerable antagonism existed between him and the *monyomiji*. After the takeover by the Condominium Government in 1914, Lohide initially received its political support even to the extent that the colonial army assisted him in settling some accounts with Chalamini, a village which, according to Lohide, had defied his authority.

After Lohide had personally killed an emissary of the *monyomiji* of Chalamini who was on his way to the British commander to demand the return of the cattle

---

14   Prince Kamiru was interviewed by Baker on his religious beliefs. Some of Kamiru's statements are quoted in Ch. 4, p. 98.

15   Kamiru's apotheosis as a miraculous bringer of fish is a rare case of a king whose violent death results in a miraculous collective blessing. While the miracle confirms the ultimate positive transfiguration of the victim of collective aggression as predicted by Girard, most regicidal victims stall in their negative transfiguration leaving a curse to the survivors, (cf. p. 368, 379, 420).

that had been raided by the patrol, the Inspector of Torit summoned Lohide to come and give him an explanation. When Lohide ostentatiously tore up the summons, a patrol was sent to arrest him.

9.9 *The heroic death of King Lohide* (Khartoum archives)

When Lohide heard of the approach of the patrol, he collected his army [the *Awusa*] to defend himself. When the two armies were face-to-face and Lohide's extradition was demanded, Lohide chose to fight. His army commander, Motong, however, deserted him at the last moment. Lohide was now alone, faced with the army detachment. He refused to surrender. Instead, he climbed the roof of his palace, and succeeded in killing two of the government soldiers, firing from the top of the house. He was finally mortally wounded by a bullet fired by a soldier from inside his house through the roof. He was carried to the house of his mother, Ngajon, where he died a few hours later (archival sources and oral history; also Seligman, 1934:333).

The rhetoric of the harangue

The antagonism between the king and the people is also expressed in the formal verbal exchanges between king and *monyomiji*. If both parties come face-to-face in public, the tone may, depending on the nature of the meeting and the conjuncture of the relationship, be respectful, authoritative or openly aggressive and confrontationist.

For each rhetorical position, the Lulubo have a special form of address. If the tone of the king is respectful, he will address his people as "my husband". If the tone is paternal, commanding, the mode of address may vary from "my children" to "my stable" or, more aggrandising "my ants", the king being equated with the queen-ant.

When the situation demands confrontation, the *monyomiji* are called by their collective name and addressed as a single body, singular verbal forms [I and you] are then employed in the verbal exchanges.

The following extract of a speech delivered by the Rainmaker of Ngulere at the occasion of the New Year celebration of 1986 ['*Odhurak*' which in Ngulere has been fixed on the first of January] is typical of the latter rhetorical position.

Odhurak marks the transition from the cultivation season to the hunting season. It is the occasion for the *monyomiji*, the king and Masters of Disasters to make statements reflecting the state of the nation. An assessment is made of the prosperity of the community, and the performance of the *ohobwok*, the king and the Masters, on the one hand, and that of the *monyomiji*, on the other. The year 1985 had been particularly disappointing mainly because of the poor rains. The intervention of the Rainmaker was in reply to two speeches by spokesmen of *Lofohitu* ('Immune to Witchcraft') the generation-set which had retired in 1975 and *Taruha* ('-Vultures-'), the ruling generation. *Lofohitu* blamed *Taruha* for mismanagement of the country. *Taruha* thereupon defended itself against the accusation by putting the blame on the failing performance of the different Masters of Disaster: the Rainmaker, the Master of the Mountain (who in Ngulere combines his office with that of government chief), the

Master of Grain, the Master of the Land and the Master of Worms. The Rainmaker was the first to formulate a reply to the allegations of *Taruha*:

9.10 *Harangue by Lokepo, Rainmaker of Ngulere* (live recording)

"Taruha, I am pleased to notice how well you organise yourself. I feel happy and grateful about the harmonious way in which you conduct your affairs. But we should be frank as to where we stand. You asked the kings (*ohobwok*)[16] to clarify themselves. Is there anybody here who is treated like a king? I am not asking you to tell me that I am the king. One day I was put on the throne. Now I have come here just because my wife brought some food here for me to eat. I am here just to eat, like on Christmas day last week. I was not aware that I had come here as a king. As far as the kingship is concerned it has been emptied of its meaning since the days of Wanditio [1940s]. Okwir came scraping some leftovers from the grinding stone. After Okwir, Lofohitu scraped the grinding stone completely clean. What is left of kingship today? Nothing! I don't mind! That is life!"

"You Taruha have a God. God is amongst you [The Rainmaker refers to the Roman Catholic parish priest who comes from Ngulere and is a member of Taruha and is present during the meeting]. But now, don't come to me and tell me: You, our God, please talk to us. Don't poke fun out of a black person [*omoliha*][17]. I have eyes and ears. Don't deceive me. A king is not above God...."

"You, Taruha, are not the first to handle this country. Alangure handled its affairs. Kalang administered it. Wanditio and Okwir ruled. But a weak administration like that of you has never existed. You are useless administrators, selfish and without regard for your brothers."

If at least you had discussed village matters, the country would not have fallen in such disarray.

"I appeal to you, *monyomiji*, never put it into your head again that you have a king. You are free. Pray to God. I too pray to Him.
I appreciate that you requested the royal family to explain itself. But did you ever treat me as a king during my presence amongst you? Did you ever render me any *amopwa*? Did you ever honour me with a goat so that I could regard you as mine? You are stingy. What have you given to me? I have no food. I have no beer. Purificatory sacrifices are performed at my own initiative and costs!
If I said something wrong I ask forgiveness. But as far as I can see you are the cause of the fall of this community. You put this community down!"

When *monyomiji* and Rainmaker come face-to-face, when community matters are to be settled, positions are defined in polar terms and the content of the verbal exchanges is predominantly accusatory or justificatory. Insinuations and 'beating about the

---

16   *Ohobu* (pl. *ohobwok*) in Lokoya is the title that the Rainmaker/King shares with the other 'Fingers of God' (*ovalahojok*, see Ch. 13, p. 289): the Master of the Mountain (*ohobu lodonge*), the Master of the Land (*ohobu lahap*), the Master of Grain (*ohobu lohimai*), the Master of Bows (*ohobu latang*) and the Master of Wind and Worms (*ohobu loriri*).

17   *Omoliha*, 'black person', is used here in the general sense of 'human being'. More on this term in Ch. 2, note 4, p. 49.

bush' are disapproved of. During meetings, no appreciation is shown for speakers who indulge in the expression of indirect incriminations and vague suspicions. People doing so are told to either shut up or come to the point and speak the 'plain truth', meaning that they should formulate their point as a clear-cut accusation.

When there is uncertainty as to how one's words will be received, it is better to take a position which expresses opposition to the audience than to try to please them. In 1936, when Chief Lolik was imposed on the Lulubo as their new Paramount Chief, there was some resistance among certain sections in Lokiliri who supported a candidate from the Kursak rain family. In his inaugural speech, Chief Lolik did not make promises that would lessen the resistance (for example, promises with regard to the rights of the Lulubo and its rain clan). He recalls that he addressed the meeting of Lulubo in the following words:

> "You, Lulubo, why do you accept me? I am brought to you to trouble you. I am very rough. I will beat you every day. I will mistreat you and make you work hard for long hours."

Chief Lolik told me that the Lulubo liked his tough stand and that after the speech there was no more resistance to his appointment.

Mediators between king and people

Most interactions between king and people are not face-to-face. Both the king and the *monyomiji* have their delegates to transmit messages and to carry out negotiations on their behalf. The way these interactions are structured shows a striking resemblance with interactions between enemies.

In Lotuho, each village section has its own emissary to the king (*aboloni hobu*) whose task it is to represent the worries and interests of the *monyomiji* of the section to the king, and who will transmit information and advice on rain to the *monyomiji*. At the *Nefira*, the sections choose a new *aboloni hobu*. The emissaries are picked out by force from their fellow *monyomiji* who are members of the royal Igago clan. After their capture, they are laid down flat on the ground to receive their consecration. The procedure followed in their selection and consecration is similar to that of the installation of the king, discussed in Chapter Eighteen (p. 399–403).

For his part, the king is assisted by a number of 'ministers' (*labusi*, sing. *labusuti*), assistants, most of whom are recruited from families of the Omini clan on a strictly hereditary basis. They are responsible for the execution of the rain rituals and the rituals surrounding royal installation, marriage, burial and exhumation. The *labusuti hobu* was considered the most senior and acted as the second-in-command to the king. In the past, this 'Prime Minister' was buried alive with the dead king. Besides the ministers, the king has a deputy in each village (*ohidak*) who communicates his wishes to the *monyomiji* of the place.

In Lokoya, the office corresponding to that of the Lotuho *aboloni hobu* is that of the Guardian of the Calabash (*obidhi*) who is an official at the level of the village. He is one of the three officials appointed by the *monyomiji*. The others are the 'Head' (*nahu*) who has the power to call for emergency meetings and the 'Heart' (*odhaji*) who leads in battle. The Guardian of the Calabash mediates in the relations with the different Masters of Disaster (*ohobwok*), not only with the Rainmaker but also with the Master of the Mountain and the Master of the Land. If the villagers are worried about drought or other calamities, the Guardian of the Calabash is to prepare beer and invite the Rainmaker or one of the other Masters to his house to ask for an explanation and for suggestions to remedy the crisis.

The king of Liria appoints a deputy (*oihejek*) for each village section. The deputy acts and mediates on behalf of the king. Each of the six Masters of Disaster (Rain, Land, Mountain, War, Grain and Winds) in Liria has his deputy. They are selected from among the sister's sons of the respective Master.

The Lulubo *monyomiji* do not have a special official to represent them in their dealings with the Rainmaker. Each of the Masters of Disaster, however, has a *jaigo* (plural *jai*), a ritual assistant whose highly valued position is hereditary in a particular family.

The Pari *mojomiji* choose as mediator, in contacts with the king, a man who is a paternal cousin of the king and, therefore, a likely rival. Very significantly, he bears the title of *pem*, which means 'opponent'. The fact that a rival is selected to negotiate with the king on behalf of the *mojomiji*, and that this mediator bears the title 'opponent' indicates that among the Pari, dynastic rivalry and the antagonism between king and people are merged into a single antagonistic relationship.[18]

The Bari elders seem to have dealt with their Rainmakers through councils of clan-based elders (*temejik*) rather than through age-class based representatives. The kings of Shindiru who were *kimak 'duma*, 'big rain kings', delegated powers to minor Rainmakers (*kimak nadit*) who practised under their auspices, to relatives who were appointed as local deputies of the *matat 'duma'* (great king) while '*dupi* (slaves) were sent to outlying villages to perform rituals, to convey messages and to collect tribute.

Particularly revealing in this context is the use of women to mediate between the king and the *monyomiji*, a custom recorded for the Lulubo, Lopit and Lotuho. In Lopit, women were used in times of crisis when negotiations between the *monyomiji* and the king had reached a deadlock. They were sent to the king to investigate the cause of the drought and to find a solution. In Lulubo and Lotuho, women go to the Rainmaker before the rainy season with some presents to induce him to make rain. In Lulubo, the delegation usually consists of a poor and a rich man's wife so as to represent the community as a whole. In Lotuho, elderly women are the first to bring some small presents to the king. Later, in mid-April, every section sends a delegation of women who bring firewood, some tins of grain or a goat while singing songs to praise the king.

The choice of women as mediators is significant since, together with blacksmiths, they are the only persons who can move unharmed between enemy lines. Baker and

---

18   Personal Communication by Eisei Kurimoto.

Gordon both conducted their negotiations with the Bari through women. Baker's peace negotiations with Bilinyan were conducted by way of the sister of the chieftain of Mögiri, while Gordon sent a well-dressed woman to negotiate with the Muggi. Vinco made use of the services of blacksmiths when he sued for peace with the Lokoya on behalf of the Bari.[19]

An analysis of the procedures of interaction of king and people makes clear that the position of the king cannot simply be defined on a continuum between a *primus inter pares* and an official occupying the top of a hierarchy. The king's position is not conceived as merged with or emerging from his people but rather as an outsider standing in opposition to them. There is a clear contrast between the ascribed position of the king and the 'achieved' positions in the age-class organisation. The Lokoya Guardian of the Calabash, for example, could be removed and replaced any time the assembly of *monyomiji* felt his performance was poor. I was witness to one such reshuffle during the New Year Festival (*Odhurak*) of Langabu in 1985 when all three officials (*Nahu, Odhaji* and *Obidhi*) were removed from their posts for negligence of duty. This negligence was, according to the *monyomiji*, the main cause of the poor rains.

The marriage between king and people

In accordance with the adage "we marry those whom we fight" the principal means to surmount the antagonism of king and people was through marriage. The Lotuho, Lulubo and Lokoya kings were given wives by their *monyomiji*. Among the Bari, in the days of Lugör, every clan was expected to contribute one cow and one calf to the king's bridewealth.

Abilli (1925–1934) was the last of the Lirian kings to be provided with a wife at his installation. The following procedure was followed:

> **9.11 *The marriage of a wife to the king by the* monyomiji** (Liria, living memory)
>
> The *monyomiji* select the bride to be given to the king. She never refuses. It is believed that if she did, she would become barren. The morning after she has been brought to the king the *monyomiji* go to him and inquire whether he has accepted the girl and whether the girl has accepted him. If the answer is affirmative, the *monyomiji* will go and pay the bridewealth.

In Lulubo, the union of the king and his official wife is given more elaborate ceremonial expression:

> **9.12 *The wedding of king and people*** (Lokiliri, living memory)
>
> The newly selected king and his bride are locked up in a hut in which a fire of ebony wood is burning. The smoke of burning ebony is very prickly and it is believed that, if the king or his bride sneezes, the royal office (*opopi*) is not compatible with him or her, or that (translating another Lulubo expression) "the office does not like them". When they come out after successfully having stood the test, the

---

19 Baker, 1874, Vol.I:331; G.B. Hill, 1881:120; Vinco, 1940:307. The custom has also been recorded by Von Harnier (1866:35) for the Tsera and Mandari, and by Kaufmann (1974:181).

monyomiji, who have meanwhile kept the house surrounded, seat the two on special stools in front of the house and perform the purificatory sacrifice that marks the installation of the king. After this, the queen is sent to the royal enclosure to assume her duties as a cook, while the *monyomiji* go around collecting the livestock and other valuables for the queen's bridewealth.

The prickly smoke, according to one informant, not only symbolises the conjunction between the power of royal office and the royal couple, but also the fusion of the *monyomiji* and the king. The power of office (*opopi*), in this case, is at least, to some extent, conceived as an agency independent of the king. There is no conception among the Lulubo of royal power as a divinity, whether totemic as the *ring* of the Dinka Masters of the Fishing Spear, or ancestral as the Shilluk Nyikang. Ebony is a type of wood associated with kingship and used for the payment of tribute.[20]

In Lotuho, the heir to the throne should descend from a father and a mother who both have rain. So, the queen married off by the *monyomiji* is usually the daughter of a king in a neighbouring kingdom. Her bridewealth is paid by the *monyomiji* of her future husband. This bridewealth is not added to the wealth of her father. With the exception of a few special objects it is distributed among his *monyomiji*, so that the marriage expresses not only an alliance between the king and his *monyomiji*, who provide the bridewealth, but also between the two kings and between the ruling generation-sets of both kingdoms.

The unity between king and people is further expressed in the following sacrifice in which the sacrificial bull is 'shared' between king and people.

9.13 *The royal wedding in Lotuho* (Novelli)

In Loronyo, as a preliminary to the royal wedding, the bride has to follow the itinerary by which the culture hero and royal ancestor, Imuhunyi, entered Lotuholand. She pays a visit to all of the villages until the site of ancient Imatari is reached, near present-day Hoding, the sacred hill for the Lotuho kingdom of Loronyo. There, the bridegroom and bride will be sprinkled with the stomach-contents of a black bull which is brought by the people of Lobera, the easternmost Lotuho village. The bull is eaten by the *monyomiji* while its skin is used by the couple to lie on during their first night together. Their being united in this particular way is believed to bring prosperity to the country. If the queen becomes pregnant, a period of *edwar* (state of non-violence) is proclaimed in which all violence and all things reminding of violence — including dancing, beating of children by parents, drumming — are prohibited. If the taboo is broken, the well-being of the country and that of the child are in jeopardy (Novelli, 1970:606).

The king and the people do not only relate to each other as receiver of the bride and as bridegroom, but also, as we noted above, as wife (the king) and husband (the people). *Mari agosi* ('my husband') is one of the titles of address used by the Lulubo king. And indeed, most of the items given and the activities performed by the *monyomiji* in the

---

20 For another informant, the smoky session in the hut was only a test for the royal bride to find out if the *opopi* was compatible with her. This compatibility was important since the queen might rule after her husband's death.

way of tribute have a male character within the sexual division of labour: clearing the king's land, building his palace, and hunting — the king being entitled to specific parts of many types of game: the tail of the crocodile, one hind leg of an antelope, the trunk and (since the beginning of the ivory trade) one or two tusks of the elephant, the claws of lions and leopards, etc.

Conclusions

I have endeavoured to show that there is considerable structural continuity in the dualist organisation of territorial and age-based groups, on the one hand, and the relationship between the king and his people, on the other. This similarity is not only a manifest in the antagonistic character of the relationship but also in the ways in which the antagonism is mediated.

The centralist mode of achieving social consensus at first sight appears to function as just another form of dualism. While sections, moieties, age-sets and generation-sets are constituted and reproduced in a process of antagonistic balancing between equivalent social segments, the antagonism of a collection of these segments with a king constitutes and reproduces this collection of social units as a 'people'.

We have seen that once we accept this principle, a number of aspects of Nilotic kingship which at first sight defy analysis become more easily understandable: the frequent occurrence of rebellion, the destructive punishments meted out by kings on their subjects, the alliances of kings against their people, and the easy betrayal by kings of their people.

The role of the king as 'symbol of unity' of the people, is not, in the last instance, rooted in the positive identification of the people with their king, but derives from two superposed antagonisms: the external antagonism of the kingdom with its enemies and the internal antagonism between king and people. It is the possibility of the king's vengeance that holds his people together. The Nilotic polities, in which the balance of power between king and people is still a largely open-ended affair, can afford to dramatise the reciprocal antagonism. 'States', namely polities in which the balance of power has irreversibly tipped towards the holders of central power, repress the open expression of the antagonism, at least in its reversible form, and require their citizens to positively identify with the power that has conquered them.

The government-chief of Hiyala (in casual dress) celebrating New Year (Nalam) flanked by notables who are appropriately dressed for the occasion and covered with sorghum flour, 1982.

10

The King as Unifier of the People

Since he is in opposition to the community as a whole, the king transcends the oppositions existing inside the community: between clans, sections, villages and generations. The tension underlying the community's relationship with its king to a greater or lesser degree absorbs the tensions of inter-clan, inter-sectional and inter-village rivalries. With respect to these rivalries, the king is the unifying factor, a shared focus of attention, a *centre*. The unity between the different groups that constitute the kingdom is generated and reproduced in a process of confrontations with the common king.

In this chapter, I analyse some institutions which derive directly from the king's structural position as the unifying factor, *the centre*, of the society: his role as a commander in war, his judicial role and his leading role in rituals that aim to create and maintain unity on the level of the kingdom.

The king as supreme commander in war

Within a political system that is structured by the complementary opposition of equivalent segments, the king's role as war leader follows directly from his position as the most inclusive segment of the society. The king is the only political actor capable of making a cogent appeal to all segments of the political body. When the antagonism between king and people is suspended in confrontations with the enemy, the role of leading the people automatically falls to the king. Any other segment that would take the lead would run the risk of alienating itself from the others, breaking up the unity and weakening the polity.

The king's position in relation to the segments of his kingdom and to the enemy can be perfectly visualised by the diagram designed by Evans-Pritchard to account for the operation of complementary segmentary opposition among the Nuer (Diagram D.) which was reproduced in Chapter One (p. 22). The diagram models a situation of complementary opposition of segments at four superposed levels of inclusion. In Diagram L, a centralist configuration is projected on Evans-Pritchard's diagram. The fact that the same model can be used to clarify the dynamics of fission and fusion in a political field organised as a kingdom when the king and the people are inserted as the higher level complementary segments, suggests a fundamental continuity between the consensual antagonism at work in dualist and centralist configurations. This chapter will examine other evidence of this overarching, unifying role of the king, first of all his role in confronting enemies, the level of opposition at which the identities of king and people fuse.

L. The king as a segment in a political field structured by dualism (a sequel to Diagram D.)

A	B		
King A and People B are united in their opposition to external enemies who may be organised as kingdoms or otherwise (*the enemies are not represented in the diagram*)	**X1** The sections X1 and X2 are united as moiety X in their opposition to moiety Y	**Y1** The dualism of the sections Y1 and Y2 unites their sub-sections including z1 and z2	**Y 1**
The dualism of king (A) and people (B) unites the moieties X and Y into a single people	**X2** The dualism of sections X1 and X2 unites the sub-sections of X2	**z1** The dualism of z1 and z2 unites the clans (*unnumbered*) occupying the sub-section z1	**Y2**
		z2 The dualism of z1 and z2 unites the clans (*unnumbered*) occupying the sub-section z2	

The actual participation of the king in the war activities varied. In Lotuho, the king declared war by sending a spear to the enemy. The spear was carried by a woman. To the *monyomiji,* the signal to go to war was given on the royal drums of which there were only three sets in Lotuho: in Loronyo, in Tirangore and in Loguruny.

The control of the royal drums — used only to call the people to war, to announce the annual cultivation day for the king (*ekubo*) and to announce the king's death — was one of the main privileges associated with kingship and only consecrated kings were entitled to their use.[1]

Apparently, there was no strict rule as to the king's presence on the battlefield. According to my Lotuho informant, the king should be well protected by his elite force if he joined the *monyomiji* in battle.

Sources[2] on the Bari report that the king did not go to war himself but that he appointed a war leader (*walogor*). During the fighting, he and the elders waited outside the village, at the outskirts of the cultivated land, for the party to return with the booty. All cows, goats, captives (only young boys and girls) and other spoils were handed over to the king for distribution. A portion was kept by the king; the rest went to the warriors. Haddon adds that women — who accompanied their husbands carrying

---

1   Lomoro Hujang, who was a regent on behalf of his elder brother's son, never enjoyed this privilege. It was held by his mother Queen Iloyi.

2   Accounts of Bari warfare have been given by Baker (1874), Gordon (in G.B. Hill, 1881), Haddon, (1911: 38) and Kaufmann (in Toniolo & Hill, 1973:181–182).

food — who had excelled in preparing food and beer for their husbands might also be given a cow from the takings (*Thesis*, Ch. 1).

The procedure among the Lulubo and Lokoya was similar. In Ngulere, each of the *ohobwok* (Rainmaker, Master of the Land, Master of Grain, Master of Bows, Master of Worms and Master of the Mountain) received a share in the spoils. An aged informant who was a boy when the war with Moli took place, not long before the pacification in 1914, remembered that each *ohobu* received two head of cattle.

According to Lirian informants, the king as a rule did not go to war. It was the duty of the Master of the Mountain to give the *monyomiji* the blessing before they set off, while the Master of Bows (*ohobu latang*) blessed the weapons. The war party was led to the battlefield by the *Othulo lo operudhi*, the Guardian of the Firesticks. At the return from war, both the warriors and the king were purified (*avulyo*) lest the rain be endangered.

In Lulubo, both the king and the Master of the Land played a role in war. The king, if he was not old, was the war leader while the Master of the Land stayed at home praying for the success of the war. The king moved in the middle surrounded by the *buluka*, the elite warriors. At the return, the warriors were purified by the Master of the Land who also received a portion of the spoils of war.[3]

Although many Bari and Lokoya informants state that the king should stay away from the battlefield, it appears from archival records and oral history that kings were frequently present on the scene of fighting.[4]

Peace negotiations were initiated and carried out by the king who made use of women or blacksmiths to carry messages to the enemy. Not only war and peace, but most transactions with other communities, whether trade or the reception of foreign visitors, were the domain of the king. At the arrival in Equatoria of traders and conquerors from the North in the mid-nineteenth century, contacts with the newcomers were invariably claimed and monopolised by the rain kings.

---

3   This division of responsibilities is respected up to the present day: In 1975, there was an affray between Lokiliri and Liria, triggered off by a dispute over game in a hunting ground used by both communities. It left three Lirians dead. When the confrontation reached the point of using violence, it was the Kursak, Rainmaker of the Lokwe moiety, who took the lead of the Lulubo *monyomiji*.

4   The following examples may suffice:
   - King Nyiggilo of Bilinyan took the lead in the sudden outburst of violence against the traders in Gondokoro in 1854 when the Sardinian Consul Vaudey, was killed (Case 4.1).
   - King Bepo, Nyiggilo's son, led the revolt against the Egyptian garrisons in 1885. After 1889, he led the Ansar in raids (Case 15.2-third round).
   - King Wani of Loronyo guided the Ansar in war against Tirangore (ca.1890).
   - King Lomiling of Liria led the raid on Aru in Lulubo in 1906.

   Some of the important warring kings at the end of the 19th century are remembered together with their war leaders: Lomoro and Lohide with general Motong; Könyi-lo-Jalinga of Tombur with Kulang.

The king as bridge across social cleavages

The structural position of the king in the internal affairs of the community was defined by the fact that he transcended its divisions. Above, we have seen how his antagonistic presence as such created a political constellation in which intra-communal rivalries were relegated to a second plane. We shall now examine the role of the king when these rivalries threatened to upset communal peace and unity.

In the societies studied, the major lines of fracture are either 'vertical', between descent groups and sections, or 'horizontal', between successive generations. I will show that on both lines of potential social fission, the king played a unifying role. First, I consider the role of the king in mending disputes between villages, sections and clans. Next, I discuss his role in bridging generational divisions.

It is difficult to make a reconstruction of the actual peacemaking procedures and court sessions as they obtained prior to the days of foreign intervention.[5] Contemporary informants, when asked about the role of the chief in the past, tend to make extrapolations from the (more powerful) position of the colonial chief. This makes the pre-colonial king look more powerful in judicial matters than he really was. The colonial state has generally strengthened the position of the chief as judge, not only by backing his decisions, but also by reducing the number of office holders involved in dispute settlement and by reducing the possibility for litigants to resort to physical force if they disagreed with the court's verdict.

Before the introduction of effective colonial rule, a greater variety of office holders — Masters of the Land, Masters of the Mountain, and so on — as well as *Big Men* with a reputation in settling disputes were involved in resolving conflicts. There was no monopoly on peacemaking just as there was no monopoly on the use of physical force.

A second obstacle in determining the king's pre-colonial judicial role is the bias in the reports of Western observers. They understood Nilotic royal office in terms of the more elaborate forms of monarchism they knew at home. Nilotic kings were either seen as very powerful: as absolute rulers who used their power arbitrarily, or as very weak: as mere ritual figureheads without any power over worldly affairs. The first assessment was usually based on observations or stories concerning the arbitrary use of violence by the king, whether these be raids or summary executions, the second on the observed absence of well-defined legislative or executive powers.

By carefully sifting the contradictory assessments of foreign observers and the biases of oral tradition, the following description may be a fair approximation of pre-colonial judicial practice. In the king's intervention in social conflicts between different clans or between sections, we can distinguish three stages:

---

5   Similar difficulties were encountered by P. P. Howell (1952a:102) in reconstructing the role of the Shilluk *reth* in the administration of justice.

M.	The judicial role of the king

- the king offered sanctuary to persons who feared revenge for an act of violence committed by them and who desired a settlement;

- the king brought the parties in the conflict together for negotiations and presided over the peace talks

- the king used certain sanctions to reinforce the observance of the terms of the settlement

The king's judicial role can be summarised as one of initiating, facilitating and monitoring peace processes — the success of which depended on the willingness of the conflicting parties to reach a settlement.

The king's palace as a sanctuary

The homestead of the king, even his physical proximity, offered asylum to persons fearing to become victims of an act of revenge. Violence in the presence of the king, wherever he might be, was taboo. Once the persecuted person had entered the royal enclosure, or grabbed the king's body (if he found the king outside his residence), he was safe. This is how a Lulubo informant described the procedure of *runepa* (seeking asylum) as it was practised during his childhood, in the days of King Ali Bey:

> **10.1** *Demanding asylum at Ali Bey's in Lokiliri* (living memory)
>
> In Lokiliri, a person whose life was in jeopardy because he had killed or committed adultery would run to Ali Bey (the Rainmaker during the first decades of the twentieth century) and kneel in front of him, grabbing his leg.[6] After he had explained his case, the king would order for water and would make the fugitive drink. After this ceremony, anybody who would try to do harm to the refugee would be considered to harm the king. People would warn one another with the words: "The king has touched him." After this, Ali Bey would ask for a ram or a goat to safeguard his house against misfortune since 'blood' had been brought to it. He would invite both parties to his house and lead the negotiations, appealing to all parties to forgive one another and reconcile. "You are all my children. By bad luck you have brought yourselves in this trial. Please reconcile!" Ali Bey would plead with Jada Lualla (the government chief whom the government expected to deal with criminal cases or to refer them to a higher court) for clemency for the fugitive since "he had held his leg".[7]

---

6   The fugitive might also lick the king's feet, or alternatively remain standing, depending on the gravity of his crime.

7   Statement by Bishop Benjamin Yugusuk who spent his childhood in the immediate vicinity of the Rainmaker.

Other prominent members of the community also offered sanctuary, in Lulubo and Bari, the Master of the Land,[8] in Lotuho, the prime minister (*labusuti hobu*), the sectional emissaries to the king (*abollok hobu*) and the Master of the Village (*amonyemiji*). In Bari, any *Big Man* could in principle offer asylum. Among the Pari, both the king of Kor and his counterpart in Boi did so, but in a dispute between a clan from Wiatuo and one from Kor, sections whose relationship was marked by frequent hostilities, the persecuted person would seek asylum on neutral ground, in Pugeri. Its *rwath* was considered impartial so that both parties could meet there for negotiations without fear of being molested.

Examining these practices, we find that three criteria determined the choice of a particular authority as asylum-giver: He should have sufficient political leverage to support the defence of the asylum-seeker. His residence should be acceptable to the enemy as a venue for negotiations. And he should not be biased in favour of the asylum-seeker's enemy. All three conditions were fulfilled in the following case which occurred in Lokiliri in 1983:

> **10.2 *Sanctuary for a man accused of homicide*** (contemporary case)
>
> A prominent member of the rain clan accused a poor young commoner of having caused the death of his daughter. The girl had died while delivering her first child which had been begotten by the young man. The affair had been against the girl's father's will. The father had refused to allow the two to marry even after his daughter became pregnant.[9] At the girl's death, the young man ran to Chief Lolik, the Lokoya government chief, and not to the rain or government chief of Lokiliri because they were members of the same clan as his prosecutors. Chief Lolik who was the government chief of the Lulubo from 1938 till 1976 and still a generally respected person in 1983, had enough leverage to influence the elders of the rain clan in Lokiliri to accept a settlement of the young man's case. Such a settlement was eventually reached after almost two years had passed. During this time the young man did odd jobs in the compound of his protector.

The Lulubo compare the chief to a 'dam' or 'buffer' (*rari*), since he prevents a situation of conflict from getting out of control. That the king could be a buffer in a very literal sense is demonstrated by an incident witnessed by Baker during his stay in Tirangore in 1863.

> **10.3 *The person of the king as a mobile sanctuary*** (Baker)
>
> It appeared that a native of Kayala [Hiyala, the town that was attacked by the Turks during Baker's stay in Tirangore] had visited Tarrangollé [Tirangore] to inquire about a missing cow. The chiefs Moy [Hujang] and Commoro [Kamiru], brought him to the Turkish [all foreigners from Khartoum and beyond were

---

8   Nyiggilo was given asylum by the Master of the Land, Mödi-lo-Busok (Case 17.10—2nd round).

9   The father objected arguing that the marriage would not only be a *direct exchange* but also the duplication of an already existing alliance. He had paid the bridewealth for the suitor's sister who had been married by his sister's son. Since the family was poor, it was to be expected that the bridewealth given on the first occasion would return to him.

labelled 'Turks'] camp, merely to prove that he had no evil intention. No sooner was it announced that he was a native of Kayala than the Turks declared he was a spy, and condemned him to be shot. The two chiefs, Moy and Commoro, feeling themselves compromised by having brought the man into such danger, unwittingly threw themselves before him, and declared that no harm should befall him, as he belonged to them. Tearing him away by the combined force of many men, the prisoner was immediately bound and let forth by his bloodthirsty murderers to death (Baker, 1866, Vol. I: 225).

Kamiru (who had taken part in the raid) and Hujang obviously expected immunity from attack for the man in their company. They emphasised this by throwing themselves in front of him—as a dam.

If kings themselves were in danger, they would go to a more powerful authority. The offices of colonial administrators were often used to this effect by local royalty. Mountenay-Jephson (1890:143) mentions that Emin Pasha offered asylum to a member of the Lotuho royal family for over six months, while Queen Tafeng of Loronyo, after having been chased from Loronyo and Hatiha, stayed with Mr. Haddon, the Assistant District Commissioner in Gondokoro, from July to November 1910.[10]

The king as arbitrator

We possess an account by the trader Brun-Rollet of an attempt at arbitration by Subek and Nyiggilo when a person accused of theft sought asylum in his boat when both royals were paying him a visit.

10.4 *Arbitration by the king* (Brun-Rollet)

One day, when Nyiggilo and Subek were visiting me, a resident of Bilinyan came to seek refuge in my boat. The man had been accused by the people of Marju (the place where we were) of having stolen their cows, so they wanted to kill him. The court was held next to our camp. The accused was free to move among his enemies and judges. I observed the changing expressions on his face which reflected his feelings. One moment, he looked full of assurance and hope when the words of Nyiggilo and Subek, who had taken up his defence, were met with an approving mutter. However, despite the lack of evidence and the eloquence of his defenders, his enemies prevailed and succeeded in having him sentenced to death. This outcome caused a general uproar. Nyiggilo regained control over the commotion by threatening to have the village burnt by my crew if the sentence would be executed. At this ultimatum, the assembly dispersed grumbling; the accused returned to my boat. He was not molested as long as he remained there, but when he wanted to go back to his village some days later, he was killed on the way or in the forest. The sentence had to be respected. The unfortunate fellow had been spied on to make sure the sentence was carried out (1855:238–239).

---

10   Monthly Reports, Gondokoro District, August 1910, October 1910 and November 1910; Uganda National Archives, Secretariat Minute Papers 189.

It is clear that the influence of Nyiggilo and Subek on the course and outcome of the procedure was limited. They failed in their objective to reach a settlement without bloodshed although the accused was a subject from their own village. We are left to guess for the reasons of their failure: rivalry between Ilibari and Bilinyan, caused over their respective share in the trade with the North? The incapacity of the accused to return or compensate the stolen wealth?

The choice of the word 'sentence' by Brun-Rollet is, I think, based on his perception of the meeting as a court session in the European sense. The accused is not killed by order of the court. He is killed by his accusers to whom the court has not offered an acceptable settlement. It is his bad luck that he had to find sanctuary and be judged in the middle of his enemies.

The case highlights the role of the king in stopping bloodshed, but also its limitations. The usual procedure of arbitration in Lulubo is described in the following statement:

> **10.5 *Arbitration by the king in a case of homicide*** (Lokiliri, living memory)
>
> The king will ask the killer: "What possessions do you have?" He may answer: "A child." The king may then ask: "Do you have any goats?" He may answer "I have ten." The king will call for the elders and address them saying: "Have you heard he has a child and ten goats for *oggi* [a chain with beads that a widow puts around the waist to mark the end of the mourning period]?" If the elders agree to the deal, the killer and his brothers will take the child and the goats to the homestead of the brother of the victim who will say: "Why take revenge of our brother, since a child has already been offered." After the compensation has thus been accepted, *tomora* [reconciliation ritual] is performed.

Sanctions

The king's presence during a negotiated settlement was in itself a sanction. His endorsement of the settlement changed it from a more or less trivial deal — so many heads of livestock for so many lives — between two private parties into a communal concern for peace. Compliance with the king's will was not just the acceptance of the outcome of the negotiations but also the recognition that the conflict had been a danger to the peace of the community at large rather than a mere private quarrel.

After agreement was reached on the terms of the settlement, it was the responsibility of the elders of the clans of the disputing parties to perform the reconciliation ritual which formed a further sanction against renewed outbursts of violence:

> **10.6 *Reconciliation after a conflict in which one or more persons were killed***
> (Lulubo, living memory)
>
> The party of the killer provides a goat. After it is killed[11], its blood and stomach contents are mixed in a calabash. The parties to the conflict position themselves face to face in two rows, each person applying the mixture to all members in the

---

11   In Kudwo, the goat was killed by slitting its throat; in Edemo, it was killed bloodlessly by a blow on the head.

opposite row uttering the words: "Let your body be cool." Then the meat of the goat is consumed in a common meal. After washing their hands, all participants spit in the calabash with the remainder of the washing water. Then, the calabash is put between the two rows and an elder of each group sprinkles the mixture of water and saliva on the members of the opposite party.

In Lulubo and Lokoya, the custom is that the party of the killer gives one goat to purify (Lulubo: *'bulo*; Lokoya: *avulyo*) the rainstones. Sometimes, a goat is also given to the Master of the Land for the purification of the land. These payments are also made if the Rainmaker and the Master of the Land have not helped in the arbitration, since any act of violence is believed to have an adverse effect on the rain. Even after minor fights — not resulting in serious injury or death, but serious enough to draw blood — the *monyomiji* of the section concerned usually order the fighters to take a goat to the Rainmaker to have it sacrificed on the rainstones.

In Lulubo and Lokoya, the king did not receive a share from the animals paid in compensation. In some cases the king took care of the transfer of the goats from the killer's family to that of the victim. In others, the brothers of the killer would bring the bloodwealth, the transfer of goats coinciding with the reconciliation ritual.

On two occasions during the judicial process, a sacrificial animal was given to the king: at the beginning, when offering sanctuary, and at the end of the peacemaking process. The first one served to ward off evil from the house where asylum was offered since 'blood' had been brought to it. The second marked the end of the violence and re-established cosmic order, averting any drought that might result from the bloodshed.

The sanctions applied to prevent a renewal of the violence were threefold: the fear of the curse that would result from breaking the pact sealed by the sharing of each other's spittle, the fear of a renewed disturbance of the restored cosmic order (drought) and the fear of arousing the king's anger which could lead to acts of aggression on his part.

Evidence concerning arbitration among the Bari and Lotuho indicates that in addition to the animals given for sacrificial purposes, considerable fines were paid to the king. Emin Pasha, who visited both Mayya in Loronyo and Hujang in Tirangore, reports that out of a total payment of bloodwealth which amounted to fifteen head of cattle, the king received five. According to the same source, the king also received half of the compensation paid for theft, which amounted to four times the value of the stolen goods. The king also received the properties of persons killed because of witchcraft, while in cases of adultery, two-thirds of the confiscated property of the adulterer would be passed to the king (Emin Pasha, 1894:774–802).

The amounts mentioned by Emin Pasha seem very high and may reflect an attempt on the part of Hujang and Mayya to impress the Egyptian Governor with a powerful image of themselves. Emin's remark that blood-feuds did not exist in Lotuho seems to confirm this interpretation. The amounts may also be initial claims made by the king at the height of his anger. We may assume that during the process of negotiation, these would normally be reduced to more manageable proportions.[12]

The early reports on the Bari are vague and contradictory. Beaton (in his contribution to Nalder, 1937) mentions that the bloodwealth for a member of the Bekat clan was paid to the Rainmaker. His role as the recipient of the fine could also be attributed to the Rainmaker's role as clan elder rather than to his role as king. It is not clear from Beaton's information whether the Rainmaker took a share of the latter payment.

The fact that among the Lotuho, and possibly also among the Bari, fines were paid to the king reflects their kings' greater power compared to their counterparts among the Lulubo and Lokoya, who did not derive any immediate material benefit from their role as arbitrators.

Whatever the share of the king in the bloodwealth paid among commoners, there is abundant evidence that the value of the bloodwealth paid as compensation for a person with rain was higher than that paid for commoners.

The use of physical force as a sanction

Unwillingness to accept the terms of a settlement proposed by the king was no longer a simple choice in favour of one's interests as against those of the opponent. It constituted, rather, a morally and politically reprehensible act in which one let one's own pride prevail over respect for the king. From the point of view of the interests of the wider community, submission to the king equalled willingness to put public interests, peace and 'rain' before private interests. From the point of view of the king, non-acceptance of the terms of a settlement achieved by his mediation equalled disrespect and a challenge to his power.

Following the dualist logic of balanced opposition, the king normally reacted to such challenges by a display of aggressiveness, either militarily or meteorologically. The examples of acts of aggression of kings against their subjects given in the preceding paragraph all fit in this pattern. These demonstrations of violence were not punishments in a narrow sense as they bore no relation to the gravity of the felony committed by the punished group or person. They were motivated by the king's intention to restore the balance of respect between himself and his subjects.

If Nyiggilo, in the case related by Brun-Rollet, had set the houses of Marju alight, it would not have been a punishment for the killing of the poor cattle thief, but rather

---

12   Emin's account on the administration of corporal punishments among the Lotuho when they had already grown obsolete according to other information, seems to belong to the category of tales in which the excessive strictness of rules in the olden days is used to make compliance by contemporaries look like a minimal concession. In the past, Emin was told, the right hand of thieves was cut off while in case of relapse the thief was blinded. The custom had, allegedly, been replaced by the four-fold restitution of the value of stolen goods, half of the value going to the king. Emin adds that theft of food in times of famine went unpunished (Emin Pasha, 1894).

a show of force in revenge for not having been taken seriously by his Marju subjects and an attempt to readjust the balance of power.

This principle is exactly what Prince Adang of Tirangore (Case 9.2) tried to get across to Baker when justifying the raid on a subject village: "the people are rather rebellious, and it will do them good to kill a few, and to take their molotes." The same principle seems to underlie the administration of capital punishment by the king, a practice reported for the Bari by Werne and by Morlang.

Executions at the hand of the king, whatever their interpretation, seem to have been the exception. Lulubo and Lokoya informants deny that such practices ever existed among them and contend that all forms of physical punishment are *gela* (resp. *ogala*), innovations that arrived with the foreigners via the Nile. Emin was told that the practice had long been abandoned among the Lotuho. Most executions were carried out either by the aggrieved party (in the case of homicide and theft, as in Case 10.4, or by the community (in the case of evil-doers such as witches, sexual deviants and drought makers).

If arbitration had taken place and the killer or thief failed to pay the compensation agreed upon in the arbitration, it was up to the party who had suffered the loss to exact its right by force. In a case recorded among the Kuku, neighbours and close cultural relatives of the Bari, by Vandenplas, a Belgian colonial officer in the Lado Enclave (Vandenplas, 1910:258), even the sentence of mutilation — namely castration and cutting off of ears — was to be carried out by the person whose goods had been stolen.[13]

A person stigmatised as intrinsically evil would be subjected to an ordeal, or killed in an outburst of mob violence. According to information collected by Haddon on the Bari, persons suspected of witchcraft would be captured unawares, preferably by having a rope thrown around their neck in the midst of a dance. The wizard would then be dragged outside the circle, speared, decapitated and his body would be thrown into the river or into the bush (*Thesis*, Ch.3).

The following is Werne's account of the Bari king's role as executioner:

10.7 *The Bari king as chief executioner* (Werne)

Jurisdiction in Bariland is organised in a peculiar way. We were told that King Logunu killed criminals with his own hands. He did so very quickly (*goâm, goâm*) without any fuss: he would be seated under a big tree with a heavy spear in his hand, to administer justice and would exhibit great anger. Maybe, people believed he was inspired by the great spirit in the tree while he was thus presiding over the court, or maybe, it was rather his own feeling of justice that put him into righteous anger and that made him into the chief executioner of the wrongdoer, although normally the latter's fate had already been sealed by the collective will....

---

13   During my fieldwork, I have found no indications that mutilation was ever practised as a punishment at the community level. It is probable that the verdict by the Kuku chief was inspired by examples set by strangers: possibly the Turkish or Mahdist rulers, the authorities of the Congo Free State or by the Zande kingdoms where mutilation was not unknown.

So, the great king does not smash the skull of the criminal with his ordinary club-sceptre, as I believed at his first visit, similar to the Shilluk where the captured Arabs are not killed by the honourable spear but beaten to death like a dog with the assagai. It seems that also in this domain, a definite idea prevails not to dispense an ignonimous death (1848:322).

The clue in this account of Logunu's role as executioner, I believe, is his show of anger. What is described is not the implementation of a court decision but rather the stage-acting of the king's anger against a person who has already been stigmatised by the community. There is no indication that the royal anger is provoked by the seriousness of his 'crime'. On the contrary: Werne speculates (or reiterates informants' speculations) that it might originate from the tree-spirit or from the king's 'feeling of justice'. The decision that the man should die had already been taken by general consensus. What Werne describes seems closer to theatre than to the administration of justice.

The same theatrical element is present in the only other mention of Bari chiefs acting as executioners. It is found in a footnote in a travelogue by Morlang (1862–3:116, note 2), one of the Austrian missionaries at Gondokoro, and relates to the period of exceptional drought between 1855 and 1860. In the fourth year of the famine, Morlang briefly mentions, Medi [Mödi-lo-Bosuk], the Master of the Land of Ilibari[14] and Burgodschi[15] and Tchoáka [Swaka] *kimak* of Marju and Libo[16] used to kill thieves with their own hands and throw their bodies into the Nile. I suspect that this chiefs' campaign against theft must have been a rather exceptional and desperate emergency operation. The normal settlement of theft in Bari was by means of payment of compensation, one such case — which occurred during the same famine—being

---

14   Mödi-lo-Bosuk was "without doubt the most important chief" (Kirchner, Tagebuch: 277, Comboni Archive, Rome, Typescript, A/127–7/3), "the *Gran-capo* to whom the mission paid rent" (Beltrame, 1881:311). He lived in Kujönö and was the Master of the Land (*monyekak*) when the first traders arrived (Whitehead, 1936:156). Beaton (Southern Records Office, Historical Notes on Bari Chieftainships, p. 83) notes a treaty between Mödi-lo-Busok as leader of the Panyigilo and Lumbari clans and Dere of the Bekat that fixed the boundaries between the two zones of influence. He was the person who stopped the missionaries from taking one of their converts to Khartoum (Beltrame, *idem*). He killed the Sardinian Consul Vaudey (Lejean, 1865:78; Case 4.1) and he offered sanctuary to Nyiggilo before he was killed (Morlang, 1862/3:117, note 2). At the beginning of the twentieth century, his spirit was still invoked in rainmaking (Haddon, 1911: 143).

15   "Burgadsch" (or "Burkodschi") was the chief of "Libo" or "Ulibari" where Vinco was buried (Kirchner, idem: 276). According to Brun-Rollet, Vinco's house, where he had been buried, was at Marju (1855:202).

16   According to Lejean, who visited Gondokoro in the winter of 1860/61, Tchoka or Tchoba [Swaka] was the chief of the blacksmiths in Ulibo who owned half the village. To Lejean, he declared that his father had killed Nyiggilo with his own hands, and had so become Nyiggilo's successor. De Bono, writing in 1861, gives Shoka as the name of *chef principal* of the Bari (1862:11–12). The fact that a blacksmith killed the king and subsequently succeeded to the position of head-chief, raises some intriguing questions which I am unable to answer with the information at my disposal.

recorded by Kirchner.[17] In normal circumstances, if the object stolen was food, and the motivation of the theft appeared to be hunger, the only sanction applied was ridicule and abusive songs.[18]

Haddon, who made his observations on the Bari in 1909, states that only in case of a relapse the thief had to pay a fine to the *matat*. The same rules applied to the settlement of a case of theft as to the payment of bloodwealth. If a person was unable to pay in livestock, he could give his son or daughter, whom he could redeem by payment of the ransom in instalments, or alternatively, he could give up his freedom and bind himself to a *Big Man* (Haddon, 1911:105).

Since information on the role of kings as executioners is extremely scarce, we are justified to look further afield for additional data that may throw light on the practice. Apart from Werne's mention of a similar practice among the Shilluk in the quotation above, I only found one more reference to the role of the Shilluk king as executioner in a footnote of an article by Pumphrey: "The *Reth* is said to have had the enviable privilege of killing a tiresome litigant with a club." (Pumphrey, 1941:19, note 29; also quoted by Howell, 1952a:105). Despite the brevity of the comment, it clearly suggests that among the Shilluk, too, the king's intervention as executioner was not motivated by the gravity of the misdemeanour of the 'criminal' but by the way the king chose to feel antagonised (by finding him 'tiresome').

The three cases of capital punishment at the hands of central authorities fit into a scenario of theatrical display of royal antagonism. The king's anger was not so much aroused by homicides and raids, which were a common phenomenon among the Bari and the other Nilotic peoples, but by acts, gestures and insinuations which, in his eyes, indicated a lack of respect for his power. The capital punishments administered by the king fit in the same category as the outburst of royal anger of Lomoro and Logunu which were analysed in Chapter Nine.

The king as bridge of generational cleavages

After this presentation of the role of the king in restoring normal relations between conflicting clan groups and territorial sections, we shall now examine his role in maintaining the unity between rivalling age-classes.

In all the societies in our field of study, the position of the king is defined in such a way that he, at least in theory, transcends generational divisions. He is the leader of the society as a whole and not the protagonist of any particular grouping in it. In practice, though, the king was not always above generational divisions. Frequently,

---

17 According to Kirchner, who in 1858 spent one month in Gondokoro, thieves were killed, mutilated and thrown into the river. He does not say that the chiefs were responsible for these executions. In a later diary entry, he mentions that the brother of Master of the Land, Mödi-lo-Busök, had been caught stealing cattle from the Mission. This case was settled by the restitution of the cattle minus a compensation charged to the mission for driving the cattle back, clearly another indication of the powerful position of Mödi (see Kirchner, Tagebuch: 275).

18 Emin specifically states that theft of food in times of hunger was not prosecuted (1894:779); note 10–12.

he belonged to a generation older than that of the *monyomiji*, and there are plenty of indications that it was difficult for him to stand outside the process of generational polarisation, especially during the period preceding the transfer of power.

Old kings easily became scapegoats of the aspirations of the new ruling generation. Many assaults on the king were initiated by a generation junior to that of the king. Ngalamitiho, the last king of Imatari, was the victim of an attack by 'Tome' which was led by his son Ohurak. Mayya was chased from Loronyo after ruling it for many years as the result of a coup by his son Wani who — we may assume — had the support of his age-mates. Mayya was eventually killed by the *monyomiji* of Ilyeu. King Nyiggilo of Bilinyan was chased from his sanctuary at the *monyekak*'s in Kujönö and killed by "a numerous group of armed young fellows from far and near" (Morlang, 1862/3:115, note). Morlang's choice of words suggests that this was an operation of the *teton*, the age-class of junior warriors. In the recent regicide cases of Lowe (Case 9. 6) and Lafon (Case 17.11), the killers also belonged to a younger generation than that of their victims.

While ambitious princes like Ohurak and Wani used the generational antagonism to mobilise support for their cause, impatient generations used dynastic rivalry to speed up the process of transfer of power. Among the Lulubo, Lokoya and Pari, the generation aspiring to take over power usually claimed their own king, preferably a person of their age. The attempted coup by the generation of Limojo in Lokiliri against Taruka (Case 8.2) is a good illustration of this strategy. The near-killing of his father Alikori by Kidi of Lafon (Ch. 6, p. 143–5) was also due to generational pressure. When Tome took over power in Liria in 1956, it dismissed and almost killed the Rainmaker Himang. He was accused of drought and put next to a burning stack of wood, from which ordeal he was saved, only at the last moment, by Chief Lolik. He was chased from the village to make place for Abilli's son Logwek who was Tome's favourite and ruled till the outbreak of the war in 1964.

Despite this tendency towards a close association of the king with a particular generation, the king remains the only person who is, in principle, above the generational dichotomy. This makes him the obvious person to monitor and supervise the transfer of power from one generation to the next. Among the Lotuho, Pari and Bari, the king indeed plays a central role in the ceremonies of handing over power. Among the Lulubo and Lokoya, he intervenes during the last stage of the ceremonies, which follow a predominantly dualist scenario.

Let us first briefly examine the role of the Lulubo and Lokoya Rainmakers in these ceremonies and then that of their Lotuho and Pari counterparts.

After the incoming and outgoing generations are reconciled (*tomora*) in the bush — which is done without the intervention of the king (see Ch. 8, p. 202) — the new *monyomiji* enter the village from the bush and conquer the drums in a mock-battle with the retiring generation. After the first dance around the village shrine, they are sprinkled in purification (*avulyo, 'bulo*) with the rumen of a sacrificial animal by the Rainmaker (Lokoya) or by the Master of the Land (Lulubo).

This purification by the Rainmaker and the Master of the Land respectively is analogous in its form and content to that administered to the *monyomiji* when they return from war. It marks the opposition between the peaceful order of the village and violence and warfare associated with the bush. By sprinkling the dancers the violence of the generational trial of strength is neutralised and the boundary between the two worlds reaffirmed.

The Lotuho, the Pari and also the Bari give a more prominent role to the king. The Lotuho king officiates during the great *Nefira*. The following is an abridged description of the *Nefira* at Hoding (the centre of the *Mayya dynasty*) presided over by King Patricio Ohucoli.[19]

10.8 *The* Nefira *at Hoding in 1955* (Novelli)

Before daybreak, the king spun the new fire that was carried to the seventeen villages of the kingdom to light the fires that had been extinguished the previous night.

After the runners carrying the torches with the new fire departed to their respective villages, the king ceremonially smoked a pipe which was lit with the new fire. After the candidate *monyomiji* had killed the sacrificial bull in the bloodless and noiseless way described above in Chapter Eight (p. 203), the king slit its stomach and addressed the *monyomiji* throwing the rumen of the bull at their faces.

Four new drums which had been prepared by the new generation were brought and sounded by the king. This sounding was the sign for the *monyomiji* to start surrounding the mountain while dancing. Six men climbed the mountain to toll 'the bell of Mocaram'. This bell, named after a king of Imatari, is fixed inside a cave. After tolling the bell, the six men on top of the mountain blew their bugles as a sign for the *monyomiji* to return to the ceremonial ground to receive their generation name from the king. The name given was *Iru*: 'swarm of birds', a name emphasising the numerical strength of the generation. After finishing his speech in which he advocated the importance of brotherhood and co-operation, the king started sounding the drums again. The *monyomiji* arranged themselves according to generation, age-set, village and section and paraded in front of the king, thus offering a demonstration of Lotuho social order. While marching to the rhythm sounded by the king, they dispersed in the direction of their respective home villages (Novelli, 1970:680).

The royal *Nefira* of the Lotuho combines elements from a number of rituals, the performance of which in other areas is the prerogative of specialist Masters: the ritual of the bell in the cave, a typical ritual for the promotion of the birth rate, is usually the responsibility of the Master of the Mountain; the extinguishing of old fires and the spinning of a new fire is a cleansing ritual which, in other places, is performed by the Master of the Land.

---

19   Based on eyewitness accounts by E.K. Mulla, Executive Officer Torit Rural Council ('A Report on the *Nefira* of 1955', Council Monthly Diaries, May 1955; Southern Records Office, Juba, File TRC/24.B.1) and by Father Pazzaglia, related by Novelli (1970) Appendix I:633–680).

If we compare the Lotuho scenario of the transfer of generational power with that of the Lulubo and Lokoya, we see that the Lotuho king has not only taken control of the reconciliatory sacrifice but also of some of the ritual functions of other Masters of Disaster. In Lulubo and Lokoya, the *monyomiji* bypass the Rainmaker and make their own arrangements for the killing of the reconciliatory bull and the conveyance of the blessing, for example in the overtly dualistic way of the cross-wise exchange between moieties and generation-sets in Edemo (see Ch. 8, p. 202).

The Pari scenario stands midway between that of the Lulubo/Lokoya and that of the Lotuho. It establishes a close connection between the king and the bull of reconciliation. The bull is offered by the king from his own herd and before it is sacrificed, the king smears the bull with grain, beans and sesame seed as a good omen for the rule of the next generation. In Chapter Eight (p. 202–3) we have seen how the bull — as a vehicle of the spitted blessing of the retiring generation — is made into a bridge between the generations. Next to being a link between the generations, it also points towards the central, unifying role of the king in society.

The little we know of the operation of the Bari age-class system indicates that the role of the *matat* was of considerable importance in the constitution of a new age-set. The focal group of the Bari age-class system were the *teton*, the unmarried young men. They were mainly associated with life in the wet-season cattle camps. Their role in the management of village affairs was limited, not comparable to that of the *monyomiji* among their eastern neighbours. Village affairs were in the hands of the council of elders (*temejik*). There was no large-scale ceremony of transfer of power in which generational antagonism was enacted. The formation of a new age-class depended on the number of young men who had reached the age to be a warrior (Beaton, 1936:131–145; Beaton, in Nalder, 1937:126–128).

According to Spagnolo (1932:393), if there was a chief's son among the initiates — which must usually have been the case in view of the chiefs' polygamy — he became the *matat-lo-ber*, the leader of the set. His father provided him with the bull for the initiation of himself and his age-mates. The initiation took place at the house of the chief or of that of a *Big Man*. The *matat-lo-ber* had the privilege to announce the name of his group. He also had the duty to invite his age-mates for an annual celebration. If he were to succeed his father to the chieftainship, his age-mates would become his bodyguards.

The scarce evidence indicates that the age-classes among the Bari, to a much larger extent than their counterparts to the east, were extensions of royal power. By hosting the initiation and by providing the bull for their inauguration, the chief exercised an important degree of control over generational antagonism. The selection of the chief's son as leader of the *teton* simultaneously created a bridge between the political leadership in the village and the young men in the cattle camps.

These controls did not exclude all antagonism between the *teton* and the Rainmaker as we have seen in the case of Nyiggilo's death. We are also informed by Haddon (1911) that in periods of drought, the *teton* would take the chief's son — most probably the *matat-lo-ber* — hostage in order to force the father to make rain.

Conclusion

The role of the king as the *centre* of the society has been the subject matter of this chapter. We have seen that the term 'centre' is not a mere geometrical metaphor. As a peace-maker the king places himself in between the conflicting parties, if necessary using his body as a buffer.

Compared to the dualist mode of reproducing consensus in which group unity continues to depend to a large extent on its antagonistic relationship with an external enemy, the centralist mode of maintaining consensus offers opportunities for a greater degree of autonomy of the community in relation to the outside world. Group unity no longer depends on the vicissitudes of armed confrontations with outsiders. With the antagonist at home, as a *centre*, the amount of violence necessary to maintain the unity between the groups at different levels of segmentation can be reduced considerably. At the same time, the capacity of the political community to expand by the inclusion of new groups, increases.

In the next pages, I shall show how the kings of the Equatorian east bank of the Nile made use of their centrality to reduce their dependence on the people.

The royal mode of locomotion: the king peeking over the shoulder of the man carrying him 'like a vulture'. Depicted is King Kachiba of Obbo, Acholi (Baker, 1866, Vol. I, p. 333).

11

Tipping the Balance of Power from the People to the King

A crucial difference between the political systems studied here and state systems is the fact that the use of physical force was not monopolised by the king, not even in theory. Much of the confusion of early observers, anthropologists among them, derives from the assumption that this monopoly did exist. When they met with kings who used physical force against their people, they assumed he held absolute sway, but if the same king was seen to be challenged by his people's behaviour, disobeyed, or even molested, they concluded that this king was weak or only had 'ritual' power.

In the preceding chapters, I argued that the king and the people used violence to define their reciprocal relationship. This relationship was structured as a balance of power in which the threat of physical force against the king was more or less matched — at least in the perception of the participants — by the military and cosmological violence that the king might unleash against his subjects.

If there was reason for the people to feel that the balance dipped in favour of the king, for example when the tokens of respect offered were not commensurate to the blessings delivered, his subjects would retaliate, chase him away or kill him as it happened to the two sons of the Queen of Segele (Case 9.4). If the king discovered signs that segments of the society assumed too much 'power', for example when his arbitration was not respected, the customary tribute was not paid, or when he was the target of acts of insolence, the king reacted — or was believed to react — by upsetting the cosmological order, by sending drought, or other disasters. If he was strong enough militarily, he might decide to raid his disobedient subjects.

Because of the belief in the king's cosmic powers, king and people perceived one another as potentially equally destructive. Chances were, though, that in the eventuality of a head-on confrontation between the two, which could be triggered off any time by an apparent failure of the king's cosmic powers, the king would be the weaker party. And he would be sure to be the loser if the rebellion were supported by a majority of the people. So it was in the king's interest not to depend on his subjects' beliefs alone, but to strengthen his position by additional means. In this chapter, I examine the economic and political strategies employed by the centre to this end.

The following strategies can be distinguished:
- The increase of the number of royal dependants;
- The creation of an army;
- The conclusion of alliances with clans, sections and villages inside his kingdom as well as with powers outside;

- The attainment of a dominant position in the division of labour and in trade;
- The levy of tribute in order to reinforce the centre's position in social and economic exchange.

The king's men

Since in these societies power depended primarily on the number of able-bodied men one controlled, the most obvious strategy aimed at consolidating the king's power was increasing the number of his dependants. There were a number of established procedures to do this: by contracting multiple marriages, by offering the opportunity for a matrimonial career to young men without wealth, by attracting fugitives and refugees as clients.

In using these procedures, the king acted like other *Big Men* in the community. Compared to *Big Men*, the wider network of relationships and the tribute received placed the king at an advantage in attracting clients and in contracting marriages. He was the 'biggest man', the head of several households, while his principal residence was usually by far the largest.

The king possessed many wives. Logunu of Bilinyan had forty wives (Werne, 1848:291), Nyiggilo, at a younger age had 22 (Brun-Rollet, 1855:190), Legge of Liria between thirty and forty (Morlang, 1974:112), Alikori of Lafon forty[1], Lomoro fifty, thirty of them living with him in Loguruny (Powell-Cotton, 1904b:459). In Lotuho, the king had a wife and a residence in each of his subject villages. This meant that the royal family grew at a much faster rate than other families. As a rule, the royal clan was bigger than any of the other clans in the village. I estimate that in most 'capitals' the members of the royal clan constituted between one-tenth and one-third of the total population.[2]

The houses of the king's dependants and clients usually were sizable agglomerations located in the centre of the built-up area near the principal ceremonial ground. The king recruited his messengers, servants and bodyguards there. In Pari, these people were collectively called 'the legs of the king'. These agglomerations sometimes developed into separate sections. The settlement which grew around the Lualla's palace in Lokiliri as a result of an influx of refugees from Bariland during the last decade of the nineteenth century became a section of its own called Gulumere, named after the stretch of high

1   *Reports on the Finance, Administration and Condition of the Sudan, 1909*, Annual Report Mongalla Province: 758–759, Sudan Archive, Oriental Library, University of Durham.

2   Beaton made a count of the size of the Bari clans using the data of the 1932 census. Out of a total of 5,903 households, 681 were Bekat, and 792 were Nyori, the other major rain clan in Bari and probably the leading clan before the Bekat achieved hegemony (see Ch. 2, p.63–4). This means that one quarter of all Bari households had a rain connection through their clan, excluding minor rain clans such as the 'Dung'. In the course of time, the Bekat and Nyori have split up into sub-clans whose members are allowed to intermarry. Again, among these sub-clans, the royal clan of Shindiru and Bilinyan (Bekat Limat) is by far the largest: they have 443 out of 681 Bekat households. The Nyori Kimak ('Nyori royals') account for 214 households out of 792 (Southern Records Office, Historical Notes on Bari Chieftainships).

ground on which the government post of the Uganda Protectorate administration at Gondokoro was located.

The king's dependants made for a considerable fighting force deployable in conflicts between the royal clan and any of the other clans. Their labour meant a considerable source of wealth which could be used by the king as a political tool, in staging feasts, in showing hospitality to potential clients and, in general, by rendering his subjects beholden to him through his generosity. Informants invariably point at this magnanimity when asked for the cause of the political success of chiefs like Lualla in Lulubo and Lomoro in Lotuho.

The creation of armies

The introduction of firearms opened another era in the relationship between king and people. Soon after the first firearms appeared in the area armies were formed by the kings. Loro-lo-Laku, the cargo chief of Gondokoro kept 25 guns, found when his house was searched after his execution by Emin Pasha's men in 1884 (Hassan, 1893, Vol. I: 111).

The warlords who controlled Bariland between 1885 and 1898 had far larger armies. King Könyi of Tombur was found to possess 132 guns, 65 of which were breechloaders.[3] Owing to these guns, many of them received or captured from the Ansar, he had been able to remain where he was during the period that most other Bari went into exile.

Lomoro in Lotuho had a large army, called the *Awusa*. It greatly impressed American explorer Donaldson-Smith when he visited the Lotuho king in 1899:

11.1 *The Awusa* (Donaldson-Smith)

We were rather taken aback at the display made by this commander of perhaps 25,000 warriors on his visit to our camp. He was accompanied by a flag-bearer and about 200 soldiers with rifles, and clad in various kinds of uniforms, principally white with gay-coloured sashes and turbans, and by a much larger following of archers and lancers, naked except for their quick-flashing, bright helmets. Everything about Amara [Lomoro] was 'spick and span', from his dark blue uniform of a Uganda rifleman to the European saddle upon his mule (Donaldson-Smith, 1900:621).

Even if the explorer's numbers are not accurate,[4] Donaldson-Smith's description does show that Lomoro was able to manage an impressive military pageant. If his display

---

3   'Arrest of Kenyi', *Secretariat Minute Paper* 1356, Uganda National Archives, Entebbe.

4   Captain Barlow who visited Lotuho in 1903 on behalf of the Uganda Administration judges that Donaldson-Smith's statements are "highly exaggerated, and in many cases purely imaginary", and puts the number of men that Lomoro could bring in the field between 5,000 and 10,000 (Uganda National Archives, Entebbe, *Uganda Protectorate Intelligence Report*, no. 21, App. C. p. 7); *Foreign Office Correspondence, East Africa*, Confidential, 1904, Vol. II); Spire, the Collector in Gondokoro, who accompanied the same expedition, was clearly disappointed by what he saw in Lotuho. The impressions of Barlow and Spire may have resulted from a deliberate low profile kept by Lomoro, Tafeng and Issara (the Loudo king) since they had an interest to pretend that

of power could impress the American explorer, we may safely assume that his military might had even greater impact on the Lotuho and the surrounding peoples, where concentrations of military force on this scale were rare.[5]

Lomoro had copied the idea for his *Awusa* from his ally Ogwok, the king of Padibe in Acholi, who kept a similar fighting force called the *Buchura*. The Danagla traders, who for a long time had a trading post in Padibe, had helped him in setting it up (Onyango ku Odongo & Webster, 1976:199–208).

The loyalty of the men who formed these armies went to the person from whom they received the guns rather than to the *monyomiji* or to a particular clan or village section. These soldiers were king's clients. They had joined the army for good fortune whether it be a share in the booty or the hope their patron might pay their bridewealth. Among the *Makatub* of the Lulubo prince Wani-lo-Jele, who had twelve guns, most men were bachelors, which may be an indication of their client status.

If these were not armies of the *monyomiji*, even less were they 'people's armies'. Lomoro's army contained non-Lotuho elements (see Ch. 5, p. 131). The foreignness of his army was further accentuated by its uniform: the *jibba*, the dress of the Mahdists whose support Lomoro had won after outmanoeuvering his rival Wani, king of Loronyo.

The *Awusa* enabled Lomoro to extend recognition of his sovereignty temporarily to the Lango, Logir and Imatong to the south of Tirangore. This expansion related to the king's power only. It should not be seen as an extension of the power of Tirangore as a whole. Despite his conquests, Lomoro's position in Tirangore itself was weak, as we noticed (Case history 9.1). From the circumstance that the *monyomiji* expelled him from Tirangore shortly after Donaldson-Smith's visit, we may draw the conclusion that the *monyomiji* did not identify with his political and military success, and that the old-time antagonism between king and people went unabated.

Among the Bari, the warlord's armies of the end of the nineteenth century largely replaced the indigenous military organisation of the *teton*, the warrior age-class. The last documented event in which *teton* played a prominent military role was the storming of the Rejaf garrison by the *Lubere* age-set of Tokiman in 1885 as auxiliaries of the insurgent forces led by King Bepo of Bilinyan. The result was that well before the turn of the century the balance of power between the Bari warlord-chiefs and the people had irreversibly shifted to the side of the chiefs.

Among the Lulubo, Lokoya and Pari, during that same period, the *monyomiji* remained the main military and political force, largely independent of the will of the local kings. In Lotuho, the situation was more complicated. Although there can

---

they did not own any firearms (Spire, 'Brief Report from Gondokoro to Tarangole', *Foreign Office Correspondence, East Africa*, Confidential, 24/7/1904, section 9, Appendix G., p. 17).

5　King Ogwok of Padibe (Acholi), King Könyi of Tombur (132 guns, 60 of which were breechloaders; 'Arrest of Kenya', Secretariat Minute Paper 1356) and Warlord Mödi Adum (1,500 men under arms, Report on Nile Province, 1900–02, *Shuli Correspondence*, A/16/2:52, Uganda National Archives), were the only leaders of comparable military strength in the area.

be little doubt that Lomoro's *Awusa* played a decisive role in making him the *de facto* sovereign of the Lotuho — especially as far as his recognition by foreign powers is concerned — yet the *monyomiji* were strong enough to suspend him from the kingship and chase him away from his palace.

The conclusion of alliances

Alliances with insiders and outsiders helped to broaden the base of royal power or, using a formula which is more in line with the perspective on kingship defended here, helped to reduce the expression of antagonism towards the king.

According to Emin, the Lotuho kings had a wife in each of the villages of their realm.[6] The present successors to the throne of the *Mayya* dynasty still customarily marry wives from each village. Chief Lolik Lado who started his career as a *mukungu* of a single village, eventually became the chief of twelve Lulubo, Lokoya and Bari villages, marrying ten wives, each one from a different village in his chieftainship.

Alliances with outsiders, fellow kings, *monyomiji*-sets of villages and sections of villages belonging to one of his rivals, as well as age-classes of communities outside the *monyomiji* area (Toposa, Boya) were an important factor in the consolidation of royal power. The importance of Tirangore's network of alliances (Liria, Obbo, Loudo) in offsetting its small numbers as compared with the kingdom based at Loronyo was examined in Chapter Five (p.126, note 6).

The king's allies not only played a role in the defence against common enemies, but, more importantly, these allies were mobilised when the king's position was threatened by internal rebellions. In previous chapters, a number of alliances of this type were noted: King Ngalamitiho, who asked the help of the Toposa against the rebellious *Tome* generation of Imatari (Case 8.2); Queen Mulak of Segele, who called upon King Ngalamitiho to fight the *monyomiji* of Segele (Case 9.4); King Lugör who conspired with Köri against their common subjects (Case 9.5); prince Adang of Tirangore who invited Baker, and later the traders, to raid one of his subject villages (Case 9.3); and others.

Such alliances between kings against a rebellious people can be understood as a corollary of the persistent dualist structure of kingship. When the king felt his position threatened, he looked for political actors he could combine with in order to restore the balance, or tip it to his advantage. For kings, fellow kings would be the obvious allies — although not necessarily the only ones. The position at the apex of their kingdoms which entailed the control of its external affairs gave kings a decisive advantage over their peoples in mobilising allies. While it should have theoretically been possible for *monyomiji*-sets of different kingdoms to make a common front against their combined kings, I have not come across such cases. As a result, when severe imbalances developed in the relationship between king and people and when these did not converge into a regicidal runaway, the eventual outcome of the crisis

---

6   Emin Pasha mentions that each of the thirteen villages under Mayya ('Lotomoi') contained a number of huts inhabited by wives of the king (*Tagebücher*, Vol. II: 189).

was mostly in favour of the position of the kings. *Monyomiji*-sets that would want to stage a political rebellion against their king would soon enough find a royal ally willing to embrace and exploit their cause. The result was an *introversion* of the dualist antagonism that was constitutive for the unity of the polity. Instead of uniting the polity in function of an external adversary, opposed blocks consisting of both royals and commoners from the same polity would start fighting one another, thus leading to a split of the polity. Things would really turn bad when the fighting factions managed to mobilise external allies. The destructive consequences of this conflagration of dualist and centralist dynamics are the topic of a separate chapter (Chapter Fifteen).

The keen interest of Nilotic kings in concluding pacts with foreign invaders from the middle of the nineteenth century onwards should be understood in terms of their structurally weak position. The kings sought alliances with the colonial governments not so much to offset external threats (although this certainly played an important role, especially in the case of the Lokoya threat to the Bari) as to consolidate their position *vis-à-vis* their own subjects and in relation to rivals who could take these subjects away from them.

The king and the social division of labour

The iron industry on the east bank of the Nile — mining, smelting and the production and distribution of finished products — was largely controlled by the kings. Shindiru, the home of the Bekat, was an old iron working centre. As recently as 1905, blacksmiths, who had an unfree social status (*'dupi*), were melting iron ore in the valley of the Kaya for the king of Shindiru. In return for their iron production, the king gave them sorghum flour (Powell-Cotton, 1908:156).

The power of the Bekat of Bilinyan must to a large extent have been based on the production and trade of iron objects. When stopping over in Bukö, a village on the section of the Nile bank inhabited by the Tsera, Werne witnessed the exchange of iron objects for slaves by agents of King Logunu. The slaves were put to work in the mines in Bilinyan. The iron industry must have been a very profitable activity at the time: six iron bracelets, not thicker than a finger, fetched one slave (Werne, 1848:291, 360, 363, 365–6). In 1860 in Nyangbara, whose blacksmiths, too, were immigrants from Bari, the value of one hoe equalled that of an elephant tusk. Few people could afford an iron hoe and used shoulder blades of elephants to turn the soil (Morlang, 1974:124).

The Bilinyan Bari also traded iron with the Pari in exchange for salt, copper, textiles, tobacco and products of game (giraffe fur, hides; Werne, 1848:299, 314, Vinco, 1974:85).

The blacksmiths in Lokiliri were closely associated with the rain clan and shared in some of its prestige. The location for their blacksmithery, Bongilo, was given to them by King Tira and was part of Goke, the section where the king used to stay. Members of the clan of blacksmiths call members of other clans *bomo*, 'commoners', just as the rain clan does. To underline the special relationship with the blacksmiths, King Lualla used to give them a share of the tribute he received.

There are reasons to assume that the rise to power of Imuhunyi and the subsequent prominent position of Imatari was due to the introduction of ironworks by the Cor, blacksmiths who had accompanied Imuhunyi at his return from Bari. The importance of this connection is emphasised by the fact that the sacred spears of the Lotuho royalty were those given by the Bari king to Imuhunyi.

By way of this control of the iron industry, the king exercised control over the distribution of essential productive tools (hoes in agriculture, arrows and spears for hunting and war) and of important means of exchange: hoes, spear and arrowheads were generally used in bridewealth payments throughout most of Equatoria.

Lotuho brass helmet made of recycled bullet cartridges

Brassworks in Lotuho was also a royal monopoly. The brass helmets made of bullet cartridges were the property of the king. At the death of the owner, the helmet was passed to another person designated by the king (Powell-Cotton, 1904:467).

The hunters and fishermen in Bari were also dependants of the king or of chiefs. They were *tomonok* (sg. *tumunit*) like the blacksmiths, and their social status was unfree. The hunters provided the king with honey, *heglig*, tamarind fruits and ants; the fishermen supplied him with the tail of every crocodile killed, two legs of every hippo, and hippopotamus oil. In return, the chief paid the bridewealth of hunters, fishermen and blacksmiths, just a cow and a calf, the rate for the servile classes (Whitehead, 1929:93–4).

Certain trees were the monopoly of the chief. Chaillé-Long mentions a tree the bark of which was used to make a fragrant red powder which, mixed with oil, was applied to the body. Again the chief was the sole distributor of the powder (Chaillé-Long, 1876:31/1/1875).

Tribute

Wealth was transferred from the people to the king by way of regular and coerced services and by gifts of agricultural produce, game and cattle. Among the Bari and Lotuho, these gifts were quite substantial, a genuine material tribute. Common to all the peoples in the area was (and still is) the annual day of cultivation for the Rainmaker (Bari: *kuruket*; Lulubo: *mobo*; Lokoya: *amopwa*; Lotuho: *ekubo*). Cultivating for the Rainmaker was the principal procedure by which a village or village section expressed its recognition of a particular sovereign. "We dig for X" is synonymous with "X is our Rainmaker". A refusal by the *monyomiji* to perform this duty or negligence in its performance was, therefore, not taken lightly by the king and even today provokes an immediate political crisis.

Regular forms of tribute further included supplying the king with choice parts of hunted game. The rules determining the selection of the part of the animal to be given to the king differed from place to place. In Lokiliri, the hind part of most types of hunted animals was given. In Lotuho, it was the head and the breast. From the collection of termites, Lulubo Rainmakers also received a substantial share. This tribute was justified as an acknowledgement of the Rainmaker's role in sending *tobu*, the early morning rain that made the termites leave their anthill.

Gifts of cattle and small livestock formed the bulk of the tribute (Bari, *'doket*; Lotuho, *edumit hide* ["rain-tax"] given to the king during his procession through the country. Rainmakers tried to get the best possible deal. They took advantage of their subjects' fear of drought. If we believe Vinco, his popularity among the common Bari was largely due to a speech in which he argued that rain was not given by Rainmakers but by God, because of its implicit rejection of the necessity to pay tribute (Vinco, 1974:83).

Visits to the Rainmaker to request that he perform the annual rain rituals were an important occasion at which wealth was transferred. Where the women came to beg for rain, as among the Lulubo, women's produce, beer, oil, flour and firewood were offered. Men gave cattle, goats and spearheads to the Rainmaker. At the king's request, they would rebuild or re-thatch his house. When he had visitors, the King would call on the *monyomiji* to bring flour for beer and food.

A community suffering from drought was an easy prey for a Rainmaker who wanted to enrich himself. The longer the drought lasted the more his demands were raised. This blackmailing was not without risk, however. If the drought persisted his people might turn against him and kill him. A prudent Rainmaker would try to focus the community's attention on other potential scapegoats in order not to become one himself. He would repeatedly find new reasons for the drought, on his own or by consulting his private diviner. Admitting to his subjects that nothing could be done about the rain equalled a confession of impotence that would make him redundant in the eyes of the people. Frequently Rainmakers survived by sheer bluff.

The following passage from the monthly diary of the Executive Officer of the Torit Rural Council, besides offering a lively description of the ceremonial transfer of tribute, strikingly illustrates the Rainmaker's demeanour in trying to outbid his people with his gift of rain. Patricio Ohucoli, king of Loronyo from 1945 to 1959, was given the following reception when he returned from Torit in March 1959 to perform the annual rain ritual:

> **11.2 *Tribute collection by the Lotuho King*** (Mulla)
>
> On one of the visits of the Executive Officer to Loronyo Village where the Rainmaker who is also the chief resides, he met him riding fast [on bicycle] towards his home. The Executive Officer stopped and gave him a lift. One mile before reaching the village, they were met by a multitude of women who had come to receive their New Year blessing of rain from the Rainmaker. Immediately when the scout saw the car he signalled to the rest and the rain song was sung. People rushed to the car and within less than a minute the dance was commenced. People blocked the road in such a way that the car was deprived of its usual speed. There was no way out but to observe their activities and let them alone. It took more than three hours for the car to cover the one mile. Arriving home, it was a wonder to see the Rainmaker being carefully carried and gently seated on the New Year chair which was made ready for him. When the Executive Officer inquired into the matter, he was told that those people had come from a long distance, about forty miles away. They had brought presents totalling: 10 English pounds, 10 bulls, 40 tins of *dura* [sorghum] and 40 tins of white *merissa* [sorghum beer]. Besides, they were to dance for seven complete days. The Rainmaker, while hearing this remarked: "*What these people have brought is little compared with the amount of rain that I am going to give to them during the coming year*" [italics mine]. He also said that he was sometimes unable to keep a correct account of the revenue he received for his rain business.[7]

Rainmakers, especially those of the Bari and Lotuho, permanently tried to maximise the amount of tribute, using its size as a measure of their power and, as the account above indicates, to blow their own trumpet.

In 1938, Acalili, Patricio's father, had received an American motor car as tribute. Every subject household had donated five piastres, or given meat and game trophies, which had been sold to contribute towards the cost of the vehicle. When the automobile was bought, the king asked the *monyomiji* to build a diversion in the main road that would bypass Chalamini because the place had long ago been cursed to all his descendants by King Attulang, the dynastic ancestor (Case 15.1). The road was finished very quickly on the basis of village competition. Not satisfied yet, Acalili demanded the building of garages in a number of villages. When the *monyomiji* of Buruhutule, a section of Hatiha, refused, he simply said, "Don't bother to pay me for the rain anymore, you are not my people!" A few years later, Buruhutule returned

---

7   Torit Monthly Diary, March 1959, Southern Records Office, Juba.

to Acalili. Muratori's story does not state the reason for their return or whether the garage was built.[8]

As a final remark to this paragraph, I note that there is no evidence indicating that the king was formally released of agricultural labour. Despite his numerous dependants and the often considerable tribute, both in labour and in kind, there was no conception that the king should be exempted from manual labour.[9]

Trade

Control of the trade with other communities offered another avenue to the king to consolidate his power. His control of the flow of goods that entered the community from outside was important leverage to create relationships of dependence. This position of the king as a trader was greatly reinforced after the Nile route from the north was opened up.

Before this, Eastern Equatoria was already linked to transcontinental trade routes to the east (to Ethiopia) and to the interlacustrine kingdoms in the south, especially Bunyoro (Brun-Rollet 1855:116–119; Werne 1845:299, 314). On the arrival of the Egyptian expedition in 1840, the wearing of cotton gowns originating from India had already become a distinctive mark of royalty. When meeting the expedition, King Logunu of Bilinyan wore *un mélayé de Surate*[10] (D'Arnaud, 1842:579) and King Mucarabong of the Pari in 1851 wore a similar dress when he met Vinco (Vaudey, 1852:533).

The long-distance trade was carried out by young men who may be assumed to have undertaken these journeys independently of their king (Brun-Rollet, 1855:112–113). When textiles and beads became available at the Nile banks, this trade passed into the hands of the kings and cargo chiefs controlling the river banks, who in turn traded the articles with fellow kings further inland.

The sudden demand for ivory in the nineteenth century offered an even more important windfall to the kings. It enabled them to achieve a rapid increase of their wealth and power.[11] It became the standard practice over a wide area for the king to receive one tusk of every elephant killed, while in some areas he claimed both.

8　Muratori, 'Accalili, Lotuxo Rainmaker, His Life and Exhumation', typescript, p. 7 and 'George Accalili, 1865–1944', typescript, p. 3, Comboni Archive, Rome, A/126.

9　The more powerful Shilluk Kings are also known to have worked their own fields (Riad, 1959:196).

10　The word *mélayé* is not found in French dictionaries of the period. It suggests a link with *malay* possibly referring to the textiles that were traded as *Java Prints*. Surat is an important port in Gujarat on the west coast of India.

11　The early observers agree that before the advent of traders from Khartoum in the Southern Sudan, ivory did not have a commercial value. Capitan Selim who led the first Egyptian expedition (1839–1840) and Thibaut, who took part in the same expedition, both report on the ignorance of the local people of the commercial value of ivory. They mention the use of elephant tusks as cattle pegs. Thibaut also reports on the use of tusks as a ridge around the hearth (Selim Capitan, 1842:163; Thibaut, 1856:154–55). These observations were made on the Nile bank close to the 6th parallel, not far from Bariland. Brun-Rollet who made his first visit to the South

Ivory market (Speke, 1863:589).

In the course of the nineteenth century, these new developments enabled the kings to strengthen their position as hubs in an international trade network and to become the main distributors of the new goods that reached the area via the Nile and East Africa. The kings jealously guarded these trade monopolies. In 1851, the trade of imported beads was important enough for Nyiggilo to travel all the way to Lotuho himself. Three months after his return, in the same year, he went to Lotuho again, dropping the missionary Vinco at Lafon (Vinco, 1974:89–92).

The fact that the caravan of Nyiggilo and Vinco had bypassed Liria on its northern, uninhabited side displeased King Legge so much that he attacked Vinco on his return journey at the only watering place on the route (*ibidem*). The economic rationale for this attack must have been the same as king Legge's refusal nine years later to allow the trader, De Bono, to proceed to Lafon. Despite long negotiations, De Bono, who was accompanied by the explorer Dr Peney, was stopped from proceeding, because, as Legge finally admitted to them, "we would have robbed him of the trade in ivory that the Pari tribe carries out in Liria" (De Bono, 1862:22; Malté-Brun, 1863:58).

---

in 1845 confirms these observations (1855:89–90), but also reports a story by a brother of the king of Bilinyan according to which ivory traders from Zanzibar used to visit the Bari every two or three years. After they had been massacred by the Bari seventy years earlier (*ca.* 1780) the traders from Zanzibar had not returned (1845:234).

Another reason for Legge's lack of co-operation was his trading relation with Khurshid Aga, De Bono's principal rival on the east bank. Two years later, Baker, during his search for the sources of the Nile, only succeeded in bypassing Liria by imposing himself at the last moment on a caravan of Khurshid Aga. To obtain passage, he paid the considerable sum of fifteen heavy copper bracelets, a large quantity of beads and a bottle of Nubian gin (*aragi*) to King Legge.

The main articles traded by Legge with Lafon and the Oromo merchants that frequented it were iron hoes — probably manufactured in the smithies of Bilinyan — and ivory which, according to Baker, he exchanged against cattle at the fabulous rate of twenty cows for one tusk (Baker, 1866: Vol.I, 135, 170–184).

The peripatetic character of kingship

Did the concentration of political and economic power in the hands of the king give rise to a well-defined conception of a geographical centre? Did the kingdoms have a capital?

Let us examine the situation on the level of the village first. In Liria and Lowe, the king occupied a section that was centrally located in the line of settlements at the foot of the mountain. In most villages, the section of the king was the largest. In old Lokiliri, the main meeting point of the *monyomiji* and the king's palace were located at elevated spots at both sides of the valley of the Lokiliri stream so that, as a Lulubo informant explained to me "the King and the *monyomiji* could always keep an eye on one another and notice any suspect activities on the opposite side". The same polar arrangement was found in the Lotuho villages. In Imatari, after which later Lotuho villages were modelled, the layout was such that the palace of the king and the sitting platform of the *monyomiji* of the senior section were located at opposite ends of the central ceremonial ground. In these arrangements, both the centrality of the sovereign and the duality of king and people were given spatial expression. The locations that functioned as centres in the multi-village kingdoms of the Bari and Lotuho were not in the first place the palaces of the kings but places with a ritual function. For the Bari this was the rain shrine of Shindiru (depicted on p. 300 and p. 323) I have no information on the location of the rain shrine of Shindiru before the Bari were moved inland from their villages on the Nile. When I visited the shrine in 1981, it was located deep in the bush, a two and half hour's walk from the roadside village. The rain of Shindiru is believed to serve the whole of Bariland while the Bari as a people believe to have originated from Shindiru.

In Lotuho, each of the two rivalling royal dynasties has its own shrine where the bones of the royal ancestors are kept in large urns. Both are located near or on rounded rocky outcrops rising about 100 metres above the plains, not far from the abandoned site of Imatari. The *Mayya Dynasty*, which has been based in Loronyo for most of its history, inherited the original shrine of Imatari on Mount Hoding while the shrine of the *Hujang Dynasty*, based in Tirangore, is located on Mount Loguruny.[12]

In times of severe drought sacrifices are made on the urns in which the bones are kept. Next to being a rainmaking shrine, the mountains are the scene of the *Nefira*, the ceremony in which power is handed over to the next generation of *monyomiji*. During the ceremony, the mountain symbolises the country as a whole. By surrounding and climbing the mountain, the new *monyomiji* take power for twenty-two years, after which time a new generation will storm the mountain to take its turn.

The centres of Shindiru, Hoding and Loguruny were closely associated with kingship. But their role was mainly ritual and symbolic. The political and economic nerve centres of the kingdom were formed by the villages where the king had his permanent residence. These villages can be considered *capitals*, centres distinct in their functions from other settlements, in a limited sense only. Although the coming and going of trading caravans and delegations from other villages must have given the king's village a busier aspect than the other villages, especially after the intensification of trade in the middle of the nineteenth century, the difference was one of degree rather than structural.

Traffic between the king and his people was two-way. The king was not immobilised in his palace as a pole of attraction for his people. On the contrary, there was movement in both directions. The Bari and the Lotuho kings spent much of their time travelling from village to village, performing rituals and collecting tribute. Pitia Lugör, *mor* of Shindiru (1912–1949), used to leave his village in November only to return in May. One year, he would visit his subjects on the west bank of the Nile and the next year those living on the east bank. On his journeys, the Bari king was carried on a couch by four of his *'dupi*. Pitia Yeng-ko-Piyong (*ca.* 1850) and Lugör (*ca.* 1875) are remembered as kings whose feet never touched the ground (Seligman, 1928:424).

In fact, the capital largely coincided with the physical presence of the king. Even the rainstones, the most important ritual objects of the royal cult, were mobile and carried along on the king's journeys, so that rain rituals could be performed at each port of call.

The same mobility characterised the Lotuho kings. Emin Pasha (1882:267) writes that when there was an urgent rain problem in one of the villages of his kingdom, King Mayya would go to that village, borne on a couch and accompanied by escorts carrying beer. Apart from these emergency visits, the Lotuho kings toured their villages twice a year to collect tribute. Emin gives the following description of their mode of travelling:

11.3 *The royal mode of travelling* (Emin Pasha)

In front of the procession goes a man who, in addition to his own spear, carries that of the chief. Usually, he has bells attached to his ankles. He is followed by the

---

12   Photographs of the two holy mountains form the frontispiece of Ch. 9, p.206; two photos of the shrine containing the pots with the royal bones on Mount Loguruny, one made in 1922 and another one made in 1981, are the frontispiece of Ch. 16, p.342.

chief himself who is carried on the back of a sturdy man[13] and flanked by two more carriers who take turns. Behind him goes his favourite wife with a full pot of beer on her head and then five or six men of his retinue, all fully armed. Frequent stops are made in order to have a go at the beer. Usually, however, the cortege travels at a fairly fast pace from village to village where the chief's wives welcome him in his hut with plenty of beer. During his presence, he is supplied with food and drink at the expense of the village. During his stay, the tribute is settled and stored in the king's local homestead (Emin Pasha, 1894:782).

Emin's description indicates that the tribute — in this case almost certainly grain — is not transported to the king's main residence in Tirangore or Loronyo, but left in the homestead he owns in the village. There is no mention of a tribute of cattle in Emin's description; neither do we possess information whether the royal stables were decentralised like the granaries. We do know that in the case of the Bari, the king of Shindiru returned home from his annual tour of the country followed by large herds of cattle.

The evidence suggests that, relative to tax collection, the Lotuho villages remained, to a large extent, self-contained units. The king did not relate to the villages as mere interchangeable siphoning points in a centralised system of extraction of surplus. On the contrary, between each village and the king, there was a unique relationship. With some exaggeration we could say that Lotuho society consisted of some twenty individual polities each ruled by its own council of *monyomiji*, each with its own palace, united by the fact that it was the same king who came to stay in the different palaces. The relative autonomy of the village is attested to also in Pazzaglia's description of the protocol of the welcome offered to the king upon his arrival in a village on his tribute collecting tour:

11.4 *Welcoming the king on his tribute collecting tour* (Pazzaglia)

The king's impending visit is announced well ahead of his arrival by his Prime Minister (*labusuti*) and again when his cortège approaches the village. The *monyomiji* who have donned their helmets, shields and ornaments, go to meet the king at a place half-way between their own village and the village where he has to come from. They are accompanied by the women.

Upon the king's arrival, a mock-battle is staged between the villagers and the party of the king which simultaneously expresses the capture of the king by the *monyomiji* and the defeat of the *monyomiji* by the king. The battle is accompanied with great excitement and much ululating of the women. After this show of mock-hostility the *monyomiji* throw their spears on the ground as a token of submission. The first man who surrenders has the privilege to carry the king on his shoulders. Other men take turns and bring the king to his residence, either his own house kept by

---

13   The Lotuho compared the king while he was thus seated, watching over the shoulder of the man carrying him, to a vulture sitting in a tree sticking his neck out looking to find something on the ground—a metaphor that would seem to equate the king with an exploiter (Pazzaglia, Il Capopioggia, *typescript*, p.118, Comboni Archive, Rome).

one of his wives, or the house of his deputy. The spears are picked up by one of the king's servants and taken to the same house.[14]

In this *viaggio trionfale*, to quote Father Pazzaglia's characterisation of the royal tour, the king in his role as antagonist of his people is made to theatrically reconquer each individual village anew.

The tribute collected was used for three principal purposes: for ostentatious hospitality with which allies from inside and outside the kingdom were entertained (for example, the reception of the Ansar and of MacDonald's expedition by Lomoro (cf. Ch. 5, p. 130 and Case 11.1), for the purchase of firearms[15] and the maintenance of the army, and to reward and enlarge the number of the men who owed a special loyalty to the king.

As far as the last point is concerned, it is known that both Lomoro and Lohide followed deliberate policies to attract young unmarried men who had difficulty in finding enough cattle to marry a wife. After the young man had eloped with his future wife, he sought sanctuary with the king who would then negotiate the bridewealth with the girl's parents. The Rinderpest at the end of the nineteenth century pushed many young men towards the king in this manner. The men thus made dependent on the king were called *oruri ba* by the Lulubo, 'men seized by the king'.

Conclusions

In Chapters Nine and Ten, we have seen how the royal office emerges within the context of a fragile power equilibrium between the king and his people. In this chapter, we have examined a number of procedures by which the king consolidates his office to his own advantage and at the expense of people's power. The creation of a large number of dependants and an army, the levy of tribute and the king's involvement in trade, restructured the relationship between the king and people along unequal lines, the king and his men definitively gaining the upper hand.

The Bari and Lulubo call the upper stratum that is thus formed *kör* and *opi*, respectively, while the class of commoners, the rainless majority, is called *böngön* and *bomo*, respectively. In Bari, the *kör* included the king's slaves (*'dupi*) while in Lulubo the *opi* also included the Masters of the Land and the Mountain. The word *kör* — which is now becoming obsolete — still has a distinctly exploitative ring to elderly Bari. The stratification into a class with rain and a class without rain also expressed itself in a significantly higher value of the payments of bridewealth, bloodwealth and adultery fees for persons with rain (excluding persons of unfree status).

The evidence I presented indicates that this stratification developed as a consequence of the antagonism between the king and the people. The economic privileges of the king and the rain class and the exploitation of the commoners were the consequence of this antagonism rather than its cause.

14 A. Pazzaglia, Il Capopioggia, *typescript*, p.117–119, Comboni Archive, Rome.
15 Lomoro, Lohide and Ohuyyoro bought their guns from the Nubi stationed in Gondokoro and Nimule in exchange for cattle (Case 14.2).

In the following chapters, I show that territorial expansionism and the concentration of cosmological powers in a single king also correspond to strategies aimed at the strengthening of central power. Once centralism has emerged as the lever of social consensus, its subsequent consolidation is, first of all, a political process in which all resources of power — economic, military and divine — are put to use.

The imperialist penetration in the area from the mid-nineteenth century onwards offered a wide-ranging variety of new opportunities to the kings that enabled them to make the balance of power tip towards them: firearms, potential allies with unprecedented power, the demand for ivory, and the supply of new trade goods which — at least in the case of the Bari — were delivered at the king's doorstep. These new assets of power must have offset the loss of other resources such as the monopoly of iron production.

In view of the structural uncertainty of the king's position, the complete lack of reserve of many kings in making use of the support of the foreign intruders and supporting them in return — even against their own subjects — becomes understandable. Many of the local kings welcomed colonialism as a way out. The successive imperial governments during the nineteenth century never had difficulties in finding allies in Eastern Equatoria. Whenever different powers competed for control of the area, each would find its own allies. This had disastrous consequences for Bari society during the nineteenth century, when dynastic rivals within the same polity were supported by armies of competing traders and governments (Case 15.2).

In Lotuho, the eagerness of the kings to be recognised by the colonial authorities worked out differently and assured a relatively smooth transition to colonial rule. In areas where the position of the king in relation to the *monyomiji* had remained weak (Pari, Lokoya, Lulubo) even during the latter years of the nineteenth century, the Condominium government, when it wanted to establish itself, needed a much greater show of military force before the people submitted.

The colonial period, in a general way, strengthened the position of the Lotuho kings. Since the king was entrusted with administrative responsibilities and provided with a rest house, a dispensary, a court, etc., the residence of the king acquired a more capital-like character. One of the consequences was that the tribute was taken to Loronyo, as we learnt from the account of the Executive Officer (Case 11.5), instead of being collected by the king.

It was the historical tragedy of the Eastern Nilotic kings that the very alliance that gave them immunity to their subjects' rebelliousness reduced them to petty agents of an imperial power and nullified the grandeur that had been part and parcel of their previous position, however unstable it was.

The apparent partiality of rain — and by implication of Rainmakers believed to be involved: at least three showers can be distinguished in front of the mountain range (the Lopit mountains seen from Hiyala).

12

Boundaries in the Sky:
The Territorial Dimension of Kingship

Theoretically, there is no limit to the radius of a centre. The greater the radius, the more powerful the centre. It is intrinsic to the dynamism of centralised political systems to extend their reach, to apply the centralist vocation of bridging differences to ever larger circles of people, including people of different languages and cultures. Moreover, territorial expansion is one of the major strategies to render a kingdom immune to attacks from outside. In virtue of his structural position, the king is a universalist and an imperialist.

The Nilotic kings were no exception to this rule. All of them were keen on winning recognition by ever-growing groups of followers. Since recognition of the king's power largely coincided with the belief in his control of rain, his following could very rapidly expand to include neighbouring communities and peoples. Conversely, if his claim to recognition was not supported by the right military and meteorological events, this expansion of royal power would just as rapidly be nullified, especially in the peripheral areas of the king's power zone.

As a result of this, the boundaries of the territory ruled by a king sometimes followed a very erratic course. For this reason, the ethnological literature refers to the territories under a particular king as *rain areas* (Huntingford, 1953). And in fact, the extent of the power of the king was measured in the sky and not on the ground. The Bari use the word *'diko* (singular *'dikolo*) which literally means *clouds*, to indicate the domain of a chief or king. The extent of a king's power is determined by the reach of his clouds. Places where his rain or drought does not reach are per definition outside his power. As a corollary of a king's rain fortunes, his 'clouds' may suddenly expand beyond the horizon, but they may just as easily contract. Rain careers were often ruined as quickly as they were built.[1]

This chapter deals with these processes of territorial expansion, contraction and fragmentation of royal power. As an example of expansionism, I examine the spread of the Kursak and the Bekat rain clans in Lulubo and Bari, respectively. As an example of fragmentation, I look at the division of the Lotuho kingdom. The chapter concludes

---

1   Lulubo informants told me that Lualla of Lokiliri was recognised as king by many of the Lokoya villages, including Ilyangari, one of the traditional enemies of Lokiliri. At first, I took this as mere boasting. Viewed from the perspective of control of the sky, the statement is not necessarily untrue. Taking into account a tradition according to which Lualla received tobacco from Lowe, another enemy, in payment of his rain, it would seem that Lualla, at one stage of his career, was believed to control the skies over a large part of the east bank, and was, therefore, considered superior to other kings in the area and given tribute accordingly.

with a comparison between the large-size kingdoms of the Bari and Lotuho and the small-scale polities of the Lulubo, Lokoya and the Pari.

Segmentary expansion: the Kursak

The story of how the Kursak became the Rainmakers in Lokiliri runs as follows:

12.1 *How the Kursak became the kings of Lokiliri* (Mogga Lado)

Before the arrival of the Kursak, the people of Lokiliri went to the Rainmaker in Ngangala to beg for rain. One Rainmaker was very cruel and did not allow the women who brought him ebony firewood to put their loads down while they sang songs in his praise to ask for the rain. The following year, a member of the Kursak clan advised the women to teach the Rainmaker a lesson and throw the firewood down and run away without singing. So they did. When the Rainmaker noticed the affront, he called his warriors to pursue the women. The warriors of Lokiliri who were led by a Kursak man had anticipated this response, waited for them and caught them in an ambush. The Rainmaker of Ngangala became very angry and declared that the Lulubo would forever suffer from drought. In revenge, the Kursak man, manifesting his *tomiya* (power to perform miracles), ordered that there should be no rain in Ngangala. Rain fell in Lokiliri even before the women had returned home, but none fell in Ngangala. After suffering from drought for more than two years, the Rainmaker of Ngangala acknowledged the superiority of the Kursak. This is how the Kursak became Rainmakers in Lulubo (Mogga Lado, ed., 1981:10).

The story is typical of the way the usurpation of power by a new leader is conceived. Power is won by a mixture of ruse and military prowess by an exceptional, charismatic leader in a power contest with a weak, cruel or decrepit ruler.

The Kursak protagonist of the story, according to most informants, is Tongun, the grandson of the first Kursak immigrant in the area. He was the son of Kuteng, whose father, Oni (Lokoya: Owoni), had immigrated from Fajelu and had established himself as a Rainmaker in Co'doni, one of the Northern Lulubo villages. Tongun, who must have lived around the middle of the nineteenth century, had married a girl from Kworijik, one of Lokiliri's moieties, and had stayed with his parents-in-law after the period of his bride service was over. He had five sons, all of whom became Rainmakers in their own right. Tira, the eldest, succeeded him as king of Lokiliri. Okale, his second son, followed the same marriage policy as his father and married a girl from Lokwe, the other moiety, and continued to stay with his parents-in-law after marriage. He became a Rainmaker in Lokwe. His son Lualla succeeded him and built up a vast network of alliances: with the kings of Shindiru, with the Ansar, with Mödi Adum and later with the Ugandan authorities. This network later enabled him to successfully claim the paramountcy over the Lulubo.

Tongun's younger sons, Lobijo, Langudwo and Pitia Mura, later also formed followings of their own:

Left: *Peter Tombe Lualla, Rainmaker of the Lokwe moiety, Lokiliri, beside his collection of rainstones.* Right: *Paride Tongun Lualla clad in the leaves of the* memele *tree on the occasion of the New Year* ('Kajuwaya'), *Lulubo B-Court Chief from 1976–2004.*

12.2 *The ramifications of the Kursak in Lokiliri* (oral history)

There was increasing intermarriage between the Goke and Lokwe sections which belonged to opposed moieties. Goke was the home of the descendants of the kings, Lokwe that of Lualla, the later government chief. When there was a stick fight between the two moieties Goke refused to come to the assistance of the other sections of Kworijik, because of its numerous marital ties with Lokwe and also — allegedly — because the other sections had pestered it with a song in which Goke was portrayed as the 'mother-in-law' of Lokwe. When Kworijik was defeated in the stick fight, there was further estrangement between Goke and the other sections. Two princes made use of the discontent in Kworijik. Lobijo set himself up as the leader of the section of Mögiri and Langudwo of the section of Ngerjebi. Pitia Mura stayed in his father's house in Goke and occupied it after his father's death. His descendants[2] became the guardians of *Tukure*, the central shrine and ceremonial ground of the Lulubo.

In the next generation, the Kursak further ensconced themselves not only in the different sections of Lokiliri, but also in the villages of Kudwo and Co'doni, replacing existing rain clans by making clever use of conflicts. The result was that by the beginning of the twentieth century, five generations, after the immigration of the first ancestor into Lulubo and three generations after Tongun's establishment in Lokiliri, a fairly dense network of Kursak rain power covered not only most sections of the four northern Lulubo villages, but also sections of Ngulere (Lokoya) and Ngangala (Bari speaking Lokoya).

---

2   The author is proud to be counted as one of them.

Segmentary expansion: the Bekat

The expansion of the Bekat in Bariland is of older date than that of the Kursak among their eastern neighbours. Compared to the violence of the fraternal rivalry in the Bekat clan, the Kursak story looks idyllic. The 'Golden Age' of Shindiru is associated with the name of Lokuryeje, who is most probably the founder of the Bekat dynasty in Shindiru.[3]

12.3 *The dispersal of the Bekat over Bariland* (oral history)[4]

The golden age of Shindiru came to an end as a result of fraternal rivalry between Jada and Mönöbur, the sons of King Mödi. They quarrelled over the killing of their sister, Juan, who was Mönöbur's uterine sister. She had been sacrificed to make an end to a series of disasters: drought, blighted crops and infertility of women. Mönöbur then seceded from his elder brother, Jada, who had condoned their sister's killing and started a kingdom of his own in Kuli on the west bank of the Nile.[5]

A second split occurred among the sons of Jada, Subek and Kose. Kose, the younger son, was the favourite of the people because of his rain powers. Subek, the senior son, moved off when the people selected Kose as king. He went to Bilinyan where he, or his descendants, established their own kingdom. In the story related by Beaton, Subek's motivation for migrating was to save face.

In the tradition collected by Haddon some twenty years earlier it is explicitly stated that the Rainmakers of Shindiru and Bilinyan were rivals and that both claimed the title of *matat 'duma* (great king).[6]

The Bekat of Bilinyan further separated into a group established on the east side of the mountain in Mögiri under Tombe-lo-Gwagwe and another group on the west side of the mountain under Dere and his son Muludyang, who was the father of King Logunu who received the Egyptian expedition in 1841.

---

3   In Chapter Two (p. 63–64), I have argued that the earlier rulers of Shindiru in the genealogy produced by Beaton (1934) are most probably not Bekat but Nyori.

4   This account is based on Beaton (1934), Haddon, (1911), and my fieldwork data.

5   The division reported by Werne between east and west bank Bari may very well be the aftermath of this split between Bekat Limat and Bekat Mönöbur (Werne, 1848:323).

6   It is likely that the effective centre of the Bekat kingdom moved to Bilinyan in response to the development of the iron industry there, the shrine in Shindiru being left to the younger brother. In the tradition recorded by Haddon, the split between the Bekat of Bilinyan and Shindiru is dated after the reign of Jangara and associated with the *monyekak* Mödi-lo-Busok who, we know, was still alive in 1860. The rivalry between Bilinyan and Shindiru for the supremacy over all the Bari is confirmed by Logunu's territorial claims to the Egyptian expedition: four days downstream and seven days upstream. The radius of seven days, even if taken as an exaggeration of the true size of the kingdom, easily includes Shindiru. The four days' march downstream from Bilinyan is hardly exaggerated. Werne was witness to the reality of Logunu's influence among the Tsera at Bukö. The latter, however, were quick to secede after Logunu's death which occurred before 1844. A plausible reason for this breakaway was the collapse of the iron monopoly of Bilinyan as a result of the trade with Khartoum.

Kose, in Shindiru, was succeeded by his brother, Ladu Jangara. Contemporary informants think of Jangara's rule as the dividing line between the era when the Bari were united and at peace, and the years of fragmentation and internecine warfare that characterised political life in Bari up to their inclusion in the Condominium in 1914.[7] The reign of Jangara's successor, Pitia Yeng-ko-Piyong, who received the visit of Don Angelo Vinco in 1851, was marked by the rivalry with his brother, Wulang. Legally, Pitia was Kose's son, biologically, however, he was the son of Jangara, who had inherited Kose's wife. So, in terms of primogeniture, Pitia was senior to Wulang, Jangara's own son. When Pitia grew old[8], Wulang, who feared that his turn to have a taste of power would never come, killed Pitia. Before he died, Pitia cursed him saying: "Your descendants will not inherit the kingship." And indeed, after the death of Wulang, who only ruled for a short period, the throne passed to Lugör, the son of Pitia with the wife of an elder brother.

I end this account of the expansion of the Bekat with Lugör, the last independent king of Shindiru who died in the 1880s or 1890s. After his death, the days of segmentary expansion were over. The power of his sons depended on their association with the warlord-chiefs and the colonial government.

In the Bekat tradition, fraternal rivalry in the rain clan is depicted as the main motor behind the clan's dispersal over most of Bariland. Next to the lineages mentioned there were Bekat Rainmakers in several other places. From north to south, they controlled — and to some extent still control — the rain in Pöyiti near Jebel Lado, in present-day Bungu on the west bank, in Darjur on the Nile bank further to the south.[9] There were also Bekat Rainmakers among the Nyangbara (Huntingford, 1953:72) and the Kuku (Nalder, 1937:218).

In the expansion of the Kursak and the Bekat, there was a kind of 'push' and 'pull'. The pulling factor was the reputation of a particular Rainmaker or rain dynasty. Villages or village sections which had so far been outside the power sphere of a particular clan invited a son of the Rainmaker or another rain prince to come and stay with them. In such cases, the ruling rain family might either be dethroned or relegated to a subordinate role in matters of rain. Such changes occurred especially in times of drought, in an attempt to solve a rain crisis.

The most important pushing factors were the conflicts between brothers rivalling over the succession to their father's throne. If one of the brothers set himself up as a Rainmaker in a place away from his father's centre — either inside the existing rain area or outside of it — the potential harm of the conflict over succession was mitigated. At the same time, the position of the royal family as a whole was strengthened. Despite the continuation of clan rivalry after the split, clan solidarity could be expected to

---

7   Haddon puts the rivalry over supremacy between Shindiru and Bilinyan after the death of Jangara.

8   Vaudey, who must have received his information from Vinco, described Pitia as an old man in 1852 (Vaudey, 1852:528).

9   Muludiyang of Darjur who was the host of the explorer Dr Peney in 1861 (Malté-Brun, 1863:44–45). The Bekat of Darjur were in continuous competition with the Nyori of Tombur.

prevail in conflicts with third parties. If we compare the expansion histories, it would seem that in the case of the Kursak, the accent was on the 'pull', and in that of the Bekat on the 'push'.

According to Haddon the dispersal of Bekat Rainmakers over most of the Bari-speaking area was not only the result of conflicts between brothers or between fathers and sons.

> It is stated that the king sent his sons into these dependencies to govern them and to act as local agents for collecting fees, also that he sent some of his 'boys' who knew about rainmaking to act as local rainmakers and forward the fees to him (Haddon, 1911: 98).

Haddon adds that several of Lugör's sons had found employment in this way. He gives one example of the application of the principle:

12.4 *The placement of a Bekat rain prince* (Haddon)

Jada Lugör, the son of Lugör, was asked to become the Rainmaker for the subjects of Kirba Lokole, the warlord-chief of Logo at the turn of the century. Kirba had tried to make rain himself with rainstones purchased from an Acholi man, but he had failed. When Jada took office, he had told Kirba to hide the Acholi stones under a fireplace so that their power could not interfere with his stones. Jada's rituals — despite threats by Kirba to kill him — had no result either. Finally, a settlement was reached in which Jada had to pay back all the tribute he had received (Haddon, 1911: 146).

Jada Lugör's placement as a Rainmaker in Logo can hardly be considered an illustration of the expansion through the use of agnatic ties. The initiative was taken by Kirba, who tried everything in his power to overcome the major weakness in his position: his lack of rain powers.

Above (Ch. 4, p. 119), we noted that Haddon did not realise that commoner chiefs like Kirba were a recent phenomenon among the Bari. Far from forming an instance of Bekat expansionism, the case highlights the new subordination of the Bekat to the warlord-chiefs.

Is the model of the segmentary state applicable?

If the appointment of princes to rule outlying districts was a deliberate strategy to increase the power of the centre, the system of Bekat and Kursak political domination would resemble that of the Alur (speakers of a Lwoo language living in northwestern Uganda and northeastern Congo) as described and analysed by Southall (1953, 1965, 1988). An essential feature of this system is the fact that political expansion is achieved through the placement of princes and other relatives to serve as Rainmakers among groups that have hitherto been outside the orbit of the king's power. As a result of the brotherly solidarity between the members of the rain clan, a situation emerges in which political power over a wide area is centralised such that the network of kinship relations between senior and junior segments inside the clan simultaneously functions as the political framework of what Southall chooses to call a *state*. This type of centralised authority which is based on the clan solidarity of the royals at the top and, from below, on the veneration of the commoners for the special political, judicial and rainmaking skills of the members of rain clan, is classified by Southall as a *segmentary state*, a type of political organisation that is intermediate between centralised, hierarchical states and acephalous segmentary formations. Contrary to the hierarchical character of the state where power derives from the centre and is delegated to the periphery, power in the segmentary state results from a cumulative process initiated from the bottom. As a result of acceptance of the king by ever wider circles of followers, his power has a *pyramidal* character.

As far as the process of the formation of a widening base for the power of the rain clan is concerned, the Bari and Lulubo cases fit Southall's model. There are, however, other dimensions of royal power in the political systems studied here that are at odds with the segmentary state model: first of all the competitive character of the relationship between co-ruling members of the same rain clan, and the role of brotherly rivalry in the process of expansion. Scanning my field notes and the extracts of the written sources on dynastic history of peoples on the Equatorian east bank of the Nile, it is difficult to find cases of brothers of the rain clan acting in concord; while there are plenty of examples of brothers competing or fighting with one another, also in the case of the 'milder' Lulubo. Secondly, it is difficult to accommodate the systematic antagonism between ruler and ruled in the model. Fear of the king's power to withhold the rain played an important role in the operation of his authority on the east bank. To the extent that the powers over rain have a transcendent origin, the king's relation to his subjects has a hierarchical rather than a 'pyramidal' character. Lastly, there is the more general objection against the use of the concept of the state for a constellation where the issue of the legitimate use of physical force is far from settled, let alone that such coercion was monopolised by the top.

There are good reasons to doubt that placement of sons or brothers as agents of the king was ever systematically practised in our area of study as a policy to strengthen the king's power. If the king needed agents to represent his interests, it may be assumed that he would rather choose his slaves or his sister's sons.[10] The use of slaves (*'dupi*) as agents by the Bari kings is well attested by informants. Pitia Lugör, for example, is known to have relied on them to make rain and to collect the *'doket*. When I asked a Lotuho informant if King Lomoro appointed brothers to represent his interests, the informant laughed and replied: "By doing so he would certainly have undermined his position!"

The division of the Lotuho

In Chapter Eight (Case 8.2), we saw how the escalated dispute between the ruling *monyomiji* who were faithful to King Ngalamitiho and the aspiring generation led

---

10   In Lulubo the same word is used for both statuses: *opi*, singular: *opiogo*. The relationship between sister's son and mother's brother is discussed in Chapter Three (p. 87–90).

by Prince Ohurak led to Imatari's destruction by the Toposa. In the battles between the Toposa and Lotuho, both the stubborn king and the rebellious son were killed. Ohurak's young son, Oyalala, the only heir who had rain both from his father's and mother's side, was captured by the Toposa during the fighting and believed dead until he re-appeared in Lotuho many years later as a grown-up man. In the absence of the true heir after Ohurak's death, the *monyomiji* offered the throne to Irwangi, the son of Ngalamitiho by a *black wife*, a daughter of parents one or both of whom 'did not have rain'.[11]

This choice, so Lotuho historians say, was the beginning of the division of the Lotuho into two kingdoms: Loronyo under the dynasty of Mayya, the son of Oyalala, and Tirangore under the dynasty of Hujang, the son of Irwangi's brother, Okomo.

The Lotuho traditions that I have collected picture the transition from the collective existence of most Lotuho in Imatari[12] to their scattering in twenty different villages or so as a rather sudden event in the period immediately following the Toposa incursion.

The history of the division of the Lotuho can be divided into a number of stages according to the protagonists who were the principal rivals:

12.5 *The division of the Lotuho kingdom* (based on oral traditions of both dynasties)

Round 1: Irwangi versus his brothers

The queen given to Irwangi to seal the covenant between the king and the *monyomiji* was Nyadinga, an Acholi rain princess from Obbo, the sister of Kachiba.[13] When Irwangi, who is portrayed as an old man, did not have any children with Nyadinga, his younger brother Abalu tried to seduce the queen. Irwangi discovered the intrigue and surprised the couple in the cave which served as their hide-out at the moment when Nyadinga was plucking Abalu's beard. Irwangi killed his brother on the spot.

Olutoyek, another brother, not discouraged by Abalu's fate, also tried to win Nyadinga. He met his death in the same way as Abalu.

Finally, Okomo, the youngest of the four brothers, tried his luck. Again Irwangi was informed of the affair and prepared himself to kill Okomo. One day, at sunset, when the two were making love in one of the caves at Hoding, Irwangi entered the cave and raised his spear. But Okomo saw the silhouette, thrown on the wall of the cave by the setting sun, just in time to escape.

After the elders pleaded with Irwangi not to kill yet another brother, Irwangi conceded to compromise and agreed that Nyadinga be brought before the assembly of the *monyomiji*. The *monyomiji* asked her: "Nyadinga! Whom do you love, Irwangi or Okomo?" She answered "Okomo". At this reply Irwangi decided to resign from the kingship. He asked for a black goat and water, purified himself of the kingship and gave a blessing to Nyadinga.

---

11   On the term 'black wife' see Ch. 2, n. 4, p. 49

12   The villages of Otunge, Chalamini and Ilyeu were never part of Imatari.

13   Kachiba was Baker's host on his journey from Tirangore to Bunyoro (1866, Vol. I, chapters 9 and 10); Kachiba is the king being carried on the illustration on p. 246.

Round 2: Oyalala versus Okomo

Under Okomo's rule, the Lotuho were united. He gave his subjects abundant rain for many years. This period of calm ended when Oyalala, the true heir to the throne, reappeared on the Lotuho scene.[14] Oyalala had grown into a man among the Toposa of the Nmachi section. There, he spent his time looking after cows. He had acquired a reputation for his miraculous powers. He merely needed to pull some grass from the ground for a pool of water to be formed. One day, when he came to Lohutok, the iron working centre of the Lomiya on the Lopit range, to order cowbells, he was recognised by his nurse by a scar on the forehead which he had incurred when he had fallen from his nurse's back as a baby. When Mosingo, the king of the Lomiya, who was a maternal uncle of Oyalala, heard this, he sent a message around among the Lotuho informing the *monyomiji* to come and collect their true king when he would come back to collect his cowbells. The *monyomiji* of Loronyo responded to the appeal and came to Lohutok. They cornered Oyalala in front of a steep rock pretending they were going to show him some more bells. Oyalala, who was still unaware of his true descent, cried for help because he thought they were going to kill him. The *monyomiji* quickly sacrificed four goats of different colour configurations to prevent Oyalala from turning into lightning[15] and smeared him with the stomach contents. After this, they took him home to Loronyo.

Oyalala established himself as a Rainmaker in Loronyo, while Okomo still ruled from Hoding. His reputation, however, spread all over Lotuho and not long after his appearance, the *monyomiji* decided that Nyadinga, the official queen, should be taken away from Okomo and be given to Oyalala.

Thus it happened. Okomo felt humiliated and started to brood on revenge and caused a drought (by collecting some water of the first rain and putting it under the fireplace). When Oyalala was questioned by the *monyomiji* concerning the drought and could not give a satisfactory explanation, Okomo went to him pretending to give some advice from experience. Okomo pointed at the difficulties he had experienced with Nyadinga when she was his wife. He convinced Oyalala that she was the cause of the drought and that she wanted to ruin his rain career. He circulated the same story to the *monyomiji* who decided that Nyadinga should be killed. To avoid further trouble, Oyalala agreed. Nyadinga escaped and hid in a cave near Iloli. There, the *monyomiji* found her and killed her. When Okomo heard she had been killed, he removed the spell so that there was abundant rain again. To Oyalala, he said: "As long as you stayed with that woman you could not be at peace and your royal power remained barren, but you see: now your rain rains."

---

14   The recorded version was told to me by the senior son of the present queen of the Mayya dynasty. This version has more miraculous elements than the version of the story told in the rivalling kingdom of Tirangore. No informant, however, expressed scepticism regarding the identity of Oyalala as the 'lost son'.

15   Asang, the ancestor of the royal dynasty, had first disappeared into lightning when the monyomiji of Otunge tried to catch him after they found out that he had killed and eaten their children. Only after smearing Asang with the stomach contents of four goats of different colour configurations could the *monyomiji* catch him to be their king. See Chapter Eighteen for a description and discussion of the Lotuho installation ritual (p.399–402).

Okomo's wrath was not satisfied yet. He not only wanted revenge for the loss of Nyadinga but also for the royal herds that had been transferred to Oyalala. He took *Asalak*, one of the two sacred spears brought by Imuhunyi from Bilinyan (Case 2.5), and speared a heap of cattle dung with it. When cattle died in big numbers, the *monyomiji* came to Oyalala to question him on the new disaster. Oyalala went to Okomo again to ask his advice. Okomo gave him *Asalak* to use it in a sacrifice to stop the epidemic. Oyalala did not know it was the wrong spear. To the *monyomiji*, who came back to him when the cattle continued dying, Oyalala explained the measures he had taken. "But why did you make a sacrifice with *Asalak*?" they asked. "*Asalak* can only make things worse. *Igusolemye* should have been used." Oyalala then also collected *Igusolemye* from Okomo and performed the ritual again. The epidemic stopped.

Oyalala now realised that he had been cheated by Okomo all along. He asked his wife, Ibur, to prepare beer. He stirred it with *Asalak* and offered it to Okomo while he himself and his followers drank from a different calabash. Soon afterwards, Okomo developed stomach troubles which eventually caused his death.

When Oyalala refused to come to his deathbed, Okomo made two figurines out of clay, each carrying a spear. He put them facing one another saying: "These two will never stop fighting. From now on the kingdom is broken into two!"[16]

Okomo's revenge did not end with his death, so contemporary Lotuho chroniclers say. A serious drought followed Okomo's death. Oyalala was suspected again, but he managed to influence public opinion by putting the blame on Bobit, Okomo's senior son and successor, and, therefore, Oyalala's main rival. The *monyomiji* of Hiyala then killed Bobit. Okomo's other sons, including Hujang, all fled in fear of Oyalala. When the drought persisted, the *monyomiji* of Hiyala put the blame directly at Oyalala's doorstep and sentenced him to death saying: "You caused us to kill Bobit, now it is your turn to be killed!" So, Hiyala killed Oyalala. According to my informant, the drought that caused Oyalala's death was the posthumous vengeance (*epit*) of Okomo.

---

16   There are at least two more traditions of how Okomo cursed the Lotuho. Both refer to one of the last *ekubo* (annual cultivation day for the king) in Okomo's honour in which the *monyomiji* of the whole kingdom participated. In the first one, Okomo gave the right front leg of the bull that was killed for the occasion to Tirangore and the two hind legs to Loronyo and Hatiha. By doing so, he implied that the *monyomiji* of Tirangore would be in the forefront and on top, while those of Loronyo and Hatiha would remain a disorganised lot and lagging behind. In the other story, Okomo is said to have blessed Tirangore by sprinkling its *monyomiji* with a mixture of stomach contents and iron ore after the participants in the digging party from Loronyo and Hatiha had left, thus making Tirangore to be the most powerful of the Lotuho villages.

Bokké, Queen of Tirangore, likely to be the same person as Queen Iloyi (from Baker, 1866, Vol. 1:216)[17]

▓ *Round 3: Mayya versus Hujang*

Oyalala was the last king to rule the Lotuho as a single kingdom. Mayya (Emin's 'Latomé') and Hujang (Baker's 'Moy'), the respective sons of Oyalala and Okomo, first tried to unite the Lotuho under their individual authority but these attempts failed.

The definitive split, in Lotuho conception, was the work of a woman: Queen Ibur, the widow of Oyalala, a daughter of the king of Faciti. After her husband's death, she had inherited the responsibility of the rain and, therefore, she was, at least in theory, the most powerful person in Lotuho. To keep the Lotuho united, it would have sufficed for Hujang to marry Ibur. But Ibur had set her mind on her firstborn son Mayya to become the king. She refused Hujang's offer and instead cleverly arranged that Hujang marry her sister Iloyi. She also arranged that the *monyomiji* paid for her sister's bridewealth. The fact that there were now two rain queens — and, therefore, two legitimate lines of descent — made the division of the kingdom irreversible.

---

17   Baker described Queen Bokké, wife of Hujang, as a person with natural authority. On her own authority she stopped the soldiers of the visiting traders' army from harassing a group of women who were on their way home from fetching water. Since Baker mentioned that Bokké was Hujang's 'head-wife', it is likely that she is the same person as Iloyi of whom we know that she was the wife that had been married by the *monyomiji*. Iloyi was photographed as an old lady by Powell-Cotton in 1903 (1904:464; photo on. p. 312). The name Bokké was not recognised by the members of the royal family I interviewed. In this connection: see my remark on personal names Ch. 14, n. 32, p. 316.

The Lotuho tell their history as an alternation of periods of violent rivalry between claimants to the throne and rarer periods of relative calm when the kingdom was united under a single king. During the periods of confrontation, the protagonists formed neatly polarised pairs: Irwangi/Abalu, Irwangi/Olutoyek, Irwangi/Okomo, Okomo/Oyalala, Oyalala/Bobit, Mayya/Hujang. Ideally, the protagonists end the contest by killing their rival, if not by the sword (Abalu, Olutoyek), then by poisoning (Oyalala against Okomo) or by poisoning one's rival's rain (Okomo versus Nyadinga; Oyalala versus Bobit; Okomo, posthumously, versus Oyalala).

In the stories I collected, the focus is on the duelling heroes. Not much is said about the nature of their following, although it seems plausible that in the rivalry between Okomo and Oyalala, a certain antagonism between the northwestern and the southeastern Lotuho played a role. The boundaries between the two kingdoms are erratic and have shifted repeatedly in response to the ups and downs in the rainmaking reputations of their kings.

Although the Lotuho were staunchly centralist, expecting their kings to play a unifying role in their social life, and despite the institutional checks to limit the rivalry for the throne — the rule of primogeniture, the requirement that the successor should have 'double' rain descent, and the rule that there could only be one queen at a time — these principles and checks could not stand up to the forces of division. Lotuho political reality reverted to a *de facto* dualist formation, the two rival kingdoms being structured in a way analogous to moieties on the village level. There was one crucial difference with the moiety scenario, however. The two kingdoms considered themselves sovereign and felt no impediment to fight each other with the spear and with the help of foreign allies.

In the aftermath of the division of the Lotuho, an opportunity offered itself to reunite the rain of Lotuho after King Wani of Loronyo had been killed and his widow Tafeng was not immediately remarried to one of Wani's brothers. Three of Hujang's sons (Lomoro, Onik, and Lohide) made an attempt to marry her. This story is told in Chapter Fourteen (Case 14.1).

As I said, the boundaries between the twin kingdoms of the Lotuho shifted many times, villages having few scruples to turn their back on the king if the rival from the other kingdom looked more promising. Hatiha, the area around the present-day administrative centre of Torit, changed its allegiance four times within half a century. In the 1860s, it performed *ekubo* (annual cultivation for the king) for Kamiru when he resided in Tirangore. At the turn of the twentieth century it recognised Queen Tafeng of Loronyo, while around 1905, they were followers of Lohide, one of the sons of Hujang of Tirangore. After Lohide's death, they returned to Acalili in Loronyo. Changes of allegiance also occurred at the sectional level as the case of Imeni in Hiyala proves (cf. p. 135).

If we compare the history of the Lotuho and the Bari, we see a degree of inverse symmetry in the way the history of their respective kingdoms unfolds. While the history of the Bekat Kingdom is a process of expansion, branching out from a single source (Shindiru) and resulting in inevitable fragmentation, the point of departure of the historic Lotuho kingdoms is the powerful unity in the days of Imatari, which was lost and which, despite repeated attempts by successive kings, could not be restored. The inverse symmetry goes further, for while Shindiru remained the main single source of rain power for a large number of small rivalling rain areas, the centre of Imatari was eventually lost and replaced by two comparatively large, permanently rivalling kingdoms.

The arena within which the Lotuho princes competed for power was limited to the existing Lotuho communities. I have no evidence that Lotuho princes set themselves up as Rainmakers in communities that had so far been outside the orbit of the rain of Igago. Segmentary expansion was not a safety valve of dynastic rivalry as it was among the Bari and Lulubo.

The territorial span of the centre

Between the Nile and the Kidepo, the territorial scope of kingdoms stabilised in two typical ways: as a single conglomeration of settlements located at the foot of a mountain or as a string of many villages located along the banks of a river. The first situation is that found among the Lulubo, the Lokoya and the Pari. The second is the situation among the Lotuho and the Bari. Let us first examine the first type of territorial scope.

In the Lulubo villages, rain power is most dispersed. In Aru, for example, each of the four sections has its own Rainmaker, each of them from a different rain clan. In addition, there is a Rainmaker of the village as a whole. Above, we noted that although the senior lineage descending from Tongun-lo-Kuteng provided the Rainmaker-kings of Lokiliri, many sections had their own Kursak man who acted largely independently of the king. In the two northern villages, a situation similar to that in Lokiliri prevailed.

The kings of Liria control the rain on Mount Opone, which includes both Liria and Ilyangari, a village which is an offshoot of Liria. Kamuturu (Langabu), once part of the same kingdom, had its rainstones stolen by Liria (cf. Case14.5) and invited a Rainmaker from Bilinyan to take care of its rain. In Ngulere, the Onyati control the rain, but until recently Kursak also had a following. The Kursak Rainmaker has recently sold his stones to the Rainmaker of Liria. In the kingdom of Lowe, which consists of a string of settlements on and around the Lowe Mountain, a single family had the hegemony, but there are at least two subordinate rain families with a following of several sections (cf. Case 9.6). Lafon is a single agglomeration consisting of six sections united by their joint recognition of a single rain dynasty. However, it is generally believed that the *rwath* of the Kor moiety also has rain powers.

In all these cases, the territorial radius of the king's power was limited to a single agglomeration, or to a group of adjacent settlements located at the foot of the same mountain.

Among the Bari and Lotuho, the hegemony of the ruling dynasty covered a far wider area. The power of the kings of Shindiru and Bilinyan stretched over the whole length of Bariland (some 150 kilometres from south to north) and even included areas of neighbouring peoples. The Lotuho Kingdom of Loronyo extended over a distance which could not be covered in a single day's march. That of Tirangore was smaller, at least during most of the colonial period. In Bari, there were a number of rain areas belonging to non-Bekat Rainmakers, especially in the south of Bariland. These Rainmakers, whose areas were relatively small, recognised the sovereignty of their big brother in Shindiru. The conception of the relationship that existed between these echelons had a definitely hierarchical character. According to a comment by Haddon, the minor Rainmakers (*kimak nadit*) went to the major Rainmaker (*matat 'duma*) when there were problems with their rain, while the major Rainmaker went directly to *Ngun-lo-Ki* (God of Heaven) to solve his problems (Haddon, 1911: 97).

Why this difference between the Bari and the Lotuho, on the one hand, and the Lulubo, the Lokoya and the Pari, on the other? I want to suggest two answers: one based on military considerations, the other on the difference in the opportunity to levy tribute in the two situations.

Since the plain-dwelling Bari and Lotuho lacked the strategic defence the mountains provided for their enemies, they were more vulnerable to attack. As single village units, they had an interest in compensating for their greater vulnerability by forming larger units as to be a match for their enemies, be they mountain-dwelling Lulubo or Lokoya as in the Bari case, or plain-dwelling Toposa, as in the Lotuho case. On the other hand, with their 'mountain fortresses' as bases, the Lokoya, the Lulubo and the Pari could afford smaller political units.

The chronicles of the kings of Shindiru, which consist of an enumeration of wars against the Lulubo, the Lokoya and the Pari, confirm this connection. All the kings of Shindiru immediately preceding the era of foreign intervention—Kose, Jangara and Pitia Yeng-ko-Piyong — waged war with their eastern neighbours. Their names in Bari history are mainly remembered in association with the tricks they employed in warding off the feared mountain-dwellers.

Interestingly, Beaton's stories also mention that the different Lulubo and Lokoya villages created alliances to fight the Bari. Kose, for example, had to cope with a combined force of Liria, Ilyangari and Lulubo. Jangara had to defend himself against joint attacks of Liria, Ilyangari and Lowe.

The establishment of the Bekat in Bilinyan is associated with Lokoya attacks as well. According to Haddon (1911, Appendix VII: 15), the Bekat settled there in the days when Mödi-lo-Bosuk was the Master of the Land. The Bekat joined forces with the local clans in order to fight the Lokoya. The fact that many of the wars with their eastern neighbours ended in defeat explains the eagerness of the Bari kings of Bilinyan to seek alliances with the 'Turks' when these arrived.

The pressure put on the Lotuho by their Toposa neighbours may be held accountable for the formation and continued existence of the Lotuho kingdoms. A second factor that may have facilitated the creation of more large-scale political units among the Lotuho and the Bari was their cattle. Cattle, as a form of wealth, can be accumulated and transported over long distances. Among the Lulubo and the Lokoya cattle were rare, even before the period of foreign intervention and the spread of sleeping-sickness. Tribute to the Lokoya and Lulubo Rainmaker was mainly in the form of agricultural labour; while among the Bari and the Lotuho cattle seemed to have been the principal item of tribute. The combination of existing centralist institutions with the need for unified defence and the availability of a form of wealth that allowed for a centralisation of tribute over a wider area created conditions favouring the emergence of political units that encompassed several villages. On the other hand, the strong strategic locations of the Lokoya and Lulubo and their capacity to create effective alliances, if necessary, created conditions which favoured smaller-scale political units.

The uniformity of the age-class system among the Pari, the Lokoya and the Lulubo, and the synchronic timing of their ceremonies of transfer of generational power created an ideal basis for the formation of military alliances. Since the structure of command, the ranking of the age-sets, and the rules of commensality and division of the spoils were similar for the different communities, joint ventures could quickly be organised.

Between the Lokoya/Lulubo, on the one hand, and the Bari/Lotuho, on the other, the Pari occupy a somewhat anomalous, intermediate position. They had large herds, but lived in a single, vast conglomeration (today more than 10,000 people) which coincided with the Pari Kingdom. Although Lafon was located on a hill, the tiny size of Lipul hardly offered the kind of protection that the mountains further south offered to the Lulubo and Lokoya. The mainstay of Pari military strength must have been the size of their settlement and the number of their fighters. In this respect, Lafon may be the last surviving specimen of a type of settlement of cattle owners that was more common in the past, judging from the legends concerning the size of Imatari and Segele.

The evidence from Eastern Equatoria presented here would contradict the thesis of Schneider, according to which more evolved forms of social inequality, including state formation in East Africa, correlate with mainly agricultural societies, while pastoral systems tend to resist central authority and remain more egalitarian (Schneider, 1979). Between the Nile and the Kidepo, the Bari, who were more cattle-oriented than the other societies, were also the least egalitarian.

Conclusion

In this chapter, we noted that the balance of power between king and people in the Bari and the Lotuho political systems tilted towards the king, more so than among the Lulubo, the Lokoya and the Pari. This difference between the two types of polity is also reflected in the territorial scope of power. We have examined some explanations for the contrast. In the next chapter, we shall see that this difference in the people/king power balance is also reflected in the social distribution of powers over disaster. The Lotuho and the Bari concentrate these powers in one person. The Lulubo and the Lokoya offer an example of a more egalitarian solution.

The Fingers of God 'ovalahojok' of Liria taking off in solemn procession to the community shrine up the mountain......

....kneeling at successive stations during the climb, praying and putting their hands together moulding heaps of soil for fertility and abundance (Liria, 1986).

13

The Fingers of God:
The Cosmological Dimension of Kingship

The confrontations between the king and his people involve political issues; above all, however, they have a cosmic dimension, in which the stakes are rain and drought, disease and fertility, abundant harvests and plagues etc. Whenever the community is struck by disaster, king and people accuse each other and press the other to take away the cause of the adversity.

Rather than just saying that the king's power has a cosmological aspect — as is customary in studies of both the Frazerian and the structural-functionalist tradition — it would be more correct to say that the whole of nature, its order and disorder, its capricious favours and calamities, is one grand stage on which king and people battle for power.

Nature, as a location outside ordered life, is the cosmological zone where the expelled forces of violence dwell. Culture coincides with the zone of ordered social interaction, ritually purged of these forces. Nature and culture are locations in a ritual drama. It is the prime responsibility of the Nilotic king to keep the forces that lie in wait to re-invade ordered life in the form of plagues, pests, diseases and drought at bay. His task it is to keep the disorder outside, far away from the peace within. When the boundary between inside and outside is maintained, and the subjects enjoy relative prosperity, the king is "the dynamic centre of the universe" — to use Seligman's classic characterisation of the power of the 'divine king' (1934). But when the boundary is blurred, when the community is beset with disaster, the antagonism in the relationship between king and people comes to the surface and dramas unfold of the sort described in the regicide case of Lowe (cf. Case 7.6).

The presentation and analysis of the dramatic escalations in the relationship between king and people during rain crises is the subject matter of Chapters Sixteen and Seventeen. The focus of this chapter is the social distribution of cosmic power over different persons and offices. More than once in this study, we met with officials called 'Masters' (Master of the Land, Master of the Mountain, etc.). It is time to introduce these bearers of special offices and to situate their power in relation to that of the 'Master of Rain', the king.

Compartmentalisation of powers: Lokiliri

The importance of the role of these Masters can be appreciated by listing the offices that exist in Lokiliri. Each of these offices is hereditary within a particular lineage of a particular clan. Practically, each clan has an *opopi*, a 'power' or 'office', which is a generic term also used to refer to the royal office.

N. Masters of disaster and blessing, Lokiliri

Office	Clan	Power of office *(opopi)*
Rain	Kursak , lineage of Tira	• rain in Lokiliri as a whole • rain in Kworijik moiety
	Kursak , lineage of Okale	• rain in Lokwe moiety, including the power over termites
	Kursak, lineage of Okale, other sub-lineage	• rain in Loronyo section of Lokwe
	Kursak, lineage of Lobijo	• rain in Lomega section of Kworijik
Land/Soil	Loo	• fertility of the land in Lokiliri, Co'doni and Kudwo • 'cooking of the land' (ritual preparation of the land before the cultivation season) • purification of the land of bloodshed • annual consecration of Tukure (central shrine of Lokiliri) • annual blessing of the *monyomiji* before the hunt of the New Year festival • annual expulsion of diseases to the Bari (*rozwa*) • protection against snakes and scorpions
	Modungi	• fertility of the land between Lokiliri and Langabu
Mountain	Kokajin	• promotion of human fertility as *Master of Lukedini* , the bell-shrine which is a dependency of the more important mountain-shrine of 'Dujo in Co'doni • protection against certain epidemics • protection against crop-eating insects (*onga)*
	Onyoko	• fertility of the land around Kelio Mountain • protection against baboons, snakes and scorpions
In'di	Onyati	• protection against *in'di*, a harmful crop-eating insect, possibly a species of aphis
Locusts	Ongairo	• protection against locusts
Tsetse fly	Okare	• protection of the health of cattle, in particular against the tsetse fly
Leopards	Okare, originally Kokajin)	• control of leopards in the bush surrounding Lokiliri (The office was inherited maternally after Kokajin was forced to resign from it after causing a fatal incident)
	Paole	• control of leopards in the bush surrounding Ngulere
Lions	Kutunot (clan of blacksmiths)	• control of lions
	Koluba	• control of lions

Office	Clan	Power of office *(opopi)*
Bows	Okare	• control of the directionality of arms and projectiles so that one's own hit enemy targets and those of the enemy miss their aim or boomerang • ceremony of sharpening spears and arrows before war and hunt • ceremony of lighting the grass before the hunting season
Grain	Kanamu	• proclamation of *edwar*, the state of exception during the ripening of the first crop when all violence, drumming, shouting, etc. is forbidden • ceremony of lifting *edwar* • ceremony of eating of first crop that he cooks in dew
Worms	Orupi	• protection against worm-pests (The Master of Worms was discontinued by the *monyomiji* but reinstated after an infestation of worms in 1985)
Winds	Kursak, lineage of Okale	• protection against winds that destroy crops, particularly the gusts of wind blowing from a gap in Kilifomu Mountain (maternally inherited)
Birds	Unknown clan in Aru	• protection against bird invasions for the whole Lulubo area

Each of these Masters is believed to control a specific threat to the well-being and the survival of the community. The position of the Master rests on the belief that he has the power to allow the misfortunes under his custody to enter the community. Except for the power over spears and arrows and the power to provide immunity to enemy attacks, most of the offices listed concern powers over 'natural disasters' (if we include disease in the realm of nature). It is significant that the protection of human and natural threats is faced and handled by practices from a single ritual repertory.

The powers attributed to the different Masters correspond to the most common misfortunes the Lulubo face in their struggle for survival. Table O classifies these disasters according to three criteria: their economic specificity (the number of branches of production affected, that is, agriculture, livestock, etc.), the duration of the disaster, and its spatial distribution.

Drought scores highest as a disaster; attacks of leopards and lions lowest, since they rarely affect the community as a whole. The disasters in between all affect the survival of the community or a part of it, for a longer or shorter period of time, either in a single branch of production (agriculture, animal husbandry, hunting, fishing, etc.) or in several branches at once.

The table provides a partial explanation why the power over rain and drought should be the attribute of the king. In a later chapter, I show that rain is important not only economically but also symbolically. The Lulubo address the Masters of the Land and of the Mountain with the same title as the king (*osi*). The elevated status of the Master of the Land derives from his concern with bloodshed and his role as a peacemaker. Blood may cause the land to be infertile (*avwa*). The land, I was told, is like a quick-tempered, highly sensitive child. If it is not treated well it may refuse to yield its favours. It is the duty of the Master of the Land to ensure that this important partner to the survival of the community is not upset and remains well-disposed towards the people who take their livelihood from it.

O. The relative gravity of common disasters

Disaster	Economic specificity + = more than one -= only one branch of production affected	Duration + = long -= short	Spread + = wide -= limited	Score
drought	+	+	+	3
epidemics in man	+	+	+	3
epidemics in livestock	-	+	+	2
infertility in man	+	+	-	2
floods	-	+	-	1
soil infertility	-	+	-	1
crop pests (worms, insects)	-	+	-	1
locust and insect plagues	-	-	+	1
crop-eating animals (birds, baboons, etc.)	-	+	-	1
predatory man-and livestock-eating animals	+	-	-	1

In previous chapters, I pointed at the importance of population numbers for the survival of the community in times of war. The Master of the Mountain is the guardian of the birth rate. He performs rituals to promote fertility in human beings. He is also responsible for the control of epidemic diseases. These are sometimes kept in pots in a cave in the mountain and released when the anger of the Master of the Mountain is kindled.

The 'mountain' is frequently used as a metaphor for the village community. In Lotuho, where villages are not necessarily located on mountains, the office equivalent to that of Master of the Mountain is that of *amonyemiji* ('Master of the Village'). The mountain itself with its caves, crevices, snakes and sheer volume provides a powerful image of reproductivity. The shrine of the Master of the Mountain is usually a cave inhabited by snakes. In some places, a bell is fixed in the cave. It is tolled during fertility rituals. In other caves, pots are placed. In some places (Kudwo) these pots symbolise the communities for the benefit of which the fertility rituals are performed, in others (Shindiru, Kajobo)[1] each pot is believed to contain a specific disease controlled by the Master of the Mountain.[2]

---

1   Kajobo Mountain is located between Ilyangari and Lokiliri. It is now deserted. The Onyati clan is still held responsible for the cave shrine.

2   The Rainmaker of the Lokuriaba clan of Ngangala also possessed sacred pots which he kept in his house. These contained rain, grasshoppers, worms and crop-eating insects.

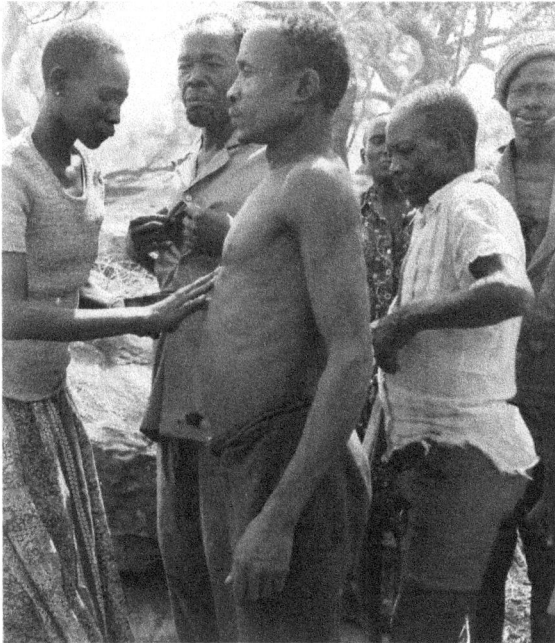

The Mistress of the Mountain of Langabu administering a blessing for fertility; applying an ointment that has been touched by the snakes of her mountain.

During the ritual for the promotion of human fertility, the Master climbs up to the cave and anoints himself, or two figurines that represent a man and a woman, with oil, beer or milk. He then has himself or the figurines licked clean by the snakes.[3] After this, he descends into the village imitating the crying of a baby. A goatskin used to carry babies is suspended from his shoulders with an effigy of a newborn child in it.

In many places, there is overlap between the Office of the Mountain and the Office of the Land; the care for the land at the foot of a mountain is then included in the Office of the Mountain.

The Masters controlling other disasters are not addressed as 'king'. The Lulubo refer to them as *modi* (person) of a particular disaster, for example: *o'duri modi*, 'the man of the leopards', or *omuri modi*, 'the man of worms'. In Lokoya the title *ohobu* is used for a slightly larger number of office holders. In addition to the Lulubo triad, they honour the Masters of Winds, the Master of Bows and the Master of Grain with the title *ohobu*. The word *ohoboloni*, meaning *elder* or *Big Man*, is used for the minor offices. From the point of view of the disasters controlled by them, the main difference between men addressed as 'king' and the others seems to be the more permanent character impact on the community's well-being of the disorders *kings* are dealing with, the minor offices generally being associated with calamities of short duration.

The boundary between Master and king is not sharp. The use of the honorific title depends on the context and is subject to individual interpretation. When I addressed the 'Queen of the Mountain' in Liria as *ohobu*, she objected saying she was a mere

---

3   The Mistress of the Mountain of Lowe is herself licked by snakes. I do not know whether male Masters of the Mountain subject themselves to the same practice.

ohoboloni and that only the Rainmaker was *ohobu*. But later in the interview, she did not brush off the suggestion that in virtue of her control of population numbers she was probably the most important of the six 'kings'.[4] Her initial reservation did indicate that the relative importance of the different offices is subject to jealousy and rivalry.

The more prominent officials have an assistant (Lulubo: *jaigo*, pl. *jai*) whose office is also hereditary in specific clans. The Nyori, for example, provide the *jaigo* for the Rainmaker of Lokwe. The first Nyori Rainmaker had come from Bari during the last half of the 19th century, carrying rainstones from his native home. Lualla, who was busy setting himself up as a Rainmaker welcomed the Nyori migrant and asked him to pool the rainstones with his own and to become his *jaigo*. In this way, he neutralised a potential rival while mobilising for his own cause the powers the Nyori man represented.[5]

Assistants are usually responsible for the manual priestly work: they hold the calabash with the oil that is sprinkled on the land and do the actual washing and oiling of the rainstones. The Loo Master of the Land of Lokiliri used to have two assistants. Case 3.1 showed that the office of assistant is important enough to occasion considerable rivalry.

Disaster and power

Ideally, each clan has a specific power with which its members claim to contribute to the well-being of the community, and to which they may appeal when threatening others. Only three out of the nineteen clans represented in Lokiliri do not have an *opopi*. Two of these are relatively recent immigrants from Bari. A member of the third clan jokingly confessed to me that "his clan was only there to love others", implying that the powers of the others were often used to negative ends.

Clan powers play an important role in conflicts between descent-based groups. Members of clans which control monkeys, for example, are believed to send their monkeys to eat the crops of a person who has insulted them, or who has not repaid a debt. The standard way to utter such a threat is the elliptic expression: "The *monyomiji* will question me." The implication is that the community, or part of it, will be hit by a misfortune, serious enough to call for an emergency meeting (*paluko*) of the *monyomiji* who will summon the clan associated with the particular calamity to provide an explanation. Persons who feel neglected or who are the victims of repeated misfortune are believed to use the powers of their clan to attract the attention of the community to their plight. When a disaster strikes the village, such persons may try

---

4   In two Lokoya villages, Ngulere and Ilyangari, the *mukungu*-ship (lowest governmental level under the A-Court chief) is hereditary in the family of the Masters of the Mountain, an indication of the relative importance of the Office of the Mountain at the time of the first contacts with the colonial administration. In Ilyangari the first government appointed chief was Minge (cf. Case 8.4); the Master of the Mountain Lopiti was the first government chief of Ngulere; he was the leader in the war with Lokiliri (cf. Case 7.1).

5   The photo on p. 267 (left) shows Lualla's collection of rainstones.

their luck and admit that they are the cause of it. Normally, the *monyomiji* will arrange for the appeasement of the aggrieved person.

Paride Okollo, the Master of the Land of Lokiliri, carrying his staff with tinkle bell, flanked by his pipe holder ('dangunaziri modi').

The powers may also be mobilised against private enemies for payment, especially those that can hit precise targets. The Master of Leopards of Ngulere was reputed to have a wide circle of customers, some of them as far away as Mandari. Although the rain usually falls over areas wider than a single plot, there are Rainmakers who accept assignments to make drought to take revenge on a particular individual. It is up to the victimised community to settle the case. The powers are also deployed in battle. The war between Ngulere and Lokiliri (cf. Case 7.1) broke out directly after a leopard attacked. When in 1908 the government army was stopped from marching on Lafon by a huge swarm of bees and by floods, everyone believed that it was the work of King Kidi. Kudwo's Master of Bees became famous when during the civil war in 1965, a detachment of the National Army on its way to Kudwo had to return half-way when it was attacked by a swarm of bees.

When a calamity strikes the village, one of the first questions to ask is who is responsible for it. The Lulubo phrasing of this question is: "Who is the king (*osi*) of the disaster?" The person to whom a calamity is attributed is its *osi* ('king') or *osinde* ('queen') for as long as the disorder lasts. Once the king of the disaster is known, steps towards the resolution of the crisis can begin.

*Tombe Kenyi, Master of
Leopards, Lokiliri*

The core meaning of the Lulubo verb *ososi*, which is a derivative from the noun *osi*, refers to this dimension of the operation of power as well. It denotes the antithetical but related processes by which the king reduces the existing order to chaos and reinstates a new order out of disorder. In the conception of the Lulubo the conversion of cosmic order into disorder and vice versa is the dynamic core of *opopi*, the power of office. Taking this reasoning one step further, one might define the king as a person who is at the centre of communal attention because of the hope that he will maintain order and because of the fear that he may unleash disorder.

In Lulubo, every individual could, through the power associated with his clan, be a king for a brief span. The period of his *ososi* would last from the moment he was designated by the community as the cause of its misfortune until the disaster was over or suspicion had shifted to someone else. As the *osi* of a disaster, a person could keep the community in suspense for as long as his grudges or demands were not satisfied and he was able to keep the others thinking that he was its cause. The aggrieved person placed himself in an antagonistic position towards the community, just like the king, simultaneously receiving its blame and the satisfaction of his wishes. In Chapter Sixteen, I examine in greater detail these transactions of anger and appeasement, specifically in connection with the power of the king.

Disasters are called up as part of ongoing political struggles, to support demands for a better deal in transactions between persons and groups, and to define the balance of power between competing clans.

The control of temporal order and disorder: Liria

While the variety and range of offices controlling specific disasters in Liria is similar to the situation in Lokiliri, there are not less than six officials who are addressed as *ohobu*. In addition to the king (called *ohobu* without further qualification, occasionally also *ohobu lohide* (King of Heaven) or *ohobu lohuju* (King of Rain), there is the King of the Land (*ohobu lahap*), the King of the Mountain (*ohobu lodonge*), the King of Bows (*ohobu latang*), the King of Grain (*ohobu lohimai*) and the King of Winds (*ohobu loriri*) — six in all. As a group, these kings are referred to as the *ovalahojok*: "the Fingers of God".

The masters referred to as Fingers of God derive their royal and divine title from their role in the annual ritual calendar. Each of them controls a seasonal transition or the economic activities during one of the seasons. Each king, in effect, plays a narrowly circumscribed role in the annual ritual calendar.

At the start of the rainy season, after the Rainmaker has made the sacrifice for rain, the *monyomiji* assemble (*avaluho*) to discharge the Master of Bows who has been in power during the dry season, and to order the Master of the Land to take his hoe and ritually turn the soil to open the cultivation season. Before sowing, the Master of Grain anoints the seeds as a blessing. When the sorghum is about knee-high, the Master of Winds closes the *ahaduhe*, the House of Winds and Worms, located high on the mountain, in order to prevent the wind from destroying the crops, and the worms from eating them. After the Master of Winds has locked up the winds, the Master of the Mountain performs the sacrifice for the fertility of human beings at the sacred cave and feeds the sacred snakes.[6] When he descends from the cave, he proclaims *edwar*, the period when all forms of violence, including shouting, ululation, drunkenness, drumming and dancing, are forbidden. *Edwar* lasts until the first harvest when the Master of the Mountain lifts the state of exception. The lifting of *edwar* coincides with the expulsion of all evil (which the Lokoya push off in the direction of the Bari), a ritual which is accompanied by much noise and ululation. The following day, the Master of the Mountain anoints all women so that that they may give birth.

After the last harvest (in December), the Master of Grain will sound the drums to hand over responsibilities to the Master of Bows, who calls for the Guardians of the Firesticks (*abollok lopirudhi*) to set fire to the dry grass. Soon after this, it will be time for the New Year Festival (*Odhurak*).

At *Odhurak*, the Master of Winds unlocks the House of Winds and Worms, while the Master of Bows gives a blessing to the *monyomiji* who are sent to the bush. There, they set out the policies for the coming year and review the performance of the kings, Masters and other notables. After that, they go on a divinatory hunt which prefigures the course of events in the new year. When the *monyomiji* have returned from the hunt, the six *Fingers of God*, followed by the local notables (*abollok*, pl. *aboloni*) and

---

6   The present *ohobu lo donge* informed me that nowadays the ritual was only carried out at the special request of the *monyomiji*.

other elders, solemnly ascend the mountain to the central ceremonial ground, located at a height of about a hundred metres above the plains. When the kings have reached the ceremonial ground, the *monyomiji*, lined up according to sections and age-sets, are allowed to start their race towards the ceremonial ground to be the first to start the New Year dance. The rule of the Master of Bows lasts until the end of the dry season, the season of war and hunting. After the first rains, he hands his power over to the Master of the Land.

Although the ritual calendar as outlined above is not unique to Liria, no other community known to me has worked it out with so much sophistication or gives it greater emphasis. Royal power is not only divided according to a scale of more or less serious disasters but also on a temporal scale, each period of the year corresponding to the 'rule' of a particular 'king'. In the balance of power between king and people, the five other *Fingers of God* make for an important counterweight against the single commanding Finger of the Rainmaker. Here, as well as elsewhere, priority should be given to underlying rivalry over seeming co-operation as an explanatory context for the phenomenon of kingship.

The division of royal powers in Liria is not a prefiguration of a bureaucratic structure of command (as educated Lirians like to argue, comparing the *ohobwok* to a ministerial cabinet and the *monyomiji* to a parliament). Using Durkheim's concepts: the dynamic behind this political arrangement is not derived from 'organic solidarity' but is inspired by the 'mechanical solidarity' of competing antagonistic groups of which the class of royals is just one, although a very important one.

Concentration of powers: the Bari

Although the kings of Shindiru were first of all Rainmakers, they were also feared for their powers over diseases. These were kept in a collection of pots in a cave in the Midi Mountain, each disease in its own pot: scabies, smallpox, chickenpox, measles, yaws, syphilis, conjunctivitis, spinal meningitis and dysentery.

The king would open a pot if someone came to complain to him about injustice suffered at the hands of another party. He would point the pot's opening in the direction of the alleged wrongdoer. Formerly, an annual sacrifice was made in which the blood of the sacrificial animal was smeared over the outside of the pots. The blood was believed to be consumed by snakes.[7]

These powers over fertility and health proper to the Bari royal office were complemented with a wide range of other powers. Let us examine the protocol of a visit of Pitia Lugör to one of the villages during his annual procession along the Nile:

---

7   The pots have not been taken care of since Pitia Lugör died. My proposal to go and see what had become of the pots was met with rather mixed feelings. Because of their long neglect, it was feared that the sudden interest in them prompted by the visit of the anthropologist might be harmful. The number of livestock demanded to be sacrificed for the pots and as access fee was increased at every reminder so that the project was eventually abandoned.

13.1 *The protocol of a visit of the Bari king to a subject village* (living memory)

Villages wishing to host the king would send emissaries to collect him. In the days of Lugör (*ca.* 1870), the king was carried on a couch as his feet should not touch the ground. He was accompanied by twenty to forty people including his servants (*'dupi*). His rainstones were carried along in a small bag.[8] As he arrived, everyone from far and wide would come to see the *juök* (divinity). To welcome him, the leader of the village, a Rainmaker, a *Big Man*, or the government chief, speared one bull for the king. He also presented him with a live cow. Each village in the vicinity sent at least one he-goat and one ewe.

The washing and oiling of the rainstones was the first ritual the king or his *'dupi* would attend to. A goat was sacrificed and its rumen was used to purify the stones. During the ritual, one of the rainstones would be fixed in the king's hair (which was never cut). If there was a drought, the king and the local Rainmaker would 'pour themselves', throwing water up in the sky and making it fall on their bodies.

A mandatory part of the visit was the expulsion of diseases (*yangande*) which took place early in the morning. Pitia Lugör was seated on the lap of a prominent female member of the community who had to be beyond child-bearing age, usually the senior wife of the local chief. Thus ensconced, he would be washed and smeared with sesame oil pressed by the old women of the village, each individual lady providing a small quantity. The ceremony was accompanied by the singing of praise-songs for the king, by clapping of hands and much ululating. After the washing was over, all the villagers would be lined up facing west. The *'dupi* of the king would pass behind the row, touching each individual with an iron rod dipped in the mixture of oil and water that dripped from the king's body, saying: "Let all diseases go with the sun."

Barren women would take advantage of this ritual. They would come to the king or his female attendants to ask for a cure. Usually, they would be oiled or given some oil to swallow. Payment for this service was only expected after the birth of the third child.

Pitia Lugör also blessed the seeds of the new crop. Every household brought one head of sorghum. Pitia Lugör removed the seeds, put them in a large calabash and rubbed them as a blessing. Every household would then collect some seeds from the king to mix with his own.

According to an informant from Pöyiti, a village near Mount Nyerkenyi (Jebel Lado), Pitia Lugör was also involved in the distribution of new land, his *'dupi* helping in the demarcation and blessing of new plots. He settled disputes which the local authorities had not been able to solve.

Informants from Mongalla and Pöyiti mentioned the lighting of new fire as one of the rituals performed by Pitia Lugör on his journeys. All fires were extinguished, the hearth cleaned and the ashes thrown into the bush in a westward direction or

---

8   According to an informant in Mongalla, twelve stones were carried in an earthen pot. Another informant, in Tokiman, said only four stones were carried in the king's bag. The present Rainmaker showed me his *kupenga*, a bag made of the skin of a squirrel, which contained six stones: four green stones and two white ones, four males and two females.

into a river. The king's *'dupi* would spin a new fire from which every household would light its hearth.

After three days, the king left the village again, carrying with him not only the *doket*, but also the diseases of the community. After his departure from the village, there would be outbreaks of smallpox and chickenpox. But these incidents were considered a good omen for the next crop. In the trail of the departing *juök*, leopards and lions would be found to roam.

By the time Pitia Lugör reached home again, the grain would be knee-high. Pitia Lugör had become fat from all the meals offered to him and he was followed by a large herd of cattle and smaller livestock.[9]

The *Mor* was not only a Rainmaker but he also had the powers which the Lulubo and Lokoya attribute to their Master of the Mountain (fertility, diseases), the Master of the Land (land demarcation, expulsion of evil), the Master of Bows (the lighting of new fire), the Master of Grain and the Master of the Leopards.

The number of offices involved in the control of disasters was limited among the Bari. Next to the local Rainmakers, of which there could be several in one location, only one other official played an important role in the division of ritual labour among the Bari: the *monyekak*, the Master of the Land. He was responsible for the allocation and fertility of the land and he controlled diseases and, according to Spagnolo (1933:321), he was believed to have powers over rain as well. In his quality of main officiant in the annual *yangana* ritual — when the old ashes, together with diseases and other evil are expelled from the village — he is referred to as *monye kurök*, 'Master of Ashes'. Frequently, his office is combined with that of *monye yöbu*, Master of the Bush, because his blessing extended to hunters. The *monyekak* is a descendant of the first settlers in the area and in most places, his office antedates that of the Rainmaker. The reach of his powers is strictly local and in most of the ritual activities he performs, reference is made to the earth and to what is below its surface, especially the spirits of the dead.

Because the powers of office in Bari can be categorised on a vertical scale, some observers have postulated an underlying dual classification of powers between *Ngun lo Ki* ('powers of the above') and *Ngun lo Kak* ('powers of the below'), the former considered as fundamentally 'good' and the latter as basically 'evil'.[10] But the evidence at my disposal indicates that the suggested cosmological division connected with the two offices is less neat than these authors suggest. There is considerable overlap between the office of *monyekak* and that of *matat lo piyong*, while the Manichean division of the two offices is without foundation. Both officials send their followers both blessings and disasters. The main difference between the two offices seems to lie in the territorial dimension of the power invested in them. That of *monyekak* has a

---

9   During the last journey in 1964 by Mauro Lugör, Pitia's successor, which reached as far as Tombek in Mandari land, twelve head of cattle and twenty-five goats were collected. Mauro Lugör never equalled his uncle in popularity. Since the independence of the Sudan, the Bari interest in their Rainmakers has greatly diminished.

10   Haddon, 1911: 113; Seligman (quoting a personal communication by Whitehead), 1932:274.

strictly local character as it is connected with a well-defined stretch of land and with the history of a particular village. The autochthony of the *monyekak* also manifests itself in his connection with the graves of the dead and his responsibility for the pole-shrine ('*bilili*) at the centre of the ceremonial ground (Spagnolo, 1933:324).

The Rainmaker's domain, his '*diko*, the stretch of earth served by his clouds, has no well-defined boundaries. It moves with the person of the Rainmaker and its circumference depends on the Rainmaker's effectiveness. A Rainmaker receives gifts as signs of recognition from every community that believes it has been watered by the king's '*diko*.

Concentration of powers: the Lotuho

The tendency towards a concentration of powers in one office and in one person is as evident among the Lotuho as it is among the Bari. When I described the royal *Nefira* (cf. Case 10.5), I pointed at the accumulation of the ritual responsibilities (making of new fire; the bell shrine) in the hands of the king. The Lotuho king presides over most of the calendrical rituals that in Liria are distributed over the six *ohobwok* ('Fingers of God'). In Lotuho, only the king carries the title of *hobu*.

> **13.2 *The calendrical duties of the Lotuho king*** (living memory, Seligmans)
>
> At the beginning of the agricultural season the *monyomiji* of each village send an emissary to the king with a gift of a cow, a sheep or money, and ask the king for permission to start cultivation.[11] The king gives permission by ceremonially digging the soil with four blows of his hoe (Seligman&Seligman, 1932:332). This is done after he has sent the *monyomiji* of his village on a divinatory hunt to determine the general prospect for the coming season. Two weeks later, the *monyomiji* perform their annual day of agricultural labour for the king (*ekubo*). Before sowing, the king or his prime minister mixes and blesses the seeds of the people. When the plants are about one metre high, the king performs a special sacrifice to firm up the fragile stalks so that the winds will not break them. Around the same period, he performs a ritual to keep the worms and grain eating birds at bay. King Acalili of Loronyo was famous for his power over birds. The halting of a plague of birds in Lafon is remembered as one of his major miracles. At the first harvest, the king leads the ceremonies of lighting the new fire and that of tasting the food of the new harvest. Finally, the king is the central figure in the New Year Festival (*Nalam*) at the end of the harvest, which marks the beginning of the hunting season. The spoils go to him.

There are a few other officials who have power over disasters. First of all, the Master of the Village (*amonyemiji*) controls human fertility and disease. Like the Bari *monyekak*, the *amonyemiji*—and on the sectional level also the *amonyemangat*—is usually a descendant of the first settlers (Paolucci, 1970:122; Novelli, 1970:628). The same applies to the Masters of the Land (*amonye fau*), the Masters of the Bush

---

11 Pazzaglia, 'Il Capopioggia', p. 108-113, Comboni Archive, Rome, A/26/11/3; most of this summary of the ritual duties of the Lotuho *hobu* is derived from this text.

(*amonye mur*) and the Masters of the River (*amonye hari*) (Nalder, 1937:94; Paolucci, 1970:124–129). The intervention of their powers is required for successful cultivation, hunting and fishing. Like the office of the Bari *monyekak*, these offices are linked to well-defined stretches of territory or to particular villages. Frequently, these different powers controlled by specialists are united in a single office. They may also be included in the duties of the *amonyemiji* (Nalder, 1937:90). In contrast to their counterparts in Lokoya and Lulubo, the Lotuho Masters of the Land, the Bush and the River deal with private groups or individuals who want to use a particular piece of land for cultivation or hunting, not with the *monyomiji* as a body.

The allegiance of the *monyomiji* is with the *hobu* and so are their confrontations with central authority. Only the Master of the Village receives a reward from his subjects in the form of agricultural labour by the non-initiated young men.[12] Despite the importance of the *amonyemiji*'s local role, I have found no evidence that he could be considered a rival to the authority of the *hobu*, or a political factor in the succession struggles for the kingship.

As far as the division of labour among the Masters of Disaster is concerned, the Lotuho arrangement is very similar to that of the Bari. On the one hand, we have a king associated with heaven and rain who has monopolised ritual control of the important seasonal transitions and over a wide range of collective misfortunes. On the other hand, there are a number of strictly local offices, associated with the earth and concerned with the maintenance of order and well-being on the level of the village, the village-section or just catering for the ritual needs of resident households.

The Pari are an intermediate case between the high concentration of powers of the Bari and Lotuho and the systematic compartmentalisation of the Lokoya and the Lulubo. They have three kings each with a specific power: the Rainmaker, the Master of the Mountain (fertility and diseases) and the Master of Birds. There is no plurality of minor offices as is the case among the Lulubo and the Lokoya.[13] It looks as if the Lotuho and the Bari kings had neutralised all potential rival claims to power over cosmic order by a unilateral declaration of omnipotence.

The social distribution of divinity

The difference between the two power constellations is not unlike that between a polytheistic pantheon in which deities — one of whom is usually considered the most senior — rival for the attention of the believers, and monotheism, which attributes omnipotence to a single god and condemns rival claims to divinity as sinful heresy.

The analogy between our Kings of Disaster and Divinities, whether polytheistic or monotheistic, does not halt at this distributional dimension of divine power. It also extends to its operation. The confrontations and exchanges between the king and his followers and those between the divinity and its believers follow an identical

---

12　Lilley in Nalder, 1937:92; in his account, the roles of the *amonyemiji* and the *aboloni hobu* seem to have been confused.

13　The Surma-speaking Tenet in Northern Lopit conform to the Lulubo/Lokoya pattern.

pattern. Lack of attention on the part of the people is reciprocated with disasters, the outbreak of diseases and other disorders, while reverence for the king is rewarded with prosperity, bliss and peace of heart. Just like gods, displeased kings are appeased by gifts and demonstrations of humility.

Frazer objected to this. Basing himself on rather incomplete ethnographic information, he called the kings of the Bari, the Lulubo, the Lokoya and the Lotuho 'magical kings' (Frazer, 1913, Part I, Vol. 1:345) and reserved the label 'divine' to kings who were conceived as incarnations of a spirit which was independent of the person of the king, as for example the divinity *Ring* by which the Dinka Rainmakers are possessed, and Nyikang, the dynastic ancestral spirit of the Shilluk which takes possession of each king at the moment of his enthronement.

I would like to contend that the relative independence of the king's divine power from his person, from which Frazer draws far-reaching evolutionary conclusions, is only a secondary elaboration; the fundamental similarity between kingship and divinity lies on the level of the operation of the powers. Among the peoples in our area of study, the relationship between the power and its human agent is conceptualised in the following three ways:

- The human agent is defined as the possessor of the power.

- The power is defined as the possessor of the human agent.

- The power and the agent are defined as identical.

The first variant is met with most frequently in our area of study, probably because, when divine power is defined as an entity which can be possessed, it is easier to accommodate the power socially. The 'rain' of kings and the *opopi* of the Lulubo belong to this category.

The relationship between the divinity *Ring* and the Dinka Masters of the Fishing Spear[14] and between Nyikang and the Shilluk kings belong in the second category. By defining the power as an independent agent, the possibility of competing for possession of the power is drastically reduced, — in fact it is 'theologically' impossible. The configuration of a divine incarnation more effectively protects the exclusiveness of royal office than constraining rules of descent and royal achievement. Once Nyikang has taken possession of the Shilluk king, contriving to remove him is a complex affair. Similarly, as incarnations of the active principle of sacrifice (*Ring*), the Dinka Masters of the Fishing Spear were able, by arranging for their own burial alive, to take control of the victimary process on which their leadership depended and avoid the regicidal dramas of the Equatorian east bank. While the Lulubo kings are assumed

---

14   The main source on the religion of the Dinka and on the custom of the burial alive of their Rainmakers or Spear Masters is Lienhardt (1961) who carried out extensive fieldwork among the Rek Dinka during the late 1950s. Earlier references to the burial alive and killing of Dinka Spear Masters are: Seligmann (n.d.:29–32) presenting information collected on the Cic, Agar, Nhiel and Bor Dinka during his field trip of 1910; Titherington, 1925:196–7, on the Dinka of Bahr-el-Ghazal; Seligman, 1932: 195–200, again on the Bor, Agar and Nhiel; Bedri (1939:125–131, 1948:50–51), on the Padang Dinka; Howell (1951:271, 273 n.1) on the Ngok Dinka.

to be owners and managers of their *opopi*, the installation ritual has one hint of the second type of understanding the relationship: in order to test the suitability of the would-be queen, the royal couple is confined to a hut in which ebony wood is burnt. The smoke is considered 'bitter' and as such associated with the bitterness of the power of the king (cf. below Chapter Nineteen *The bitter stomach of the king*). The royal *opopi* is believed to take possession of the couple through the medium of the smoke of burning ebony. If the would-be queen cannot stand the smoke, this is a sign of her rejection by the *opopi*. Apparently, such a rejection is not anticipated for the Prince Royal (cf. Case 9.12).

The identification of the custodian with his power applies when the powers manifest in a person are believed to be extraordinarily strong. The Bari called persons of great power *juök*, the Lotuho *ajok*, and the Lokoya *ojok*, a word from a root which in most Nilotic languages is used for the power of the divine. Informants usually translate the word as "god", but in some contexts also as "devil". The prophet Lado-lo-Moyok who led the resistance against the Egyptian occupation of the Bari, the Rainmaker Pitia Lugör (cf. Case 9.5), and the missionary Angelo Vinco (Vinco, 1940:306) were all three considered *juök* by the Bari. Missionary Augusto Pazzaglia was also addressed as *ajok* by the inhabitants of Tirangore, where he enjoyed great popularity (Paolucci, 1970:310). In the harangue of the Rainmaker of Ngulere (cf. Case 7.10), the Roman Catholic parish priest of the Lulubo and the Lokoya was called *ojok* by the Rainmaker. Since *juök*, etc. is also used to denote persons with a power to do evil; many people will take it as an insult when they are referred to as a *juök*.

Juök, however, may also be conceived as an attribute of a person. When a Rainmaker is successful in making rain at the right moment, he is said to possess *juök*, and persons like myself, whose arrival in a village more than once coincided with a long-expected shower, were also said to be in possession of *juök*. Uncommon technological skills, as those brought by the Europeans, were also referred to as *juök* or *ajok*. (Molinaro, 1940:179).

The belief systems of the peoples in our field of study do not have a clear dividing line between the divine in living human beings, in tangible objects, and in intangible divinity. Before the advent of Islam and Christianity in southern Sudan, local theological speculation was primarily focused on the king and not on invisible deities. For some observers, this was sufficient reason to conclude that the Bari did not have a religion.[15]

Conclusions

The role of the king in maintaining or disrupting the boundary between order and disorder corresponds exactly to what we should expect on the basis of the scapegoat scenario formulated in the first chapter. The king's cosmological role is defined as a

---

15   See the remarks of Kirchner quoted in Chapter Four (p. 99). Both Seligman and Haddon complained about the difficulties they had in extracting consistent statements from the Bari concerning their beliefs in God.

balancing act on the borderline between good and evil, between the order within and the disorder outside: the balance tips to the good side and the king is hailed in his benevolent transfiguration; the balance tips towards disaster, and the king is exposed in his evil transfiguration and turned into the target of his people's blame.

The king's political art is that of 'brinkmanship'. As watcher at the gate through which disaster and violence enter the community, the king may at times deliberately put the door ajar to awaken the community to the central importance of his person. But if the door would happen to be blown wide open, the king should be seen to do everything in his power to close it again, simultaneously defusing the tension building up against him.

The idiom which expresses the operational dimension of the king's power, the process by which disorder is converted into order and vice versa, is the concept of 'bitterness' (Pari: *kec*, Lulubo: *angana*, Lotuho/Lokoya: *odwa*, Bari: *pötwör* — words usually translated as 'sacred'). This use of images from the metabolic process will be discussed in the last chapter of this book.

The second conclusion to this chapter is that the comparatively more advanced centralisation — territorially as well as in terms of the volume of tribute levied–of the Bari and the Lotuho is mirrored by a greater concentration of the divine powers in the hands of the king, while in the small-scale polities of the Lulubo and the Lokoya the divine powers are distributed over a large number of kings and masters and are used as a weapon in the general competition between clan groups and factions.

I add a comment on one kind of 'Master' not mentioned yet: the Master for Relations with the Government (Bari: *matat-lo-gela*, Lokoya: *ohobu logala*, Lulubo: *osi gelari*, etc.) — the 'Chief'. At the arrival of foreign powers in the region, relations with the government were included in the office of the king who was traditionally in charge of foreign affairs. After the establishment of colonial administration, a division of labour developed between the rain king, the incumbent of the sovereignty of old, and a member of the rain family who acted as liaison with the Khartoum traders and the government. In Tirangore, Prince Kamiru and later, Ajaru, dealt with the traders while Hujang took care of the rain. Later, in 1908, when the relationship with the government had gained in importance, we see that the rivalling brothers, Lohide and Onyong, reached a compromise over the division of powers, Lohide, the more ambitious brother, taking *gala* and Onyong, the rain. In the same period in Liria, we find Lomiling looking after the relations with the government while Lojing was responsible for the rain. A similar division of labour existed between Lualla and Ali Bey in Lokiliri where it was ratified by the colonial authorities.

The 'Master of Government' (Paride Lado, the B-court chief of Lokiliri and Paramount Chief of the Lulubo; in white shirt on the extreme left) subjecting a suspect to the ordeal of licking the sacred spear, Lokiliri.

There is no indication that this division of powers is a sequel to an older idea of 'dual sovereignty', a division of the sacred and secular powers over two offices, which Needham (1980) assumes to have existed among the Shilluk — the *reth* being invested with the sacred sovereignty while the sectional chieftains wielded secular power. Rather, the evidence suggests that the new office developed in response to what was perceived as a threat, a new kind of disorder calling for a new type of brinkmanship.

The rain shrine of Shindiru, the ritual centre of the Bekat kingdom as photographed in 1903 by Fred Spire, an official of the Uganda Protectorate stationed in Gondokoro. In 1903 the shrine was fenced with megaliths. (From Spire, 1905).

The rain shrine of Shindiru as photographed by the author in 1981. The grinding stones interconnected with iron rods contain different collections of stones catering for different types of rain events. Posing in the picture are the Chief Rainmaker of Shindiru, Pompeio Lado (with the collar), the grandson of Pitia Lugör (Illustration, p.120) and three of his assistants ('dupi).

14

Rain Queens and Rainstones: Symbols of the Centre

The royal office in the Nilotic kingdoms largely coincides with the person of the king. When the king has died the Shilluk say: "The country is lost".[1] And indeed, there were few attributes of central power other than the person of the king: there was no capital to speak of, no bureaucracy, and no military establishment; there were no extensive public buildings.

The fear that with the death of the king the kingdom would fall to pieces was not just a rhetorical expression to underline the central importance of the king. It was an assessment based on a realistic understanding of the nature of the kingdom's cohesion. The centre unifies the different segments of the society through its singularity and through the oppositional balance it maintains with those segments. When the king dies, this balance is lost. The centre can no longer hold and the society falls apart, reverting to its constitutive segments. The country as a holistic entity is, for all intents and purposes, 'lost'. Even today, the sense that without the king the people cannot durably stay together still exists, as the words spoken by the lame man, the blind man and the cripple before Queen Nyiburu of the Pari was killed prove (cf. Case 17.11).

It was important, then, to find ways and means to represent the continuity and singularity of the centre so that it would at least *seem* independent of the person of the king. In this chapter, I examine two such means of representing the kingship as a reality in its own right: the role of the queen and the rainstones.

The Lotuho queen as source of legitimacy and as ultimate prize of dynastic rivals

While it was by no means rare among the Lulubo, Lokoya and Pari that queens succeeded their husbands — or sometimes their brothers — the institution of queenly office was most elaborate in Lotuho. Concerning the Bari I have no information indicating that women could succeed to the royal office.

In Lotuho the queen played a key role in determining the legitimate successor to the throne. This she did in two ways. First, in her capacity of legitimate mother of princes, she limited the number of rightful heirs. Only the wife who had been married by the *monyomiji* was a full or *red* queen. To be selected both her parents needed to be of rain descent. The sons of a *black queen* were excluded from succession even if their mother was senior to the *red queen* in terms of the duration of her marriage to

---

1   *Piny bugon*, Howell & Thomson, 1946:18; Arens, 1984:358.

the king. This, of course, did not mean that these sons did not try to win the throne and that in some cases (Okomo, Acalili) they have been successful. Secondly, at the king's death, the *red queen* was the first in line to take responsibility for the rain, not the brothers of the king or his sons. She would keep that responsibility till her senior son was old enough to take over. During her regency the queen-widow was *de jure* the most senior authority in the kingdom.

The benefits of the rules that restricted legitimate succession to the sons of one royal wife only, becomes evident when we take a look at the succession struggles among the Bari. Although the rule of primogeniture limited the number of potential successors, large-scale polygamy and the practice of begetting sons in the name of deceased brothers and fathers made it inevitable that rivalling claims arose concerning the seniority of princes. Earlier in this book we encountered several cases where the ambiguity surrounding the seniority of the heirs to the throne was a cause of bloody conflict: the rivalry between Subek and Nyiggilo in Bilinyan (Ch. 4, p. 101) and (Case 15.2), in Shindiru the rivalry between Pitia Yeng-ko-Piyong and Wulang (Case 12.3) and also in the regicide case in Lowe (Case 9.6). In each of these cases the unresolved issue is: Who is more senior, the father's own biological son or or a son — who could very well be older than the biological son — who has been sired in the name of one's deceased father or elder brother?

While the restrictions on the eligibility to the Lotuho throne must certainly have reduced the number of rivals, the second rule that made the queen the custodian of the rain powers as long as no suitable candidate was available from among sons of the king, created another kind of rivalry: the competition to marry the queen-widow because marrying a queen widow offered a shortcut to succession to the kingship.

In our examination of the division of the Lotuho kingdom (Case 12.5) we encountered several cases of brothers competing for the legitimate queen. The first case was that of the brothers of King Irwangi, considered impotent, for Queen Nyadinga, resulting in Nyadinga's transfer to Okomo. The second case is the wrangling of the kings Okomo and Oyalala over the same Nyadinga, and the third case is that of Hujang, Okomo's son, to marry Ibur, the 'red queen' married by Oyalala after Nyadinga's death. The competition between the two dynastic lines that was triggered by this wrangling for queen-widows lasted for almost a century. It is clear that queen-widows derived considerable power from their position as potential wives of their late husband's would-be successors. Queens used this position in different ways: some agreed to be inherited — as did Queen Sabina Ihure, the queen-widow of Patricio Ohucoli of the Mayya dynasty (1944–1959) who married one of her husband's brothers. Others chose not to remarry to ensure that their own son would one day become the king: Queen Ibur, Oyalala's rain-widow, for example, rejected Hujang's offer to marry her for the sake of her son Mayya. Other queens pursued a different strategy and tried to find a suitable partner by themselves.

In the last category was Tafeng of Loronyo, a daughter of full rain descent of king Iyuru of the Lomiya and the widow of Wani, the son of Mayya, who disappeared after he was taken prisoner by the Ansar. Tafeng — at that time still in her teens or early twenties — stayed behind as Wani's widow-successor.[2] A Ugandan official who met with her in 1903 described her as "a woman of hardly middle-age with a certain force of character and with considerable control over her people".[3] In 1914 — after a career full of frustrations — a Condominium official characterised her as "a firebrand and hot tempered".[4]

14.1 *Queen Tafeng* (Uganda Archives; oral history)

Not long after Wani's disappearance, Tafeng received two marriage proposals: one from Acalili, a son of her father-in-law Mayya and a 'black wife' and her main rival in Loronyo, and another one from Lomoro, the king of Tirangore, who in this way hoped to *corner the rain*, to reunify Lotuho under a single rain centre. He was not far removed from that goal since after the death of Wani, even Hiyyu, the section of Loronyo where the royal palace was located, paid its rain tribute to Lomoro. Lomoro's kingdom had greatly expanded at the cost of that of Mayya which was beset by division.[5] Tafeng rejected both proposals; her refusal of Lomoro she justified by his role in her husband's abduction and death.

Tafeng's mind was set on a more powerful consort. In 1903, she asked Mr Fred Spire, the British Administrator in Gondokoro, to marry her. The proposal was sent shortly after Spire's departure from a visit to Lotuho where he had both met Queen Tafeng and King Lomoro.

"About one march out from Tarangole, a Makungu (*sic*), or Headman of Queen Tafaing arrived with a deputation to Mr Spire asking him to return and offering him her hand in marriage. She was anxious to have a son, especially a white one, as heir to her throne, and said there was no man in all her state who was sufficiently worthy to be her husband. This, Mr Spire declined, at the same time thanking her for the great honour she had done him, and said he must return to his work in Gondokoro".[6]

The refusal to marry Lomoro and Acalili had earned her two dangerous enemies, or rather three, since Issara, King of Loudo on her western borders was a staunch ally of Lomoro. Tafeng tried to keep the military initiative by carrying out repeated attacks on villages supporting Issara and Lomoro. In 1903, she blocked the road between Tirangore and the government stations on the Nile.[7] Shortly after that, Lomoro

---

2   Donaldson-Smith who met her in 1899 describes her as a woman in her early twenties. The story of Wani's disappearance is summarised in Chapter Five (p. 129–130).

3   Uganda National Archives, Entebbe, *Foreign Office Correspondence, East Africa* , Confidential, Appendix J, Letter by Wilson, Sub-Commissioner Nimule to Commissioner Entebbe, 24/7/1904:25.

4   From a government report quoted by Muratori (Comboni Archive, Rome, A/126/4, 'Acalili, the Lotuxo Rainmaker', p. 5).

5   Muratori, *idem*, p. 3.

6   Central Records Office Khartoum, *Foreign Office Correspondence, North East Africa and the Sudan*, Report by Governor Owen of Mongalla Province, Sept. 28, 1903.

7   Uganda National Archives, Entebbe, *Foreign Office Correspondence, East Africa*, Confidential, 24/7/1904:23, Jennings-Bramly, 'Report of Journey to Latuka and back, July 13 to August

and Issara filed a complaint against her with the Uganda authorities accusing her of complicity in an attack on a Swahili caravan travelling between Lafon and Loudo in 1904 and of involvement in the kidnapping of one of Lomoro's wives. When the queen heard this, she immediately sent a delegation to Gondokoro to deny the allegations, and promised the government administrator that she would take steps to return the goods stolen from the traders.[8]

Queen Tafeng of Loronyo, widow of king Wani who was enslaved by the Mahdists. She was courted by the pretenders to both Lotuho thrones (Acalili Mayya and Lomoro Hujang) but chose to court Fred Spire, the British Commissioner of Bari District (Cunningham 1904:365)

Her next power contest, this time with Acalili, had more far-reaching consequences. In 1905, he launched an offensive against Tafeng; killed her son; and had her expelled from Loronyo.[9] She was forced to flee to Hatiha where she was welcomed by the *monyomiji*. With Labalwa as her base she continued to fight Acalili, leading the *monyomiji* of Hatiha in a destructive attack on Loronyo for which she is still remembered.

After Lomoro was assassinated, Tafeng reacted favourably to the overtures of Onik, one of Lomoro's brothers who controlled Tirangore. By this marriage, the rain would finally have been 'cornered'. However, the plan did not materialise because

3, 1903'; Uganda National Archives, Entebbe, *Shuli Correspondence*, A/16/4/81, Letter Sub-Commissioner Nimule to Commissioner Entebbe, 14/11/1903.

8   Uganda National Archives, Entebbe, *Shuli Correspondence*, A/16/5/1905, Letters Collector Gondokoro to Commissioner Nimule, 24/8/1904 and 27//12/1905 and Letter 1/11/1905 ('Agora and Tarangole Tour Escorts'), *Secretariat Minute Paper* 67/06, pt. 1.

9   Uganda National Archives, Entebbe, *Shuli Correspondence*, A/16/5/1905, Letter Collector Gondokoro to Sub-Commissioner Nimule, 27/12/1905.

Onik was killed in the succession war before the marriage could take place. Lohide, another brother of Lomoro, now asked the queen's hand in order to strengthen his claim to the throne. Tafeng refused. Lohide, who controlled some of the sections of Hatiha, then chased her away from her stronghold in Labalwa. She found temporary refuge in Mura-Hatiha but after some time she had to flee back to her home area in Lomiya. There, she played a leading role in the war with queen Ikuma of Iboni, the leader of the rivalling dynasty among the Lomiya, without lasting success.[10]

After all these trials and errors, her power base had eroded to almost nothing. Tafeng fled to Gondokoro in a last attempt to get support from the government for her case as queen of the Mayya Dynasty.[11] Haddon, the Collector at the time, was not particularly charmed by her visit:

"She wants help and refuses to go back and has already sent her escort home.... In the meantime, she considers herself my guest and as she has no food (or clothes) she has reduced me to a state of bewilderment and some anxiety. I have already reported the reasons why I could not order her back to her country, and her feet are badly knocked up by her travel. It will be observed that her strong will, coupled with her claims give her the distinction of being the first black African suffragette."[12]

After three months, she returned to Lotuho without any tangible results. All she obtained from Haddon was a used gun.

In April 1914, nine days after Torit was selected as the District Headquarters of what was then called Latuka District, she once more presented her claims to the throne of Mayya, this time to Mr Beaumont, the first Inspector of Latuka District under the Condominium. Beaumont, however, decided to support Acalili.[13]

A few years later, Tafeng's name is mentioned in the Chief's Register as the chief and Rainmaker of Buruny,[14] the village where the assassinator of Lomoro and his followers had settled. So, very appropriately and in good style, Tafeng eventually became the leader of those who had killed the man who betrayed her husband. She must have had some success as a Rainmaker because her death, a few years later, is attributed to the rivalry over her gift of rain between Lobera and Ilyeu, villages not far distant from Buruny. Lobera is said to have poisoned her when she was suspected of favouring Ilyeu with her rains.[15]

Tafeng's story highlights the extent to which Lotuho queens could use their position to play an independent political role. The Lotuho rules of succession were not watertight. Acalili — a war hero with seven victims on his record, including Tafeng's son and a

---

10 Comboni Archive, Rome, File A/126/4, Muratori, 'Acalili, the Lotuxo Rainmaker', p. 5.

11 Uganda National Archives, Entebbe, *Secretariat Minute Paper* no.189, Gondokoro Monthly Reports, August–November 1910.

12 *Idem*, August 1910.

13 Muratori, quoting files from the Torit District Archives, in Muratori, 'Acalili, the Lotuxo Rainmaker', Comboni Archive, Rome, File A/126/4, p. 5.

14 Central Records Office, Khartoum, CIVSEC II/44/1/1,' List of Lotuko chiefs 12/12/1918'

15 Her death must have occurred before or in 1921 since Tafeng's name no longer figures in the list of chiefs contained in the Latuka Intelligence Report of December 1921 (Central Records Office, Khartoum, *Mongalla Files* 1/4/27, Monthly Intelligence Reports, Latuka District.

lion, and a respectable rain reputation, although not of full rain descent — eventually won the competition for power.

Lomoro's assassination[16]

Our next case is the aftermath of the assassination of Lomoro Hujang in the rival kingdom of Tirangore. Here again, royal widows played a decisive role.

Lomoro was the second son of King Hujang of Tirangore and Queen Iloyi. After the death of his brother King Ajaru, the control of the war drum and the responsibility for the rainstones were entrusted to queen Iloyi while Lomoro handled most secular matters. Iloyi wanted Ajaru's son, Ohuyyoro, to succeed to the rain of Tirangore. Lomoro seemed to have agreed to the temporary character of his occupation of the throne. He groomed Ohuyyoro to be the successor. To the Uganda Administration in Nimule, where Lomoro had taken his nephew along on several occasions, Lomoro's position had been defined as that of the regent of Ohuyyoro.[17] Whether we should view this arrangement as an application of the principle of primogeniture or as compliance with the wishes of the queen who is said to have had a special liking for Ohuyyoro is now difficult to determine. Informants agree that despite Lomoro's prominence in political and military matters, the ultimate sovereignty rested with Iloyi.[18]

During the first years of his rule, Lomoro's power was uncontested. His dealings with the Ansar had been a resounding success and with his *Awusa*, he had considerably extended the area over which he held sway. His expulsion from Tirangore not long after 1900 notwithstanding, the outside world, in particular the Colonial Administration continued to see him as the sovereign of the Lotuho.

In 1906, Lomoro was assassinated in Iloli, a village under the Mayya Dynasty.[19] Among the many versions of the story concerning the motive of the assassination,

---

16   In describing the succession wars following Lomoro's death in 1906, I have used both oral tradition and documents written by the Ugandan authorities. The wars took place without foreign intervention. The Ugandan authorities were firmly established along the Nile but considered the extension of their administrative control to the hinterland too tricky and too costly at the time. Since the east bank was considered a British zone of influence a keen interest was taken in what was going on. From their side, the Lotuho royals did their best to maintain good relations with the British administrators on the Nile, mainly in the hope to be able to count on their support when they would need it. On the whole, the archival documents confirmed the reliability of the stories as they were related to me by informants.

17   The D.C. of Nile District describes him in his letter of 12/1/1909 to the Chief Secretary in Entebbe as "a nice-looking and intelligent fellow of, I should say, 20 years of age" (Uganda National Archives, Entebbe, Secretariat Minute Papers 1357).

18   When the Seligmans visited Loguruny in the dry season of 1921/2, Iloyi still controlled the rain shrine. If she is the same person as Bokké (Note 12.4) she must have been in her early nineties as she was accompanied by an adolescent daughter when she visited Mr and Mrs Baker when they were in Tirangore in 1863.

19   According to the report sent to Nimule by King Ogwok of Padibe (Acholi), his ally Lomoro was killed because of popular opposition to his decision to send a man accused of murder to be judged and punished by the colonial administration in Nimule. The Ugandan authorities

the one that attributes it to revenge for an adultery affair seems the most plausible. The offended husband, a certain Omeyuk, killed Lomoro during a dance:

> Omeyuk suddenly emerged from the dancers, and threw his spear at Lomoro who was playing the drums. He [Omeyuk] escaped to the hut Acalili possessed in that village where everybody had the right of sanctuary. From there, he moved to Buruny where he lived for another thirty five years (Novelli, *thesis*: 200).

In fact, the village of Buruny was founded as a result of the conflict that broke out after the killing of Lomoro, those supporting Omeyuk moving away from Iloli to Buruny.

The cast of the succession struggle is the following: at the time of Lomoro's death, there were three Queens in Lotuho who fulfilled the requirements (ceremonially married by *monyomiji* and of double rain descent) to produce an heir. Besides Tafeng, there were Iloyi, Hujang's wife, who wanted Ohuyyoro, the son of Ajaru, to succeed, and Ikang, Ajaru's wife, who had been inherited by Onik, the senior son of Hujang and Haworuho, Hujang's second wife.

Alongside Ohuyyoro, three of his uncles pretended to the throne: Onik, the senior son of Haworuho—who was of rain descent and married to Hujang before he became king; Onyong, the son of Husuro, Hujang's third wife; and Lohide, the son of Hujang and Ngajon who was a daughter of the King of Liria. All of these wives of Hujang were of rain descent, but only Iloyi had been married by the *monyomiji*.

The competition for the succession is best described as a game consisting of successive rounds in each of which one protagonist is eliminated. I reproduce the facts as they can be gleaned from the retelling of the drama by the descendants of the different protagonists and from the reports of the administrators of the Uganda Protectorate:

14.2 *The succession of Lomoro* (Uganda archives; oral history)

The first round: The elimination of Onik by Ohuyyoro
After Lomoro was chased out of Tirangore and went to stay in Loguruny together with Iloyi and Ohuyyoro, Onik had become the *de facto* leader and king in Tirangore. At Lomoro's death, he inherited queen Ikang, who was originally the widow of Lomoro's elder brother Ajaru who had only ruled for one year. Ikang

---

in their correspondence with Entebbe seem to accept the story at face value, possibly because it corresponded to some wishful thinking on their part (compare this with Owen's conceited interpretation of Kidi's request to kill Alikori related in Chapter Six (p. 144). From the context of the events, the story seems merely invented to throw dust in the eyes of the Sub-Commissioner, in the expectation that the British would support Ohuyyoro, the candidate who also had Ogwok's blessing (Uganda National Archives, Entebbe, *Secretariat Minute Papers*, no. 257, Letter Sub-Commissioner Nimule to the Acting Commissioner & Commmander-in-Chief in Entebbe, May 8, 1906). According to Muratori the killer was bribed by Lomoro's brother Onyong who wanted to take the throne (Muratori, 1949:109). Another informant told me that Lomoro's death was due to Iloyi's curse because she wanted her favourite grandson, Ohuyyoro, to take power. Put against other evidence, the last two stories make little sense. What they prove is that when there is a royal victim in Lotuho, all survivors, including mothers, may be suspects, because all are considered potential rivals.

was a key asset in Onik's ambition to succeed to the throne of Tirangore. Even more important were the promising negotiations with queen Tafeng of Loronyo which brought the dream of re-unifying all the Lotuho under his kingship within Onik's reach.

If the marriage would take place, both Tafeng's and Onik's chances to be victorious in their respective succession struggle would be excellent, since by their marriage *the rain would be cornered*. All the Lotuho would be unified under the joint clouds of the re-united royal family. (cf. Case 14.1 '*Queen Tafeng*').

Ohuyyoro, the son of Ajaru, was an ambitious young man. He was of giant stature, a wrestling champion and rather short-tempered. His aspirations to take over power immediately after Lomoro's death went directly against his grandmother's admonitions. She wanted him to wait until his father's brothers had had their taste of power.

Ohuyyoro counted on the connections Lomoro had made for him with the British officials in Nimule. One of his first deeds after his uncle's assassination was the settlement of the many outstanding debts of Lomoro with the Nubi soldiers in Nimule and Gondokoro. This was obviously intended to substantiate his claims as heir in the eyes of the British officials. He was so keen to pay all the bills the soldiers presented to him that the Collector felt it necessary to organise a public auction for Ohuyyoro's cattle and settle the debts on his behalf to protect Ohuyyoro against excessive demands.

The settlement of Lomoro's debts may also have been a precondition for the Nubi to sell him more guns, a business which had to be kept hidden from the administrators. Whatever the case, in December 1908, the Sub-Commissioner of Nile Province formally requested the Chief-Secretary in Entebbe to recognise Ohuyyoro as rightful King of the Lotuho.[20]

The first clash between Ohuyyoro and Onik had occurred during Lomoro's funeral. Onik had wanted the funeral to take place in Tirangore, in Lomoro's former palace which Onik now occupied. Iloyi and Ohuyyoro had opposed this location since they feared that by playing host at Lomoro's funeral and the subsequent rituals, Onik would gain a decisive advantage in the succession struggle. Onik gave in, but when he arrived at the funeral in Loguruny, Ohuyyoro slapped him in the face and knocked him to the ground.

In August 1908, it came to a full-scale confrontation between both protagonists and their followers. Ohuyyoro had persuaded the *monyomiji* of Hiyala to join him in an attack on Tirangore. When both armies stood face to face outside Tirangore, led by the two rival princes, Onik fired his gun as soon as he saw the tall Ohuyyoro. The bullet blew the *fez* off his rival's head and caused him to retreat. Obehe, Ohuyyoro's younger brother, who was at his side, snapped at Ohuyyoro: "Collect your courage, if you flee now you can just as well forget your kingdom!" While

---

20   Uganda National Archives, Entebbe, Secretariat Minute Papers 1357, Letter Sub-Commissioner Nimule to Ag. Commissioner Entebbe, dated 7/8/08. In a letter dated 8/1/09 the Acting Commissioner advises the Sub-Commissioner to act at his own discretion.

Onik was still poking the gunpowder in his muzzleloader for a second bullet for Ohuyyoro, the latter aimed his gun, fired and killed Onik.

Ohuyyoro stopped the *monyomiji* of Hiyala from proceeding to Tirangore and attacking it as they had anticipated, explaining to them: "We are only here to seize the kingship." He immediately proceeded to assume his role as King of Tirangore by ordering its *monyomiji* to collect Onik's body, announcing that he would come for the funeral the following day.

But Ohuyyoro never came for the funeral. That very day, Lohide, the third rival to the succession, entered Tirangore in triumph. When Lohide had received the information that Onik was dead he had called the *monyomiji* of Hatiha and said: "The situation is critical. Be men! I am the king! Follow me!" Lohide had set off for Tirangore right then, and was received enthusiastically by the *monyomiji* because of his former connections with that village.

▓ *The second round: The deal between Ohuyyoro and Onyong*
Before confronting Lohide, Ohuyyoro wanted to make sure that Onyong, the third uncle with a claim to the throne, would not choose Lohide's side. Lohide and Onyong were considered close since their mothers were sisters (Osuru and Ngajon). With Onik dead, Onyong was a formidable rival for Ohuyyoro: it was he who would likely inherit Queen Ikang. Lohide himself could not marry his uterine sister.[21] Ohuyyoro and Onyong agreed to divide the sovereignty. Ohuyyoro would take care of the relations with the colonial government while Onyong would be responsible for the rain.[22]

As soon as this agreement was reached, Ohuyyoro went to Nimule to buy the guns needed to fight Lohide. But before Ohuyyoro returned from Nimule, he sent the following message to Loguruny: "Onyong, if I still find you at Loguruny at my return, it will be your death." Oral tradition and archival records give no reason for this *volte-face*. Perhaps, Ohuyyoro felt he could do without Onyong's support since the Sub-Commissioner had been most accommodating. Onyong was no fighter. He fled to Ilyeu, then to Logir, and from there to Lofe.

▓ *The third round: Ohuyyoro is killed while making preparations to kill Lohide*
Lohide had lived in Tirangore until the day he was chased away by Lomoro. Lomoro had had affairs with two of Lohide's wives and feared his revenge. The *monyomiji*

---

21   Both Lohide and Ikang were children of Ngajon, a former wife of Lewat (King of Liria), who had run off to her sister Osuru, Hujang's third wife. When Osuru discovered that Ngajon had had an affair with her husband, she ran away from him to Mayya. Ngajon was given a house in Haforyere where she won the respect of the people by the successful performance of fishing rituals. When Lewat demanded the restitution of the bridewealth, the *monyomiji* of Haforyere paid it, so that in a limited way, Lohide's mother had also been married by the *monyomiji*.

22   Seligman describes Onyong as easy-going and of uninspiring, little authority. In one incident witnessed by Seligman (1932:309), Onyong had his thumb severely bitten by a man being lashed by him. Onyong did not have an appropriate answer to this. In the eyes of his environment, he must have saved his face when the culprit — by accident according to Seligman — broke his thigh while running away.

of Hatiha — part of Mayya's Kingdom at the time — had accepted Lohide to stay with them as their leader.[23]

Before facing one another in the battlefield, Ohuyyoro and Lohide did their best to increase the number of guns in their possession. Lohide levied a tribute in goats and sheep from Hatiha and with these, he went to Gondokoro and Nimule to buy the weapons. From the archival records, we know that it was Lohide who communicated the news of Onik's death to the Collector in Gondokoro.[24] On his return journey, he ordered the *monyomiji* of Tirangore to come and meet him in Liria, the place of his maternal uncles. During the night, he played a trick on his followers of Hatiha by ordering the *monyomiji* of Tirangore to seize their guns.

At the same time, Ohuyyoro sent his brother, Obehe, to Gondokoro to buy guns. On his way to Gondokoro, he was attacked by the Lirians, Lohide's allies. Most of his wealth was stolen: one Egyptian donkey, ten head of cattle, two hundred sheep and goats, two tusks of ivory, nine guns, and six hundred Rupees. One of his men was killed.[25]

After this failed journey, Ohuyyoro and Obehe put another request to the Ugandan authorities in Nimule for support to no avail. The British did not want to be involved in peacekeeping or administration in the territory east of the Bari. So, Ohuyyoro and Obehe had to look for new sources of wealth to buy guns. On their return journey from Nimule in December 1908, they raided the people of Chief Luluri of Imotong, justifying the attack as a punishment for his secession from Lomoro's kingdom after the latter's death. Both brothers got killed in the attack.[26]

The final round: Compromise between Lohide and Onyong

After Ohuyyoro's elimination, the only protagonists still alive were Lohide and Onyong, sons of the same father and of two sisters (Osuru and Ngajon). At Onik's death, Onyong, as the next senior son of Hujang, had inherited Queen Ikang. Lohide had tried to outbid Onyong by asking Queen Tafeng to marry him and so 'corner the rain'. But his request had been refused, since Tafeng, the story says, was still attached to the memory of Onik.

It was due to Ikang's influence on both men, one her uterine brother and the other her husband and mother's sister's son that both men agreed to peaceful coexistence. The deal proposed by Ohuyyoro to Onyong was now implemented in the relationship between Lohide and Onyong. The ambitious Lohide settled in

---

23   On his journey to Lotuho in 1903, the Collector of Gondokoro, Spire, met with Lohide in Torit, one of the villages of Hatiha. Lohide was also recognised as Paramount Chief of Labalwa (Uganda National Archives, Entebbe, *Shuli Correspondence*, A/16–2, F. Spire, 'Brief Report on a Journey from Gondokoro to Tarangole, 1902–1903').

24   Uganda National Archives, *Secretariat Minute Paper* 1357, Letter from A/Collector Gondokoro to Collector Nile District Nimule, dated 7/8/1908.

25   *Idem*, Letters District Commissioner Nile District to *Ag.* Chief Secretary, Entebbe, dated 7/12/1908, 8/12/1908, 4/1/1909, 12/1/1909.

26   Uganda National Archives, *Secretariat Minute Paper* 786, Gondokoro Annual Report 1908/09, p. 29 and Nile District Annual Report 1908/09.

Tirangore and took the government chieftainship, while Onyong settled in Lofe taking the queen and the rain.

Despite the support he received from the Condominium government, which took over affairs in 1914, Lohide's rule did not last long. The alienation of Hatiha, more important now because it was selected as the location of the District Headquarters, and the violence used in his dealings with Chalamini—former allies of Ohuyyoro —led to his death at the hands of the colonial army (cf. Case 9.9, *The heroic death of King Lohide*). From 1917 to his death in 1928, Onyong was the government chief. After a short interval during which a son of Lomoro was the government chief, the responsibility for both rain and government went to Queen Ikang who acted as regent for Lomiluk (Lohide's son and Ikang's sister's grandson) to succeed her. Ikang died in 1936, after having been closely associated with six kings of Tirangore (with Ajaru, Lomoro, Onik and Onyong as wife, with Lomiluk as regent, and with Lohide as a sister).

In the succession war after Lomoro's death, all the protagonists were successively eliminated, tasting but briefly or not at all the power they had risked their lives for. Each of the players in this knockout race had his own assets: the blessing of the late king, the backing of the queen-mother, the possession of the queen-widow, the recognition by the government, guns, seniority, powerful in-laws, a greater or lesser degree of purity of blood, luck with the rains, and personal charisma. Each one also had certain handicaps: juniority, non-eligibility to inherit the queen, no 'rain' on the maternal side, weak allies, etc.

Each player in the game also controlled certain villages, or sections of villages: Ohuyyoro had Loguruny, Hiyala and Chalamini; Onik had Tirangore; Lohide controlled Hatiha and Onyong counted on Lofe and Ilyeu.[27]

The extended case story clearly shows the great stability of office enjoyed by the queens compared to the kings. Iloyi, Hujang's wife, survived four of her husband's sons and two of his (and her) grandsons who made a bid for the kingship. Ikang survived four of her first husband's brothers and two of his sons (by a different wife). Queen Ikang herself was barren. The queenly office was a more enduring symbol of the singularity and continuity of the centre than the kings were. While the king, his brothers and sons, one by one fell victim to the internecine rivalry for power, the continued presence of the queen offered a semblance of permanence to the existence of the centre. I believe that this aspect of the role of the queen-mother in African kingdoms has not been taken into consideration as a factor that could explain her importance in royal courts.

The events that followed Lomoro's death also demonstrate that the struggles for succession cannot be interpreted as a simple sequel of a controversy over the interpretation of the rules of succession, nor can the violence of the Lotuho interregnum be considered a ritual reversal of norms — as it may have been in other

---

27 These, at least, were the main participants in the game. Since certain villages were divided in their allegiance, the support of each of the princes was larger and more complex than this.

African kingdoms. What we find here are cases of full-blown competition in which the rules, although they help to limit the number of rivals, play a subordinate role and are used as assets in the hands of the rivals.

Queen Iloyi, widow of Hujang, mother of Lomoro, possibly the same person as Queen Bokké pictured on p. 275 (Powell-Cotton, 1904:464; the scan of the photo was kindly made available by the Durham University Library).

The outcome of these struggles was not ritually predetermined either. For the most part, the outcome depended on historical vicissitude, as did the violence which is an inevitable side effect of the struggle rather than a programmed reversal of order. It is possible that the Nilotic rivalry described here is a more direct expression of the same tensions that in the more institutionalised kingdoms in other parts of Africa, have become largely ritualised. I am confident that a comparative study from this angle could also throw new light on the role of the queen-mother and on the significance of royal incest in African kingdoms. We can imagine that if the Lotuho had been allowed to accumulate more historical experience with their kingship, the rules would have come to provide a more effective protection against abuse by rivals while the tension of the transfer of power would have found more ceremonial forms of expression.

The Shilluk, whose history of kingship had greater continuity, provide an example of this. Although political competition continued to play a decisive role in the succession to the throne, it was more predictable. Prescribed was that the royal office had to alternate between two lineages, two generations of the royal family and two moieties of Shillukland.

The value of rainstones

Rainstones are the most important objects used in rain ritual. In routine rituals, they are washed with water and anointed with an oily substance, usually sesame oil. When the rain situation becomes critical they may be washed in the stomach contents of a sacrificial animal and smeared with the body fats of the animal.

All pieces of stone or rock with a remarkable shape or colour, of a size such that they can be held in one or both hands, may serve as rainstones. Most stones I have seen were between three and ten centimetres in diameter. Pieces of white quartz on which condensation forms when the humidity in the air rises are the most desirable kind.[28] The value of a particular rainstone depends first of all on its history: the manner of its acquisition, the kings who used it, the rains and prosperity it once helped to bring about.

Each Rainmaker owns a collection of stones. Some have just one, others a dozen. In the rain shrine of Shindiru (Illustrations p. 299, 300) there are more than a hundred. Normally, most of a Rainmaker's stones are inherited from his predecessor's collection, but collections are incidentally enlarged by finding, buying or stealing new stones. If a commoner finds a rainstone in his field or in the bush, he should bring it straightaway to the Rainmaker under whose authority he is placed. If he kept the stone for himself serious misfortune might befall him (dropsy) or his family (sterility).

According to a Lulubo belief, the stones originate on small anthill (*ituki*) when fungus forms on them after a period of heavy rain. When the fungus is touched by the end of the rainbow, a rainstone comes into being. The soil of the same type of anthill is swallowed by persons who have killed a human being, as an antidote to the disturbance that the homicidal act may cause to their physiological and psychological equilibrium. The Lirians say that they brought their rainstones with them on their migration from the east. The stones are said to have originated in the Itaraba pool, the sacred lake of the Lotuho. Their substance is a kind of gum, a sticky liquid (*angenge*), which develops on the rocks overhanging the pool. When the gum drops into the water, it coagulates and hardens into stone. The Lotuho believe that their rainstones were brought by the mythical ancestor of the rain clan Asang when he was fished from the pool.

During the rainy season, the stones are kept in pots with water or in old, hollow grinding stones. During the dry season, they are usually buried or kept in a pot inside the Rainmaker's house.

Stones are transferable, but their exchange, sale or theft is always a risky business (cf. Cases 14.3, 4, 5; 17.1, 6). They circulate in the same sphere of exchange as brides

---

28   Reymes Cole, Assistant District Commissioner in Gondokoro District during the first decade of the century had some rainstones inspected in England. They were found to be pieces of rock crystal, amethyst, and aventurine (Cole, 1910:91).

and payment of bloodwealth. During the early 1900s the Madi paid for a rainstone the same price as for a girl of rain descent (five head of cattle),[29] while the transaction turned the buyer into a sister's son to the seller (Middleton, 1955:34). At times the value of rainstones is held to be superior to that of a bride, as the following case shows:

14.3 *The Kanamu rainstones given as bloodwealth to Kursak* (Kanamu clan lore)

Before the Kursak clan, the Kanamu clan was responsible for the rain in Lokiliri. They used their own set of stones. One day, Kursak decided to intermarry with Kanamu and brought a girl to the home of Jogo, the Rainmaker. Soon after her brothers' departure, the girl fell dead while grinding sorghum flour. When the Kursak heard about it, they accused Kanamu of having mistreated and killed her. Bloodwealth was claimed.

Kanamu could not reject the claim because of Kursak's superior power. They offered all their cows, two stables full, but Kursak did not accept. Kursak wanted nothing but the rainstones. So, the rainstones were given in *lonya* (bloodwealth). Since that day, Kanamu can no longer make rain, although they can still cause drought. After the payment of the stones they were robbed of their cattle as well.

The following story, about the seizure of the sovereignty over the Bari village of Logopi by an Acholi dynasty also shows the great value of rainstones: [30]

14.4 *The extortion of the rainstones of Logopi by Mila* (published, archival and oral sources)

One day, Mila, the leader of the Pandiker clan from the Acholi chieftaincy of Parabongo, found the Rainmaker of Logopi fallen in the water of a hot spring and stuck in the mud up to his waist. He had been there for many days and begged to be pulled out. Mila asked for a reward. The man offered him many things ranging from sheep and goats to a bride. These were all refused by Mila who asked for the rainstones the Rainmaker of Logopi was carrying with him in his bag. Since his skin was already becoming flabby from the hot water and the skin of his head had become red he agreed to hand them over. Mila then took a creeper and pulled the man out saying, "You are my subject now." This is how the Pandiker became the rulers of Logopi.[31]

29　Rogers (1927:83) mentions the price of one bull, one cow, one goat and three hoes for a set of stones purchased in Lokai at the beginning of the twentieth century.

30　Logopi was the Southernmost Bari village in 1851 when Vinco made his exploratory journey southwards in search of the sources of the Nile (Vinco, 1940:320). It has now been absorbed in a mixed Madi-Acholi village. Mila lived around the turn of the twentieth century. The historical core of the story, then, is the transfer of Logopi from a Bari-dynasty to the Pandiker Rainmakers, an event that must have occurred in the last quarter of the nineteenth century.

31　The same story is related by Rowley, an Administrative Officer of Torit District in the 1930s (1940:291–293; also Rowley, Notes on the Madi, *manuscript*, Southern Records Office, Juba, E.P.66.B.42). The Acholi chief in Rowley's version is called 'Ker' who in the genealogy provided by Rowley, is thirteen generations removed from his informant chief. My informant, a native from the chieftaincy, attributed the extortion to Chief Mila, who was government chief during the days of the Uganda Protectorate. In 1910, he was reported as being "very old, very loyal and a celebrated Rainmaker" (Uganda National Archives, Entebbe, *Intelligence Report* 40,

The two stories attest to the supreme value of rainstones. In addition, the message is that the transfer of rainstones is a transfer of power.

The rainstones of Liria as a focus of rivalry and an archive of history

Added to their value in making rain and in legitimising the power of the king, the collection of rainstones at any Rainmaker's disposal is an archive of the history of the expansion of his family's power. The most important stones have their own name and history. Many of them tell a story of conquest, migration, past alliances, dynastic rivalry and intrigue. The following case recounts the history of the major rainstones of Liria over the past 150 years.

> **14.5 *Liria's dynastic history from the point of view of its rainstones*** (oral history)
>
> By tracing the origin and the successive owners of rainstones, a fairly complete history of dynastic rivalry is obtained as the following accounts of some of the famous rainstones of Liria prove:
>
> *1. The acquisition of the great Mosidik —by hook or by crook*
> Mosidik, a green stone, came from the Itaraba pool, the sacred lake of the Lotuho royal clan. When ritually activated, the stone would cause the sky to turn black, and rocks would roll down the mountain carried by the rain-caused floods. Before washing and anointing Mosidik, Rainmakers used to warn their people to stay indoors. The stone was considered the main instrument that enabled the Ohoyo rain dynasty to achieve hegemony over the other clans in Liria.
>
> When Hatulang, the leader of the Ohoyo immigrants, conquered the mountain of Liria, his elder brother stayed in Kamuturu, south of Liria, where he was in charge of the stone. This brother died, and Liria suffered a period of drought. Hatulang sent his son to visit the successor at Kamuturu. While taking dinner with his hosts Hatulang's son went to relieve himself in the bush and stole the most important rainstones which were kept some distance away from the house. He took the mother-stone, Mosidik, and its husband. After returning to Liria he provokingly called the people of his brother's son *awang ohobu*: "those without a

---

Appendix 64). Mila was a contemporary of Lugör with whom Rowley's Ker had undertaken war expeditions (1940:291). As *ker* means 'power of kingship' in Acholi, Rowley's story has been affected by mystification, as the 'thirteen generations' between the rescue of the Logopi chief and Rowley's interview also indicate.

The Bari chief of Logopi met by Vinco in 1851 is called Gwandoca. He stopped Vinco from proceeding further south to Bunyoro ('Quenda') because of the alleged warlike character of the Madi. This offers another clue to the timing of Mila's rule since the name of Mila's father and predecessor is Andoga, a name closely resembling that of Gwandoca. Andoga,in Rowley's genealogy is Mila's father and predecessor. Our case then provides a neat example of the way historical traditions obscure past violence and are altered to reinforce claims to legitimacy of rule. It is to be expected that this bias is especially strong in stories about chiefly lineages is collected by colonial officers. A similar case is the alleged continuity in the dynastic line of Shindiru presented to Beaton by his Bekat informants (Ch. 2, p. 63–64).

king." This nickname later contracted to *Ongabu* and *Langabu*, which remained the name of the people and village of Kamuturu to the present day.

2. The theft of the rainstones from the indigenous minority

After Hatulang had conquered the mountain of Liria, the Omoholony or Ongole, the native inhabitants of the place, had refused to accept the new dispensation although Hatulang allowed them to follow their custom and to keep their Masters. During the reign of Hatulang's successor, Aderi Ringwat[32], the fields of Liria were affected by drought, while those of the Ongole were well watered. Aderi proposed to Madhaira, the Rainmaker of the Ongole, that they should put their rainstones together in order to make it rain. At first, Madhaira refused, but when Aderi insisted, he complied. The night after it had rained, he ordered Madhaira to come and collect his stones. Before Madhaira arrived, Aderi hid the most powerful stones. Madhaira noticed that some were missing and demanded them back. Aderi is said to have answered with a play on words: "You stay as Ongole" (*Ongole* meaning 'food leftovers' in Lokoya). Today, the Ongole receive their rain from the Ohoyo Rainmaker, but they still have their own Masters of Bows, Grain and the Soil.

3. Jur Bende, the cause of Legge's death

At Aderi Ringwat's death, his wealth and power were divided between his two sons Legge and Lewat. Legge received Jur Bende and his father's cattle and Lewat, who happened to be away in Bilinyan when his father died, received Mosidik, and from the cattle only one cow and a calf.

Jur Bende[33] was round, metallic white, and is said to have had 'elbows'. It was about five centimetres in diameter. Legge relied on Jur Bende for his rains. Legge was a very wealthy, astute leader and his victory over a traders' army earned him a notoriety that reached Europe. His rain achievements were less impressive. He was accused of drought and beaten to death by the *monyomiji*. Since the drought that caused King Legge's death, Jur Bende was left unattended. It was lost when Liria was burned by the Sudanese Army in 1965.

4. Mosidik's days of glory

Legge's brother Lewat took over. The days of Lewat and his son Rugang are remembered as 'the reign of Mosidik', a time of great prosperity. After Lewat's death, Mosidik was inherited first by Rugang, who ruled Liria during Emin's days, and later by another son of Lewat named Lorwungo. In 1903, Rugang's sons who were coming of age began to challenge Lorwungo's power.

---

32   An important obstacle in reconstructing Lokoya history, and to a lesser extent that of Lotuho as well, is the fact that the same person appears under different names while informants are often ignorant of the equivalences. In Liria, this problem is even greater because of its recent turbulent history. It is quite possible that Aderi Ringwat and Hatulang are one and the same person. In another version of the story I collected, the person who seized the stones of the Ongole is named Lowiyang. He should be the same person as Aderi, while his son Luruböt must be Legge who was met by Baker. The fact that Luruböt inherited his father's herds, according to this tradition, would confirm this equation, since Morlang (1862/3:117), Peney (Malté-Brun, 1863:58) and Baker (1866, Vol.I:179) report on Legge's numerous herds.

33   *Jur Bende* is apparently a word of Lwoo origin. An informant translated it as: "all the enemies".

In 1903, Lomiling, only 22 years old,[34] staged a coup. Lorwungo sought sanctuary with Lualla in Lokiliri, carrying the stone with him on his flight. Drought followed in Liria and soon afterwards, Lorwungo was collected back by the *monyomiji*, who attributed the drought to Lorwungo's and Mosidik's absence. Lorwungo was restored to power.

In 1909, Lomiling was killed by a falling tree; Lorwungo was accused of having caused his death. Lomiling's brother, Okellong, took it upon himself to revenge his brother by eliminating Lorwungo. Getting wind of the planned assassination, Lorwungo made sure that neither Okellong nor Jada, his brother, could get hold of Mosidik. Only Lojing, a son of Rugang by another wife, was informed about the hiding place of the stone: it was rolled in a blanket and tucked away in one of Lorwungo's houses. Okellong killed Lorwungo. A few years later he, too, died, allegedly from the same disease Lorwungo had suffered from in his lifetime.[35]

5. Tulili and Gumar: the rainstone couple of the first government chief

Okellong was succeeded by Jada Rugang who became the first government chief of Liria.[36] For his rains, Jada relied on Tulili, a small stone of pure green, which — together with its female counterpart–produced rains lasting for as long as twelve hours and gave a lot of fish, and on Gumar, a small green stone with white speckles, which gave gentle rains. But neither of the two was as powerful as Mosidik which remained in Lojing's hands. A *de facto* division of labour developed whereby Jada concentrated on relations with the government and Lojing on rain matters. With Lojing's death, sometime during the early 1920s, Mosidik got lost. Lojing died on the way to Mongalla where he went to look for medical treatment, probably carrying Mosidik along. Today, the whereabouts of Mosidik are still a subject of speculation and controversy.[37]

---

34   Age estimated by Spire who visited Liria in 1903 (Uganda National Archives, Entebbe, *Shuli Correspondence*, A16 2, 1902–03, F. Spire, 'Brief Report on Journey from Gondokoro to Tarangole').

35   Liria's neighbours were worried that the internal violence would sooner or later turn against them and prepared for the worst. Haddon, the British Administrator in Gondokoro, comments:"The inter-tribal war alarm may to some extent account for the absence of inter-tribal friction between the Bari chiefs" — a fine example not only of what anthropologists later called the dynamic of fission and fusion in a segmentary system based on complementary opposition (Uganda National Archives, Entebbe, Gondokoro Station, File 644, Annual Report, 1909–1910), but also of the local understanding that communities are likely to rid themselves of internal violence and chaos by turning against an external enemy-as the enemy scenario (Table 1.3) postulates.

36   Central Records Office, Khartoum, *Sudan Monthly Intelligence Reports*, INTEL 6/8/25, January 1915; Mongalla files, 1/2/6, 'Report on the Lokoiya Patrol by Governor Mongalla to War Office', 31/1/1915.

37   Some say Mosidik was lost on the way to Mongalla. Others say that Lojing's wife lost the stone. After her husband's death, she used to carry Mosidik around fixed to the ring which she put on her head for carrying firewood. Others again say that Lojing's wife did not lose it but handed it over to the wife of Abilli, the Rainmaker and government chief succeeding Lojing and that Abilli's wife gave it to her son who lost it in the confusion of the civil war.

6. Itit, Abilli's kickstart capital

Abilli, son of Legge, succeeded to the rain after Lojing's death. Mosidik was lost and Jur Bende evidently useless (his father was killed due to its ineffectiveness). Tulili was kept by Jada Rugang. In short, Abilli had to start all over again. To acquire an initial rain capital he went to Acalili, the Lotuho King in Loronyo, who had a reputation for his rain powers and with whom Abilli had stayed as a young man. After much begging, Acalili conceded to give him 'Itit', a dozen white silvery stones, known to provide brief, heavy showers. Abilli used to carry Itit in the pockets of his trousers warning the people immediately surrounding him never to empty his pockets because of the pluviometric consequences. The Lirians were satisfied with Abilli's performance and in 1931, they proposed him as government chief. Captain Cooke, however, thought he was too soft and had him replaced by Chief Lolik Lado (cf. Case 6.2)

7. The Frog: postwar erosion of rain powers

During the civil war, many of the rainstones of Liria were lost, including Abilli's Itit. Of the famous stones of the past, only Tulili remained. When the civil war was over, new stones were needed. In search of them went Loselik, the son of Lojing who was given the government-chieftainship when Liria was a government controlled 'peace-village' during the civil war and Lolik was with the Anyanya. The Kursak Rainmaker in Ngulere who wanted to give up his rain responsibilities (mentioned in Case history 12.2) was prepared to sell him Hidudwuk, 'the Frog'. The vagueness of the terms of the transaction later became a source of trouble. The original owner, a poor man who grew very old, made fresh claims for payment every time the stone changed hands. When Loselik died and 'the Frog' went to his widow, she had to make an extra payment to the original owner to avoid that the stone would turn against its owner and against Liria. When at her death a few years later, her daughter inherited the stone, she was asked to pay one hundred Sudanese pounds, a considerable sum during the famine of 1986. She paid since the discontent of the original owner could have serious consequences for the rain.

When I left the Sudan in 1986, the rain office of Liria was still vacant. The main candidate for the vacancy was another son of Lojing, a government employee in Juba. Loselik's widow first, and later his daughter, had been reluctant to part with 'the Frog' and Tulili although Loselik had given clear instructions that his brother should succeed to the rain.

Since the *monyomiji* had arrested and interrogated him shortly after his brother's death on suspicion of causing drought even this brother became reluctant to take up the rain office. The last time I interviewed him, he admitted to me that he did not want to take the responsibility: "But if Mosidik were still around, I would become king without any hesitation."

The rainstones are the principal tangible and enduring symbols of kingship. When the stones are lost, sovereignty is lost, too, as the stories of the stones of Ongole, Kamuturu, Logopi and the Kanamu of Kudwo make quite clear. The stones as symbols of kingship are the focus of the rivalry for succession. A Rainmaker can claim the royal office credibly only if he has rainstones. These are the concrete, imperishable, embodiment of the kingdomship. The Bari underline this by using the same word *'diko* (singular *'dikolo*, lit. 'cloud') for the stones as well as for the kingdom as a geographical unit.

To be an effective Rainmaker, one needs a collection of rainstones which, however small, demands respect because of the association of the stones with the rain powers of a well-known Rainmaker or because of their attested effectivity. In this respect, there is a striking parallel between the East Equatorian rainstones and the royal necklaces of the Anuak described by Evans-Pritchard (1940c).

The sexual symbolism of rainstones

The stones are sacred. They are surrounded with tales of their miraculous power. The Madi, for example, believe that when a Rainmaker or his wife is about to die, his stones give off light (Williams, 1949:206). If the stones are stolen or lost, they are believed to return to their owners of their own accord. The rainstones swallowed in anger by the Rainmaker of Aru (Lulubo) before he died returned to the surface of the earth through a power inherent in them, and ended the drought invoked by their gruesome burial.

The stones should be handled by the Rainmaker and his assistants only. Commoners run serious risks if they touch or see them. Those who do so inadvertently (or for purposes of research, for that matter) have to undergo a special purification ritual (as I had to do several times); otherwise they will be struck by blindness, by sterility, or by a disease that makes the body swell with water. Because of this dangerous quality, rainstones are sometimes used for swearing oaths on.[38]

The belief, held in Liria for instance, that stones of different substance, shape, size and colour produce different types of rain, is widespread. The classification of types of rain is quite elaborate and takes into account: the presence or absence of thunder, lightning and hailstones, the force of the wind, the duration of the rain, the colour and the heaviness of the clouds, the density of the rain, the size of the drops, the rain's destructiveness, the time of the day and the time of the year, the direction it comes from, the smell of the earth when the rain falls, its effect on the appearance of ants, and many other conditions and circumstances.

The homology between the classification of rainstones and that of types of rain, and the way the stones are believed to influence the elements[39] would be a subject for a separate study. Here, I restrict myself to the sexual symbolism of the rainstones in relation to the power of kingship.

In most collections the stones are classified as male and female, husband and wife, or father(s) and mother(s). Sometimes, there are children as well while the Bari also have *'dupi* (slaves) in their collection. To make rain, the Bari do not wash and oil the children. The male and female stones can easily be distinguished by their shape, the

---

38 Among the peoples of the Central Sudanic Bongo-Baka group this practice also exists (Baxter, 1952).

39 For example, the Bari believe the stones *drink* the clouds (Spagnolo, 1933) while the Lugbara call their rainstones *nostrils*, since through them the drought making power breathes (Avua:1968).

male ones are elongated; the female stones are round. The Rainmaker of Shindiru demonstrated to me with his portable set of stones how the sexuality of the stones was put to use. To 'pull' the rain the male and female stones have to be arranged such that the male stone points in the direction of the clouds in between two female stones, the arrangement suggesting the act of sexual intercourse.

Rainstones kept in pots with water, Lowe, Lokoya

At the change of the season, all of the stones, about a hundred, in the shrine of Shindiru are rearranged according to the direction of the expected rain. From March to June, the male stones point east, from July to September, to the north and from October to the end of the rainy season in December, they pull the rain from the west.

It is widely believed that during rains, the rainstones jump up and down in the pots and grinding stones in which they are kept. After a night of heavy rain they may even be found outside their pots because of too much frolicking about. The positioning of the male stone in between the female ones is an obvious sexual metaphor, and so is the jumping movement of the stones. Lack of movement, sitting still, is associated with barrenness. The Master of the Mountain of Ngangala who is responsible for the fertility rituals would sit still if he was angry and wanted to harass the people. The sexual nature of the dance performed by the stones is confirmed by the belief that they dance *kore*, the courting dance in which a man and a woman together jump as high as they can.

Rainstones kept in grinding stones, Aru, Lulubo

The king's body and the rainstones are of the same symbolic stuff, and are, from a ritual point of view, interchangeable — except that the king's body is more potent than rainstones are. When the routine washing and oiling of the stones do not result in rain, the Lulubo wash and anoint the Rainmaker instead. A similar equation is made by the Bari when they wash and anoint their king during his tour of the country. The circumstance that the king is seated on a woman's lap when he is washed points to this sexual symbolism as well. The same equation is made when people suspect Rainmakers who do not wash themselves regularly of wanting to cause drought, and, again, when they warn those who splash too much while taking bath, not to cause heavy downpours.

The identity of the Rainmaker and rainstones is also manifest in a belief, recorded in Imatong that each true Rainmaker is born together with a rainstone, the stone being born before the baby. The custom of putting a rainstone in the hair of the Bari Rainmaker, and in his armpits and knee joints when he lies in state, and that of tying rainstones around the waist of the Rainmaker (practised in rain rituals in Aru) all point in the same direction.

The sexual dimension of the power of the Lulubo and Lotuho kings was also manifest in the royal marriage rituals recorded in Chapter Seven (p. 225–227). The Lotuho ceremony highlights the connection between the prosperity of the country and the sexual union of the king and the queen. 'Washed' with the stomach contents of the sacrificial bull (just as rainstones are purified), the new royal couple has sexual intercourse on the skin of the same bull. The couple's position on the bull's skin is homologous to that of the rainstones in Edemo after a rain ritual. During the nuptial night of the royal couple of Edemo, the rainstones are placed inside the stomach of the goat that has served as a rain sacrifice.

The same sexual meaning must, I think, underlie another Edemo practice. After performing the rain ritual, the Rainmaker — or his assistant — spends the night in a prostrate position. The custom has also been recorded for the Madi. Interestingly, among the Madi, the wife of the person who is to perform the ritual must not be pregnant — as if the Rainmaker's procreative power at the time of the ritual should be exclusively devoted to public ends (Rogers, 1927).

Conclusion

Among the peoples inhabiting the Equatorian east bank of the Nile, rainstones and the rain queen are the most important external embodiments of the centre other than the dead or the living king. Because of the queen's uniqueness and the risks involved in tampering with the sacred rainstones, these attributes of kingship may have limited the number of effective rivals over the succession. On the other hand they also provided the rivalry with a clear focus.

There are other regalia, however. In the competition for power between Okomo and Oyalala, we noticed the important role played by spears. Spears, the skull and bones of the dead king, and the royal tomb, are all repositories of rain power. In the case-study of Lomoro's succession the location and ownership of the tomb of the deceased king became a serious issue in the rivalry between Ohuyyoro and Onik.

We noted that the imagery surrounding the use of rainstones is essentially sexual. From this symbolic angle, there is a close connection between rainstones and the rain queen who is the most immediate recipient of the king's force of procreation. The possession of either brought the pretender to the throne closer to the power of kingship itself. While the connection between rainstones and the power of kingship is essentially metaphorical — the rainstones being substitutes of the king — the relationship between the rain queen and royal power is metonymic — the rain queen being the person most intimately connected with the operation of the king's procreative power.

The Master of Lipul Mountain (Pari) performs the annual blessing of spears, 1986. Photo by Eisei Kurimoto.

15

The Spear and the Bead:
The Fragility of Kingship

I concluded Chapter Ten with the observation that centralism makes it possible to unite greater numbers of people in a permanent political community than dualism does. In this chapter, I want to show that centralism also creates the preconditions for more lastingly destructive divisions inside the political community. If the centre is incarnate in a single mortal person, as in the polities examined in this book, the need of succession applies by definition. Usually, there is more than one candidate, which complicates the succession. Even elaborate rules such as those pertaining in Lotuho are unable to forestall rivalry. To be sure, the divisive potential of rivalry can be channelled into segmentary expansion and hence need not always be harmful to the integrity of the centralist polity. In that scenario, the general position of the ruling clan is strengthened by a multi-village network of dynastic ties which serve as a basis for co-operation between a growing number of communities united by the same rain.

However, rivalry does become harmful when the pretenders to the throne surround themselves with a following and use their father's kingdom as an arena for competition. This is what happened after the deaths of Lomoro (cf. Case 14.2) and of Mayya (cf. Case 12.5; 14.1). Within the two kingdoms, each rival heir to the throne was supported by a group of communities, ready to march against other groups. When Tafeng was chased out of Loronyo by Acalili, she went to Hatiha, from where she launched an attack on her former subjects whom she now treated as enemies. The showdown between Ohuyyoro and Onik pitted Tirangore and Hiyala against each other.

The effects of dynastic rivalry become quite destructive if, to overcome their opponents, rivals enter into alliances with outsiders. King Ngalamitiho of Imatari brought in the Toposa against his son and rival, Ohurak. Things are even worse when outsiders whose power is vastly superior come to the 'aid' of dynastic rivals. This sort of disastrous escalation of internal dynastic quarrels occurred at several points in the history of the east bank. In this chapter, I examine two such cases, looking at them in terms of the well-known Nilotic myth of The Spear and the Bead.

The myth of the spear and the bead

This story of fraternal rivalry and its deplorable consequences is, in various versions featuring different heroes, known by most Western Nilotic peoples. The Lotuho have incorporated a rather elaborate version of the myth into their dynastic history. A comparative analysis of distinct versions of the story, as found among the Dinka, the Nuer, the Shilluk, the Shilluk-Luo, the Acholi and the Alur, was made by Lienhardt

(1975). He interprets the myth as expressive of the contradiction between altruism and self-preservation and, in the case of the 'royal Nilotes', more specifically as a reflection on dynastic conflict (The bead and the spear are both symbols of royal power.). Interestingly, Lienhardt notes a rising scale of intensity from the version as told by the Nuer, the Dinka, up to the versions adhered to by the Shilluk and the Alur. He relates this to the nature of the political systems of these societies. The former being less centralist than the latter.

Among the Pari and the Madi, too, the myth is current. The Pari version (cf. Case 2.2) depicts Nyikang and Dimo as the main protagonists, as do the Shilluk and the Shilluk-Luo versions. The Pari use it to explain their separation from the Shilluk and, in another version, the Pari story accounts for the parting of ways between them and the Lokoya and the Lopit. Another version still is told by the Madi of Kerripi, to explain the migration of a branch of the leading rain family, which is of Fajelu origin, upstream from Metu (Rowley, 1940:289). The fact that the story occurs in far-flung areas[1] and is used to account for many separations and dynastic conflicts should warn us against a narrowly historical interpretation as suggested by Crazzolara (1950, Vol. I: 62–66; Vol. II: 113–114).

The Lotuho storyline is fairly close to that of the Shilluk, Acholi and Alur and is a sequel to the myth of their founding king Asang (cf. Case 18.2). Asang was collected from a pool by the villagers of Otunge, a village at the southern tip of the Lopit Range. When it was discovered that he secretly killed the children of Otunge to eat their livers, the people tried to kill him, but he escaped by turning himself into lightning. He left Hitiho, his wife, behind while she was pregnant with a son, who was named Owarra.

The first step in the chain of successions to the Lotuho kingship was simple enough. There was only one heir and since the king had disappeared, there could be no other. The problems began with the second succession. Owarra, who had married a princess from Lomiya named Abalyare, had two sons, Facar, who succeeded his father in Otunge, and Attulang, who became a famous warrior and hunter and established himself with a following in Chalamini after a conflict over their father's inheritance. According to one version of the myth, there was a third brother, Isifoi, who, after repeated quarrels with Facar, established the village of Lolyanga. While in the other versions of the myth the separation of the protagonists puts an end to the rivalry, this is not the case in the Lotuho story:

15.1. *The spear and the bead* (Lotuho version of the myth as recorded by Pazzaglia)[2]

One day, Facar visited Attulang in his house. While they were drinking beer, a man came running to Attulang to warn him that an elephant was roaming in his

---

1   The story is also known in Central Africa. An elaborate version from Malawi is 'The boy who visited the elephants' in: Schoffeleers and Roscoe, 1985:207–222.

2   This version is mainly based on Pazzaglia: 'Omuk eyabita to hobwok Otuho', p. 18–23, Comboni Archive, Rome, A/126/10. Although I recorded two versions of the same story myself, this one seemed more complete and consistent. I thank Constantine Bartel for his translation

field and destroying his crops. Attulang ran outside taking Facar's spear and hit the elephant. But the animal ran away with the spear in his body. Facar was very angry about the loss of his spear. He refused to accept any replacement or compromise, and told his brother to bring it back. After long and dangerous wanderings through the forest, following the track of elephants, Attulang, one day, walked into a large square where the elephants were dancing the mourning dance (*oburye*) for their speared brother. He saw the spear standing against the pole-shrine (*alore*) in the middle of the square. Attulang joined the mourning dance. He made a show of deep grief and anger as if he had lost an intimate relative. As is customary during funeral dances, he performed *iratara*, running with a spear to the corners of the dancing ground, brandishing it in aggrieved anger against the forest, the abode of hostile forces. For this purpose, he used the spear standing against the shrine. He did so four times. The elephants said: "Look at our friend! How aggrieved he is about our brother!" Then Attulang took the spear for the fifth time and ran away with it. When some time had passed and he did not return, the elephants wondered who he was. One said: "He must be the murderer of our brother." Immediately, the elephants put their tusks, which they had put down for the dance, back into their mouths and followed Attulang on his way to Chalamini. When he had reached the top of the mountain before descending to Chalamini, he shouted to the elephants who followed him: "You elephants, do not return to this area, otherwise you will die." And to the people of Chalamini he said: "You men of Chalamini, never again spear any elephant." The spear was returned to Facar.

Not much later, Facar's daughter swallowed a bead that had fallen from Attulang's girdle of blue beads (*ajwangijwangi*) while he was repairing it in preparation for the New Year Festival (*Nalam*). Now, it was Attulang's turn to insist that the bead be returned. Facar killed a cow for his brother but Attulang refused any substitute. The girl was made to defecate and vomit, but the bead, which could be felt under the navel, did not come out. Facar then decided to cut his daughter's belly saying: "My child, it is not I who is going to kill you; it is my problem with my younger brother." Facar returned the bead to Attulang who immediately put it on his girdle. Facar's anger was boundless.

Attulang further pronounced a curse on Otunge saying that no king would ever be brought forth by that village. In fact, all Facar's sons died before him.

Facar took revenge on his brother by sending a messenger to the Toposa: "Go and bring the enemies who will make Attulang pay for my daughter's death." The Toposa came and killed many people from Chalamini before they found Attulang in the cave where he was hiding. Before Attulang died he cursed (*epit*) the people of Chalamini for having revealed his hiding place: "There will be no more king in Chalamini after my death. Any Igago man who sets himself up as a king will certainly die."

This story was first told to me on a night in August 1982 as I drove the Lotuho Queen on a journey from Lobera, where she had solved a rain problem, back to her palace in

---

of Pazzaglia's Lotuho text. Another version, apparently based on the same material, is found in Paolucci (1970:496–503).

Hiyala. A mile or so before reaching Chalamini, which is half-way between the two villages, the queen asked me to stop. She descended from the vehicle with her son and entered the bush, taking a direction away from the nearby village. After about 45 minutes, she reappeared on the road and the journey continued. When I inquired about the reason for the walk, I was told that it was in order to avoid Attulang's curse.

There are some significant differences between the Lotuho story and the other versions inside and outside South Sudan. In a sense, the Lotuho version begins where the others end. In all other versions, the cutting of the girl's belly triggers off the separation of the brothers. In Lotuho, the two brothers have already fallen out and created their own kingdoms before their quarrel over the spear begins.

The elephant funeral and the *iratara* of the dancers add a typical Lotuho touch to the story not found in the other stories of the protagonist's quest in the land of elephants. Elephants are likened to humans to a degree (cf. Case 2.1) and when they are killed, the Lokoya hunter should dance a funeral dance. The partial humanity attributed to elephants may be due to their possession of tusks which are equated to spears. In swearing oaths, elephant's tusks and spears tend to be interchangeable, as in the story: people are made to jump over a tusk or swallow some powder scraped from it for the same reasons as they are made to lick spears.

In the versions of the Shilluk, the Acholi and the Alur, the elephants cooperate with the hero in the retrieval of the spear, or there is an old woman helping the hero. In the Acholi version, the old woman in the land of the elephants even provides the hero with a token of his royal title: the bead which will later be swallowed by his brother's daughter. In the Lotuho version, the hero gets the spear back by way of a trick played on the elephants. The ensuing confrontation leads to a final separation of the elephants and the villagers.

In the other versions, the sequence of the swallowing of the bead leads to the separation of the protagonists. In the Shilluk version, Nyikango and Dimo exchanged curses, sending death to one another and limiting the number of their subjects and offspring. The exchange of violence of the Lotuho brothers goes much further. When Attulang pronounces his curse on Facar and on the kingship of Otunge, Facar reciprocates by bringing the Toposa enemies in to destroy his brother's village. During the attack, the people of Chalamini — after suffering many casualties — desert their king who takes revenge by cursing them: never will they have a king again. The Lotuho version of the quarrel ends in a spiral of violence which destroys kingship itself.

Contrary to the versions of the myth in other societies, all of which end up justifying the power of a particular dynasty and the migration of one of the protagonists to a new land, the Lotuho version casts doubt on the usefulness of kingship as such. Going by the events related in the story, kingship creates more problems than it solves: the rivalry between the two centres, the division of men and elephants, the invasion of enemies and the ominous curse of the king against his own people, not to mention the poor princess who was cut open.

According to oral tradition, Otunge and Chalamini never had kings of their own again. Facar died childless and Attulang's curse on Chalamini precluded the restoration of the kingship there. It even prevents current royals from setting foot on Chalamini soil. Upon his return from exile among the Bari, Attulang's posthumous son, Imuhuny, a single heir, established his kingdom in Imatari, in the plains across from Chalamini.

In the following, I want to show that the violent rivalry that characterised the relationship between Facar and Attulang is not just a mythical theme but also a comment on the dynamics of early kingship in the area we have selected for our study. I shall first examine the dynastic rivalry between the Bekat kings in Bilinyan during the last half of the nineteenth century and then look at the rivalry between the two Lotuho dynasties in the context of the beginning of the first civil war.

The spiral of violence in Bilinyan

Bilinyan lies in the vicinity of the nineteenth century trading post and mission station of Gondokoro. For this reason, written documents on its history are more detailed than for any other area in Bariland. A careful reading of them allows for a reconstruction of the course of events, especially relative to dynastic rivalry. Although I made several appointments to corroborate the written documents with testimonies from oral tradition, for a variety of reasons the hoped-for interviews never took place.

The earliest observations on dynastic rivalry in Bilinyan regarded the tensions between Subek and Nyiggilo, the two sons of King Logunu, who both accompanied their father in welcoming the Egyptian expedition in 1841. Subek's support base were the villages on the western side of Bilinyan Mountain, collectively named Indöru, while Nyiggilo was supported by Gitong, the ring of villages on the eastern side. The rivalry between the two was continued by their sons. In the early 1890s this rivalry appended itself to the war between the Egyptian government and Mahdist insurrection — Subek's son receiving support from the Egyptian troops while Nyiggilo's son fought on the side of the Mahdists — with disastrous results.

Several 'rounds' can be distinguished in this feud which lasted for almost half a century:

15.2 *Dynastic rivalry in Bilinyan, 1841–1888* (various published sources)

▨ *First round: Nyiggilo versus Subek (1841–1859)*
King Logunu died soon after the visit of the Egyptian expedition. Subek, Logunu's son by Wasuk, Logunu's senior wife, was the recognised successor and was introduced as such to Werne[3]. Nyiggilo was biologically the son of Logunu and Ide, a wife Logunu had inherited from his father Muludyang. Legally, therefore, he was the son of Muludyang, Subek's grandfather and, in this respect, senior to Subek. While Subek had inherited the rain on the basis of his seniority from the point of view of the rule of primogeniture, Nyiggilo, who also possessed some rain

---

3   Her name is written 'Ischok' by Werne. She was the lady who presented the statues to Selim Capitan (Werne, 1848:317).

powers, sought to reinforce his position through his relations with the newly arrived foreigners. Subek's rain failed him at several occasions, but Nyiggilo's contacts with the foreigners were a resounding success.

Nyiggilo closely associated himself with the Savoyard trader, Brun-Rollet, during the latter's first visit to the Bari in 1844. Nyiggilo seems to have treated Brun-Rollet as a kind of age-mate. Both shared their meals and spent time together. Brun-Rollet was taken sightseeing by Nyiggilo and after a while, Nyiggilo moved in with Brun-Rollet on his boat, together with two of his wives and some servants. He followed Brun-Rollet on his return journey to Khartoum at his own request, rendered by Brun-Rollet as follows:

"I leave myself in your hands. I want to know the country that produces the fruits and drinks that you have given me to taste; I want to see how woven fabrics and the other objects in your possession that I admire are manufactured. They prove that your people are superior to us who cannot produce anything of the like. If you give me some of these articles, I will return to my country as a rich and powerful man either with you, if you wish so, or with the people you confide to me to buy ivory" (Brun-Rollet, 1855:188).

Subek adopted a stand that was opposed to Nyiggilo's foreign contacts. When Nyiggilo allied himself with the missionaries and with some of the European traders, Subek associated himself with the traders who had the blessing of the Governor in Khartoum, who was opposed to the missionary action in the south and to independently operating European traders like Brun-Rollet. Nyiggilo struck a deal with Knoblecher, the leader of the missionary expedition visiting the Upper Nile in 1849, allowing the missionaries to settle in Bilinyan in return for firearms. Subek vetoed the plan. Nyiggilo then tried to help the missionaries out by offering them his mother's village, Ferica, as a location for their activities. The missionaries were first welcomed but then, suddenly, the mood of the villagers changed and Yugusuk, the local chieftain, ordered them to quit the village.

According to Knoblecher, Yugusuk had been brainwashed by Gumbiri[4], who served as interpreter to the missionaries and was under the influence of the Turkish traders. One year later, Angelo Vinco, a member of the first missionary party, evaded the orders of the Governor and sailed south again hoping that Nyiggilo would accommodate him as a friend. As Nyiggilo was away on a trading journey in Lotuho, Subek offered him hospitality in Marju and cultivated a friendship with the priest, possibly in the hope of taking over Nyiggilo's foreign connections. After ten days, Nyiggilo returned from Lotuho. At the sight of the cordial embrace of Vinco and Nyiggilo, Subek withdrew to Bilinyan, not hiding his jealousy of Nyiggilo, whom he scorned as "the favourite of the whites" (Vinco, 1974:76–78).

Shortly afterwards, Vinco and Nyiggilo jointly attended the meeting in which an ultimatum was put to Subek to make rain or else be killed (cf. Case 16.15). This was the second major accusation of drought during his career (Brun-Rollet, 1855:227).

---

4   This Gumbiri, a Tsera who spoke both Dinka and Bari, had been picked up by the first Egyptian expedition and apparently had established close relations with the traders in the nine years between the expedition and the arrival of the missionaries (Werne 1848:355).

According to Brun-Rollet, he had gone into hiding in 1849 to save his life after being blamed for drought. This time, Subek fades from the scene. No mention is made of him in the writings of the missionaries who stayed in Gondokoro up to 1860. All the transactions with the Bari were conducted through Nyiggilo.

In 1859, Nyiggilo was killed for the rain. His death did not end the rivalry. If anything, it took on greater scope

Second round: Laku-lo-Subek versus Bepo-lo-Nyiggilo

After the missionaries had left, the traders took full control of Gondokoro. From the mid-1860s Muhammad Abu Sa'ud al-Aqqad, the manager of the official trade monopoly of the Egyptian firm of Aqqad, was the most powerful man. Abu Sa'ud found an ally in Loro-lo-Laku, who was an in-law of Bepo, the son of Nyiggilo, and an adversary of Laku the son of Subek. Laku had on two occasions successfully destroyed patrols of Abu Sa'ud. Loro was an in-law of Bepo, Nyiggilo's son.

In 1871, when Baker arrived in Gondokoro to turn it in an Egyptian government post, he found the country in a state of anarchy after the recent murder of "the *sheikh* of Bilinyan". He was told that Abu-Sa'ud had invited the *sheikh* and his dignitiaries to a party at his house where he had killed all in cold blood. The celebrations on the occasion of the annexation of Equatoria to Egypt were attended by his successor. Shortly after this, Baker got wind of a conspiracy of Abu Sa'ud, Loro-lo-Laku ('Alloron' in Baker's text), the 'cargo chief' of Gondokoro, and another not yet named, Bilinian chief to undo the establishment of the government station.

Inferring from our knowledge of the rivalry between Nyiggilo and Subek we can safely assume that the *sheikh* killed by Abu Sa'ud was Laku, the sòn of Subek[5] and that the chief who was plotting with Abu-Sa'ud against Baker was Bepo, the son of Nyiggilo. Like their fathers before, Laku and Bepo ended up with allies who were each other's enemies. Baker must not have been aware of the complexity of the internal politics in Bilinyan as he did not make use of the internal division during his thirty-five days siege of Bilinyan a few months later.

The peace that made an end to the siege was the result of an initiative of the third Bekat-Limat Rainmaker resident on Bilinyan Mountain, Jada of Mögiri, located on the eastern side. Baker narrates that the first overtures were made by his "exceedingly clever sister" who led a delegation of headmen and informed Baker in the name of the women of Bilinyan that they were tired of the war and wanted a settlement. A peace treaty was concluded with *sheikh* Wani who figures in Baker's narrative as "the sheikh of the mountain" (Baker, 1874, Vol. II: 338). Both names, Jada and Wani, appear in Beaton's genealogy of the Mögiri rain family.[6] The agreement

---

5   Beaton (1934)'s story that Laku-lo-Subek had been seized and beheaded by 'Mimbe' (the Bari name of Emin Pasha; from 'Emin Bey') at an auction of raided cattle held in his compound is not correct. Emin made one trip to Lotuho in 1881. Even if he had brought some cattle back, he would have used them to feed his troops. It would, therefore, seem that Beaton's informants confused the story of the death of Loro-lo-Laku in 1883 ordered by Emin Pasha (related in Chapter Four) with that of Laku-lo-Subek at the hands of Abu Sa'ud.

6   Baker, 1974, Vol. I: 331. This 'Jarda' must be the same as the 'Giada' who offered hospitality to the party of De Bono and Peney in April 1861 on their first stop on the journey to Liria (De

between Bilinyan and Baker apparently did not include Bepo since the attacks on Baker's camp continued. When Baker asked Wani how he could best impose a grain tax to feed his troops, Wani suggested that he should to join forces and raid "Oom Nikla", the village of Nyiggilo's mother's brothers who must have been Bepo's closest allies.[7] Baker, however, turned the suggestion down because of the village's former connection with the Austrian Mission (Baker, 1874: Vol. I: 337).

Baker Pasha's thirty-five days siege of the stockades of Bilinyan, August-September 1871 (Baker, 1874, Vol. I, p.327).

After Baker had neutralised Abu Sa'ud during his operations in Acholi and Bunyoro, Loro-lo-Laku offered his allegiance to the government, and helped him to retrieve a number of slaves who had fled to Bilinyan (Baker, 1874, Vol. II, Ch. XXVI., April 1873). A period of relative calm followed. Loro, supported by Bepo, became the virtual sovereign of the Bari and was on good terms with Emin Pasha.

The successor of Laku-lo-Subek, on the western side of the hill, was Lado-lo-Ide, a son of Subek by Ide, a woman who had first been married to Muludyang and had successively been inherited by Logunu and, at the latter's death, by Subek. Lado was Subek's biological son and Logunu's legal son (He is also known as Lado Logunu).

Bono, 1862:18). To express his relief about Baker's withdrawal, Wani named his brother's son "Ali Bey" the name by which Baker was known among the Bari (Beaton, Southern Records Office, Historical Notes on Bari Chieftainships, Mögiri). Ali Bey became a popular given name in Equatoria. *"Ali Bey* was the usual designation of any white officer in command, and among the Bari, the Governor General bore this title as well as myself", Chaillé-Long, one of Gordon's army commanders, informs us (1876:3/2/1875).

7   The tie between a man and his sister's children is extended to the children of the sister's son.

To Bepo, he was the uterine brother of his father and his father's brother's son — by coincidence, both legally (via Logunu) and biologically (via Subek).

The peace was broken at Loro's execution on Emin's orders in 1884.

Third round: Bepo-lo-Nyiggilo versus Lado-lo-Ide

After the execution of Loro by Emin Pasha, Bepo emerged as the leader of the anti-government rebellion (Emin Pascha, *Tagebücher*, Vol. III, entry 30/7/1885) which united Bari, Nyangbara and Aliab Dinka. In the decisive battle of Lado in 1885, Bepo escaped while the leader of the rebellion, the prophet Deng Tonj, was captured and burned alive. Bepo continued to defy the Egyptian garrison. At the beginning of 1888, the garrison of Rejaf carried out an attack on Bilinyan, which according to Casati, resulted in a defeat for Bepo (Casati, Vol. II: 139; Emin Pascha, *idem*, entry 11/4/88). Throughout the year 1888, Bepo continued to wage war against the government posts at Kiri and Muggi (Emin Pascha, *idem*: entry 19/7/88).

Circumstantial evidence suggests that Lado-lo-Ide was on the side of the government troops at the beginning of 1888 when Bepo's villages were ransacked. We know that Lado was an ally of Lugör, the king at Shindiru, whose villages remained faithful to the Egyptian government during the revolt led by Bepo.[8]

When finally, at the end of 1888, the steamers from Khartoum managed to break through the *sudd* filled with Ansar soldiers, Bepo chose the side of the Ansar and assisted them in the attack on the government station of Rejaf (Emin Pascha, *idem*, Vol. IV, entry 22/10/88). In return, the Ansar assisted Bepo in carrying out an attack on Indöru, Lado's villages. After recovering from the heavy losses, Lado collected his remaining forces, and once more hit back, destroying Gitong and killing Bepo.[9] Because of this attack, Lado was arrested and imprisoned in Rejaf by Bepo's Ansar allies. He escaped later and was reportedly killed in a dispute over an unpaid bridewealth.

Despite a number of gaps in the information, the general pattern of interaction between the two rivalling royal families and the new intruders in the area is clear. Because of the existing internal rivalries Bilinyan became an arena where comprehensive imperialistic rivalries were fought out for over half a century:

In the days of Subek and Nyiggilo, Bilinyan was divided between a party supporting the Egyptian Governor of Khartoum and one supporting the Catholic Mission and

---

8   Beaton, Southern Records Office, Juba, 'Historical Notes on the Bari Chieftainships', *typescript*, p. 2.; Emin Pascha, *Tagebücher*, Vol.III, entry 31/7/1885. The fact that Lugör's name does not appear in any of the reports, diaries or travelogues of the period is another indication that he chose to stay aloof of the changes brought about by the foreigners. The only exception is the mention of his name, written as 'Luga' on Chaillé-Long's route map (Chaillé-Long, 1876).

9   This revenge must have taken place between 1891 and 1893 when the Mahdist forces evacuated Rejaf under the threat of the steamer cult led by the prophetess Kiden. At the end of 1893, when Rejaf was re-occupied by the Mahdists and the new Emir, Arabi Dafa'alla, selected seven loyal chiefs to be sent to Omdurman, Bepo's name is not on the list, which may indicate that he had already died (Letter Arabi Dafa'alla to Khalifa, 12 Jumada 1311, Central Records Office, Khartoum, *Mahdiyya* I/32/48; I thank Mr Bol Deng Chol for his assistance in reading and translating the text).

its allies. In the 1860s and early 1870s, the focal points of the division were, on one side, Bepo, the son of Nyiggilo, and, on the other, Laku, the son of Subek. Bepo was allied to Abu Sa'ud of the Aqqad company. Abu Sa'ud killed Laku. Loro-lo-Laku ('Alloron'), the 'cargo chief', was initially in the same camp. He made peace with Baker after the siege and had no problem with Gordon who relied on Abu Sa'ud's network but was ultimately killed by Emin for sympathising with Bepo's rebellion. It is likely that Morbe who was put forward by the Bari chiefs as their contact person with the Egyptian Government was in the Indöru camp. In the late 1880s, Bepo continued to lead the anti-government camp allying himself with the Ansar while the pro-government camp was led by Lado-lo-Ide. While the names of the protagonists and the interests they served changed, the polar division between the two camps remained a constant. The fact that the rivaling leaders of the Bilinyan communities received support from state armies fighting for control of the southern Sudan had a most destructive effect on these communities.[10]

The rivalry between the Lotuho kingdoms

The rivalry that led to the split between the dynasties of Mayya and Hujang (Case 12.5) persisted throughout the Condominium period, albeit in a less violent way than in the Turco-Egyptian and Mahdist periods. In Chapter Five, we saw that it focused on the control of villages and village sections. The rivalry also extended to more mundane domains. At his appointment as chief in November 1938, Lomiluk bought a motorcycle.[11] Less than a year later, Acalili acquired a motor car for which a special tribute had been levied.[12] In 1940, one of Acalili's wives fled to Lomiluk. Although Lomiluk officially married her in 1941, paying the then considerable sum of fifty English pounds as bridewealth, Acalili continued to look for ways to get her back. Finally, in 1948, after Acalili's death, his son and successor, Patricio Ohucoli, succeeded in kidnapping her from Tirangore.[13]

Patricio and Lomiluk adopted different attitudes to the colonial administration. While Ohucoli struck the British administrators as a traditionalist at heart,[14] Lomiluk's

---

10   Bambu, the grandson of Subek who became the Rainmaker and government chief of Bilinyan after the withdrawal of the Ansar, fled to Lafon together with many other villagers.

11   Tribal Appointments and Dismissals of Chiefs: Entry on Lomiluk, 1939; *Torit District Files*, Southern Records Office, Juba.

12   Torit District, Annual Report 1939, *Torit District Files*, no. 57/C/3, Southern Records Office, Juba.

13   Torit District, Monthly Diary, March 1948, Southern Records Office, Juba, E.P.57/D/5/Vol. I: 624.

14   In 1950, the D.C. of Torit has this to say about Patricio: "Chief Patrizio of Loronyo is a standing argument against the appointment of a rainchief to a Government Chieftainship. He is conservative to a fault, deeply opposed to any new ideas and mainly concerned in consolidating the power he derives from the rain at the expense of and by means of the power given to him by the Government. Education strikes at the Rainchiefs and he knows it with the result that schools in his area are discouraged" (Annual Report, Torit District, Southern Records Office, Juba EP/57/3/1/2). In 1953, another District Commissioner characterises him as "the most powerful

leadership was distinctly modern and even seemed charismatic to them.[15] While Patricio was mainly concerned about the rain, Lomiluk took an active interest in the political developments that led to Sudan's independence. He was one of the chiefs openly opposing the amalgamation of southern Sudan with the north. By 1954, when the internal administration of the country was transferred to Sudanese civil servants, Lomiluk had established a reputation of being 'anti-Arab'. The following case shows how, in the events that mark the beginning of the civil war — the first five years Lotuholand was the major battle ground, the two kings end up occupying antagonistic positions and do not hesitate to call on outsiders to punish their rival, much like their forefather Facar did in mythical times:

15.3 *The rebel and the informer king* (Juba archives; living memory)

In 1955, during the *Nefira* of the Kingdom of Mayya at Hoding, over which Patricio Ohucoli presided,[16] Lomiluk, taking with him a following of armed *monyomiji* of Tirangore, posted guards at the sacred Itaraba pool, which belongs to Tirangore, to prevent Patricio's people from bathing the ceremonial ox in its sacred water before sacrificing it.

King Lomiluk of Tirangore, patron of the early resistance to a united Sudan, government chief from 1936–1955 (Photo kindly made available by his son Vitale Aburi Lomiluk, king of Tirangore since 2010).

Mr Basit, the new Northern District Commissioner, who was aware of Lomiluk's political ideas and who, since his arrival in Torit, had been faced with a series of unclarified acts of sabotage — including the setting on fire on his own house

rainchief ... idle, reactionary and obstructive to all ideas of progress" (Chiefs Appointments and Dismissals 1953, Torit District, Southern Records Office, Juba, file TD.66:186).

15 "Lomiluk has natural command and authority", *idem,* 1944; Lomiluk evinces "plenty of personality", *idem,* 1942.

16 Earlier in the book (Ch. 8, p. 203; Case 10.8) reference was made to this *Nefira*. The *Nefira* of Tirangore had taken place earlier in 1953.

— decided to take the matter seriously. He sentenced Lomiluk to two years imprisonment and suspension from the chieftainship "to close the curtain on his career which played such an important part in the history of the primitive and backward Latuka".[17]

Basit miscalculated. Lomiluk gained in popularity because of his imprisonment and, to most Lotuho, the detention amounted to still another proof of the hostile intentions of the new government.

During the mutiny of the second company of the Equatorial Battalion in August 1955[18], the prison doors were opened and Lomiluk was among those who were freed. Shortly afterwards, he became one of the leaders of a group of mutineers and local warriors who staged armed resistance to the government. Between 1955 and 1959, a series of attacks were carried out against government targets and chiefs who were regarded as collaborating with the government.

The rebel action that drew most attention was the attack in March 1957 on a lorry carrying a delegation of government officials and loyalist chiefs from a meeting with British authorities in northern Uganda. At the meeting, the colonial administrators in Uganda had offered assistance in rounding up Lomiluk's gang, which used to cross the Ugandan border for safety. When the convoy entered Sudan, one of the lorries was fired upon. Five people were killed, three of them chiefs.[19] Seven other passengers, including three chiefs, were injured. The acting District Commissioner, a certain Mr Youssif, who was in the same vehicle, saved his life by hiding himself in a culvert under the road.[20]

After the incident, measures to liquidate Lomiluk's rebel army, estimated at some 400 armed men, were intensified. Villages suspected of harbouring 'outlaws' were severely fined. In April 1959, Haforyere, a village belonging to Lomiluk, was burnt down by the army for having accommodated Lomiluk's gang. The following year, the village was transferred on government order to a new site on the Torit–Kapoeta road.[21] When the government directed an appeal to the chiefs for help in rounding up Lomiluk and his followers, Ohucoli personally went to see the police inspector in Torit and offered detailed information on the hiding places of Lomiluk, located within his own kingdom. He also revealed to the police that he knew that he,

---

17   Torit District, Annual Reports, 1954/55; Southern Records Office, Juba, 57/C.3, p. 173.

18   The Torit Mutiny was the immediate reaction of the Equatorial Corps to the order issued by the newly autonomous — but not formally independent yet—government in Khartoum to transfer the southern troops to the north of the country. It is conventionally considered as the beginning of the first civil war which lasted until the Addis Ababa Agreement of 1972.

19   Among them were Lapwenya, since 1914 chief of Ikotos and chairman of the District Court and Ingong Loliha, chief of the Logir since the early 1920s.

20   Reports and Correspondence on the Border Incident 26/3/1957; File *Southern Corps Mutiny*, pp. 6572, 158161, Southern Records Office, Juba.

21   Torit Rural Council, Monthly Report, April 1960; *Torit District Files*, Southern Records office, Juba.

Ohucoli, and some other chiefs — among them Petro Issara of Loudo—were on the top of the rebels' black list to be killed.[22]

After the death (1958) of Latada Lokiya, the military leader of the rebel group, the movement lost military momentum. Lomiluk died on 9 April 1960 in exile in Uganda. After his death, the rebel army was dissolved. Patricio had died of dysentery in Juba Hospital one year earlier (24 June 1959). His body was transported home from Juba, the state footing the bill.[23]

For four years, Lomiluk had been the driving force behind the major armed offensive in protest against the terms on which the southerners were included in the independent Sudanese state.

To obtain a full picture of all the forces at play during the period, more historical research is needed on the recruitment and the operation of the rebel army and its relation with the *monyomiji* and the local-level administrators during the four years of its existence.[24] It is clear from the episode of the civil war related above that the kings adopted political stands which were to an important extent motivated by the old divisions between the *Mayya* and the *Hujang Dynasties*. This rivalry formed a major obstacle to a common approach against a government which was disliked by all.

Conclusions

The institutions underpinning the uniqueness of the centre that were discussed in Chapter Fourteen are often not capable of containing the rivalry between pretenders to the throne. Once the unity of the royal family is broken, there are no mechanisms to stop the rivals from recruiting a following on the basis of the existing dualist divisions in the society, neither does the sectional rivalry have a brake that stops the sections from connecting their fight to the causes of foreign princes, governments and warlords.

Among the Bari, segmentary expansion made for a safety valve for dynastic rivalry. The malcontent prince was given a chance to test himself in an outlying district. Where this safety valve — for whatever reason — was not an option, as in Lotuho, the conflagration of dynastic and dualist antagonism resulted in an alignment of forces that not only split the kingdom but caused serious destruction to the very constituencies of the rival leaders. The reversal of a centralist configuration into dualism is far more destructive than the switching of dualist antagonism between superimposed segmentary levels in an acephalous society. Unlike competing segments, dynastic rivals who entrench themselves behind internal sectional dividing lines tend to bring in outsiders that are disproportionately powerful to the level at which the

---

22   Letter Torit Committee to Minister of Interior, *d.d.* 27/11/1957; Letter D.C. Torit to Governor Equatoria *d.d.* 2/12/1957 and 13/2/1957; File *Southern Corps Mutiny*, pp. 1211–1221; Southern Records Office, Juba.

23   Torit Rural Council Monthly Diary, June 1959; Torit District Files p. 144; Southern Records Office, Juba.

24   Scholarly studies on the civil war have focused on the political and diplomatic side of it. So far, there has been no study of the civil war as it was fought on the ground.

conflict is fought. An ever deepening rift is cut in the society until a point is reached that it can no longer be bridged, not even in the face of an outside enemy.

Let us once more have a look at the diagram used earlier to elucidate the unifying role of the king (Table 10.1) and insert one more kingdom in the diagram to get the full range of relevant actors for this demonstration:

P. The collapse of centralism into a dualist deadlock (a sequel to Diagrams D and L)

Kingdom A	Kingdom B		Kingdom C
King and people can jointly benefit from the succession war in kingdom B, not only for the spoils and the glory but also as a boost to the bond between king and people;	King B has died and his power is being disputed between his rivalling sons B1 and B2		King and people can jointly benefit from the succession war in kingdom B. not only for the spoils and the glory but also as boost to the bond between king and people.
King A chooses to support pretender B1	Pretender to the throne B1, supported by kingdom A	Pretender to the throne B2 forced to get help from kingdom C	King 3 (= old time enemy of king A)
People A, divided into sections 1a, 1b, etc. but unified by their king	Following of prince B 1 consisting of sections Ba, Bb, etc. fighting the opposite sections Bx, By, etc.	Following of prince B2 consisting of sections Bx, By, etc. fighting the opposite sections of Ba and Bb, etc.	People 3 consisting of sections 3a, 3b, etc., unified by their king
Kingdom B becomes a battleground, not only of its rivalling princes and their sectional constituencies, but also of the rivalry between Kingdom A and C.			

When the sons of king 2 rival for power both of them mobilise constituencies maximising their following. In the case of prince 2A, this following will consist of sections of division 2 of his father's kingdom, for example, 2a, 2b, and 2c. Prince 2B receives support from the sections 2x and 2y. If there is not a quick winner and no compromise, the conflict will continue escalating. The princes will find allies outside the kingdom. If king 1 and his warriors are supporting prince 2A, prince 2B is forced to look for help. Since he wants a quick and positive response, he will look for an ally among the enemies of his rival. There is king 3, an old-time enemy of king 1. The internal conflict between the two princes and their supporters has now grown into an external, inter-communal conflict with its battlefield right inside what used to be a single political community:

When the rivalry between two dynastic protagonists escalates, it becomes a pole of attraction for other hostilities in the area. There is an inherent tendency in the early kingdoms discussed in this book to drift back into a dualist deadlock by turning internal rivals into enemies and by embroiling external enemies into a local stalemate. The latter may be kingdoms, as in the case of Imatari and Segele (cf. Case 9.3); acephalous political groupings, such as the Toposa in the myth of the Spear and the Bead, and in the destruction of Imatari or statal actors rivalling for regional hegemony as in the cases of Bilinyan (Ansar vs. Egyptian army) and the Lotuho kingdoms in the 1950s (pro-Khartoum chief vs. anti-government rebels) discussed in this chapter.

The potential for endemic internecine violence in these kingdoms, based on a combination of dualism and centralism, seems to be larger than that in plainly dualist formations. Going by Evans-Pritchard's analysis of Nuer complementary segmentary opposition, it is difficult to conceive that non-Nuer groups would be invited by a Nuer tribe to help settle its accounts with another Nuer tribe, or that two primary sections would get involved in a conflict between secondary sections of another primary section. In the polities on the Equatorian east bank of the Nile, this 'introversion of dualism' was a common political hazard. The peoples in the area were aware of its dangers, as the Lotuho myth of the Spear and the Bead shows.

PART IV

The Scapegoat King:
The People as Aggressor of their King

King Legge of Liria, killed for causing drought, ca. 1875 (Baker, 1866, Vol.1, p.175).

*"Upon the King! Let us our lives, our souls, our debts, our careful wives,
our children, and our sins, lay on the King!'*
(Shakespeare, Henry V, Act 4, Scene 1)

The shrine with the pots containing the bones of the Lotuho kings in the line of Hujang in Loguruny.

Above: *the shrine as photographed by the Seligmans (1925, plate II). According to the Seligmans, the pots contain the bones of kings Hujang, Ajaru, and Lomoro, and queen Osuru, the mother of Onyong, as well as other relatives not mentioned in the book.*

Below: *The same shrine as photographed by the author in 1981 when the shelter was in dire need of renovation.*

16

The King as Victim in Suspense

The antagonism that is constitutive for the formation of political groups and for the bond between king and people also rules the relationship between the community as a whole and the forces that impinge on it from outside. Disasters are experienced as attacks from outside that need to be neutralised. To organise this defence, or to launch a counter-attack, procedures are followed which are similar to those employed in facing the enemy: the war drum is sounded and the *monyomiji* gather for an emergency meeting (Lul. *paluko*, Lok. *avaluho*, Lot. *ewaha*) to decide on a course of action.

Incidental disorders are cursed and driven away by the *monyomiji* during the meeting. This was the approach adopted in 1984 by the *monyomiji* of Lokiliri against a plague of armyworms and again to counter the spread of *Jok-jok*, a possession cult originating among the Acholi and Madi which affected the girls of one of the village-sections.

Disasters and disorders with a recurrent character are the special domain of the king or of another Master of Disaster. The *monyomiji* approach the king/Rainmaker or the relevant Master to discover the cause and to find a remedy.

In this chapter, I examine the interactions between the community and its Rainmaker in times of drought. Most of the cases presented here refer to the drought that ravaged the east bank of the Nile in the mid-1980s.

The anger of the king versus the sins of the people

In the traditional worldview, natural and social events which, to the modern mind, belong to different realms and are subject to different modes of explanation are but one text to decipher. Nature and society are conceived as part of a single system ruled by the same principles. Rain and drought, health and disease, plagues and good harvests are elements in a single socio-political drama. Its principal actors are the community and its different sub-divisions, on the one hand, and the Rainmaker and the Masters of Disaster, on the other. A third actor who only appears on the scene when the other two have exhausted the means at their disposal to combat disaster is 'God'.

There are many ways in which a group or an individual member of the community can open the door to calamity: fighting, especially if there is bloodshed, hatred, incest, unreconciled deaths, the breaking of solemn treaties. Transgressions of specific taboos may also cause drought: bodies of slain warriors should not be buried inside the village. Women should not deliver their children — an act in which blood is spilt — in a place other than their own. If this happens nonetheless such women should give the Master of the Land a goat to purify the land. Tombs should be levelled before the rainy season starts. Drought is also believed to be caused by deliberate anti-social acts, by individuals or groups, with or without the help of specialists.

In Chapter Thirteen, the king was described as playing the central role in protecting his subjects against the hostile forces from without, be they enemies or natural disasters. If a drought occurs, there are two possible explanations: the king has either taken the side of hostile forces in a move against his people, or he is lax, dissatisfied or angry because of the way his subjects treat him.

If all 'normal' remedies fail, a drought may be attributed to God (Bari: *Ngun*, Lul. *Ori*, Lok. *Ojok*, Lot. *Ajok*, Pari: *Juok*). Admitting that the disaster is from God is an act of resignation in the face of defeat. In the traditional worldview, God is a presence which it is wise to keep at a distance. He is first of all associated with disease and disaster. Each year, at the harvest festival (*nekanga*), the Lotuho offer some of the first food to God and then chant a curse to send Him away from the village. Everyone, including the children and old women, takes a piece of wood, a stone, or anything they can lay their hands on and shout: "God, go away, leave us in peace, go to the north, go to the Nile, go to the Bari and drink milk there!"[1]

The curse is repeated during the night. God, as the source of disease and death, is told to go and stay with the enemies. The relationship of the community with God is structured along dualist lines. God is conceived as an antagonist one rather keeps at bay.[2]

The aetiology of disaster delineated here leaves plenty of room for controversy and disagreement as to who is to blame for a particular disorder. Once the most obvious causes for hostility and hatred within the community have been reviewed and remedied, the king and the people take antagonistic positions in the discussion as to who is responsible. The king will point an accusing finger at his subjects, while the people hold the king responsible. The king will blame the people for negligence or disrespect in its dealings with him, for the small size of the tribute, for quarrelling too much, for harm done to someone who has drawn the king's attention to his predicament. The people, in return, may accuse the king of only thinking of his own interests, of being merciless and relentless, or of plain ineffectiveness.

Confrontations over rain are not only started by the people. The Rainmaker may also mount an offensive and threaten to stop the rain if certain of his wishes are not fulfilled or if the terms of settlements presided over by him are not respected.

The Bari and Lulubo call the ominous state of mind of an aggrieved or angry Rainmaker and of other Masters of Disaster *wiwinya*, translated by Spagnolo as "to murmur because of suffered injustice". It refers to an unspoken curse in which the desired effect is not made explicit. The same term is used when individual misfortune

---

1   "*Ajok, ilo, Ajok, ilo; Ajok ilooo, ilo o wor, ilo karitogol, ilo Pari, ilo Mata le!*" (Molinaro, 1940/41:184; Paolucci, 1970:199–200).

2   For a discussion of the concept of the Supreme Being among the Lotuho, see: Molinaro, 1940/41:179–187; Schmidt, 1940:495–530 (largely based on Molinaro); Paolucci, 1970: 300–330.

is attributed to the discontent of a family member. A Rainmaker's grievance is usually discovered once its effects have become manifest. He usually admits the charge and will accept a gift as appeasement. The Rainmaker may also *wiwinya* on behalf of another person, usually a clansman or a relative who requests him to intervene. In such cases, according to a group of elders I interviewed in Shindiru, the rain cannot be stopped for more than seven days. After that, the Rainmaker has to convene an assembly of elders (*momoret*) to arrange for the settlement of the case.

The Lokoya and Lotuho name *aduvio*, the subversive use of power by the king or another Master of Disaster, which may be translated as 'to convert the blessing attached to the power of office into a curse'. The powers of the *adufani* are more redoubtable than those of the wizard (*adyamani, afarani*), which have a more private character. The disasters believed to be caused by *aduvio* are held to be intentional acts of sabotaging the cosmic order. The Rainmaker is believed to have opened the door to the external forces he is expected to shield the community from.

Aduvio is usually perpetrated to draw the community's attention to some injustice towards the Rainmaker or someone under his protection. The Lokoya term *elamwön* refers to a more serious state of affairs. It was translated to me as "to cause havoc by a curse" and refers to an all-out destructive attack by the Rainmaker against the community. The redress of the injustice and the appeasement of the Rainmaker by the *monyomiji* should normally put an end to the disaster caused by *aduvio*. Unlike the effects of *aduvio*, *elamwön* cannot be overcome via negotiation but needs to be counteracted by force.

A third category of evil influences emanating from the Rainmaker is referred to by the term *omahio*. It refers to disorders which are the unintended consequence of the breaking of a taboo or of an act of disrespect towards someone or something sacred.

During the nine months of the year that crops are in the field, the Rainmaker and his people continually keep an eye on each other. The amount of rainfall, its territorial distribution and its timeliness are seen as an index of the state of their relationship.[3] Unwelcome spells of drought and floods are interpreted as symptoms of a disturbance of the relationship. The weather is the central issue in a perpetual debate in which king and people take turns in playing the role of accused and accuser.

When the king is the accuser, the people try to mollify him by taking away the cause of his grievances. Just as the Rainmaker may point at certain well-timed rains as his gift to the community, he may claim a spell of drought that supervenes at the right moment as a punishment meted out by him. But willingness to please the Rainmaker has limits. Sooner or later, the Rainmaker will have to deliver the goods.

---

3 Pazzaglia, in his account of Lotuho rainmaking, states that it is only as a last resort that the Rainmaker brings up his own dissatisfaction with lack of respect of the *monyomiji*. My material indicates that this view is not correct. Before sacrifices are made on the bones and tombs of ancestral Rainmakers, all potential extant causes have normally been reviewed and remedied, especially the grudges the Rainmaker might hold. Was Pazzaglia who was a good friend of Acalili too tolerant in his judgement of the abuses of the divine profession he and his friend shared? ('Il Capopioggia', p.110, Comboni Archive, Rome, file A/26/11/3).

When the people adopt the role of accuser, there are two courses of action open to the king. Either he accepts the allegation and allows himself to be appeased, or he rejects it by offering a substitute explanation on which the *monyomiji* can work. Whatever the stand adopted by the king at this stage, the invariable result of the confrontation will be that a procedure is set in motion which, as the participants believe, will restore the natural and social order. When king and people agree on the source of the disaster, social unity is reaffirmed and — as a consequence of the resolution of the crisis — rain is bound to fall.

If the rain does not fall, the accusation will bounce back to the king. If the Rainmaker keeps blaming the community, he will in time be considered merciless. His acceptance of additional gifts for rain now enlarges his responsibility for the drought and he may be accused of blackmailing the community to further his own interests. Should he deny responsibility, he would admit his impotence in the face of the drought, spoil the game and make himself look redundant. In all three eventualities, force will be used against the Rainmaker, either to break his resistance or to extract a redeeming confession. If even this does not help and the king has not fled, regicide remains as the only solution.

The process of confrontation set in motion by the drought has many stages of escalation and is full of suspense. There is one practice that slows the pace of escalation down: sacrifice. In sacrificial ritual, both parties substitute reciprocal accusations for co-operation in the killing of an animal victim and the invocation of a higher power — the ancestor of the rain clan or, as a last resort, God — to bring the rain back. There are several types of sacrifice for rain. They are believed to vary in effectiveness and importance, the latter being a function of several factors: the value represented by the victim, the status of the *sacrificer*, the sacredness of the location of the sacrifice and the ancestor invoked. Given these step-by-step differences, sacrifice can create its own suspense and act as a powerful buffer and temporiser in the open antagonism between the Rainmaker and the people.

In the following pages, I first examine the process of confrontation between the Rainmaker and his people as triggered off by accusations of drought. After that, I consider the mitigating role of ritual.

Emergency meetings

When enemies or disasters threaten the community, the big drum is sounded to call the *monyomiji* for a general meeting to discuss the emergency and to take appropriate action. These meetings (called *avaluho* in Lokoya, *paluko* in Lulubo, *ewaha* in Lotuho and *momoret* in Bari)[4] may also be convened by women. This happens especially when they see that the crops are in danger and when they are of the opinion that the men are not doing enough to solve the problem.

---

4   Unlike the emergency meeting of the peoples practicing *monyomiji* rule, the *momoret* of the Bari is only attended by the elders (*temejik*).

During such meetings, everyone is encouraged to speak openly and to hide neither grievance nor suspicion, so that the cause for the disaster can be determined. All rumours concerning the cause of the drought are reviewed, both those relating to wrongs in the community and those relating to the power of the Rainmaker. Special attention is paid to persons who have suffered personal misfortune — death of wife or children — and those involved in disputes over the inheritance of widows, livestock or offices. Should grudges be uncovered, the *monyomiji* may impose a solution if the disputing parties involved are not able to do so by themselves.

All should attend these meetings. If one shirks this duty, suspicion is raised as to one's involvement in the disaster. If a person knows he is suspected of the drought and his defence is weak, it is better for him to leave the village altogether than to attend the meeting. One acquaintance of mine who had been accused of drought by the women of Lokiliri stayed in Juba for more than six months before it had rained enough to believe that the women would have forgotten their case against him.

Some of these meetings have a distinctly victimary ambience, as evident from the following extracts of an account written by a recent school-leaver who witnessed his stepmother being interrogated in connection with a drought which was attributed to her husband, the Rainmaker.

> **16.1 *A women's* paluko *for rain*** (diary notes of the son of the woman accused)
>
> "Before we could finish our discussions [in the bar] four women came and ordered O. [emissary of the women sent to the Rainmaker to obtain his advice] to come [to the women's paluko] and be a witness. K. [a *Big Man* in the settlement] and others had also been told to attend O.'s testimony on what the Rainmaker [who could not attend since he lived some fifty kilometres away] had said to him. Women are known for action in such meetings. Nobody had dared to disobey their order. Even K. had to put on his great coat, take a spear in response to the order. The meeting was held under a tree near the road and as I passed by, I looked towards my mother standing in the middle of the crowd, apparently being interrogated. Some women pointed at me and my mother looked in my direction with the helplessness of a hope [*sic*]. That moment, I felt sorry for her and wished I had power to deliver her from the crowd. But I was equally helpless and I moved on to save myself from having to witness cruel remarks about my mother and about the entire [rain] clan....
>
> The next morning, I was relieved to see her in Juba and I nearly wept in indignation. She accused me of conspiring to betray her, and that I had not come to the village for seeds, but to watch her humiliation....
>
> It was not easy to make her understand my situation during that meeting. She was lucky that nothing serious was done to her compared to some suspects who were tortured by sitting in the sun with a fire around them while drinking salt....
>
> She told me that after hearing the testimony of O., some bottles of liquor had been produced by the women to be drunk by all the good people of the village who did not have the intention to punish the land with drought. Those who would have refused to drink would without exception have been suspected of bad intentions. If

the bad person had been among those who drank, the liquor would have remained in his stomach and caused him a terrible death. Everybody drank including those who never drink alcohol because nobody wants to be on the wrong side".

The statement of the Rainmaker as communicated by O. denied the suspicions that his wife had aroused his anger by settling in the village where the *paluko* took place. The accused woman was acquitted and the meeting had been concluded by an ordeal. In this way, the *paluko*, at least, gave a new impulse to the village consensus by exposing the innocence of all present.

In the dry season of 1983–84, I sent out a brief questionnaire which was addressed to the spokesmen of the *monyomiji* in the six Lulubo villages. One of the questions concerned the *paluko* that had taken place during the previous rainy season. In total, twenty-two *paluko* were recorded. Eighteen of these concerned the drought. The subject of the other four were a plague of insects, a storm at the time the sorghum was ripening, a plague of monkeys and a suspicious stranger reported as moving about in the vicinity of the village. The following were the causes attributed to the drought:

Q. Causes of drought as identified by eighteen women assemblies in Lulubo in 1983

Number	Causes of drought
1–3	disrespect towards the Rainmaker
4.	failure of the *monyomiji* to perform the customary annual cultivation for the Rainmaker
5.	the resettlement of a section of the village away from the old village and their Rainmaker
6.	adultery with a woman of the rain clan
7.	injuries suffered by a member of the rain clan in a fight
8.	elopement of a girl of the rain clan
9.	failure to return the bridewealth to the Rainmaker after divorce
10.	theft of the Rainmaker's goat
11.	failure to settle a debt in money to the daughter of the Rainmaker
12.	amputation of a leg of the son of a widow who belonged to the rain clan
13.	the anger of the Rainmaker about the failure of the killer of his sister's son to make a reconciliatory sacrifice on his tomb
14.	violence between the Rainmaker and his son
15.	outsider from Acholi accused and acquitted
16.	incest between brother and sister (same father, different mothers)
17.	lack of unity in the village
18.	after rejecting all rumoured accusations the women performed a collective rain ritual by throwing water up into the air

In the majority of the cases (1–11 and 14), the local Rainmaker was held responsible for the drought. His *wiwinya* was in seven cases triggered off by harm done to his private interests (4, 6–11): his properties, his nubile daughter, the bridewealth.

In five cases (1–5), the Rainmaker's recognition was at stake (the cultivation of his field, the migration of people away from the central village, open challenges to his authority). In one case (14), drought had been caused by domestic violence in the house of the Rainmaker, a particularly dangerous situation.

In five cases, the accused was not a member of the rain clan (13–18). In one case (13), the drought was caused by a sister's son to the rain clan; in another case (15), an outsider was accused; while in two others (16 and 17), the 'sins' of the community or of some of its members were seen as the cause. In the last case, no one in particular was blamed and affirmative ritual action was taken to bring the rain back. I shall now examine some of these cases in more detail.

Drought, a Rainmaker's weapon

In most of the cases listed above, the Rainmaker was quick in affirming the rumours concerning his involvement in the drought. From the point of view of his reputation, this might have been the best course of action. Waiting to be summoned by the *monyomiji* and play the humiliating role of the accused suspect, as in Case 16.1, reflects unfavourably on a person. On the other hand, by creating the impression that he uses the rain to advance his private interests, the Rainmaker is at risk to acquire a reputation of being an exploiter and of not having the community's best interests at heart. This is what worried the Rainmaker of Lokwe in the following case:

> **16.2 *Drought as a means to force the repayment of debts*** (contemporary case)
> The daughter of the Rainmaker had sold distilled liquor on credit. When her customers continued to postpone the settlement of their debts, she said to one of them "Lobole will collect it on my behalf," implying that one day the *monyomiji* [called Lobole] will have to discover the unpaid debts through a *paluko* to resolve a drought crisis. When there was a spell of drought at a critical point in the agricultural cycle a few weeks later, a *paluko* of the *monyomiji* seriously discussed her case. It ruled that all debts to her should be paid with immediate effect. A delegation was sent to question the Rainmaker on the case. The Rainmaker pleaded that he had nothing to do with the case. As a gesture of good will, he washed and oiled his stones the next morning. Immediately afterwards, he went to the village where his daughter lived and gave her a scolding for having appealed to his powers without good reason. The moment he entered the village, some rain began to fall. *Lobole* received him with a show of hospitality.

Under favourable weather conditions, a trivial threat like this one uttered by a young lady would have passed unnoticed. In a situation of crisis, the community seizes upon it in the hope that it will proffer a way out.[5]

---

5   The powers of rain control among the Uduk in southern Funj (Blue Nile Province) have been described and analysed by Wendy James (1972) as a means to reinforce claims on debtors, not unlike the case described here. There are some important differences between the use of rainstones and drought by the Uduk and by the peoples who are my topic. First of all, the ownership of rainstones is not limited to a special rain clan as in Eastern Equatoria. Among the Uduk, every household can, in principle, become the owner of rain powers. The destruction

Five of the cases (1–5) listed involve the recognition of the Rainmaker's power. In the first three, there had been an exchange of words in which the Rainmaker was ridiculed or his power played down by one of his subjects. That this is a dangerous thing to do is shown by the subsequent droughts, immediately claimed by the Rainmaker and recognised by the *monyomiji* as his just revenge. In one case, the Rainmaker received a compensation of fifty Sudanese pounds — a considerable sum in the village,[6] in another case the grievance pay was ten pounds.

The reason for the Rainmaker of Kudwo to claim the responsibility for a drought (No. 5 on the list) was more complex:

16.3 *Drought caused with the aim of keeping the village together* (contemporary case)

The Rainmaker of Kudwo had long been unhappy about the fact that his people moved away from their village at the foot of the mountain to settle along the Juba–Torit road. They settled there in order to do petty business with passing traffic. In 1983, the part of the village right next to the road experienced a long spell of drought. When asked for an explanation, the Rainmaker declared that they should not have moved away from him and that, if they wanted rain, they should return to the original village. A *paluko* was held during which the issue was discussed. The meeting resulted in the Rainmaker accepting the *status quo*. He also agreed to take some of his rainstones to the road and keep them with his late brother's wife so that he could make rain on the spot. He hoped that the transfer of the stones would help to raise the status of the wife of his late brother (the former Rainmaker).

Two years later, his brother's wife died and the stones were given to her daughter. When the drought reached a critical stage again, the Rainmaker was summoned to a *paluko* of the *monyomiji* and interrogated on the question whether the division of his collection of stones might have caused the drought. The Rainmaker replied that it was not the division of the stones that had caused the drought but the fact that the people of one section of the village had not come to his late brother's wife's funeral. The *monyomiji* accepted the allegation and one of the sections immediately offered to pay a compensation of five Sudanese pounds to the Rainmaker for not having come to the funeral dance. A few days later, it rained.

On both occasions that the Rainmaker was given an opportunity to use his influence, he advocated a course of action that would counteract the process of disintegration of the village. In both instances, he failed to achieve his objective. The *monyomiji* contented themselves with paying obligatory respect. But the Rainmaker of Kudwo

---

caused by the activation of the stones in Uduk is believed to affect the settlement of the debtor alone, which is usually different from that of the owner of the powers. In contrast, in Eastern Equatoria it is usually the village of the Rainmaker that suffers the consequences of the Rainmaker's anger. The use of different clan powers in Lulubo and Lokoya — each clan deploying its own power (fertility, locusts, mosquitoes, etc.) to exact its demands — may offer a closer parallel to the way the Uduk use their rainstones. Even then, we should not overlook the fact that the East Equatorian power holders are, first of all, custodians of public interests, which are defined in opposition to private clan interests.

6   In Juba in 1983, this sum equalled the monthly wage of an unskilled labourer.

provided his community with an explanation of the drought on which further action could be taken. It helped to maintain the village consensus and allowed him to retain a semblance of power. This power, already curtailed from the days the village had a government chief, was further eroded by the growing involvement of his people in cash-oriented activities in Juba. The lack of interest shown for the funeral of the late Rainmaker's widow reflected this as well.[7]

In the next case the rain also functioned to support the interests of the community as a whole. It was brought before the court of the government chief of Ikotos (Lango) in August 1981. I happened to be present at the time.

16.4 *Demanding justice by staging a drought* (contemporary case)

A man (A) had injured another man's (B) foot with a spear. The two lived in different villages (X and Y). Between the families, no compensation had been paid and no revenge taken. The victim went to his Rainmaker and told him about the injustice that had befallen him. A long spell of drought in village X followed. The diviner, consulted by the *monyomiji*, pointed at the possibility that the Rainmaker in Y might be demanding justice for the uncompensated injury of his fellow villager. The *monyomiji* of X then sent a delegation to Y. The Rainmaker demanded five cows — three for the wounded man and his family and two for the rain. On hearing the demand, the clansmen of A hid their brother so that the *monyomiji* were powerless to enforce a settlement.

When the drought persisted, the women of X went to see a diviner and found out about the unsettled case involving villager A. They rounded A up, took him prisoner and led him — under much commotion and ululating — before the government chief at Ikotos. When A pleaded that he did not have any cows, the chief ordered his in-laws to return five of the cows paid to them in bridewealth by A in order to stop the drought in the village.

In pre-government days, the *monyomiji* or the women would have brought the culprit in front of the Rainmaker himself, who would have pronounced the final verdict. Apart from the greater power and popularity of the contemporary government chief, the fact that village X was not within the rain area of the Rainmaker of Y was a reason for the women not to deal directly with him. The case offers a good example of the intervention of women in a dispute that the *monyomiji* were unable to solve. The restraint, or powerlessness, of the *monyomiji* in such cases is due to their fear of the possibly violent consequences of arresting the culprit in case his section would decide to support their man.

Drought may also result from bereavement and injustice suffered by a member of the rain clan. In this case, the drought is interpreted as an appeal for attention and help from the community. One of the cases listed above fits into this category: that of the grief of a mother about her son who returned home from Western Equatoria with one leg amputated. The following case is also in this category.

---

7   Part of this village is located at the junction of the Juba–Torit–Kenya and Juba–Nimule–Uganda roads which, in the early 1980s, was an important centre for 'informal trade' in imported essential commodities such as engine fuel.

16.5 *Demanding social attention by causing drought* (contemporary case)

A widow who was a sister's child to the rain clan lost her only daughter and was deeply aggrieved. At her daughter's death she had tucked away the clothes of her late daughter without even washing them. Divination by means of wild cucumbers[8] indicated that she had caused the drought. The *monyomiji* gave her a goat in appeasement and ordered her to wash all the properties belonging to her daughter.

In cases like this one, there is no elaborate speculation on how the poor widow could have arranged for the drought. Her grief and her close connection with the rain clan were sufficient cause for problems with the rain to arise.

I would like to highlight one more case on the women's list because it shows an accused who plays his role as scapegoat very well and to the benefit of the community. The protagonist is widower Wodiya (fictitious name), who is a sister's son to the rain clan. He is widower who had never remarried, not because of poverty, but out of choice. He was considered an eccentric because, despite his advanced age, he continued to be a big-game hunter (*liggogo*), a lonely and dangerous profession. The fact that he had been the village leader during the rebellion may have added to the ambivalence of his reputation.

16.6 *The drought of the old elephant hunter* (contemporary case)

The researcher arrived in his village the day Wodiya had been interrogated by the *monyomiji*. Three weeks before his arrest, the women had performed *logi logi noga* (ritual simulation of regicide described in Cases 17.8 and 9) which had resulted in a few days of rain. Since then, drought conditions had resumed. The *monyomiji* had made *paluko* and Wodiya's name was mentioned as a serious suspect. Some hotheads even demanded his burial alive. Wodiya had immediately confessed his complicity in the drought and demanded a goat for the grave of his sister's son who had been killed a year earlier. Since the burial, the family of the killer had not made a sacrifice of reconciliation on the victim's grave. Wodiya confessed that he had smoked his pipe on top of his cousin's grave and that he had made a sign of the cross, both of which were acts that, in the given situation, could cause drought. The goat was soon produced and sacrificed. Wodiya received a severe warning. If he caused drought again, the *monyomiji* would go straight to the chief to ask permission to bury him alive. The same night "Wodiya's rain rained". Although the rain was very mild, the villagers were visibly relieved and convinced it proved that they had found the right solution to the rain conflict.

I had no opportunity to ask Wodiya whether he really intended to cause a drought on behalf of his sister's son. The days following his accusation and confession, he was the focus of praise for his good rain. Talk about the incident that had made him the object of everybody's attention was avoided. Since he struck me as a sober and responsible man, I am inclined to believe that his confession concerning the unreconciled cousin was invented on the spot. From a sociological point of view, Wodiya played his role as

---

8   Several fruits of the wild cucumber, each representing one of the suspects, are put on a rat trail overnight. The person whose cucumber has been gnawed at is guilty.

a scapegoat very well. He had given the community an opportunity to reinforce the consensus by allowing the tension against his person to build up to a certain point. At the critical moment, he had found a way out of his plight, and simultaneously obliged two formerly hostile families to reconcile.

Turning the tables on the Rainmaker

In the previous cases, the demands of the Rainmaker were met and peace between the *monyomiji* and the agent stopping the rain was restored. Although appeasement may be the most frequent course of action taken by the community, it is by no means the only outcome of a rain conflict.

The next case from Lotuho shows how the willingness of the *monyomiji* and the Rainmaker to reach a compromise can turn into unwillingness and to open confrontation if the drought persists.

16.7 *The expulsion of a Lotuho Rainmaker from his village* (Grüb, contemporary case)

The Rainmaker had inherited his brother's widow who was a rain-queen. He had never been consecrated because of the disturbances of the civil war. When his brother died, he was in prison on the Red Sea as one of the soldiers who mutinied in 1955. After his release from prison, he went into exile in Uganda and only returned to Lotuho after the war. In his dealings with the *monyomiji* over rain, he relied heavily on his diviner who read the intestines of sacrificial animals for him to identify the cause of drought. Through the years, the diviner put the blame for drought on the *monyomiji*. According to his divination, they had neglected their Rainmaker. They were repeatedly ordered to provide more tribute and services to their Rainmaker. According to the Rainmaker himself, the drought was due to a lack of belief of the *ahou* (the leading age-set of the *monyomiji*, lit. 'head') in his powers.

In 1982, after a spell of drought, the tension between the Rainmaker and the *ahou* erupted into open conflict. At a discussion at their meeting point, the *monyomiji* had, in an attempt to break the deadlock in their relationship, offered the Rainmaker a wife and a day's labour (*ekubo*) to cultivate a larger field for him. The Rainmaker refused the proposal saying: "I no longer want your gifts."

Not long after this, the two strongest sections of the village sounded the drum for *ewaha* (emergency meeting); collected the Rainmaker from his palace and dragged him to the central ceremonial ground, without giving him a chance to put on his clothes. There, they questioned him on the drought. The Rainmaker, as usual, immediately demanded a ram for his diviner to read. The *ahou* refused, saying that the diviner's interpretations always laid the blame on the same party and never offered a solution. The Rainmaker then proposed that the *monyomiji* wash away his rain powers (by a ritual of purification)[9] and select someone else. He suggested the name of one of his rivals who had a following in the village. The *ahou* did not immediately have an answer to this countermove. Some said: "He has no powers, so how can they be washed away?" Others feared the consequences his dismissal might have for the rain.

---

9   Such a ritual was performed on King Irwangi (Case 12.5).

At this stage of the debate, some members of the retired generation intervened, advising that it would be better for the Rainmaker to leave the village and go into exile. So the Rainmaker went, escorted by the police in order to avoid any violence, and followed by the queen who feared that she might be abducted by one of her husband's rivals whose possession of the queen-widow might reinforce his claim on the kingship.

When later rain-medicines that could cause drought were discovered in the house of the diviner he was expelled as well.[10]

This case shows how at a certain point, depending on the popularity of the Rainmaker, the patience of the *monyomiji* and the actual rainfall, accusation shifts from community negligence to a Rainmaker at fault. By refusing new gifts from the *monyomiji* and by demanding to be relieved of his rain duties, the Rainmaker avoided an escalation of the conflict which could have brought him into a situation similar to that of Rodrigo in Lowe (Case 9.6). By accepting the gifts, he would have accepted further responsibility for the rain and risked his life.

Perhaps, he might have taken the risk if he had been properly consecrated or if he had had more confidence in his powers himself. It seems that his long stay away from Lotuho, as a prisoner and later as an exile, had turned him into a sceptic in rain matters.[11] It is also clear from the case that in the confrontation between the Rainmaker and his subjects, much depends on the Rainmaker's diplomacy. If he is out to receive always greater signs of respect, materially as well as symbolically, he might very quickly find himself in a head-on clash with his subjects. The more he is given, the greater his culpability if the goods are not delivered. The preceding story has a sequel in another village of the same kingdom. Normally, Lotuho Rainmakers get away with having adventures here and there but when their rain fortunes turn, their transgressions are less easily forgiven:

16.8 *The use of ritual to reduce tension* (contemporary case)

In February 1982, the Rainmaker had an affair with a married woman. When her husband detected the affair, he gave the adulterous Rainmaker a sound beating. The latter fled to the sub-chief for safety, who took him to a nearby police station for protection against violence. During a long spell of drought in August 1982, the local deputy (*ohidak*) of the Rainmaker was interrogated by the *monyomiji* and confessed that he had been instructed by his superior to collect some scoops of the first rain

---

10   I thank Andreas Grüb who carried out anthropological fieldwork in Hiyala for relating this case to me and Toby Martyrio and Eluzai Mogga for assisting me in following up on the case.

11   Such skepticism about one's own powers should not be too openly expressed. Spire, the Ugandan Administrator who knew Leju, the Rainmaker of Shindiru writes: "Ledju confessed to me that neither he nor any of his assistants really believed that they were able to make rain but their fathers before them were supposed to possess such powers, and the inhabitants consequently believed them to be possessed of the same. What, therefore, could they do? Some time ago, Ledju publicly announced his inability to make rain and, in consequence, the population seriously threatened his life, and he was obliged to flee to the Government Station for protection" (Spire, 1905:20).

and to put it in a gourd. On receiving this information, the *monyomiji* wanted the Rainmaker for further interrogation. The sub-chief in the meantime detained the *ohidak* as the key witness in the drought case.

These events coincided with the expulsion of the Rainmaker as described in the previous case (16.6). By the time a delegation of the *monyomiji* came to look for the Rainmaker, he was on his way to Yei on the west bank of the Nile, a safe distance away from the scene of rain conflicts. The queen who had first accompanied her husband into exile had been allowed by the *monyomiji* to return on probation. No services (collection of firewood, cultivation, repairs on the palace) were to be offered to her by the *monyomiji* until she had proved to have the interests of the community at heart.

She agreed to come and look into the rain problem for which her deputy was still under detention. When she finally arrived, the deputy had fled. The queen then stated that the deputy had no power of his own over rain. She ordered the *monyomiji* to collect a black he-goat from her deputy's stable. It was killed near a stream, its stomach contents being sprinkled into it. The next day, there was rain.[12]

The cases above show that the rain continuously forces king and people to redefine their relationship. The power over rain is not just an ideological superstructure, justifying and mystifying the power relationship. It is the subject matter of daily transactions by which king and people test the balance of power between them. The dramatic potential of the rain may be one of the deeper motives why kings in the climatic zones of tropical Africa depending on unpredictable rainfall are makers of rain.

There are two more elements that demand our attention in the last case: the danger of using violence against the Rainmaker and the neutralising role of rain ritual. In the next paragraph, I examine the problems that are believed to arise when a Rainmaker is closely associated with acts of violence. After that, I discuss the political function of rain ritual.

Violence and the Rainmaker

One of the cases in my survey of Lulubo emergency meetings on drought involved a fight between the Rainmaker and his son as the cause of drought. Normally, the Rainmaker should be screened off from all violence in the community. Among the Bari and Lulubo, the Rainmaker should, as a general rule, not be exposed to the sight of fighting and of blood. For this reason, quarrels in the Rainmaker's family are considered particularly ominous.

The following case from Lulubo, dating from 1985, provides another example of a Rainmaker blamed for drought because of alleged mismanagement of his household:

16.9 *The Rainmaker's domestic quarrels and the rain* (contemporary case)

The two wives of the Rainmaker were jealous of each other. The second one was inherited from the Rainmaker's late elder brother. Each wife was the recipient of

12 I thank Luis Oduho for the reception given in Lobera, and Eluzai Mogga for his assistance as an interpreter on the journey in Lotuho in August 1982.

mobo, the annual cultivation day for the king, one moiety cultivating for the first wife and the other moiety for the second one.

In 1982, the first wife brought her grievances against her co-wife into the open by refusing to provide the *monyomiji* with the seeds they had come to sow as part of *mobo*. She explained that her refusal was in protest against her husband since he took care of the second wife to the exclusion of herself.

When drought followed the sowing of the first crop, the *monyomiji* convened a meeting (*paluko*) in which the Rainmaker was blamed for failing to keep the peace in his house and for allowing one of his wives to cause the drought. The Rainmaker was tied, beaten and ordered "to wash the drought away" by washing and anointing the rainstones and to restore peace in his house. Some elderly *monyomiji* went with him to his house and performed the ritual to reconcile the husband and his wives.

As a result of the violence, the Rainmaker could no longer use his right arm for work. Three years later, there was another crisis in the family. Because of his handicap, the Rainmaker was not able to take proper care of his wives. The second wife now decided to leave the house and settle on the main road where she could earn some money by selling firewood and grass to passing traffic. In April 1985, she cleared some land to cultivate for her own subsistence. She told everyone who wanted to listen to her complaints how she had been neglected by her husband. When there was a spell of drought after the first sowing, the women of the settlement where she stayed convened a *paluko* in which the suspicion was raised that she had left her husband against his wish and that the drought was her husband's revenge on the roadside community for having offered hospitality to his wife. She was sent back to the Rainmaker with the understanding that she would only be allowed to return if her husband would come in person to explain the reasons of her moving to the roadside. Her departure was followed by two days of heavy rain. To the women, this confirmed their theory concerning the cause of the drought.[13]

Since the primary role of the Rainmaker is to create peace and to control violence on the level of the community, it is obvious that a Rainmaker who cannot even contain the violence in his own household is considered a liability to his people. The same applies to Rainmakers with a taste for competition in the field of rainmaking. One drought in Lokiliri in the late 1970s was attributed by the women of Lokiliri to a rain contest between the Rainmakers of the two moieties of the village. As part of the contest, according to the women, one of the Rainmakers had tried to stop his rival's rain and thus caused the drought. He received a vigorous beating at the hands of the women and was forced to perform a sacrifice to bring the rain back.

---

13   The case also illustrates the present destitution of the rain family. The lack of control of the Rainmaker over his affairs is better understood when we look at the contradictions that mark his position. Being the direct, most senior descendant, of the formerly powerful kings of Lokiliri, he has mounted the throne in a period when the government chief is by far the most important man in the community. While his early career prepared him to be an agent of modernisation— he was not only among the first five Lulubo to be baptised and to follow primary school but also, prior to being a Rainmaker, Lokiliri's first, government-employed dresser—he accepted a position that was traditional *par excellence*. Being a rather quiet man without gift for haranguing and bluff he ended up in a more or less chronic victim role without ever giving enough offence to be severely mistreated.

If there is strife in the royal family, the *monyomiji* of the section where the royals reside are held partly responsible. They are expected to take the initiative to restore order in the family before the conflict affects the village as a whole. If they do not take proper measures, they may be attacked by the *monyomiji* of their fellow sections, as events which occurred in the late 1930s demonstrate:

16.10 *The role of the* monyomiji *in maintaining peace in the royal family* (contemporary case)

A rain prince, son of the king of Lokiliri [biological son of the former Rainmaker, legal son of the Rainmaker's elder brother] lost his wife at an early age. When his [biological, but not legal] father died his possessions went to his [legal and biological] children. The prince had hoped to at least inherit one of his father's wives since his own wife had died. But the wife on whom he had set his heart was given to his elder brother, who also inherited the kingship. Because of this double misfortune, the loss of his own wife and the failure to inherit his father's wife, he was strongly suspected of having had a hand in the drought which occurred after the inheritance was settled.

When the *monyomiji* of Kworijik, the moiety of the king, proved unable to find a solution to the problem of inheritance which satisfied all parties, the *monyomiji* of Lokwe, the other moiety, convened a *paluko* at which they decided to attack Kworijik in order to put pressure on it to solve the quarrel in the royal family. The two moieties had a stick fight. The following night, there was heavy rain. Shortly afterwards, the new king provided his unfortunate younger brother with the means to marry a new wife, thus making an end to their conflict.

As a last illustration of the rule that the royal family should project a peaceful image to its subjects, I quote an intelligence report written by the Governor of Mongalla on the killing of the great Bari Rainmaker, Wani Matat:

16.11 *The marital problems of Wani Matat* (Khartoum Archives)

In 1902, when she [Wani's wife] had run away from her husband, there had been a serious drought in Mankaro where Wani stayed. The people would have killed him if the government chief of Mankaro had not taken him to Bambu, king of Bilinyan, for protection. In 1909, there was another drought which coincided with a quarrel between Wani and his wife who had run away. This time the people of Mankaro could not be stopped and Wani was killed on 24/8/1909.[14]

The buffer of ritual

Most rain rituals are carried out in response to the rain situation of the moment, usually at the request of the community. During periods of abundant rains, ritual activities at the rain shrine are few. In times of poor rains, the Rainmaker and his assistants may be quite busy. The calendrical rituals performed at the beginning of the rainy season are usually light, elliptic, versions of the complete ritual sequence.

---

14 Monthly Diary Mongalla Province, August 1909, Central Records Office, Khartoum, Intelligence Reports Mongalla, 19051909, INTEL 8/2/13, p. 80.

All the Lotuho Rainmaker does at the beginning of the season is crush a fruit of the wild cucumber over the rainstones and invoke his ancestors. The Bari and Lulubo Rainmakers just collect their rainstones from the place where they were stored during the dry season; wash them with water; and, if the women happened to have brought some oil, anoint them. The Pari Rainmaker simply selects a black cow from the herds of the community; sprinkles some water on its back; and returns it to its owner. More elaborate rituals are only performed in response to an express demand by the community. Their performance is situational, not calendrical.

When the Lotuho Rainmaker gets his rainstones out in March or April and squeezes a wild cucumber over them, or when his Pari counterpart sprinkles water over the black cow's back, they are just preparing for the year's rain game, the actual course of which is unpredictable and resembles a game of chess. The Rainmaker and the community sit at opposite sides, making their moves. The game is unexciting when the rains are regular and the harvests satisfactory. When the rains are poor and the harvest is threatened, tension mounts and both the moves on the board and the activities at the rain shrine become more frequent.

Rain ritual cannot be understood in isolation of the antagonism between Rainmaker and community. It functions as a safety valve in the relations between the two; directing the reciprocal anxiety and aggressiveness towards the ritual and to its sacrificial victim. The more critical the rain situation, the more elaborate the ritual for rain. The more intense the collective mood of anxious expectation, the more drastic the ritual measures taken. Rain rituals are either elaborations or elliptic reproductions of a scenario which can be summarised as follows:

R.	The basic scenario of rain ritual
1.	an act of elimination of the evil influences believed to inhibit the fall of rain by applying a purifying substance taken from a sacrificial animal (*e.g.* stomach contents) or a substitute (*e.g.* the liquid squeezed from the wild cucumber) to the rainstones or any other tangible symbol of the rain powers);
2.	an act boosting the beneficial operation of the rain powers usually by applying an oily substance to the body of the Rainmaker(s), the rainstones, the skull or bones of ancestral rainmakers, or to specific, named, rocks and mountains;
3.	a celebration of renewed consensus, frequently in the form of a communal meal in which the animal victim of the rain sacrifice is eaten;
4.	simulation of the desired rainfall by splashing water up into the air, by imitating the behaviour of people fleeing for shelter from an imminent shower, etc.

In ritual practice, the entire sequence is not necessarily followed through. In the ritual performed by the Lotuho and Lulubo Rainmakers to open the rainy season, an elliptic version of step one is performed: the squeezing of the cucumber and the washing of the rainstones with water, both being acts of ritual purification. The Pari practice can be seen as an elliptic contraction of steps one and four. Between these 'minimal rituals' and the rituals performed in times of crisis which may involve multiple animal — or even human — sacrifices, there is a scale of increasingly radical interpretations of the basic scenario.

It is not difficult to elicit an enumeration of these steps from informants. The following steps taken by the Rainmaker when facing a rain crisis were recorded for the Lotuho by Father Pazzaglia:

S.	Escalation in Lotuho rain ritual (as recorded by Pazzaglia[15])
1.	When the community is affected by drought, its *monyomiji* see the Rainmaker; he orders them to bring a black he-goat, has it slaughtered and reads the intestines for an interpretation of the drought.
2.	The interpretation usually warrants a demand for an extra payment for rain to the Rainmaker (*edumit hide*), usually a cow or two goats.
3.	If the weather does not improve, more gifts will be brought; the Rainmaker will make a sacrifice on the rainstones and has the intestines of the sacrificial goat read by his diviner.
4.	If there is no result the same evening, a ram is sacrificed and the fat of its tail is smeared on the rainstones.
5.	If there is no result within three days, the Prime Minister (the second-in-command after the Rainmaker), accompanied by a Lomini girl (the clan of the attendants to the King), go to a particular stream to fetch pure water to wash the rainstones. The king now invokes God (*Ajok*): "God come and help me, the people have paid me."
6.	If rain does not fall, the *monyomiji* may conclude that God is "bad", since he refuses the rain–a conclusion signifying the defeat of the Rainmaker by the forces of disaster.
7.	As a last resort the king may make a sacrifice on the bones of his ancestors, which for the Hujang dynasty are kept in pots in Loguruny (Illustration, p. 342), for the Mayya dynasty in Iloli. The prayer spoken by Acalili on such an occasion was: "God, You Lord of Disasters! [16] What is wrong with you? Why do you not chase the sun away? Let rain come! Let the sorghum turn red. Don't treat us so mean! If you want to be harsh punish us in a different way! Let us have food to eat!" The goat is cooked, eaten by the elders and its bones are put in the shrine (near the pots with the bones of the dead Rainmakers) with the words: "Take the bones; eat them so that you may help us." After that the king and his aides wash their hands and throw the wash-water inside the shrine.

15 'Il Capopioggia', *typescript*, p.110, Comboni Archive, Rome.

16 'Lord of Disasters' is the translation of *Hollum*, a Lotuho epithet that refers to the violent, punishing aspect of divinity. *Hollum* is the name of God that was adopted by the Catholic Mission.

Haddon recorded the following enumeration of ritual steps, also seven, taken by the Bari Rainmaker after he has made a sacrifice on the rainstones to open the rainy season:

T.	Escalation in Bari rain ritual (as recorded by Ernest Haddon, *Thesis*, 1911)
1	The people assemble at the start of the rainy season under the village tree and are welcomed by the Rainmaker who pours water from special pots over their feet. A sacrifice is made and the rainstones are washed and oiled.[17]
2	If rain does not fall, a second sacrifice is made on the grave of one of the ancestors of the rain clan in the presence of all the elders of the rain clan; the rainstones are washed and oiled a second time after they have been placed on top of the ancestral grave; the blood of the sacrificial animal is drunk by those present and an extra fee is paid by the community to the Rainmaker; if the rain does not fall immediately, all present wash themselves over the grave.
4	The ceremony may be repeated at the grave of another more powerful ancestor.
5	A sacrifice is made to feed the mountains. The liver of the goat is cut in portions which are shared between the Rainmaker, the elders of the rain clan, and the surrounding mountains. A piece is thrown towards each mountain in the neighbourhood with the words: "What is the matter with you, (name of the mountain), take your food!"
6	The stones are taken out of their pots, put in the sun to dry, then washed with rumen and oiled.
7	As a last sacrificial resort people go and sacrifice on the grave of Mödi-lo-Busok, the Master of the Land of the area around Gondokoro in the middle of the 19th century.

The name of Mödi-lo-Busok indicates that Haddon collected his information close to his office in Gondokoro. Richardson, who collected his information in Bilinyan, states that the grave of King Subek was the ultimate location for rain sacrifice.[18]

---

17   Spire, one of the first British administrators in Gondokoro, left us a description of the ritual procedure in Shindiru. He recorded the text of the invocation that Leju Lugör made when demonstrating the ritual to Spire. After the rainstones had been washed by his '*dupi* (slave assistants), Leju anointed them, praying:

"I am the son of Lugar, my home is near the mighty Nile. Shobi [Subek] has brought me a fine fat fowl; we have had a very good feast. Shobi wants rain for his crops; if he does not get rain, all his crops will fail and he and all his women will either die of hunger or migrate to some distant land and become the slaves of strangers. Oh, the rain must come! Oh, my father, send the rain! Send the rain! Send the rain! You were in your day a mighty Rainmaker; many people believed in your power, brought you many goats and sheep and you became rich. Your flocks were as numerous as the grass which now covers the surface of these lands. Now you are dead; and I am left to make rain in your stead! Oh send the rain! Send the rain!" (Spire, 1905:15–21).

18   According to Richardson's information, the village demanding a sacrifice at this most sacred spot had to send a delegation consisting of five representatives, each of them bringing a bull in payment for the performance of the ritual. The bull that was sacrificed was provided by the Bekat themselves (Richardson, Notes on Belinian, Typescript, joined to Beaton, 'Historical Notes on Bari Chieftainships', Southern Records Office, Juba).

The succession of stages does not suggest an underlying systematic order. The list of Pazzaglia puts more emphasis on the payments to the Rainmakers (Lotuho 1, 2, 3, and 5, Bari 3 and the note by Spire) which, we know from other sources, were important in Bari as well, while the Bari list emphasises the role of ancestral graves (Bari 3, 4 and 7, Lotuho, 7). The significance of the graves of ancestral Rainmakers will be discussed in Chapter Eighteen.

The element of purification is well represented in both. As an ultimate purification, the Lotuho bring water from a special stream to wash the stones. The Bari do a complete 'overhaul' by putting the stones in the sun. Under normal conditions, rainstones should not be exposed to direct sunlight.

The list of Father Pazzaglia has more references to the co-operation — or rather the lack of it — on the part of God (4, 5 and 6). The Bari of Gondokoro treat the mountains as divinities who control rain and drought. The fact that the Bari postulate relations of kinship and affinity between mountains, just as they do with rainstones, and the fact that rocks and mountain walls are sometimes smeared with stomach contents of sacrificial animals would suggest that they are identified as giant, super effective rainstones.

When the rain situation becomes more critical, the Lotuho sacrifice a ram. According to Richardson's account, the Bekat Rainmakers of Bilinyan perform a rain ritual in which the rain spears and the rainstones are stirred together in stomach contents taken from a live ram. The rationale for sacrificing sheep under more critical conditions is their greater 'coolness' in comparison with the more common goat.[19]

Consensus, 'being of one heart', is a precondition for the fall of good rains. The first stage in Haddon's list is in fact a reconciliation ritual (*tomora*). After a dispute is resolved, the two parties are made to spit in a calabash with water which is then thrown by the officiating elder at the feet of those present.

All splashing with water is to some extent an imitation of rain. More dramatic than the use of water in the *tomora* ritual is the conclusion of the rain ritual, recorded by Richardson (*idem*), where a community delegation that comes to ask the Bilinyan Rainmaker for rain is urged, after the performance of the ritual, to return home running in order to reach before the rain falls.

The ritual domain offers a series of increasingly radical steps to which a Rainmaker has recourse in overcoming and surviving a prolonged rain crisis. Because there is a variety of rituals, the Rainmaker may bring the safety valve of ritual into play at successive occasions, thus reducing the pace of escalation of tension between himself and his people. By making clever use of the internal hierarchy of ritual alternatives, it is possible for him to transfer some of the tension against his person to the field of ritual. However, when the ritual alternatives are exhausted and the drought still persists, the full blame will be placed on the Rainmaker.

---

19   The reasons for this comparative coolness are discussed in Ch. 19, p. 441.

The apocalyptic time-frame of rain ritual

The Bari had one more, final, ritual step if the rain continued to fail. This step was not included in Haddon's inventory. We have two descriptions of it, the first one from an eyewitness, the missionary Don Angelo Vinco, the second one from Jennings-Bramly, an officer in the colonial army:

16.12 *The ultimatum to King Subek — 1851* (Vinco)

Generally speaking, the rains were abundant this year, and the crops and fodder for the cattle were in plentiful supply. There was only one period of eight or nine days, when the sky remained clear and there was no rain, whilst the *dura* [sorghum] which is their national grain crop began to wither. The natives went to see Subek and declared that if he had not caused the rain to fall within three days, they would kill him. The next day, all the *Big Men* (*grandi*) assembled at Subek's house, where I was also invited. I thought it wise to accept the invitation, especially since the people demanded it unanimously. I went accompanied by Nyiggilo and one of my servants. We entered in a large hut where all the chiefs had already gathered. I greeted them with the customary "*Ta dotore!*", and sat down on a very small chair[20] observing the development of this new spectacle. Several oxen were brought, one of which was given to one of their priests who are called *bunit* ['diviners'] in their language. The others were slaughtered, and all the people, without distinction, men and women, ate from the flesh, while the *Big Men* together with Subek and the *bunit* discussed the problem of rain. A bell[21] was brought in. It was filled with water. With the water, Subek washed a green stone, many times, while the other chiefs spat in that same water. When this was done, everyone assured me, without showing a shred of doubt that on that very day rain would fall (Vinco, 1940:306–7).

The rain sacrifice described by Jennings-Bramly belongs to the same category of rituals as that attended by Vinco:

16.13 *The ultimatum to the Bari Rainmaker* (Jennings-Bramly)

There comes a time when the need is too great, and he [the Rainmaker] is given a last chance. Then an ox, if they can afford it, is slaughtered and a great feast prepared, and some of the blood,[22] with some round pebbles, is put in one of the hollowed stones used by the women for grinding corn. This is left on one side, I presume as an offering to some higher power. The feast is held with much drumming; at its conclusion, on a given signal, amid dead silence, all retire to their huts, and not a sound is made till morning. If no rain comes in three weeks from that day, the

---

20   The one-legged seat of ca. 15 centimetres high that people on the east bank used to carry along strapped to their upper arm; nowadays only the people to the east of the Lotuho still carry their seat along.

21   This is the heavy cow bell offered by Selim Capitan to King Logunu (Werne, 1848:297; Brun-Rollet, 1855:229).

22   During my fieldwork, I have not come across instances of blood being used on rainstones. In Nilotic cosmology, blood is closely associated with violence and is a substance endangering the effectiveness of rainstones. I, therefore, think that Jennings-Bramly, because of his unfamiliarity with the use of rumen in ritual, mistakenly assumed that the substance applied to the stones was blood.

Rainmaker is killed and his son rules in his stead, his cattle being divided among the villagers (Jennings-Bramly, 1906:102).

Both rituals end in an ultimatum to the king to make rain. As far as the duration of the ultimatum is concerned, the missionary must be right. Three more weeks of drought would have finished off a crop which undoubtedly was withering by the time the ultimatum was set. The sudden transformation from noise to silence, from exuberant sociality to silent expectation in Jennings-Bramly's description creates a formidable suspense and a powerful sense of unity which must be a very potent threat to the Rainmaker. The scene of indiscriminate commensality at Subek's house was apparently also aimed at creating a sense of primeval unity between those present. Normally, men and women eat separately, each one taking the portion of the animal to which he or she is entitled on the basis of age and gender.

Striking is the certainty of the participants that the ritual will have a positive result. This assurance that I have found in many informants' descriptions of rain rituals is present also in the exhortation with which the ritual ends: to run home in order not to get wet. The combination of the suspense of expectation, the willingness to eliminate perpetrators of evil (the Rainmaker, for instance), the suspension of status differences and the unshakable belief that the expected blessing is coming within a specified length of time, is reminiscent of the mood of millenarian movements and cargo cults. There is an unmistakable similarity between the drought stricken community waiting for rain and the followers of the Bari Steamer Cult waiting for the steamers filled with trade goods on which I touched briefly in Chapter Four.

The time-frame of rain ritual is not cyclical. There is not much in it of the 'eternal return' that characterises calendrical ritual. On the contrary, its time-frame is that of suspense. From the first conciliatory and purification rituals of the Lotuho and Bari to the last sacrificial festival at the tombs of powerful ancestors, there is a gradual build-up of suspense, each step inaugurating a collective state of mind which is more 'apocalyptic' than the previous one: more marked by impatient expectation of rain and by the willingness to take drastic measures to eliminate obstacles — in the community or in the person of the king — that may delay the coming of the rain.

To conclude this discussion of the role of ritual in the antagonistic relationship between the Rainmaker and his community, I offer a description of the pattern of escalation in rain crises among the Dongotono. While the lists of rain rituals by Haddon and Pazzaglia almost exclusively focused on the interventions of the Rainmaker[23] the following description — based on informants' statements and a paper by Father Pazzaglia — presents an integrated picture of the successive, alternating steps taken by both the community and by the Rainmaker. Apart from the temporising ritual inputs already discussed, this schema includes community initiatives: renovation

---

23   Probably because the accounts were collected from Rainmakers. Father Pazzaglia was a good friend of Acalili while Haddon collected much of his information from King Bambu of Bilinyan (Haddon, 1911: 139ff).

of religious structures, communal searches of conscience, reconciliation meetings, etc., in which the Rainmaker is not he officiant.

U.	**The course of a rain crisis among the Dongotono** (Pazzaglia)
1.	*Reminder of the Rainmaker followed by a minimal sacrifice at the pole-shrine* If the rains delay the *monyomiji* send their contact person to the Rainmaker (*loikojin lo hobu*) to ask for the reason. Normally the Rainmaker will give him an *olorose* fruit (wild cucumber), spit on it while invoking God and his ancestors, and instruct the contact person to crush it on top of the sacrificial stone at the foot of the pole shrine (*balacar*) while saying: "God (*Jok*) if you care for our land at all let the rain fall."
2.	*Identification of wrongdoers* If the drought persists the *monyomiji* consult a diviner. He will read his divinatory stones to detect the wrongdoer (*afarani*) to whom the drought can be attributed, often a person involved in violent conflict or other anti-social or sinful behaviour. The diviner may also discover that the Rainmaker has caused the drought.
3.	*Community reconciliation with sinners* Detected wrongdoers will be ordered to mend their ways, settle any conflicts that could stir violence and arrange for a reconciliatory sacrifice with the community. Each of the villages affected by the drought receives some of the stomach contents of the sacrificial goat that are applied to the sacrificial stone next to the village pole-shrine.
4.	*Community reconciliation with the Rainmaker* In case the Rainmaker is the cause of the drought, the *monyomiji* will have to make the heart of the Rainmaker turn *cool* again. It is the task of the women to find out from the Rainmaker what went wrong and how to repair the relationship. (Cf. Ch. 9, p. 224–225 on the role of women as mediators).
5.	*Assembly of all men to ritually expel the forces hostile to the rain — using spears.* If the drought persists, all men, including uninitiated young men and old men, assemble in front of the rock 'Imatahi' in the Sacred Wood (*Sawa*) a patch of high altitude forest high up the Lomohidang Mountain (2,623m). The meeting can only be held if *all* men are present. The Master of the Sacred Wood, from a clan different from that of the Rainmaker, presides over the meeting and concludes the meeting by beating Imatahi with a twig, praying: "Let rain come, let your hearts be cool." This is the sign for all men to get up, take their spears and shields and simulate a fight against an imaginary enemy. After that the men of the clan of the Master of the Wood will run into the forest shouting: "The sky is covered with clouds, completely covered!"
6.	*Reconciliation of all men and animal sacrifice — strictly non-violent.* If drought persists, all men led by the Master of the Wood climb the mountain again now to a rock which has a natural basin. This time no weapons are allowed, not even sticks. Beer is made inside the basin. The root of *aturlele*, a wild eggplant, is put in the beer. Everyone, beginning with the Master of the Wood, takes a sip from the mixture and spits it back into the basin. In this way all grudges between members of the community are neutralised and replaced with positive social feeling, *coolness*. After this one or more goats are sacrificed. Branches of the *iporwoi* tree are dipped in the stomach contents and taken back to the villages downhill. The stomach contents are sprinkled all over the villages, especially on the sacrificial stone.

7.   *Rebuilding of the Rain Shrine and consecrating it with a human sacrifice*
    Pazzaglia relates an alternative course of action: four unmarried young men go up to
    the rock Imatahi, accompanied by two adults. They kill three goats which are roasted
    inside the skin and eaten. They spend the night with the Master of the Wood and go
    up again now taking two goats. After these have been killed "one of the young men
    will lay down on the ground mouth-to-mouth with one of the slaughtered goats while
    another man pours water on the touching faces". After this the Rain Shrine containing
    the pot with the Sacred Iron Dish is rebuilt. This happens "in a great hurry and in a
    mood of sacred terror". The Sacred Iron Dish is a piece of iron three cm thick and three
    cm in diameter with a hole in the middle, "cold and humid as a hailstone". This is the
    holiest spot of Sawa. When they are leaving the sacred forest they shout: "The sky is
    covered, it is black with clouds. Let the rain come!"

The measures taken by the Dongotono to combat the rain crisis begin with a standard
sacrifice. If that is not enough, the attention first turns to the sins of the members
of the community, then to any expressions of ill-feeling and disrespect against the
Rainmaker. The sinners are socially reintegrated and neutralised by means of a sacrifice
at the pole-shrine, and the king, if need be, is appeased. If this does not help, another
attempt will be made, in open discussion among the men, to rid the community of
any division of heart that might still exist. After the discussion, consensus is boosted
by a mock fight against an imaginary enemy.

The next step constitutes an even more radical attempt to expel all bad feeling from
the community. It is staged in an emphatically non-violent manner (no weapons)
and it establishes a more intimate bond between the men (by the mouth-to-mouth
connection of spittle, water and the *aturlele* fruit).[24] A sacrifice concludes this stage.

The account of the last option to remedy the rain, by Pazzaglia, has an enigmatic
character, especially the scene of the men and the goats lying flat on the ground.
Since the piece of iron, cold and humid as a hailstone is clearly a substitute for
rainstones,[25] we would expect the performance of an act of purification — using a
powerful ritual cleanser such as the stomach contents of a black ox — followed by
an act of consecration — in which a high-grade sacrificial oily substance, such as the
chyle, the milky fluid secreted by the small intestines of the ox — is applied to the
Iron Dish. Nothing of the sort is mentioned except the sacred tremor of those present.
The only way we can make sense of the scene of the young man and the goat lying
mouth-to-mouth is by assuming that Pazzaglia's informant hesitated to tell the full
story wanting to spare the missionary the graphic details of the violence to which the
young man had been subjected. The "sacred tremor" of the officiants and the funny
position of the boy on the ground face-to-face with a dead goat only makes sense if
we assume that the boy has been killed. The mouth-to-mouth positioning of the goat
and the boy suggests a contrivance to neutralise a posthumous curse comparable to

---

24   I have had no opportunity to determine the *aturlele* fruit either botanically or symbolically.
25   Iron is considered a rain-generating element. In the form of rain spears, it is frequently used in
    rain ritual.

the piercing of the tongue of the Pari Queen (Case 17.11). The circumstance that the young men had to be 'virgins', that is human beings unaffected by the violence of sex and war, adds to the likelihood that the four were potential sacrificial victims. Apparently, only one was selected to die. How the selection took place, Pazzaglia's story does not tell

My assumption that a scene of human sacrifice has been censored away by Pazzaglia's informant is not just an educated guess. Three years before I read Pazzaglia's text, a person from the area had related to me that one of her childhood playmates, a boy from the rain clan, had been taken up the mountain and killed for the rain.

Conclusions

Between the moment when the first suspicions concerning the causes of the drought are rumoured and the final act of regicide, there is a whole range of transactions between king and people that temporise the confrontation and increase its suspense. These activities are of two sorts: transactions that restore the peace between king and people and rituals.

In the first type of transaction, the people blame the king and demand an explanation. If the explanation is acceptable, they repair any wrongs the king may have indicated and allow him to continue to live. From the side of the king, it is important to have a series of plausible counter-accusations at hand and present them one by one, so that he will not put himself in a situation in which no further suspense is possible.

Ritual plays a mitigating role in this game. It offers the possibility to create suspense on a different plane. The arsenal of ritual at any Rainmaker's disposal consists of a range of procedures which vary in effectiveness and importance. This variation depends on: the value represented by the victim, varying from the fruit of a wild cucumber to a human victim, the status of the sacrificer (the king, a minor Rainmaker or an assistant Rainmaker), and the sacredness of the location of the sacrifice: the domestic shrine, the tomb of an ancestral Rainmaker who may also vary in importance, or the Sacred Wood. Given this capacity of sacrifice to create its own suspense, it acts as a powerful buffer in the open antagonism of king and people.

The course of a rain crisis can be summarised as follows:

V. Typical course of a rain crisis

Actions of the people	Actions of the king
1. make sure the customary sacrifices are made; if necessary request the Rainmaker to make extra sacrifices	perform the necessary sacrifices in the customary order, keeping the more complex and powerful sacrifices till later;
2. do a collective search of conscience and take remedial action for any violence or infringement on the rules that may have caused drought	demand remedial action for breaches of peace and non-observance of taboos; solve any disputes and sanction their settlement

	Actions of the people	Actions of the king
3.	blame the king and appease him	demand more tangible signs of respect from the people; accept the responsibility for drought and allow yourself to be appeased
4.	use divination to find out if no other drought maker has been at work; check on rivalry and violence within the royal family	identify another scapegoat (a rival, a foreign Rainmaker, a wizard) and promote the idea among the people
5.	perform the ritual of simulated regicide (Case 17.7; 17.8)	make more demands, increasing the suspense
6.	present the king with an ultimatum to make rain or be killed	perform the most powerful sacrifice available in the dynastic repertory;
7.	use physical force so that the king releases the rain he is reluctant to give	declare the drought as coming from God; diffuse the tension by focusing on other issues (war for instance)
8.	accept the drought as a punishment of God, or kill the king	surrender to the anger of the people or flee and get sanctuary from a friendly king

All stages of this scheme will be traversed only if the drought continues for a considerable length of time. The order in which successive interventions take place varies and depends on the particular circumstances of the drama and the 'style' of wielding power adopted by a particular *monyomiji*-set or Rainmaker. In the following chapter, I turn to the discussion of the final steps taken (5, 7, 8) by the people in dealing with a king who is considered utterly obstructionist.

Bura, one of the villages of the kingdom of Queen Nyiburu who was killed on 8 July 1985 for causing drought after an escalation of tension between her and the monyomiji *that lasted for over three years. The photo (by Eisei Kurimoto) was taken from Lipul Mountain not long before sunset at the time cattle are returning to the stables.*

17

The King as Victim

In the previous chapter, we looked at rain conflicts which were amenable to a solution through the appeasement of the Rainmaker, by negotiations resulting in the payment of reparation to aggrieved parties, by the settlement of debts, by sacrifices to purify the land of drought attracting bloodshed, etc. We emphasised the role of ritual as a buffer in the escalation of tension between a Rainmaker and his community. This chapter traces the escalation of the antagonism between the Rainmaker and the community when the drought has gone beyond appeasement of the Rainmaker and peace-building in the community, and all sacrificial options have been exhausted. The community becomes more and more obsessed by identifying a wrongdoer and eliminating him or her. Solutions are conceived in terms of unilateral action by the community and not as the outcome of negotiations or ritual. We shall successively examine the range of common targets of blame besides the Rainmaker, the use of oracles and ordeals to detect drought makers, the use of torture in forcing drought makers to release the rain, and the rituals in which a substitute of the unknown drought maker is killed — which are believed to have real effects. A list will be presented of twenty-four historic cases in which a king or Rainmaker was deliberately killed by his people. The discussion of one of these cases — that of the killing of the rain-queen of the Pari in 1985 — will conclude this chapter.

Targeting the blame

The most immediate suspects of drought are the Rainmaker himself, his agnatic relatives and other members of the rain clan, his sister's sons, his assistants in the performance of rain ritual as well as other dependents. In Bari, the *'dupi* of the Rainmaker and the Master of the Land may stop the rain (Spagnolo, 1933:322–32). In Bari and Lulubo, the many persons who are related to the rain clan through their mother (*ngörinyi*) are especially distrusted. According to informants, they are the favourite accomplices of Rainmakers with evil designs.

In some places, the designation of a scapegoat is complicated by the fact that there are several recognised rain clans (in Ngangala, for example). All over the east bank, persons professionally dealing with sacred matters — diviners and healers, frequently a combined profession — are believed capable of influencing the rain. Their machinations with the rain are especially distrusted in Lotuho and among the Pari.

Drought can also be caused by the dead. The posthumous anger[1] of Rainmakers is considered to be an important cause of drought. Three cases in this category were discussed in previous chapters: the curse left by Okomo that caused a drought for which Oyalala was blamed and killed (Case 12.5, Stage 2); the curse attributed to the Rainmaker of Lowe who was buried alive (Case 9.6); and the alleged curse of Sardinian Consul Vaudey which, according to Lejean, was held responsible by the Bari for the great drought in 1855–1860 (Case 4.7, note 28).

Apart from people with more or less official rain connections, there is a vaguer category of anti-social elements (Lot. *afarani*) including incestuous couples, wizards and commoners who have acquired rain-medicines. As a result of the increased circulation of these medicines, mainly originating from Acholi, this category of drought makers has become larger in recent years.

Between rival sections, generations and villages, there is a perpetual fear that the other group will 'steal the rain'. The grave of a recently deceased Rainmaker should not be left unattended, lest the *monyomiji* of another village or section come and take the rain along. Generations also take precautions against their rain being sabotaged by ill-disposed retiring elders.[2]

Sometimes, the suspect is a collective body. Drought is used as a weapon between enemies on different levels of segmentation. In Chapter Four, we made mention of the drought over Lafon in 1911 (p.144) which was first blamed on their exiled king, but later when he had returned home, on their Bari enemies.[3] In 1933, the Tirma and Toposa raided each other's rain. A Tirma party was accused of having stolen some of the first rain when visiting the Mogoth section of the Toposa. In revenge, the Mogoth went to steal some water from a watering place of the Tirma.[4]

Foreigners were sometimes accused of causing drought. According to Knoblecher, the founder of the Austrian mission, the fear of drought was the main argument the traders used to persuade King Subek not to allow the missionaries to settle among them (Toniolo & Hill, 1974:53). Vaudey and Nyiggilo were blamed for the great drought in Bariland, as were traders, missionaries, diviners (*'bonok*) as a group (Morlang, 1862/3:115; Hansal, 1876:300) as well as a French expedition of Nile explorers which entered Bariland by river in 1856. The leader of the expedition, the Duke of Aumont,

---

1   Pari: *cien*, Lokoya: *acen*, Lulubo: *cieng*, translated as 'ghostly vengeance' by Evans-Pritchard (1956:288–292) and Lienhardt (1962:34–86). I have not been able to ascertain whether the related Bari word *sendya* ('to curse') is used with special reference to posthumous curses. The Lotuho equivalent *epit* has a different range of meaning since it also includes blessings that are bestowed posthumously.

2   During the Pari transfer of power, the retiring elders have to show the contents of their mouth to the new *monyomiji* before spitting a blessing into the mouth of the bull of generational reconciliation. Spitting wild fruits into the bull's mouth would be a curse causing drought (Ch. 8, p. 203). See also the last phase of Case 8.13.

3   *Reports on the Finances, Administration and Conditon of the Sudan*, Annual Report, Mongalla Province, 1912:200, Sudan Archive, Oriental Library, Durham.

4   *Sudan Monthly Record*, January–February 1933, 1/3/80 91, Central Records Office, Khartoum.

was given an ultimatum by Yugusuk, Chief of Ferica, to make rain. When the rain did not fall, the Frenchman was faced with a declaration of war. A small shower at the right moment was the Duke's good fortune. He escaped unharmed (D'Aumont, Duc, 1883:200).[5] It is clear that in these cases of collective scapegoats, it is difficult to draw a boundary between 'scapegoats' as such and 'enemies'. In the last case, the Bari did not make that distinction either.

Among the ethnic groups discussed here, I have not come across sweeping designations of socially arbitrary categories as 'the short people' who were accused among the Mandari of Tali in 1958[6] and the 'old people', the social category customarily blamed by the Lango of Uganda.[7]

Oracles, ordeals and divination

The principal means employed to detect unknown drought makers are divination and ordeals. Divination is performed by specialised diviners or, if the number of potential rain stoppers is limited, by an oracle implemented by the *monyomiji*. The latter alternative is practised in Ngangala, which receives its rain from three Rainmakers, each of whom belongs to a different clan.[8] If among the three there is no obvious wrongdoer, a collective hunt is organised. It is divided in three rounds, each held in the name of one Rainmaker. The Rainmaker in whose name an animal is killed is designated as drought maker. The animal is then given to this Rainmaker to eat. If he is indeed guilty he will die soon after eating it.

A less strenuous alternative to this divinatory ordeal, is to put three fruits of the wild cucumber (Bari and Lulubo: *loroso*) in the house of the clan elders of each of the three rain clans. The rain clan whose cucumber is eaten by rats is made to confess guilt, if not by persuasion, then by force. Similar oracles are used in Lulubo. The women put fruits of the wild cucumber, representing suspects, near rat trails. If the animal killed and the suspects are of the same gender, the latter's guilt is established.

A more discreet way to determine the cause of drought is to consult a diviner (Bari: *'bunit*, Lulubo: *ozo*, Lotuho/Lokoya; *iboni*, Pari: *ajua*). This is probably the most frequently employed method. The *monyomiji* or the women appoint a delegation; collect some money; and ask the diviner for advice. Diviners use a wide variety of

---

5 Foreigners, as a category, have often been the target of the blame. In 1982, traders of Nigerian origin in Juba, the so-called 'Fellata', were accused of the drought. The shades that protected them and their merchandise from the sun were torn down by a local crowd "in order that they may feel the sun". Being a minority among the Northerners, the marginality of the Fellata explains their selection as a scapegoat group.

6 Juba District Annual Report, 1958/9, Southern Records Office, File 57.E.3/1, p. 10.

7 "Should the drought continue ... it is suspected that one or more of the old men have maliciously hidden the rain, and endeavours are made to find the culprit.... The old men first search among themselves.... If they are unable to find the culprit, all the old men are mercilessly beaten by the *awobi* [the uninitiated young men] and are mulcted of innumerable goats" (Driberg, 1923:261).

8 Lokuriaba (considered senior), Moje, and Kursak, a branch of the same clan as the clan of the Lulubo Rainmakers.

divinatory methods, the most common of which are the throwing of stones and shells (Bari, Lulubo, Lokoya) and the inspection of the intestines of sacrificial animals (Lotuho, Logir, Lango).

In Lulubo, Lokoya and Pari, the diviners are independent individual specialists who owe their position to an individual career.[9] In Lotuho, the king relied on more or less permanent diviners. In Case 16.6, we saw that the Lotuho diviner functioned as a buffer between king and people, screening the king off from direct challenges to his power and obliging the people to pass through the diviner before approaching the king directly.

In a serious accusation, the suspicions of the public are usually tested against the utterances of the diviner. So, the diviner plays an important role in the management of the flow of accusations in the community by endorsing, invalidating and temporising them.[10] The following case illustrates the temporising influence the diviner may have:

17.1 *The temporising role of the diviner in a rain conflict in Liria* (contemporary case)

In 1985, the women of Liria suspected the queen (the wife of the late Rainmaker) of being responsible for the drought. Her late husband had bought some rainstones from the Rainmaker in another community. The original owner asked for a payment on the occasion of the transfer of the stones to the queen to ensure their continued effectiveness under the new caretaker. The queen refused, arguing that the stones had been fully paid for.

The women collected money to ask advice from the diviner. They received the following recommendation: "Go to the queen and ask her if she has caused the drought. If she answers 'yes' give her a black goat, but if she says 'no' come back to me." When the queen answered "no", they were told by the diviner to make the queen swear an oath that she was innocent in her transactions with the Rainmaker who had owned the stones before. The queen took the oath in front of the meeting of women, stating that she was innocent of any *aduvio*. One month later, she died from a disease that only lasted for one day. There was heavy rain to 'mourn her'. (Case 14.5-7 deals with the same events but from the viewpoint of the rainstones.)

---

9   The experience required to qualify as a diviner is either a personal crisis in which the aspiring diviner is 'attacked' by the power that enables him/her to become a diviner, or a period of apprenticeship with a more experienced person. It is common for a child of a diviner to inherit the profession from one of his or her parents, either through possession by the power after the parent's death, or through a deliberate initiation by the parent. It is a career open to both sexes. The spread in the 1930s of an offshoot of the Bari possession cult, Yakanye, has been responsible for quite a few callings as diviner among the nubile girls in Lulubo. More recently, the Acholi *Jok-jok* possession cult has triggered off a new trickle of callings.

10   Diviners could accumulate considerable power. The Lotuho remember the name of Hodoliyang, the diviner who led King Ohori on a disastrous expedition to the east, just before the definitive desertion of the site of Imatari. Lokuryeje, the ancestor of the Bekat royal clan, was a diviner before he usurped the throne (Ch. 2, p. 63).

The vulnerability of royal widows

A category of community members that is particularly vulnerable to drought accusations is that of the royal widows. Among the Lulubo and Lokoya, it is not usual for a wife to succeed her deceased husband. But as a successor is normally only installed at the beginning of the next rainy season, the wife is supposed to have *de facto* control of the rain shrine during the interim period. These widows, who combine a certain degree of social marginality with a direct responsibility over the attributes of rain control, account for a disproportionally large percentage of drought accusations, including those leading to a full-blown regicide.

In the list of twenty-four cases of deliberate regicide which is presented below, seven of the victims are women: a number that is disproportionally high in comparison to the number of female Rainmakers at any one time, especially if we subtract the four cases from Bari, where succession by women is most exceptional.[11] Of these seven women, three are sisters of the Rainmaker and four are wives married from other communities. All were widows.

The following factors can be put forward to explain the preponderance of women: It is more difficult for them to defend themselves against allegations. They live away from their own clansmen so that their opportunities to mobilise support are limited especially since they do not have direct access to the male age-class system, including the *monyomiji*, the main regicidal agent. Because they are women, they also lack the access to resources and manpower that would enable them to build an economic position — as *Big Men* do. Livestock is divided between the male members of the family. Women cannot expand family membership and their social networks by way of multiple marriages as the men can.[12] One informant bluntly stated that Nyikale (the eighth case in the list of Case 17.11) was killed because she was *likico*, a person without wealth or dependants. The fact that widows are economically dependent on male members of the family makes them 'sitting ducks' for accusations. The assumption is that their grief over the loss of their husband, brother or son easily overrides their concern for the rain or, even worse, affects the rain directly.[13]

Torture

The mode of torture applied to rain stoppers follows the logic of 'an eye for an eye and a tooth for a tooth.' The Rainmaker is made to feel the heat of the sun he is allowing to shine uninterruptedly. He is made to sit in the midday sun for long hours, or close to a hot fire. Sometimes, fire is placed all around him. Emin Pasha reports that in order to make the torture worse, salt may be forced down the throat of a Lotuho drought maker. His head may be shaven and smeared with honey and his hands tied

---

11   As far as royal succession is concerned, Ngangala follows the practice of the Lulubo and Lokoya.

12   'Woman-marriages' in which a woman marries a wife and becomes the *pater* of the children, as occur among the Nuer, do not exist in the part of Eastern Equatoria studied here (Evans-Pritchard 1951: 108–109).

13   There is an obvious parallel here with witchcraft accusations in late-medieval Europe.

so that he cannot drive away the bees and the other insects attracted by the honey. The drought maker may also be exposed to the sun with his body in the ground up to the neck. Emin adds that these punishments were not applied to kings. Kings were attacked at night and raided of all their properties and either killed or expelled from the village (Emin Pasha, 1894:780).

Putting fire around the Rainmaker and beating him have been the most widely used forms of torture in recent years. They sometimes cause the death of the Rainmaker as in the following cases:

17.2 *The torture of the man who caused 'Akudi'* (contemporary case)

Around 1930, Lado, the younger brother of Yugusuk, the Rainmaker of a section of Lokiliri, was accused of the drought that was later wryly called *Akudi* ('when buttocks were so thin that the anus could be seen'). Yugusuk was infuriated when Lado's son, Loro, committed adultery with his wife. "Have I not paid your mother's bridewealth?" he said to the son of his much younger brother.

Since this case divided the rain family, it was brought before the chief's court in Liria. During the court session, there was a fight with the chief's guards in which Lado's teeth were broken. Lado was sentenced to paying a considerable adultery fee to his brother while Loro was banned from the village. He enrolled in the Equatorial Batallion but died a few months later of pneumonia. His death was attributed to a curse of Yugusuk.[14]

Lado was deeply hurt by his son's death and full of resentment against his brother. When there was a spell of drought, the suspicion fell on Lado. The women rounded him up and sat on top of him collectively. When Lado had been made to feel "that he was just a human being" — to use the expression used by my informant — the women said: "You are bringing death to us, now it is our turn to bring death to you, you man of death." He was questioned by the *monyomiji* while the women set a fire around him. After much torture, he confessed that he had indeed caused the drought because of his hatred for his brother. He said he had painted an ochre cross on a potsherd and put it up in a tree. After this confession, the *monyomiji* took him away from the fire and ordered him to provide a goat to perform the ritual of reconciliation (*tomora*) with his brother Yugusuk. A few days after both brothers had reconciled, Lado died. His body had become swollen before his death. After he died, his stomach burst and water came out. People said it was the rain Lado had wanted to prevent. After Lado's death there was abundant rain.[15]

---

14   Yugusuk was said to have taken the arrow-head used in cutting the umbilical cord of his father (who was also a grandfather to Loro) and with it stirred the beer which he offered to Loro before he left. The arrow-head called *otonga* is kept throughout life and inherited by the elder son. Put in the quiver with other arrows it brings luck. If it is mixed with 'cool' substances such as food, beer and water, it becomes very dangerous since the arrow is associated with fire and with killing.

15   Stories of the event are contradictory as to the disposal of the body. According to some it was thrown in a dry river bed. I was once shown the location. According to others, the body was buried and mourned.

The cause of the *Akudi* drought belongs in the category 'violence and rivalry in the rain family'. The policy of the *monyomiji* was aimed at eliciting a confession that could be used in redressal action, in this case the reconciliation of the two rain brothers.

The expression "when he had been made to feel that he was a human being", used by my informant who had witnessed the scene, refers to the breaking of the stubborn hostility of a Rainmaker towards the community. Obstinacy and relentlessness are typical motivations attributed to a Rainmaker turned drought maker. The torture is believed to reduce the rain stopper to human proportions and make him amenable to a negotiated solution.

Torture does not usually lead to death. Frequently, clouds appear on the horizon at last, and the victim is released. Another way to escape one's fate is a promise to the torturers to show and hand over the rain charm that caused the drought. The two following cases illustrate this:

17.3 *Deliverance from torture of a Kuku rain family* (contemporary case)

In 1981, the widow of one of the Rainmakers of Kajo-Kaji was placed near a fire, together with her assistant Rainmaker (*kedi*), his wife and her mentally deranged husband's brother. Later, she told me that during the torture, she prayed very intensely, looking towards the sacred grove where her husband and his ancestors were buried. After a while, some wind started to blow and small clouds appeared from the direction of the forest. All four were released because the torturers considered that the ordeal had served its purpose.

In the following case from Lulubo the transfer of the rain charms made an end to the torture.

17.4 *The confession of two tortured drought makers* (contemporary case)

When the first civil war began to affect the Lulubo (ca. 1965), a man and a woman were accused of causing drought and put near fire by the women of Lokiliri. The man, a member of the rain clan, could not accept the death of his son who had been killed by the rebels for being an informer of the National Army. There was no way to avenge his death, nor was it possible for the father to claim bloodwealth (*lonya*).

The woman, whose husband was a member of the rain clan, lost her son when he was killed in a fight by a clansbrother in Khartoum. It is not customary for bloodwealth to be paid inside the clan. In both cases, normal procedures to claim reparation for suffered injustice were blocked.

The man and the woman, who were in-laws, were accused of having joined hands in causing the drought.

After they had been tied, the woman promised to show the evil charm and to remove it. There was rain not long afterwards. The story does not mention what kind of charm it was.

The production of the rain charm or the rainstones that have been instrumental in causing the drought is frequently used as a last resort for the accused to delay the execution of the death sentence as the rain dramas in Lowe (Case 9.6), in Pari

(Case 17.11), and also the fate of the young, inexperienced Rainmaker of Nyongkir (Southern Bari):

> **17.5 *The burning and death of an inexperienced Rainmaker*** (contemporary case)
>
> In September 1983, during a period of drought, the Rainmaker of Nyongkir, who had just succeeded his father, and his father's sister were blamed for the drought. The young man was accused of not taking his work as Rainmaker seriously. Both he and his father's sister were beaten and put in the sun. During a second round of torture when the Rainmaker was put in the middle of four fires, he confessed that he had sold the two most powerful rainstones in his collection to a befriended *Big Man* in the neighbouring chieftaincy of Kelang. The latter wanted them in order to generate more respect among his co-villagers. He had offered twenty-five goats in payment and paid in cash because the Rainmaker was afraid that his fellow villagers would question him about his newly won wealth.
>
> The stones were retrieved from the *Big Man*. The next morning, a sacrifice was made and the stones were washed and oiled. There was rain from morning till evening. It rained again during the night and the whole of the following day. In the evening of that day, the Rainmaker died of the beating and the burns. His aunt had a dislocated hip as a result of the beating. She has since taken over the responsibility for the rainstones.

On the west bank, torture seems to play a more prominent role in the way communities relate to their Rainmakers. Torture is not just applied to elicit a confession from the victim; it is believed to have a direct positive effect on the generation of rain. This instrumental attitude towards torture already transpired in the case of the torture of the Kuku rain family (Case 17.4). If we can believe Mrs Brown's report, the way the Mundu treat their Rainmakers is even more instrumental:

> If there is no rain, the Rainmaker is fetched, beaten and tortured by the chief's police. Rainmakers themselves believe that if they are not beaten their lives will be shortened. Being beaten is not only thought to make them live longer but also to make them fatter and in better health. They, therefore, stop or withhold rain to prolong their lives (Brown, 1984, Appendix E: 27).

Among the Jur 'Beli, torture of the Rainmaker is considered to be a method to break his resistance:

> The culprit is seized, bound, and afterwards thrown into water to withdraw his opposition. Only when the rain falls is he anointed with oil and given food to eat (Seligman, 1932:478).

The simulation of regicide

If the individual responsible for the drought cannot be detected by the means described above, the community may enact a ritual drama in which the killing and burial of the Rainmaker are simulated. A specimen of the animal or tree associated with the rain clan is selected. While it is killed or cut, the people recite the names of the rain clan members suspected of having hidden the rain. This is the scenario of the ritual called *kilitandi* or *logi logi noga*, the cursing and cutting of the Rainmaker[16] as the Lulubo practise it:

17.6 *Collective curse of the* monyomiji *to kill the king* (Lulubo, living memory)

In Kudwo and Lokiliri, the *monyomiji* first demand that the Master of the Land give them the axe (*tolu*).[17] The Master of the Land hands the axe to the Rainmaker who hands it to the *monyomiji*. They go some distance from the village and select a *lucuri* tree.[18] The *lucuri* is the totem[19] of the Kursak rain clan. They hit the stem with the axe and with the iron-tipped rear ends of their spears (*bidi*), reciting curses (*rilemi*) against the potential rain stoppers. The leader of the ritual (who could very well be the Rainmaker himself, the Master of the Land or one of the assistants) begins:

"The person who is trying to kill us"

The crowd answers:

"Let him die!"

The leader may continue:

"Let him fall down!"

Or names may be mentioned of potential rain stoppers:

"If it is A." the crowd answers: "Let him die!"
"If it is B." the crowd answers: "Let him die!" etc.

The tree is cut into pieces and burnt.

Around the heap of ashes, moulded into the shape of a tomb, the dance to mourn royals (*owilara*) is danced and sung. The *monyomiji* return home convinced that the person who has hidden the rain will die when he eats from the new harvest. A guard is left at the scene to prevent the person who has stopped the rain from pouring oil on the ashes and so undo the effect of the ritual.[20]

---

16   I could not find the word-by-word meaning of the term from Lulubo informants. Most likely the terms are Bari. *Logi* (Spagnolo, 1960:144) means 'with a lefthanded stroke' or 'to the left' which fits nicely with the rule that the spear with which the substitute victim is hit should be held in the left hand. *Noga* (idem, p. 208) means 'to burn, incinerate, carbonise'.

17   *Tolu* is an old type of axe, no longer used except for rituals like the one described.

18   According to Spagnolo's Bari Dictionary (1960:173) the *lusuri* (pl. *lusuryet*) is the *Combretum aculeatum*, a climbing shrub.

19   Totemism is fragmentary among the Lulubo. More important in distinguishing the clans are the powers (*opopi*). The members of the rain clan are not allowed to cut the *lucuri* tree.

20   In the report of the Project Development Unit for the Regional Ministry of Agriculture in Juba, Dr Jean Brown reports on a similar custom among the Kakwa of the Rainmaker of Rubeke near Mount Otogo: "When the rains fail or stop during the wet season and the rainmaker is thought to have stopped it because he is angry, the people of the neighbourhood gather and cry: "The rainmaker is dead. The rainmaker is dead." The three *bura* [assistants to the Rainmaker] confer with the Rainmaker to try to find out what might have upset him to stop the rain; frequently he has been upset by not being asked for a beer party" (Brown 1984, Appendix A: 29).

Owilara songs are believed to be very potent. It is not allowed to sing them other than at funerals of members of the royal clan. When they are sung in front of a living member of the rain clan, they amount to an assault on that person's life.

There is a women's version of the same ritual which is more frequently performed. In 1983, the year at the end of which I circulated a questionnaire among the *monyomiji* spokesmen, Lulubo women had performed *logi logi noga* twelve times in five out of the six villages. The basic scenario is the same as that of the men's ritual. There are local variations, depending on the rain clan in the area. I have combined accounts of the ritual from Bari (Lyeparang, Ngangala), Lulubo (Kudwo, Lokiliri and Edemo) and Lokoya (Liria).

17.7 *Collective curse of the women to kill the king* (Liria, Lokiliri, contemporary practice)

The day before they intend to perform the ritual the women ask the Master of the Land for the axe to cut the tree: a *lucuri* in Lokiliri and Kudwo; mahogany tree (*kir*) in Bari; or a type of acacia (*okokwe*) in Liria. The women put on their husband's helmet and take his shield, spears, and bow and arrows. The Bari women dress in leaves.

They also take drums and horns which are normally only played by men. Before entering the forest, a meeting is held in which their suspicions are discussed and confessions made.

As they march, the women blow the horns using the tunes owned by their husbands. They arrive at the tree that fulfils the requirements to serve as a substitute victim. They cut and burn it. In some performances, two women may be sent to collect a breadfruit. It is pulled towards the fire with a rope, and then thrown in. The ashes are swept together to form a tomb-like shape on which a small grass roof is erected as on royal graves. Alternatively, the ashes are disposed of inside a cave in a nearby rock. The women sit around the grave weeping, showing excessive grief while they shout

> "The king is dead!
> The king is gone!"

In Lulubo, *owilara* is danced around the tomb.

The wife of the assistant of the Rainmaker will pour water over the place of the fire, saying: "Rain is falling to mourn the King!" The women then run back to the village to reach home before the rain falls.

Different communities select different substances for the ritual killing of the rain stopper. The mahogany tree that the Bari use is a tree classified as 'bitter' (*pötwör*), possibly because Rainmakers, especially powerful ones, are also considered 'bitter' (see Ch. 19, p. 443–445). According to my informant, the relationship was more direct: the mahogany is selected because its own 'bitterness' would enhance the effectiveness of the ritual. In Liria, the *okokwe* tree is chosen because of the speed with which its leaves wither. My informant said that the withering of the leaves evoked the rapidity with which the rain stopper would pass away. The following curse against rain stoppers in Edemo establishes another connection between withered leaves and the death of the Rainmaker:

17.8 *Curse to kill the king by pounding withered leaves* (Edemo)

The leaves of sorghum that have withered because of the drought are put in a mortar and pounded with the stem of the *lucuri* tree. During the pounding, the following curse[21] is recited.

> "May the leaves of our sorghum gaze at you!
> May the blood of our children burn you!"

A person to whom this curse was directed some thirty years ago died of an unexpected disease. At his death, liquid dripped from his body. The people said that it was the rain that he had withheld.

The breadfruit (Lulubo: *lo'do*) is used as an effigy (*ngöjino*) of the unknown Rainmaker.[22] It is also used in the collective ordeal against the rain clan: all clan members of seven years and older are assembled in one place and made to jump over a fruit of the breadfruit tree (*lo'do*) that is still hot to indicate the effect of the scourging heat which, in the absence of the real culprit, is now applied to a substitute. Any clan member with evil intentions is expected not to survive the ordeal.

The women of Edemo kill a frog (*ododu*) in lieu of the Rainmaker. The frog, they say, is the ancestor of all kings. In Bari, the frog is the totem of the Nyori clan of which the Edemo Rainmakers claim to be a branch. The animal caught is killed as if it were a Rainmaker: its stomach is slit open, the frog is buried and a tomb is made in the same way as when a *lucuri* tree is burnt. If the women of Edemo do not succeed in catching a frog, a *lucuri* tree is cut and burnt. As a result, the stomach of the guilty Rainmaker is believed to swell to the point that he dies.

The drama of simulated regicide is usually executed as an extension and conclusion of an emergency meeting of women (*paluko*) in which existing suspicions have been aired and reviewed. The women have the reputation of being more radical in their dealings with anti-social elements than the men. Their radicalism in rain matters is motivated by their more immediate concern with the next harvest because of their responsibility to feed the household. They, therefore, are less patient in their dealings with the king. The Lulubo saying: *Women do not have a king!* means that since they are further removed from the institutions that maintain peace between men, they are less restrained when there is an opportunity to manifest themselves as an oppositional political force.

---

21 This type of cursing is called *cuko*.

22 The breadfruit as the equivalent of a person. If a grave has been dug for a person who was wrongly assumed to be dead, a breadfruit is thrown into the grave before it is closed. Nalder (1937:85) reports a Lotuho legend in which the ancestor of the Loudo clan was stolen as a baby from the goatskin in which it was carried while its parents were taken into captivity. A fruit of the sausage tree wrapped in a leopard skin was put back instead of the baby to deceive the parents and their Anuak captors.

The scenario of these ritual dramas is that of an attack against a collective enemy. Its location is outside the village where there is no taboo on the shedding of blood. The women put on the war attire of their husbands: weapons, helmet, shield and they sometimes even put on war paint. By taking their husbands' weapons, drums and horns, they shed their roles as housewives and unite as women of a particular community to attack the enemy and to defend their common interests. From the perspective of the life-cycle of women, it represents a return to the militant solidarity that characterised the age-sets of the unmarried girls (see Ch, 19, p. 175).

The transvestism and the wearing of leaves by the Bari women signifies the effacement of status differentiation, similar to the suspension of the rules of commensality when King Subek was given a rain ultimatum (Case 16.13). The women rally section by section, while the wives of the village leaders (king, Master of the Land, Assistant to the Master of the Land) adopt the role that their husbands play on the masculine side of village affairs. The women's activism blends in with the antagonism between king and people, the women playing the role of the *monyomiji's* backbenchers, more alarmist and more inclined to radical measures than the *monyomiji* themselves.

This is why the men supervise the proceedings of *logi logi noga* from beginning to the end. After the Master of the Land has given the green light by giving the axe[23], the *monyomiji* closely monitor what is going on as the following story recorded by a secondary school-leaver who witnessed a women's *paluko* shows:[24]

17.9 *The interruption of a women's* paluko *by the* monyomiji (diary notes villager)

Following some weeks of drought, a delegation of the *monyomiji* had gone to the diviner for an explanation. They received the following oracle: "You men, why do you look for some queer misfit? The one you are looking for is one of your wives, and a widow at that." One of the women (from section A) had overheard her husband discussing the result of the visit to the diviner. When the drought continued the women of section A decided to go and see the diviner themselves to corroborate their suspicions. When the diviner revealed that the widow was from section B the women knew enough.

Paluko of women was announced to be held under a big tree located in the centre of the two camps [sections]. The next morning, the whole village was alive with the action of the women. Those who were married adorned themselves with the garments of their husbands and carried weapons while some others blew horns to the tunes of their husbands. Even the unsuspecting Juan [the widow and inherited wife of the Rainmaker] was yelling her *mamare* [war song in praise of oneself] and demonstrated to her colleagues that she was as warrior-like as a man. When the noise did not seem to stop as each woman was outdoing her friends, the leaders blew their whistles and shouted for silence. That done, one of the women was

---

23   In Edemo, the axe is kept by the Rainmaker himself. He rarely refuses to give the axe. By doing so, he would certainly attract suspicions to his own person. If the *monyomiji* are of the opinion that the ritual is inappropriate, they back the Rainmaker against the women.

24   Where possible, I have retained the lively style of my informant because it does justice to the excitement characteristic of the activities described.

called to tell from whom she heard the story of Juan being responsible for the drought. The women now had to come out in the open with their stories which were traced back to Kenyi, a neighbour of Juan. There seemed to be no end to the revelations as the women continued to uncover to each other the most trivial and irrelevant circumstantial evidence.

Kenyi's wife was called forward to state where she got the story from. She refused, fearing perhaps what her husband would do to her if she opened her mouth.... Instead, she preferred to endure the humiliating insults of the sympathisers of Juan while the extremists were already taking position for an attack, clan by clan, camp by camp.

The men had to interfere to restore peace. Gore [the spokesman of the *monyomiji*] brought the women to their senses with his powerful gift of expression. He warned them against hasty judgements and rumour-mongering. The assembly broke up and the disappointed women dispersed shaking fists against invincible adversaries.

The women who had put the gossip against Juan into circulation had underestimated the sectional solidarity she could count on despite the rumours started by her immediate neighbour. The intended joint offensive against the rain stopper stranded in sectional rivalry. Since they are not party to the pact that binds king and people, the women are less inhibited to express their anxieties. The *monyomiji* condone the women's initiatives as a means to put pressure on the Rainmaker, but if they threaten to upset village peace, they interfere and stop their process.

Deliberate regicide

Two types of regicide should be distinguished: regicide as a result of conflict with rivalling members of the dynasty or an insurgent section of the kingdom; and regicide as the outcome of the build-up of tension in a long-term confrontation between the king and the collectivity of his subjects. In the first type of regicide, the killing takes place in a battle or in an act of assassination. In the other, the king is faced with an overwhelming majority of his people. Although he might try to fight back (Case 9.7) or escape (Case 16.7), his fate is normally in the hands of those staging the attack. In the first type of regicide, a change in the occupancy of the throne is the main objective. In the other, it is a change in the community's conditions of survival, often narrowed down to a change in the weather conditions. In previous chapters, we have discussed several cases of regicide of the first type. Now let us turn to a discussion of the second type.

Regicide of this type is the violent culmination of an escalation of conflict between the king and the people. Such conflicts are the recurrent and necessary manifestation of the antagonism that, as this book demonstrates, is constitutive for this relationship. The victimhood of the king is implied in the staging of the installation ritual and is anticipated at every outbreak of conflict. Threats that the king should be killed are uttered at the first signs of popular discontent (Case 17.12). Whether such threats materialise depends on the diplomacy that the two opponents, king and people, are able to muster and, of course, on the rains. It is with regicide as with war. The threat of it has more far-reaching political consequences than the actual waging of war. While the potential outbreak of war is a permanent concern of every government, warfare as a sequence of military operations is episodic. Similarly, the possibility of an assault on the king is never completely absent from the minds of his subjects. It has a structural character and is constitutive for the exchanges between king and people, also when these are cordial.

Missionary Francesco Morlang who was witness to the murder of King Nyiggilo on 21 June 1859, conversing with a group of Bari. The Mission Station of Gondokoro is visible in the background. Drawing by Wilhem von Harnier, in: Adolph von Harnier (ed.), 1866, Plate XIV).

When the relations cool — for example because of a drought incident — the immediate fear of both parties is that it may lead to further damage and an eventual breakdown of the relationship with all its undesirable consequences of a disruption of the social order. In such a situation, the community has an interest to reduce the pace of escalation and reach a compromise even when the demands of the king are excessive.

The following are cases of accomplished regicide that I have recorded within the boundaries of my field of study, from oral testimonies and written sources. I have excluded cases where the actual killing failed to take place (escape of the king, sudden shower), neither do I include cases where the king died of the after-effects of torture or as a result of having taken an oath. I suspect that a more thorough and more extensive search of oral history would bring to light many more cases, especially in the eastern part of the area of study.

W.   List of confirmed cases of accomplished, deliberate, regicide

c.1840   **Nyadinga**, *queen of all Lotuho, successive wife of kings Irwangi, Okomo and Oyalala*:
The Boro *monyomiji* killed her in Iloli for a drought believed by some to have been engineered by Okomo out of spite for Nyadinga leaving him for King Oyalala (Hino, 1980:75ff.; Case 12.5, round 2).

c.1845   **Bobit**, *king-elect of Lotuho, successor to Okomo*:
The Ollongo *monyomiji* killed Bobit, the son of Okomo, in Hiyala. Oyalala had persuaded the Ollongo that the drought had been caused by Bobit. Others attributed it to the posthumous curse of Okomo Oyalala in revenge of his poisoning of Okomo. It was Oyalala who had persuaded the *monyomiji* that the drought had been caused by Bobit (Case 12.5, round 2).

c.1845   **Oyalala**, *last king of all-Lotuho*:
The Ollongo *monyomiji* who had killed Bobit eventually, when the drought lasted, also killed Oyalala (Case 12.5, round 2).

c.1850   **King of Jabur**, *east bank Bari*:
His stomach was cut open. Only a brief mention by Brun-Rollet (1855:227).

c.1860   **Gulundo,** *widow of Manya, Rainmaker of the Mero section of Lokiliri, Lulubo*:
Manya belonged to the Kokajin clan who were Rainmakers in Lokiliri before the Kursak. According to one source, Manya had earlier been killed for the rain. He left a wife, a son and two daughters behind. When there was drought a few weeks before the first harvest, the *monyomiji* of Mero encircled the house of the Rainmaker and asked for Manya's son. When he did not appear, they questioned his mother, Gulundo, on the drought and asked her for the rainstones. When these could not be found, Gulundo suggested: "It is better that you kill only me." She also stated that with her death the rain office (*opopi*) should disappear from the family. The *monyomiji* dug her grave while she was grinding sorghum. She was made to try out the hole. When it fitted she was pushed inside. She had to be kept down with sticks while the earth was thrown into the grave. After she died, the daughter unearthed the rainstones, Tomeja and Likuka by name, from underneath the fireplace. While *kilitandi* (mourning dance of women for the Rainmaker) was danced, there was a very heavy rain. The people of Lokiliri still remember the drama with the following song put in Gulundo's mouth while grinding sorghum at the side of her grave:

> "Where am I to go, son of Manya, owner of rain?
> Laba, daughter of Gulundo. Find me Likuka and Tomeja!
> Likuka that feeds Mero. There is nowhere I can go.
> Where am I to go, son of Manya, owner of rain?
> Ibila, daughter of Gulundo. Find me Likuka and Tomeja!"

Likuka and Tomeja were transferred to the Kursak Rainmaker, Tongun. This is how the Kokajin clan lost its rain.

1859   **Nyiggilo,** *king of Bilinyan, east bank Bari*:
He was killed near the Catholic Mission of Gondokoro. According to Von Harnier, who had taken the missionary as a passenger from Khartoum, Francesco Morlang had been present at the scene of the lynching (1866:49). Nyiggilo had successfully resisted two earlier assaults on his person using his gun (Case 9.7). In Morlang's published diaries, one footnote is devoted to the killing: "He had to flee from Bilinyan where his livestock was plundered and his houses were set alight. For some time, he wandered the countryside, persecuted by all, until he found refuge with his relative Mödi near Gondokoro, where he wanted to wait for the ships going to Khartoum, to save his life. But on June 21st, a large group of armed young men assembled from far and near in Kujönö [Mödi's residence] and impetuously demanded the Rainmaker, Nyiggilo. He fled again but he was captured in Swakir, a nearby village. He was thrown to the ground with four spear thrusts and some blows of clubs. His stomach was slit open, and he was left to be eaten by the vultures.... After his murder, all cattle belonging to his family and relatives were collected and driven off. His old mother died of fear and anger; his wives and children fled, some here others there. Otherwise all of Nyiggilo's progeny would have been exterminated" (Morlang, 1862/3, p.115). Lejean, who visited Gondokoro the following year, reports that his body had been thrown into the Nile. (Lejean, 1865:75).

1875   **Legge,** *king of Liria, Lokoya*:
He was beaten to death by the *monyomiji* because of drought. No further details are available. Legge's death at the hands of his people was confirmed by Emin Pasha who visited Liria in 1881(1882:262); see also Case 14.5–3.

c.1890   **Lohilong** and **Lorwata**, *Rainmakers of Longairo, Horiok*:
Lohilong, the great-grandfather of the Rainmaker of Longairo I interviewed in 1985, and Lorwata, the brother of his grandfather, were beaten to death by the *monyomiji* for causing drought. No further details.

c.1897   **Mayya,** *son of Oyalala, king of Loronyo, exiled in Ilyeu, Lotuho*:
The *monyomiji* of Ilyeu accused Mayya of causing drought in Ilyeu while giving abundant rain to Lobera and Buruny, villages across the valley. They killed him inside a closed hut, his neck being put between two pieces of wood which were tied on one side and then pressed together.[25] After Mayya's death, Ilyeu paid bloodwealth to the royal family.

c.1900   **Kaku-lo-Loringa,** *daughter of Loringa-lo-Lowong, the Rainmaker of the Lokuriaba clan in Ngangala during the Mahdiyya; former wife of Logunu, government chief of Bilinyan 1914–20*:
Logunu had sent her home because he could not cope with her *miyan* (thaumaturgic powers). The Kurjuman *monyomiji* accused her of drought and buried her alive.[26]

---

25   Novelli, 1970: 195. The same mode of killing is practised by the Atuot on their *gwan riang* (Master of Flesh), a pestle being used to suffocate him (Burton, 1976; 1981:448).

26   The oral evidence I collected in Ngangala is rather fragmentary. For the information on Loringa: Beaton, 'A Short History of Ngangala', typescript: 11, Southern Records Office, Juba.

c.1900 Lo-Jima, *Rainmaker of the Ngerjebi section of Lokiliri, Lulubo*:
He could not pay the bridewealth that his in-laws demanded when his newly
married wife died shortly after marriage because his livestock had been raided.
Custom requires full payment of bridewealth when one's wife dies. Lo-Jima
refused, saying: "I shall open my anus to the rising sun!" — a powerful drought
curse. When the dry season continued into April, the *monyomiji* beat him to death
and raided all his possessions.

c.1900 Nyikale, *queen-widow, Edemo, Lulubo*:
Nyikale was a *likico* (a poor widow) who had inherited the rain powers from her
father because the only male heir, her brother Muryeki, was still too young to take
over. The Lonyume *monyomiji* accused her of a drought which lasted for over two
years and buried her alive. She sat beside the grave on a small portable chair (*gara*)
smoking her pipe while the hole was being dug. The *gara* was put in the grave as a
headrest. Before she was lowered into the grave, the people discovered a rainstone
in her long hair. Nyikale's grave is still used as a rain shrine. Some rainstones and
the pipe she was smoking are kept in the grinding stone on the tomb. When there
is severe drought, the Rainmaker goes to the old location of Edemo, higher up
on the mountain where she was buried, and washes and anoints the pipe and the
rainstone with honey and oil.

c.1900 Lojigba, *Rainmaker of the Ololoru clan, Edemo, Lulubo*:
He was blamed for a drought that hit Langabu after a Langabu man had killed
his brother. The *monyomiji* of Langabu abducted him from his home and buried
him alive in Langabu. Since then, the Ololoru Rainmakers, formerly rivals of the
Panyangiri Rainmakers are their assistants and classified as their sisters' sons.

1902 Igwana, *queen-widow of King Mayya, Ilyeu, Lotuho*:
The *monyomiji* of Ilyeu killed her five years after her husband's death (Cf. Case
14.1).

1909 Wani Matat, *Rainmaker in Mankaro, northeastern Bari*:
Wani had been a roving Rainmaker for the Mahdist troops for whom he had made
"floods of rain".[27] The people of Mankaro considered his never-ending marital
problems a liability for the rain. They caught and killed him one day as he was
chasing his wife who had run away from him. The Condominium Administrator
reported: "It seems that every man in the village took a hand in the murder in order
that no man could be said to have done it. The body was then thrown in the river.
I have all the offenders under arrest but one, whom I hope to catch shortly." What
kind of punishment was meted out is not mentioned (Case 16.10). The report
dates the killing as 24 August 1909.

c.1910 Laku, *'dupiet of Leju Lugör, king of Shindiru, southern Bari*:
Although legally of slave status, the political role of the king's *'dupi* was comparable
to that of the *labusuti hobu*, the Master of Ceremonies and Prime Minister, in the
Lotuho kingdoms. Laku was characterised by Collector Spire as "an intelligent
man of about thirty years of age with long hair" (Spire, 1905:15). The prohibition

---

27 Central Records Office, Khartoum, Mongalla, Monthly Diary, August 1909, p. 80; 'Intelligence
Reports Mongalla 1905–09'; INTEL 8/2/13.

on hair-cutting apparently applied not only to the Rainmaker but to his *'dupi* as well (Illustration, p. 120). Laku was not only accused of stopping the rain, but also of causing smallpox and infertility in women. According to oral tradition, he had taken a horn used for sucking blood from the body, and put grain and menstrual blood in it, hiding this inside a thatched roof. King Leju extradited Laku to the *teton* (warrior age-grade) to be killed after the following exchange with Lika, possibly the leader (*matat-lo-ber*) of the *teton*: "Leju, the sun is shining strongly ... why?" And Leju said: "No one is shining strongly. God is shining." And Lika said: "It has nothing to do with God.... Give us Laku to kill." And Leju gave them Laku and said: "Kill him!" And forthwith he was taken away to the stream (Lomoata) and killed and the rain fell. And when the rain fell, he was forthwith buried, and Leju said: "Now you have killed him, compensate me with 100 goats and 5 cows and 2 guns; now you have killed him, do not come here again." (Seligman, 1928:476; 1934:289; based on notes by Whitehead).[28]

1910   **Lualla,** *king of Lowe, Lokoya*:
Blamed for 'torturing' his people with recurrent droughts; he never stopped smoking his pipe and continued doing so while his grave was being dug. He tried to escape from his imminent burial but was hit by an arrow and hauled back.

1956   **Rainmaker in Central Lopit,** *no name recorded*:
The case came to the attention of the administration one year after the Rainmaker was buried alive for holding the rain back. When the rains did not improve, the *monyomiji* threatened to bury the son of the Rainmaker. He ran to the police post in Imehejek and reported not only the death threat, but also that the drought was caused by the fact that his father had been buried in a dry spot which prevented his body from decomposing.[29]

1957   **Rainmaker of the Logir,** *no name recorded*:
He was tied, beaten and buried alive. Twenty-six men who had taken part in the killing were judged by a special chief's court in Ikotos; no details on the name and the village of the Rainmaker.[30]

1981   **Rodrigo** (fictitious name*), the Rainmaker of the Iyata section, Lowe, Lokoya*:
His burial alive is described and analysed as Case 9.6. According to the police reports case the date of the killing was 16 July 1981.

1984   **Nyiburu,** *queen-widow of the Pari*:
She was beaten to death and thrown into the fire. The story, recorded by Eisei Kurimoto, is related and discussed as Case 17.11 below (8 July 1984).

1986   **Rainmaker of Ihirang,** *no name recorded, Ngotira, Lopit*:
The victim who was a woman had succeeded her father as Rainmaker after considerable rivalry with her father's widow who was said to have concocted the

---

28   Seligman's observation that the Bekat were too powerful to be killed is simply wrong. A decade before his visit, Wani Matat, the most senior heir to the rain in the Shindiru lineage, was killed. And of Leju Lugör, we are told by Spire that he stayed with him in Gondokoro as a refugee when he was persecuted for causing drought (Spire, 1905:20).

29   Southern Records Office, Juba, Monthly Diaries, Equatoria Province, September/October 1957, File 57/C/2; Monthly Reports, Torit District, Sept./Oct. 1957, pp.204, 211.

30   Southern Records Office, Juba; P.H. 52.57.E3/1; Torit District, Annual Report 1957/58, p.14,

drought accusation. She was tied, beaten and thrown into a dry riverbed. Her brother reported the *monyomiji*-set responsible to the Sudan People's Liberation Army (SPLA) who controlled the area at the time. All men who had participated in the killing were lashed (fifteen strokes) and a fine was imposed (six cows and ten goats). The village was forced to pay compensation to the family of the woman (12 April 1986).

1986   **Rainmaker of Logunuwati,** *Dorik, Lopit*:
He was buried alive for not taking care of the rainstones which, after an investigation ordered by the *monyomiji*, had been found in the bush (14 April 1986).

The distribution of our cases over time shows a remarkable gap: between 1910 and 1956 no cases were recorded. This span coincides precisely with the period of active colonial intervention in the area. The first patrols began in 1910 and Independence was won in 1956. Rather than attributing this to the effectiveness of the colonial police — regicide was and is, of course, forbidden — I suggest that during the forty years of colonial impact, the antagonism between the colonial rulers and the rest of society — with its own victimary logic — overruled local-level antagonisms. Immediately after independence, the grip of the centre weakened, and local-level antagonism became of overriding significance again, particularly in remote villages.

By far, the most frequently practised method of putting the Rainmaker to death is burying him or her alive (nine cases). The popularity of this mode of execution can be explained by its collective character. Every member of the community participates and no one in particular can be blamed for the deed. The joint digging and filling of the grave creates a context of status undifferentiation which underlines the unanimity of the killers. The fact that no blood is shed is a symbolic advantage of this mode of killing. This advantage also applies to strangulation, the method employed by the Lotuho.

Causing death by beating (five cases) lacks this advantage, but it offers opportunities for wide participation. This aspect is explicitly mentioned in the report of the British administrator concerning the killing of Wani Matat.

None of the twenty-four victims was — as far as we know — fully cooperative. Most of them offered considerable resistance. A recurring theme in accounts of the live burial of Rainmakers is their unperturbed pipe smoking at the edge of the grave and their descent into it in order to measure the hole. No informant has suggested that these practices should be interpreted as connivance of the victims with their executioners. The practice of making the victim descend and re-emerge from the grave would rather seem to be the ultimate stage in keeping and increasing the suspense of the regicidal process. Where possible, the victims resisted until the very end.

On the one hand, there was no bad conscience about these killings such that the participants would tend to cover up the violent dimension. "He (or she) is killing us, so why should we not kill him (or her)?" is the standard justification given by informants. Many informants' accounts of regicidal dramas provide details of the killing that would have been censored had the community felt uncomfortable about the events. On the other hand, the violent character of the execution made the graves of the killed Rainmakers unsuitable as shrines, unlike the graves of the Rainmakers who die a natural death. The only exceptions to this rule are Nyikale who, being a *likico*, may have been an exceptionally meek victim, and Mayya, whose bones were later transferred to the shrine in Hoding (Case 18.4). Concerning the aftermath of Mayya's killing, we have little information.

The facts indicate, though, that generally speaking, the fear of revenge (*cien*) by the killed Rainmaker was greater than the hope of a blessing from his death. This fear explains that in four cases (and probably more) the body of the killed Rainmaker was just thrown away in the bush, in a river, or in a dry riverbed — places where the victims of war are left and to which evil is expelled in ritual. The violence of the killing of the king precludes a positive transfiguration of the victim, unlike his dying in peace, as we shall see in the next chapter.

From the little information we have, it appears that there were two procedures to deal with the property of the king who had become a victim of regicide. The possessions of the king were either raided by his killers and no bloodwealth could be claimed by the family of the late king, or bloodwealth was paid and the king's properties were inherited in the usual way. In cases 10, 17, 21 and 23, the killed Rainmaker is still considered a member of the same juridical community. In cases 6 and 12, he is treated as an enemy. The raiding of the possessions of the king, also mentioned by Jennings-Bramly (Case 16.14), is coherent with the disposal of his body in the bush or in a dried-up riverbed — namely, treating him as an enemy. It is a reversal of the direction of the flow of tribute of which the king has been the beneficiary during his lifetime.

The Lowe case indicates that the payment of compensation for the killing of the Rainmaker may also depend on the attitude taken by the successor and on the pattern and the amount of rainfall in the period following the event. It may be assumed that a successor who is a direct descendant of the king would take more trouble to demand bloodwealth from the *monyomiji* than a more remote relative. Poor rains, even after the king has been killed, may lead to a review of the cause of the drought, and become a lever for relatives of the king to demand compensation — as Aristo did in Lowe, although without success.

In most cases, the act of killing was a public event. There was no attempt to surround it with the mystery and secrecy that is typical for regicide in West African kingdoms. Only the Lotuho screened the execution of the king from the public eye. Informants could not give me a satisfactory explanation for this. Possibly it should be interpreted as an attempt to contain the contagious violence of the regicidal act — a concern which is also present in the Lotuho preference for strangling as a method of killing.

The answer to the question why the stomachs of the killed king of Jabur, of Nyiggilo and also of Queen Nyiburu of the following case-study were slit open will be postponed to Chapter Nineteen.

The killing of the queen of the Pari

The most detailed record available of a case of regicide is the account of the death of the Queen of the Pari, by Eisei Kurimoto of the Institute for the Study of Languages of Asia and Africa in Tokyo. Kurimoto, who carried out fieldwork in Lafon during different periods between 1978 and 1986, returned from a break in his research to the village one month after the drama had taken place. His account and analysis of the event was published in Japanese in the Bulletin of the National Museum of Ethnology in Osaka (1986). Eisei Kurimoto kindly made an oral English translation for me of the pages of his article that describe the course of events.

Queen Nyiburu had succeeded her husband, Fidele Ongang, after his death in 1980. During her first year in power, the rains were very poor. When I tried to pay her a visit in July 1981, she was in hiding (or being screened off from me) because of the conflictual situation in which she found herself. I was told that a few weeks earlier, she had received a thorough beating from the *mojomiji* (to use the Pari term), something which according to my informants had never happened to her husband. She had looked for refuge at the police post but had been dragged away from there. Anyala, the *rwath* of Kor, the moiety opposite to that of the Queen, was also blamed for the drought.

17.10 *The rain conflict in Lafon, 1982–84* (Kurimoto)

📷 *1982*

After the Pari had sown in April 1982, the rains were very poor. By the end of May, the lack of rain caused a conflict between the *mojomiji* of the sections of Wiatuo and Bura (see Diagram 7.2 for the arrangement of the sections and moieties around Lipul Hill) As a result, two *mojomiji* of Bura were killed.[31] Nyiburu together with Anyala, the *rwath* of Kor, were summoned by the *mojomiji* of Wiatuo and blamed for the drought. They were forced to jump over the *likweri* [the sacred stick of the peacemaker which punishes lies by death], Nyiburu four times and Anyala three times, to prove their innocence. The rains remained scarce even in June, causing Anyala to flee to Torit for fear of being killed. Nyiburu was summoned by the *mojomiji* again and told: "If you cannot make it rain, we shall exhume Fidele [her husband] and you will be killed." She fled to Mongalla on foot [about 75 kilometres, through uninhabited plains] and from there went to Yei where she stayed with her elder son. In June, there was nobody left to control the rain.

The *mojomiji* invited a Rainmaker from Lobone in Acholi, named Rodolfo (fictitious name). He arrived in Lafon at the beginning of August. He had been a friend to Fidele before and had given rain-medicines to him. Upon his arrival, the rains started. There was too much rain because his rain medicine was too powerful. Because of its power, more than thirty children died of measles. When the rain continued to fall uninterruptedly even during harvest time in September, the

---

31   In March, a man from the Bura section had been caught trying to bury the hind part of a dog in the fields of Wiatuo, while disposing of its head in Bura, thus trying to cause drought over Wiatuo. Wiatuo took revenge and in the ensuing stick fight two men were killed.

mojomiji asked Rodolfo to stop the rain. When the rain did not stop the *mojomiji* sent Rodolfo packing. He returned to Lobone.

The harvest of 1982 was very poor because of the combination of drought and flooding. To make things worse, there was a plague of weaverbirds (*iru*) in August.

1983

The early rains of 1983 (April–May) were again very disappointing. The *mojomiji* of Wiatuo decided to call Anyala and Nyiburu back to Lafon at a time that both of them happened to be in Torit. A delegation of elders was sent to meet them since the *mojomiji* were on bad terms with the two. They accepted, but their return did not bring the rain back. The annual period of hunger was very severe because of the poor harvest of the previous year.

The *mojomiji* assembled again and decided that the *cien* of Fidele held back the rain. In June, his grave was exhumed and the corpse was thrown into the River Hos. Then, the rain started but in July, it stopped again.

The grave posts erected on the burial site of the Pari kings descending from Ocudo, the dynastic ancestor and culture hero who created cattle and the bridewealth institution. In 1983, the remains of king Fidele Ongang were exhumed and removed from this site in order to stop the drought, believed to be caused by the king's cien. Photo by Eisei Kurimoto.

Nyiburu and Anyala then decided to go together to see a diviner named Iriha, a Lotuho woman from Torit who occasionally visited Lafon on business. They went accompanied by two elders belonging to Kilang, the retired age-sets from the Kor and Pugeri sections. The diviner told them that it was Anyala who withheld the rain. The two Rainmakers and two elders did not tell this to anybody, keeping it a secret. The *mojomiji* also went to see a diviner since they doubted the interpretation according to which the drought was due to the *cien* of the late Rainmaker. The diviner denied that Fidele was responsible for the drought, saying that the cause lay elsewhere.

In July, the *mojomiji* of all six sections assembled. In their meeting, the visit of the four to the Lotuho diviner and Anyala's complicity in the drought were brought to the attention of the public. The elders who had accompanied the *rwadhi* to the diviner were accused of not having reported the matter immediately and were fined one ox each. The oxen were brought and slaughtered on the spot and the meat was divided among the *mojomiji* and the elders. Both Nyiburu and Anyala were put under house arrest and ordered to concentrate on making rain only.

Anyala escaped by making a hole in the wall of his house and fled to Torit. After his departure, the rains became regular. The people were convinced of his complicity in the drought. The early harvest of 1983 was good because of the rains in July and August. The late harvest in October was one of the best.

1984

The rains of 1984 began in April, as normal, but they failed in May and June. The *mojomiji* of Wiatuo reached consensus that the stoppage had been caused by the *cien* of a member of the Kilang generation. The corpse of the elder was exhumed and thrown away.

In June, the *mojomiji* of Wiatuo called for two successive meetings of all the *mojomiji*. Both times, Nyiburu was interrogated: "Why don't you make proper rain?" Both times she replied: "I have done my best, but *juok* [god] is preventing the rain from falling." The *mojomiji* then accused her of deceiving them: "You are cheating. You don't do your best. At home you are only drinking. If you don't want to make rain, give the rain-medicines to us." She answered: "I only received rainstones from my husband, and I do not know where they are now."

The interest of the *mojomiji* was now focused on finding the rain-medicines, since they believed it would be better if they controlled them, instead of Nyiburu, although they were not certain whether she possessed any.

During the month of June until the day of her death (July 8), Nyiburu went on drinking daily. In fact, the *mojomiji* themselves were the ones who gave her the beer to drink, each section contributing fifteen Sudanese pounds in cash and one tin of sorghum flour.

Her state of mind at the time can be inferred from the following incident that was related to me by someone who knew her well. One day, while she was sitting in her house, several bats [an ominous animal for the Pari] fell down from the roof in front of her feet. She said: "I am going to die this year."

In July, there was still no rain. At the beginning of that month, the *mojomiji* called for a third general meeting. Nobody was allowed to go to the field that day. Everyone had to stay home.

The first and the second meeting had been held at a place between the Pugeri and Kor sections. The third meeting was at a place outside Wiatuo where more critical problems were usually discussed. If a crime is discussed in that place, the accused should be prepared for serious punishment.

The meeting was held on 7 July. Everyone participated, including children, elders and women. The *mojomiji* asked Nyiburu: "Why don't you make the rain?" She answered: "I have tried my best but I cannot!" The *mojomiji* then said: "You refuse to make rain. You are trying to overturn the hill. We shall kill you. After that we shall leave this place. The children who are not able to endure the hardship of the journey will die."

The expression "overturning the hill" means: the whole community will be destroyed, spoilt. Without food, there is no reason to stay at the foot of Lipul hill; so, people would have to migrate to another place.

Some excited youngsters of Madang, the age-set immediately junior to the *mojomiji*, then started to beat Nyiburu with sticks and whips. The *mojomiji* stopped them. Nyiburu now confessed about the rain-medicines in her possession: "They are with me. I will hand them over to you if you request me so." The *mojomiji* then answered: "No, we are not the Rainmakers. We don't know how to use them even if you gave them to us. You are the one to make rain." Despite this refusal, Nyiburu was taken back from the meeting place to her house to hand over the rain-medicines. Only a few leading *mojomiji* of Wiatuo followed her inside the house. Nyiburu took out nine rainstones. Some angry *mojomiji* tried to beat her but they were stopped. Then the *mojomiji* told her: "Give us your rain-medicines, otherwise we shall kill you. If you give them, we won't kill you." It is not clear whether Nyiburu handed over any medicines since only a limited group was present.

The next day, the *mojomiji* assembled again in the bush at a place opposite Wiatuo. This place was further away from the village than the one they had come to the previous day. This time, only the *mojomiji* were present. There were no elders, children or women. A fire was set behind Nyiburu's back who was sitting on the ground. The *mojomiji* said to her: "You will die in these flames." Nyiburu then said: "It is alright. My death will not interfere with your harvest. I shall not cause problems. If someone has left *cien*, find out who it is. If the drought is from *juok* [god], there is no solution. But I, myself, I will leave no *cien*."

Three disabled men now placed themselves in front of her, a blind man, a lame man and a leper. The blind man touched Nyiburu's body saying: "If people leave Lipul, who will lead me on the journey? If you die we shall also die." The lame man (a case of polio) then spoke: "If the people leave the hill I will stay behind. If you die I shall also die." Lastly the leper came up to her, saying: "If the people abandon the village I will still not be able to cultivate. If you die I shall also die."

On hearing this, Nyiburu stood up and tried to run away. But she was beaten by the stick of the lame man and thrown backwards into the fire. This was the start of a series of acts of violence that caused her death. When she tried to get away from the fire, she was beaten by sticks and whips and kicked and thrown back into the fire. After she got out of the fire a second time, she was beaten again and thrown back into the blaze. After a while, she died as a result of the burning and the beating.

Her body was carried into the bush at some distance of the place of the ordeal. It was stretched down on the ground. Her belly and stomach were cut open. The *mojomiji* brought a fruit of the *ucok* (a cultivated melon). It was crushed and mixed with the stomach contents and blood of Nyiburu. The mixture was put back into the stomach. Then her tongue was pierced with thorns on both sides. The body was left in the bush.

The *mojomiji* returned to the village. Before entering it, the *mojomiji* slaughtered a goat and took out its stomach contents. These were smeared onto their bodies together with a mixture of anthill soil, water and crushed wild cucumber (*akarajo*).

After Nyiburu's death, the rain started. I went to check the rain gauge at the Rural Development Centre. There was no rain in the first week of July, but on the day of the murder, the gauge was registered as containing 7 mm. On the 9th and the 11th of July both 10 mm of rain fell. On 13 July about 15 mm, and on 18 July 60 mm! Only after that, the sorghum started to grow.

Nyiburu's killing is the climax of a process of escalation of conflict that lasted over four years, the suspense of the antagonism intensifying at every spell of drought. Although the *mojomiji* tried other solutions (the appointment of an interim-Rainmaker, the exhumation of the corpses of the former Rainmaker and of the elder of Kilang), after each attempt the ball returned into Nyiburu's court and the confrontation between the *mojomiji* and Nyiburu (sometimes flanked by her royal kinsman Anyala, who had become her companion in misfortune) became increasingly merciless. It took two years before the threat to kill her, openly uttered in 1982, was carried out.

The escalation in the process of polarisation of the community against the queen is marked by the size of the meeting and by the choice of the location. In 1982, the rain conflict was limited to the sections of Wiatuo and Bura. At the second meeting, in 1983, the *mojomiji* of three sections were invited. In 1984, there were four meetings, the first one by the *mojomiji* of Wiatuo, the second by all *mojomiji*, the third by all the people (including women, children and old people) and the final one again by the *mojomiji* of the six sections.

The cast of the third meeting emphasises the effacement of social differences in the confrontation of evil — as in the meetings in which an ultimatum was given to the Bari king and in the rituals of simulated regicide carried out by the women. The meetings were held at increasingly remote places in the bush, making the confrontation increasingly warlike.

The purification the *mojomiji* applied to themselves after the deed points in the same direction. A person who has killed an enemy should, at first opportunity, eat some soil of an anthill to prevent him from fainting, since killing is supposed to produce a quasi-physical reaction in the body of the killer. A goat or chicken must be killed before one enters one's house to neutralise the contamination with enemy blood. The crushed wild cucumber served the same purpose. In short, the *mojomiji* returned to the village as if they had come from battle.

In the end the unanimity of the village to kill the queen was complete. There was nobody who stood up to defend her. Even after the act, there was no one who put an accusing finger in the direction of Anyua, the *mojomiji*. When Kurimoto discussed this matter with participants in the drama, he was told that, had the elders been present and had Nyiburu asked them for protection, she would not have been killed. The absence of the elders should, therefore, be considered as their silent approval of the deed. It is significant that, while Kurimoto had no difficulty in eliciting detailed information on the killing of the queen, his informants were reluctant to talk about the decision-making process in which the *mojomiji* of the section of Wiatuo had played a leading role. This reluctance may have been motivated, on the one hand, by the wish to present the killing as an act of the collectivity as a whole, on the other, by the unwillingness to point at any one in particular as the responsible agent, since this would have amounted to breaking up the newly regained consensus.

The participants were struck by the queen's resignation to her fate. In the first years of the rain crisis, she had tried to escape from Lafon on at least two occasions. She could very well have tried to run away again during the weeks before her death. Instead, she made things worse for herself. By accepting the drinks of the *mojomiji* and by allowing herself to be accused of being a drunkard, she made herself increasingly guilty of the suffering of her people. Indeed, she seems to have connived in becoming her people's scapegoat. The Pari attributed her resignation to her fate, to *cien*. They did not consider it normal that a person should not fight back.

The intervention of the three handicapped men just before Nyiburu was killed is remarkable and puzzling. Was their appearance stage-managed by the *mojomiji*? Were they brought in to make it clear to all participants that the killing conformed to the law of revenge: "Since you are killing us, we have all the right in the world to kill you!" is the gist of what they said. Or did they act on their own initiative, happy to get an opportunity to play an active role in fighting an 'enemy', a role their handicap otherwise precluded them from playing?

Recorded fragments of the speeches delivered during the meetings also indicate that the killing was conceived as a revenge for 'turning the mountain upside down'. The last precautions taken on her body — the cooling substance applied to the stomach and the immobilisation of the organ of articulate speech — were also intended to prevent counter-revenge by means of *cien*.

Conclusions

Regicide as a deliberate act of the community is the tragic *denouement* of a protracted confrontation with its king. It is not a ritual and it is not a political assassination. It is a last resort, an inevitable step in a process of increasing suspense. The Pari would have preferred the rain to the death of their queen, but when the rain did not come there was no way back, no silent exit from the built-up antagonism.

Most rain conflicts between king and people have a happier ending: an agreement is reached, the king escapes or, most frequently, rain falls. From a statistical point of view, the number of times regicide has actually taken place is only a fraction of the number of times it could have occurred had circumstances been more adverse.

Regicide as an event is not only the last stage in a process of escalating conflict. It is also the dramatic summary of the relationship between king and people. The possibility of regicide structures the relationship between king and people, not only their conflicts, but also their transactions in time of peace. Regicide has the same function as the institution of the feud in political systems based on complementary segmentary opposition. Just as the possibility of vengeance is essential to the operation of a segmentary system, the possibility of regicide is a precondition for the functioning of the centralist political systems in the communities studied.[32]

The gradual build-up of suspense against the king reinforces the consensus of the people as a whole. In Lafon, in the course of the escalatory process, the number of sections that was mobilised against the queen increased step by step. But the process of escalation is easily arrested, especially in its earlier stages, when its momentum is still weak, as a result of the resurgence of sectional differences, as in the first phase of the rain conflict when the rain became an issue in a conflict between Bura and Wiatuo.

In the process of tightening consensus around the victim, not only the differences between the sections and moieties recede: gender, age and status differences become secondary as well. The rules of commensality are suspended, men and women, young and old sharing the same dish (Case 16.12) while women put on their husbands' war attire when simulating to kill the king (Case 17.7). The undifferentiated unanimity of the Pari community in the regicidal process was achieved by the compulsory presence of women, children as well as old people at the meeting in the bush the day before the queen was killed.

The violent character of regicide is hardly suppressed or mystified. There is very little that reminds us of the serene attitude that marks the way the Dinka Masters of the Fishing Spear face the prospect of being buried alive (Lienhardt, 1961:298–319). Most of the victims fight back until the very end, the details of their resistance being remembered by later generations. When they do not put up a fight, their resignation to their fate is explained as due to a curse (*cien* in Nyiburu's case).

Because of the violence of their death, the spirits of killed Rainmakers do not become the object of a cult. They are dealt with as a potentially negative influence. After their death, everything possible is done to avert their posthumous revenge. Positive effects are expected only from kings who died under non-violent conditions. This is the topic of the next chapter.

---

32   The following quotation by Evans-Pritchard provides a summary of this role of the feud in maintaining ordered relations between segments: "The balanced opposition between tribal segments and their complementary fission and fusion, which we have seen to be a structural principle, is evident in the institution of the feud which, on the one hand, gives expression to the hostility by occasional and violent action that serves to keep the sections apart, and, on the other hand, by the means provided for settlement, prevents opposition developing into complete fission." (1940b:161).

Regicide in the polities described in this book cannot be categorised as a ritual as it can among the Dinka. Community control over the eventual outcome of the process is too weak for this. It is, rather, an inevitable, recurrent tragedy imposed on the society by its antagonistic, centralist structure.

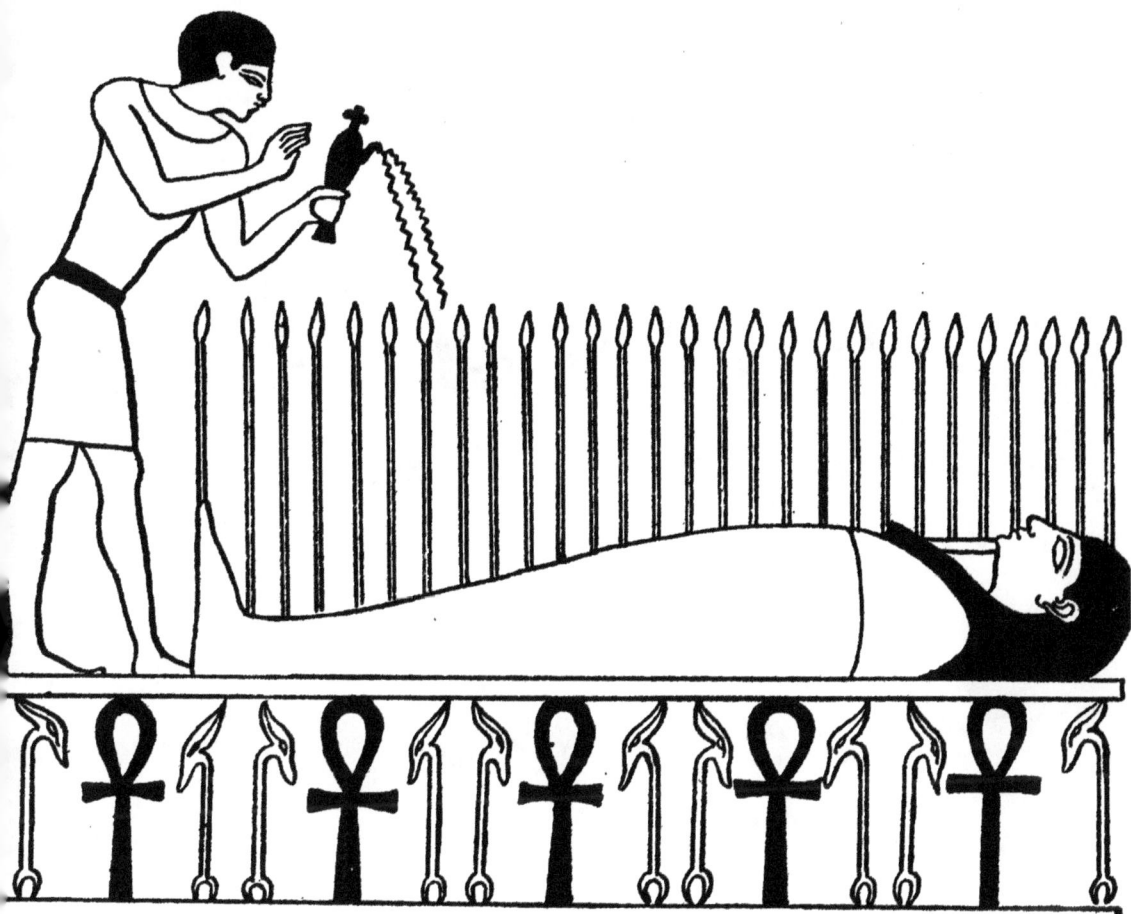

Grain sprouting from the mummified body of Osiris as it is being sprinkled by Isis; bas-relief from the Osiris temple in Philae (Wallis-Budge, 1973, Vol. I: 58).

18

"Catching Life in the Spell of Death": The Ritualisation of the King's Victimhood

When rain falls out of season, or in remarkable quantities, people immediately suspect that some Rainmaker has died. In the middle of the dry season of 1948, at the end of January, a sudden shower fell in Torit. Everybody was convinced that this was the sign that Queen Ikuma of the Lomiya, who had been in agony for some time, had finally passed away. The interpretation proved wrong. She died a full month later on 28 February.[1]

In this chapter, I would like to examine this beneficial effect of the king's death. In contrast to the death of kings who end their lives violently as scapegoats for the rain, the non-violent death of the king is generally believed to be a source of blessings. This corresponds to the positive transfiguration of the victim predicted by the scapegoat mechanism. We shall see that not only the customary practices following the king's death, but also those surrounding his inauguration correspond to an underlying victimary scenario. I begin with an examination of the installation ceremonies and then move to a discussion of the royal funeral and exhumation.

The installation of the king

When the Lulubo discuss the selection of their Rainmaker or chief, they may use an expression in which the new official is compared to a domestic animal that will be sacrificed. They say he is "taken to be cut". The same reasoning underlies the customary demand of the maternal uncle for compensation when his sister's son is designated as king. He will bring his claim to the attention of the *monyomiji* saying: "My sister's son has been put in the midst of evil." At the installation of a Rainmaker in the 1960s, for example, the *monyomiji* paid seven goats to compensate his maternal uncle. Informants say that the evil in which the king is put refers to the fact that he is destined to be a target of accusations and a focus of rivalry.

In the installation ritual in Shindiru, the identification of the king-elect with evil is even more blatantly expressed. After he is put on the skin of a bull that has been killed for the occasion, the 'owners of the village' (*monyejur*, the Bari equivalent of *monyomiji*) wash him with water. While they move their hands over his body, the different powers of office, especially those over diseases, are transferred to him by an act of cursing *(lömbu)*. They say:

> Let measles be with you!
> Let syphilis be with you!

---

1   Southern Records Office, Juba, Monthly Diaries, Torit District, E.P.57.D5 Vol.I: 615, 619.

Let smallpox be with you!
Let conjunctivitis be with you!
Let scabies be with you!
Let dysentery be with you!
And so on.[2]

At each curse, the public present repeats in chorus "Let it be with you!" After the curses have been pronounced, the king is oiled by elderly women. He then addresses the people present saying: "You are my stable; you are my dependants (*langet*);[3] I accept you!"

The Lulubo and Bari use words with the root *lem-*and *löm-*for expelling evil (diseases, pests) from their midst to the enemy, and also to keep the enemy at bay. *Wila* is another type of cursing that is practiced during the installation of a king. The *monyomiji* of Ngangala recite the following invocation during the installation of their Rainmaker:

We are putting you as king [*matat*].
May your body be cool!
May the powers [*miyan*] of your fathers and grandfathers become you [*rukö*]!
May you live long among us!
And take care of our stomachs!
We want to eat!
We share the bitterness [*tupötwör*] of our stomachs with you.
The bitterness of each of our stomachs it is yours!
May your body be cool and the powers of your ancestors fit you!
Hold us!

The invocation [*wila*] expresses the expectation of the people that the king should be of a balanced and peaceful disposition ("cool") and that the special powers [*miyan*] of which he is the incumbent will not derail him but generate the food for their stomachs. The concern is not only the stomach's digestive function, but also the symbolic stomach whose bitterness stands for the capacity to transform a 'hot' temper and an inclination to violence into 'coolness' and orderly coexistence (Ch. 19: Table X).

While invocations referred to by terms derived from the root *lem-*or *löm-*denote a disjunctive operation—malevolent diseases being removed from the people and transferred to the Rainmaker, *wila* operates a positive conjunction — the people being held in peace by their king (Ch. 19, p. 443–445).

---

2   The cursing by which diseases are transferred to the new king evokes the modern technique of inoculation. While the transfer of diseases to the Bari king was aimed at immunising the social body, the purposeful infection of a person with a specific pathogen is aimed to protect the human body. Interestingly, it was an American slave originating from the Central Sudan who, during a period of recurrent smallpox epidemics at the beginning of the eighteenth century, introduced the idea of inoculation ('variolisation') to the North American settler colonies (Behbehani, 1983:464).

3   *Langet* includes the wives, children, clients, and affines belonging to the household of a *ngutu 'duma* (Big Man).

While for the Bari and Lulubo the first step in the installation of their king is an act of negative transference, the Lokoya and Lotuho have a very different conception:

18.1 *The royal installation ritual in Liria* (living memory)

The ceremony begins by sounding the drums to call the *monyomiji* for an emergency meeting (*avaluho*). The message is passed around that a wild carnivorous animal has been spotted at *orek* (the place between the village and the bush where the *monyomiji* hold their security meetings). Everybody including the king-elect, who is supposed to be ignorant of what is going to happen, will run to *orek* fully armed.

After some speeches on miscellaneous issues, some of the *monyomiji* will walk up to the new king to congratulate him. This will be the start of a confrontation between the royal family and the *monyomiji*. The brothers of the new king will tell the *monyomiji* to keep their hands off their brother while the *monyomiji* will hold on to him for fear that he might escape. In the end, the prince and his brothers will be overpowered and the new king is carried on the shoulders of the *monyomiji* into the village. There, he will be put on the outstretched legs of the Master of the Bows, to be consecrated. First, shoes of giraffe skin, specially made for the king-elect, will be put on his feet while giraffe fat will be rubbed on his body. After that, a he-goat is killed and its rumen is applied to the king-elect's body. The *monyomiji* will then raise him and carry him to his house where he has to stay indoors for three days, without taking a bath, seated on the legs of the *monyomiji* who take turns in holding him. When the three days have elapsed, another goat is killed, and its rumen is applied to the body of the king.

Then *edwar* (the state of non-violence when fighting, noise, drumming and dancing are taboo) is proclaimed for three months. Anyone who breaks the *edwar* will be fined at least five goats, whose rumen will be smeared on the king's body in purification (*avulyo*).

After three months, the king's hair is shaven by his *oihejek* (ritual assistant) and taken to the rock where the skulls of former kings are kept.

The new king of Liria is captured from the bush, the sphere of violence, as if he were a feline monster.[4] He and his brothers are expected to put up a good fight but finally accept to be overpowered by the majority. Seated on the lap of the Master of Bows who controls the armed operations of the *monyomiji* in the bush (war and hunting), he is made to undergo a metamorphosis from a carnivorous into a herbivorous animal, from a violent predator into a harmless animal of prey (giraffe). He is ritually purified twice, not counting the emergency sacrifices, and for three months he is surrounded by absolute non-violence. The transfer of his hair to the shrine of the skulls of the ancestral Rainmakers establishes a link between the installation ritual and the king's ultimate victimary destination.

---

4   The capture scenario continues to be observed even when the prince-elect lives and works — as is not unusual — in a government office. The recent successor to the kingship of Tirangore was abducted by the *monyomiji* while leaving his office in Juba, put on their shoulders and taken by car to Tirangore.

The Lotuho installation ceremony closely follows the myth of the capture of Asang, the dynastic ancestor of the Igago rain clan. The story is a typical 'mythical charter' that Lotuho may consult if there is any disagreement on installation procedures and on the role of the different clans during the ceremonies. I present the story of Asang in lieu of a description of the Lotuho inauguration ceremony:

18.2 *The capture of Asang* (Lotuho dynastic myth)

Asang first revealed himself to a group of young shepherds of Otunge. He emerged from the water of a small stream called Dongak,[5] played with the shepherds and asked them for milk. The boys told the story about the water man to the *monyomiji*. They only believed them after they had sent four men (from the Igago, Lomini, Lomiya and Labalwa clans) to observe the man from the treetops. The elders told the *monyomiji*: "This is the true king. Get four goats of four different colour configurations (*omoli, egara, orrege, ohidangi*) and go to the river. The Igago man should kill the goats. The Lomini man should sprinkle the rumen (*amwaha*) on the king. The women of the Labalwa clan should ululate four times; and the four horn blowers should blow their horns four times."

The next morning, all *monyomiji* accompanied the shepherds to the riverside, taking the goats. While they were hiding in the grass and the boys were milking the goats, Asang came out of the river to play with the boys and to drink milk. Suddenly, the *monyomiji* rushed at him and grabbed him. Asang fell down half dead. The *monyomiji* followed the instructions of the elders. All four goats were killed and their rumen was applied to the king's body. The women ululated and the horns were blown.

Asang came back to life sitting in the middle of all the people who started to praise (*etabuyo*) him.

The four goats were now roasted. Each of the clan elders chewed his chunk of meat four times, together with the piece of charcoal that had been put on top of the meat, and spat it out again. Before eating, the elders of Igago, Oudo, Abalwa, Omiya and Omini made a holy pact with the new king. All present spat in the calabash and rinsed their mouth with the water (*ejaha*). The repast finished. The *monyomiji* marched back to the village bringing their new king.[6]

Here too, the king is captured from a place of violence, outside of ordered life. Instead of putting up a fight, the Lotuho king-elect simulates death when captured — possibly to underline the end of his existence as an aquatic monster (the crocodile is the totem of the royal clan). Yet, the eating of charcoal by the elders would imply that they are not convinced yet of the completeness of the metamorphosis achieved by the four-fold sacrifice, the trumpeting and the ululating. Charcoal, on the east bank, is used to protect oneself against predators and enemies. We can now draw a comparison between the different practices. While for the Bari and Lulubo the installation of the

---

5   The name of the stream varies with the different versions: Yolik seems to be another name for Dongak: Yasi, Obelet or Ibong are all names of (a) stream (s) near Isohe.

6   Pazzaglia, 'Omuk eyabita to hobwok Otuho', *typescript*: 1–8, translation from Lotuho by Constantine Bartel.

king is a procedure by which a sacred power is conveyed onto the person of the king by his subjects, the idea underlying the installation ritual of the Lokoya and Lotuho is the socialisation of a sacred power originating outside of ordered life.

Using the distinction between sacralising and desacralising rituals made by Hubert and Mauss in their pioneering work on sacrifice (Hubert & Mauss, 1968: 251–255), we see that the Bari and Lulubo conceive the inauguration primarily as a 'sacralising' operation, while for the Lokoya and Lotuho it is an operation of 'desacralisation'.

The sacrifice of the four goats for the Lotuho king aims to rid him of his initial superhuman (or infra-human) state of being and locks him up in a sacrificially generated human metamorphosis, like Oyalala who would have turned into lightning had the four-fold sacrifice not been made in time (Case 12.5 Stage 2). This does not contradict one informant's interpretation that the four-fold sacrifice for the new king is as a measure to prevent him from bringing diseases to the village.[7]

While the Bari Rainmaker is invested with the diseases by the community, the Lotuho Rainmaker is purified of the diseases that cling to his wild persona. The same inverse symmetry is found in the attitude to hair. While the hair of the Lokoya Rainmaker is shaven at his installation and placed in his family's skull gallery, that of the Bari Rainmaker should remain uncut until his death.

The contrast between the 'wildness' of the Lotuho and Lokoya kings and the 'culturedness' of the Bari and Lulubo is corroborated by the respective myths of dynastic origin. While Asang emerged from the water attracted by the cow milk of the villagers (Case 18.2), Oni, the dynastic ancestor of the Kursak, attracted the villagers of Co'doni to his camp by his possession of cow milk — a product previously unknown to them.

The Pari myth of dynastic origin takes a mediate position.

18.3 *The capture of Ocudo* (Pari dynastic myth)

Ocudo, the dynastic ancestor of the Pari kings, was discovered by children playing at the waterside. The people wanted him to stay with them but he did not want to. Only after two failed attempts did they manage to take him to the village. When he had made a girl pregnant, he found himself in problems with the parents of the girl. He escaped again but before disappearing, he created cattle to compensate the parents of the girl, thus instituting the practice of paying bridewealth. The girl became the mother of the first legitimate successor to the kingship.

The Pari dynastic ancestor places himself at both sides of the line separating inside and outside. He sticks to his transcendent existence but he also lays the basis for ordered social life. Besides cattle, he also left tobacco and beer behind.

---

7   In fact, this comment is in line with a slightly different version of the Asang myth: "Asang was found in the fishing net of a woman of the Lomini clan. The Lomini woman was frightened and threw him back into the water. The next time an Igago woman fished him up and called the *monyomiji* to take him to Otunge. Before entering the village, Asang requested that four goats (of the four colour configurations already mentioned) should be killed. All four were killed and the rumen thrown at Asang's feet" (Pazzaglia *idem*: 8–10). This version of the myth explains why the Lomini are closely associated with the Igago and act as their servants and messengers.

The royal funeral

The missionary Pazzaglia left us a detailed eyewitness account of the procedures followed during the funeral of Queen Ikang of Tirangore which occurred on 1 November 1938. Since it contains all of the major elements of the scenario of royal funerals, I use it as my point of departure for analytical and comparative comments.

18.4 *The death and burial of Queen Ikang* (Pazzaglia)[8]

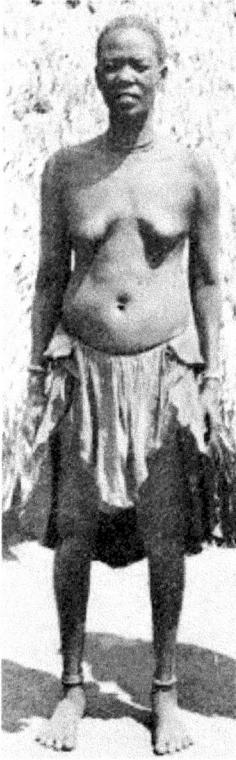

When Ikang was about to die, the family, the emissaries to the *monyomiji* (*abollok*), the royal attendants (*labusi*), and other officials were informed that their presence was needed to receive the last will of the dying queen. People hurried to the deathbed of the queen as they would do to an ordinary person: without ornaments and crying. When they arrived at the palace, they were told to stop wailing. An elder asked the queen to give her last will. Amidst deep silence, the queen spoke: "I am now dying. Recognise and obey the king I am leaving you. Do the things he asks you to do. Listen to him whenever he speaks to you. If you treat him badly, he will be useless as a Rainmaker. If you have conflicts with him, I know that in the end you will always return to him voluntarily. If you listen to him, he will give you abundance of food and you will live in peace." Immediately after these words were spoken, all present expressed consent: "You have spoken well. We agree."

After this, those in attendance joined the group of people waiting for the queen's death under the trees in front of the palace. When the queen entered her last agony, the *labusi*, male and female, returned to her deathbed taking a variety of agricultural products along. Ears of sorghum of different varieties and small calabashes with sesame oil, groundnut oil and butter were carefully and reverentially put in her hands, so that they would receive a lasting blessing; also as a homage since these were the products that had matured thanks to the queen's rain.

Queen Ikang of Tirangore (Seligman, 1932: frontispiece).

At the signal *Aye Hobu* ("The queen is dead"), shouted in a piercing voice by an attendant of the Lomini clan, all the people ran to the palace. A drum had been placed in the middle of the courtyard. The drum was sounded at intervals, four beats each time, and the people, in complete silence, proceeded on hands and feet to the queen's house to pay their last respects. After the last person had left, two ladies of the Lomini clan went inside to lay out the corpse. The whole body was anointed with butter. Necklaces of blue beads were placed around the neck and loins. Groundnut paste was rubbed in all orifices of the body: eyes, ears, nose, mouth, vagina, anus and under the nails. A new blanket was put over the body and on top of that a leopard skin. In the meantime, the elders of the Lomiya and Lomini clans had started to dig the grave near the wall of her house, while the *monyomiji* had brought a black cow for the funeral sacrifice. The cow's

---

8　The following is a summary of Father Pazzaglia's account, 'La Morte della Capessa della Pioggia "Ikang"' (Tirangore 1 November 1938)', *typescript*: 129–134, Comboni Archive, Rome, A/26/11/3.

stomach was slit with a spear and the rumen taken out while the cow, still alive, was kept down with large poles. The grave was sprinkled with it. The skin of the cow was removed and put inside the grave on a dung-covered platform. The body was put on top of the skin. Her rings and other ornaments were removed, including the necklaces of blue beads. The queen was buried naked. A dung-plastered roof was placed over the body so that the soil would not fall on it. Then the grave was filled up. On top of the tumulus, different agricultural products were laid out as a symbol of the power of the queen. A grey goat was sacrificed on the tomb. While sprinkling the tumulus with rumen, the *monyomiji* solemnly proclaimed the onset of *edwar*: "Nobody to dance with the drums until the queen is exhumed from the grave..." Finally, a straw roof was erected on top of the tomb.

After the burial, the royal drums were brought to the court of the palace to be 'made bitter' (*itadwara*). A Lomini man sounded the drum while a woman of the same clan sang the following song:

> The king is dead.
> The king has turned into a lion.
> Tell the son to come and watch his father.
> The king is dead, son of the king.
> His eyes shine red.

After the drumming had stopped, suddenly, as if a signal had been given, all the women seated in the courtyard jumped up and danced with a staggering step, towards the drums and back, four times.

After this, the drums and the *ametere* [the effigy of the deceased person][9] were brought to the pole-shrine (*alore*). Now it was the turn of the *monyomiji* 'to make the drums bitter'. They were again sounded by a Lomini man. After midday, the women and the uninitiated young men also arrived, the dance lasting until late in the night. The second day was a repetition of the first: in the morning more people came to the palace to pay their respects to the dead queen made present by the *ametere*; the *itadwara* of the drums was carried out again, and later in the day the *ametere* was taken in procession to the pole-shrine. The ornaments of the queen, her rings, the necklaces, a horn and the skins of a leopard and black goat were put on top of the *ametere* just as they had been on the queen's body. On the third day, the *ametere* was removed and thrown into the bush while the royal compound, including the queen's house, were cleaned.[10]

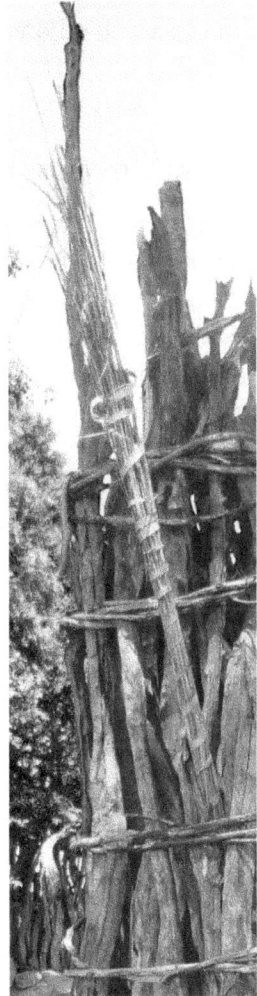

Ametere.[10]

---

9   The *ametere* in the illustration was made of a bundle of grass tied with goatskin. The *ametere* is addressed as if it were the deceased. Throughout the daylight hours, during the funeral dance, it is attached to the shrine-poles. After three days, it is thrown away in the bush. An *ametere* is, in principle, made for every villager except for men killed in battle (Seligman, 1925:34).

10   This is what normally happens on the third day of a funeral. Pazzaglia writes that it was a day of rest.

On the fourth day, a meeting of the *monyomiji* (*ewaha*) was convened to discuss the succession and the inheritance of the queen's properties.[11]

The *edwar*, the state of non-violence, lasted until the start of the rainy season of 1940, well after Ikang's exhumation which took place in November 1939. For dances, only the *natar* (a long horn) was used. During this period, it was also forbidden to sell any grain to foreigners, since it had been obtained with rain received from the late queen. The sign for the end of *edwar* was given by the successor, the new King Lomiluk, who ceremonially beat a dog to death saying: "I break the *edwar* on this dog's body."

In the ritual sequences that constitute the funeral, two simultaneous operations can be distinguished: on one side an operation that aims to safely dispose of the negative, dangerous charge of the king's body, 'the king's evil', and on the other, an operation that ensures and optimises the collection of its positive charge, the king's blessings.

The safe disposal of the king's evil

Wailing at the king's death is subject to strict rules. Among the Lotuho, one should refrain from it altogether and create a complete silence around the dead body. In Imatong, a rain chieftaincy at the eastern foothills of the mountain of the same name, people wail only briefly in response to four blows on a horn made of elephant tusk. In Liria, people are allowed to wail once the body orifices have been closed; while among the Bari, the Kuku and the Nyepu, one should wait with wailing until the body of the king, which has been placed on a platform, bursts.

The taboo on wailing is justified by reason of the dangerous forces that are present in the dead body and might be activated by the tumultuousness of the wailing. On the west bank (Kuku, Nyepu), people expressed the fear that the body might jump up as a leopard or as a *kanyaba* (an imaginary feline monster). The Bari believe that *gworong* (feline man-eaters) and insects might come in large numbers from the bush to visit the grave and cause damage; while the Kakwa and the Nyangbara hold the opposite belief: they think that the wailing is likely to frighten the lions, tortoises, snakes and fireflies so that they do not come to mourn the body of the Rainmaker. If they do not, he will not rest in peace and his spirit might enter the body of a lion and cause harm to the village.[12] Nyangbara elders warn young people that they should not obstruct these animal mourners in any way, since they are the brothers of the dead Rainmaker.

---

11   Since it was clear that Ikang wanted Lomiluk, her half-sister's grandson, to succeed her, the meeting was fairly straightforward. The only opposition came from Otuyek, the son of Ajaru (sired by Lomoro) who had been Ikang's favourite during an earlier period. Otuyek had been government chief in the late 1920s, but had fallen in disgrace when he had demanded that the *monyomiji* should do *ekuboi* to him and not to Ikang. Lomiluk had already taken over the government chieftainship in 1937 and had regularly assisted Ikang in the execution of her government duties over a longer period of time.

12   Jean Brown for Project Development Unit & Regional Ministry of Agriculture, Juba, *Report*, Appendix A, p.31.

The return of the king to his former feline status also seems a concern among the Lopit. Before the king's grave is closed, a leopard's skull is held out and moved towards the face of the dead Rainmaker four times. This can be understood as a gesture impressing on the dead person that his human metamorphosis is over and that he is again surrounded by his feline brothers.

The uncontrolled utterances and the loud demonstrations of anger that are part of wailing are a threat to the delicate balance between violence and order which has become even more delicate as a result of the death of the king. The dead king has always played a crucial role in maintaining order. The ordering faculty is located in the stomach. Strong external stimuli may set unpredictable and dangerous body processes in motion. Therefore, bloodless and noiseless sacrifices are prescribed at the funeral: the black bull or goat slaughtered to purify the grave is suffocated by closing its mouth and nostrils (in Loudo, Logir and Imatong) or strangulated (among the Kuku).

To ensure that the dangerous charge in the body does not escape through its orifices the royal corpse is plugged, a custom followed by all peoples in our area of study except the Pari. In most areas, the body orifices are plugged with the thick paste of sesame which remains after the oil has been extracted.[13]

The Lulubo believe that, if the king were not plugged, his *opopi* (power of kingship) might leave the body, and cause all sorts of disorders such as pests of worms and crop-eating insects (*in'di*). The Lopit, who start to seal the body even before the Rainmaker has died, believe green grasshoppers (*ibi*), worms (*huti*) and weaverbirds (*iruti*) (three notorious crop-pests) may leave the body if it is not closed. They also fear that the rain might be affected. For the Bari-speaking Nyangbara, the insects escaping from the king's body are blessings. They are white ants (*konga*) and white soldier ants (*koloro*) both of which are considered delicacies.

In Lokoya, each of the six *Fingers of God* is closed up in this manner, and in Lulubo, the three *opi* (Rainmaker, Master of the Land and Master of the Mountain) as well as the clan elders of Onyati who are the 'Masters of *In'di*' (crop-eating insects)[14] are so treated.

---

13   Among the Lopit of Mura, the Bari of Kelang, the Kuku, the Fajelu (Limbe) and the Nyepu, the soil of the anthill (Lopit: *masala*, Bari: *luduiri*) is used; in Liria, bees' wax; and in Logir, butter from cows' milk. The Lulubo stuff the leaves of the castor oil plant (*kulugo, Ricinis Communis*) into the orifices of the Kursak. The choice of the *kulugo* leaves may be motivated by the 'oily' texture of the tree which places the leaves in the same category as sesame paste and butter. Castor oil is in some places used to anoint the rainstones (in Imatong) and so is bees' wax (in Edemo). The Fajelu use leaves of the black plum tree (*konyuki, Vitex Doniana)*; the Kakwa, leaves of the *laro* tree (possibly *Afromomum*); and the Nyangbara, the leaves of a species of *Combretum* (*nyalibi*), a plant classified as 'cool'. To identify some of these plant names, the lists of plants with names in Kakwa, Kuku, Fajelu, Avukaya and Käliko collected by Hamo Sassoon has been of help. It is kept in the East African Herbarium in the National Museum in Nairobi, Kenya.

14   *In'di* are probably the insects the Lotuho call *neguru*, a species of Aphididae. The insects are closely associated with Lotuho kingship (cf. Case 18.5; Seligman mentions that the *neguru* are believed to swarm around tombs of Lotuho *hobwok*. He quotes a piece of information provided

The Lulubo (and the Fajelu and the Nyangbara) remove the leaves used for plugging the body (*imuture*)[15] before the grave is closed and take them to a stream or to a cave in the mountain. The *imuture* is removed from the corpse by old men, preferably a sister's son to the deceased, and given to old women to dispose of. These receive the *imuture* in a kneeling position, in an attitude of intense respect. They carry the sacred package to a river or a cave in a solemn procession, kneeling at successive stations during the procession, their heads bent down and singing royal mourning songs (*owilara*); while they move their hands as if they were harvesting sorghum and millet.

The Lulubo say that the *imuture* is thrown away "so that the power (*opopi*) may not cause death to the successor". The disposal of the *imuture* allows the dangerous charge resident in the king to be transported from the ordered human world to the sphere of violence where it ultimately belongs. In this way, it will not interfere with the induction of the new king.[16]

The Bari perform a ritual which is analogous to the Lulubo disposal of *imuture*. Before burial, the hair of the dead Rainmaker (which was never cut, and characterised by Beaton, without further comment, as "defiling") is shaven off, put in calabash and thrown away in the bush by an elder sister of the deceased. A goat is taken along into the bush to absorb any polluting effects of the sacred hair. It is killed a few days later. Its urine will be used to wash the rainstones (Beaton, 1932:87).

So, the objective of the taboo on wailing, the plugging of the orifices and the disposal of the *imuture* and royal hair is to safely ferry the violent aspect of the king's power to a place where it can do no harm to ordered life.

Collecting the blessings from the dying king

When Ikang entered her last agony, agricultural products were put into her hands "so that they might be blessed". The products were brought by commoners and given to the attendants to be put in contact with the queen. Pazzaglia observed that they were freshly harvested or prepared.

The death of the queen re-sacralises (*itadwara*) the drums. The re-charge of the drums is confirmed by a succession of rounds of dancing, the first round immediately

---

by Driberg: "It is an insect always associated with a *kobu*, which is natural, as the *kobu* is concerned with crops, whose greatest pest is aphis"(Seligman, 1932:312).

15   The similarity in word form suggests a connection with the Lotuho *ametere*. The *ametere* may be made for each person and represents a particular, named individual, while the *imuture* is the dangerous substance of the supra-individual power of kingship. The *ametere* is a substitute for the king as an individual while the *imuture* is a receptacle of impersonal royal power. Common to both is that in the end they are thrown away, expelled.

16   Seligman quotes an informant's statement recorded by Whitehead which makes exactly the same point about the plugging of the royal orifices. The objective is "that the spirits may not go out, so that the son may manage the father so that he obeys [him], so that the spirits obey the son" (1932:292). If we assume the Bari word *rukö*: 'to interact without conflict', was used by Whitehead's informant where Whitehead translated 'obey', the Lulubo and Bari interpretations of the plugging are identical.

after the queen's burial inside the palace by her female attendants. It is followed by a dance of the whole community in the central, ceremonial ground of Tirangore, the queen being represented by the *ametere*, her effigy, stuck in between the poles of the shrine. The *itadwara* of the drums will be repeated on the two following days so that all the communities of the kingdom can participate in the ritual renewal of the bond between king and people.

The Bari have a different way of linking the body of the dead king to the processes and objects that need the king's blessing. After the body of the king is closed, it is anointed with sesame oil, and red sorghum and sesame seeds are sprinkled over it. According to Haddon, the body is slashed with a knife. Sesame is ground and the mixture of oil and husks is rubbed into the cuts (Haddon, *thesis*: 79). The body is put on a platform normally used to dry the sorghum crop before it is stored in the granaries. It is left there until the abdomen bursts and liquid starts to drop from it. In the case of the Kuku Rainmaker Jibi-lo-Kajo, of whose burial we have an eyewitness account (Yunis, 1924:19–21), it took four days before the abdomen broke. By the bursting of the body, peace, rain and food were believed to spread over the land "like the air from a punctured ball", as one informant explained. This is the moment that the king is considered truly dead.

Drying platform with sorghum ears, in some communities also used to lay out the corpse of the king.

A *'dupiet* (slave) is left under the platform to wait for this so that he can give the signal of the king's death when 'the oil of the king' drips on his body. Once the body has burst, wailing and dancing are allowed again. The prescribed dance is *kore*, the jumping dance associated with the period of plenty after the harvest. The Nyepu ritual is a variation on this theme: after the stomach has burst it is removed by the chief assistant of the Rainmaker and shown to the people as evidence of the king's death.

While the Lotuho royal funeral articulates the relation between the royal body and food metonymically by bringing both in physical contact, as during the funeral of Queen Ikang, the Bari, the Kuku and the Nyepu *equate* the royal body to food.

Among the Lulubo, the connection between food and the dead king is given expression in the public distribution of seeds after the burial during the last funeral dance. At sunrise, after a night of dancing around the tomb, the wife or sister of the deceased distributes seeds for the next crop among the participants who will mix them with seeds of their own. While giving the seeds the woman distributing them says: "Squat down and receive the oil of [name of the late person]." In funeral speeches, the body of the late member of the rain clan is frequently referred to as "our food".

The Lirians express the same idea in a more playful way. While the Rainmaker is lying in state in his house surrounded only by his close relatives, the *monyomiji* will come and knock on the door. At the question of the brothers of the late king: "Who are you? What do you want?", they answer: "We are the Lotuho. We want food. We want grain!" The *monyomiji* say they are Lotuho because in times of famine people from Lotuho often visit Liria in search of food. The door opens and some grain is poured into the hands of the *monyomiji*. The ceremony is repeated three times. The *monyomiji* chew the unthreshed sorghum on the spot.

The reign of the dead king

Among the Bari and the Lulubo, the grave of the Rainmaker consists of a shaft leading to a chamber with a recess in which a platform is placed on which the body is put. The burial is completed when the shaft is filled and a tumulus is formed on top. A forked ebony pole is erected at the head of the grave. When moving the body of the Rainmaker out of the house, the door should not be used. A special opening is made in the wall. This practice may also be motivated by a concern to avoid acts that could cause shock to the dead Rainmaker. By using a hole in the wall he is deceived with respect to the destination of his last journey.

The Lulubo and the Lotuho build a fence around the royal tomb and put a thatched roof similar to that covering a granary on top to highlight the fact that there is 'food' underneath. During the dry season, one or more flags are unfurled on the grave. During the rainy season, the flags are kept under the roof "lest they should blow the rain away".

The Lotuho kings are buried under their doorstep or next to the door, the head pointing outside the perimeter of the house. While the Lulubo seem to want to leave their deceased kings in uncertainty as to their whereabouts, the Lotuho place him on the boundary of inside and outside. Female relatives of the deceased guard the tomb. As a precaution against evil influences escaping from the grave, they caulk whatever cracks may appear in the tumulus.

Exhumation is practised both by royals and commoners among the Lotuho and the Lokoya, either as the ceremonial ending of the funeral period, or on the advice of diviners who recommend it as a remedy against the misfortunes that the dead might send. For members of the Lotuho royal family, exhumation is a 'must'. The Lokoya only exhume the skull and one of the leg bones. Although the Lotuho call the exhumation *nahuccyo hou tulo* (lit. excavation of the head), they, and most of the other Lotuho speakers, exhume the whole skeleton. Among the Pari, exhumation of the body only takes place when there are compelling reasons to suspect a posthumous curse (*cien*).

The Bari and the Lulubo equivalent of exhumation is the levelling of the tomb. The tumulus, called *'di* (head) by the Lulubo, is removed. Only the ebony pole remains to mark the grave. All tombs should be levelled before the new rains.

The royal exhumation and the levelling of royal tombs is made to coincide with the end or with the beginning of the rainy season. If it takes place at the end of the rainy season, the installation will take place at the beginning of March when the rains start. If the burial happened during the last months of the rainy season or during the dry season, more than a year will elapse before levelling or exhumation is undertaken. This rule is aimed to ensure that the community will have the full benefit of the blessings of the king's death since these are believed to peak during the rainy season that follows his death.

In fact, as far as the rain is concerned, the dead Rainmaker continues to rule. His rain power is believed to be greater than that of the fresh king-elect. It is believed to be especially active and beneficial immediately after his death. Then rain falls 'to mourn the king', like the animals of the species associated with the kingship (lion, leopard, *neguru* insects[17]) that will flock and swarm around the grave to mourn their brother.

If rain falls out of season — as in Torit in the example at the beginning of this chapter — people invariably conclude that a Rainmaker must have died. If the king died taking his grievances with him into the grave, the period following his burial may be beset by drought. In that case, reconciliatory sacrifices (Lotuho, Lokoya: *emuara;* Bari, Lulubo: *tomora*) must be performed and the body should be exhumed without delay.

During the funeral period, the tomb of the dead king is the appropriate location for rain sacrifices. People in need of rain may come and kill a goat on the grave and spread its stomach contents over the mound, or crush the fruit of the wild cucumber on it. Frequently, the rainstones are kept on top of the tomb during this period. In Lotuho, a small shrine (*edurore*) is constructed as a shelter for the container with the stones.

In Lulubo, a drum should be at hand near the royal tomb so that mourners can dance around the grave. People visit the tomb, section by section, to sing the *owilara* songs for dead rainmakers, dancing to the tunes and rhythm of *kilitandi*. While dancing, they 'capture' the rain for their section. The age-set of nubile girls of a section may also come to dance *nyale* on the grave for the same purpose.

During the funeral period, the tomb should always be well guarded since groups of foreigners could come and dance around it and so steal the rain. When Yokwe Kerri, the Bari chief of Koggi, died during a period of drought for which he and Pitia Lugör

---

17   Aphididae; see note 18.5.

had blamed each other, Yokwe's son informed the District Commissioner, Captain Cooke, that although he and "his brother Beaton" (who was the Assistant District Commissioner and who wrote an article on the funeral proceedings) were welcome to attend the funeral, they did not want to invite all the chiefs "because they will take our rain" (Beaton, 1932:84–95). The fear that the rain may be stolen is also the reason for putting a guard on the tomb.

The *owilara* songs of the Lulubo, a special repertory of funeral songs and tunes, are believed to increase the beneficial effects emanating from the dead king. However, if these songs are addressed to a living member of the rain clan, the singing is considered an assault on that person. One can be sued in court for having sung *owilara* against a Kursak.[18]

The texts of the *owilara* songs are rather hermetic, not only to the outsider, but also to the people who sing them. They are a mixture of obsolete expressions and recent innovations and accretions. Many songs have different versions. Often, they refer to specific social contexts, the words being ascribed to named persons who have a joking relationship (in-laws, mother's brother/sister's sons). When *owilara* is performed, its incessant rhythm, called *kilitandi*, the lamenting and accusatory tone, the effervescent unanimity of the dancing singers circling the tomb on which the bereft sisters of the late king are seated, make the content of the song texts secondary.[19]

For at least one year, the rains and the harvests depend on the dead king. To emphasise this point, the Lotuho forbade the sale of crops to outsiders "as they were produced with the rains of the late queen". The Tsera of Gemmeiza go a step further in highlighting the power of the late king. A successor is not appointed until four years after the king has died, because, as my informant stated: "After he dies, it will rain for four years and there will be enough food."

The belief that the king's greatest blessings are produced after and as a result of his death is exactly what the scapegoat mechanism predicts. The rain and the food produced by the king's death are the positive transfiguration of the scapegoat after his successful elimination (*see* Model A, p. 14).

---

18   I attended a court case in which the inappropriate singing of *owilara* was the main issue. A poor old woman (*likico*) had sung *owilara* to her son-in-law, a member of the royal Kursak clan, after he had insulted her. On hearing the song, the son had tried to spear her. Afterwards, one of the children of the man had died while the man himself had felt sick for a whole year. He had now come to court to accuse the woman of his misfortune. The court, in this case, chose to protect the poor old lady and sentenced the young man to pay a fine to the government and compensation to his mother-in-law — for having taken her to court.

19   Attempts to achieve translations and interpretations with the help of informants have so far failed. Muratori, author of a grammar and dictionary of Lotuho, facing the same obstacle in translating the set of *hobu* songs he collected, remarked: "To understand them (*netadwäriti hobwok*) a good knowledge of the Lotuxo Language is needed too, because of elisions, cohesion of sounds, and use of old forms or of rather obsolete words" (Muratori, 'Accalili, Lotuxo Rainmaker', *typescripts*, Comboni Archive, A/126/4:30).

The live burial of the king's assistants

In Bari and Lotuho, the king's servants who had been most closely associated with his life and work were buried together with their master. In Lotuho, the person buried with the king was the *labusuti hobu*, the 'Prime Minister' or 'Master of Ceremonies'. His relationship was "so close that it could be broken only in death" (Paolucci, 1970:110 quoting Pazzaglia who refers to the situation during the 1940s). His responsibilities were considerable: he assisted the king in rituals; deputised for him; accompanied him on his journeys; and acted as a kind of intermediary between the king and the people. Because of this close association and his subordinate status, he was called the "king's dog". Like the king, his person was sacred: his spittle was sought as a blessing; his house was a place of refuge and his tomb was venerated as a rain shrine (*idem*: 110–112). Prior to colonial days, he was buried alive alongside the king. Since the Prime Minister was expected to offer resistance to his fate, his arms and feet were tied. A cowbell was hung around his neck. When it had stopped ringing, people concluded that he was dead. His family received a generous compensation for the death of their kinsman.[20] Seligman (1932:339) made inquiries about this custom and wrote that the *labusuti* was put on a bed of leaves covered with the hide of an ox and that his bones were exhumed and put in pots like those of a king.

Among the Bari, the man selected to wait for the 'death' and the 'oil' of the king was the young *'dupiet* who had carried the king's pipe. He was considered very close to the king. The fact that he had 'seen the king's death' and had been sprinkled by his body fluids made him particularly sacred. His curse was considered very potent. After his emergence from the royal grave to announce the king's death, there were two options for him: either return into the grave immediately and be buried together with his Master, or be allowed to survive as a person with respectable rain powers. If he chose the first option, the *'dupiet's* family was compensated. The *'dupiet* was even allowed to express his wish as to how he wanted his relatives to be treated. If he chose the second route, he was first purified of the king's body liquids and washed by the king's senior surviving wife. He was expected to spend the year after the king's burial on top of the grave of his Master. Eventually, he would become the chief assistant to the king's successor on whose selection he even exercised influence.[21] The only written evidence of the burial alive of a *'dupiet* in the grave of the Rainmaker is a footnote by Beaton, in which he states that in the past, two *'dupi* would be buried with the Rainmaker, the one carrying his pipe and the other carrying his seat (Beaton, 1932:87, note 4).

---

20   Pazzaglia, 'La morte della capessa della pioggia Ikang', *typescript*, Comboni Archive, A/126/11/3, pp. 130–131.

21   Among the Kuku, the man determining the moment of 'death' of the Rainmaker stays in a special shelter near the entrance to the grave. In the morning and the evening, he goes down to check on the condition of the corpse. As a compensation for this duty, he was given two cows and a bull. In the old days, a wife was given to him (Yunis, 1924:19).

For an interpretation of these customs, we should not immediately look towards the tombs of the Pharaohs as do Beaton and Lewis (for the same custom among the Murle, 1971:82). The servant buried alive with the king had, on account of his close association with the king and with rain ritual, accumulated a great deal of experience and a considerable amount of power. For the successor, he would be a particularly difficult person to deal with, the more so because of his sacredness and the power of his curse. The alternative offered by the Bari seems logical: either consolidate his status so that he is supportive of the new regime, or do away with him.

The exhumation of the king's body

Missionary Carlo Muratori left us an exceptionally detailed eyewitness account of the exhumation proceedings of the Lotuho King Acalili which took place on 10 December 1945.[22] The king had died on 26 November 1944. On his deathbed he had been baptised in response to his demand "to put the flag of the mission [the cross] on his tomb". The conversion of the king, which was an important victory for the spread of Catholicism among the Lotuho, explains the interest taken in this exhumation by the missionaries.

Judging from Muratori's description, the exhumation ceremony is even more elaborate than the burial itself. It is an occasion at which all officials of the kingdom are given an opportunity to play their official role and during which the whole hierarchy is brought to life. Muratori lists about twenty persons who, by hereditary right, play a role in the exhumation ritual as singer, drummer, excavator, sacrificer, shrine-builder, carrier of the royal bones, or as rainstone advisor.[23] They were from different villages and different clans, although most of them were *labusi* of the Lomini clan living in Loronyo. The officials were recruited on the basis of their membership of certain families within particular clans and not on sectional membership. The *abollok*, the sectional contact persons of the king, for example, did not play a role in the ceremonies. The following is a summary of Muratori's account:

> **18.5 *The exhumation of King Acalili*** (Muratori)
>
> When Father Muratori arrived the evening of 8 December, the *labusi* had started to pull down the fence around the tomb and the small roofed platform over the head of the tomb in which the rainstones were kept (*odurore*). The demolition was interrupted for the crushing of the fruits of the wild cucumber and by the ritual blowing of puffs of tobacco smoke towards the fence — purification rituals. The roof and the poles were thrown in an open place some distance away from the palace where, in between some rubble, Muratori was shown a broken pot which contained the bones of Ibur, Acalili's grandmother. The pots with rainstones were

---

22   Carlo Muratori, 'Accalili the Lotuxo Rainmaker and his exhumation' (32 pp), and 'Accalili, Lotuxo Rainmaker, His life (c. 1865–1944) and his exhumation (1945)' (42 pp), *typescripts*, Comboni Archive, Rome, A/127/17/4 & 5.

23   Muratori admits that it was impossible to get a clear idea of the duties of some of these specialists, as for example the *ehuhumak hisihi* (the rainstone advisors).

transferred to a completely new shrine. While the tumulus was being swept clean, a *neguru* (crop-eating insect associated with the kingship) jumped up to Muratori. One of the *labusi* immediately shouted: "The spirit (*ajok*) of the king sprang up to the Father!"

At 3:00 am, the exhumation started with the immolation of a black goat, the first one in a series of four which were of the same colour configurations as those killed at the king's installation ritual (Case 18.2). The killing was done by suffocation. During the sacrifice, the king-elect told those present to squat "in order that the crop-eating birds may stay quiet; that the winds will not come with violence and the rains come down gently". The stomach contents of the first goat were sprinkled at the four corners of the grave by the four *labusi* who were to do the excavation. At the same time, the four horn blowers blew their horns, four times, another man blew a whistle and a woman *nabusuti* ululated at a low voice.

After some ceremonial knocks with their hoes (of locally produced iron), the *labusi* started digging from the four corners of the tomb, two working inside the house and two outside.

When the slabs covering Acalili's grave were uncovered, the second goat (*egara*: "green") was killed on the same spot and in the same fashion, but by a different group of *labusi*. Its stomach contents were sprinkled on the slabs. After that, the slabs were removed, starting with those at the foot end.

The third goat (*okidangi*: khaki brown) was slaughtered. Its stomach contents were thrown on the bones, since most of cowskin in which Acalili had been wrapped had been eaten by worms. The corpse was inspected and as the tendons and nerves were still holding the bones together it was necessary to cut them apart. This was done inside the tomb.

The fourth goat was now cut open with the same ceremony (horn-and whistle-blowing, ululating) and its stomach contents thrown inside the tomb. The bones were removed, first put in a calabash and then in a pot, working upwards from the legs to the head. The skull was washed with a mix of stomach contents and water before it was put in the pot.

Then, the *nehuhumani*, a female official described by Muratori as "an arbitrator in Rainmaker matters" came in with a fresh gourd filled with water. She collected the powdered dust from the bottom of the tomb and the mixture of stomach contents and water in which the skull had been washed. These were put ready for the reconciliation (*emwara*) between the dead king and his surviving wives and children, to take place the following morning.

By 4:00 am, all the bones had been put in one urn. A woman came and sprinkled sorghum seeds over the urn and everyone stood up to take the urn with bones to the newly built shrine. Over the short distance over which the urn was transported, eight stops were made, at four step intervals, the first one on the threshold of the burial hut. At each stop, the procession squatted, blew the horns and whistles, ululated, and sprinkled rumen. The four *labusi* who had removed the bones from the tomb had their hands anointed with some oil of the *ahohoi* tree (*Strychnos Spinosa*). The urn was put in the shrine and closed by placing a small pot on top.

Then two pots containing the bones of Acalili's sons were collected from an old shrine and placed next to those of their father.

The four *labusi* who had opened the grave then performed *nejaha,* four rounds of rinsing their mouths with a mixture of water, their spittle and charcoal concluded by the drinking of old beer.

Around 5:00 am, the *monyomiji* of Lobera arrived. They brought a black bull. They suffocated it by tightening a thick rope around its neck. Its stomach contents were sprinkled on the urn that contained Acalili's bones and on the two pots with rainstones. While the *labusi* were adding finishing touches to the new shrine, the reconciliation ritual was performed for one of Acalili's widows and for two of his children.

During the morning hours, people arrived from all over Lotuho, from Loudo, Lomiya, Lopit and Lafon, dressed in full dancing gear. The dance to consecrate the new shrine (*etadwara,* lit. to make [the shrine] bitter) started at 2:00 pm in the courtyard where the shrine with the bones and rainstones was located. Then, the drums, eight in number, were brought out. Because of *edwar,* they had been silent for a whole year. At a signal given by the king-elect, Patricio Ohucoli, four drummers, all senior *monyomiji* of Loronyo, started to sound the rhythm of the opening tune during which the singers had to squat down in silence eight times. After this, the dance developed very soon into what is described by Muratori as a "a mighty unison of some few hundreds of people singing by full voice mixed with the nervous cadenced rhythm of eight drums echoed through the air till far away, electrizing [*sic*] and exciting the later comers". After this consecration dance, people moved around at very fast speed characterised as "galloping" by Muratori. After the last galloping rounds, everybody moved to the ceremonial ground of Hiyyu, the royal section. At the ceremonial ground, the same *etadwara* was performed, the people squatting down only four times. After dancing a few rounds in Hiyyu, people moved to the ceremonial ground of Ingorwai which is the joint dancing ground of the other five sections of Loronyo. They performed *etadwara* there as well, and sang the *netadwäriti hobwok,* the songs to make the new king 'bitter'.

While the dance was going on until late in the night, Acalili's widows stayed in the burial hut next to the open grave from which the bones had been removed. They were visited by wailing women who threw ashes and fine soil over their heads "in order to obtain a good harvest".

The next day, the ceremonial hunt for the king was held.

On the fourth day, the tomb which had been left empty for four days "so that the wind could blow Acalili's spirit away", was, without further rituals, filled up with black earth from the Ohuleleng Stream. This was a special request by Acalili's. The black earth was also put around the fence of the new shrine. On the same day, the *labusi* went to the ancestral shrine of Hoding to perform a sacrifice on the bones of Acalili's father (Mayya) and on those of a son of Acalili which had been kept at the ancestral shrine.[24]

---

24   Muratori fails to tell us why the bones of Acalili were not transported to the shrine in Hoding where the bones of his ancestors are kept. Another conspicuous omission in the account is the

The year of the reign of the dead king was marked by the observation of great restraint in the use of violence and in the activities associated with violence (drumming, dancing, shouting). It was ended with a ceremony in which social order was ostentatiously reaffirmed with all the ceremonial and ritual sophistication available. The forces of disorder that could have been unleashed by the exhumation of the king were met by a massive and seamless defence of order. This emphatic negation of violence and disorder was present at all levels: the humble body posture of those present, the regulation of sound signals, the division of the itinerary of the pots with bones in stages and the division of the distances between the stages into steps.

All means of purification are put to use in order to neutralise potential disorder: tobacco smoke, fruits of the wild cucumber, the stomach contents of the four goats and those of the black bull — all killed in a bloodless way, the mixture of water and stomach contents in which the skull was washed and the mixture of charcoal and water used for cleansing the mouths of the *labusi*.

All these measures indicate and define the dangers attributed to the exhuming operation — the principal danger being associated with a possible resistance of the king to his death and decomposition. At the exhumation of King Okong of Tirangore in November 1985, his bones were reported to be extraordinarily clean. No cutting was needed to take them apart. This was generally interpreted as evidence of kind-heartedness to his people. The cleaner the bones, the better the dead king. The meaning of this particular belief becomes clear if we see the decomposition process as the last stage in the surrender of the victim to his elimination. The more cooperative the victim, the more easily he relinquishes his body substances and the greater the benefits for the community.

The reverse reasoning — the more reluctant the victim, the more his body will expand and retain the benefits for the community — is also valid. Rainmakers who are accused of drought are said to show body swellings. The Lulubo call these swellings

---

political aspect of the succession. There is no record of the official consecration of the king-elect, Patricio Ohucoli, who, at the time of his succession, was the favourite of the colonial government but whose support among the *monyomiji* was divided. This may explain the limited attendance by members of the royal family—noted with surprise by Muratori. Only one of Acalili's widows and two of his children came to perform *emwara*.

Muratori also notes that Acalili had not given a formal blessing to Patricio as his successor. Before his death, Acalili is said to have communicated the name of the true successor to a trusted *aboloni* from Mura-Hatiha who was to keep the name hidden for two years after Acalili's death. In 1948, when Muratori left Sudan for good, Acalili's decision had not been revealed yet. Present-day Lotuho believe that another son was Acalili's favourite, but that Acalili had resigned himself to Patricio's succession because of his acceptability to the government. Patricio had been to school and had drifted away from the Lotuho tradition. As the Master of Ceremonies of his father's exhumation, he had to rely on a written script of the proceedings. During his career, he must have considerably improved his performance in rain matters (see Case 11.2 and 15.3).

Patricio's rivals took their chance at his death in 1959. His brother won the support of most sections of Loronyo, while the son of Acalili's senior brother Wani, who had 'rain' from both parents, found a following in Loming and Lalanga, so that the brother who inherited Patricio's senior wife was left with a significantly reduced kingdom.

apaba (a category roughly coinciding with the symptoms of oedema). Although they know that *apaba* is usually caused by exposure to fire and hot objects, they attribute the *apaba* of the Rainmaker to his reluctance to release the rain. When the *lucuri* tree has been cursed, cut and burnt as a substitute for the king in the ritual simulation of regicide (Case 17.6 and 17.7) , the stomach of the Rainmaker guilty of stopping the rain is believed to swell with the water he has 'held back'. He is said "to die of water".[25]

A similar victimary logic informs the reasoning of the Lopit Rainmaker whose father and predecessor had been buried alive for causing drought Table W. no.19). When the Rainmaker-son was threatened to be buried alive like his father, he demanded a reburial of his father. By burying him in a dry place, his father's body did not decompose. This, according to the son, hampered the rainfall and was the cause of the drought.

Once the king's bones have been given their final resting place, the *edwar* is lifted and normal life with all its exuberance and risk-taking can resume: dancing, warfare, stick-fights, the shouting of self-praise songs, including unrestrained wailing over the dead king which had been suspended for the duration of *edwar*. The transition from the obsessional order of the exhumation to the electrifying togetherness of the dance, is the defining moment of the exhumation celebrations.

The protocol of the exhumation ceremony in Lopit (Mura) follows a reverse timeline from that of the Lotuho. Here, the exhumation is preceded by three months of dancing for the late Rainmaker. Then, a short but very strict *edwar* is proclaimed: no one is allowed to burn grass, or cut trees, to collect firewood or use the grinding stones for a period of two days. The third day, after a full night of dancing *burata*, the funeral dance for Rainmakers, the bones are taken out of the graves and put in pots which have been prepared by the in-laws of the rain clan and kept in a house in the compound of the Rainmaker. The day after the exhumation, the late king's *ametere*, which had been kept at hand to be used in rain rituals and to ward off insect plagues, is thrown away in the bush.

The relics of the dead king

In the models S. and T. (Ch. 16, p. 359–60) describing the stepwise ritual response to a rain crisis by Bari and Lotuho communities, the importance of the relics and graves of historic Rainmakers as a last ritual resort was pointed out. Here follow some more instances of the ritual use of relics as substitutes of the victim-king.

In Liria, only the king's skull and one bone of the lower leg are exhumed. They are taken in a solemn procession of the *monyomiji* and the members of the royal family to the rock-pool in which the skulls of the former Rainmakers are kept. A sacrifice is

---

25   The Lulubo distinguish two types of swelling: *apaba* and *toku*. The first can be the result of cursing (*lemi*); the other is the domain of the *arigi*, a technical medical specialist. If *toku* occurs, the body is exhumed for fear that the puss will cause disease to the descendants. This is the only occasion when the Lulubo practise exhumation. An informant from Mura (Lopit) told me that a man who dies of *abalaca*, a swollen stomach, will not be buried until after his stomach has been cut open.

made near the pool and the stomach contents of the victim are applied to the skull and the leg bone. The branch of the creeper (called *imolyeti*) growing near the pool will be cut and bent into a ring that is put around the neck of the successor Rainmaker when he returns from the pool, thus linking the new man's powers to those of his ancestors. While walking back to the village in a procession, the Rainmaker should, under no circumstance, look back in the direction of the pool. The installation ceremonies are completed with a final sacrifice at the new Rainmaker's return to the village.

The skull and bones of the Rainmaker will only be used for important rain sacrifices, in case of persistent drought. When the new Rainmaker performs his first rain ritual, he sends for water from the pool of the skulls to wash his rainstones.

In Lulubo, some of the most powerful rainstones are kept at the graves of the Rainmakers. *Cololo*, a large, ball-like piece of rock, is kept on the grave of Tira, the great-grandfather of the Rainmaker in charge at the time of the field work. *Ngulere*, the main stone of the Panyangiri of Edemo, and *'Dubo*, the stone of Ololoru, are also kept at the ancestral graves.

The different ritual practices postulate a close relationship between the body of the Rainmaker, the remains of Rainmaker's ancestors and the rainstones. When placed on top of the grave, they are treated as a substitute for the Rainmaker's body or rather his skull since they are placed over the head. The tumulus, which in, at least, one language (Lulubo) is also called 'head' (*'di*), is purified with stomach contents, or with crushed wild cucumber, just like the rainstones are in a routine rain ritual, and like the skull of Acalili during the exhumation ceremony.

The equation of a stone and a skull is also made in funerals of commoners. If a Lulubo man has died away from home, his son (or his nearest male relative) has the obligation to 'bring his father's skull home'. To that effect, he collects a black stone from a place near the original grave, cuts a creeper and ties it to the stone as a rope. Pulling the stone behind him, he walks home and puts the stone near the ebony pole (*poi*) which he has erected as a grave post for his father, tying the creeper around the pole. The funeral is completed with the sacrifice of a goat and the oiling of the stone and the *poi*.

In addition to these relations of substitution, the rainstones and the dead king are also connected metonymically. The stones are placed on top of the tomb or next to the urn containing the bones of the king in this way absorbing some of the power of the ancestral Rainmakers. The Bari elaborate on this connection by putting rainstones in the armpits of the dead king while he is lying in state, waiting for the abdomen to rupture. The stones that are so placed are two specimens of *Muryesuk*, yellowish stones that bring rain in heavy drops, and two specimens of *Munda*, green stones, whose rains make the world turn green. They are removed before the king is buried. The stones are equated with the end product of the dying of the king. Like the bones and the skull, they are the residue of the king's power after death and 'victimage' have done their work.

Taking the stones along in the Rainmaker's grave is a reversal of this process generative of rain and causes drought. This may be the logic behind the story of the rainstones of Aru which returned to the surface of the earth on their own, two years after the Rainmaker, in an attempt to punish his people, had swallowed them while dying. It also corresponds to the reasoning of those who put the blame of the drought, following the live burial of the Rainmaker of Lowe, on the fact that his rainstones had been thrown into the grave together with their owner (Case 9.6).

Conclusions

In contrast to the necessarily violent character of regicide, the funeral of the king is surrounded by rules prescribing the strictest non-violence. While the aftermath of regicide is beset by worries whether the killing was the right thing to do, the mood following the unprovoked death of a king is generally euphoric although utmost care is taken not to disturb the state of non-violence proclaimed after the king's death. While regicide creates a sense of unity and suspends all conflicts *before* the king is killed in the collective drive against him, the funeral of a king who died a natural death is followed by the imposition of a state of social peace by prohibiting the expression of all conflicts *after* the death of the king. In regicide, the victimary process stalls in the negative transfiguration of the victim: the killed king becoming the focus of concerns regarding his possible revenge and his body the object of rituals to neutralise any curse it might carry while those who killed the king are subjected to purification rituals.

In the royal funeral, the positive transfiguration predominates: the king's body is equated with food. Crops and rainstones are brought in contact with the body of the dying king in order that their efficacy is increased. Both scenarios, that of regicide and that of the royal funeral are inversely symmetric realisations of the more fundamental scapegoat scenario, in which the negative and positive transfiguration are two sides of the same coin. This undivided scenario sometimes suddenly crops up in practices surrounding the death of the king, as when the Lulubo consider the singing of the royal funeral songs (*owilara*) as an act of quasi-regicide

The installation and funeral ceremonies are complementary enactments of the same scenario. They mark the beginning and the end of the victimary career of the king. The career of the king is conceived in two fundamental ways: among the Lotuho, the Lokoya and the Lopit, the king is a monster, half-man and half-feline. He is seized from a location outside ordered life, made fit for the role of king by rituals of domestication and purification; and after having fulfilled his victimary task, he returns to his feline brothers outside the realm of culture. This last element is expressed in the Lotuho song, sung right after the burial of the king: "The king has turned into a lion ... his eyes shining red" and in the leopard skull moved in front of the eyes of the dead Lopit king before his grave is closed.

The Bari and Lulubo king is selected from inside the social community and invested with the powers of kingship in what could be called a "ritual of collective negative transference". The powers thus transferred stay with the king until his death, when they are carefully disposed of in the form of the king's hair that was never cut (in the case of the Bari) and the *imuture* in the case of the Lulubo.

The dying of the king is conceived as a productive process — not a momentary event — generating rain and good harvests. The Bari king 'dies' in three stages. After his 'clinical' death, he goes on dying until his stomach bursts and releases its 'oil'. After that, when he is buried, his dying continues to produce spontaneous effects up to the moment the tomb is levelled. In the case of the Lotuho king, dying and decomposition are a single process lasting up to the exhumation. It is as if the societies in our field of study try to prolong the moment of death in order to derive maximum benefit from it — the Lotuho and Tsera even placing the year, or years, following the king's death under the formal authority of the dead king.

With respect to this attribution of ultimate sovereignty to the dead king, there is a striking parallel in the Nile Valley — ancient Egypt. In Egypt, the dead and the living king ruled simultaneously. The dead king was equated with Osiris, who was responsible for the progression of the agricultural seasons; while the living ruler was identified with Osiris's son Horus. The motor behind the annual flood and the regeneration of the crops was the power (*ka*) released at the king's death and equated with the divine power of Osiris, the dismembered king who was resurrected annually in the flood of the Nile. In *Kingship and the Gods*, Frankfort defines Osiris's power as "life caught in the spell of death", a characterisation that could very well also apply to the power of the dead Nilotic kings (Frankfort, 1978:185).[26]

---

26 While the renewed edition of this book underwent its last round of editing, Eisei Kurimoto sent me newly collected information about the practices surrounding the death of the Pari king. In 1980, when king Fidele Ongang was about to die, his body and face were covered with the freshly removed skin of a bull especially killed for that purpose. The skin was pressed against the mouth and nose of the king by a close kinsman so that the king died of suffocation. Kurimoto was told that this was done "to preserve the power of the final blessing (*gweth*) of the king".

Gweth is the opposite of *cien*, the posthumous curse left by a person who dies while in discord with his family or community — as in the case of Fidele's widow, Nyiburu, whose death and the precautions taken against her *cien*, were described in Case 17.11.

The Pari practice of suffocating their king is clearly a more archaic form of the practice reported for their Shilluk relatives further north who spread a cloth over the body of their king when he is about to die, applying it to his face till he dies of suffocation (Seligman, n.d., p. 221, 1932:91).

In anthropological discussions the Shilluk practice has often been labelled as *regicide*. Set against the funeral procedures presented in this chapter the custom of suffocating the Pari and Shilluk king belongs to the same category of practices as the plugging of the Bari, Lulubo, Lokoya and Lotuho kings, their common purpose being the optimisation of the king's posthumous blessings. These practices in which the transfigured victimhood of the king was given ritual expression were reserved for kings who died a non-violent death and were loved by their people, not an act of *regicide*.

The failure to distinguish the different modes of royal dying: in a contest with rivals, as a scapegoat in a confrontation with his people, or glorified in a royal funeral — which cannot avoid to give, in one way or another, ritual expression to the scapegoat mechanism — have caused a lot of confusion in the anthropological debate on regicide from Frazer, via Evans-Pritchard to Arens.

Tying the new pole-shrine (alore) *with the rain creeper that once linked heaven and earth, Loronyo, 2012.* Photograph by Naoki Naito.

19

The Metabolism of Violence and Order: The King's Stomach at Work

Two questions still need a clearer answer. The first one is of a general nature: what is the connection between rainmaking and peacemaking, the two major responsibilities of the sovereign in the polities on the Equatorian east bank of the Nile? Is there a more intimate connection than the potential of rain to dramatise the balance of power between king and people, and the sheer fact that of all disasters, drought is feared most? The second question is more specific: why is the stomach of the Rainmaker cut after his death and why, in the case of Queen Nyiburu, was a 'tasteless' cucumber applied to it? To answer these questions we need a brief excursion into the cosmology of the Equatorian east bank. For this purpose, I would like to examine some aspects of the festival that marks the transition from the cultivation season to the hunting season, from the rainy to the dry season. Because of its diverse names (*Löri* in Bari; Lulubo: *Kajuwaya*; Lokoya: *Odhurak*; Lotuho: *Nalam*; Pari: *Nyalam*), I refer to it as the New Year Festival. Its ritual and symbolism provide a synopsis of the social values and cosmological ideas of these Nilotic communities.

The festival lasts one day. It starts early in the morning and culminates in a dance of the whole community in the afternoon. The following sequences can be distinguished:

- Consecration of the pole-shrine by the responsible Master or guardian, before sunrise;
- Meeting of the *monyomiji* in their meeting place deep in the bush where the previous year is evaluated and measures for the new year are discussed;
- Village-wide divinatory hunt in which all sections co-operate — the hunt is believed to predict the fortunes of the community in the new year;
- Formal welcoming of the *monyomiji* by the women at the meeting ground at the boundary between village and bush;
- Administration of blessings (for food, for a hunt without mishaps, for the birth of children) by the respective Masters of Disaster;
- Re-appropriation of the ceremonial ground by the *monyomiji*, followed by the other members of the community, sometimes on the basis of sectional competition; and
- Joint dance of all the members of the community.

Let us briefly examine each of these sequences.

The New Year festival

The preparations for *Kajuwaya* celebrations of 1986 started with a visit to the diviner (*ozo*).[1] I joined the delegation of the *monyomiji* of Lokiliri. They were worried because in 1985 fighting had broken out during the first preparatory dance. A connection was suspected between that untimely violence and the poor harvest. The diviner threw her stones. Her reading held no special warning: people should be 'of one heart' and keep their celebrations sober-in fact the only option considering the situation of famine.

A few days later, before dawn, the Master of the Land and his deputy, the Guardian of the Shrine (*kaciri modi*) and the Speaker of the *monyomiji* congregated at the pole-shrine to pray. After pouring a mixture of beer and oil at the foot of the pole-shrine, all present took a sip from the calabash praying to their ancestors that "that the bodies of the people who were going to celebrate might be cool".

After the prayer, a fresh liana (Lulubo: *uno*, Bari: *dölöngi*, Lokoya: *odyalang*) was tied around the poles of the shrine. This creeping plant is a variety of the wild vine tree (*Cissus mossambicensis*, Spagnolo, 1960:28), a woody climber used by the Bari as a rope for pulling boats. The lianas are watery inside. It is certainly because of this quality that they play an important symbolic role. Following Buxton in this, I shall refer to this plant as 'rain creeper' (1973:116).

At daybreak, more *monyomiji* arrived and started clearing the ceremonial ground of weeds. In the afternoon, when the weeding was finished, the first *ira* of the season was danced and sung. *Ira* is accompanied by songs that commemorate past war feats recalling the names of enemy victims and evoking the circumstances of the victory. Between the opening of the ceremonial ground and the day of *Kajuwaya* — a warming-up period when people dance a few rounds every night — the shrine should be well guarded. In the past, in Ngangala and Ngulere, the guardian of the shrine slept next to it to prevent enemies from performing sacrilegious acts on it to harm the village.

The responsibility for the village shrine and for the New Year's festival is, in some villages (Kudwo and Edemo), an office in its own right. In others, it rests with the Rainmaker (Ngulere), the Master of the Land (Ngangala, Lokiliri)[2] or the Master of Bows (Liria; illustration p. 430) .

Before dawn on the day of the New Year's festival, libations of unfiltered beer and oil are poured at the foot of the shrine. In Kudwo, water is poured in a receptacle which is located in a cavity underneath the poles of the shrine. In Lokiliri, both the Master of the Land and his wife rub oil and spit beer on the ebony poles.

In Liria and Ngulere, the *anggat*, a rectangular structure made of bare branches, placed to the east of the pole-shrine at the outer circle of the ceremonial ground, is

---

1   *Kajuwaya* is celebrated on a fixed day, 28 January. This date was fixed by the generation of Kwara (1956–1975). They also ruled that *Kajuwaya* should henceforth be danced during daytime and not at night, during the new moon with torches as was the old custom.

2   In Lokiliri, the *opopi kajuwayari* is under a junior lineage of the rain clan which also keeps the drums. Rituals at *Tukure*, the central village shrine, are performed by the *Osi Buri*, the Master of the Land.

the focus of ritual attention at *Odhurak*. The structure represents the community's eco-system in microcosm. It is placed in an east-west direction because the most important rains come from the east. In the middle, some sorghum seeds are sown. When the sorghum is ripe, it will only be used to provide the seeds which will be sown on the same spot for the next harvest.[3] In and around it are the *omunu* ('snakes'), sets of wooden pegs planted in the soil, also referred to as *ahabusi* ('queens'), used for thanksgiving after the hunt and the harvest. The catch of the New Year's divinatory hunt is deposited at the shrine (Illustration, p. 428). The *anggat* is renewed on New Year's day, according to strict building prescriptions as to which materials should be used and where these should be collected, every beam having its own name and type of wood. The Rainmaker, the Master of Grain and the Master of Bows jointly consecrate and administer this 'eco-shrine'. On New Year's day, the Master of Bows is in charge (Illustration, p. 430). Since the eco-shrine is susceptible to enemy curses (*elamwön*), it is well guarded during *Odhurak*.[4]

After these ritual preparations, the drums are sounded and the *monyomiji* come for blessings before they go on the hunt. A mixture of roughly ground sorghum flour, oil and water is applied to the head as a blessing. In preparation for the hunt, the spears and arrows are put together on one heap and are touched with a thorny branch (Lulubo: *ropiko*, Lokoya: *akadavi*). The Master of Bows takes red grain and white ashes from a calabash, spits on it and throws the mixture on the weapons saying: "May your hands be red!" — referring to the blood of the animals that will be killed. One arrow is taken out from the heap and sharpened on the stone next to the shrine while a prayer is uttered: "My father, and you my brothers, we ask for food, we look for our stomach, You father, let our spittle blend!" In Lafon, the New Year's blessing of spears is carried out by the Master of the Mountain and his assistants (Illustration, p. 324).

On New Year's day of 1986, before the *monyomiji* left the village for the hunt, the following words were spoken by three village leaders: the Assistant (*jaigo*) of the Master of the Land, the *mukungu* (headman) who is an elder of the rain clan and by a member of the senior age-set of Lomini, the generation in power.

19.1 *Invocations before the hunt, Kajuwaya 1986, Lokiliri* (live recording)

Jaigo: "Please let there be no misunderstanding. You know there is nothing to eat. But we should not give up. Let us not give others a chance to say: "Those there have surrendered because of hunger." We dance Kajuwaya as usual. This year we ask you, Serafino Okollo, owner of the village: "urinate on our land!" We ask you: "let our land be wet! The coming year when I put my seeds in the ground, please urinate on it.

---

3   There is an interesting parallel here with the ancient Egyptian Osiris beds. On the festival that opened the cultivation season, effigies in recess of the god Osiris were made and used as nurseries for grain seeds whose germination symbolised the resurrection of the god.

4   The Lulubo also use the peg shrines in their hunting ritual. Informants tended to be evasive about their significance. Seligman comments briefly on the peg shrines of the Lokoya (1932: 343–45) and the Acholi (1925:32–34; 1932: 123–4).

By myself, I have no power (*goa*).[5] Father, if there is hostility (*tongica*)[6] in your heart, let it go! Ask your God! Let your children have food this year. When they go to the bush let the grass not cut their feet."

Mukungu: "Let their face be white![7] Let them stay nearby and come back safely and find me here! Let evil vanish from our hearts. Let God see to it. Let food appear!"

All: "Let it come! Let it appear!"

Lomini: "All evil, let it go from your hearts, let it go with its wood![8] I want your bodies to be cool!"

Jaigo: "When the boys have come back from the forest, I want them to work hard and clear large plots."

Lomini: "I only have this to say: let your body be cool!"

All: "It is cool!"

Lomini: "This year all of you will be one body with a good heart; let your body be cool!"

All: "It is cool!"

Jaigo: "Food has come. Wherever God may have gone, let him hear us. Let God accept."

Mukungu: "Let God hear us. Let God accept! God has accepted your prayers."

Jaigo (business-like now): "Don't go to *re* (the assembly point at the boundary of village and bush). We have two tamarind trees here and one mango. They are big enough. Some food will be served there. Now, tell the children to go to the bush."

That year no guests from outside (government, aid agencies, church) were invited because of the famine, which in the speeches was treated as an enemy to whom the community should not surrender. The significance of the symbolism of urine and spittle, heat and coolness, red and white, will be discussed in a later paragraph of this chapter.

The New Year deliberations

In 1986, the *monyomiji* of Liria and Langabu convened the annual meeting to discuss the state of the community at the fixed meeting ground in the forest. Those

---

5   *Goa* (from Arabic): power based on secular resources especially on wealth, different from the (sacred) power of office.

6   Word from Bari root *ngisa*, translated by Spagnolo as: 'to be a foe, to be an adversary, to have anger against, sever any friendly relation with' (Spagnolo, 1960–224).

7   Standard formula meaning "Good luck!" in an enterprise, especially in hunting.

8   The expression "Let it go with its wood" refers to a ritual in which evil is expelled by throwing a piece of wood (*kwe*), usually of the *itubi* tree (a *Combretum* species), over the fence into the bush.

of Ngangala, Ngulere and Kudwo held their discussions at the outskirts of the village (Lulubo: *re*; Lokoya: *orek*; Bari: *rek*), at their return from the hunt; while the people of Lokiliri exceptionally met in the village, under the tamarind and mango trees as stated in the recorded speech. I was present at all the meetings except that of Liria. The common message of all speeches was to start the New Year with a clean sheet, to settle any unresolved issues that could cause division in the coming year, and not to give in to the famine.

In Ngulere and Langabu, the policies of the *monyomiji* were heavily criticised. In Langabu, *Mura* (the ruling generation) replaced all its appointed officials. A second point on the agenda was the poor attendance of the *monyomiji*. The last matter to be dealt with was the control of bloodshed in the village. The old rule that persons guilty of bloodshed should be raided by the *monyomiji* of the opposite moiety in case they failed to pay the fine imposed on them was reaffirmed and the fine was raised to fifty piasters plus one goat for the purification (*avulyo*) of the two fighting parties. The new rate was implemented the same day (see below).

The speeches at Ngulere escalated into an exchange of accusations between the Rainmaker, the other Masters of Disaster and the retired elders, on one side, and the *Taruha monyomiji*, on the other (Case 9.10).

In Kudwo, the main topic of discussion was the division of the village since an ever larger group of people was moving to the roadside. The majority of the speakers fulminated against this division and compared it to *kokora*, the re-division by the government in Khartoum of the southern Sudan into three regions — one of the immediate causes of the civil war. Most speakers blamed the famine on God.

19.2 *Kajuwaya speech 1986, Kudwo* (live recording)

Hunger has spread to all the villages now. It is not in one village only. So, all we can say is "God is killing us with hunger, let him help us." As you know, we are cutting trees [for charcoal and cash]. Let the trees help to cool your body. Be cool!

Tell the children to moderate their drinking habits. Let them get wiser. What is the point of fighting? It is bad when you beat your brother and kill him. Taking the number of fights into account, the drought could very well be a punishment of God to all the villages. This year, we hope to live in peace. Our children will help us through as much as they can until the start of the rains. My friend, let hunger go away. Let food come to the village. Let it come. Let my child's body be cool, let it be cool. This is all I have to say.

The tenor of the speeches in Ngangala was similar, although more bitter in tone because of the severe famine. Only two calabashes of beer were brought to *rek* and these were given to the parish priest and the visiting anthropologist. The speeches in Lokiliri had a tone of resignation.

The New Year hunt and the 're-conquest' of the village

All the *monyomiji* and youngsters participate in the hunt. The way the hunt is conducted and the game killed is considered a prefiguration of the way in which 'food will come to the village' in the New Year. Accidents and discord during this hunt are inauspicious. The number and colour of the animals killed is an indication of the fortunes of the next year — a black animal being considered a good omen and a red one being considered a bad omen.

The catch of the New Year's hunt was deposited at the eco-shrine (anggat) *of Ngulere. The catch of this duiker was considered ominous because of its red colour.*

The Lirians were happy with the black warthog they killed in the 1986 hunt. The red colour of the duiker killed by Ngulere was problematic. By redefining it as a border case of khaki brown its value as a forecast was played down. Ngangala bagged ten animals and Lokiliri had none.

When the *monyomiji* return from the bush, they first gather at the meeting ground at the outskirts of the village (*orek* in Lokoya, *rek* in Bari, *re* in Lulubo). They sit age-set by age-set and enjoy the drinks brought to them from the village by the women (Illustration, p. 80).

In Liria, the *monyomiji* are only allowed into the village after the solemn procession of the *Fingers of God*, followed by elders and other officials, has reached the main ceremonial ground. The procession stops at a number of stations where everyone squats down, each person using his right hand to make a small heap from the loose soil beside him on the path, in order to 'make the food of the coming year heavy' (Illustrations, p. 280).

Solemn procession of monyomiji *to the ceremonial ground of Ngangala. While singing the songs of warriors coming home from the battlefield, they stop at regular intervals to squat and mould heaps of dry soil in order to promote fertility and abundance, 1986.*

In Ngangala, the *monyomiji* themselves make the heaps while marching from *rek* to the ceremonial ground. In Ngangala and Langabu, they sing marching songs, known as *nyakarumo(ng)* which are sung when returning home from the bush (after war, or after the period of seclusion of the newly initiated generation).

In Lokiliri, Liria and Ngulere, the ceremonial ground is reoccupied in a race from the open ground outside the gates of the village (*re* respectively *orek*) In the past, Lokiliri was divided into four competing divisions for that purpose. In Ngulere, the race in 1986 was between the two moieties — the best runners being sent ahead with the sectional flags (Illustrations, p. 25, 198).

*The Master of Bows of Liria, next to the eco-shrine (*anggat*) keeping a pot of ointment warm to bless late-comers to the New Year celebrations.*

At the eco-shrine, those who had not received their blessing in the early morning lined up to have a mixture of flour and oil rubbed on their head by the wife or the assistant of the Master of the Land or the Master of Bows. In Kudwo, the calabash that had been used for the blessings before the departure to the hunt, was repeatedly refilled so that late-comers could also be served.

In Langabu, the blessing by the Mistress of the Mountain was scheduled after the return of the *monyomiji* from the bush. She and her aide had positioned themselves near a rock crevice where snakes have their abode. She poured beer to attract the snakes so that they might drink from her calabash. The same container was used for the oil with which she blessed the people. The oil was applied to the chests of those who wanted to receive this blessing of fertility and health (Illustration, p. 285).

The New Year dance

The celebrations culminate in the dance, in which all members of the community participate, including old people who would otherwise not take the trouble to dance, and young boys and girls. While to the east, the choreography of the dance seems to conform to that of the war dance (Lotuho: *erremoti*; Lokoya: *itholu*), in Ngangala, Ngulere, Kudwo and Lokiliri it has a number of unique features, first of all with respect to the attire of the people during the dance.

The carnivalesque side of the Lulubo New Year celebrations: left: *the Catholic parish priest allowing himself to be engaged by a daring young lady in a buttock bumping dance;* right: *inversion of gender roles, Kudwo, Lulubo.*

In Lokiliri and Kudwo, everyone should come dressed in the leaves of the *memele* tree (*Lonchocarpus laxiflorus*) — a species which gets fresh leaves before the start of the new rains; its vivid green contrasts sharply with the surrounding brownish colour of the dead dry season vegetation (Illustrations, p. 267, 431, 432). The *memele* is associated with rainmaking. After the Rainmaker has been ritually washed (Cf. Ch. 14, p. 321), he dips a branch of *memele* in the water and sprinkles it up into the air. The spray is believed to condense into a cloud. The twigs of the *memele* tree are also used to stir the rainstones. The Lokoya Rainmakers keep their stones under a *lokebek* (Lokoya for *memele*) tree.

The Lulubo explain the custom of wearing leaves as a survival from the past when *Kajuwaya* was danced at night at the new moon. Some say the leaves served to protect the bodies of the dancers against sparks falling from the torches. Others say that it was to make people, especially the members of the opposite sex, indistinguishable and that it served as a preliminary to sexual promiscuity. The latter explanation would also clarify why *Kajuwaya* is a 'bumping' dance, in which men and women are expected to hit one another with their backsides (Illustration 19.6). Because of the sideways gait that goes with the bumping, the dance is also referred to as 'the dance of the hyena'.

In Lafon, groups of dancers (age-sets usually) smear themselves with black mud on New Year's Day — the black colour possibly signifying the immunity from danger, or evoking the colour of the clouds in the year to come.

New Year's ('Kajuwaya') dance in Kudwo, Lulubo, 1986. People wear spring leaves and put winnowing trays as head covers. The leaves of the memele *tree are the first to sprout, long before the start of the rains.*

On their head, the dancers in Lokiliri wear, upside down, a miniature *keti*, a square basket to carry flour, or, increasingly so nowadays, all sorts of headgear which are products of *bricolage* and phantasy (p. 431, photo on the right). In the past, the dancers brought their own beer along to the dancing ground. In Ngulere, Kudwo and Ngangala, a winnowing tray is carried on the head. There, the dance ends in a fast galloping around the pole-shrine, by couples or small groups consisting of a man and one man and one or more of his sisters. The sister(s) hop(s) at the side of her/ their brother waving coolness to his face with a cloth. The explanation given for these customs is that they show the prosperity of the family — the sisters constituting its most important source of wealth.[9] If we compare the dance between brother and sister to the customs observed by their neighbours in Lokiliri, a more fundamental meaning appears: the leaves, the bumping and promiscuity, the drinking of one's own beer and the dance of brother and sister are all activities in which the social obligation to exchange has been abolished or reversed. The dancers enact a return to a pre-cultural state where the straightjacket of marriage and hospitality is taken off. At the same

---

9   Men without sisters are excluded from this last galloping round.

time, the visible signs on the body of blessings of oil and flour, and the grain baskets and winnowing trays on the head express abundance of food.

To this return to the age of plenty good rains belong as well. During the dance, the Rainmaker and his assistant go around in the crowd with a calabash with water and produce a fine spray over the dancers using branches of the *itubi* tree (Bari: *gwögwötit*, *Combretum undulatum*) shaped into a kind of brush. In Kudwo, the water used is that which has been kept in the cavity underneath the shrine. The *itubi* tree is associated with peace and good health. A stick of *itubi* is thrown between two parties to stop them from fighting. Popular belief holds that whoever will first step over the branch will lose the fight. *Itubi* is further used by the Lulubo to ward off plagues or enemies and to expel evil influences from the house.

While in the past the dance went on for a full night, nowadays only a few tunes (three or four) are played. This restriction of the number of dances is motivated by the fear that violence may break out. Despite the ambience of transgression in the past, there were fewer incidents, informants say, because of the tighter social controls. After the dance, people disperse and continue the celebrations by exchanges of visits at their private homes.

The containment of violence during the New Year festival

The execution of the programme of New Year's day is taken as a prefiguration of the course of events during the year to come. The outbreak of fights is, therefore, the main worry of the organisers. Any breach of peace on this day is believed to have repercussions for the year that has just started. The limitation on the number of dances, the change of the timing of the dance, the abolition of the promiscuous element from the dance, are all measures aimed at avoiding violence. Fights between individuals easily escalate in confrontations between villages, sections, clans and generations.

As in 1985, during the dance following the clearing of the ceremonial ground in Lokiliri, a fight broke out. This year the antagonists were the age-sets of uninitiated young men of two different sections between the non-initiated age-sets of young men of two sections. The whole age-set of the section that had started the fight was arrested by the police of Ngangala where they were kept until the wounds of the man who had been hit by a stone had healed. The fight eventually led to a re-evaluation of the relations between the section of the victim and the other sections of Lokiliri. The section of the victim was offered a *mukungu*-ship of its own so that in the future it could defend its interests better.

During the *Odhurak* of Langabu, no fewer than four violent incidents were brought to the attention of the *monyomiji*. Immediate action was taken. Three people who had been caught fighting — including a married couple — were fined twenty-five Sudanese pounds each. The fourth case was considered more serious since blood had been shed. The man who caused the blood to flow was fined fifty pounds in accordance with the new rate ratified by the *monyomiji* that very morning. In addition the culprit was ordered to kill a goat to purify (*avulyo*) the drums. The man did not accept the charge.

His refusal kept the whole village waiting for the dance could not start without the purification done. Finally, the man gave in and killed the goat. He rubbed some of its stomach contents on the drums, the rest being thrown to the waiting crowd. His wife was seen carrying the carcass around as a sign that her husband had complied with the order of the *monyomiji* and that the dance could begin. During the dance, the dead goat was tied to the pole-shrine in the middle of the dancing crowd. It was later eaten by the retired elders, the only ones who can eat a goat that has expiated blood (*amwödidha*) since they are already on the brink of death.

The pole-shrine

The pole-shrine is the focal point of the New Year celebrations. It is where the festival begins with libations in the early morning and around which it culminates in the dance. Its poles serving as drum posts, the shrine is the pivot around which the community, reduced to a single, undifferentiated mass, rotates, striding, bumping or galloping, throwing up clouds of dust (Illustration p. 432). Because of its central ritual importance, we should have a closer look at it.

In the eastern part of our field of study, the shrine consists of a bunch of between ten and thirty ebony poles. Among the Bari, only a single stake is erected. The bundle of ebony poles stands man-high in the middle of the ceremonial ground. Ebony wood, which is also used for grave posts and palisades, is very durable. *Tukure*, the shrine of the old Lokiliri village up the mountain, which was abandoned in 1936, is still standing firm in the middle of the bush. Ebony gives a prickly smoke when it burns. The smoke is classified as 'bitter' (Lulubo: *angana*; Lokoya/Lotuho: *odwa;* Pari: *kec*; Bari: *pötwör*), a word that in certain contexts is best translated as *sacred*. Ebony is associated with kingship (Case 9.12).

Ebony poles fresh from the forest ready to be erected and bundled as the new shrine of Loronyo, Photograph by Naoki Naito.

When the shrine in Lokiliri is in need of renovation the Guardian of the Shrine brings the poor state of the old poles to the attention of the *monyomiji*. On an appointed day, the *monyomiji* go to the forest to collect new poles. They return singing *nyakarumo* songs, songs that are sung when marching home from war or from the forest after initiation. When arriving at *re*, the Guardian of the Shrine purifies ('*bulo*) the *monyomiji* as if they were warriors returning from the battlefield, slaughtering a goat from his own stable. For the ritual fixing of the poles, the *monyomiji* provide their own goat. While the *monyomiji* stand around the hole, each man holding a pole, the goat's stomach is opened and its contents, mixed with blood and oil, are poured into the hole. When the poles have been fixed, the remainder of the stomach contents and the oil is smeared on the poles. The water that the elders have used to wash their hands after the sacrifice is poured in between the poles. Then, a liana of the rain creeper (Lulubo: *uno;* Bari: *dölöngi;* Lokoya: *odyalang*) is brought and tied around the poles. One end of the liana is crushed so that the fibres form a brush, which the assistant of the Rainmaker uses to sprinkle water up into the air. After planting the poles, the inaugural dance starts which may last for several days.

In Liria, when the men who have collected the poles arrive at *orek*, they are welcomed with food and beer. A very strict state of non-violence (*edwar*) is proclaimed. The poles are heavily guarded during the night to prevent any malevolent act. No one is allowed to eat, drink or smoke before the poles have been fixed. All villagers participate in the planting of the poles. The poles are purified (*avulyo*) as in Lokiliri and consecrated (*ajohiyo*) with unfiltered beer, mashed sorghum flour, a broth of beans and blows of tobacco smoke. Water is sprinkled over the participants and *itholu*, the war dance, is danced after the poles have been planted.

Among the Bari who erect single pole shrines the scenario is different. In the past, the Bari buried a girl, a cow-calf or a lamb of the female sex under or next to the shrine of a new ceremonial ground. The Bari word *wore* refers to the shrine as a whole — the ebony pole, the victim buried underneath and the ceremonial ground. The family offering the girl was highly respected "for having offered the blood of the land". Its male members were exempted from going to war because their family had already shed its blood. I was assured that even today, it made a difference for a family if it had, in this way, contributed to the foundation of the community.

Spagnolo informs us that the victim was selected from among the daughters of the slaves ('*dupi*) of the Master of the Land. Two holes were dug — one for the calabash with sesame oil in which the pole would stand and one for the girl. The girl would be tied to the pole with specially manufactured iron bracelets or chains. The sesame oil that was put in the calabash was also applied to the members of the community (Spagnolo, 1933:324). The grave was later covered with black and white stones.

The Bari *wore* was used for war dances (*kore lo mörö*) before going to war. The dance served to boost the morale and offered a clue as to the outcome of the war, According to one informant, if blood appeared on Piateng, the shrine-pole of the *wore* of Darjur under which a '*dupiet* daughter had once been buried, it was a sign that people would die. If Piateng did not bleed, the victims would be on the side of the enemy.

While I have no information whether the eastern multi-pole shrines were ever used for pre-war dances, they are currently used for the postwar celebration, in song and dance, of the victories of the *monyomiji* past and present.

The contrasting ritual practices connected with each type of pole-shrine correspond to the two scenarios of consensual antagonism. The Bari war dance around a single pole that is intimately linked to the sacrifice of one of the community's members follows the scapegoat scenario. The easterners (Lulubo, Lokoya, Pari, Lotuho) who collect substitute victims from a quasi-battlefield and erect them as a shrine of ebony poles in the central ceremonial ground of their community practice an interpretation of the enemy scenario.

The single pole of the Bari shrine expresses the identity of the community and the victim, while the multiple poles of the easterners express the identity of a plurality of enemy victims with the community as a whole. In the Bari scenario, the link between the shrine and the victim is metonymical. The tying of the victim to the pole by an iron chain achieves an unbreakable contiguity while the relationship between the community and the victim is metaphorical — the victim's blood being shed on behalf of the community. This substitutive role is underlined by the rule that the victim's death absolves her brothers from becoming victims of war.

The relationship between multiple poles erected by the easterners and enemy victims is metaphorical and so is the circumspection with which the poles are handled and the purification of the *monyomiji* who collected the poles as if they were enemy victims. The holding of the poles by the *monyomiji* during the planting ceremony establishes the desirable contiguity with the victims.

The inverse symmetry between the sacrifice of the pre-war single victim and the celebration of the postwar multiple enemy victims, underscores the fact that sacrifice and war share a common victimary logic.

The rain creeper

At the inauguration of a new shrine (p. 435) and in the early morning of the New Year festival (p.424), it is custom to tie the bundle of ebony poles of the shrine with fresh lianas of the rain creeper. Why the rain creeper? The watery inside of the liana explains its use in rainmaking. Cut, its fiber shaped into a brush, dipped in water and swung into the air, the rain creeper produces a fine sprinkling that resembles rainfall. The lianas of the rain creeper are also used to tie the branches of a high tree to wooden pegs fixed in the ground like anchors. When clouds suddenly approach and there is no time to prepare the rainstones, the ropes are pulled in such a way that the branches sway in the direction one wishes the rain to fall (Spire, 1905b:18; Spagnolo, 1933:299).

In 1861, when Peney and DeBono were the guests of Muludyang, the Bekat Rainmaker of Darjur, they slept under a tamarind tree that was used for this rainmaking procedure. Under the tree was a basket with earth and 'pebbles' (These must have been the rainstones.) in which three lianas were planted that went all the way up to the top of the tamarind tree. Muludyang claimed to be the inventor of this particular rainmaking device which he said was very effective (Malté-Brun, 1863:43–44). The rain creeper is also used in fertility and healing rituals. In Aru, people are made to pass under a rain creeper liana which has been tied between two poles before receiving the oil from the Master of the Land.

To understand the full significance of the use of the creeper in rain rituals, we should look at the Nilotic myth of the separation of heaven and earth. The basic plot of this widespread story is well known:

19.3 *The separation of heaven and earth* (basic plot of the Nilotic myth)

Long ago, people from heaven and earth had regular intercourse. They intermarried and danced together. There was plenty of food and women only needed to grind one seed of sorghum to give the household a full meal. Due to greed, over-diligence or the intervention of an animal hostile to man, the rope along which people travelled up and down was cut or broken and the present regime of scarcity and death commenced.

The Guardian of the community shrine of Kudwo has finished the New Year oiling of the implant of the poles and is devotedly holding the rain creeper that keeps the shrine, and the community, together in peace

In the translated recordings of the various versions of the myth, the nature of the rope is usually not specified.[10] In the Nyangbara and Kuku versions I collected, the

10 Spagnolo, 1933:271, Crazzolara, 1953:68; Evans-Pritchard, 1956:10; Buxton, 1963:19–26, 1973:2; Lienhardt, 1961:33–4; Zanen & Van den Hoek, 1987:170–197. In the Didinga version

rope between heaven and earth is explicitly identified as a *dölöngi* liana, that is, the rain creeper.

19.4 *The separation of heaven and earth* (Nyangbara–Kuku version of the myth)

The Nyangbara say the rain creeper grew on top of Mount Luli (1318 m., in the north of Yei River District). There had been a big feast in heaven and meat and bones were left near the rain creeper (*dölöngi*) that was fixed between heaven and earth. The lion found the meat and started eating it. He did not pay attention to the liana in between the heap of bones and accidentally bit it. At that moment heaven jumped up beyond reach. Forever.

We can now understand why the Bari and Lulubo Rainmakers tie the branches of high trees. By so doing, they restore the connection between heaven and earth and call forth the conditions of plenty that characterised life before their separation. It should cause no surprise that another Nyangbara myth tells how the 'rain hoes', which, in Nyangbara, take the place of rainstones, were brought from heaven by a man who descended along a rain creeper. It is to be anticipated that further research will confirm that the Bari Rainmakers who, according to a tradition recorded by Haddon (1911: 147) used to go up and down to heaven, must also have used the rain creeper as a ladder.

There is a negative counterpart to the rain creeper. The Bari and Lulubo believe that the rainbow is a reddish snake that from time to time emerges from a cave or an anthill. When it leaves its hole, drought follows and the rainbow becomes visible. While the rain creeper connects heaven and earth, the rainbow separates the two. The Lotuho version of the end of the age of abundance confirms this opposition between the rain creeper and the snake:

19.5 *The end of the age of plenty* (Lotuho myth)

In the past, not very long ago, the earth was covered with water and mud, and, therefore, uninhabitable. Only the highest peaks of the mountains were inhabited and that is where the first people lived. They were happy. There was no suffering and working was not necessary. For their living, they only had to pick the ripe fruits off the trees. One day, a huge snake (*namunu ajok*, the snake of god in his evil transfiguration) swallowed all the water and vomited it out in the north so that only a little water was left in the rivers and streams. On that day, man lost his primeval happiness and started to cultivate and suffer (Molinaro, 1940/41:181).

While in the Bari myth the celestial waters were once accessible to the people living on earth via the rain creeper, in the Lotuho myth the people, who once lived in a kind of heaven, lost access to the terrestrial waters as a result of the intervention of the god-snake. When on New Year's Day the pole-shrine is tied with the rain creeper, the act evokes not only the unity of the people but also that of heaven and earth. Water, the unifying substance transmitted by the creeper, not only mediates between

---

recorded by Kronenberg (1972:132), the connection between heaven and earth is specified as being a liana. In the Didinga story, the liana was bitten by a hyena after the first people had descended from heaven.

heaven and earth, but also between the different divisions of the community and between communities divided by war. Cosmologically speaking, there is a great deal of overlap between rainmaking and peacemaking so that the king's role as a mediator between heaven and earth effortlessly merges with his work as a peacemaker between the sections of his kingdom as well as with enemies.

A cosmology of violence and peace

Having established the relationship between peace and rain, we now examine some of the other cosmological notions employed in the New Year ritual. First, there is the already familiar notion of blood as a correlate of violence and the opposite of rain. The empirical evidence of blood is an important criterion in judging the seriousness of a fight, as the four cases of violence during *Odhurak* in Langabu demonstrated. Blood, including the blood spilt in giving birth, endangers the rainfall. Even if a homicide has occurred in the bush, the *monyomiji* may order for a purificatory sacrifice on the spot of the violence. Blood is highly contaminating. Encounters that may lead to violence must, therefore, as much as possible, be planned outside the village. In the escalation of tension around Queen Nyiburu of the Pari, the meetings of the *monyomiji* with the queen were held at increasingly remote spots in the bush. The discussions of the *monyomiji* on New Year's Day should ideally be held at a spot well away from the village. Only the *monyomiji* of Liria and Langabu observed this custom in 1986. Those of Liria went to a place more than an hour's walk away from the village and those of Langabu stayed relatively near.

The bush is the location of violence. Among the Lotuho and the Lokoya, the corpses of men who have been killed are left in the bush. If the body is taken home (for example, if death occurred on the way) it should be buried outside the fence, to avoid *aret*, the repetition of death in the family. The grave of the war victim is covered with *akadavi*, the thorny bush, also used by the Master of Bows to make weapons 'hook', to block the inauspicious emanations from a victim of war. Before the rains begin, a brother of the dead man is expected to purify the path along which the body was carried into the village, otherwise drought may follow. The same procedure is followed when men are killed in hunting. To avoid *aret*, one should avoid shaking hands with persons who have been speared and who are still living (or rather: still dying), and also with persons who have just successfully speared a person. The latter should stay outside the house, at the *obali*, for three days, and be purified (*avulyo*) either using his own hands or with the help of a brother.

It is, therefore, appropriate that the homicide should phrase his wish to be given asylum by the Rainmaker as a request for water (Case 10.1). It is also appropriate that the Rainmaker should first demand a goat to prevent his rainstones from being affected by the violence the asylum-seeker is associated with (*idem*).

The settlement of cases of bloodshed is also marked with the splashing of water. After the transfer of bloodwealth, the party of the victim and that of the victimiser perform the reconciliation ritual (Bari, Lulubo: *tomora*; Lotuho, Lokoya: *emwara*).

Each of the participants takes a sip of water from a calabash; rinses his mouth; and spits the mixture of spittle and water back into the calabash. When everyone has had his turn, the water is poured over the feet of the participants who are then considered reconciled. Meetings of the *monyomiji* in which conflicts in the community have been discussed are normally concluded with a ritual 'to unite the bodies' (Lulubo: *runi omiya*) by mixing and applying water and spittle in the same way.

The fundamental opposition between violence and order that finds expression in the elemental symbolism of water as the antidote to drought and violent division is replicated in other symbolic domains: in colour symbolism, sonic symbolism, somato-sensory symbolism, in the symbolism of body liquids, and in the classification of animals and plants. Finally, we shall see that in conceptualising the conversion from a state of violence to one of peaceful order, the people in our area of study make use of digestive and gustatory symbolism.

Colour symbolism

The standard blessing of the Master of Bows for the *monyomiji* who go to the bush to hunt or to confront the enemy is "Let your hands be red; let your face be white!" The colour red alludes to the blood of the hoped-for victims while white refers to the absence of obstacles in one's undertakings. Black, the third colour of the colour triangle, symbolises the obstacles that should prevent the enemy from reaching his goals. Black lines are drawn on the ground with charcoal to stop predatory animals, plagues or enemies from entering the village. Charcoal is also chewed to avert evil (Case 18.4). Black and white are two sides of the same beneficial action (Case 19.4).

In divinatory hunts, the most favourable omen for the rains is a black animal. Participants justify their preference for a black victim by the resemblance between the animal and dark clouds. Black is also the colour that averts influences that might impede the rain. There is a belief that Rainmakers have a darker complexion than others (Kronenberg, 1972:139). Bari Rainmakers used to blacken their faces with charcoal,[11] and many Rainmakers perform their sacrifices and say their prayers for rain in the darkness of the night.[12]

Rainstones may be white, black or green, and the stone that the Master of the Land dips into oil and presses on the stomachs of his people in time of famine, is black. During the New Year celebration (*Nyalam*) in Lafon, the junior age-sets rub black mud onto their bodies. I observed the same practice in Lulubo where it is done on an individual basis. Finally, we noted above that the stones used to close the grave of the slave-girl buried under the Bari pole-shrine were black and white.

---

11   On his march from Gondokoro southwards, Baker was guided by a Rainmaker whose face had been blackened with charcoal (1874, Vol. I: 45).

12   The son of Pitia Lugör told me that his father performed the rain sacrifice at night and in deep silence. The Rainmaker of Lafon makes his annual invocation for rain at night, the spear of Ocudo pointed upwards. King Okong of Tirangore confided that he used to pray for the new seasonal rains in the night of the 12th of March.

Somato-sensory and sonic symbolism

In the rhetoric of peace and rain, the opposition of 'hot' and 'cool', plays an important role. A 'cool heart' or a 'cool body' is a disposition free of envy, hatred and violence. A 'hot'-tempered Rainmaker is a danger for the community. The Rainmaker's body should be thoroughly cool, and indeed informants assured me that the handshake of the Rainmaker could be remarkably cold.

Victims are classified as 'hot' and 'cool'. A cool victim is cooperative. Its immolation does not cause violence, before or after the sacrifice. A female victim is 'cooler' than a male one. This was the justification given for the choice of a girl, bovine calf or female lamb as victim to be sacrificed under the Bari pole-shrine (*wore*). My suggestion that a male slave (*'dupiet)* could be taken instead, was brushed from the table, since a slave was a particularly 'hot' victim. Being involved in the cooking in the house, he, or his associates, could concoct a particularly violent revenge. Between the he-goat and the ram, the latter is the cooler animal and preferred for rain sacrifices.

The opposition between noise and silence is homologous to that between hot and cool. When the state of non-violence has been proclaimed (*edwar*), no unnecessary noise should be made. Drumming is forbidden and people who shout their praise-names (*mamare*) are fined. This silence is observed from the moment the crops are knee-high up to the time of the first harvest in July. The end of *edwar* is celebrated with a massive outburst of noise, people beating iron utensils against one another, drumming and shouting. Above, we quoted Jennings-Bramly's observation on how the Bari made rain by a sudden conversion of noise into silence (Case 16.14).

Sacrifices for rain should ideally be bloodless and noiseless. The suffocation and strangulation of the victim is frequently justified as a method to circumvent the gurgling noise of the dying animal. The same concern to surround the sacrificial animal with the least possible violence underlies the prescription that the animal should be roasted in its skin and that its bones should not be broken (Table U).

Blood is a body liquid that is bound to transmit harm if it is outside the body. It is the medium for curses. A man may invoke his own blood in pronouncing a curse over others: "Let my blood finish them!" Spittle fulfils the opposite role. It is the conductor of benign sensations between people. The spittle of the Rainmaker is considered particularly potent. It is sometimes used to bless the rainstones.[13] The first travellers were amazed about the eagerness with which people competed for drops of the king's spittle as was Powell-Cotton:

> …when Limoroo [Lomoro] wished to spit, many eager hands would be thrust out competing for the favour of being used as a spittoon, and the lucky one would rub it into his leg with every sign of satisfaction (Powell-Cotton, 1903:463).

The Verona fathers who travelled in the area as part of an exploratory mission in 1920 were also struck by the custom. The spittle of Ikuma, Queen of the Lomiya,

---

13   The present (at the time of the study) Lotuho Queen in Hiyala told me that she used to rub the stones with spittle.

was collected every time she spat, by a person in her following who rubbed it on the ground (Pedrana, 1921:110). This intentional application of spittle to the ground is the diametrical opposite of the bloodying of the soil by violence. The same opposition is found between the rituals of reconciliation in which spittle and water are shared from mouth to mouth and the avoidance of a handshake with a person — victim or victimiser — who has been in contact with violence.

The cosmological notions that have been passed in review can be summarised in the following list of homologous oppositions:

X.   Fundamental cosmological oppositions

drought	rain
heaven and earth separated	heaven and earth connected
rainbow/snake	rain creeper
hunger	food
hot	cool
red	black/white
noise	silence
blood	spittle
bush	village
predatory animals	domestic animals

All oppositions ultimately express the opposition between violence and peace. The king is identified with the qualities listed in the right-hand column. He should not go hungry and should be kept away from bloodshed and noise. In some areas, he should not go to war and the sight of blood is strictly taboo to him. When the *monyomiji* of Liria return from war and bring their booty to the king for redistribution, both the *monyomiji* and the king need to undergo a purification ritual. On the west bank of the Nile, this avoidance of violence was even more marked and Rainmakers were not expected to attend funerals.

The king has an intimate relationship with water. Some Rainmakers are said to have been able to produce water in their hands by merely closing and opening them; others are said to suffer from permanent perspiration. Pitia Yeng-ko-Piyong, as a baby, survived in a pool of water and needed a sacrifice before he became 'normal' and accepted the milk of his mother's breast. When King Oyalala was a cowherd, he only had to tap the earth with his staff for a pool of water to appear, even in the middle of the dry season when the land was parched.

While the Bari Rainmakers were associated with the heavenly waters to which they were believed to have access via the rain rope, the ancestors of the Lotuho and the Pari rain dynasties, Asang and Ocudo, emerged from terrestrial waters.

All dynastic ancestors are associated with cattle: Asang emerged from the water because he was attracted to their milk. The Bekat and Kursak introduced cattle to those who later became their subjects. And Ocudo created cattle to solve the conflict with the parents of the girl he had made pregnant. In the role cattle play in marriage, they represent the 'cool' alternative to the 'hot' conflicts caused by the contradiction between the rights of the husband and those of the father and brothers of the bride.

The bitter stomach of the king

With an understanding of the principal categories used by the participants to conceptualise order and violence, a last question is: how is the transformation conceived from one state of being to the other? What are the images used to define and interpret the conversion from drought and hunger to a state of prosperity, from a state marked by heat, redness and noise to a 'cool' state?

The principal metaphor used in our field of study to understand and articulate this transformation is the digestive process. The organs involved in human and animal metabolism, their functions and the different stages in the processing of that which has passed the mouth are used as signifiers.

In the course of this study, I have repeatedly touched on the stomach and on stomach contents (also 'rumen' or 'chyme') as ritual elements — the stomach contents of goats and cows being one of the most frequently employed ritual substances. When questioned on the reasons why the content of the animal's stomach was selected for purification, informants could never give me a satisfactory explanation except for the repeated statement that they were used to make things 'cool'.

I think a meaningful explanation is possible when we take the transitory character of the rumen as its ritually relevant quality. The rumen in its half-digested form is a substance undergoing transformation. It is still recognisable as grass but at the same time it is already on its way to be partly absorbed by the body, partly transformed into dung. It may be worth mentioning that the dung of domestic animals has many practical uses: as plaster in housebuilding, to close and cover wounds, as fuel and as manure. It is collected and exchanged or traded and not just thrown away. The 'trans-substantial' quality of rumen makes it particularly appropriate as a metaphor of a process of conversion from one state of being into another.

The circumstance that the stomach contents are taken out while the animal is still alive confirms this interpretation: if what people think to take out is 'processual' rather than substantial, it is better to remove it when the metabolic process of the animal is still intact. After its stomach has been emptied of its contents, the sacrificial goat is sometimes left walking about with its stomach open to die a slow death.

After the rumen has been processed by the successive stomachs of the sacrificial animal, it reaches the small intestines where it forms a milky fluid technically called 'chyle' (Lul.: *kele*). Chyle is used as the ritual vehicle of positive blessings, for example to boost a healing process. Chyme and chyle are metaphors of different stages of transformation. While the acidic chyme is used for the elimination of impurity, the chyle, product of a more advanced stage of digestion, is a catalyst of a process of positive transformation. The contrast in the sacrificial uses of chyme and chyle is homologous to that between the use of the watery juice squeezed from the wild cucumber (Bari, Lul.: *loroso*; Lok. Lot.: *orese*) in cleansing rituals and the use of vegetal oils used in blessing rituals.[14] At this point of the demonstration there is no need to emphasise that the master recipe of all these ritual operations is provided by the successive stages of negative and positive transference postulated by the scapegoat mechanism (Table 1.1)

Not only the substances processed by the alimentary tract are used in ritual, but also the organs of digestion. In Edemo, to make rain, the Panyangiri Rainmakers keep 'Ngulere', their leading rainstone, overnight inside the stomach of the animal sacrificed for the occasion. The intestines are used in, at least, two different ways. In rain divination, the position of the bowels give an indication of the blend of 'hot' and 'cool' forces at work at any particular moment. During the village *Nefira* of the Lotuho, the intestines of the sacrificed animals are made into rings and hung around the necks of newly initiated *monyomiji*. Their usage as an attribute and catalyst in the social transformation the initiates undergo confirms my interpretation that the ritual significance of the alimentary tract lies in its capacity to symbolise processes of transformation from a state of relative disorder to a state of order.

We can now answer the question why the stomach of a Rainmaker who has been killed for causing drought is slit open and why the Bari wait for the stomach of the dead Rainmaker to burst. If we take the stomach of the Rainmaker as the organ that converts social 'heat' into 'coolness', the community has an interest not to interrupt the process prematurely. The conversion process that takes place in the stomach is believed to continue after the moment of death — the bloating of the stomach providing empirical proof of this. It is, therefore, logical that the Bari should wait for the stomach to burst and consider the liquid dropping from it as a beneficial substance, a blessing ointment, since it is the final product of the 'cooling work' of the king. If the king dies in a state of anger, as when he is killed by his subjects for causing drought, his stomach that had already stopped fulfilling its expected cooling function, is assumed to work in reverse, converting coolness into heat. Hence, it is necessary to interrupt its ominous operation. Slitting the stomach open is one method of disabling its posthumous effectiveness.

The belief in the capacity of the stomach to work in reverse is also manifest in witchcraft beliefs. In a person of a peaceful disposition, the operation of the stomach neutralises 'hot' emotional states, 'cooling' them. But in an anti-social, resentful person the stomach is believed to be full of blood. The Lulubo say a wizard has blood (and also a snake) in the stomach and red eyes. The quantity of blood in his body is said to be larger than in normal people and he is said to dispense his blood in different places in order to harm his fellow human beings.

There are, however, situations when a 'hot' temper is socially desirable, when there is an imperative need to mobilise and exploit the raw violent energies. War is such a

---

14   A similar distinction in the ritual use of the two semi-fluid substances resulting from different stages of the metabolic process is made not only by the Eastern Sudanic Nuer (Evans-Pritchard, 1956:212) and by the Central Sudanic Lugbara (Middleton (1960: 96, 110), but also in Bantu sacrifice (De Heusch, 1985:201).

situation. An effective warrior is driven by anger and should not suppress his violent impulses. When the *monyomiji* of the Kworijik moiety of Lokiliri go to war, they perform a ritual that lowers the moral inhibition to the use of violence. They invoke the power called *Pirigaga*. *Pirigaga* was given to them by a Bari wizard who threw up blood from his stomach which was collected in a calabash and mixed with beer. The mixture was then swallowed by the men of Kworijik. When they tried its power out by touching a thorn tree, the thorns just became limp and the tree fell over. In the story of the acquisition of *Pirigaga*, the desirable 'cooling' function of the stomach had been inverted, the inversion being manifest by the vomiting of blood.

Before she was left behind in the bush, Queen Nyiburu's open cut in the stomach was rubbed with the fruit of the cucumber variety called *akaraja* by the Pari. The Pari classify the fruit as *böth*, "tasteless", which is the opposite of *kec* ("bitter"). Kurimoto's informants told him that the fruit was applied to neutralise the effects of *cien*, the posthumous anger of the queen (Kurimoto, 1992).

'Bitter' (Lotuho and Lokoya: *odwa*, Bari: *pötwör*, Lulubo: *angana*) and 'tasteless' are gustatory signifiers. 'Bitter' is one of the words most frequently used in referring to the power of the king. Contrary to European usage, the Nilotic concept 'bitter' refers to a quality of both the food as it is tasted and the organs signalling the taste. The core meaning seems to refer to a condition in which both food and body interact such that the effectiveness of the digestive process is maximised.

It is no coincidence that Rainmakers who have been cursed are often said to die as a result of dysentery. Dysentery is a condition in which the alimentary track has lost its grip on the ingested food, a state that is the opposite of 'bitterness'. It is therefore to be expected that the curse of a wizard intent on maximising the damage to a royal victim will target his stomach, the organ that transforms heat into coolness—the core function of the operation of royal power.

It is clear now why 'bitter' is a term applied to the power of the king. A king is bitter when he comes to grips with the problems of his subjects; when he contains the potential violence in his realm. His word 'bites' (using the etymology of the English word) if it breaks a deadlock in negotiations; arrests a process of escalating violence and gives new directions in a situation of confusion. The imagery used in the invocation at the installation of the Rainmaker of Ngangala: "we give the bitterness in our stomachs to you" (Ch. 18, p. 400) now also makes sense.

Conclusions

The New Year celebrations among the peoples of the Equatorian east bank of the Nile are no different from annual feasts of renewal in other parts of the world in that they stage a recreation of social order. The basic scenario is a sequence of unifying confrontations with evil forces outside, aimed at procuring victims, followed by a sequence of celebration of social unity focused on a positively transfigured victim-substitute.

In the bush, all issues that caused division in the previous year and that might occasion conflict in the year to come are settled and left where they were discussed. The new spirit of unity is tested in the hunt. The animal victims acquire a special significance in relation to the way in which the boundary between inside and outside will be maintained in the coming year.

The homecoming from the hunt is staged as a return to the age of undivided abundance. After the distribution of welcoming gifts by the women and blessings by the Masters of Disaster, the community dissolves into an indistinct mass joyfully gyrating around the community shrine, enjoying the beer of the new harvest and the company of the opposite sex, unhindered by the rules of property and exchange.

The central value expressed in the speeches and prayers is that of 'coolness of heart' — a state of non-violent togetherness undisturbed by hunger and disease. Coolness is not only a moral disposition in individuals but also a social and cosmological state of being. Rain is the principal cosmic signifier of coolness and the king is its main agent. The desirability of coolness and rain in the New Year finds expression in the tying of the village shrine with the rain creeper and in the spraying of water on the dancing crowd. The application of watery elements also helps in averting any upsurge of violence.

In the transformation from violence to order, from 'heat' to 'coolness', every member of the society has a role to play. 'Heat' is conceived as a primary condition which is transformed to 'coolness' by the digestive process. If the digestive process is inverted, violence and disorder will result. A wizard is defined by his inverted metabolism.

The effectiveness of this digestive process, whether for good or for evil, constitutes the 'bitterness' of a person — what one could call his 'sacred power'.

In the generation of coolness for the community as a whole, the king plays a central role, so that the bitterness of his stomach — and the anxious question whether it functions for good or for evil — is a public concern.

In terms of the metabolic imagery used here, the fundamental moral imperative of the societies in question can be summarised as: *do not upset the normal process of digestion of* heat *into* coolness *and of* blood *into* water.

King Muteesa of Buganda making a show of his capacity to unilaterally and irreversibly victimise his subjects (Chaillé-Long, 1876:106).

Conclusion

The scapegoat mechanism and Nilotic kingship

We have seen that Girard's scapegoat mechanism helps to throw fresh light on a wide range of phenomena varying from warfare and age-class organisation to regicide and digestive symbolism to conceptualise the operation of kingship regicide to the study of annual festivals. The strength of the concept is the postulation of a connection between collective aggressiveness, victimisation and social consensus.

Apart from providing additional proof of the hermeneutic value of the victimary mechanism, I believe this study also enlarges and refines Girard's theory on three points. First, it demonstrates that the scapegoat scenario should be seen as part of a wider range of phenomena of consensual antagonism. In defining the scapegoat mechanism, Girard based himself exclusively on contexts in which the victim, whether an individual or group, was significantly weaker than the victimiser. Processes of generation of consensus by means of victims ('*victimage*') are not limited to a majority/minority context. From a global historical point of view, there are good reasons to suppose that victimage between parties of unequal strength is only a special case of victimage between antagonists of roughly equal strength.

To account for cases where the strength of victimiser and victim is balanced, I have defined what I called the 'enemy scenario' which is more open-ended with respect to the sacralisation resulting from the scapegoat scenario. In Chapters Seven and Eight, I demonstrated that this model can be successfully applied to the analysis of the social organisation of the people who are the subject of study of this book. We also saw that the assumption of an underlying dualist structure in the age-class organisation resolved a number of analytical difficulties met by other researchers in studying comparable systems.

The enemy scenario also took us a long way in explaining the antagonism between king and people. The scapegoat king emerging from the pages Girard devoted to him is a ritual or theatrical figure who passively accepts the role attributed to him. Most of our Nilotic kings, however, were extremely active and enterprising men, keen on reinforcing their power, wherever they could, at the cost of their subjects and rivals. Girard's model one-sidedly accentuates the role of the king as victim to the detriment of his role as political entrepreneur and victimiser.

King and people in the societies we have studied were alternately victimiser and victim in relation to one another. The king's brinkmanship on the boundary between the ordered life inside and the human and natural enemies outside gave him a host of opportunities to victimise his subjects, or to credibly claim that he was doing so. Oral history repeatedly blames kings of the past for bringing the enemy home.

The king's role as scapegoat — in the narrow sense of a powerless individual who is blamed for many evils and eliminated in a common drive of the people against him — is subsumed in this scenario of reciprocal victimisation. Although the king's position was culturally defined as that of a victim throughout his royal career, he only became a real victim of communal violence under special circumstances. But, at least in the societies studied in this book, even as a victim, he remained active, resisting his killers to the end.

A second rejoinder to Girard's theory, coming forth from this study, is the observation that the 'live' elimination of the royal scapegoat does not necessarily produce a positive victimary transfiguration. Although the death of a king killed for withholding the rains is generally believed to result in rainfall, the violence of the death itself is feared to counteract the hoped-for effect.

The positive effects of the scapegoat mechanism are attributed to the dying of kings who passed away in a non-violent manner. In fact, an inverse symmetry between the two types of royal death and their respective consensual effects is postulated. While in the drive against the king *before* committing regicide an extraordinary sense of consensus is reached, a state of strict non-violence (*edwar*) is proclaimed *after* the death of the king who died a natural death. The opposition between the two types of dying was underlined culturally by the absolute non-violence imposed at the moment of the natural death of the king.

The two ways of achieving social consensus, that preceding regicide and that succeeding natural royal death have a different quality, however: one is inspired by the scapegoat mechanism, the other builds on the scenario of the aborted violence. One is 'automatic', the other imposed. Counter to what the scapegoat mechanism predicts, the negative transfiguration of the king-victim is, in our area of study, rarely followed by a positive transfiguration. The dominant mood surrounding the killing of the king is one of anger, anxiety and, if the rains do not fall, remorse. If they do fall, there are no demonstrations of gratitude towards to the dead Rainmaker, no positive transfiguration.

Being posthumously positively transfigured is the destiny of the king whose death was not provoked. His blessings are believed to be particularly vivid during the period immediately following his death. Because of the dead king's continued generativity, no successor was appointed until some time after his death.

A third rejoinder to Girard, closely connected with the former, concerns the mystification of the violence used against the scapegoat. Girard has repeatedly pointed at the moral contradiction posed by the fact that the scapegoat mechanism stops violence by making use of it. To make the procedure morally acceptable, the violence is often ignored or mystified, so that the members of society keep a good conscience about their cultural arrangements, and the scapegoat mechanism can do its work unhampered by moral objections.

The peoples on the Equatorian east bank of the Nile have solved the awkward dilemma posed by the violence of regicide by adopting two complementary interpretations of the scapegoat scenario: an auspicious, preferred variant staged in the funerals of kings who die peacefully, and an ominous regicidal variant practised in times of crisis when the discrepancy between the expectations that the people have regarding their king and the blessings delivered by him can no longer be bridged. His death is considered a just retribution for the harm the king has done. The mystification, in this case, does not hide the violence itself but consists in shifting the blame for the violence from the people onto the king.

There are, however, other solutions to this moral and logical dilemma. It is instructive to have a brief look at the way related peoples in the Nilotic Sudan have solved this problem. The ideal form of death of the Dinka Masters of the Fishing Spear, who are Rain and Peacemakers as well as incarnations of the divinity *Ring* (sacrificial flesh), is, according to Lienhardt (1961:298–319), to be buried alive. They make their wish known at what they consider an appropriate moment. Their burial is a festive event that draws a wide public. The scenario has elements that remind one of the regicidal scenes on the east bank of the Nile: the men wear arms, as if they are going to war. The atmosphere is described by Lienhardt as "a concentrated public experience of vitality and, in the Dinka world, aggressiveness" (*idem*: 317). In fact, at a certain stage during the ceremony, the young men throw themselves collectively on a calf — which, up to this moment, has been treated with much respect — and trample and suffocate it under their joint weight. The Dinka Master is victimiser and victim simultaneously. The grave is closed at his own request and before the Master is covered with soil, he solemnly sings songs from under the roof of the platform on which he is seated in his grave.

Social unity during the proceedings is marked by the effacement of all signs of status differentiation (no distinction between hosts and guests, between agnatic and affinal relatives; there are indications of former sexual promiscuity during the ceremony). The live burial is believed to keep enemies at bay and to have a beneficial effect on crops and health in humans and cattle.

The Shilluk also limit themselves to a single, auspicious, enactment of the scapegoat scenario on the death of their kings. They solve the dilemma by simultaneously minimising the violence of the act of regicide and generalising it to all kings dying a natural death. The practice, which is surrounded by some mystery, seems to be that the wives of the king suffocate him with a cloth when they expect the king is going to die. The ancestor of the royal dynasty, Nyikang, is believed to have been the first to suffer this type of death. According to a myth recorded by Hofmeyer, Nyikang requested to be suffocated when he noticed that his subjects wanted to kill him.[1] The

---

1   "Nyikang had to experience that his people did not know love, did not respect him and insulted him..... They made him tired of life and looked for an opportunity to put him to death — a death which he then gave himself. One day, he called all his people together for a sumptuous feast: it lasted for four days and uncountable numbers of sheep and oxen were slaughtered. The praise of the host was on everyone's tongue. On the last day a whirlwind arose and dispersed all the people. Nyikang used the opportunity to part with this life; he had his face tied with a cloth so that breathing was no longer possible" (Hofmeyer, 1910:330; my translation).

myth confirms our view that the minimal regicidal act of the Shilluk — which comes close to euthanasia—is a substitute for violent regicide. The killing of the Shilluk king is justified by the blessings it procures for his subjects. An ordinary natural death is believed to have adverse effects on the crops and the health of his subjects.

Contrary to Evans-Pritchard's opinion, according to which the stories about regicide among the Shilluk belong to the category of royal myth, I found that the custom is well attested in the literature,[2] not only for the Shilluk kings, but also for the related Shilluk-Luo (Santandrea & De Giorgi, 1965:27). According to my Shilluk colleagues in Juba, the custom has not been abandoned.

In the way they ritualise the dying of their 'kings', the Dinka and the Shilluk stick to an expurgated interpretation of the scapegoat scenario. While the Dinka solve the moral dilemma posed by the killing of the king by expecting their Master of the Fishing Spear to take the initiative for his being killed, the Shilluk divest regicide of its patently violent character by making the act of killing coincide with the natural death of the king.

In retrospect, the solutions of the Dinka and Shilluk add weight to my view that regicide and the royal funeral among the Equatorian Nilotes of the east bank are complementary interpretations of the scapegoat scenario, necessitated by the moral and logical difficulty of attributing a peacemaking effect to violence.

Dualism and centralism as alternative forms of political structure

I must return to the claims made at the beginning of this book. First, I stated that in the theoretical perspective defended here, the methodological necessity to make an *a priori* distinction between segmentary political organisations and centralised states as separate fields of anthropological analysis can be disposed of. If it is true that king and people interact in the same way as complementary segments in a system of balanced opposition, the theoretical distance separating political systems with centralised authority from those who lack such authority becomes small indeed. In Chapter

---

2   The first published record of regicide among the Shilluk is in a letter (dated 28 October 1842) by the French Consul in Alexandria to the *Bulletin de la Société de Géographie de Paris* based on his conversations with the explorer D'Arnaud who had joined Mohamed Ali's first expedition to discover the sources of the Nile. If the Shilluk king suffered from a mortal disease, the Consul reports, he was strangled by his female guards. The next testimonies on Shilluk regicide are from the missionary Beltrame and the trader Poncet. Beltrame, who visited the Shilluk capital in 1859, reports that when *Reth* Nyidok (*ca.* 1845–1859) was about to die, a few months before Beltrame's visit, he was finished off with three thrusts of a spear administered by a close relative. He was killed, the Shilluk told the missionary, "because it does not befit such a great Monarch to die a common death." Poncet, whose information must also have been based on the story of Nyidok's death, makes mention of the same mode of killing, three or four thrusts with a spear (Poncet, 1863:19). When he gave his Frazer Lecture (1948:10), Evans-Pritchard was not aware of these early accounts. The oldest testimonies he knew of were those of the missionaries P.L. Banholzer (Roman Catholic Mission in Lul) and J.K. Giffen (American Protestant Mission on the Sobat) who contributed to the Compendium on the Anglo-Egyptian Sudan edited by Lt Col Count Gleichen (1905, Vol.1:198).

Nine, I have adduced evidence that the relations between the people and its king are to a large extent structured as relations between enemies: exchanges of violence occur and negotiations are carried out by the same categories of intermediaries, while peace between both is sealed by means of marriage. In Chapter Ten, I showed that the maintenance of the unity of the kingdom is a function of the antagonism between the king to his people. Lack of respect for the king's powers and internal divisiveness are punished by disaster or by raids. In the last arrangement, the difference between the centralist punishments of the king and dualist punishments as, for example, the Lokoya practice of collecting unpaid fines by means of a raid by the *monyomiji* of the opposite moiety, is minimal.

The material presented in this book suggests that we have to take another look at systems of early kingship. Does the antagonism which we have discovered to be a structuring device in the political systems discussed above operate in the political systems of neighbouring peoples as well?

In two societies that are neighbours to our field of study and culturally closely related to it, the Shilluk and Anuak, the antagonism between king and people also receives overt expression, and has been the subject of anthropological debate. Frazer's famous image of the Shilluk king spending the night waiting for his rival "as a sentinel on duty ... prowling round his huts fully armed, peering into the blackest shadows" (1913, Part III: 22), is certainly exaggerated and romanticised. However, judging from early travellers' reports, the rivalry for the Shilluk kingship must have been intense. Brun-Rollet, who visited Shillukland in 1844, tells us that the king's palace was constructed as a labyrinth and that the king never spent more than two nights in the same apartment (1855:93–4). Beltrame, who visited the royal capital in 1859, reports that there were strong fortifications around the royal enclosure, which contained not less than sixty houses, and that fifty guards were stationed at each of its corners (1881:78).

The attacks on the king were organised by princes who were supported by a following recruited from their own village (Princes grew up in their mother's villages), section, and maternal kin. Evans-Pritchard gave the following, paradoxical interpretation of these rebellions in his celebrated Frazer Lecture on the kingship of the Shilluk:[3]

> Shilluk rebellions ... were made to preserve the values embodied in the kingship which were being weakened, or it was believed so, by the individual who held office. They were not revolutions but rebellions against the king in the name of kingship (1948:83).

Although Evans-Pritchard's intuition of the general positive effect of these rebellions is far-sighted, he underestimates the importance of the 'taste of power' desired by the rival princes. One of Seligman's informants assured him that he would be glad

---

3   Needham, for example, is highly appreciative: "an excellent example of sociological explanation" (1980:66).

to accept the kingship even if he were killed the next day.[4] Evans-Pritchard's widely acclaimed formula is in fact a *tour de force*: it is difficult to see, at least from the structural functional perspective that underlies the analysis, how subversion of a particular authority could simultaneously strengthen it. To make it theoretically possible for this to happen, Evans-Pritchard must make a distinction between the institution of kingship and the person of the king. This separation of person and office, the hallmark of bureaucracy, seems a far cry from the personalised rivalry that characterised succession in the pre-colonial Nilotic Sudan.

The model of centralist antagonism proposed in this book provides a less involved interpretation of the rebellions and their generally beneficial effect on the unity of the society. Lienhardt's interpretation of the frequent rebellions in the Anuak villages is much nearer to my point of view:

> The Anuak speak of *agem*, rebellion, with great enthusiasm; and it is possible even for a stranger to see eventually that it is by virtue of constant ostracism of headmen that the Anuak are able to avoid diffused and uncontrolled conflict within the village, and to rule themselves, rejecting any submission to the symbol of their implicit contract which they themselves have created (Lienhardt, 1957:32).

Consensus in centralist systems is generated in the same way as in dualist systems: by way of violent confrontations. In its simplest form, centralism is only a transformation of dualism with a different cast: one of the social segments is replaced with the king.

We have seen in Chapter Fifteen that the advantages of centralism, in terms of an increase in political and military strength of the polity, are by no means guaranteed. Because of the dualist oppositions between villages, moieties and sections, kingdoms easily fall prey to internal antagonism when princes vie for power. As a result, the strife between the segments constituting the kingdom exacerbates and the society is brought to the brink of self-destruction, especially if external allies become involved in the competition for power.

There is one society in the political laboratory of the Nilotic Sudan that appears to have turned its back on the centralist solution: the Nuer. While Nuer social structure has often been treated as an expression of a primeval sense of social equality, there are indications that their egalitarianism has emerged from a pre-existing situation that was marked by the same kind of inequalities that are found among their Nilotic neighbours. The office of the Master of the Land (*kuaar muon*)[5], for example, combines most of the attributes that among neighbouring peoples are the appanage of the Rainmaker or king: he offers sanctuary to men who want his arbitration in conflicts; he punishes with drought those who do not respect the terms of agreements or who are not willing to compromise; he is believed to have powers over the fertility of the land and also over rain; he wears a leopard skin in a similar way as kings elsewhere; he is an incarnation of *ring* in a similar way as his Dinka counterparts; and similar

---

4   In letters to Frazer dated 8 February and 9 March 1911, quoted by the latter in *The Golden Bough* (1913, Part III: 23).

5   In the literature frequently referred to as 'leopard-skin chief'.

to the Bari and Shilluk kings, he is buried in a recessed grave so that his body is not touched by soil. What makes the *kuaar muon* different from other Nilotic royals is that his responsibilities are not exercised over a domain which can be defined as a political unit; he does not even belong to the dominant clans of the political units in which he operates. His position is that of an outsider, an immigrant, and his relation to his constituency is defined as that of a mother's brother to a sister's son, that is, as a relationship which is per definition non-antagonistic. An obvious corollary to this is the fact that he is not killed. From the way Evans-Pritchard writes about the Nuer Master of the Land, it looks as if his informants systematically tried to play his political role down in favour of the dualist dynamics of inter-sectional relations–as if they were aware of the centralist power potential of the office.

The Nuer case within the Nilotic Sudan shows that dualism and centralism may, at certain times and under particular circumstances, have been alternative options. The Nuer brand of it was militarily very successful and allowed them to expand at the expense of these neighbours (Sahlins, 1961; Kelly, 1983, 1985). Between centralism and dualism, the former was not necessarily the type of political organisation that offered its society better chances for survival as simplistic evolutionist schemes might suggest. Between the Lotuho and their acephalous Toposa neighbours, for example, the balance of power repeatedly favoured the Toposa side, the rivalry of the Lotuho princes being one of the main causes of the relative weakness of the Lotuho.

The king, the sacred and power

When we study kingship as an ongoing drama rather than a particular mode of distribution of power or a system of beliefs, the political and sacral aspects of kingship can be accommodated in a single explanatory model. Chapters Nine and Sixteen, especially, showed that in the transactions between king and people, political and sacral elements jointly determine the position of both partners to the transaction. The relationship is, first of all, defined as a balance of power. When king and people are face-to-face they seldom omit to probe the degree of power possessed by each. The people look for signs of weakness in their king, and the king for signs of reduced respect in his people. If these signs are present, sooner or later reciprocal acts of aggression follow.

The relationship between people and king is also defined as that of a victimising majority to a victim. This dimension receives ritual expression in the installation ceremonies. When the country is hit by disaster or enemies, the king is there to receive the blame. In theory, he can be killed for each failure to maintain the community's immunity. In practice, the sentence is suspended as long as there is a possibility to restore the relationship between king and people. Moves to this end, which include procedures to appease the king and a range of rain rituals, are graded according to the effectiveness attributed to them, and deployed in accordance with the seriousness of the crisis. In this way, it is possible to build up the suspense of the confrontation over a considerable period of time, from the first respectfully phrased interpellation to the final assault on the king.

The ongoing relationship between king and people is at once a balancing of power and a victimary process. A politically weak king runs greater risks of being made a victim for the rain than does a successful one. On the other hand, rain power can become a formidable instrument in the hands of an ambitious king who is lucky with the rain.

The cosmology associated with the victimary role of the king orders the political and the natural world in a single projection. Taking the basic cosmological distinctions: inside-outside, before-after and good-evil (Table B.) as our template, we see that between each of the spheres defined by these oppositions, the king plays a mediating role.

Spatially, the king's position is coterminous with the boundary between inside and outside. Balancing on this boundary, the king maintains the separation between the violence outside, which may present itself in the form of enemies but also of disasters, and the order inside. This cosmological brinkmanship defines the king's role as supreme commander in war and as a sovereign controller of disaster, who lays exclusive claim to protecting a particular group of subjects. Negatively, his power is defined as the capacity to allow enemies and disasters to enter the community. Positively, he is the community's patron defending it against these dangers. The divinity attributed to him is his faculty of turning protection into destruction and vice versa. It is this faculty which plays a prominent role in the power politics between the king and his subjects.

On a temporal scale, the king's death is the lever of cosmological order. It is the central generative and rejuvenating principle in the local world view, tacitly assumed in all interactions between king and people. The possibility of the king's death gives direction to the feelings of anxiety and frustration in the community and so enhances its unity and resilience in the face of adversity.

On the moral plane, the king's input in the community is defined by his role in promoting processes of mutual understanding and forgiveness and the resolution of conflicts. The cosmological and political roles of the king are also merged here. The reconciliation of conflicting parties is not only the result of the practical talents of the king as a judge, but also the work of the 'bitterness of his stomach', the sacred effectiveness of which makes dissension shrink propagating a sphere of 'cool' consensus.

The state as irreversible centralism

I denied the status of *state* to the rain kingdoms of the Equatorian Nile. The principal reason for taking this stand was the fact that in none of the polities discussed in this book did the centre have an unequivocal monopoly on the use of physical force. The relationship between king and people was defined as a changing balance of power which depended on reciprocal acts of aggression. In Chapter Eleven, we examined the strategies the kings employed to consolidate their position in relation to their subjects. In Chapter Twelve, we saw that the balance of power had stabilised in ways that show significant differences in its territorial, economic and divine scope. In Lotuho and Bari, the king united villages in a wide area and collected a considerable amount of tribute, while in the other areas, the political units were smaller and, it seems, less exploitative as well. In Chapter Thirteen, we noted that the greater degree of centralisation of the Bari and the Lotuho was mirrored by a greater concentration of divine powers in the hands of the king. These facts led me to suggest that when conditions were favourable, the Nilotic kings used all the resources available — territorial expansion, tribute, and the propagation of the belief in their omnipotence — to increase their power at the cost of that of their subjects.

The coming of foreign powers to southern Sudan in the middle of the nineteenth century offered many new opportunities to the kings to reinforce their position *vis-à-vis* their subjects. Many kings made eager use of these opportunities: the trade intensified, armies were created; and alliances were sought with the invading superpowers. The kings did not need to be taught the way to statehood. Perhaps, if more time had elapsed between their incorporation in international networks of trade and the establishment of colonial administration, the balance of power would have irreversibly gone to the king, and a permanent apparatus of domination would have developed, as in many parts of Africa under similar circumstances. Kings would have become victimisers only and their subjects a reservoir of potential victims, as in some of the interlacustrine kingdoms.

Or maybe, things would never have reached that stage in the Nilotic Sudan, not because of a deep-rooted sense of egalitarianism that made the peoples in the area resist the spectre of the state, but because of their great taste for competition and their irrepressible belief that power and victimage should be reversible.

Appendix I:
Chronology of Key Events

also mentioning the presence or visits of observers who have documented past conditions and events

1841	The second Egyptian expedition to discover the sources of the Nile reaches Bariland and is received by King Logunu and Prince Nyiggilo of Bilinyan. The expedition is accompanied by the engineers Werne and D'Arnaud and by the trader — later French Vice-Consul—Thibaut. All of them report on their observations, Werne with a book of over 500 pages.
1853–1859	The Apostolic Vicariate of Central Africa is established by the Pope. The Mission Post in Gondokoro is built in 1853 but is already closed down in 1859. It made few converts among the Bari, but caused many deaths of disease and hardship among the missionaries. Revds. Beltrame, Kaufman, Kirchner, Morlang and Vinco have left accounts of their life as missionaries in Gondokoro.
1851–1852	Angelo Vinco, the priest assigned to prepare the quarters for the Austrian Mission carries out exploratory journeys into the interior. He stays in Bilinyan, Lafon (3 months), Southern Bari, and Loudo.
1855–1860	Protracted drought and severe famine in Bariland. King Nyiggilo is killed as a scapegoat of the drought (21–6–1859).
1856–1862	The race to discover the source of the White Nile brings many explorers to Gondokoro most of whom left reports on their observations (Duc d'Aumont, Lejean, Miani, Peney & DeBono, Petherick). Peney and De Bono stranded in Liria on an aborted trip southwards.
1860	The first inland trading post of the Egyptian firm Shenuda is established in Loronyo the capital of the Lotuho kingdom of Mayya. Shenuda's troops burn and plunder Liria in revenge for the murder of five of their soldiers. A joint force of *monyomiji* from Liria, Ilyangari and Ngangala carry out a counter-attack, killing 117 of the traders' troops as well as a large number of Bari auxiliaries. A similar, but even bloodier, scenario unrolls in 1863 in Imehejek whose *monyomiji* are reported to have killed 100 traders' soldiers and 200 Loronyo *monyomiji*.
1862	The outlet of Lake Victoria into the Nile is discovered by Speke and Grant who had travelled inland from Zanzibar. They returned via Gondokoro. Baker who had been sent to Gondokoro to meet them completes their work by exploring Lake Albert as a part of the Nile system.
	Making a detour to avoid the risky direct route through Southern Bari and Madi, Baker visits Liria and spends two months in Tirangore (Lotuho) on his way to the Bunyoro kingdom and to Lake Albert. His two volume travelogue (1866) on this trip becomes a best-seller.

1871	Samuel Baker, who has been appointed as Governor of Equatoria by *Khedive* Isma'il, formally annexes Equatoria to Egypt, selecting Gondokoro, renamed Ismaïlia, as its capital. When Bari, Lokoya and Lulubo attack Gondokoro shortly after the proclamation, Baker lays a prolonged siege to Bilinyan, the centre of resistance. His governorship is the subject of another two-volume bestseller.
1874–1876	Charles Gordon succeeds Baker as Governor. He builds a line of government stations along the Nile and moves the capital to Lado on the west bank of the Nile. Two government stations are established in Lotuho, in Ohila (kingdom of Mayya) and Tirangore (kingdom of Hujang). Gordon's death at the hands of the Mahdists turns him into a hero and martyr of the British Empire. Most of his papers and letters have been published.
	During his governorship, the Bari prophet Moyok leads an anti-government rebellion.
1876–1888	Emin Pasha succeeds Gordon as Governor of Equatoria. The first years of his rule bring about a degree of political stability. The commodities brought by the government steamers serve Emin to buy the loyalty of the chiefs who in turn use them to underpin their own power.
1882	The blockage of the *sudd* stops the supply of commodities and is an important factor in the disaffection of the chiefs. A cargo cult preaching that the *Khedive* will miraculously send steamers with fresh supplies of goods as well as another governor takes hold of the Nile stations.
1884	The conquest of Amadi by the Mahdists ('Ansar') is for Emin a signal to abandon Lado and move his command centre to Wadelai, the southernmost Nile station. To pre-empt a general rebellion he has Loro-lo-Laku, the most powerful Bari chief, beheaded before leaving Lado. Bepo, Nyiggilo's son, becomes the leader of a widespread anti-government rebellion which links up with the movement of the Dinka prophet Deng Tonj and later with the Ansar.
	The diaries of Emin Pasha are a rich source of information on the period 1876–1888.
1888–1897	When the *sudd* reopens, the Ansar finally arrive and conquer the government stations north of Dufileh (near Nimule). In Southern Bari the Ansar face strong resistance from an armed movement led by the prophetess Kiden. In 1891 she forces the Mahdists to withdraw to Bor. They only return in 1893.
	In Lotuho Lomoro Hujang is the key ally of the Ansar, in Lulubo it is Lualla-lo-Okale.
1897	The troops of the Congo Free State defeat the Ansar in the Battle of Bedden and occupy the government stations of Lado and Rejaf. These become part of the Lado Enclave (1897–1910) which is administered by the Congo Free State and includes the west bank Bari.

1898–1914	British troops occupy the east bank of Equatoria, one group entering from Uganda following the Nile and another from Mombasa entering Lotuho from the south-east.
	The east bank area south of the 5th parallel is annexed to the Uganda Protectorate. The area north of the 5th parallel is included in Mongalla Province of the Anglo-Egyptian Condominium. For a period of 15 years the Pari and the east bank Bari living north of the 5th parallel are under a different administration from the Lotuho, Lokoya, Lulubo and the southern east bank Bari. Only the Bari and Madi receive a degree of protection and administration from the Uganda protectorate. Their eastern neighbours are considered as only a 'zone of influence' meaning that the colonial authorities do not interfere in local politics, yet keep a keen eye on developments, a situation that results in a coverage of events by the British Administrators in Gondokoro and Nimule that yields interesting material for the anthropologist and the historian.
1914	The east bank Bari, Lulubo, Lokoya and Lotuho are transferred to the Condominium Government and are for the first time brought under effective administration. Torit District is established. The pacification of the Lokoya is particularly violent, each Lokoya community being served by its own sequence of punitive patrols.
1947	During the Juba Conference, convened to discuss the willingness of southern communities to join Northern Sudan in a shared independence, the Lokoya Chief Lolik Lado stands out as one of the few southern delegates to oppose unity.
1954–1956	During the transitional period of internal autonomy preceding full independence, hardly any of the government vacancies created by the departure of the colonial masters go to southerners.
1955	Torit Mutiny: the refusal of southern soldiers to be transferred to the North is generally considered the beginning of the first Civil War.
1955–1960	Guerrilla warfare against the new administration by a group of combatants consisting of mutineers and *monyomiji* operating in Torit District under the patronage of king Lomiluk.
1963–1972	The Anyanya is established as a united movement and coordinates the armed rebellion against the government in Khartoum. Much of the fighting takes place on the east bank of Equatoria.
1972–1984	The Addis Ababa Peace Agreement of 1972 gives a degree of autonomy to the Southern Region and creates an environment sufficiently safe for field research.
1983–1989	The Khartoum Government increasingly favours policies that undermine the autonomy of the Southern Region. In response the Sudan People's Liberation Army (SPLA) is formed in Jonglei. Around Christmas 1984 the Zendiya battalion makes its first incursion into Eastern Equatoria, recruiting large numbers of young men, especially from among the Pari. They are trained in Ethiopia. When they return as trained soldiers in 1986, they take over control of most of the countryside of the east bank of Equatoria. By the end of the 1980s all the communities that form the subject of this study are under SPLA control. In 1989 the SPLA captures Torit as the last government bastion in the area. For three years Torit will be the command centre of the SPLA.

Appendix II:
Linguistic affinity between the ethnic groups figuring in the text

N I L O S A H A R A N	**EASTERN SUDANIC**	E A S T E R N N I L O T I C — *Bari*	Bari Fajelu Kakwa (also in DR Congo and Uganda) Kuku Mandari (incl. Köbora, Böri, and Tsera or Shir) Nyangbara Nyepu
		Lotuho	Horiok (also Ohoriok) Lango (Dongotono, Logir, Lokwaa, Ketebo, Lorwama, Imotong) Lokoya ('Ohoriok') Lopit (Lomiya, Ngotira, Dorik, Ngaboli) Lotuho
		Maa	Maasai, Samburu and Il-Chamus (in Kenya and Tanzania)
		Karimojong	Nyangatom (also in Ethiopia) Toposa Turkana (Kenya)
		W E S T E R N N I L O T I C — *Dinka-Nuer*	Atuot (Reel) Dinka (Jieng) Nuer (Naath, also in Ethiopia)
		Lwoo	Acholi (also in Uganda) Alur (in Uganda and DR Congo) Anuak (Anyuak, Anywaa, also in Ethiopia) Jur-Luo (Jo-Luo, Bahr-el-Ghazal) Lango (in Uganda) Luo (in Kenya) Pari ('Lokoro') Shilluk (Chollo) Shilluk-Luo (Jo-Luo, Bahr-el-Ghazal)
		S U R M A — *Surma*	Boya (Narim, Longarim) Didinga Murle Tenet Tirma
		Nubian	Danagla (sg. Dongolawi), largely Arabised (in Sudan, Northern State)

NILO-SAHARAN	**CENTRAL SUDANIC**	*Madi-Moru*	Avukaya
			Käliko
			Lugbara (incl. Aringa) (mainly in Uganda and DR Congo)
			Lulubo (Olu'bo)
			Madi (also in Uganda)
			Moru
		Bongo-Baka	'Beli (Jur 'Beli)
	KOMAN		Uduk (in Blue Nile State, Sudan)
NIGER-CONGO	**UBANGIAN**		Adio ('Makaraka')
			Mundu
			Zande (also in DR Congo and CAR)
	BANTU		Banyoro (in Uganda)
			Baganda (in Uganda)
			Gikuyu (in Kenya)
	ATLANTIC		'Fellata' (Fulani, widely spread from Atlantic to Red Sea coast)
AFRO-ASIATIC	**CUSHITIC**		Oromo ('Galla'; in Ethiopia, Kenya)
	SEMITIC		Arabic, official language of Sudan; many colloquial varieties
			Nubi, creolised Arabic, also in Uganda and Kenya
			Juba Arabic, lingua franca in South Sudan

N.B. The names of the ethnic groups that are the focus of this study have been highlighted.

Archival Sources

Central Records Office, Khartoum

Mahdiya files
—Letter Ali Mukhtar Bakr to Khalifa, dated 13 Dhul Qa'dah 1310, Mahdiya files, I/32/9.
Letter Arabi Dafa'alla to Khalifa, dated 12 Jumada 1311, Mahdiya Files, I/32/48.

Foreign office correspondence
Correspondence respecting Abyssinian Raids and Incursions into British Territory and the
    Anglo-Egyptian Sudan. Foreign Office Correspondence, Abyssinia No. 1,
    1928:1–20.
Report by Governor Owen of Mongalla Province, Sept. 28, 1903, North East Africa and
    the Sudan.

Civil secretary files
 Equatoria Province Monthly Diary, November 1944. CIVSEC 57/20/43.
List of Lotuko chiefs d.d. 12/12/1918. CIVSEC II/44/1/1.

Intelligence files
— Letter from D.Z. Carré from Dufile, 1/2/1899. INTEL/5/5/49.
— Intelligence Reports Mongalla, 1905–1909. INTEL 8/2/13.
— The Bari and Berri, by H.D.E. Sullivan, Act. Gov. Upper Nile Province, Sudan
    Intelligence Report, Sept. 1906, Appendix B, INTEL, 6/4/23).
— Sudan Intelligence Report no. 98, 118 (INTEL 6/4/15), 138 and 224 (INTEL
    6/7/23).
— Mongalla Province, Monthly Diary, August 1909.
— Mongalla Intelligence Report, September 1909. INTEL 6/5/18.
— G. Donne, Report on Punitive Expedition against Chief Minge at Ilyangari.
    INTEL 91/57.
— Sudan Monthly Intelligence Reports, January 1915 (INTEL 6/8/25), 1916, and 1917
    (INTEL, 6/7/23).
— Mongalla Province, Intelligence Reports; July, August and September 1918.
    INTEL 2/48/408.
— Uganda Reports: Lotuko Intelligence Reports, August 1923 & March 1924.
— Sudan Monthly Record, 1933. I/3/80–91.

Mongalla files
— Monthly Intelligence Reports. Latuka District, Mongalla 1/4/27.
— Report on Punitive Patrol no. 14; Letter Bimbashi Beaumont, d.d. 9/12/1914; Report
    on the Lokoya Patrol by Governor Mongalla to War Office Khartoum, 31/1/1915,
    Mongalla, 1/2/6.
— Report Lotuko Patrol no. 19, Mongalla 1/2/8.
— Report Small Patrols Latuka, Mongalla 1/2/9.

Juba District Files
— Chiefs Evaluations, Juba District Files 1/1/2.

Uganda National Archives, Entebbe

Shuli correspondence
— Transport and Road Clearing Arrangements Nimule/Gondokoro. Shuli Corr. A/16/1, Inward, vol. I.
— Macallister, Sub-Commissioner Nimule Province, Report on Nile Province, 1902. Shuli Corr. Inward: A16/2/52.
— Brief Report on Journey from Gondokoro to Tarangole. Shuli Corr. A/16/2, 1902–03.
— Letter Sub-Commissioner Nimule to Commissioner Entebbe, 14/11/1903, Shuli Corr. A/16/IV/81.
— Letters Collector Gondokoro to Commissioner Nimule, 24/8/1904, 27//12/1905. Shuli Corr. A/16/5/1905.
— Gondokoro Monthly Reports, January 1905–October 1908. Shuli Corr. A/16 Vol. III.
— Letter Collector Gondokoro to Sub-Commissioner Nimule, 27/12/1905. Shuli Corr. A/16/5/1905.
— List of Chiefs on the Bari Dewan, 1905. Shuli Corr. A/16/IV.
— Bari District Reports for 1905/1906. Shuli Corr. Inward, A/16/III.
— 'Raid Lummelum on Rugun," File 67/06 Vol. I, containing a.o. Letter Fowler to Acting Commissioner from Camp Kiriloo, 15/1/1906, and letter Capt. Fletcher, OC Nile District to Sub-Commissioner in the field, Nimule, 9/1/06; Shuli Corr. A/16/5, 1905/06.

Secretariat minute papers
— Letter 1/11/1905. Agora and Tarangole Tour Escorts, Secretariat minute paper 67/06 Part I.
— Letter F. Spire to Commissioner Entebbe, d.d. 5/5/1906, Secretariat minute paper 257.
— Letter Sub-Commissioner Nimule to the Acting Commissioner & Commmander-in-Chief in Entebbe, May 8, 1906; Secretariat Minute Papers 257.
— Gondokoro Annual Report 1908/09 and Nile District Annual Report 1908/09. Secretariat minute paper 786.
— Letter from A/Collector Gondokoro to Collector Nile District, Nimule, 7/8/1908, Secretariat minute paper 1357.
— Letter D.C. Nile District to Chief Secretary Entebbe 12/1/1909. Secretariat Minute Papers 1357.
— Letter A/D.C. Gondokoro to Chief Secretary Entebbe, 21/10/1910. Arrest of Kenyi. Secretariat minute paper 1356.
— Monthly Reports, Gondokoro District, August, October and November 1910; Secretariat minute papers 189.
— Letter D.C. Nimule to Chief secretary Entebbe, dated 13/12/1910, Secretariat minute paper, 2092, B/13.
— 'Return of Capital Sentences in the Uganda Protectorate during the Year 1912', Secretariat minute paper 809/08.
— Northern Province Annual Report, 1911–1912, Secretariat minute paper 2135A.
— Monthly Report Bari District, July 1912, Secretariat minute paper 1859.

Foreign office correspondence
— Letter Macdonald to Foreign Office, 7/11/98 (Despatch 40); For. Off. Cor., East Africa
   Confidential, 26/9/1904, Appendix D, Enclosure 3.
— Letter Macdonald to Foreign Office, Debasien River, 9/12/98 (Despatch 44), For. Off.
   Cor., East Africa Confidential, 26/9/1904, Appendix D, Enclosure 5.
— Lt.Col Martyr, Report on the Nile District of the Uganda Protectorate. Enclosure 1, in
   Despatch 76 from Acting Commissioner Kampala; For. Off. Corr. East Africa,
   May 18, 1899.
— Map of Uganda, reproduced at Intelligence Division, War Office, from a map compiled
   by the Lt Col J.R.I. Macdonald, ass. by Maj. H.H. Austin and Lieut. R.T. Bright,
   from Surveys during the Macdonald expedition, 1897–1898 in: Brevet Major E.M.
   Woodward, 1902.
— Uganda Protectorate Intelligence Report no.23, For. Off. Corr., Inward, Vol. III, East
   Africa, 1899.
— Lt Col Macdonald, Report of his Expedition from the Uganda Protectorate, May 3,
   1898 to March 5, 1899, Africa, no. 9, (1899), For. Off. Cor., Inward, East Africa, 1899.
— Col J.R.L. MacDonald, 'Memorandum respecting Proposed Boundary between
   Egyptian Soudan and Uganda Protectorate, For. Off. Cor., 11/9/1902.
— Foreign Office Correspondence, North East Africa and the Soudan, Sept. 28, 1903.
— Foreign Office, East Africa Confidential, 1904, vol. II, Uganda Protectorate Intelligence
   Report, no. 21, App. C.
— Spire, Brief Report from Gondokoro to Tarangole, For. Off. Corr., East Africa
   Confidential, 24/7/1904, section 9, Appendix G.
— Letter by Wilson, Sub-Commissioner Nimule to Commissioner Entebbe. For. Off.
   Corr., East Africa Confidential, 24/7/1904, Appendix J.
— Jennings-Bramly, Report of Journey to Latuka and back, July 13 to August 3, 1903.
   Foreign Office Corr., East Africa Confidential, 24/7/1904.

Intelligence reports
— 'Notes on the Tribes in the Nile District' by P.W.Cooper, Uganda Protectorate
   Intelligence Report, no.28, Appendix 8, August 1906.
— Northern Province Monthly Reports, July 1911; Intelligence Report , no. 40,
   Appendix M.
— Annual Report, 1909–1910. Gondokoro Station, File 644.

Southern Records Office, Juba

— Beaton, A.C. (1930–34). Historical Notes on Bari Chieftainships, *typescript.*
— Richardson, Notes on Belinian, *typescript,* joined to Beaton 'Historical Notes on Bari
   Chieftainships'.
— Chief's Register. Reports on Chiefs, 1923, 1925 & 1933, File SCR/66.I/8.
— Mulla, E.K. (1955). A Report on '*Nefıra*' 1955, by the Executive Officer of the Torit
   Rural Council, file TRC/24.b.6.
— Rowley. Notes on the Madi, *manuscript,* E.P.66.b.42.
— Chiefs Appointments and Dismissals, Annual Report, Torit District, EP/57/3/1/2.
— Equatoria Province, Monthly Diaries. Sept/Oct. 1957. File 57/C/2.
— Reports and Correspondence on the Border Incident 26/3/1957; File 'Southern Corps
   Mutiny, pp. 65–72, 158–161.

— Letter Torit Committee to Minister of Interior, 27/11/1957; Letters DC Torit to Governor Equatoria, 2/12/1957 and 13/2/1957; File 'Southern Corps Mutiny', pp. 1211-1221.
— Juba District, Annual Report, 1958/59, File 57/E/3/1.

Torit district files
— Torit District, Annual Reports, 1939, 1954/55.
— Torit District, Monthly Reports, 1942.
— Torit District, Monthly Diaries. March 1948, March & June 1959 E.P.57/D/5/vol. I.
— Tribal Appointments and Dismissals of Chiefs', T.D.66; including Letters DC Torit to Governor Equatoria 26/6/1945 & 17/11/1945.
— Lafon Area Trek File, Reports on visits 5/4/48, 23–25/8/48, 13–14/4/49, 14/3/1975, Torit District Files no. 4.
— File on border issues Torit District/Eastern District, including a letter of the Governor of Equatoria Province to the DC Torit & DC Nagichot, July 11, 1952; E.P.66/B/41, vol. I.
— Annual Reports, 1939, 1954/1955, File 57/C/3.
— Annual Reports, 1957/58, P.H. 52. 57.E.3/1.
— Torit District, Monthly Reports, Sept/Oct. 1957.
— Torit Rural Council, Monthly Report, April 1960.
— Torit People's Rural Council, Monthly Report, January 1976.

Comboni Archive, Rome

Pazzaglia, A.
— La morte della capessa della pioggia 'Ikang' (Tirangore 1 Nov. 1938*), typescript,* A/26/11/3.
— Omuk eyabita to hobwok Otuho. *Typescript,* A/126/10.
— Il Capopioggia, A/26/11/3.

Muratori, C.
— Accalili, Lotuxo Rainmaker, *typescript,* A/126/4.
— Accalili the Lotuxo Rainmaker and his exhumation, *typescript,* A/127/17/4.
— Accalili, the Lotuxo Rainmaker, His life (1865c.–1944) and his exhumation (1945). *typescript,* A/127/17/5.
— Accalili, the Lotuxo Rainmaker and his exhumation, Observations made during the exhumation of Accalili. *typescript,* A/127–7/3.

Kirchner, M.
— Tagebücher, *typescript,* A/5:3.

Sudan Archive, Oriental Library, Durham

— *Reports on the Finances, Administration and Conditions of the Sudan,* 1908, 1909, 1912. Each of these annual publications contains an "Annual Report on Mongalla Province".
— Kenrick, Correspondence with his Parents, 1937, 647/5/1–91.

Published Titles and Theses[1]

ABRAHAMS, R.G.
1986 'Dual Organization in Labwor?' *Ethnos*, 1(2):88–104.

ACHTERHUIS, Hans
1988 *Het rijk van de schaarste, van Thomas Hobbes tot Michel Foucault*, Utrecht: Ambo.
2011 *Met alle geweld: Een filosofische zoektocht*, Rotterdam:Lemniscaat.

ABURI, Vitale
1986 Lotuko Dynastic History. *Typescript*, written for the present research, 5 pp.

ADELBERGER, Jörg
1987 'Sakrales Königtum und politische Macht.' *Anthropos*, 82:216–225.

ADLER, Alfred
1979 'Le dédoublement rituel de la personne du roi.' In: M. Izard & P. Smith, *La function symbolique, Essais d'anthropologie*, pp. 193–207. Paris: Gallimard.
1982 *La mort est le masque du roi, La royauté sacrée des Moundang du Tchad*. Paris: Payot.

ALBAN, A.H.A.
1923 'The Langu.' *Sudan Notes and Records*, vol. 5:49–51.

ALBERTIS, E.A. D'
1908 *Une croisière sur le Nil, Khartoum–Gondokoro*, Cairo:D.Diemer (Fink & Baylaender Succ.), Paris: H. Falque.

ALFIERI, Luigi
2008 'Le Tiers qui doit mourir: Aux fondements de la relation politique.' In: Anspach (ed.), pp. 91–97.

ALLEN, Timothy
1984 Acholi Decision Making, A paper for the Norwegian Church Aid Sudan Programme. Torit, *mimeograph*.

ALMAGOR, U.
1992 'The Dialectic of Generation Moieties in an East African Society'. In: Maybury-Lewis & Almagor, pp.143–169.

ANSPACH, Mark R,
1984 'Tuer ou substituer: L'échange des victimes', *Bulletin du MAUSS*, 12 (4) : 69–102
1993 'De la foule à la folie', *Psychiatrie Française*, XXIV, 3, pp. 45–53.

---

1   For readers who are interested in the theoretical perspective of this study I have included titles of publications touching on the application of mimetic theory in anthropological research that have appeared since Kings of Disaster first went to press 25 years ago. While general interest in mimetic theory has exponentially grown over this period, the share of social and cultural anthropological work in this growth has remained limited. New titles relating to the ethnography of the peoples studied have also been added. Because of the war that has continued for most of the last 25 years these are also few.

1995 'Le sacrifice qui engendre le don qui l'englobe', *Revue du MAUSS semestrielle* 5, pp. 224–47.

2002 *À charge de revanche, Figures élémentaires de la réciprocité*, Paris: Seuil.

2008 'Trying to Stop the Trojan War: Prophesying Violence, Seeing Peace, *Western Humanities Review*, vol. 62 (3):86–97.

2008 'Naissance du divin et psychose naissante.' In: *Intellectica* 50(3): 93–101.

2010 *Oedipe mimétique*, Paris: Éditions de l'Herne.

2011 'Imitation and Violence: Empirical Evidence and the Mimetic Model'. In Garrels (ed.): 129–154.

2017 *Vengeance in Reverse: The Tangled Loops of Violence, Myth and Madness*, Studies in Violence, Mimesis, and Culture. East Lansing: Michigan State University Press.

ANSPACH, M. (ed.)

1992 *Vengeance*, Special issue of the *Stanford French Review*, 16 (1).

2004 *Oedipus Unbound: Selected Writings on Rivalry and Desire (by René Girard)*. Stanford: Stanford University Press.

2008 *René Girard*, Cahier de L'Herne, Paris: Éditions de l'Herne.

ANTONELLO, P. & P. GIFFORD (eds.)

2015 *Can we Survive our Origins: Readings in René Girard's Theory of Violence and the Sacred*. East Lansing: Michigan State University Press.

APTER, Andrew

1983 'In Dispraise of the King, Rituals "against" Rebellion in South-east Africa". *Man* (N.S.), 18: 521–534.

ARBER, H.A.

1936 A Simple Lotuko Grammar and Lotuko Vocabulary. Juba, *mimeograph*.

ARENS, W.

1979 'The Divine Kingship of the Shilluk: A Contemporary Re-evaluation.' *Ethnos*, 44 (3–4):167–181.

1984 'The Demise of Kings and the Meaning of Kingship: Royal Funerary Ceremony in the Contemporary Southern Sudan and Renaissance France.' *Anthropos*, 79:355–367.

ARNAUD, Joseph-Pons d'

1842 '1ère Lettre de M. d'Arnaud à M. Jomard.' In: Jomard (ed.), 1842:376–379.

AUMONT ET DE VILLEQUIER, L-M-J, Duc d'

1883 'Du Caire à Gondokoro et au Mont Redjaif, Notes de voyage.' *Bulletin de la Société Khédiviale de Géographie* (Le Caire), Série II:191–202.

AUSTIN, H.H.

1903 *With Macdonald in Uganda, A Narrative Account of the Uganda Mutiny and Macdonald's Expedition in the Uganda Protectorate and the Territories to the North*. London: Edward Arnold.

AVUA, L.

1968 'Droughtmaking among the Lugbara.' *Uganda Journal*, 32(1)29–38.

BAKER, SAMUEL WHITE

1866 *The Albert N'Yanza: Great Basin of the Nile and Explorations of the Nile Sources*, 2 vols. London: MacMillan.

1874 *Ismailia, A Narrative of the Expedition to Central Africa for the Suppression of the Slave Trade*, 2 vols. London: MacMillan.

BANTON, Michael (ed.)
1965 *Political Systems and the Distribution of Power.* A.S.A. Monographs 2, London, etc.: Tavistock.

BARTH, Fredrik
1959 *Political Leadership among Swat Pathans.* London: Athlone Press.

BATESON, G.
1972 *Steps to an Ecology of Mind, Collected essays in anthropology, psychiatry, evolution, and epistemology.* Chicago: University of Chicago Press.

BAUDRILLARD, Jean
1977 *Oublier Foucault,* Paris: Éditions Galilée; translated as *Forget Foucault,* 2007, Semiotext(e). Cambridge (MA) and London: MIT Press.

BAXTER, P.T.W. & A. BUTT.
1952 *The Azande, and Related Peoples in the Anglo-Egyptian Sudan and Belgian Congo.* London: International African Institute.

BAXTER, P.T.W. & U. ALMAGOR (eds.)
1978 *Age, Generation and Time: Some Features of East African Age Organization.* London: C. Hurst & Company.

BEATTIE, J. & G. LIENHARDT (eds.)
1975 *Studies in Social Anthropology.* Oxford: Clarendon.

BEATON, A.C.
1932 'Bari Studies.' *Sudan Notes and Records,* 15(1)63–95.
1934 'A Chapter in Bari History, The History of Shindiru, Bilinian and Mögiri.' *Sudan Notes and Records,* 17(2)169–200.
1936 'The Bari: Clan and Age-Class Systems.' *Sudan Notes and Records,* 19(1)109–145.

BEDRI, I.
1939 'Notes on Dinka Beliefs in their Heriditary Chiefs and Rainmakers.' *Sudan Notes and Records* 22(1)125–131.
1948 'More Notes on the Padang Dinka', *Sudan Notes and Records,* 29 (1):40–57.

BEEK, Wouter van (ed.)
1988 *Mimese en geweld: Beschouwingen over het werk van René Girard,* Kampen: Kok-Agora.

BEHBEHANI, Abbas M.
1983 'The Small-pox Story: Life and Death of an Old Disease[1]. *Microbiological Reviews,* Dec. 1983:455–509:464.

BEIDELMAN, T.G. (ed.)
1971 *The Translation of Culture.* London: Tavistock.

BELTRAME, G.
1881 *Il Fiume Bianco e i Dinka,* Memorie. Verona: G. Civelli.

BESWICK, Stephanie
2010 'The Nineteenth Century Rise and Fall of the Bari: War, Local Trade and the
    Destruction of the Bari'. In: Spaulding, J, S. Beswick, C. Fluehr-Lobban & R.A.
    Lobban Jr. (Eds.), pp. 177–200.

BINSBERGEN, W.M.J. van
1992 *Tears of Rain: Ethnicity and history in western central Zambia.* London & Boston:
    Kegan Paul International.
2003 *Intercultural Encounters: African and anthropological lessons towards a philosophy of
    interculturality.* Berlin etc.: LIT.
2004 '"Then give him to the crocodiles": Violence, state formation, and cultural
    discontinuity in west central Zambia, 1600–2000.' In: Van Binsbergen (ed.) *The
    Dynamics of Power and the Rule of Law: Essays on Africa and Beyond, in Honour of Emile
    Adriaan B. Van Rouveroy,* pp. 197–219. Münster, etc.: LIT.

BOCCASSINO, R.
1951 'Il contributo delle antiche fonte sulla religione dei Latuca, Obbo, Bari, Beri, Denca,
    Neer e altre popolazioni.' *Annali Lateranensi,* 15:9–52.
1966 'Il sacrificio umano praticato dagli Acioli dell'Uganda e da altri popoli nilotici e
    nilo-camiti.' *Anthropos* 61:637–678.

BOON, J.
1983 'Functionalists write too: Frazer/Malinowski and the Semiotics of the Monograph.'
    Semiotica, 46, 2–4:131–149.

BREIDLID, Anders (ed.)
2014 *A Concise History of South Sudan.* Kampala: Fountain Publishers.

BROWN, J.
1984 'Report on Agricultural Practices in Yei River District', Report, Regional Ministry of
    Agriculture and Project Development Unit, Juba.

BRUN-ROLLET, A.
1855 *Le Nil Blanc et le Soudan, Etudes sur l'Afrique Centrale, Moeurs et Coûtumes des
    Sauvages.* Paris: Librairie de L. Maison.

BUCHTA, Richard
1881 'Meine Reise nach den Nil-Quellen im Jahre 1878.' *Petermann's Mittheilungen,*
    27:81–89.

BUET, Charles
1887 *Les premiers explorateurs français du Soudan Équatorial, Alexandre Vaudey, Ambroise et
    Jules Poncet.* Paris: Letouzey et Ané.

BURENG NYOMBE, G.V.
2007 *Some Aspects of Bari History: A Comparative Linguistic and Oral History
    Reconstruction.* Nairobi: University of Nairobi Press.

BURKERT, Walter
1983 *Anthropologie des religiösen opfers, Die Sakralisierung der Gewalt,* München: Carl
    Friedrich von Siemens Stiftung.
1986 *Homo Necans, The Anthropology of Ancient Greek Sacrificial Ritual and Myth.* Berkely,
    etc. University of California Press.

BURTON, J.W.
1976 'Death by suffocation'. *Man* NS, Vol.11: 388–391.
1981 *God's Ants, A Study of Atuot Religion*. St. Augustin: Anthropos Institute.

BUTT, A.
1952 *The Nilotes of the Anglo-Egyptian Sudan and Uganda*. Ethnographic Survey of Africa, London: International African Institute.

BUXTON, Jean C.
n.d. The Bari: Social and Political Structure. *Typescript* kept at the Institute of Social Anthropology in Oxford.
1963 *Chiefs and Strangers, A Study in Political Assimilation among the Mandari*. Oxford: Clarendon.
1973 *Religion and Healing in Mandari*. Oxford: Clarendon Press.
1975 'Initiation and Bead-sets in Western Mandari.' In: J. Beattie & G. Lienhardt (eds.), 1975:310–327.

CAILLOIS, R.
1950 *L'homme et le sacré*, 3rd edition. Paris: Gallimard.

CASATI, G.
1891 *Zehn Jahre in Aequatoria und die Rückkehr mit Emin Pascha*, 2 vols. Bamberg: Buchner.

CASTELLI, Enrico
1987 'Bari Statuary, the influences exerted by European traders on the traditional production of figured objects', *RES: Anthropology and Aesthetics*, No. 14, pp. 86–106.

CHAILLÉ-LONG, C.
1876 *Central Africa: Naked Truths of Naked People, An Account of the Expedition to the Lake Victoria Nyanza and the Makraka Niam Niam, West of the Bahr-el-Abiad (White Nile)*. London: Sampson Low, Marston, Searle & Rivington.

CLAESSEN, H.J.M.
1987 'Kings, Chiefs, and Officials: the Political Organization of Dahomey and Buganda Compared'. *Journal of Legal Pluralism*, nrs. 25 & 26: 203–241.

CLAESSEN, H.J.M. (ed.)
1988. 'Variant Views. Five Lectures from the Perspective of the "Leiden Tradition" in Cultural Anthropology' *ICA Publications*, 84, Leiden: Instituut voor Culturele Antropologie.

CLAESSEN, H.J.M. & P. SKALNIK (eds.)
1978 *The Early State*. The Hague: Mouton.
1981 *The Study of the State*. The Hague: Mouton.

CLASTRES, Pierre
1974 *La société contre l'état*, Paris: Minuit.

COLE, W.E.R.
1910 'African Rain-making Chiefs, the Gondokoro District, White Nile, Uganda.' *Man*, 10(49)90–92.

COLLINS, Brian
2014 *The Head beneath the Altar: Hindu Mythology and the Critique of Sacrifice*, East Lansing: Michigan State University Press.

COLLINS, Robert.
1962 *The Southern Sudan, 1883–1898, A Struggle for Control*, New Haven: Yale University Press.
1968 *King Leopold, England, and the Upper Nile*, New Haven: Yale University Press.
1971 *Land beyond the Rivers: The Southern Sudan, 1898–1918*, New Haven: Yale University Press.
1983 *Shadows in the Grass: Britain in the Southern Sudan*, 1918–1956, New Haven: Yale University Press.
2008 *A History of Modern Sudan*, Cambridge: Cambridge University Press.

COMAROFF, J.L. & S. ROBERTS
1981 *The Cultural Logic of Dispute in an African Context*, Chicago & London: University of Chicago Press.

COOKE, R.C. & A.C. BEATON.
1939 'Bari and Fur Rain Cults and Ceremonies.' *Sudan Notes and Records*, 22(1)191–193.

CRABITÈS, Pierre
1933 *Gordon, the Sudan and Slavery*, London: Routledge.

CRAZZOLARA, J.P.
1950 *The Lwoo*, Part I, 'Lwoo Migrations'. Verona: Missioni Africane.
1951 *The Lwoo*, Part II, 'Lwoo Traditions'. Verona: Missioni Africane.
1954 *The Lwoo*, Part III, 'Lwoo Clans'. Verona: Missioni Africane.

CUNNINGHAM, J.F.
1905 *Uganda and its Peoples, Notes on the Protectorate of Uganda especially the Anthropology and Ethnology of the Indigenous Races.* London: Hutchinson & Co.

CUNNISON, I. & W. JAMES (eds.)
1972 *Essays in Sudan Ethnography, presented to Sir Edward Evans-Pritchard.* London: Hurst.

DAHRENDORF, R.
1957 *Soziale Klassen und Klassenkonflikt in der modernen Gesellschaft.* Stuttgart.

DE BONO, ANDREA
1862 Voyage au Fleuve Blanc, *Nouvelles Annales des Voyages*. No. 3:5–38.

DIELS, Hermann,
1957 *Die Fragmente der Vorsokratiker*, (Nach der von Walter Kraus herausgegebenen achten Auflage), Hamburg: Rowohlt.

DEGUY, M. & J-P. DUPUY, Jean-Pierre
1982 *René Girard et le Problème du Mal*, Paris: Grasset.

DONALDSON-SMITH, A.
1900 'An Expedition between Lake Rudolf and the Nile.' *The Geographical Journal*, 16:600–625.

DOUGLAS, M.

1978 'Judgments on James Frazer.' *Daedalus,* winter:151–164.

DOUIN, G.

1936–41*Histoire du Règne du Khédive Ismail,* 3 vols. Cairo: La Société Royal de Géographie d'Egypte.

DRIBERG, J.H.

n.d. Further little known tribes of the South Eastern Sudan. *Typescript* kept at the Institute of Social Anthropology, Oxford.

1919 'Rainmaking among the Lango.' *Journal of the Royal Anthropological Society.* 49:52–73.

1923 *The Lango, A Nilotic Tribe of Uganda.* London: T.F. Unwin.

1925 'Lafon Hill.' *Sudan Notes and Records,* 16:47–57.

1930 *People of the Small Arrow.* London: George Routledge & Sons.

1932 'Lotuko Dialects.' *American Anthropologist,* 34: 601–609.

1939 'Clan Functionaries.' *Journal of the Royal African Society,* 38(150)65–74.

DUMOUCHEL, P. & J-P. DUPUY (eds.)

1985 *Violence et Vérité, Colloque de Cerisy, Autour de René Girard,* Paris: Grasset.

DUMOUCHEL, Paul

1999 *Émotions: Essai sur le corps et je social,* Le Plessis-Robinson: Synthélabo pour le progrès de la connaissnce.

2011 *Le sacrifice inutile, Essai sur la violence politique,* Paris: Flammarion.

2014 *The Ambivalence of Scarcity and Other Essays.* East Lansing: Michigan State University Press.

2014 'From Scapegoat to God'. In: Dumouchel, 2014, pp. 259–273

2015 'A Covenant among Beasts: Human and Chimpanzee Violence in Evolutionary Perspective'. In: Antonello & Gifford, pp.3–24.

DUPUY, Jean-Pierre

1982 *Ordres et désordre, Enquête sur un nouveau paradigme,* Paris: Seuil.

2003 *La panique,* Paris: Les Empêcheurs de penser en rond.

2008 *La marque du sacré,* Paris: Carnets Nord.

2008 *Dans l'oeil du cyclone, Colloque de Cérisy,* Paris: Carnets Nord.

DURKHEIM, Émile

1893 *De la division du travail social: étude sur l'organisation des societies supérieures,* Paris: Felix Alcan.

1912 *Les formes élementaires de la vie religieuse, Le système totémique en Australie,* Paris: Félix Alcan.

1915 *The Elementary Forms of Religious Life.* London: George Allen & Unwin.

DURKHEIM, Émile & Marcel MAUSS

1963 *Primitive Classification,* translated by Rodney Needham. London: Cohen and West.

DYSON-HUDSON, N.

1966 *Karimojong Politics.* Oxford: Clarendon Press.

EHRET, Christopher
1974 *Ethiopians and East Africans, The Problem of Contacts.* Nairobi: East African
    Publishing House.
1982 'Population Movement and Culture Contact in the Southern Sudan, c. 3000 BC
    to AD 1000: A Preliminary Linguistic Overview.' In: J. Mack & P. Robertshaw (eds.),
    1982:19–48.

EKHOLM, Kajsa,
1972 *Power and Prestige, The Rise and Fall of the Kongo Kingdom.* Uppsala: Skriv Service
    AB.

ELIAS, Michael
1995 'Neck-Riddles in Mimetic Theory: The Two Faces of the Scapegoat'. *Contagion
    Journal of Violence, Mimesis and Culture* 2(1):189–202.

ELIAS, M. & A. LASCARIS (eds.)
2011 *Rond de crisis: Reflecties vanuit de Girard Studiekring.* Amere: Parthenon

ELIAS, M. & R.REIS (eds.)
1998 *Getuigen ondanks zichzelf. Voor Jan-Mathijs Schoffeleers bij zijn zeventigste verjaardag,*
    Maastricht; Shaker Publishing.

ELIOT, C.N.E.
1902 'Notes of a Journey through Uganda, down the Nile to Gondokoro.' *The
    Geographical Journal,* 20(6)611.

EMIN PASCHA
1882 'Reisen im Osten des Bahr-el-Djebel, März bis Mai 1881.' *Petermann's Mittheilungen,*
    Heft VII:259–272 & Heft IX:321–329.
1888 *Eine Sammlung von Reisebriefen und Berichten Dr. Emin Pascha's aus der ehemals
    Aegyptischen Aequatorialprovinzen und deren Grenzländern,* herausgegeben von G.
    Schweinfurth & F. Ratzel. Leipzig: F.M. Brockhaus.
1894 'Land und Leute in Latuka.' In: Stuhlmann, 1894:774–802.
1917–27 *Die Tagebücher von Dr. Emin Pascha* (edited by Franz Stuhlmann), 5 volumes.
    Berlin, Braunschweig & Hamburg: Georg Westermann.

EVANS-PRITCHARD, E.E.
1940a 'The Relationship between the Anuak and the Föri (Sudan).' *Man,* No. 62, April
    1940:54–55.
1940b *The Nuer: A Description of the Modes of Livelihood and Political Institutions of a
    Nilotic People.* Oxford: Clarendon Press.
1940c *The Political System of the Anuak of the Anglo-Egyptian Sudan.* London: London
    School of Economics, Monographs on Social Anthropology no. 4.
1947 'Further Observations on the Political System of the Anuak.' *Sudan Notes and
    Records,* 27: 62–97.
1948 *The Divine Kingship of the Shilluk of the Nilotic Sudan.* Cambridge: University Press.
1971 'Reigning and Ruling.' *Man* (N.S.) 6:117–118.

FALLERS, L.A. (ed.)
1964 *The King's Men: Leadership and Status in Buganda on the Eve of Independence,*
    London, Oxford, Nairobi: Oxford University Press.

FORTES, M. & E.E. EVANS-PRITCHARD (eds.)
1940 *African Political Systems*, London, etc.: Oxford University Press.

FOUCAULT, Michel
1991 'Governmentality', Lecture delivered at the Collège de France, February1978. In: *The Foucault Effect, Studies in Governmentality*, edited by G.Burchell, C.Gordon and P. Miller. Chicago: Chicago University Press, pp. 87–104

FRANKFORT, Henri
1978 *Kingship and the Gods, A Study of Ancient Near Eastern Religion as the Integration of Society and Nature*. Chicago & London: University of Chicago Press.

FRAZER, J.G.
1913 *The Golden Bough, A Study in Magic and Religion*, 13 Volumes. London: MacMillan.

FROBENIUS, Leo V.
1923 *Das unbekannte Afrika, Aufhellung der Schicksale eines Erdteils*, München, C. H. Becksche Verlagsbuchhandlung.

FROST, J.W.
1974 A History of the Shilluk of the Southern Sudan. *PhD. Thesis*, University of California, Santa Barbara.

FUKUI, K. & J. MARKAKIS (eds.)
1994 *Ethnicity and Conflict in the Horn of Africa*. London: James Currey; Nairobi: E.A.E.P., Kampala: Fountain Publishers; Athens: Ohio University Press.

GANS, Eric
1981 *The Origin of Language, A Formal Theory of Representation*. Berkeley, etc.: University of California Press.
1985 *The End of Culture, Toward a Generative Anthropology*. Berkeley, etc.: University of California Press.
2008 *The Scenic Imagination: Originary Thinking from Hobbes to the Present Day*. Stanford: Stanford University Press.

GARRELS, Scott R.(ed.)
2011 *Mimesis and Science: Empirical Research on Imitation and the Mimetic Theory of Culture*. East Lansing: Michigan State University Press.

GELLNER, E.
1969 *Saints of the Atlas*. London: Weidenfeld.

GESCHIERE, Peter
1995 *Sorcellerie et politique en Afrique, La viande des autres*, Paris: Kharthala.

GEYER, F.X.
1914 *Durch Sand, Sumpf und Wald: Missionsreisen in Zentral Afrika*. Freiburg im Breisgau: Herder.

GIRARD, René
1961 *Mensonge romantique et vérité romanesque*, Paris: Grasset.
1970 'Une analyse d'Oedipe Roi', *Critique Sociologique et Critique Psychanalytique*, pp. 127–163, Brussels: Institut de Sociologie, Université Libre de Bruxelles.

1972 *La Violence et le sacré*. Paris: Grasset.

1977 *Violence and the Sacred* (translation by Patrick Gregory). Baltimore & London: Johns Hopkins University Press.

1978 *Des choses cachées depuis la fondation du monde, Recherches avec Jean-Michel Oughourlian et Guy Lefort*, Paris: Grasset.

1982 *Le bouc émissaire*, Paris: Grasset.

1987 *Things hidden since the foundation of the world* (with Jean-Michel Oughourlian and Guy Lefort; translated by S. Bann and M. Metteer). East Lansing: Michigan University Press.

1989 *The Scapegoat*. Baltimore: Johns Hopkins University Press.

2002 *La Voix méconnue du réel, Une théorie des mythes archaïques et modernes*, Paris: Grasset

2003 *Le sacrifice*, Paris: Bibliothèque nationale de France.

2004a *Oedipe Unbound, Selected Writings on Rivalry and Desire*, Edited and with an Introduction by Mark R. Anspach. Stanford: Stanford University Press.

2004b *Les origines de la culture, Entretiens avec Pierpaolo Antonello and João Cezar De Castro Rocha*, Paris: Desclée Brouwer.

2007a *Evolution and Conversion: Dialogues on the Origins of Culture*: by René Girard, Pierpaolo Antonello and João Cezar De Castro Rocha. New York: Continuum International.

2007b *De la violence à la divinité*, Paris: Grasset (including Girard's first four books: Girard, 1961, 1972, 1978 and 1989, with a new introduction by the author).

GIRLING, F.K.

1960 *The Acholi of Uganda*. Colonial Research Studies No. 30. London: Her Majesty's Stationery Office.

GITHIGE, R.M.

1978 'The Religious Factor in Mau Mau with Particular Reference to Mau Mau Oaths.' *M.A. thesis*, University of Nairobi.

GLEICHEN Count

1905 *The Anglo-Egyptian Sudan: A Compendium Prepared by Officers of the Sudan Government*, 2 vols. London: Harrison & Sons.

GLUCKMANN, M.

1954 *Rituals of Rebellion in South-East Africa*. The Frazer Lecture for 1952. Manchester: University Press.

GOODALL, J.

1986 *The Chimpanzees of Gombe*. Boston: Houghton Mifflin Publishing.

GOODHART, S., J. JORGENSEN, T. RYBA & J.G.W. WILLIAMS (eds.)

2009 *For René Girard, Essays in Friendship and Truth*. East Lansing: Michigan State University Press

GORDON, C. G. (edited by M.F. Shukry)

1953 *Equatoria under Egyptian rule. The unpublished correspondence of Col C.G. Gordon with Ismail, Khedive of Egypt and the Sudan, during the years 1874–1876*, edited by M.F. Shukry. Cairo: Cairo University Press.

GOULDNER, Alvin W.
1960 'The Norm of Reciprocity: a Preliminary Statement', *American Sociological Review*, 25 (2):161–178.

GRAEBER, David,
2011 'The divine kingship of the Shilluk: On violence, utopia, and the human condition, or, elements for an archaeology of sovereignty.' *HAU, Journal of Ethnographic Theory*, www.haujournal.org, 1, No 1.

GRAY, R.
1961 *A History of the Southern Sudan, 1839–1889*. Oxford: University Press.

GREENBERG, J.H.
1955 *Studies in African Linguistic Classification*. New Haven: Compass.
1963 *The Languages of Africa*. The Hague: Mouton.

GRÜB, Andreas
1992 *The Lotuho of the Southern Sudan, An Ethnological Monograph*. Stuttgart: Franz Steiner Verlag.

GULLIVER, P.H.
1953 'The Age-Set Organization of the Jie Tribe', *Journal of the Royal Anthropological Institute of Great Britain and Ireland*, 83: 147–168.
1958 'Turkana Age Organization.' *American Anthropologist*, 60:900–902.

GUTHRIE, W.K.C.
1950 *The Greek Philosophers: From Thales to Aristotle*. London: Metuen & Co.

HADDON, E.B.
1911 'Notes on the Ethnography of the Bari.' *M.A. thesis*, University of Cambridge, kept in the Haddon Library, Cambridge.
1911 'The System of Chieftainship amongst the Bari.' *Journal of the Royal African Society*, 10(40):457–472.

HAMERTON-KELLY, Robert .G.(ed.)
1987 *Violent Origins, Walter Burkert, René Girard, and Jonathan Z. Smith on Ritual Killing and Cultural Formation*. Stanford: Stanford University Press.

HAMERTON-KELLY, Robert G.
1996 'The King and the Crowd: Divine Right and Popular Sovereignty in the French Revolution'. In: *Contagion: Journal of Violence, Mimesis, and Culture*, Volume 3, Spring 1996, pp. 67–83.

HANSAL. M.L.
1876 'Die Bari-Neger', *Mittheilungen der kais. und kön. geographischen Gesellschaft in Wien*, 19 (neue Folge):294–307.

HARNIER, Adolph von (ed.)
1866 *Wilhelm von Harnier's Reise am Oberen Nil nach dessen hinterlassenen Tagebüchern*. Darmstadt & Leipzig: Eduard Zernin.

HARRISON, Simon J.
1993 *The Mask of War: Violence, Ritual and the Self in Melanesia*. Manchester: Manchester University Press.
2006 *Identity and Mimetic Conflict in Melanesia and the West*. New York & Oxford: Berghahn Books.

HARTMANN, R.
1884 *Die Nilländer*. Leipzig: G. Freytag & Prag: F. Tempsky.

HASSAN, Vita
1893 *Die Wahrheit über Emin Pascha, die Aegyptische Aequatorialprovinz und den Sudan*, 2 vols. Berlin: Dietrich Reimer.

HATULANG, A.V.O.I.
1978 An Outline of Otuho History, 1820–1918. *B.A. thesis* (Honours), University of Khartoum.

HEINE, B.
1976 *The Kuliak Languages of Eastern Uganda*. Nairobi: East African Publishing House.

HÉRITIER-IZARD, Françoise
1973 'La Paix et la pluie. Rapports d'autorité et rapport au sacré chez les Samo.' *L'Homme*, 13(3) :121–138.

HERSKOVITS, M.J.
1926 'The Cattle Complex in East Africa.' *American Anthropologist*, 28:230–272, 361–388, 494–528 & 633–664.

HEUSCH, Luc de (*et alii*)
1962 *Le Pouvoir et le Sacré, Annales du Centre d'Etude des Religions I*. Brussels: Université Libre, Institut de Sociologie.

HEUSCH, Luc de
1981 *Rois nés d'un coeur de vache*. Paris: Gallimard.
1982 *The Drunken King, or the Origin of the State*. Bloomington: Indiana University Press.
1984 'Sacraal koningschap als een symbolisch-politieke structuur, Frazers interpretatie opnieuw bekeken.' *Sociologische Gids*, 31(4):301–326.
1985 *Sacrifice in Africa, A structuralist approach*. Manchester, University Press.
1986 *Le sacrifice dans les religions africaines*, Paris: Gallimard.
1997 'The Symbolic Mechanisms of Sacred Kingship: Rediscovering Frazer.' *Journal of the Royal Anthropological Institute*, 3 (2), pp. 213–232.
2005 'Forms of Sacralized Power in Africa.' In: Quigley, pp. 25–37.
2005 'A reply to Scubla.' In: Quigley, pp 63–66.

HILL, G.B. (ed.)
1881 *Colonel Gordon in Central Africa, 1874–1879, from Original Letters and Documents*. London: Thos. de la Rue.

HILL, Richard
1959 *Egypt in the Sudan 1820–1881*, London, etc. Oxford University Press.

HINO, Abannik O.
1980 The History of the Plains Lotuko, 1860–1920. *M.A. thesis,* University of Khartoum.
1982/3 ' "Latuka Country"; An Outline of the Process of Colonial Encroachment and Reaction to it, 1840–1900.' *North East African Studies,* 4(3):39–49.
1999 Eastern Equatoria and the White Nile Trade: The Political History of a Frontier, 1840–1900, *PhD thesis,* Department of History, Michigan State University.

HOCART, A.M.
1927 *Kingship.* Oxford University Press, London: Humphrey Milford.
1970 *Kings and councillors: An Essay in the Comparative Anatomy of Human Society.* Edited and introduced R. Needham, Chicago, University of Chicago Press.

HØDNEBO, K.
1981a *Cattle and Flies, A Study of Cattle Keeping in Equatoria Province, the Southern Sudan, 1850–1950.* Bergen: University of Bergen.
1981b *Cotton, cattle and crises, A Historical Study of Cash crop Production in East Equatoria Province, the Sudan 1920–1955.* DERAP Working Paper no. A245. Bergen: Chr. Michelsen Institute.

HOFMAYR, P.W. (also 'HOFMEYER')
1910 'Zur Geschichte und sozialen und politischen Gliederung des Stammes der Shillukneger.' *Anthropos,* V:328–333.
1925 *Die Schilluk, Geschichte, Religion und Leben eines Niloten-Stammes.* Mödling: Anthropos Verlag.

HOLY, L.
1979a 'Nuer Politics.' In L. Holy (ed.) 1979:23–48.
1979b 'The Segmentary Lineage Structure and its Existential Status.' In L. Holy (ed.) 1979:1–22.

HOLY, L. (ed.)
1979 *Segmentary Lineage systems Reconsidered, The Queen's University Papers in Social Anthropology.* Belfast: The Queen's University.

HOWELL, P.P.
1944 'The Installation of the Shilluk King.' *Man,* 44:146–147.
1951 'Notes on the Ngork Dinka of Western Kordofan". *Sudan Notes and Records,* 32 (2): 239–293
1952a 'Observations on the Shilluk of the Upper Nile and the Legal Functions of the *Reth.' Africa* (London), XXII(2):97–119.
1952b. 'The death and burial of Reth Dak wad Fadiet of the Shilluk.' *Sudan Notes and Records* 33: 156–65.
1953a. 'The election and installation of Reth Kur wad Fafiti of the Shilluk.' *Sudan Notes and Records* 34: 189–203.

HOWELL, P.P. & W.P.G. THOMSON
1946 'The Death of a *Reth* of the Shilluk and the Installation of his Successor.' *Sudan Notes and Records,* 27:5–85.
1952a. 'The death of Reth Dak wad Fadiet and the installation of his successor: a preliminary note.' *Man* 52: 102–4.

HOWELL, P.P. & J.O. UDAL.
1953 'The Election and Installation of *Reth* Kur *wad* Fafiti of the Shilluk.' *Sudan Notes and Records*, 34(2):189–204.

HUBERT, H. & M. MAUSS
1968 'Essai sur la nature et la function du sacrifice (1899)'. In: Mauss, *Oeuvres*, Vol. 1, *Les fonctions sociales du sacré*: pp. 193–354, Paris: Éditions de Minuit.

HUNTINGFORD, G.W.B.
1953 *The Northern Nilo-Hamites, Ethnographic Survey of Africa*, Part VI. London: International African Institute.

JAMES, Wendy
1972 'The Politics of Rain-Control among the Uduk.' In: Cunnison & James (eds.), pp. 31–57.

JENNINGS, C. H.
2005 Scatterlings of East Africa: Revisions of Parakuyo Identity and History, c.1830–1926, PhD thesis, University of Texas, Austin.

JENNINGS-BRAMLY, A.W.
1906 'The Bari Tribe.' *Man*, 6 (65):101–103.

JOHNSON, Douglas H.
1994 *Nuer Prophets, A History of Prophecy from the Upper Nile in the Nineteenth and Twentieth Centuries*. Oxford: Clarendon Press.
2011 *The Root Causes of Sudan's Civil Wars*. Oxford: James Currey

JOMARD, E.F. (ed.)
1842 'Second voyage à la découverte du Nil-Blanc.' *Bulletin de la Société de Géographie* (Paris), Série II, no. 18:367–384.
1845 Voyage au Bahr-el-Abiad. (Extrait d'une lettre de M. le Dr. Perron). *Bulletin de la Société de Géographie* (Paris), Série II, no. 4:159–168.

JOSSELIN DE JONG, J.P.B, de
1977 'The Malay Archipelago as a field of ethnological study' (1935). In: P.E. de Josselin de Jong (ed.), pp. 166–188.

JOSSELIN DE JONG, P.E. de
1977 *Structural Anthropology in the Netherlands: A Reader*. The Hague: Martinus Nijhoff.

JUNKER, Wilhelm J.
1889/91 *Reisen in Afrika, 1875–1886*, 3 vols. Vienna: Carl Fromme.

KAPTEIN, Roel
1993 *On the way to freedom* (Foreword by René Girard). Dublin: Columba Press.

KAPTEIN, R. & P. TIJMES (eds.)
1986 *De ander als model en obstakel: Een inleiding in het werk van René Girard*, Kampen Kok Agora.

KAUFMANN, A.
1861 *Das Gebiet des Weissen Flusses und dessen Bewohner*, Brixen (Bressanone): Weger

1974 'The White Nile Valley and its Inhabitants.' In: Toniolo & Hill (eds.) 1974:140–195.

KELLY, R.C.
1983 'A Note on Nuer Segmentary Organization.' *American Anthropologist*, 85:905–916.
1985 *The Nuer Conquest: The Structure and Development of an Expansionist System*. Ann Arbor: University of Michigan Press.

KERTZER, D.I. & O.B.B. MADISON
1980 'African Age-set Systems and Political Organization: The Latuka of Southern Sudan'. In: *L'Uomo*, IV (1):85–109.

KNOBLECHER, Ignaz
1974 'The Official Journey of the Missionary Expedition in 1849–1850.' In: Toniolo & Hill (eds.) 1974:47–54.

KRONENBERG, A.
1972 *Logik und Leben, Kulturelle Relevanz der Didinga und Longarim, Sudan*, Wiesbaden: Franz Steiner.

KUPER, Adam
1977 *Regionaal Vergelijkend Onderzoek in Afrika*, Leiden: Universitaire Pers.
1982 *Wives for Cattle: Bridewealth and Marriage in Southern Africa*. London, etc. : Routledge & Kegan Pau.

KUPER, Hilda
1944 'The Ritual Kingship among the Swazi'. *Africa*, 14–95.

KURIMOTO, E.
1984 'The Multiple Subsistence Economy of the Pari.' In: *Agriculture and land Utilization in Eastern Zaire and the Southern Sudan*, edited by K. Sakamoto, Kyoto: University of Kyoto, Faculty of Agriculture.
1986 'The Rain and Disputes: A Case Study of the Nilotic Pari.' *Bulletin of the National Museum of Ethnology* 11 (1): 103–61 (in Japanese). In: 1985 read as a public lecture at the University of Juba.
1988 'On the Concept of Jwok among the Nilotic Pari: Folk Cognition of Ultra-human Forces'; translation of his article in Japanese article by the author. *The Japanese Journal of Ethnology*, 52(4), 271–298.
1988 'A Short History of the Pari.' *Unpublished paper.*
1992 'An Ethnography of "Bitterness": Cucumber and Sacrifice Reconsidered'. *Journal of Religion in Africa*, XXII (1):47–65.
1994 'Civil War and Regional Conflicts: The Pari and their Neighbours in South-Eastern Sudan'. In: Fukui & Markakis, 1994.
1995 'Trade Relations between Western Ethiopia and the Nile Valley during the Nineteenth Century'. *Journal of Ethiopian Studies*, XXVIII, No. 1:53–68
1996 'New Year Hunting Ritual of the Pari: Elements of Hunting Culture among the Nilotes'. *Nilo-Ethiopian Studies*, No. 3–4:25–38.
1998 'Resonance of Age Systems in Southeastern Sudan'. In: Kurimoto & Simonse, pp.29–50.

KURIMOTO, E. & S.SIMONSE (eds.)

1998 *Conflict, Age and Power in North East Africa: Age Systems in Transition.* Oxford: James Currey/Nairobi: E.A.E.P./Kampala: Fountain Publishers /Athens: Ohio University Press.

LAFARGUE, J.

1845 'Extract of his letter of 1/5/1845, included in 'Voyage au Bahr-el-Abiad (Extrait d'une lettre de M. le Dr. Perron, datée 1/9/1845).' *Bulletin de la Société de Géographie* (Paris), Série III, 4:159–160.

LASCARIS, André

1993 *Het Soevereine Slachtoffer, een theologisch essay over geweld en onderdrukking,* Baarn: Ten Have.

LASCARIS, A. & H. WEIGAND (eds.)

1992 Nabootsing. In discussie over René Girard, Kampen: Kok.

LAYE, Camara

1954 *Le regard du roi,* Paris: Plon; translated as *The Radiance of the King,* 2011. New York: New York Review Books Classics.

LEJEAN, Guillaume

1860 'Nouvelles de M.G. Lejean, voyageur au Nil Blanc.' *Nouvelles Annales des Voyages,* Série VI, Vol. 6, sept. 1860:364–367.

1863 'Gondokoro, Esquisse d'un voyage au Nil Blanc, 1861.' *Le Tour du Monde,* 8:397–400.

1865 *Voyage aux Deux Nils (Nubie, Kordofan, Soudan Oriental), Exécuté de 1860 à 1864, Par ordre de l'Empéreur,* Paris: Hachette & Cie.

LEONARDI, Cherry

2013 *Dealing with Government in South Sudan: Histories of Chiefship, Community and State.* Oxford: James Currey.

LEVERENZ, I.

1983 '*Luak Nhialic,* Anmerkungen zum Stall Gottes der Agar Dinka.' In: F. Kramer & B. Streck (Hrsg), *Zwischenberichte des Sudanprojekts.* Institut für Ethnologie der Freien Universität Berlin.

LÉRY, Jean de

1578 *Histoire d'un voyage faict en la terre du Brésil, autrement dit Amérique,* Genève: Eustache Vignon; many recent republications *e.g.* in 1994 in *Le Livres de Poche* (Paris).

LÉVI-STRAUSS, Claude

1958 *Anthropologie Structurale.* Paris: Plon.

1967 *Les structures élementaires de la parenté* (2nd edition). Paris/The Hague: Mouton; translated in 1969 as *The Elementary Structures of Kinship* and published by Beacon Press in Boston.

1971a 'Rapports de symétrie entre rites et mythes de peuples voisins.' In Beidelman (ed.), pp.161–177.

1971b *L'hommme nu, Mythologiques 4.* Paris: Plon.

LEWIS, B.A.

1972 *The Murle, Red chiefs and Black Commoners.* Oxford: Clarendon Press.

LIENHARDT, Godfrey

1954 'The Shilluk of the Upper Nile.' In: D. Forde (ed), *African Worlds, Studies in the Cosmological Ideas and social Values of African Peoples: 138–163*. London: Oxford University Press.

1955 'Nilotic Kings and their Mother's Kin.' *Africa*, 25(1):29–41.

1957 'Anuak Village Headmen, Headmen and Village Culture.' *Africa* (London), XXVII(4):341–355.

1958a 'Anuak Village Headmen, Village Structure and Rebellion.' *Africa* (London), XXVIII(1):23–36.

1958b 'The Western Dinka.' In: J. Middleton & D. Tait (eds.), *Tribes without Rulers: Studies in African Segementary Systems*, pp. 97–135. London: Routledge & Kegan Paul.

1961 *Divinity and Experience, The Religion of the Dinka*. Oxford: Clarendon Press.

1962 'The Situation of Death: An Aspect of Anuak Philosophy.' *Anthropological Quarterly*, 35:74–85.

1975 'Getting your own back: Themes in Nilotic Myth.' In: J. Beattie & G. Lienhardt (eds.), 1975:213–237.

LIVINGSTON, Paisley (ed.)

1984 *Disorder and Order, Proceedings of the Stanford International Symposium (Sept. 14–16, 1981)*. Stanford: Anma Libri.

LOMODONG LAKO, Philip

1995 *Lokoya of Sudan: Culture and Ethnic Government*. Nairobi: Act Print.

LOTAR, I.

1946 La grande chronique de l'Uele, Brussels: Insitut Royal Colonial Belge.

LUSCHNIG C. A. E. & Deborah MITCHELL

2007 *An Introduction to Ancient Greek: A Literary Approach*. Indianopolis: Hackett Publishing company.

MACDONALD, J.R.L.

1899 'Journeys to the North of Uganda.' *The Geographical Journal*, 14(2):129–148.

MACK, J. & P. ROBERTSHAW (eds.)

1982 *Culture History in the Southern Sudan, Archaeology, Linguistics, Ethnohistory*. Nairobi: Britisch Institute In Eastern Africa.

MADDEN, J.F.

1940 'The Exhumation of a Latuka Rain-Chief.' *Sudan Notes and Records*, 23(2):351–354.

MAIR, Lucy P.

1934 *An African People in the Twentieth Century*. London: Routledge.

MAKARIUS, Laura

1970 'Du roi magique au roi divin', *Annales, Économies, Sociétés, Civilisations*, 25(3) : 668–698

1973 'Une interprétation de l'*Incwala* Swazi', *Annales, Économies, Sociétés, Civilisations*, 28(6):1403–31

MALINOWSKI, B.

1922 *Argonauts of the Western Pacific*. London: George Routledge & Sons.

MALTE-BRUN, V.A. (ed.)
1863 'Le Dr. Alfred Peney et ses dernières explorations dans la région du haut Fleuve Blanc, 1860–1861, Extraits de ses notes et de son journal de voyage.' *Bulletin de la Société de Géographie* (Paris), 5(6):5–74.

MATTI, Severino M.K.
1973 The Concepts of Beauty among some Tribes of Northern Uganda and Southern Sudan. *M.A. thesis*, Makerere University Kampala.

MAUSS, Marcel
1990 *The Gift, The Form and Reason for Exchange in Archaic Societies.* New York & London: W.W. Norton.

MAYBURY-LEWIS, D. & U. ALMAGOR
1992 *The Attraction of Opposites: Thought and Society in the Dualistic Mode.* Ann Arbor: University of Michigan Press.

MERCER, P.
1971 'Shilluk Trade and Politics from the Mid-Seventeenth Century to 1861.' *Journal of African History* 12:407–427.

MÉTRAUX, Alfred
1967 Religions et magies indiennes d'Amérique du Sud, Paris: Gallimard.

MIDDLETON, John
1955 'Notes on the Political Organization of the Madi.' *African Studies*, 14(1):29–36.
1960 *Lugbara Religion: Ritual and Authority among an East African People.* Oxford: Oxford University Press.

MIDDLETON, J. & D. TAIT (eds.)
1958 *Tribes without Rulers.* London: Routledge & Kegan Paul.

MILNE, A.D.
1899 'Notes from the Equatorial Province.' *Scottish Geographical Magazine*, vol. 480–483.

MITTERRUTZNER, J.C.
1867 *Die Sprache der Bari in Central Afrika, Grammatik, Text und Wörterbuch*, Brixen (Bressanone).

MOGGA LADU, Eluzai
1981 *Lulubo in Perspective, An Account of Cultural, Social and Religious Development in the Area.* Juba: University Printing Unit.
1988 *The Cultural Ceremonial Dance of the Lulu'bo: Kajuwaya.* Juba : New Day Publishers.
2002 Religion and Change in Tribal Cultures: The Case of the Lulu'bo of Southern Sudan, PhD Thesis, University of Khartoum.

MOLINARO, L.
1940/1 'Appunti circa gli Usi, Costumi e Idee religiose dei Lotuko dell'Uganda.' *Anthropos*, 35(36):166–201.

MORLANG, Francesco
1862/3 'Reisen östlich und westlich von Gondokoro, 1859.' *Petermann's Mitteilungen*, Ergänzungsheft II:115–124.

MOUNTENEY-JEPHSON, A.J.
1890 *Emin Pasha and the Rebellion at the Equator*. London: Sampson Low, Marston, Searle & Rivington.

MÜLLER-DEMPF, Harald K.
1989 *Changing generations: dynamics of generation and age-sets in Southeastern Sudan (Toposa) and Northwestern Kenya (Turkana)*, Saarbrücken/Fort Lauderdale: Breitenbach Verlag.
1991 'Generation-Sets: Stability and Change, with Special Reference to Toposa and Turkana Societies'. *Bulletin of the School of Oriental and African Studies*, 54(3): 554–567.
2009 'The Ngibokoi Dilemma: generation-sets and social system engineering in times of stress — an example from the Toposa of Southern Sudan.' In: *Zeitschrift für Ethnologie*, 134:189–211.

MULLER, J.C.
1980 *Le roi bouc émissaire, Pouvoir et rituel chez les Rukuba du Nigéria Central*. Québec Serge Fleury.
1981 'An ideological model of 'divine kingship.' In: H.J.M. Claessen and P. Skalník (eds.), p. 239–250.
1983 'Contrepoint ritual pour deluge et sécheresse: Traitement des perturbations atmosphériques chez les Rukuba et leurs voisins (Nigeria central)', *L'Homme*, 23 (4):55–73.

MURATORI, Carlo
1938 *Grammatica Lotuxo*. Verona: Missioni Africane.
1949 'Lomoro Hujang (1853–1912), A Lotuko Chief, Tirrangore.' *Sudan Notes and Records*, 30(1):107–109.
1952 'A Case of Magical Poisoning in a Lotuko Village.' *Sudan Notes and Records*, 33:133–135.
1954 'Ikang, Queen of Tirrangore.' *Sudan Notes and Records*, 35(1):144–147.

MURDOCK, G.P.
1959 *Africa, Its People and Their Culture History*. New York: McGraw-Hill.

NAILO N. MAYO, David,
1985, The Changing Universe, A Narrative Social History of the People of Southern Sudan, 1890–1953, *manuscript*.

NALDER, L.F. (ed.)
1937 *A Tribal Survey of Mongalla Province, by Members of the Province Staff and the Church Missionary Society*. International Institute of African Languages and Cultures, London (etc.): Oxford University Press.

NEEDHAM, R.
1980 *Reconnaissances*. Toronto: University of Toronto Press.

NOVELLI, B.
1970 'Ergologia ed Etnosociologia Lotuho.' *Thesis*, Università Cattolica del S. Cuore, Milano.

OHISA, Affwonni Lais
1992 *God the Master, An Outline of Otuho Religion.* Khartoum: St. Paul's Major Seminary.

OKENY, K.
n.d. Royal Drums and State Formation, c. 1679–1802: A Reconsideration. *Research Paper*, History Unit, College of Education, University of Juba.

ONYANGO-KU-ODONGO, J.M. & J.B. WEBSTER
1976 *The Central Lwo during the Aconya.* Nairobi: East African Literature Bureau.

OTTO, R.
1917 *Das Heilige.* München: C.H. Beck.

OUGHOURLIAN, Jean-Michel
2007 *Genèse du désir.* Paris: Carnets Nord.

OWEN, R.C.R.
1908 *Bari Grammar and Vocabulary.* London: J. & E. Bumpus.

PALAVER, Wolfgang
2004 *René Girards mimetische Theorie, Im Kontext kulturtheoretischer und gesellschaftspolitischer Fragen,* Vienna: LIT.
2015 *René Girard's Mimetic Theory.* East Lansing: Michigan State University Press.
2002 'Sakrales Königtum, Todesstrafe, Krieg: Der Ursprung politischer Institutionen aus der Sicht der mimetischen Theorie René Girards'. *Revista Portuguesa de Filosofia*, 28 (2), pp. 359–378

PALMISANO, A.L.
1989 *Mito e società. Analisi della mitologia dei Lotuho del Sudan. Antropologia culturale e sociale.* Milan: Angeli

PAOLUCCI, T.
1970 'Animologia Lotuho.' *Thesis*, Università Cattolica del S. Cuore, Milano.

PARSONS, Talcott
1949 *The Structure of Social Action, A Study in Social Theory with Special Reference to a Group of Recent European Writers.* Glencoe: The Free Press.

PAZZAGLIA, A.
1950 'Sawa, il bosco sacro della tribù Dongotòno.' *Nigrizia*, 152–154.

PEDEMONTE, E.
1974 'A Report on the Voyage of 1849–50.' In: Toniolo & Hill (eds.), 1974:55–73.

PEDRANA, G.B.
1921–22 'Attraverso I Latuka, Alla Fondazione della Stazione di Torit.' *La Nigrizia*, 1921:54–60, 70–75, 86–94, 108–111, 140–143, 154–156, 172–175, 189–191; 1922:11–14, 29–31, 47–49, 63–64.

PERNER, Conradin
1992 'Living on earth in the sky.' *Journal of Religion in Africa*, 22(1):21–46.
1992 'Anyuak Religion and Language.' *Journal of Religion in Africa*, 22(2):152–8)

1994 *Living on Earth in the Sky: the Anyuak; An analytic account of the history and the culture of a Nilotic people*, in 8 volumes, the first four of which have so far been published. The publication of Vol. 6 *The Political Body—Power and Authority* has been announced by the Publisher Schwabe in Basel for 2015.

PETHERICK, John and Mrs.
1869 *Travels in Central Africa and Explorations of the Western Nile Tributaries*. London: Tinsley Brothers, 2 vols.

POLANYI, Karl
1944 *The Great Transformation, The Political and Economic Origins of our Time*. Boston: Beacon Press.

PONCET, Jules
1863, 'Notice géographique et ethnologique sur la Région du Fleuve Blanc et sur ses habitants', *Nouvelles Annales des Voyages*, 4:5–62.
1864, *Le Fleuve Blanc, Notes géographiques et ethnologiques et les chasses à l'éléphant dans le pays des Dinka et des Djour*. Paris: Arthus Bertrand (contains a reprint of Poncet, 1863).

POWELL-COTTON, P.H.G.
1904 'A Journey through Northern Uganda.' *The Geographical Journal*, 24/1:56–65.
1904 *In Unknown Africa, A Narrative of Twenty Months Travel and Sports in Unknown Lands and among New Tribes*. London: Hurst & Blackett Ltd.

PUGACH, Zoja
1993, 'On the Purpose of Bari figurines'. *St. Petersburg Journal of African Studies*, No.2: 134–145.

PUMPHREY, M.E.C.
1941 'The Shilluk Tribe'. *Sudan Notes and Record*, XXIV: 1–45.

QUIGLEY, Declan (ed.)
2005 *The Character of Kingship*. Oxford: Berg.

RAGLAN, Lord (also publishing under the name Fitzroy Richard Somerset)
1926 'Tribes of the Southern Sudan.' *Man*, 6(14):22–23.

RAY, Benjamin C.
1991 *Myth, Ritual and Kingship in Buganda*. New York/Oxford: Oxford University Press.

RIAD, M.
1959 'The Divine Kingship of the Shilluk and its Origin.' *Archiv für Völkerkunde* (Wien), 14:141–284.

RICCARDO, Gaetano
1997 *L'immortalità provvisoria: Antropologia del regicidio rituale in Africa*. Turin: L'Harmattan Italia.

RICHARDS, Audrey I.
1964 'Authority Patterns in Traditional Buganda'. In L.A. Fallers (ed.) pp. 256–293.

RIDDER, R. de & J.A.J KARREMANS (ed.)

1987 *The Leiden Tradition in Structural Anthropology: Essays in Honour of P.E. de Josselin de Jong*. Leiden: E.J.Brill

ROBERTSHAW, Peter & Ari SIIRIÄINEN,

1985 'Excavations in Lakes Province, Southern Sudan.' *Azania*, XX:89–161.

ROGERS, F.H.

1927 'Notes on some Madi Rain-stones.' *Man*, 27(58):81–87.

ROLLAND, Miguel B. de las Casas

2012 Intra-ethnic Conflict and Violence: Exploring Mimetic Desire as Practice Among the Maya Tzotzil Chamula of Chiapas, Mexico'. *PhD Thesis*, Arizona State University.

2014 'From Fracturing Resemblances to Restorative Differences: Identity, Conflict and Mimetic Desire among of the Chamula Tsotsil of Highland Chiapas, Mexico.' In: *René Girard and Creative Reconciliation*, edited by Thomas Ryba, Plymouth: Lexington Books, pp.353–386.

ROSCOE, John

1911 *The Baganda: An Account of their Native Customs and Beliefs*. London: Macmillan.

ROWLEY, J.V.

1940 'Notes on the Madi of Equatoria Province.' *Sudan Notes and Records*, XXIII: 279–294.

SAHLINS, M.D.

1961 'The Segmentary Lineage: An Organization of Predatory Expansion.' *American Anthropologist*, 63:322–345.

1962/63 'Poor Man, Rich Man, Big-Man, Chief: Political Types in Melanesia and Polynesia.' *Comparative Studies in Society and History*, 5:283–303.

SALOKOSKI, Märta

2005, 'Ritual Regicide versus Succession Strife. Political Decision-Making through Ritual in Pre-Colonial Owambo Societies'. In: *Hémisphères*, No. 20, pp. 7–37

SALZMAN, P.C.

1978 'Does Complementary Opposition exist?' *American Anthropologist*, 80:53–70.

SANTANDREA, Stefano

1938 'Minor Shilluk Sections in the Bahr-el-Ghazal'. *Sudan Notes and Records,* 21:267–289

1944/48'The Luo of Bahr-el-Ghazal', *Annali Lateranensi*, VIII: 91–145 & XII: 181–205.

1948 *Bibliografia di Studi Africani*. Verona: Missione Africane.

1964 *A Tribal History of the Western Bahr-el-Ghazal*. Bologna: Editrice Missionaria Italiana

1969 'Praise-songs for "Killers" in Jur-Luo.' *Annali Lateranensi*, 24, 2(3):182–216.

1981 *Ethno-Geography of the Bahr-el-Ghazal (Sudan)*. Bologna: Editrice Missionaria Italiana.

SANTANDREA, S. & L. DE GIORGI, L.

1965 'Morte violenta per i "Re Divini" Scilluk e Dinka-Sudan.' *Africa* (Roma), XX:15–32 & 163–187.

SCHMIDT, Wilhelm
1926 *Der Ursprung des Gottesidee, Eine historisch-kritische und positive Studie*, 12 vols. Münster: Assendorffsche Verlagsbuchhandlung.

SCHNEIDER, Harold K.
1979 *Livestock and Equality in East Africa, The Economic Basis for Social Structure*. Bloomington: Indiana University Press.

SCHNEPEL, Burkhard
1988 'In quest of life Hocart's scheme of evolution from ritual organization to government.' *European Journal of Sociology*, 29: 165–187.
1990 'Shilluk Kingship. Power Struggles and the Question of Succession.' *Anthropos* 85:105–124.
1991 'Continuity despite and through death: regicide and royal shrines among the Shilluk of southern Sudan.' *Africa*, 61(1):40–70.

SCHOFFELEERS, J.M & W.M.J. van BINSBERGEN (eds.)
1985 *Theoretical Explorations in African Religion*. London: Kegan Paul International.

SCHOFFELEERS, J.M. & A. ROSCOE
1985 *Land of Fire, Oral Literature from Malawi*. Limbi: Montfort Press.

SCHOFFELEERS, J.M.
1991 'Twins and Unilateral Figures in Central and Southern Africa: Symmetry and Asymmetry in the Symbolization of the Sacred.' *Journal of Religion in Africa*, 21(4):345–372.
1992a 'De zieke als zondebok: gebedsgenezing en politiek in Zuid-Afrika. In: Lascaris & Weigand (eds.), pp. 119–35.
1992b *River of Blood, The Genesis of an African Religious Cult, ca. 1600*. Madison: Wisconsin University Press.
2000 'The Story of the Scapegoat King. On the Interplay of Therapeutic and Political Ngoma in Southern Malawi.' In: *The quest for fruition through Ngoma: Political aspects of healing in southern Africa*, edited by Rijk van Dijk, Ria Reis and Marja Spierenburg. London, James Curry.

SCUBLA, Lucien
1982 'Contribution à la théorie du sacrifice'. In Deguy & Dupuy (eds.), pp. 103–167
1985 'Logiques de la réciiprocité', *Cahiers du CREA*, 6 : 7–273.
1992 'Vindicatory System, Sacrificial System'. In: Anspach (ed.), pp.55–76.
1993a 'Vengeance et sacrifice: De l'opposition à la reconciliation'. *Droit et Cultures*, No. 23: 77–101.
1993b 'Vers une anthropologie morphogénétique. Violence fondatrice et théorie des singularités.' *Le Débat*, 77 (November-December 1993), pp. 102–120.
1998 *Lire Lévi-Strauss: Le déploiement d'une intuition*. Paris: Odile Jacob.
1999 '«Ceci n'est pas un meurtre» ou comment le sacrifice contient la violence'. In *Séminaire de Françoise Héritier, De la Violence II*. Paris: Odile Jacob, pp.135–170.
2003 'Roi sacré, victime sacrificielle et victime émissaire', *Revue du MAUSS*, no. 38 : 65–68.
2005a 'Le sacrifice a-t-il une fonction sociale'. *Pardès*, no. 39 :143–149.

2005b 'Sacred King, Sacrificial Victim, Surrogate Victim or Frazer, Hocart, Girard'. In Quigley, pp. 39–63.

2008 'René Girard ou la renaissance de l'anthropologie religieuse'. In Anspach (ed.), pp. 105–110.

2014, *Donner la vie, donner la mort : Psychanalyse, anthropologie, philosophie*, Paris : Editions Le Bord de l'eau.

2016, *Giving Life, Giving Death : Psychoanalysis, Anthropology, Philosophy*, Studies in Violence, Mimesis and Culture. East Lansing: Michigan State University Press.

SEGAL, R.A.

2007 'The Frazerian Roots of contemporary theories of religion and violence.' In: *Religion* 37:4–25.

SELIGMAN, C.G.

n.d. *Report on Totemism and Religion of the Dinka of the Sudan*. Khartoum: Sudan Press.

1911 'Cult of Nyakang and the Divine Kings of the Shilluk.' *Wellcome Tropical Research Laboratories*, Report 4, B:216–238.

1925 'Some Little-known Tribes of the Southern Sudan.' *Journal of the Royal Anthropological Insttute of Great Britain and Ireland*, 55:15–36.

1934 *Egypt and Negro Africa, A Study in Divine Kingship*. London: Routledge.

1966 *Races of Africa*, London, etc. Oxford University Press.

SELIGMAN, C.G. & B.Z.

1925 'The Lotuko Social Organisation'. *Sudan Notes and Records,* VIII:1–45.

1928 'The Bari.' *Journal of the Royal Anthropological Institute of Great Britain and Ireland*, 58:409–479.

1932 *Pagan Tribes of the Nilotic Sudan*. London: Routledge.

SELIM, CAPITAN

1842 'Premier voyage à la découverte des sources du Nil Blanc ordonné par Mohammed-Aly, vice-roi d'Egypte.' *Bulletin de la Société de Géographie* (Paris), Série II, no. 18:5–30, 81–106, 161–185.

SERINA, Antonino

2002 *Miti e riti dei Lotuho del Sudan Meridionale: Attualità dell'analsi morfologico-strutturale di V. Ja. Propp e dello strutturalismo di C. Lévi-Strauss*, Trapani: Di Girolamo Editore.

SHUKRY, M.F. (ed.)

1953 *Equatoria under Egyptian rule. The unpublished correspondence of Col C.G. Gordon with Ismail, Khedive of Egypt and the Sudan, during the years 1874–1876*. Cairo: Cairo University Press.

SIGRIST, Christian

1967 *Regulierte Anarchie, Untersuchungen zum Fehlen und zur Entstehung politischer Herrschaft in segmentären Gesellschaften Afrikas*, Olten & Freiburg im Breisgau: Walter Verlag.

SIMEONI, Antonio

1978-*Päri, a Luo Language of Southern Sudan: Small Grammar and Vocabulary*. Bologna: Editrice Missionaria Italiana.

SIMONSE, Simon

1988 'De slaperigheid van koning Fadiet, Regicide en het zondebokmechanisme in de Nilotische Soedan.' In: W. van Beek (ed.), pp.172–208.

1993 'The *Monyomiji* Age-class Systems of the Southern Sudan.' *Nilo-Ethiopian Studies Newsletter* 1:6–11.

1994 'The Burst and the Cut Stomach: The Metabolism of Violence and Order in Nilotic Kingship.' *Nilo-Ethiopian Studies* (Kyoto) 2: 1–13

1998 'Age, Conflict and Power in the *Monyomiji* Age Systems.' In: Kurimoto & Simonse, pp. 51–78.

1998 'Conflict, Accommodation, and Avoidance: From Gregory Bateson to René Girard.' In: Elias & Reis, pp.131–155.

2005 'Tragedy, Ritual and Power in Nilotic Regicide: The Regicidal Dramas of the Eastern Nilotes.' In: Quigley (ed.), 2005:67–100.

2006 'Kings and Gods as Ecological Agents: Reciprocity and Unilateralism in the Management of Nature.' In: *Contagion: Journal of Violence, Mimesis and Culture,* 12–13 (2006):31–46.

2008 'À la recherche des derniers rois bouc-émissaires'. In: Anspach (ed.) pp. 98–110.

2013 'Sacrifice as a Game-changer between Negative and Positive Reciprocity.' In: *The Ambivalence of Sacrifice,* edited by L.C. Susin, D. Irarrazaval & D.F. Pilario, *Concilium, International Journal of Theology,* London: SCM Press, pp. 36–49.

2014 'Can We Be at Peace without Sacrifice? The Connection between Sacrifice and Crisis in the Work of René Girard.' In: *The Actuality of Sacrifice, Past and Present,* edited by A. Houtman, M. Poorthuis, J. Schwarz and Y. Turner, *Jewish and Christian Perspectives* 28, Brill: Leiden/Boston, pp. 323–340.

SIMONSE, Simon and Eisei KURIMOTO,

2011, *Engaging* Monyomiji: *Bridging the Governance Gap in East Bank Equatoria,* Proceedings of the Conference, 26–28 November 2009, Torit, Nairobi: Pax Christi Horn of Africa.

SMITH, M.G.

1956 'On Segmentary Lineage Systems.' *Journal of the Royal Anthropological Institute,* 86(2):39–80.

SOMERSET, F.R. (also publishing as Lord Raglan)

1918 'The Lotuko.' *Sudan Notes and Records,* 1:153–159.

SOUTHALL, A.W.

1953 *Alur society, A Study in Processes and Types of Domination.* Cambridge: Heffer.

1965 'A Critique of the Typology of States and Political systems.' In: Banton (ed.), pp. 113–140.

1974 'State Formation in Africa'. *Annual Review of Anthropology,* 1974 (3):153–164.

1988 'The Segmentary State in Africa and Asia.' *Comparative Studies in Society and History,* 30(1):52–82.

SPAGNOLO, Lorenzo M.

1932 'Some Notes on the Initiation of Young Men and Girls in the Bari Tribe.' *Africa,* 5:393–405.

1933 *Bari Grammar.* Verona: Missioni Africane.

1960 *Bari English Italian Dictionary*. Museum Combonianum no. 9, Verona: Missioni Africane.

SPAULDING, J, S. BESWICK, C. FLUEHR-LOBBAN & R.A. LOBBAN Jr. (Eds.)
2010 *Sudan's Wars and Peace Agreeements*. New Castle upon Tyne: Cambridge Scholars Publishing.

SPEKE, John Hanning
1863 *Journal of the Discovery of the Source of the Nile*. London/Edinburgh: William Blackwood & Sons.

SPENCER, Paul
1988 *The Maasai of Matapato, A Study in Rituals of Rebellion*. Manchester: Manchester University Press.
1998 'Age Systems & Modes of Predatory Expansion.' In: Kurimoto & Simonse, pp.168–185.
2003 *Time, Space and the Unknown, Maasai configuration of power and providence*. New York, London: 2003.

SPIRE, F.
1905a 'Notes on the Madi Negroes.' *Journal of the Royal African Society* (London), 4:301–2.
1905b 'Rain-making in Equatorial Africa.' *Journal of the Royal African Society*, 5(17):15–21.

STRAUBE, Helmut
1973/74 'Die Stellung und die Funktion des Shilluk-Königs als zentrale Autorität.' *Paideuma*, 19(20):213–257.

STUHLMANN, F.
1894 *Mit Emin Pascha ins Herz von Afrika*, Berlin: Dietrich Reimer.

SWARTZ, M.J., V.W. TURNER & A. TUDEN (eds.)
1966 *Political Anthropology*. Chicago: Aldine.

TABAN LO LIYONG
1970 *Eating Chiefs, Lwo Culture from Lolwe to Malkal*, London. Nairobi & Ibadan: Heinemann.

TAPPI, C.
1894 *Cenno storico della Missione dell'Africa centrale*, Turin.
1903 'Notes Ethnologiques sur les Chillouks.' *Bulletin de la Société Khédiviale de Géographie*, pp. 111–141.
1915 'I popoli nilotoci: Saggio di studii'. *Bulletin de l'Institut Egyptien*, pp.136–161

TAROT, Camille
2008 *Le symbolique et le sacré: Théorie de la Religion*, Paris: Édition de la Découverte/M.A.U.S.S.

TESTART, Alain
2004 *La servitude volontaire, Vol.1, Les morts d'accompagnement*, Paris: Éditions Errance
2004 *La servitude volontaire, Vol.2, L'origine de l'État*, Paris: Éditions Errance

THIBAULT, G., (also G. THIBAUT , also known as IBRAHIM EFFENDI)
1841 'Extrait d'un lettre de M. Thibault, voyageur français écrite d'El-Kharthoum (Sennâr) le 28 avril 1841.' *Bulletin de la Société de Géographie* (Paris), Série II, no. XVL:127–132.
1856 'Journal inédit d'un voyage fait au Fleuve Blanc du 16 novembre 1839 au 26 mars 1840.' *Nouvelles Annales des Voyages*: 5–53; 141–191.

THOMSON, W.P.G.
1948 'Further Notes on the Death of a *Reth* of the Shilluk.' *Sudan Notes and Records*, 29(2):151–160.

TITHERINGTON, G.W. (also "G.W.T.")
1925 'Burial Alive among the Dinka of the Bahr-el-Ghazal Province.' *Sudan Notes and Records*, 8:196–197.

TONIOLO, E. & R. HILL (eds.)
1974 *The Opening of the Nile Basin, Writings by Members of the Catholic Mission to Central Africa on the Geography and Ethnography of the Sudan 1842–1881*. London: C. Hurst & Company.

TORNAY, Serge
1975 'Générations, classes d'âges et superstructures: à propos de l'étude d'une ethnie du cercle karimojong (Afrique orientale).' Equipe écologie et anthropologie des sociétés pastorales (ed.), *Pastoral Production and Society*. Cambridge/Paris: Cambridge University Press/Editions de la Maison des Sciences de l'Homme.
2001 *Les Fusils Jaunes. Générations et politique en pays nyangatom (Éthiopie)*. Paris-Nanterre: Société d'ethnologie.

SWARTZ, M.J., V.W. TURNER & A.TUDEN (eds.)
1966 *Political Anthropology*, Chicago: Aldine Publishing Company.

THE SACRAL KINGSHIP/LA REGALITÀ SACRA: Contributions to the Central Theme of the VIIIth International Congress for the History of Religions (Rome, April 1955), 1959, Leiden: E.J. Brill.

TURNER, Victor W.
1957 *Schism and Continuity in an African Society: A Study of Ndembu Village Life*, Manchester: University Press.
1969 *The Ritual Process, Structure and Anti-Structure*. Harmondsworth: Penguin Books.

TVEDT, Terje
2004 Southern Sudan: An Annotated Bibliography, 2 Vols. London: I.B. Tauris & Co.

UDAL, John
1998 *The Nile in Darkness, Conquest and Exploration 1504–1862*. Norwich: Michael Russell.

VALPY, F.E.J.
1860 *The Etymology of the Words of the Greek Language*. London: Longman, Green, Longman & Roberts.

VANDEN PLAS, Joseph
1910 *Les Kuku*. Collection de Monographies ethnographiques 6, publié par Cyr. Van Overbergh. Brussels: Albert Dewit.

VAUDEY, A.
1852 'Notes sur les Barrys et sur quelques peuplades voisines du Fleuve Bleu et du Fleuve Blanc.' *Bulletin de la Société de Géographie* (Paris), Série III, no. 4:525–535.

VERMEULEN, H.F.
1987 'P.E. de Josselin de Jong and the Leiden Tradition: A Short History.' In: Ridder & Karremans (eds.), pp. 64–84.

VINCO, Angelo
1940 'Relazione del viaggio del Reverendo Sacerdote Don Angelo Vinco, Missionario Apostolico fra le varie tribù equatoriali del Fiume Bianco dal principio dell'anno 1851 fino alla metà del 1852.' *Annali Lateranensi*, IV: 300–328.
1974 'Angelo Vinco, First Christian to live among the Bari. His Journeys, 1851–1852.' In: Toniolo & Hill (eds.) 1974.

VIVEIROS DE CASTRO, Eduardo B.
1992 *From the enemy's point of view: humanity and divinity in an Amazonian society.* London/Chicago: University of Chicago Press

VOSSEN, R.
1982 *The Eastern Nilotes, Linguistic and Historical Reconstructions*. Berlin: D.Reimer.
1983 'Comparative Eastern Nilotic.' In: M.L. Bender, *Nilo-Saharan Language Studies*. East Lansing: Michigan State University.

WALL, L. Lewis
1976 Anuak Politics, Ecology, and the Origins of Shilluk Kingship. *Ethnology*, 15:2 p.151–162.

WALLIS BUDGE, E.A.
1973 Osiris & the Egyptian Resurrection, 2 vols. New York: Dover Publications, Inc.

WEBER, Max
1947 *The Theory of Social and Economic Organization* edited and introduced by Talcott Parsons. New York: The Free Press & London: Collier-MacMillan.
1985 *Wirtschaft und Gesellschaft, Grundriss der verstehenden Soziologie*. Studienausgabe. Tübingen: J.C.B. Mohr (Paul Siebeck).

WEBSTER, J.B. (ed.)
1979 *Chronology, Migration and Drought in Interlacustrine Africa*. New York: Africana Publishing Company/Dakhousie University Press & London: Longman.

WEIGAND, Hans,
2008 'Complex Mimetic Systems'. In: *Contagion, Journal of Violence, Mimesis and Culture*, 15–16:63–87.

WERNE, Ferdinand
1848 *Expedition zur Entdeckung der Quellen der Weissen Nil (1840–1841)*. Berlin: G. Reimer.

WHITEHEAD, G.O.
1929 'Social change among the Bari.' *Sudan Notes and Records*, 12(1):91–97.
1936 'A Note on Bari History.' *Sudan Notes and Records*, 19(1):152–157.
1953 'Suppressed Classes among the Bari and Bari-speaking Tribes.' *Sudan Notes and Records*, 34(2):265–280.
1962 'Crops and Cattle among the Bari and Bari-speaking Tribes.' *Sudan Notes and Records*, 43:131–142.

WILLIAMS, James G. (ed.)
1996 *The Girard Reader*. New York: Crossroad Publishing Co.
2012 *Girardians, The Colloquium on Violence and Religion 1990–2010*, Vienna: LIT.

WILLIS, Roy
1981 *A State in the Making: Myth, History, and Social Transformation in Pre-colonial Ufipa*. Bloomington: Indiana University Press.

WILSON, C.T. & R. W. FELKIN
1882 *Uganda and the Egyptian Sudan*, 2 Vols. London: Sampson Low, Marston, Searle & Rivington.

WILSON, Monica
1939 *Divine Kings and the 'Breath of Men'*. The Frazer Lecture for 1959. Cambridge: University Press.

WOOD, G.
1982 'Frazer's magic wand of anthropology: interpreting "The Golden Bough".' *Archives Européennes de Sociologie*, 23:92–122.

WOODWARD, E.M.
1902 *The Uganda Protectorate, Précis of Information*. London: Intelligence Division, War Office.

WRIGLEY, Christopher
1981 'The Problem of the Lwo.' *History in Africa*, 8:219–246.
1996 *Kingship and State: The Buganda Dynasty*. Cambridge: Cambridge University Press

YUNIS, Negib
1905 'Tribes on the Upper Nile: the Bari.' *Journal of the Royal African Society* (London), 4(14):226–231.
1924 'Notes on the Kuku and other Minor Tribes.' *Sudan Notes and Records*, 7/1:1–41.

ZANEN, Sj.M. & A.W. van den Hoek
1987 'Dinka Dualism and the Nilotic Hierarchy of Values.' In: Ridder & Karremans (eds.), pp. 170–196.

Map of the Peoples of South Sudan

Sudan

Kordofan

Nuba

Darfur

Baggara

Dinka

Blue Nile

Maban

Uduk

Koma

Shilluk

Abyei

Bentiu

Malakal

N

D

Aweil

Kuacjok

i

Fertit

Kreish

Shilluk-Luo

Wau

Jur-Luo

Atuot

n

N u e r

Gambela

Central African Republic

Belanda

Rumbek

k

Murle

Anuak

Suri

Ethiopia

a

Bor

Jiye

Jur 'Beli

Mandari

Nyangbara

Pari

Lopit

Toposa

Nyangatom

Azande

Bongo

Baka

Moru

Bari

Lulubo

Lokoya

Kapoeta

Democratic Republic of Congo

Yambio

Avukaya

Juba

Lotuho Didinga

Turkana

Fajelu Mundu

Madi

Acholi

Lango

Dodoth

Jie

Kakwa Kuku

Lugbara

Alur

Uganda

Kenya

497

Map of East Bank Equatoria

Mountains

International Boundary

Town

Road

N

Pari

Mongalla
Lado

Lafon

Ngaboli

Dorik

Tenet

Lopit

Boya

Nyerkenyi
(J. Lado)

Ilibari/Gondokoro

Segele

Kinyeti

Juba

Mura

Imehejek

Oponi Mt.
1253m

Lohiri

Ngotira

Lomiya

Tokiman/Rejaf

Ilyangari

Ohila

Iboni

Lohutok

Boya Hills

Logo

Ngangala

Longairo

Loronyo

Hoss

Ilyeu

Kudwo

Liria

Loudo

Iloli/Hoding

Shindiruo

Ngulere

Lokoya

Murahatiha

Chalamini

Lobera

Codoni

Lowe

Torit

Haforyere

Tirangore Hiyala

Kiri

Lokiliri

Langabu

Hojovi

Imurok

Loguruny Buruny

Logir

Koggi

Edemo

Iyata

Ifotu

Kidepo

Tombur

Aru

Horiok

Imatong

Lohutoh

Isohe
2823 m.

Muggi

Kit

Magwi

Obbo

Lokwa

Ikotos

Kellang

Uma

Ayi

Keteb

Moli

Imatong
Mountains

Mt. Kinyeti
3187 m.

Lorwama

Lango

Kuku

Nile

Panyikwara

Kerripi

Madi

Opari

Pajok

Lobone

Kajo Keji

Nyepu

Loa

Acholi

Madi-Opei

Metu

Aswa

Nimule

Uganda

Laropi

Padibe

Koya

Bari

Lulubo

Nile

Name Index
of the
Kings, Queens, Masters and Other Overlords
Figuring in the Dramas of this Study

Abalu, son of King Ngalamitiho of Imitari, killed by his brother King Irwangi for committing adultery with the Queen Nyadinga, 272, 276

Abalyare, wife of King Owarra of Otunge, 326

Abilli Kömiru (also Abilli Legge), King of Liria, c.1925–1942, in 1934 replaced as government chief by Lolik Lado, 95, 152, 155, 225, 317, 318

Abu Kuka, nickname of Laku-lo-Rundyang, 'cargo-chief' of Tokiman, 1870s, 106, 107, 110, 112, 114, 115, Lualla etc. part of previous entry (Ali Bey) 117; killed by his warrior class which joined Bepo's rebellion; see also Laku-lo-Rundyang

Abu Sa'ud, (Muhammad Abu Sa'ud al-Aqqad), manager of the Egyptian Aqqad trading firm which from the mid-1860s had an official monopoly on trade in Gondokoro, 106, 107, 128, 331, 332, 334

Acalili, king of Loronyo, c.1890–1944, 132–136, 255–256, 276, 293, 302–305, 307, 318, 325, 334, 345, 359, 363, 414–417, 419

Adang, Tirangore prince, 1860s, 210, 238, 251

Aderi Ringwat, king of Liria, father of Legge and Lewat, 316; see also Ringwat, Hatulang

Agora, son of Lorwungo, chief of Liria, c. 1942–1955, lived latter part of this period in exile in Lafon after being prosecuted for murder; returned at the beginning of the war but joined Anyanya, c.1964–1985, 242

Ahimang, son of Lorwungo, usurped the rain when his brother Agora was in exile fleeing prosecution for manslaughter; his bid was rejected when the new Tome generation took power (1956) and he was expelled from Liria, 155, 175, 242

Ajaru, king of Tirangore, 1881, senior son of Hujang and Iloyi, father of Ohuyyoro, 128–130, 132, 133, 297, 306–308, 311, 342, 406

Ali Bey, the name by which Samuel Baker was known in Equatoria, 106, 332

Ali Bey Okollo, son of Tira, Rainmaker of Lokiliri after ceding his political powers to his cousin Jada Lualla, Rainmaker/king of Lokiliri, first quarter 20th century, 141, 145, 146, 151, 154, 166, 193, 233, 297

Ali Mukhtar, Bakr, Mahdist Emir of Equatoria, c.1893, 115

Alloron, name by which Loro-lo-Laku was known to the government and the traders, 106, 331, 334, see also Loro-lo-Laku

Amoya, alias of King Hujang, 125; see also Hujang

Andoga, king of Logopi, Bari, c.1850, 315; see also Gwandoca

Anyala, Rainmaker of Kor section, Pari, 1980s, 389–391, 393

Arabi Dafa'alla, Mahdist Emir of Equatoria, 1893–97, 115, 145, 333

General Index[1]

A

aboloni hobu, Lt. sectional elder responsible for relations with the king, 223, 294n

Acarok, Dorik village, 50

acen, Lk. posthumous curse, 218, 370

acephalous political systems, xiv, 5, 38, 455

Acholi, 54, 57, 67, 93, 97, 126, 326, 332, 462

Addis Ababa Agreement, 156, 336n

Adio, 179, 463, *see also* Makaraka

Adler, Alfred, 27, 28, 98

aduvio, Lt. Lk., suspension of the king's protective powers usually in an outburst of anger; turning the king's blessings into a public curse, 345, 372

age-class organisation, 55, 180–204 age-grade, 353, 406; age-set, 167, 243, 353, 392, 425, 429, 433; Bari age-system, 183, 244, 250; bullying of initiates, 190, 191, 204; generational antagonism 189, 191–193; generational moieties, 21, 209; generational succession, 189–196; generational transfer of power, 185–189, 279; generation-sets, 21, 41, 203, *see also monyomiji*; girls age–sets, 54, 172, 175, 431; initiation, 74, 209, 220, 264; Mandari bead-sets, 54; meat groups, 185; names of age-sets and generations 139, 183, 184; rite of passage, 196–203; Toposa gerontocratic system, 34, 53, 58, 184

ahou, Lt. 'head', senior age-set of the four that make up *monyomiji*-set, 353

ajohiyo, Lk. consecrate, 435

ajok, Lt. god, 296, 415, 438

Alangure, Pari generation-set, *c.*1905, 145

Alangure, Ngulere generation-set, *c.*1905, 168n, 222

Ali Bey, name used in Equatoria for the non-African staff of the Turco-Egyptian government, including the Governor, 106n, 332n

alliances between clans, 88; between communities, 63, 102, 121, 150, 178, 266, 278, 279; between kings, 6, 151,315; between kings against their peoples, 213–214, 251, 325; between kings and government, 124, 127, 136, 144, 147, 167, 178, 252, 262, 266, 457; between kings and their people's enemies, 211, 251, 327; between kings and traders,106; between sections, 171, 174; matrimonial, 32, 88, 90, 106; imperative of maximising and diversifying one's matrimonial alliances, 234n; marriage king-*monyomiji* as an alliance, 226

alore, Lt. pole-shrine, 81, 195, 196, 212, 327, 405, 422

Alur, 54, 112, 270, 326, 328

Amadi, siege of, 110

Amakuta, Pari militia allied to Ansar, 141

amangat, Lt. assembly-platform of *monyomiji,* village section, 81, 85, 185, 187

ametere, Lt. effigy of deceased person, 405, 408, 409, 418

amonyemiji, Lt. Master of the Village, 82, 188, 234, 284, 293, 294

amopwa, Lk. cultivation day for the king, 171, 215, 218, 222, 254

---

1 Terms from local languages are in *italics* followed by an abbreviation indicating the language the word is taken from. Ar. is for Arabic, B. for Bari, Lk. for Lokoya, Lt. for Lotuho, Ol. Is for Olu'boti, the language of the Lulubo and P. is for Dipari.

O

W

www.ingramcontent.com/pod-product-compliance
Lightning Source LLC
Chambersburg PA
CBHW080352030426
42334CB00024B/2849